Frontiers of Artificial Intelligence, Ethics and Multidisciplinary Applications

Artificial Intelligence is now present in numerous spheres of our everyday lives. It is poised to lead new and efficient business models for effective and user-centric services in the private and public sectors. Advances in AI in deep learning, (deep) reinforcement learning, and neuroevolutionary techniques can pave the way forward for artificial general intelligence (AGI). However, the development and use of AI also present challenges. Inherent biases prevalent within data corpora used to train AI and machine learning systems attribute to most of these challenges. In addition, multiple instances have highlighted the need for privacy, fairness, and transparency in AI-powered decision-making. This book series will provide an avenue for researchers, leaders, decision-makers, and policymakers to share research and insights on the forefronts of AI, including its use in an Ethical, Explainable, Privacy-Preserving, Trustworthy, and Sustainable manner.

The series has relevance across disciplines and be multi-disciplinary. Advances in AI, explainability AI, privacy-preserving AI, and ethical AI explored in this book series are unexplored areas for research and competence building. Such developments can reduce hesitancy for AI integration in many domains. The book series thus fits in well as an essential and growing need among those who work on artificial intelligence in academia, business and industry, and the public sector to exploit the opportunities in the constantly evolving field of AI.

The series publishes research monographs, authored works by practitioners and case studies to highlight innovative and best practices, and edited volumes putting together varied perspectives.

Rajeev Arya · Subhash Chander Sharma ·
Ajit Kumar Verma · Brijesh Iyer
Editors

Recent Trends in Artificial Intelligence Towards a Smart World

Applications in Industries and Sectors

Springer

Editors
Rajeev Arya
Department of Electronics
and Communication Engineering
National Institute of Technology Patna
Patna, Bihar, India

Subhash Chander Sharma
Electronics and Computer Discipline
Indian Institute of Technology Roorkee
Saharanpur, Uttar Pradesh, India

Ajit Kumar Verma
Faculty of Technology
Environmental and Social Sciences
Western Norway University of Applied
Sciences
Haugesund, Norway

Brijesh Iyer
Dr. Babasaheb Ambedkar Technological
University
Lonere, Maharashtra, India

ISSN 2731-8125 ISSN 2731-8133 (electronic)
Frontiers of Artificial Intelligence, Ethics and Multidisciplinary Applications
ISBN 978-981-97-6789-2 ISBN 978-981-97-6790-8 (eBook)
https://doi.org/10.1007/978-981-97-6790-8

This Springer imprint is published by the registered company Springer Nature Singapore Pte Ltd.
The registered company address is: 152 Beach Road, #21-01/04 Gateway East, Singapore 189721, Singapore

Preface

Recently, the development of artificial intelligence has shifted our horizon from the automation world to the smart world. Most of the time, it is impractical to solve issues with large data sets using an exhaustive data search. Powerful tools are available thanks to optimization methods for handling data analysis and learning problems. Several techniques are used to design and put optimization algorithms into practice, and they all work better. However, the search area expands exponentially with problem size in several applications. Moreover, the scope of applications using AI is also increasing day by day. There are various AI and machine learning algorithms which have been adapted to work in a dynamic environment. The variety of algorithms developed for automobiles, drones, road management, sensor data management and analysis etc. is motivated by new optimization research trends that are primarily founded on machine learning and artificial intelligence. The goal of AI computing method is to find a useful result out of random and dynamic data. Numerous fields, including engineering, medicine, industry, education, and the military, can handle optimization in high-dimensional real-world issues thanks to some machine learning algorithms with unsupervised frameworks.

A significant area of computational intelligence, soft computing, and optimization in general is the study of fast and effective algorithms which makes our world smarter. Since constrained and unconstrained algorithms are available, they are capable of handling a variety of problems effectively. The Internet of Things (IoTs), which uses smart devices, smart sensors, and machine learning, and cloud computing are other popular subjects. They encompass all kinds of systems, including business, finance, industry, manufacturing, management, and the environment, in addition to information and communication technology. IoT creates a significant quantity of data and links the physical world to the Internet. Big data processing is made easier by a cloud computing environment, which also uses machine learning and big data analysis to make wise choices. Additionally, the fusion of intellect and technology enables the reduction of human effort while increasing the precision and efficacy of the latter. By connecting innovative thinking with innovative action and innovative execution in nearly every aspect of human life, smart devices and systems are revolutionizing the world. A system becomes smart when it can collect data, process it, analyse it, and make right decisions. Sensors are typically used for data capture and gathering, and processing converts raw data into usable information. The task of making decisions is ultimately assisted by the analysis of data using clever algorithms.

This edited book's general goal is to compile the most recent chapter reviews on the interrelated fields of Internet of vehicles, internet of drones, and cognitive radios etc. This book is dedicated to the analysis, modelling, simulation, and applications in the interdisciplinary fields of these cutting-edge technologies, from challenges and current issues to foundations, latest research and development, and opportunities. We attempt to cover every facet of the interplay between various areas of the smart world like smart cities and smart homes etc. We intend to offer a thorough platform for researchers to present novel methods for handling various types of uncertainties in practical issues using the cutting-edge machine learning algorithms. We examine the potential future work in various domains using the internet and its novel approach to bridging the divide between theory and day-to-day practical problems. Additionally, we present a unified manifesto for applied scientists to use machine learning methods in many different engineering fields, such as IoTs and communication, as well as the difficulties they may encounter in the process. The book investigates new learning domains and includes case studies based on both synthetic and actual data from various domains. We anticipate that it acts as a one-stop resource for field researchers, scholars, scientists, and industrialists.

Chapter 1 discusses the use of AI to make communication world smarter. This chapter explains how AI has contributed to making cognitive radio smarter using various optimization techniques. The various challenges and solutions of AI driven cognitive radio network have also been discussed. The future trends of AI driven CRN and its impact on industries have also been explained in this chapter.

Chapter 2 focuses on healthcare system. Every patient wants to keep their data secure but with the development of IoT digital health records have been created. To keep this data safe while avoiding unethical access to this data is very important. This chapter explains the benefits of AI in solving various problems like remote surgery. The role of AI in various sectors of healthcare like drug discovery, radiology, and patient monitoring has been discussed.

Chapter 3 explains the enormous revolution that is happening within the healthcare industry in the 21st century with the development of Artificial Intelligence (AI). With the coming of artificial intelligence and its application in healthcare businesses, the chapter looks at the world- view move in smart healthcare. Having moved from Industry 4.0 to Industry 5.0, the healthcare industry has gone through a change that has given the industry an unused dimension and a sensational alter.

Chapter 4 explains the modern industrial environment influenced by smart manufacturing and logistics, which also drive competitiveness, efficiency, sustainability, and innovation in a variety of other sectors and industries. Businesses can detect possible hazards and opportunities using real-time data analytics and predictive capabilities, enabling them to act quickly and efficiently. The global industrial landscape is transformed by Smart manufacturing and logistics, which is often referred to as Industry 4.0 by leveraging advanced technologies to improve sustainability, efficiency, and productivity. The terms and key concepts associated with this transformation include Industry 4.0, IoT, AI, and Automation.

Chapter 5 discusses the importance of AI-powered machines in industrial automation, focusing on how they make operations more responsive and flexible in changing manufacturing environments. This chapter explores how industrial Internet of Things (IIOT) helps in performing various functions like remote monitoring and controlling, predictive maintenance, asset management, safety and compliance, and supply chain integration by analysing data, predicting challenges, optimizing processes, and introducing robotics in manufacturing. These systems can spot problems early on and prevent risks, resulting in less downtime and higher productivity. The chapter showcases case studies and success stories of AI solutions in various industries. It provides guidance for businesses wanting to capitalize on AI's potential to gain an edge in today's competitive market.

Chapter 6 deals with the applications and challenges of optimization in internet of vehicles (IoTs). It starts with the network optimization in internet of vehicle and then it covers the various cases of resource and network optimization by using computation capabilities of other devices.

Chapter 7 investigates how sensors work as IoT's sensory organs, allowing for the capture of massive volumes of data from the actual world. The chapter highlights the critical role of sensors in enabling real-time monitoring, predictive maintenance, and improved decision-making in a variety of areas, including healthcare, agriculture, transportation, and smart cities. Organizations that use sensor data can obtain significant insights into operational efficiency, resource optimization, and consumer behaviour. The chapter also discusses the problems and opportunities connected with sensor deployment in IoT ecosystems, which range from data privacy and security concerns to interoperability and scalability issues.

Chapter 8 explains the integration of smart homes. Smart homes, equipped with cutting-edge technologies and digital devices, seek to enhance safety, convenience, energy efficiency, and sustainability within residential settings. By seamlessly integrating smart homes into the broader framework of smart cities, a holistic approach to urban development can be achieved. This chapter explores the nuances of this integration, examining how smart homes contribute to the overall well-being and quality of life in urban environments. It addresses the challenges and opportunities inherent in building a connected urban habitat, emphasizing the imperative for sustainable urban development practices.

Chapter 9 explains about sorting the road traffic better, a new type of Custom Hierarchical Convolutional Neural Network (HCNN) is suggested. This HCNN uses the good parts of 1D and 2D CNNs. It can get important features from both image and video data in a big way. The use of HCNN helps make the identification of vehicle types better. This leads to a smarter study of road traffic situations. This study's findings are very important for smart transport systems, city planning, and traffic control.

Chapter 10 explores the transformative role of remote monitoring and control management systems in revolutionizing agricultural practices to achieve enhanced efficiency and sustainability. With the increasing demand for food production amidst growing environmental challenges, adopting advanced technologies becomes imperative to optimize resource utilization and mitigate risks. Remote monitoring and control systems offer a holistic approach to farm management by enabling real-time monitoring, data-driven decision-making, and automated control of critical agricultural operations.

Chapter 11 aims to explain the traffic detection system using deep learning algorithms. The goal of our deep learning-based method is to build a traffic detection system that is both quick and accurate, with no human involvement required. The study focuses on two critical aspects of intelligent traffic monitoring: accident detection and traffic flow analysis. The goal of this project is to improve future intelligent transportation systems by using TrafficNet technology. The TrafficNet system performs multiple activities, including dataset segmentation, data preparation, deep learning convolutional neural network (DLCNN) model training, traffic forecasting, and performance evaluation.

Chapter 12 delves into the foundational aspects of UANs, exploring their conceptualization, development, applications, and the challenges they present. As a multidisciplinary field, UANs incorporate principles from robotics, wireless communication, and artificial intelligence (AI) to create networks of unmanned aerial vehicles (UAVs) that can operate autonomously or be remotely controlled to perform a variety of tasks.

Chapter 13 explains the extensive integration of drones into the AI enabled IoT infrastructure also gives rise to concerns surrounding privacy, security, and adherence to legal requirements. Ensuring the appropriate and successful deployment of drone technology requires addressing crucial factors such as safeguarding data transfer, securing sensitive information, and complying with airspace rules.

Chapter 14 focuses on improving traffic sign detection and recognition (TSDR)-Net, a traffic sign recognition system for autonomous driverless vehicles that work in harsh weather conditions. The method uses multiple steps. It starts with hazy traffic sign images and uses deep learning techniques, particularly Deep Learning Convolutional Neural Network (DLCNN), to remove haze. The TSDR-Net begins by gathering hazy traffic sign images that have been affected by bad weather; using deep learning for haze removal to improve visibility; using a DLCNN to detect traffic signs; and evaluating model performance through accuracy and loss calculations. By addressing the crucial task of traffic sign recognition in harsh weather conditions, this research improves the safety and efficiency of autonomous driving systems.

Finally, Chap. 15 explores the transformative integration of artificial intelligence (AI) in higher education to build smart campuses that enhance both the learning experience and administrative efficiency. The foundation of smart campuses is laid out, emphasizing the role of technology in shaping the future of education. Various AI technologies, including machine learning, natural language processing, and predictive analytics, are examined in the context of personalized learning and student support.

Patna, India	Rajeev Arya
Saharanpur, India	Subhash Chander Sharma
Haugesund, Norway	Ajit Kumar Verma
Lonere, India	Brijesh Iyer

Contents

Editors and Contributors

About the Editors

Dr. Rajeev Arya received the Engineering Degree in Electronics & Communication Engineering from Government Engineering College, Ujjain, (RGPV University, Bhopal) India, and the Master of Technology in Electronics & Communication Engineering from Indian Institute of Technology (ISM), Dhanbad, India. He received the Ph.D. degree in Communication Engineering from Indian Institute of Technology (IIT Roorkee) Roorkee, India. He is currently an Assistant Professor at the Department of Electronics & Communication Engineering at National Institute of Technology, Patna, India. His current research interests are Applications of Artificial Intelligence (AI) and Machine Learning in Wireless Sensor Networks, soft computing techniques, 5G/6G Networks, UAV Networks, Signal Processing, Communication Systems, and Circuits Design.

Subhash Chander Sharma is a Professor in the Electronics and Computers discipline at the Indian Institute of Technology (IIT) Roorkee, Saharanpur Campus, India. He has an M.Sc. (electronics), M.Tech. (electronics & communication engineering), and Ph.D. (electronics & computer engineering) in 1981, 1983, and 1992 respectively from IIT Roorkee (erstwhile University of Roorkee). He began his career as an R&D Engineer in 1983, joining the teaching profession in January 1984 at IIT Roorkee, where he continues till date. He has more than 40 years of teaching and research experience. He has published over three hundred research papers in national and international journals/conferences, and supervised more than 30 projects/dissertations of PG students and 34 PhDs in the area of computer networking, wireless network, computer communication, applications of artificial intelligence (AI) and machine learning, internet of things (IoT), cloud & its security, and mobile computing.

Ajit Kumar Verma is a Professor in the Faculty of Technology, Environmental and Social Sciences, Western Norway University of Applied Sciences, Haugesund, Norway (since March 2012) and was Professor/HAG scale for 15 years with the

Department of Electrical Engineering/Reliability Engineering at IIT Bombay with a research focus in computational intelligence applications in reliability and safety engineering. He is also a Guest Professor at Lulea University of Technology, Sweden. He has several publications to his credit. He is the Series Editor of 5 book series, and has authored and edited several books with international publishers including Springer. He has served as the Editor-in-Chief of OPSEARCH (Jan 2008–Jan 2011), and is a Patron and Founding Editor-in-Chief of International Journal of System Assurance Engineering and Management besides being an Editor-in-Chief of Life Cycle Reliability and Safety Engineering, all published by Springer.

Dr. Brijesh Iyer is an Associate Professor in the Department of E&TC Engineering at the Dr. Babasaheb Ambedkar Technological University, Lonere, India. He is a recipient of an INAE research fellowship in the field of Engineering. His research interests include RF Front end design for 5G/6G, IoT, Biomedical Image and Signal Processing, Artificial Intelligence, and Soft Computing. He has patents to his credit, has authored five books on cutting-edge technologies such as Sensor Technology, and published over 40 research papers in peer-reviewed journals and conference proceedings. He has served as Program Committee Member of various international conferences. He holds a Ph.D. degree in Electronics and Telecommunication Engineering from Indian Institute of Technology, Roorkee, India.

Contributors

Swati Agrawal Christ University, Bengaluru, India

Bosco Paul Alapatt Christ University, Bengaluru, India

Nitin Arora Wireless Networks and Cloud Computing Lab, IIT Roorkee, Roorkee, India

Rajeev Arya Wireless Sensor Networks Lab, Department of Electronics and Communication Engineering, National Institute of Technology Patna, Patna, Bihar, India

V. Bharath Simha Reddy Malla Reddy Engineering College and Management Sciences, Medchal, Hyderabad, Telangana, India

Dara Eshwar SRKR Engineering College, Bhimavaram, Andhra Pradesh, India

Ankit Gambhir Delhi Technical Campus, Greater Noida, India

Aakansha Garg ABES Institute of Technology, Ghaziabad, UP, India

Aditi Garg J.C. Bose University of Science and Technology, YMCA, Faridabad, India

Varuna Gupta Christ University, Bengaluru, India

B. Hari Krishna St. Martins Engineering College, Kompally, Hyderabad, Telangana, India

Neha Jain Delhi Technical Campus, Greater Noida, India

Nandkishor Joshi Department of CSE, PIET, Parul University, Vadodara, India

Sapna Katiyar Impledge Technologies, Noida, India

M. Krishna Satya Varma SRKR Engineering College, Bhimavaram, Andhra Pradesh, India

Janapati Chaitanya Krishna Vardhaman College of Engineering, Hyderabad, Telangana, India

Dilip Mandloi Shri Vaishnav Vidyapeeth Vishwavidyalaya, Indore, MP, India

Vandana Mehndiratta Christ University, Bengaluru, India

Suman Mishra CMR Engineering College, Hyderabad, Telangana, India

Medhavi Pandey Galgotias College of Engineering and Technology, Greater Noida, India

U. Penchalaiah Geetanjali Institute of Science and Technology, Nellore, Andhra Pradesh, India

Ganga Rama Koteswara Rao Koneru Lakshmaiah Education Foundation, Vaddeswaram, Guntur, Andhra Pradesh, India

P. Santosh Kumar Patra St. Martins Engineering College, Kompally, Hyderabad, Telangana, India

K. Satyanarayana Raju SRKR Engineering College, Bhimavaram, Andhra Pradesh, India

Dolly Sharma ABES Institute of Technology, Ghaziabad, UP, India

S. C. Sharma Wireless Networks and Cloud Computing Lab, IIT Roorkee, Roorkee, India;
DPT, Indian Institute of Engineering and Technology, Roorkee, Uttarakhand, India

Simran Delhi Technical Campus, Greater Noida, India

N. Soumya St. Martins Engineering College, Kompally, Hyderabad, Telangana, India

Yash Thakur Christ University, Bengaluru, India

Kitty Tripathi Babu Banarasi Das Northern India Institute of Technology, Lucknow, UP, India

Swati Tyagi Dronacharya Group of Institutions, Greater Noida, India

G. Udaya Sree St. Martins Engineering College, Kompally, Hyderabad, Telangana, India

Ajit Kumar Verma Faculty of Engineering and Natural Sciences, Western Norway University of Applied Sciences, Haugesund, Norway

Hemant Yadav Department of CSE, Future Institute of Engineering and Technology, Bareilly, Uttar Pradesh, India

Neelam Yadav ABES Engineering College, Ghaziabad, UP, India

Pooja Yadav Deptt. of CSIT, FET, MJP Rohilkhand University, Bareilly, Uttar Pradesh, India

Chapter 1
AI-Driven Cognitive Radio Networks for Transforming Industries and Sectors Towards a Smart World

Nandkishor Joshi, Nitin Arora, Hemant Yadav, and S. C. Sharma

Abstract In wireless communication technology, the incorporation of Artificial Intelligence (AI) into Cognitive Radio Networks (CRNs) has become a possible paradigm change. To address spectrum scarcity and inefficiencies in wireless communication networks, the CRN can make judgments for dynamic time–frequency-space resource allocation and adapt dynamically to the radio environment. However, CRNs still face significant challenges with dynamic and real-time scenarios. Because of this, cognitive radio (CR) is usually combined with machine learning and artificial intelligence methods for efficient real-time processing. Furthermore, CRNs have entered a new phase because of the development of AI technologies, which have allowed them to progress from passive spectrum sensing to proactive, intelligent, and self-optimizing systems. However, dynamic and real-time scenarios continue to be significant hurdles in cognitive radio networks. Therefore, Cognitive radio is typically integrated with artificial intelligence and machine learning techniques for effective real-time processing. Additionally, the advent of AI technologies has ushered in a new era for CRNs, enabling them to evolve from passive spectrum sensing to proactive, intelligent, and self-optimizing systems. The revolutionary potential of AI-driven CRNs in guiding sectors and industries towards the realization of a fully smart world is examined in this chapter. AI-driven CRNs provide efficient resource allocation, safe communication, and real-time data analytics. As a result, it boosts sustainability, productivity, and safety in a variety of sectors, including manufacturing, transportation, healthcare, and agriculture. To optimize spectrum utilization and network performance, it explains how machine learning algorithms, such as deep learning, reinforcement learning, neural networks, fuzzy logic, and various AI-based optimization methodologies—empower CRNs to sense, learn, and adapt to dynamic

N. Joshi (✉)
Department of CSE, PIET, Parul University, Vadodara, India
e-mail: njoshi@pp.iitr.ac.in

N. Arora · S. C. Sharma
Wireless Networks and Cloud Computing Lab, IIT Roorkee, Roorkee, India

H. Yadav
Department of CSE, Future Institute of Engineering and Technology, Bareilly, India

R. Arya et al. (eds.), *Recent Trends in Artificial Intelligence Towards a Smart World*,
Frontiers of Artificial Intelligence, Ethics and Multidisciplinary Applications,
https://doi.org/10.1007/978-981-97-6790-8_1

spectrum conditions on their own. The current chapter delves into the obstacles that AI-driven cognitive radio networks face, outlining future research directions and highlighting persistent issues.

Keywords Cognitive Radio Networks (CRNs) · Artificial Intelligence (AI) · Spectrum utilization · Spectrum sensing · Machine learning

1.1 Introduction

Cognitive Radio Networks (CRNs) transform wireless communication by providing devices with cognitive, adaptive capabilities that challenge the traditional fixed spectrum assignment approach. Dynamic spectrum access is made possible by these networks, which let devices detect underutilized frequency bands on their own and take advantage of them in real-time without interfering with licensed users. The cognitive cycle, which consists of reconfiguration, intelligent decision-making, and spectrum sensing, is the central component of the CRN. During this cycle, cognitive radios adjust to variations in the radio frequency (RF) environment to guarantee better quality of service and effective spectrum utilization. In order to solve spectrum scarcity, reduce interference, and improve overall network performance, CRNs are essential. These networks optimize channel allocation, boost network capacity, and enable 5G and 6G technologies by dynamically managing spectrum resources. The ability to adapt and be flexible is one of CRNs' key contributions to the development of more dependable, strong, and effective wireless communication systems, which in turn opens the door to a more intelligent and connected world across numerous industries.

1.2 Integration of AI in CRNs

The integration of Artificial Intelligence (AI) in Cognitive Radio Networks (CRNs) marks a transformative leap in wireless communication technologies. AI augments the inherent capabilities of CRNs by providing advanced decision-making and learning mechanisms. Machine Learning (ML) algorithms play a crucial role in spectrum sensing, enabling cognitive radios to adapt dynamically to the ever-changing RF environment. Reinforcement Learning (RL) facilitates intelligent spectrum management, allowing devices to optimize their communication strategies based on real-time feedback. Deep Learning (DL) techniques, with their prowess in pattern recognition and signal processing, enhance the accuracy of spectrum sensing and decision-making processes. The synergy between AI and CRNs empowers networks to learn from past experiences, predict future spectrum conditions, and autonomously optimize their configurations, leading to more efficient spectrum utilization and improved overall network performance. This integration holds the potential to revolutionize how wireless communication systems operate, fostering adaptability and intelligence in the face of evolving technological landscapes. The fuzzy type-2-based cooperative spectrum sensing was introduced by Rasheed et al. (2018) for cognitive radio networks and later adopted to full duplex cognitive radio networks (Joshi and Sharma 2023). In order to ensure the QoS requirements of CR users, maximize the utilization of spectrum resources, and optimize base station (BSs) resource control strategy, Dan Wang et al. proposed the hierarchical distributed networking framework, which applies AI technologies to both channels resource allocation and base station (BSs) resources control of the 5G cellular networks (Wang et al. 2019).

In Abbas et al. (2015) and Morabit et al. (2019), the authors investigated a number of different learning approaches, such as artificial bee colony (ABC) algorithm, fuzzy logic (FL), game theory (GT), neural networks (NNs), reinforcement learning (RL), support vector machines (SVM), case-based reasoning (CBR), decision trees (DT), entropy, Bayesian approaches, Markov models (MM), multi-agent systems (MAS), and genetic algorithms (GAs).

In Morabit et al. (2019) and He et al. (2010), the authors of the study performed an in-depth analysis of state-of-the-art artificial intelligence (AI) applications in Cognitive Radio (CR). The objective was to determine workable alternatives for CR implementation and evaluate the benefits of different approaches in different scenarios. The methods covered in the review include rule-based systems (RBSs), ontology-based systems (OBSs), hidden Markov models (HMMs), artificial neural networks (ANNs), and case-based systems (CBSs). This extensive analysis provides valuable insights into the current landscape of AI applications in CR and underscores the unique strengths of each methodology for specific use cases.

In Bkassiny et al. (2013), an in-depth survey was conducted, presenting a comprehensive overview of various learning techniques, including RL, GT, NNs, SVM, and MM. The survey not only introduced these methodologies but also delved into a thorough exploration of their individual strengths, weaknesses, and the associated challenges. This meticulous examination provides a nuanced understanding of the practical implications and limitations of each learning technique, contributing to a more informed perspective on their applications in diverse contexts.

In Gavrilovska et al. (2013), the authors delved into an extensive exploration, scrutinizing game theory (GT), reinforcement learning (RL), and various reasoning approaches, including Bayesian networks (BNs), fuzzy logic (FL), and case-based reasoning (CBR). This thorough investigation illuminated the applications and interactions among these methodologies, offering a nuanced understanding of their roles and contributions within the context studied.

In Bello Salau et al. (2015), an inclusive survey unfolded, showcasing AI techniques, including genetic algorithms (GA), artificial neural networks (ANN), hidden Markov models (HMMs), and metaheuristic algorithms (MEAs). The exploration delved into a meticulous evaluation of their strengths and weaknesses, along with a thorough examination of open research issues pertinent to these techniques. This comprehensive scrutiny enhances our comprehension of the intricacies, potential, and areas for further investigation within the realm of AI methodologies.

1.3 The Potential for AI-Driven CRNs to Revolutionize a Variety of Industries

Artificial Intelligence-driven CRNs have the potential to revolutionize a wide range of sectors and usher in a new era of intelligent and flexible wireless communication. AI-driven CRNs in the healthcare industry optimize spectrum allocation for smooth medical device connection while enabling remote patient monitoring and telemedicine. The integration of CRNs improves operational efficiency in industries such as manufacturing, which can construct smart factories and use the Industrial Internet of Things (IIoT) for real-time control and monitoring. In transportation, CRNs help to create intelligent transportation systems and connected automobiles, with AI optimizing spectrum consumption for vehicle communication. To ensure adequate energy distribution, the energy sector uses AI-driven CRNs to facilitate communication and control of the smart grid. Precision farming and smart agriculture, made possible by CRNs and AI-driven sensor networks, are revolutionizing the agricultural industry. The combined influence of these sectors demonstrates the adaptability of AI-driven CRNs, which hold the promise of improved productivity, dependability, and connection and, in the end, open the door to the realization of a world that is smarter and more connected.

1.4 Cognitive Radio Networks and Artificial Intelligence

In this section, fundamental ideas of CRNs and artificial intelligence are elaborated. The incorporation of cognitive capabilities into wireless communication systems has emerged as a significant advancement in response to the constraints of traditional networks. CRNs provide a paradigm shift in dynamic and heterogeneous environments where spectrum conditions change due to different user demands and interference. The need for cognitive ability arises from the need to understand, evaluate, and adjust to the constantly changing radio frequency (RF) environment. CRNs' primary functions include sharing, adapting, and perceiving the spectrum. Real-time identification of available frequency bands through constant observation of the radio frequency environment is known as spectrum sensing. This enables CRNs to optimize spectrum utilization and prevent interference with primary users by dynamically allocating resources based on the situation. By enabling harmonious coexistence of numerous devices within the same frequency band, spectrum sharing encourages the effective use and distribution of spectrum resources. According to real-time observations, CRN adaptation entails modifying gearbox parameters, such as power levels and modulation techniques, to maximize performance. In order to overcome the drawbacks of conventional wireless communication networks and open the door for more effective and intelligent wireless communication systems, these cognitive skills work together to allow CRNs to negotiate the complexity of dynamic and heterogeneous surroundings. Due to the intelligent and dynamic behavior of CRNs, the AI methodologies are more appropriate to improve the performance of CRNs. The main fundamental concepts of CRNs and possible AI methodologies are elaborated in the following subsections.

1.4.1 Cognitive Radio Networks: An Overview

Cognitive Radio Networks (CRNs) owe their existence to the concept of Dynamic Spectrum Access.

Dynamic Spectrum Access (DSA)

Dynamic Spectrum Access (DSA) refers to a technique that enables wireless devices to access and use radio frequency spectrum dynamically, adapting to varying environmental and usage conditions (Akyildiz et al. 2006). It's a concept primarily associated with CRNs and Software-Defined Radio (SDR) technologies. DSA aims to address the issue of spectrum scarcity and underutilization by allowing unlicensed or secondary users to access and share the licensed frequency bands without causing interference to the primary (licensed) users.

In a simple way, the cognitive cycle of cognitive radio is described by Shah et al. (2012) as the seat cycle, which is an extension of the cognitive cycle. The cognitive radio SEAT cycle is shown in Fig. 1.1. "CR nodes are smart wireless equipment that can sense the environment around them, keep monitoring on network dynamics, and learn from previous encounters to make decisions that will allow them to take advantage of transmission opportunities. Constantly scanning the spectrum (S), exchanging control information (E), deciding on white space (A), and sending data (T) over the network are all part of this iterative process. This pattern, which is repeated to maximize communication efficiency, is known as the SEAT cycle" (Shah et al. 2012, 2013).

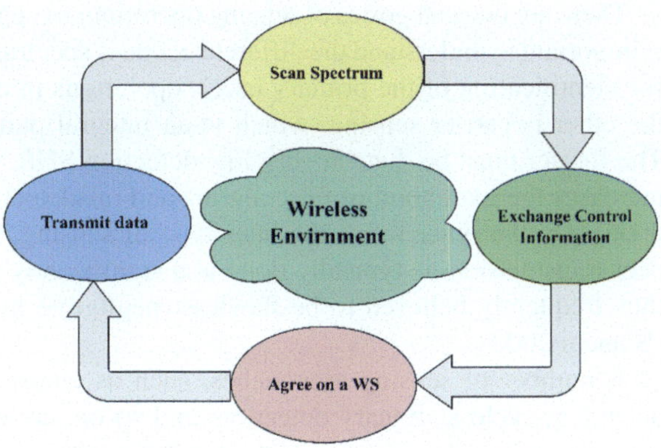

Fig. 1.1 Cognitive radio SEAT cycle. *Source* Author

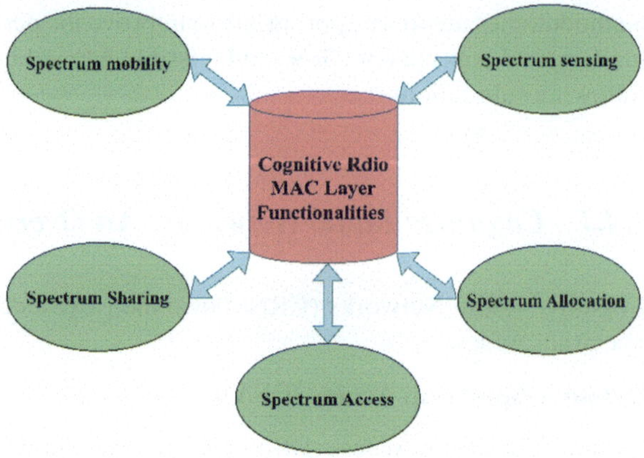

Fig. 1.2 Components of the cognitive radio network. *Source* Author

Components of Cognitive Radio Networks

The cognitive radio networks handle tasks such as channel sensing, spectrum sharing, resource allocation, and spectrum mobility (Sultana et al. 2017; Riahi Manesh and Kaabouch 2018). They are also called the primary components of the CR-MAC Protocols. Additionally, the functionality of the components is depicted in Fig. 1.2. The description of these components is described in Table 1.1.

Integration of Spectrum Sensing in Cognitive Radio Networks

Spectrum sensing is a fundamental requirement in CRNs, enabling cognitive radios to detect primary user (PUs) activities and identify vacant spectrum bands. Although spectrum sensing is part of the physical layer, spectrum sensing technologies also improve the performance of IEEE 802.11 DCF and guarantee that cognitive radios can access the spectrum when needed without negatively impacting primary users. When 802.11 DCF is used in cognitive radio networks, it can benefit from cognitive radio functionalities (components), which are described in the previous section.

There are two categories of sensing operations in cognitive radio, between which it is important to understand the difference: one is spectrum sensing, which is employed for identification of the primary user's operations in cognitive radio scenarios, and the other is carrier sensing, which is an integral part of the CSMA/CA protocol. The former must be done at very low detection SNR, which takes a lot of time and increases the likelihood of false alarms and misdetection (IEEE802.22-05/0007r46 2006). On the other hand, the later type of sensing, which is to detect an 802.11 peer transmission, is typically done at a significantly greater signal strength and is thus frequently believed to be flawless (negligible false alarms and misdetections (Bianchi 2000).

A number of sensing approaches, such as energy detection, matched filtering detection, cyclo stationary detection, and so on, are explained in detail for cognitive radio networks (Yücek and Arslan 2009; Sani et al. 2021). Although spectrum sensing is part of the physical layer, spectrum sensing technologies also improve the

Table 1.1 CR components description and functionality

CR components	Description	Functionality
Spectrum sensing	Spectrum sensing is the process of continuously monitoring the radio frequency spectrum to detect the presence of primary users (licensed users) and identify available frequency bands.	Cognitive radios use various sensing techniques (e.g., energy detection, matched filtering, cyclostationary feature detection) to detect signals from primary users and determine spectrum availability.
Spectrum access	Spectrum access involves the ability of cognitive radios to access and utilize available spectrum resources efficiently.	Cognitive radios employ policies and protocols to negotiate and request access to vacant or underutilized frequency bands, enabling secondary (unlicensed) usage without causing harmful interference to primary users.
Spectrum allocation	Spectrum allocation refers to the dynamic assignment of specific frequency bands or channels to cognitive radios for communication.	Cognitive radios can dynamically allocate spectrum resources to optimize bandwidth usage, often through negotiation or reservation mechanisms, such as time division multiple access (TDMA) or frequency division multiple access (FDMA).
Spectrum sharing	Spectrum sharing is the cooperative and non-interfering use of the same frequency band by multiple cognitive radio devices.	Cognitive radios employ sharing protocols and techniques to coexist with other cognitive radios and primary users, adjusting their transmit power, modulation schemes, or access timings to avoid interference.
Spectrum mobility	Spectrum mobility refers to the ability of cognitive radios to switch between different frequency bands or channels as needed.	Cognitive radios can perform rapid channel hopping or frequency band switching to maintain connectivity and optimize communication quality, especially in the presence of interference or changing network conditions.

Source Author

performance of IEEE 802.11 DCF and guarantee that cognitive radios can access the spectrum when needed without negatively impacting primary users.

Joshi et al. (2023) and Dappuri and Venkatesh (2018) have reported distinct sensing strategies for CRNs. Since, continuous sensing, a feature inherent in the 802.11 DCF protocol, leads to energy inefficiencies. To tackle this issue, the sensing strategy involves two specific sensing approaches: periodic sensing for detecting the ON state of the primary user, ensuring intermittent checks for their activity, and continuous sensing to monitor the OFF state, enabling a constant vigil for vacant spectrum periods. This combined approach aims to optimize energy usage while effectively identifying primary user activities within the network.

Joshi and Sharma (2023) have reported another sensing approach for FD-CRN since cooperative spectrum sensing is employed to optimize spectrum utilization and mitigate interference from licensed users. However, the multipath fading and shadowing problems are often mitigated by the detection function. Cooperative spectrum sensing uses spatial variety to improve detection, but it comes with overhead that affects overall performance in the form of delays, energy consumption, and longer operating times. The author proposed a type-2 fuzzy algorithm as a solution to address these issues, with the goal of improving cooperative sensing. It describes a type-2 fuzzy logic approach for spectrum-based energy detection that enhances cooperative sensing.

Consequently, sensing plays a critical role in cognitive radio. Its contribution to the creation of protocols that directly affect and decide the system's overall performance accounts for its significance.

1.4.2 Artificial Intelligence: An Overview

Artificial Intelligence (AI) is a field dedicated to creating computer systems capable of emulating human intelligence, encompassing tasks such as learning, reasoning, problem-solving, perception, language understanding, and decision-making. Machine Learning (ML), a subset of AI, focuses on developing algorithms that enable computers to learn and improve performance from data. Deep Learning, inspired by the human brain's structure, employs artificial neural networks, and has excelled in tasks like image recognition and natural language processing. Natural language processing (NLP) enables machines to interact with humans using language, while computer vision enables machines to interpret visual data. Robotics integrates AI for decision-making in physical tasks, and expert systems mimic human decision-making in specific domains. Reinforcement Learning involves agents learning by interacting with environments and receiving feedback. Ethical considerations, transparency, and addressing biases in AI algorithms are crucial. AI finds applications in healthcare, finance, transportation, and various industries. Ongoing trends include improving model interpretability, exploring quantum computing, and integrating AI with emerging technologies. Despite advancements, addressing challenges and ensuring ethical AI development remains a priority.

Artificial Intelligence (AI) is the engine that drives systems that replicate complex biological processes found in humans, such as self-adaptation, self-stability, self-organization, learning, and reasoning. In exploiting previous knowledge, allows intelligent machine to learn from its environment. Nevertheless, developing software that can adjust to various circumstances and adapt to deal with new limitations is a big task. The ability to learn and alter wireless signals based on the external radio environment is particularly important in the field of cognitive radios. Therefore, incorporating AI into the core of cognitive radio technology becomes crucial. Cognitive radio networks (CRNs) employ various AI techniques, including Artificial Neural Networks (ANNs), Markov Models (MMs), Federated Learning (FL), Game Theory (GT), Support Vector Machines (SVM), Multi-objective Evolutionary Algorithms (MEAs), Rule-Based Systems (RBSs), Ontology-Based Systems

(OBSs), Case-Based Systems (CBSs), Multi-Agent Systems (MASs), and evolutionary algorithms such as Genetic Algorithms (GA), Differential Evolution (DE), Particle Swarm Optimization (PSO), Bacterial Foraging Optimization (BFO), Ant Colony Optimization (ACO), Cuckoo Search Optimization (CSO), Artificial Bee Colony (ABC), and Artificial Immune Systems (AIS) (Morabit et al. 2019). The utilization of these diverse AI techniques in CRNs reflects the intricate nature of adapting and optimizing wireless communication strategies in dynamic and evolving environments.

1.5 Artificial Intelligence in Cognitive Radio Networks

In this section, we provide an overview of several AI techniques implemented in Cognitive Radio Networks (CRNs) (Morabit et al. 2019).

1.5.1 Artificial Intelligence Methodologies to Cognitive Radios Networks

1. **Artificial Neural Networks**
   Artificial Neural Networks (ANNs) are intricate networks of interconnected simple processors that do concurrent distributed processing. Each basic processor, sometimes referred to as an artificial neuron, is defined by its inputs (xi for $i = 0$ to n, weights), outputs $s = f(a)$, internal state of activation $a = F(x, w)$, transition function $f(a)$, and activation function $F(x, w)$. Every one of these artificial neurons computes an output based on the information it has received. Artificial Neural Networks (ANNs) are designed with inspiration from the behavioral principles present in the biological brain. The CRNs use three types of Artificial Neural Networks (ANNs): radial basis function networks (RBFN), and multilayer perceptron networks in both linear (MLPN) and nonlinear (MNPN) versions. Here, both MLPN and MNPN are made up of linked layers of computing units. While MNPN uses sigmoid activation functions, MLPN uses linear combinations of outputs from earlier layers. A unique family of multilayer feed-forward networks known as RBFN consists of two layers, with units in the hidden layer that use Gaussian kernels or other radial basis functions as activation functions. The centers of these functions are determined by the corresponding weight vectors (Jain et al. 1996).
2. **Markov Chains**
   In stochastic situations, Markov Models provide a mathematical foundation that extends beyond short-path techniques. These models include fundamental components such as states, which depict the agent's current state, actions that affect the dynamics of the state, and incentives related to changes in the state.

They successfully represent the temporal connections among a series of variables ($S_0 \ldots S_t \ldots$). When every variable in the series depends only on the one before it, the system is called a Markov chain, and it may be represented using the conditional probability $P(S_t|S_0, \ldots, S_{t-1}) = P(S_t|S_{t-1})$. The perspective shown here is helpful in explaining the stochastic and dynamic features of sequential processes.

3. **Game Theory**

   In the field of Cognitive Radio (CR), game theory is important because it offers a useful framework for comprehending and maximizing interactions between various entities in the wireless communication spectrum. Game theory aids in the modeling and analysis of strategic decision-making processes in the setting of CR, where several users and systems share scarce spectrum resources. Spectrum allocation game modeling is a popular use of game theory in cognitive radio. Several cognitive radio users or secondary users fight for access to the available frequency bands in a spectrum-sharing scenario. With the aid of game theory, it is possible to analyze the tactics these users use to maximize their usage of the spectrum while taking other users' needs into account. One important idea in game theory is the Nash equilibrium, which may be used to find stable places where no user has an incentive to unilaterally stray from their preferred course of action (Bkassiny et al. 2013).

   Three variables are involved in the mathematical representation of a game: $G = (N, S, U)$. In this case, N stands for the group of players, S for the group of strategies, and U for the group of utility functions. There are various sorts of game theoretic techniques, each providing distinct insights into strategic interactions. Four main classifications are frequently acknowledged (Wang et al. 2010).

   Cooperative Games: In cooperative games, players establish alliances and cooperate to accomplish shared objectives. The distribution of rewards among the participating players and teamwork are the main points of emphasis.

   Noncooperative Games: Individual players make decisions on their own in noncooperative games without overt cooperation. Every player follows their own interests, and their separate strategic decisions dictate the results.

   Auction Games: Noncooperative games that involve bidding for products, services, or resources are known as auction games. How the products are distributed and how much each participant must pay are decided by the auction regulations.

   Stochastic Games: A degree of uncertainty enters the decision-making process in stochastic games. Moreover, a stochastic game extends the Markov decision process by assessing the interactive rivalry between different actors (Wang et al. 2010). The modeling of strategic interactions becomes more dynamic because the outcomes are dependent not only on the actions of the players but also on random variables.

4. **Fuzzy Logic**

   A mathematical paradigm known as fuzzy logic addresses thinking and decision-making in the face of uncertainty. In contrast to traditional binary logic, which relies on true or false values, fuzzy logic considers degrees of truth and enables the representation of ambiguous or inaccurate data. It's ideal for systems where ambiguity and uncertainty are common since it models human-like reasoning using fuzzy sets and linguistic variables. Applications for fuzzy logic can be found in many domains, such as artificial intelligence, control systems, and decision support systems. The framework based on fuzzy logic is employed to regulate the power and MAC protocol parameters, including delay and throughput (Joshi et al. 2023; Joshi and Jharia 2014, 2015).

5. **Support Vector Machine**
   One potent machine learning approach for regression and classification is the Support Vector Machine (SVM) (Qadir 2015). In the input data space, it finds the ideal hyperplane to divide several classes. Support vectors are essential data points that specify the location and direction of the hyperplane. The algorithm uses these data points to optimize the margin between classes. SVM is frequently used for applications like pattern recognition, text categorization, and image classification because it performs especially well in high-dimensional domains.
6. **Rule-Based Systems**
   Rule-Based Systems are a subset of artificial intelligence that carry out tasks or make choices based on a predetermined set of rules. These systems have a logical structure with rules that govern the behavior of the system, usually expressed as "if-then" statements. The rules are implemented in a sequential manner by the system to accomplish a particular task or arrive at a conclusion. Each rule is composed of conditions and matching actions.
   Expert systems, knowledge-based systems, and commercial applications are just a few of the fields in which these systems are frequently utilized for decision assistance and problem-solving. Rule-Based Systems perform well in situations where rules may express explicit information and offer an understandable and transparent framework for making decisions. They work especially well on activities involving rule-driven processes and logical thinking.
7. **Ontology-Based Systems**
   An artificial intelligence system class known as Ontology-Based Systems uses ontologies to organize and describe knowledge. A formal, clear specification of a common conceptualization that establishes the terminology and connections inside a specific area is called an ontology. This organized knowledge representation makes reasoning, decision-making, and data management in ontology-based systems more efficient. These systems provide a semantic foundation for information processing and interpretation by modeling the concepts, entities, and their interactions in a specific domain using ontologies. Systems based on ontologies are widely utilized in domains like semantic web applications, natural language processing, knowledge representation, and information retrieval. They encourage more intelligent and context-aware system behavior by enabling machines to read and reason about data in a way that is consistent with human comprehension. Ontology is used in Ontology-Based Systems (OBS) to facilitate reasoning about the characteristics related to the domain of interest (He et al. 2010). An ontology consists of the following key components:

Classes: Classes stand for groups or kinds of entities within a domain, the diverse ideas or things found in the ontology are defined by them.
Individuals: Individuals are members or occurrences of a class; they are also referred to as instances. They are the real things that exist in the realm.
Properties: Properties explain the connections between classes or between a person and a piece of data. Data properties link persons to data values, while object properties link classes and individuals. These are the two primary categories of attributes.
Attributes: Features or qualities that are connected to groups are called attributes. They offer more details regarding the ontology's entities.
Relations: Relationships define the connections between classes. In the ontology, they specify the connections and relationships between various items.
Axioms: Axioms are propositions that articulate limitations, guidelines, or rational connections within the ontology. They specify the rules and semantics that control the things and how they interact.
Hierarchy: A hierarchical structure known as a taxonomy or sub Sumption hierarchy is frequently seen in ontologies, which arrange classes into them. The specialization and generalization relationships between classes are shown in this hierarchy.

8. **Case-Based Systems**
Artificial intelligence systems that use cases previous experiences to address new challenges are known as case-based systems (Gavrilovska et al. 2013). These systems work by pulling solutions from a database of instances that have already been resolved and modifying them to fit the needs of the present situation. Key components of Case-Based Systems are elaborated as follows (Gavrilovska et al. 2013):
Case Base: This is a collection of previously resolved instances kept in one location. Each case includes a description of the problem, the solution used, and the result.
Retrieval Mechanism: Based on how closely the current issue and previous cases resemble one another, the system uses a retrieval technique to find pertinent cases from the case base.
Reuse Mechanism: The system uses cases that are relevant to its current problem-solving strategy and modifies or reuses its solutions. The process of adaptation is the adjustment of the retrieved answer to the unique circumstances of the novel challenge.
Revision Mechanism: The system may go through a revision process after using the recovered solution to assess the solution's effectiveness and update the case base appropriately. In the long run, this helps the system learn and get better.
Case-based systems provide a valuable method for handling dynamic and complicated scenarios in spectrum management in CRNs. In real wireless communication contexts, these systems make decisions based on past experiences and solutions. In cognitive radio, essential features of case-based systems are as follows:

Problem Representation: First, it is necessary to define the problem with respect to the CRNs. The system contains cases, which are past examples of spectrum management problems, along with a description of the problem, an applied solution, and the results.
Adaptation to Dynamic Environments: The available spectrum and network conditions dynamically alter in cognitive radio scenarios. Case-based systems can adjust to these modifications by retrieving and modifying case-based solutions.
Spectrum Allocation: Case-based systems can help optimize spectrum allocation by bringing efficient strategies from previous cases that are comparable to the available spectrum and consumption trends now.
Interference Mitigation: In order to address interference problems, Case-Based Systems are able to obtain and modify solutions from earlier cases that effectively reduce comparable interference scenarios.
Learning and Evolution: Case-based systems in cognitive radio can continuously evolve by modifying the case based on the success or failure of implemented solutions. This contributes to the system's ability to adapt to changing network dynamics.

9. **Genetic Algorithms**
In Cognitive Radio, Genetic Algorithms (GAs) are used as optimization methods to tackle intricate and dynamic spectrum management problems. This is the application of genetic algorithms in CRNs. The genetic algorithm is a vital optimization algorithm for spectrum management in CRNs, which provides the ability to find efficient and dynamic solutions to the challenges posed by changing network conditions and spectrum availability. The mechanism for this is as follows:
Representation of Solutions: Genetic Algorithms represent potential solutions to spectrum allocation and optimization problems using encoded structures. It often occurs in the form of binary strings or other data structures. These structures represent candidate solutions that are analogous to possible frequency assignments.
Initialization: To illustrate various spectrum allocation schemes, a population of probable solutions is initialized. The efficiency of spectrum utilization, interference levels, and overall network performance are some of the factors used to evaluate each solution.
Genetic Operators: Genetic algorithms make use of critical genetic operators to evolve the population over multiple generations. Among these operators are crossover (recombination), mutation, and selection. Crossover integrates information from two parent solutions to make new offspring, selection chooses solutions for reproduction based on fitness, and mutation adds random alterations to maintain diversity.
Fitness Evaluation: The fitness of each solution is assessed based on how well it addresses the specified objectives and constraints in spectrum allocation. It also considers factors such as interference reduction, improved throughput, and efficient utilization of available frequencies.

Iterative Evolution: To do this, genetic operators are used repeatedly over a number of generations, progressively enhancing the population's solutions. By simulating natural selection and evolution, this approach produces more optimal solutions.

Final Solution Selection: The final solution, or a set of solutions, is selected from the evolving population based on the convergence of the algorithm and achievement of the desired optimization goals.

10. **Differential Evolution**

In cognitive radio (CR) networks, differential evolution (DE) is an optimization technique that has been used to address issues with resource allocation and spectrum management. A flexible and effective method for resolving dynamic spectrum allocation issues is provided by differential evolution in CRNs. It works particularly well in situations with complicated optimization circumstances. They considered that it could be challenging for conventional optimization techniques to produce acceptable results. When network conditions change, DE can be used to optimize spectrum use by exploring a variety of solution spaces. Differential evolution is used in the following ways in CRNs:

Initialization: DE starts by initializing a population of candidate solutions, each of which stands for a possible method of allocating spectrum. Usually, vectors are used to encode these solutions.

Mutation: DE introduces variety by performing mutation procedures. This mutation in cognitive radio entails influencing solution vectors and generating new trial solutions. The algorithm can consider a wider range of alternatives because the mutation process traverses the solution space.

Crossover: DE uses crossover procedures to merge data from many solutions. This entails mixing the trial solutions with the existing population to promote knowledge sharing and maybe result in better solutions.

Selection: The fitness of each experimental solution is assessed using certain criteria such as spectrum efficiency, interference levels, and overall network performance. To keep solutions that enhance the optimization goals, DE uses a selection procedure.

Iterative Evolution: Over several generations, the mutation, crossover, and selection processes are applied iteratively. The population's solutions are improved through this iterative process, leading to more optimal plans for spectrum distribution.

Final Solution: The final solution is chosen according to convergence criteria or a specified number of iterations. In the cognitive radio network, these solutions stand for efficient spectrum management techniques.

11. **Particle Swarm Optimization**

To solve the problems of spectrum allocation and optimization in Cognitive Radio (CR) networks, Particle Swarm Optimization (PSO) is a meta-heuristic optimization technique. One collaborative and decentralized method of managing spectrum in CRNs is Particle Swarm optimization (Kennedy and Eberhart 1995). Swarm intelligence ideas are utilized by PSO to find effective

ways to allocate spectrum dynamically in the face of changing user demands and network conditions. The use of PSO in cognitive radio is explained as follows:
Initialization: PSO begins with initializing a population of possible solutions, or particles, each of which stands for a potential spectrum allocation plan. These particles are described as vectors in a multidimensional space.
Updates to Velocity and Position: Based on its past performance as well as that of the top-performing particles in the population, every particle in the population modifies its velocity and position inside the solution space. Information about the global best (g_{best}) and personal best (p_{best}) is used to guide the updates of location and velocity.
Fitness Evaluation: Each particle's fitness is evaluated according to predetermined standards, including overall network performance, interference reduction, and efficient use of the available spectrum. The degree to which a specific spectrum allocation strategy conforms to the optimization goals is ascertained through this fitness evaluation.
Iterative Optimization: To approach or reach an ideal solution, the particles update their locations and velocities repeatedly. Particles can look for better solutions since the algorithm encourages exploration and exploitation of the solution space.
Dynamic Adaptation: PSO can adjust itself dynamically to evolving network circumstances. The particles modify their positions and velocities in response to changes in the cognitive radio environment, such as new spectrum availability or interference patterns.
Final Solution: Based on a predetermined number of iterations or convergence criteria, a final solution, or group of solutions, is identified. The cognitive radio network's performance is maximized by these solutions, which stand for efficient spectrum allocation techniques.

12. **Bacterial Foraging Optimization**
Bacterial Foraging Optimization (BFO) is a bio-inspired optimization algorithm that draws inspiration from the foraging behavior of bacteria (Panigrahi et al. 2011). In the context of Cognitive Radio (CR) networks, BFO has been employed to address optimization challenges related to spectrum management. Additionally, Bacterial Foraging Optimization offers a bio-inspired and decentralized approach to solving complex optimization problems, making it suitable for addressing dynamic spectrum management challenges in CRNs. BFO offers a way to effectively explore and utilize the solution space by mimicking the foraging behavior of bacteria, which enhances network performance and spectrum utilization. The application of Bacterial Foraging Optimization in cognitive radio is explained as follows:
Initialization: To begin using BFO, a population of virtual bacteria must first be initialized. Each bacteria represents a potential fix for the CRNs spectrum allocation or optimization.
Chemotaxis: Through a process known as chemotaxis, bacteria migrate along a gradient in the solution space by evaluating a fitness function. The fitness function evaluates a spectrum allocation strategy's quality in the context of CR

by considering variables, including interference levels, spectrum efficiency, and overall network performance.

Reproduction and Elimination: Bacteria go through processes of reproduction and elimination as they chemotaxis. Higher-fitness bacteria that are more successful add to the pool of bacteria that reproduce, whereas less successful bacteria might be eliminated. This is like the idea of survival of the fittest.

Swarming Behavior: BFO induces a cooperative and communicative swarming behavior in bacteria. By sharing knowledge about their encounters, bacteria facilitate the exploration and utilization of the solution space. The cooperative feature improves the algorithm's capacity to identify near-optimal or ideal solutions.

Adaptability: BFO demonstrates its ability to change its movement and reproduction rates in response to changes in its surroundings. Because of its versatility, the algorithm can react quickly to modifications in the cognitive radio network, such as shifts in the availability of spectrum or patterns of interference.

Final Solution: After a predetermined number of iterations or based on convergence criteria, a final solution or group of solutions is determined. These solutions stand for practical approaches to cognitive radio network optimization and spectrum distribution.

13. **Ant Colony Optimization**

In CRNs, ant colony optimization (ACO) is developed as a bio-inspired optimization technique inspired by ant foraging behavior (He et al. 2010). Every virtual ant in the algorithm represents a possible solution for spectrum allocation, and it starts with its initialization. By probabilistically choosing frequency bands based on pheromone levels and heuristic information, the ants construct solutions as they move across the solution space. Desirability signals, or pheromones, are left behind on the pathways and impact the decisions made by ants that come after them. A combination of local and heuristic information is used by the algorithm to constantly balance exploration and exploitation. Slow evaporation of pheromone levels encourages network conditions to be adjusted to. Towards optimal or nearly optimal spectrum allocation systems, solutions are gradually improved through repeated feedback loops. The flexible and decentralized characteristics of ACOs make them highly suitable for handling the ever-changing spectrum management difficulties in CRNs.

14. **Cat Swarm Optimization**

Cat Swarm Optimization (CSO) is a bio-inspired optimization technique that uses Cognitive Radio (CR) networks; it is inspired by the way cats hunt (Yao 2021). The algorithm starts from scratch and employs a population of virtual cats, each of which stands for a potential spectrum allocation strategy for the cognitive radio network. The search technique used by the program is based on the exploration-exploitation trade-off that is inherent in feline hunting strategies. Cats use this trade-off to dynamically alter their positions iteratively, considering both individual experiences and collective information within the pod. Scent markings are left by cats on visited locations in the solution space, which are comparable to natural territorial marking and indicate the desirability of frequency bands or spectrum distribution schemes. The algorithm adjusts its focus as it goes along, dynamically balancing local and global search tactics. CSO demonstrates flexibility in responding to modifications in the cognitive radio environment by modifying the cats' locomotion and marking techniques to investigate novel and developing spectrum allocation schemes. The ultimate solutions, ascertained using convergence criteria, are efficacious tactics for maximizing spectrum utilization and network efficiency within CRNs.

15. **Artificial Bee Colony**
Cognitive Radio (CR) networks face difficulties with spectrum allocation and optimization. One useful approach for resolving these issues is Artificial Bee Colony (ABC) optimization (Baykasoğlu et al. 2007), which draws inspiration from honeybee foraging behavior. First, ABC uses a multi-phase strategy, starting with the startup of a population of artificial bees, each representing a possible solution for spectrum allocation. Collaborative discovery is fostered in the Employed Bees Phase by the bees' dynamic positioning adjustments based on available solutions. The balance between exploration and exploitation is improved during the Onlooker Bees Phase, when workers communicate information with onlooker bees, which allows them to choose solutions probabilistically. To add randomness and variation to the population, the Scout Bees Phase regularly drops solutions that aren't working. Effective spectrum allocation techniques are chosen through a fitness evaluation that follows predetermined criteria. ABC exhibits flexibility in responding to evolving network conditions by dynamically modifying the artificial bees' exploration and exploitation tactics. The final solutions represent near-optimal or ideal strategies for spectrum management in CRNs, as assessed by convergence criteria. ABC's effective exploration and exploitation of the solution space is made possible by its decentralized and collaborative methodology, which also improves network performance and spectrum utilization.

16. **Artificial Immune System**
The Artificial Immune System (AIS) is a computational paradigm that is modeled after the complexity of the human immune system. Its use in Cognitive Radio (CR) networks provides a unique method of spectrum management. The AIS uses clonal selection algorithms, which replicate the immune system's response by cloning viable remedies according to their suitability, just like immune cells proliferate when confronted with antigens. These cloned solutions are refined via affinity maturation, which modifies their properties to increase fitness and achieve optimization goals. To help with the recall and reuse of successful solutions while avoiding previously unsuccessful ones, AIS keeps an immunological memory by storing information about successful and unsuccessful spectrum allocation schemes. Anomaly detection skills of the immune system allow AIS in CRNs to recognize anomalous patterns or interference, which triggers dynamic modifications to spectrum allocation plans. The immune

memory and response tactics of AIS dynamically evolve in response to environmental changes, learning from feedback and progressively enhancing spectrum control. Using convergence criteria, the final solutions show good practices for network performance and spectrum usage optimization in CRNs. This novel adaptive strategy improves the effectiveness and adaptability of spectrum management in dynamic and changing CR contexts. It draws inspiration from biological immune systems.

17. **Simulated Annealing**
An optimization approach called Simulated Annealing (SA) (Kirkpatrick et al. 1983), which draws inspiration from metallurgical annealing processes, has been used to solve spectrum allocation and optimization problems in Cognitive Radio (CR) networks. The algorithm starts by initializing a solution, which is a possible approach to spectrum allocation. The quality of the solution is assessed using a set fitness or objective function that considers factors like interference levels, spectrum efficiency, and overall network performance. By introducing a temperature parameter, SA makes it easier to manage the trade-off between exploration and exploitation. To encourage investigation of a wider solution space, the system is initially permitted to accept solutions that can impair performance. As the temperature drops throughout iterations, the algorithm is guided towards optimal or nearly optimal solutions and is less likely to accept subpar alternatives. SA actively adapts to changes in the cognitive radio environment by perturbing the existing allocation method and exploring neighboring options at each iteration. Convergence criteria are used to decide the final solution or collection of solutions. These solutions demonstrate effective spectrum management strategies and demonstrate the versatility and usefulness of SA in enhancing spectrum utilization and overall network performance.

18. **Tabu Search**
Glover (1986) proposed Tabu Search (TS), a potent metaheuristic optimization method that has proven useful in handling complex spectrum allocation and optimization problems in Cognitive Radio (CR) networks. The algorithm starts by initializing a solution, which is a possible approach to spectrum allocation. The effectiveness of the spectrum allocation method is assessed using a set fitness or objective function that considers factors including interference levels, spectrum efficiency, and overall network performance. To promote diversity in the search space, TS provides a tabu list, which is essential for tracking recently investigated solutions and preventing the algorithm from repeating the same configurations. With minor perturbations, Tabu Search investigates the area around the present solution at each iteration, dynamically adjusting to variations in the cognitive radio environment. The algorithm can bypass tabu constraints when aspiration criteria are included, which makes it easier to investigate possibly advantageous solutions. Convergence criteria determine the final solution or group of solutions, which represent spectrum management strategies that work well in CRNs. Effective solution space exploration is made possible by Tabu Search's flexible and strong features, such as the tabu list

and aspiration criteria, which eventually improve network performance and spectrum usage.

19. **Multi-agent Systems**

    Multiple intelligent beings, referred to as agents, collaborate to accomplish shared objectives in Multi-Agent Systems (MAS) (Hoek and Wooldridge 2008). MAS has been utilized in the context of CRNs to tackle issues related to spectrum management and optimization. Multi-agent systems provide a distributed and decentralized method of spectrum management in CRNs. In complex and dynamic CR contexts, MAS supports effective decision-making, dynamic adaptability, and cooperative optimization by utilizing the intellect and autonomy of individual agents. The following is how multi-agent systems work in this context:

    Agent Initialization: In CRNs, MAS starts with the initialization of intelligent agents, which stand in for autonomous decision-making entities that may evaluate and modify their behavior in response to the state of the spectrum.

    Collaboration and Communication: To exchange data regarding spectrum availability, interference patterns, and other pertinent factors, agents in a MAS cooperate and communicate with one another. Agents can make better decisions as a group because of this collaborative feature.

    Spectrum Sensing and Decision-Making: Agents evaluate the quality and availability of various frequency bands through autonomous spectrum sensing. Agents make decisions to minimize interference with other agents and maximize their own spectrum consumption based on this information.

    Resource Allocation and Negotiation: MAS helps agents negotiate effectively to allocate resources. Agents can bargain for spectrum access rights, adapting their plans on the fly to take advantage of shifting network circumstances.

    Dynamic Adaptation: In response to changes in the cognitive radio environment, agents in the MAS adapt dynamically. They modify their communication protocols and decision-making processes in reaction to shifts in the available spectrum or the appearance of additional network nodes.

    Learning Mechanisms: MAS frequently includes learning mechanisms that let agents adjust and get better at making decisions over time. Agents pick up knowledge through their interactions with other agents and the environment.

    Final Spectrum Allocation: The agents' joint choices and discussions produce the ultimate spectrum allocation plan. The objectives of this approach are to maximize the use of available spectrum, reduce interference, and improve overall network performance.

1.5.2 Machine Learning Approaches to Cognitive Radio Networks

Machine learning approaches in Cognitive Radio (CR) networks have revolutionized spectrum management and optimization (Bkassiny et al. 2013; Kaur and Kumar 2022). These techniques, including supervised, unsupervised learning approaches, deep learning, and reinforcement learning, empower CR systems to adapt autonomously to dynamic and diverse wireless environments. Machine learning enhances spectrum sensing accuracy, signal classification, and dynamic spectrum access, enabling CR networks to intelligently allocate resources and optimize performance. These approaches facilitate adaptive learning, allowing CR systems to continuously improve decision-making based on evolving network conditions. Moreover, machine learning contributes to interference mitigation, security enhancement, and the efficient utilization of available spectrum. By learning from data patterns and experiences, machine learning approaches in CR networks offer a versatile and effective means to address the complexities of modern wireless communication environments.

1. **Approaches of Supervised and Unsupervised Learning in CRNs**
   As illustrated in Fig. 1.3, learning can be either supervised or unsupervised (Bkassiny et al. 2013). In particular, unsupervised learning is helpful for Cognitive Radios (CRs) operating in unfamiliar radio frequencies, i.e., unlabelled types of data. In these kinds of situations, the CRs can study the environment and modify their behavior without any prior information through autonomous unsupervised learning algorithms. On the other hand, the CR can make use of supervised learning approaches if it already has knowledge about the environment, i.e., labeled type of data. For example, if the CR knows certain signal waveform characteristics beforehand, training algorithms can help it detect signals with those characteristics more effectively (Jayaweera and Christodoulou 2011; Bkassiny et al. 2012). Moreover, deep learning and metaheuristic optimization algorithms are especially useful in cognitive radio networks.
   In Dandurand and Shultz (2009), Supervised learning is defined as learning by instruction, while unsupervised learning is defined as learning by reinforcement. A third type, i.e., learning by imitation involves learning by observing the actions of similar agents. The study found that how well a learning agent performs depends on its learning method and environment. A Cognitive Radio (CR) must select the most effective learning strategy, whether it may be through instruction, reinforcement, or imitation, in order to be the best learning approach. There are certain techniques that aren't always feasible, For Example, in the absence of instructors, the CR must rely on imitation or reinforcement as a substitute for instruction. A good CR system may alternate between these techniques according to its environment, its needs, and the information at hand. How these algorithms are integrating with CRNs as follows:

   - Algorithms for machine learning (ML) are essential for improving the capabilities of CRNs, especially in the areas of decision-making and spectrum sensing. ML algorithms allow cognitive radios to analyze and understand the radio frequency (RF) environment independently in the context of spectrum sensing. These algorithms use both historical and current data to find trends, find the presence of signals, and tell occupied from vacant frequency

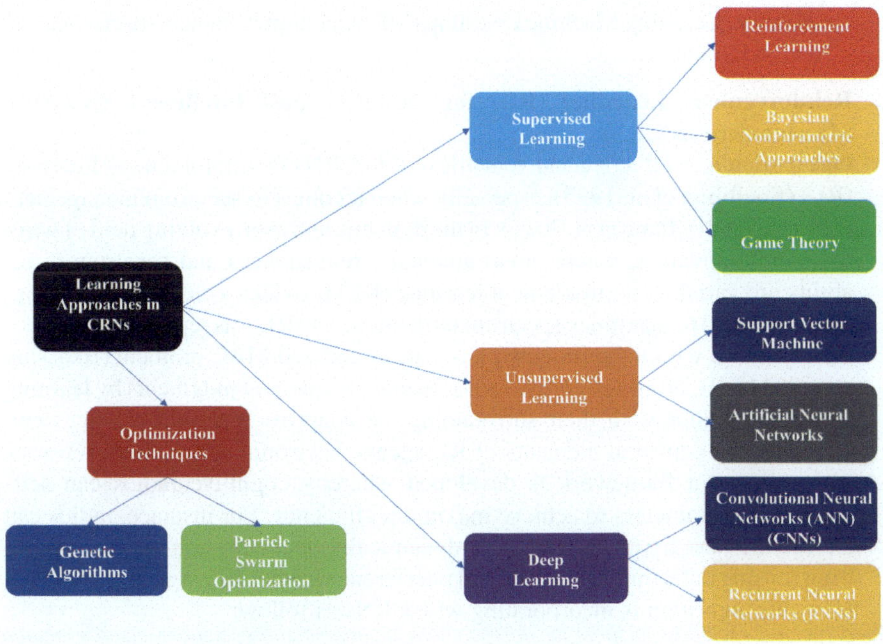

Fig. 1.3 Learning approaches to AI-driven cognitive radio networks. *Source* Author

bands. This improves spectrum sensing accuracy and makes it possible to use available spectrum resources more quickly and adaptably.

- When it comes to decision-making, machine learning (ML) techniques enable cognitive radios to make informed decisions about transmission parameters and spectrum access based on context. In dynamic and unpredictable contexts, these algorithms optimize communication tactics by learning from prior experiences and adjusting to changing RF conditions. A form of machine learning called reinforcement learning (RL) is especially important for decision-making in CRNs because it allows devices to learn the best course of action through trial and error while taking the long-term effects of their decisions into account.
- Incorporating machine learning techniques into spectrum sensing and decision-making not only improves CRNs' overall performance but also helps the network negotiate complicated and dynamic wireless environments in an autonomous and adaptive manner. In situations where traditional, static procedures might not be sufficient, this intelligent decision-making process is critical to maximizing spectrum utilization, minimizing interference, and guaranteeing dependable communication. The combination of machine learning with cognitive radio technology is anticipated to have a significant impact on how wireless communication networks develop in the future as CRNs continue to

advance. Learning Machine Learning (ML) techniques for spectrum detection and judgment.

2. **Reinforcement Learning (RL) for Adaptive and Intelligent Spectrum Management in CRNs**
   One particularly effective and versatile tool in CRNs is Reinforcement Learning (RL) (Kaelbling et al. 1995), especially when it comes to spectrum management (Yau et al. 2010; Jiang et al. 2011). In the dynamic and ever-evolving field of wireless communication, where environmental circumstances and spectrum availability are variable, reinforcement learning (RL) provides a clever and learning-driven method to maximize spectrum utilization. The RL was reported to automobile CR users within the framework of a decentralized MAC protocol (Bkassiny et al. 2011). RL allows cognitive radios to make sequential judgments by learning from interactions with their surroundings in adaptive spectrum management. Using the fundamental elements of RL agents, environments, actions, rewards, and policies, a framework is developed whereby cognitive radios can self-adapt their parameters to achieve maximum efficiency. For instance, radios can choose the best frequency channels dynamically depending on real-time spectrum sensing data, traffic patterns, and interference levels utilizing RL algorithms. How this algorithm is incorporating with CRNs as follow:

   - The capacity of RL to change with time is one of its advantages. The RL algorithm improves its decision-making policy as cognitive radios make decisions and get feedback in the form of incentives or penalties, which eventually results in more sensible conclusions. This flexibility is essential in the field of spectrum management to meet the difficulties brought on by the ever-changing radio frequency (RF) environment.
   - Furthermore, RL makes intelligent spectrum allocation and sharing schemes possible. Under the guidance of RL algorithms, cognitive radios learn to maximize their use of spectrum by considering how their actions affect the overall functioning of the network. This results in better quality of service for secondary users, less interference with prime users, and more effective use of the frequencies that are available. CRNs can provide improved performance, increased reliability, and increased overall efficiency in using the available spectrum resources by employing RL for adaptive and intelligent spectrum management (Jiang et al. 2011). By helping CRNs to function in a self-aware and self-optimizing manner, this technique complies with the fundamental goals of CRNs and advances the development of more robust and adaptable wireless communication systems.

3. **Deep Learning (DL) Techniques for Pattern Recognition and Signal Processing in CRNs**
   In the field of Cognitive Radio (CR) networks, deep learning (DL) techniques have become more popular because they provide sophisticated answers to a range of problems related to spectrum management and optimization (Bhatti et al. 2021; Hlophe 2020). The DL is a kind of machine learning that uses multi-layered neural

networks to extract complex patterns and features from data automatically. The following are some points to utilizing DL methods CRNs:

Spectrum Sensing: Deep learning methods are excellent in spectrum sensing because they use neural networks to identify intricate patterns and signals in the radio frequency spectrum. Dynamic spectrum access and more precise and effective frequency band identification are made possible by this (Shawel et al. 2018; Goyal et al. 2021).

Signal Classification: DL models can be used to classify signals, allowing for the distinction of various signal kinds, modulation schemes, and interference sources. This makes it easier for the cognitive radio to adjust intelligently to a variety of dynamic communication settings.

Dynamic Spectrum Access: By learning from past data and real-time feedback, deep learning (DL) enables intelligent decision-making for dynamic spectrum access. To maximize spectrum utilization and reduce interference, neural networks can adaptively modify transmission parameters, including power levels and channel assignments.

Interference Mitigation: The mitigation of interference is facilitated by the application of DL techniques, which learn and recognize interference patterns. This makes it possible for CR networks to dynamically modify their operations to lessen the effects of interference and provide more dependable and effective communication.

Resource Allocation: By figuring out the best ways to divide up resources, including transmission power and bandwidth, among rival users or devices, DL models help with resource allocation. This enhances the performance whole network.

Cognitive Radio Policy Optimization: DL approaches can be used to understand the correlations between different environmental parameters and the efficacy of different policy configurations, which can be used to optimize cognitive radio policies. This adaptive technique enhances the cognitive radio's ability to make decisions.

Adaptive Learning: Cognitive radios can participate in adaptive learning through DL, which helps them get better at what they do over time. This is especially helpful in ever-changing and dynamic communication contexts where experience is key to learning.

Security and Anomaly Detection: Deep learning methods improve CRN security by learning normal behavior patterns and detecting anomalies or malicious actions. This makes the infrastructure for spectrum management more resilient and safer.

Applying DL approaches to cognitive radio networks results in intelligent and adaptable solutions that lead to better interference management, more effective use of the available spectrum, and increased network performance. The combination of DL with cognitive radio technology is a promising development for managing the complexity of dynamic and heterogeneous wireless environments. The following are the main points to the utilization of DL in CRN environments.

- Deep Learning (DL) methods are essential for improving CRN performance, particularly in signal processing and pattern recognition applications. These methods, which are frequently used using multilayer neural networks, have shown impressive results in identifying complicated patterns and drawing insightful conclusions from large amounts of data, which makes them ideal for the dynamic and data-rich settings of CRNs.
- A key component of cognitive radios, spectrum sensing, is improved in the setting of CRNs by the application of DL approaches. By efficiently identifying minute patterns in the received signals, DL algorithms make it possible to identify accessible and occupied frequency bands with greater accuracy and dependability. Deep neural networks' capacity to automatically extract hierarchical characteristics from unprocessed input data enhances signal identification and categorization in.
- Moreover, cognitive radios can now carry out sophisticated signal processing tasks like interference mitigation and modulation recognition thanks to DL techniques. Deep neural networks can generalize their knowledge to recognize and adapt to different signal types and environmental conditions by training on a variety of datasets. This flexibility is especially useful in CRNs because of the dynamic and diverse RF environment there.
- Convolutional neural networks (CNNs) and recurrent neural networks (RNNs) are two examples of deep learning models that are particularly good at capturing temporal and spatial correlations in signal data. While RNNs work well for processing sequential data and are therefore appropriate for time-varying spectrum circumstances, CNNs are best suited for jobs like spectrum picture analysis.
- The incorporation of deep learning techniques into CRNs enhances the overall intelligence and adaptability of the network while also improving the accuracy of signal processing jobs. Leveraging deep learning (DL) for pattern recognition and signal processing guarantees that cognitive radios can successfully negotiate the intricacies of the contemporary wireless environment, leading to more effective spectrum utilization and improved communication performance as CRNs continue to develop.

1.6 Applications of CRNs and AI-Driven CRNs in Sectors of Smart World

1.6.1 Application of the Cognitive Radio Networks

Cognitive radio networks have many applications in various domains due to their ability to access and efficiently utilize available spectrum resources dynamically. Some major applications (Wang and Liu 2011; Iii 2000) are as follows:

- **Wireless Communication Systems**: Cognitive radio networks enable better spectrum utilization in traditional wireless communication systems such as Wi-Fi, cellular networks, and Bluetooth, leading to better data transmission rates and efficient spectrum utilization. These networks prove to be very useful in high-speed networks like 4G and 5G and so on. It also enables unmanned aerial vehicles (UAVs), V2X, IoT, satellite communications and wireless sensor network (WSN), and underwater wireless sensor network (UWSN) (Prateek et al. 2022) types of wireless systems.
- **Public Safety and Emergency Communication**: Cognitive radio networks are crucially used for strengthening homeland security and public safety in times of emergency or disaster. These networks efficiently use available spectrum bands, ensuring uninterrupted and reliable connectivity for emergency responders. As such, a natural disaster or terrorist attack could strike, destroying existing communications infrastructure and making emergency networks indispensable for search and rescue operations. Hence, in such a situation, cognitive radios can rapidly recognize spectrum availability and reconfigure themselves. Thereby providing more efficient communications and dynamic spectrum selectivity for public safety personnel. This allows reliable broadband communications and reduces information delays critical to rescue efforts. Additionally, cognitive radios facilitate interoperability between different communication systems by adapting to different network requirements and conditions. Voice, data, video, and other services can all be supported by the CR devices by means of their ability to adjust to the specifications and conditions of another network.
- **Military Communications**: Cognitive radio technology provides the Military with adaptive and secure communications capabilities in changing environments and diverse spectrums. Military communications systems often face certain limitations due to spectrum constraints, where fixed frequency assignments result in underutilization of bandwidth. Cognitive radio, through dynamic spectrum access, allocates and flexibly accesses spectrum efficiently. By doing so, it reduces spectrum congestion and maximizes the utilization of idle spectrum. Consequently, cognitive radio offers the Military a flexible, seamless, and safe communications environment.
- **Rural and Remote Connectivity**: In remote or rural areas, cognitive radio technology is a vital link to enhancing connectivity by taking advantage of available spectrum resources more efficiently. These areas often face the challenges of limited or inadequate communication services due to geographic isolation or infrastructure constraints. The adaptive nature and spectrum awareness capabilities of cognitive radio enable it to make the most of the available spectrum, thereby reducing communication gaps in these areas.
- **Agricultural Systems**: Smart farming techniques can be facilitated by cognitive radio technology, making it useful in agricultural situations. In order to improve crop yields and farming efficiency, it makes communication between diverse agricultural devices and sensors. This helps with data gathering, analysis, and automated decision-making.

- **Healthcare Systems**: Cognitive radio networks have the potential to facilitate a wide range of applications in the healthcare industry, including safe and dependable data transfer for wireless patient monitoring systems, medical imaging, and device-to-device communication.

1.6.2 Application of the AI-Driven CRNs

AI-driven CRNs can improve communication efficiency, flexibility, and dependability, which has the potential to completely transform several industries. To implement AI-driven CRNs in various industries, security, privacy, and regulatory compliance issues must be resolved. Still, there is a lot of interest in this field and continuous research because of the possible advantages in terms of efficiency, dependability, and creativity. AI-driven CRNs are being used in various industries and sectors as follows:

In Telecommunications: The following are the ways of the application of AI-driven CRNs in the telecommunication sector.

- **Dynamic Spectrum Access (DSA)**: AI-driven CRNs can optimize spectrum allocation dynamically, by allowing for efficient use of available frequencies. This enhances spectrum utilization, reduces interference, and improves overall communication quality.
- **Network Optimization**: AI algorithms can continuously analyze network conditions and adjust parameters like power, modulation, and coding schemes in real-time scenarios to optimize the network performance and energy consumption.

In Smart Cities: The following are the points to the application of the AI-driven CRNs in Smart Cities.

- **Intelligent Traffic Management**: AI-driven CRNs can facilitate dynamic traffic signal control, adaptive traffic routing, and real-time updates for better traffic management in smart cities.
- **Environmental Monitoring**: CRNs equipped with AI can be used for collecting and analyzing data from various sensors to monitor environmental parameters, such as air quality and noise levels.

In Healthcare Sector: The following are the points to the application of the AI-driven CRNs in healthcare sector.

- **Wireless Health Monitoring**: CRNs can enable the creation of wearable devices and sensors that continuously monitor health of patients at opportunistic ISM bands. AI can analyze the data in real-time, by alerting healthcare providers to potential issues and improving remote patient monitoring.
- **Emergency Response Systems**: AI-driven CRNs can enhance communication during emergencies by dynamically allocating resources and optimizing communication channels for first responders.

In Manufacturing Sector: The following are the points to the application of the AI-driven CRNs in Manufacturing Sector:

- **Industrial IoT (IIoT)**: CRNs can support the connectivity of numerous devices in smart industries, by allowing for real-time monitoring and control. AI can analyze the data generated by these devices to improve production efficiency, predict equipment failures, and optimize the processes.
- **Supply Chain Optimization**: AI-driven CRNs can optimize communication between different points in the supply chain, also providing real-time information on inventory levels, demand forecasting, and logistics.

In Agriculture Sector: The following are the points to the application of the AI-driven CRNs in Agriculture Sector:

- Precision Farming: CRNs can enable the deployment of IoT devices and sensors in agriculture for monitoring soil conditions, weather patterns, and crop health. AI algorithms can analyze this data to provide insights for precision farming, optimizing resource usage, and increasing crop yields.

In Energy Sector: The following are the points to the application of the AI-driven CRNs in Energy Sector:

- **Smart Grids:** AI-driven CRNs can enhance communication within smart grids. It also allows for better control and management of energy distribution. This includes optimizing energy consumption, predicting equipment failures, and improving grid reliability.

In Military and Defense Sector: The following are the points to the application of the AI-driven CRNs in Military and Defense Sector

- Dynamic Spectrum Allocation for Tactical Communications: AI-driven CRNs can be employed in Military and Defense Sector to dynamically allocate spectrum resources for tactical communications, ensuring security and reliable communication in dynamic environments.

In Education Sector: The following are the points to the application of the AI-driven CRNs in Education Sector.

- **Smart Classrooms**: CRNs can support the development of smart classrooms by enabling efficient communication between devices, such as interactive whiteboards, tablets, and other educational tools. AI can enhance the learning experience by analyzing data and adapting content to individual student needs.

1.7 Challenges and Solutions of AI-Driven CRNs

AI-Driven CRNs provide several advantages but they also have various challenges. Thus, the following are some of the main challenges and possible solution:

1. **Spectrum Scarcity and Efficiency**:
   - **Challenge**: The increasing demand for modern wireless communications and the limited availability of spectrum resources is a significant challenge.
   - **Solution**: Dynamic spectrum access (DSA) enabled by AI can optimize spectrum utilization by identifying and dynamically allocating unused frequencies. Cognitive radios can optimize their parameters in real-time, avoid interference, and make efficient use of the available spectrum.
2. **Regulatory Challenges**:
   - **Challenge**: Existing regulatory frameworks are often designed for static spectrum allocation. Thus, it becomes challenging to accommodate AI-powered CRNs due to their dynamic and flexible nature.
   - **Solution**: Collaboration among regulatory organizations, industry stakeholders, and researchers is crucial. Regulations should change to accommodate more adaptable spectrum access in light of developments in cognitive radio and artificial intelligence. Innovative licensing schemes and pilot programs can be utilized to investigate novel regulatory strategies.
3. **Interference Management**:
   - **Challenge**: Dynamic spectrum sharing leads to the possibility of interference between users and services, which may affect the quality of communications.
   - **Solution**: AI algorithms can be designed to predict and mitigate the interference by dynamically adjusting the parameters of transmission. Machine learning models can analyze the interference patterns and optimize spectrum access to minimize interference.
4. **Security Concerns**:
   - **Challenge**: Dynamic spectrum access gives rise to new security challenges, including unauthorized access and malicious activities.
   - **Solution**: Strong security mechanisms should be implemented, including authentication, encryption, and intrusion detection systems. AI-powered technologies can continuously monitor the network for anomalies, optimize security protocols, and even detect and respond to security threats in real-time.
5. **Privacy Protection**:
   - **Challenge**: If AI-powered CRN involves the collection and analysis of sensitive information. In such a situation, privacy concerns increase.
   - **Solution**: This requires designing privacy-preserving algorithms that will limit the display of personal information. Implement encryption and anonymization techniques to protect user privacy. The regulatory framework should also address privacy considerations associated with dynamic spectrum access.

6. **Cognitive Radio Hardware Limitations**:
   - **Challenge**: The development of affordable and efficient cognitive radio hardware with the necessary processing capabilities may be challenging.
   - **Solution**: Continued advancements in hardware technologies, such as Software-Defined Radios (SDRs), will be crucial. Research and development efforts should focus on creating cost-effective, energy-efficient, and programmable hardware to support AI-driven CRNs.
7. **Learning and Adaptation**:
   - **Challenge**: AI models in CRNs need to continuously learn and adapt to dynamic network conditions and user behaviors.
   - **Solution**: There is a need to develop adaptive machine learning algorithms that can quickly respond to changes in the network environment. This may involve reinforcement learning approaches where the system learns from its interactions and adjusts its behavior accordingly.
8. **Public Perception and Acceptance**:
   - **Challenge**: The public may be skeptical or concerned about the deployment of AI-driven CRNs, fearing potential negative impacts.
   - **Solution**: There is a need to promote public awareness and education about the benefits of AI-driven CRNs, address concerns transparently, and involve the public in decision-making processes. Hence, building trust through open communication is crucial for widespread acceptance.
9. **Resource Management**:
   - **Challenge**: Efficiently managing resources, such as power and computation, is crucial for the successful operation of AI-driven CRNs.
   - **Solution**: There is a need to Implement resource optimization algorithms that balance the trade-off between performance and resource consumption. This includes adaptive power control, dynamic modulation schemes, and energy-efficient communication protocols.

Addressing these challenges requires a multidisciplinary approach involving collaboration between researchers, industry stakeholders, and regulatory bodies. It is hoped that ongoing research, pilot projects, and iterative improvements will contribute to the successful deployment of AI-powered CRNs while minimizing the associated challenges.

1.8 Future Trends AI-Driven CRNs and Anticipated Impacts on Industries and Sectors

AI-powered cognitive radio networks (CRNs) are set to transform industries by optimizing spectrum utilization and communications efficiency. These networks, empowered by artificial intelligence, will manage resources dynamically, improving connectivity and performance. Sectors such as telecommunications, healthcare, and manufacturing will benefit, driving innovation in areas such as smart cities and IoT applications. As technology continues to advance, AI-driven CRNs are likely to see several future trends that will shape their evolution. Here are some anticipated trends in the next decade:

1. **Enhanced Machine Learning Models**:
    - **Trend**: There are continued advancements in machine learning models specifically designed for CRNs, incorporating deep learning, reinforcement learning, and federated learning techniques.
    - **Impact**: As a result, it will Improve spectrum sensing, decision-making, and adaptation to dynamic network conditions leading to more efficient spectrum utilization.
2. **Exponential Growth in IoT Integration**:
    - **Trend**: Increased integration of CRNs with the Internet of Things (IoT), leading to a massive growth in the number of connected devices.
    - **Impact**: CRNs will play a crucial role in managing the spectrum for diverse IoT applications, including smart cities, industrial IoT, and healthcare.
3. **Quantum Computing for CRNs**:
    - **Trend**: Exploring the potential of quantum computing to solve complex optimization problems associated with spectrum allocation in CRNs.
    - **Impact**: Quantum computing could significantly enhance the efficiency of spectrum allocation, leading to faster and more optimal solutions.
4. **Expedited Deployment of 6G Networks**:
    - **Trend**: Accelerated development and deployment of 6G networks, incorporating AI-driven CRNs as a fundamental component.
    - **Impact**: 6G networks will leverage AI for dynamic spectrum management, improved user experiences, and support for emerging applications such as holographic communication and immersive AR/VR.
5. **Blockchain for Spectrum Sharing**:
    - **Trend**: Increased use of blockchain technology to facilitate secure and decentralized spectrum sharing among users and devices.
    - **Impact**: Enhanced trust, transparency, and reliability in spectrum allocation, addressing security and privacy concerns.

6. **Edge AI in CRNs**:
   - **Trend**: Integration of edge computing with AI in CRNs to enable real-time decision-making at the network edge.
   - **Impact**: Lower latency, improved energy efficiency, and support for applications that require instant response times, such as autonomous vehicles and critical IoT.
7. **Experiments with Neuromorphic Computing**:
   - **Trend**: Exploration of neuromorphic computing architectures for CRNs to mimic the human brain's ability to process information.
   - **Impact**: Neuromorphic computing could bring about more energy-efficient and adaptive cognitive radio systems.
8. **AI-Driven Spectrum Forecasting**:
   - **Trend**: Development of AI algorithms for accurate spectrum forecasting, predicting future spectrum availability based on historical data and environmental conditions.
   - **Impact**: Improved planning and resource allocation, leading to better network performance and reliability.
9. **Collaborative AI in Multi-operator Environments**:
   - **Trend**: Implementation of collaborative AI models that allow multiple operators to share intelligence for improved spectrum management.
   - **Impact**: Enhanced cooperation among different network operators, leading to more efficient use of spectrum resources in multi-operator environments.
10. **Energy-Efficient CRNs**:
    - **Trend**: Integration of AI for optimizing energy consumption in CRNs, considering the increasing demand for sustainability.
    - **Impact**: Reduced energy consumption, longer battery life for devices, and a smaller environmental footprint.
11. **Regulatory Evolution for AI-Driven CRNs**:
    - **Trend**: Evolving regulatory frameworks to address the unique challenges and opportunities presented by AI-driven CRNs.
    - **Impact**: Regulatory support that will foster innovation, ensure fair spectrum access, and also address security and privacy concerns.
12. **Cross-Domain Applications and Vertical Industries**:
    - **Trend**: Expansion of AI-driven CRNs into diverse industries, including healthcare, transportation, agriculture, and education.
    - **Impact**: Solutions customized to specific industry requirements will lead to innovation and efficiency across sectors.

Trends point to a future in which artificial intelligence (AI)-powered CRNs will be key in transforming wireless communications and bringing greater intelligence, flexibility, and efficiency across a wide range of applications and sectors. It is anticipated that as these technologies advance, they will have a revolutionary impact on our interconnected world.

1.9 Conclusion

In conclusion, the integration of Artificial Intelligence (AI) into Cognitive Radio Networks (CRNs) represents a paradigm shift in wireless communications technology. The combination of cognitive radio with machine learning and AI technologies has propelled CRN into a new phase, despite the challenges faced in dynamic and real-time scenarios. This chapter explores the revolutionary potential of AI-powered CRNs, emphasizing their role in guiding various sectors towards a completely smart world. The benefits discussed in this chapter include efficient resource allocation, secure communications, and real-time data analysis. Which contribute to sustainability, productivity, and safety in industries such as manufacturing, transportation, healthcare, and agriculture. The use of machine learning and AI algorithms, such as deep learning and reinforcement learning, enables CRNs to autonomously sense, learn, and adapt to dynamic spectrum conditions, optimizing spectrum utilization and network performance. The chapter acknowledges the persistent challenges and outlines future research directions in the dynamic field of AI-powered cognitive radio networks. Additionally, this chapter provides a structured outline of the interrelationships between AI, CRN, and their transformative impact on various industries. Incorporating future trends ensures that the content is both informative and forward-looking.

References

Abbas N, Nasser Y, El Ahmad K (2015) Recent advances on artificial intelligence and learning techniques in cognitive radio networks. Eurasip J Wirel Commun Netw 2015(1):1–20. https://doi.org/10.1186/S13638-015-0381-7/TABLES/1

Akyildiz IF, Lee WY, Vuran MC, Mohanty S (2006) NeXt generation/dynamic spectrum access/cognitive radio wireless networks: a survey. Comput Netw 50(13):2127–2159. https://doi.org/10.1016/j.comnet.2006.05.001

Baykasoğlu A, Özbakır L, Tapkan P, Baykasoğlu A, Özbakır L, Tapkan P (2007) Artificial bee colony algorithm and its application to generalized assignment problem. Swarm Intell Focus Ant Part Swarm Optim. https://doi.org/10.5772/5101

Bello Salau H, Musa Aibinu A, Onwuka L, Onumanyi AJ (2015) Applications of artificial intelligence techniques in cognitive radios: a survey. [Online]. https://www.researchgate.net/publication/307935017. Accessed 26 Jan 2024

Bhatti FA, Khan MJ, Selim A, Paisana F (2021) Shared spectrum monitoring using deep learning. IEEE Trans Cogn Commun Netw 7(4):1171–1185. https://doi.org/10.1109/TCCN.2021.3071149

Bianchi G (2000) Performance analysis of the IEEE 802.11 distributed coordination function. IEEE J Sel Areas Commun 18(3):535–547. https://doi.org/10.1109/49.840210

Bkassiny M, Jayaweera SK, Avery KA (2011) Distributed reinforcement learning based MAC protocols for autonomous cognitive secondary users. In: WOCC 2011—annual wireless and optical communications conference. https://doi.org/10.1109/WOCC.2011.5872298

Bkassiny M, Jayaweera SK, Li Y, Avery KA (2012) Wideband spectrum sensing and non-parametric signal classification for autonomous self-learning cognitive radios. IEEE Trans Wirel Commun 11(7):2596–2605. https://doi.org/10.1109/TWC.2012.051512.111504

Bkassiny M, Li Y, Jayaweera SK (2013) A survey on machine-learning techniques in cognitive radios. IEEE Commun Surv Tutor 15(3):1136–1159. https://doi.org/10.1109/SURV.2012.100412.00017

Dandurand F, Shultz TR (2009) Connectionist models of reinforcement, imitation, and instruction in learning to solve complex problems. IEEE Trans Auton Ment Dev 1(2):110–121. https://doi.org/10.1109/TAMD.2009.2031234

Dappuri B, Venkatesh TG (2018) Design and performance analysis of cognitive WLAN MAC protocol. IEEE Syst J 12(3):2261–2272. https://doi.org/10.1109/JSYST.2017.2749267

El Morabit Y, Mrabti F, Abarkan EH (2019) Survey of artificial intelligence approaches in cognitive radio networks. J Inf Commun Converg Eng 17(1):21–40. https://doi.org/10.6109/JICCE.2019.17.1.21

Gavrilovska L, Atanasovski V, Macaluso I, Dasilva LA (2013) Learning and reasoning in cognitive radio networks. IEEE Commun Surv Tutor 15(4):1761–1777. https://doi.org/10.1109/SURV.2013.030713.00113

Glover F (1986) Future paths for integer programming and links to artificial intelligence. Comput Oper Res 13(5):533–549. https://doi.org/10.1016/0305-0548(86)90048-1

Goyal SB, Bedi P, Kumar J, Varadarajan V (2021) Deep learning application for sensing available spectrum for cognitive radio: an ECRNN approach. Peer-to-Peer Netw Appl 14(5):3235–3249. https://doi.org/10.1007/S12083-021-01169-4/TABLES/2

He A et al (2010) A survey of artificial intelligence for cognitive radios. IEEE Trans Veh Technol 59(4):1578–1592. https://doi.org/10.1109/TVT.2010.2043968

Hlophe MC (2020) A model-based deep learning approach to spectrum management in distributed cognitive radio networks. [Online]. https://repository.up.ac.za/handle/2263/75644. Accessed 27 Jan 2024

IEEE802.22-05/ 0007r46 (2006) Functional requirements for the 802.22 WRAN standard. [Online]. https://cir.nii.ac.jp/crid/1571698600937026304. Accessed 16 Oct 2023

Iii JM (2000) Cognitive radio an integrated agent architecture for software defined radio dissertation

Jain AK, Mao J, Mohiuddin KM (1996) Artificial neural networks: a tutorial. Computer (Long Beach Calif) 29(3):31–44. https://doi.org/10.1109/2.485891

Jayaweera S, Christodoulou C (2011) Radiobots: architecture, algorithms and realtime reconfigurable antenna designs for autonomous, self-learning future cognitive radios. [Online]. https://digitalrepository.unm.edu/cgi/viewcontent.cgi?article=1035&context=ece_rpts. Accessed 27 Jan 2024

Jiang T, Grace D, Mitchell PD (2011) Efficient exploration in reinforcement learning-based cognitive radio spectrum sharing. IET Commun 5(10):1309–1317. https://doi.org/10.1049/IET-COM.2010.0258

Joshi N, Jharia B (2014) Optimal fuzzy logic power control in cognitive radio a comparative study. In: IJARCCE, pp 8160–8162. https://doi.org/10.17148/IJARCCE.2014.31018

Joshi N, Jharia B (2015) Optimized fuzzy power control over fading channels in spectrum sharing cognitive radio using ANFIS. In: 2nd International conference on signal processing and integrated networks, SPIN 2015, pp 329–333. https://doi.org/10.1109/SPIN.2015.7095404

Joshi N, Sharma SC (2023) Switching algorithm in listen-and-talk-based MAC protocols for full-duplex cognitive radio networks with type 2 fuzzy cooperative spectrum sensing. J Supercomput 0123456789. https://doi.org/10.1007/s11227-023-05477-9

Joshi N, Kumar A, Minenkov D, Kaplun D, Sharma SC (2023) Optimized MAC protocol using fuzzy-based framework for cognitive radio adhoc networks. IEEE Access 11(January):27506–27518. https://doi.org/10.1109/ACCESS.2023.3256890

Kaelbling LP, Littman ML, Moore AW (1995) An introduction to reinforcement learning. Biol Technol Intell Auton Agents 90–127. https://doi.org/10.1007/978-3-642-79629-6_5

Kaur A, Kumar K (2022) A comprehensive survey on machine learning approaches for dynamic spectrum access in cognitive radio networks. J Exp Theor Artif Intell 34(1):1–40. https://doi.org/10.1080/0952813X.2020.1818291

Kennedy J, Eberhart R (1995) Particle swarm optimization. In: Proceedings of the IEEE International Conference on Neural Networks (ICNN'95), vol 4, pp 1942–1948. https://doi.org/10.1109/ICNN.1995.488968

Kirkpatrick S, Gelatt CD, Vecchi MP (1983) Optimization by simulated annealing. Science (80–)220(4598):671–680. https://doi.org/10.1126/SCIENCE.220.4598.671

Panigrahi BK et al (2011) Parallel bacterial foraging optimization, pp 487–502. https://doi.org/10.1007/978-3-642-17390-5_21

Prateek T, Reddy S, Chandra S, Arya R, Verma AK (2022) Malicious anchor node extraction using geodesic search for survivable underwater wireless sensor network. Sci Rep 12(1):1–11. https://doi.org/10.1038/s41598-022-17956-9

Qadir J (2015) Artificial intelligence based cognitive routing for cognitive radio networks. Artif Intell Rev 45(1):25–96. https://doi.org/10.1007/S10462-015-9438-6

Rasheed T, Rashdi A, Akhtar AN (2018) Cooperative spectrum sensing using fuzzy logic for cognitive radio network. In: 2018 Advances in science and engineering technology international conferences (ASET 2018), pp 1–6, Jun 2018. https://doi.org/10.1109/ICASET.2018.8376914

Riahi Manesh M, Kaabouch N (2018) Security threats and countermeasures of MAC layer in cognitive radio networks. Ad Hoc Networks 70:85–102. https://doi.org/10.1016/J.ADHOC.2017.11.003

Sani M, Tsado J, Thomas S, Suleiman H, Shehu IM, Shanuna MG (2021) A survey on spectrum sensing techniques for cognitive radio networks. In: 2021 1st International conference on multi-disciplinary engineering and applied science, ICMEAS 2021. https://doi.org/10.1109/ICMEAS52683.2021.9692412

Shah MA, Zhang S, Maple C (2012) A novel multi-fold security framework for cognitive radio wireless ad-hoc networks. In: ICAC 12—proceedings of the 18th international conference on automation and computing: integration of design and engineering, no September, pp 31–36

Shah MA, Zhang S, Maple C (2013) An analysis on decentralized adaptive MAC protocols for cognitive radio networks. Int J Autom Comput 10(1):46–52. https://doi.org/10.1007/s11633-013-0695-z

Shawel BS, Hailemariam Woledegebre D, Pollin S (2018) Deep-learning based cooperative spectrum prediction for cognitive networks. In: 9th International conference on information and communication technology convergence: ICT convergence powered by smart intelligence, ICTC 2018, pp 133–137, Nov 2018. https://doi.org/10.1109/ICTC.2018.8539570.

Sultana A, Fernando X, Zhao L (2017) An overview of medium access control strategies for opportunistic spectrum access in cognitive radio networks. Peer-to-Peer Netw Appl 10(5):1113–1141. https://doi.org/10.1007/s12083-016-0465-0

van der Hoek W, Wooldridge M (2008) Chapter 24 Multi-agent systems. Found Artif Intell 3:887–928. https://doi.org/10.1016/S1574-6526(07)03024-6

Wang B, Liu KJR (2011) Advances in cognitive radio networks: a survey. IEEE J Sel Top Signal Process 5(1):5–23. https://doi.org/10.1109/JSTSP.2010.2093210

Wang B, Wu Y, Liu KJR (2010) Game theory for cognitive radio networks: an overview. Comput Netw 54(14):2537–2561. https://doi.org/10.1016/J.COMNET.2010.04.004

Wang D, Song B, Chen D, Du X (2019) Intelligent cognitive radio in 5G: AI-based hierarchical cognitive cellular networks. IEEE Wirel Commun 26(3):54–61. https://doi.org/10.1109/MWC.2019.1800353

Yao C (2021) Hearing loss classification via stationary wavelet entropy and cat swarm optimization. Cogn Syst Signal Process Image Process 203–221. https://doi.org/10.1016/B978-0-12-824410-4.00014-3

Yau K et al (2010) Applications of reinforcement learning to cognitive radio networks. In: 2010 IEEE International conference on communications workshops. [Online]. https://ieeexplore.ieee.org/abstract/document/5503970/. Accessed 27 Jan 2024

Yücek T, Arslan H (2009) A survey of spectrum sensing algorithms for cognitive radio applications. IEEE Commun Surv Tutor 11(1):116–130. https://doi.org/10.1109/SURV.2009.090109

Chapter 2
Beyond the Code: Bridging Ethical and Practical Gaps in Data Privacy for AI-Enhanced Healthcare Systems

Ankit Gambhir, Neha Jain, Medhavi Pandey, and Simran

Abstract Artificial Intelligence (AI) has the potential to revolutionize healthcare in the current digital environment by providing hitherto unheard-of gains in patient care, operational efficiency, and predictive analytics. Big data connected to health is expanding along with AI's role in healthcare, which presents both immense potential and equally intimidating obstacles in terms of data protection, security, and ethical use. This thorough study attempts to find a balance between protecting patient data and improving AI applications by navigating the intricate interactions between these urgent concerns. The study closely examines the current frameworks, laws, and regulations governing data privacy and security in AI-driven healthcare applications. It does this by drawing on thorough literature reviews, real-world case analyses, expert interviews, and data breach occurrences. To comprehend the importance of big data and machine learning in healthcare, we look at how these technologies are affecting all facets of contemporary life. For example, AI can provide personalized medication, predict epidemics, and enhance the delivery of healthcare services, much like how Netflix customizes content and Amazon maximizes commerce. These advantages, meanwhile, depend on sensitive data being handled securely and morally. Our research reveals a substantial disconnect between current policy frameworks and practical implementations, highlighting the necessity of a reliable, standardized model that can satisfy the competing demands of data privacy and utility. It is anticipated that the study would provide insightful information to legislators, medical professionals, and AI developers, strengthening the AI-enhanced healthcare

---

A. Gambhir (✉) · N. Jain · Simran
Delhi Technical Campus, Greater Noida, India
e-mail: er.ankit.gambhir@gmail.com

N. Jain
e-mail: nehajain312@gmail.com

Simran
e-mail: siimran.2504@gmail.com

M. Pandey
Galgotias College of Engineering and Technology, Greater Noida, India
e-mail: medhaviipandey@gmail.com

R. Arya et al. (eds.), *Recent Trends in Artificial Intelligence Towards a Smart World*,
Frontiers of Artificial Intelligence, Ethics and Multidisciplinary Applications,
https://doi.org/10.1007/978-981-97-6790-8_2

ecosystem and making it safer and more effective. Our goal is to provide a roadmap for future research that will prioritize data privacy and security while harmonizing the integration of AI in healthcare through this comprehensive examination.

Keywords Artificial Intelligence (AI) in healthcare · Data privacy and security · Predictive analytics · Ethical AI applications · Medical imaging and AI · Federated learning · Patient data protection

2.1 Introduction

The advent of Artificial Intelligence (AI) in healthcare marks a paradigm shift promising transformative changes across multiple facets of the industry (Nolan 2024). This evolution is embedded within a broader global narrative, where the convergence of digitization and globalization is reshaping the worldwide financial landscape, presenting opportunities for the development of new business models. Businesses embracing digitalization can rapidly expand their operations into foreign markets, a phenomenon that has captured significant attention in recent years as per (Williamson and Prybutok 2024; Bekbolatova et al. 2024).

The potential of AI to revolutionize medicine is prominently witnessed in the domain of medical imaging, where the application of computer vision techniques, traditional machine learning, and deep neural networks have led to remarkable advancements (Tran et al. 2020). The driving force behind such progress can be largely ascribed to the release of large, curated corpora of images such as ImageNet, fostering performant pre-trained algorithms that facilitate transfer learning.

However, these advancements also bring forth a series of questions and challenges extending beyond the scope of mere technical implementation. Among these, the ethical considerations surrounding data privacy and security have emerged as critical issues requiring immediate attention (Khan et al. 2024). The exponential growth of health-related big data provides unprecedented opportunities for enhancing patient care, optimizing hospital operations, and enabling robust medical research. Yet, this data deluge also poses severe risks, the most pressing of which is the potential for privacy invasion and unauthorized data access (Mamede and Santos 2024; McCarthy et al. 2021).

Historically, healthcare data was confined to paper records and locked away in secure cabinets. The transition to Electronic Medical Records (EMRs) and other digital repositories has dramatically shifted this landscape. These digital repositories now hold vast amounts of sensitive data, making them attractive targets for cybercriminals (Hunkenschroer and Luetge 2022).

Moreover, AI algorithms require extensive datasets for training and validation. The need for even larger amounts of imaging and clinical data for precision medicine implementations accentuates the challenge (Dai and Abràmoff 2023). Large cross-sectional population studies like the UK Biobank, even though based on volunteer participation, fall short in bridging this data gap. The primary reason being the lack of standardized, electronic patient records, especially in underprivileged regions where the cost of electronic data management is a significant barrier.

The digital transformation, often referred to as the 4.0 industrial revolution, has not only affected the way organizations operate but has also expanded the horizons of the healthcare sector, integrating comprehensive, equitable, and integrated models to facilitate transformative changes aimed at progressive improvement and prioritizing individual needs.

The study makes the case that worries about privacy go beyond personal anxieties and incorporate wider societal standards, especially the trust that underpins doctor–patient relationships. We explore the intricacies of electronic health records, informed permission, and the conversion of personal patient data into anonymous research data, providing tactics to avoid unintentional disclosures of private health information. Furthermore, the study underscores the latest technology developments in encryption and anonymization as possible means of maintaining data security.

In addition, we provide a comprehensive overview of state-of-the-art and upcoming approaches to safe, federated, and privacy-preserving AI, with a special emphasis on applications in medical imaging. A thorough discussion is held regarding three strategic frameworks for ethical data sharing and three steps up the methodological ladder to improve privacy protection. Figure 2.1 shows applications of AI in Healthcare.

2.2 The Pivotal Role of Patient Data

In the evolving landscape of healthcare, patient data has emerged as an invaluable asset, serving as the essential fuel that powers Artificial Intelligence (AI) applications. This data plays a multifaceted role, acting as the cornerstone upon which machine learning models are built, refined, and ultimately put into practice. The adage that "an AI system is only as good as the data it learns from" holds particular resonance in healthcare, where the stakes are exceptionally high (Holley and Becker 2021).

The type of patient data utilized in healthcare AI is incredibly diverse, spanning a broad spectrum that includes but is not limited to diagnostic images like X-rays and MRIs, comprehensive medical histories, genomic sequences, biometric data, and even information pertaining to lifestyle choices such as diet and physical activity (Panayides et al. 2020). Each category of data serves a specific purpose, contributing unique insights that enhance the model's accuracy and reliability.

The digital technologies in healthcare create a profound effect on how health services are being delivered and how the entire health service operates. The latest technologies such as blockchain, cloud, and artificial intelligence (AI) and machine learning tools help the healthcare sector to identify and evaluate large volumes of patient data (Wang 2024). By 2025, the digital health market is projected to reach 38 billion (Ganapathy 2023), underlining the eagerness of the healthcare sector in implementing digital technologies in healthcare practices. These technologies, including Mobile health (mHealth), health informatics, telehealth, and electronic

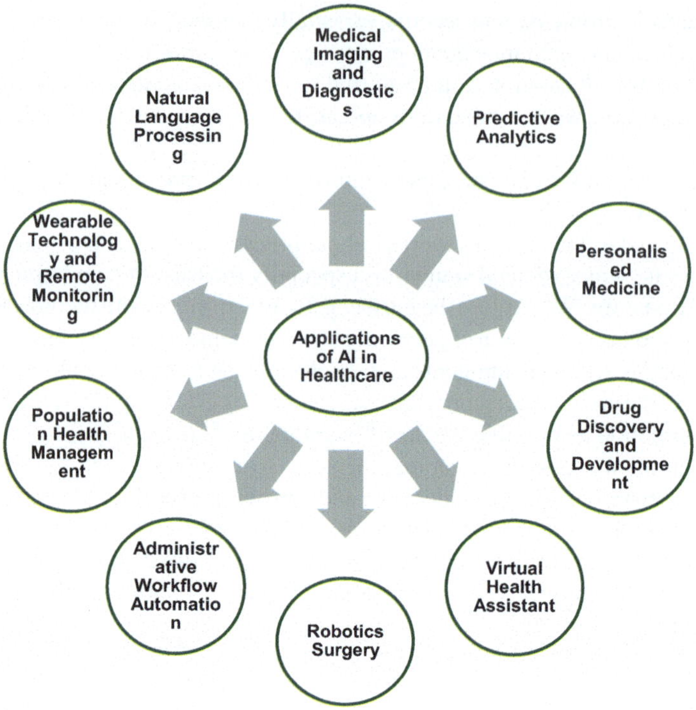

Fig. 2.1 Applications of AI in healthcare. *Source* Author

health (eHealth), facilitate the collection, analysis, and generation of significant insights to augment patient care.

2.3 Background

The healthcare sector has seen a burgeoning interest in the integration of Artificial Intelligence (AI) over recent years, with a particular focus on Machine Learning (ML) and Natural Language Processing (NLP). These AI technologies have shown promise in improving patient care, diagnostic accuracy, and operational efficiencies by harnessing the power of data. The vast amounts of clinical data generated from medical procedures such as screenings, diagnostics, and treatment tasks form the bedrock of AI's potential in healthcare (Singh et al. 2024). Figure 2.2 reflects Artificial Intelligence (AI) in Healthcare Market Size.

1. AI Technologies
    a. Machine Learning (ML): ML algorithms are known for evaluating structured data like imaging, genomics, and electronic patient (EP) data. They have been

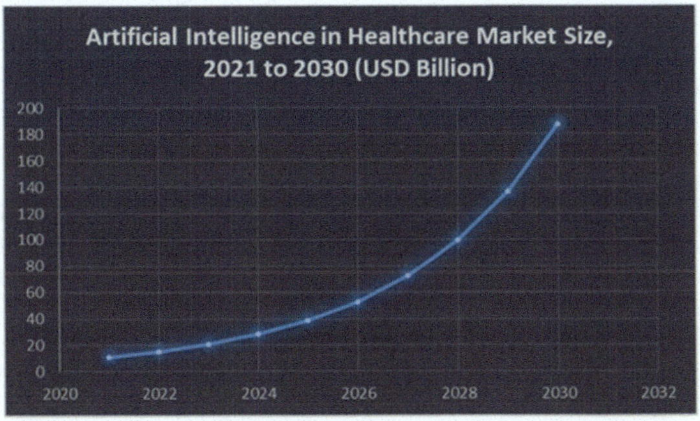

Fig. 2.2 Artificial Intelligence in healthcare market size. *Source* Precedence research Artificial Intelligence in healthcare market size, report 2022–2030. https://www.precedenceresearch.com/artificial-intelligence-in-healthcare-market

instrumental in creating predictive models for disease prognosis and treatment optimization (Dwivedi et al. 2024; Habbal et al. 2024).

b. Natural Language Processing (NLP): NLP is pivotal in extracting valuable insights from unstructured data sources like clinical notes and medical literature. It enhances the organization and accessibility of medical data, facilitating more informed clinical decisions (Just 2024).
c. AI Applications in Disease Diagnosis and Treatment: The bulk of AI research in healthcare has been oriented towards three major disease types: cancer, nervous system disease, and cardiovascular disease, largely owing to their high mortality rates. AI has notably enhanced imaging, genomics, electronic medical record (EMR), and electrophysiology (EP) research techniques, which are critical in the early diagnosis and treatment of these diseases (Sufyan et al. 2023; Bai et al. 2024).

2. **Hardware and Software Innovations**
The evolution of hardware platforms like CPUs, GPUs, FPGAs, and ASICs has catalyzed the efficient implementation of complex neural network algorithms. Simultaneously, software advancements have led to the development of deeper neural networks capable of sophisticated learning and analysis. The convergence of hardware and software innovations has significantly accelerated AI research and its application in healthcare.
3. **AI in Assisted Living and Rehabilitation**
The amalgamation of AI technologies with intelligent robotic systems has ushered in a new era of assisted living. Innovations such as man–machine interfaces have empowered disabled individuals with enhanced mobility, while fall-recognition systems are pivotal in ensuring the safety of the elderly (Ekambaram and Ponnusamy 2024).

4. **Data Privacy Concerns**
   The exponential growth in data, essential for training sophisticated AI algorithms, has concurrently exacerbated data privacy concerns. Acquiring requisite data while adhering to stringent privacy laws poses a significant challenge in advancing AI in healthcare (Habbal et al. 2024).
5. **Economic Aspects and Investment**
   The healthcare industry and investors are channeling substantial resources into AI research and implementation. The economic implications alongside the necessity for rigorous validation of AI effectiveness are paramount considerations for stakeholders (Iyke 2024).
6. **Progressive Trends in AI Healthcare Research**
   A surge in publications over the last decade, particularly post-2012, denotes a burgeoning interest and investment in healthcare-related AI research. The key technology keywords discerned from this surge include "Machine Learning", "Electronic Health Records", and "Natural Language Processing", indicative of the primary focus areas within the AI healthcare domain (Shah and Mishra 2024). Figure 2.2 represents artificial intelligence in healthcare market size based on the Report 2022–2030 published by precedence research.

2.4 Types of Healthcare Data

Medical records are just one type of healthcare data generated by our complex medical systems. Researchers with the Centers for Disease Control and Prevention (CDC) estimate that over 883.7 million office-based physician visits take place annually in the United States. According to the National Center for Health Statistics within the CDC, over 85% of office-based physicians use electronic medical record systems.

Below is an expanded discussion on the various categories of healthcare data mentioned, along with some additional insights:

1. Medical Records: These are comprehensive documents that encapsulate patients' medical histories, diagnoses, treatment plans, and outcomes. They're integral for ensuring continuity of care, supporting medical decisions, and are a requisite for insurance claims. With the advent of technology, Electronic Medical Records (EMRs) have become predominant, enabling easier sharing and management of medical information.
2. Dental Records: Much like medical records, dental records chronicle a patient's dental history. They contain diagnostic information, treatments administered, and ongoing dental care plans. These records are crucial for ensuring proper dental care and can also be pivotal in legal scenarios, like identity verification in forensic cases.
3. Surgical Records: These documents are an exhaustive record of surgical procedures a patient undergoes. They encompass preoperative diagnoses, details of the surgery itself (e.g., surgical team, techniques employed, duration of surgery),

and post-operative care instructions. Surgical records are vital for evaluating the outcomes of surgical interventions and for legal compliance.

4. Behavioral Data: This pertains to data regarding a patient's lifestyle choices and behaviors that may impact their health, such as diet, exercise habits, and substance use. Collecting behavioral data can be instrumental in devising personalized care plans and in preventive healthcare.
5. Biometrics: Biometric data includes physiological and behavioral measurements such as blood pressure, heart rate, and other vital signs. These metrics are crucial for monitoring a patient's health status over time and for detecting potential medical conditions early.
6. Living Conditions: Information regarding a patient's living environment and social determinants of health (e.g., socioeconomic status, education, neighborhood and physical environment, employment, social support networks) is also a significant part of healthcare data. Understanding a patient's living conditions can provide a holistic view of their health and can be utilized to tailor care plans effectively.

2.5 Evolution to Digital Health Records

The transition from paper to digital records marks a significant stride in healthcare data management. Initially, medical records were confined to handwritten notes or typed reports, with results from medical examinations stored in paper file systems. This practice dates back to ancient times, with the oldest case reports found on papyrus texts from Egypt around 1600 BC. Stanley Reiser's description of clinical case records as narratives where patients, families, and doctors are characters in the plot highlights the storytelling aspect of traditional medical record-keeping.

The digital revolution commenced with the advent of computer systems, transitioning the healthcare sector towards Electronic Health Records (EHRs) and Electronic Medical Records (EMRs). In 2003, the term "electronic health records" was endorsed by the Institute of Medicine, a division of the National Academies of Sciences, Engineering, and Medicine, to signify records aimed at enhancing healthcare for the benefit of both patients and clinicians. EHRs are defined by Murphy, Hanken, and Waters as computerized medical records for patients that encompass past, present, or future physical/mental health information residing in electronic systems designed for healthcare delivery and related services (Nashwan et al. 2023; Adnan et al. 2023).

Advancement and Initiatives

The "All of Us" initiative by the National Institutes of Health (NIH) stands as a testament to the growing importance and application of digital health records. This initiative aims to amass data from one million or more individuals, encompassing EHRs, medical imaging, socio-behavioral, and environmental data. The objective is to create a diverse database to fuel research and foster a new era of health science which is personalized, proactive, patient-driven, and preventive (Kucirkova and Leaton Gray 2023).

Digitization of Healthcare and Big Data

The trajectory of healthcare has been significantly altered with the advent of digital technologies, marking a shift from traditional paper-based systems to electronic platforms. This metamorphosis catalyzed the emergence of big data, which in the healthcare milieu, encapsulates a vast spectrum of data including Electronic Health Records (EHRs), Electronic Medical Records (EMRs), personal health records (PHRs), medical practice management software (MPM), and more. These digital platforms have profoundly impacted the quality, efficiency, and cost management in healthcare, also paving the way for more personalized patient care (Meenakshi et al.).

The inception of EHRs, especially, marked a significant milestone in healthcare digitization. Initially, the adoption of EHRs was gradual, but post-2009, it saw a substantial surge. This digital transition has also been bolstered by various governmental initiatives, promoting a shift towards more organized, accessible, and analyzable healthcare data. The underpinning objective is to enhance patient care, reduce medical errors, and foster preventive medicine.

Moreover, the integration of the Internet of Things (IoT) in healthcare has birthed a smart web of interconnected devices capable of real-time monitoring and data collection. Wearable devices, monitoring systems, and other IoT-enabled healthcare devices are generating an enormous amount of data, which when analyzed, holds the promise of improving health outcomes and controlling costs.

Benefits of Digital Health Records

Transitioning to EHRs and EMRs brings forth a plethora of advantages. For healthcare professionals, having immediate access to a patient's complete medical history expedites the recognition and treatment of medical conditions by reducing the time lag associated with obtaining previous test results. This has led to a noticeable decrease in redundant examinations, lost orders, and ambiguities caused by illegible handwriting, thus promoting better care coordination among multiple healthcare providers. The digitization of healthcare records has also proven instrumental in reducing medication errors, enhancing care continuity, and facilitating communication between healthcare providers and patients (Chidambaram et al. 2024).

Furthermore, EHRs have significantly streamlined administrative processes. They enable faster data retrieval, facilitate reporting of key healthcare quality indicators, and improve public health surveillance by enabling immediate reporting of disease outbreaks. By reducing paperwork, EHRs expedite electronic authorization and insurance approvals, thus diminishing delays and confusion in billing and claims management. The amalgamation of EHRs and the internet has democratized access to critical health-related information, making it readily available to millions of individuals.

Healthcare as a Big Data Repository

Healthcare is indeed a rich reservoir of data owing to its multidimensional structure encompassing health professionals, facilities, and financial institutions. The data generated spans across various health sectors like dentistry, medicine, midwifery, nursing, psychology, and physiotherapy, each holding a treasure trove of patient information.

The evolution from paper-based to digital records has not only streamlined healthcare operations but also has made healthcare a significant contributor to the big data paradigm. This data, when properly harnessed, can provide invaluable insights into patient care, disease patterns, and healthcare management, thereby improving the overall healthcare ecosystem.

Big Data in Healthcare

The healthcare domain is a rich repository of big data, courtesy of the myriad data components it encompasses. These include healthcare payer–provider data, genomics-driven experiments, and data garnered from the IoT. The initial adoption of EHRs was slow, but post-2009, it witnessed substantial growth. The burgeoning reliance on information technology for managing and utilizing healthcare data is palpable. The advent of wellness monitoring devices and related software capable of generating alerts and sharing patient health data with healthcare providers is a stepping stone towards establishing real-time biomedical and health monitoring systems. These innovations are generating a vast amount of data ripe for analysis to provide real-time clinical or medical care.

Nature of the Big Data in Healthcare

Electronic Health Records (EHRs) hold the potential to drive advanced analytics and fortify clinical decision-making by offering a vast expanse of data. However, a significant portion of this data currently exists in an unstructured form. Unstructured data refers to information that doesn't conform to a specific model or organizational framework, making its analysis more challenging. The preference for this format may arise from the flexibility it offers in recording data across diverse formats. Additionally, structured input alternatives like drop-down menus, radio buttons, and checkboxes often prove inadequate for capturing intricate data. For instance, capturing nuanced data concerning a patient's clinical suspicions, socioeconomic status, lifestyle choices, and other pertinent information necessitates an unstructured format. Grouping such diverse yet crucial data into a coherent or unified format for subsequent algorithmic analysis aimed at enhancing patient care proves to be a daunting task. Despite these challenges, it's imperative for the healthcare sector to harness the wealth of insights embedded in these data streams to elevate patient care, streamline management, and reduce treatment costs. Although the promise of big data in revolutionizing healthcare is profound, the journey towards fully actualizing these benefits and gleaning meaningful insights is still underway. Achieving these objectives demands a methodical approach to managing and analyzing big data within the healthcare landscape.

Big Data in Biomedical Research

Biomedical research has always been data-centric, but with the onset of modern technologies like Next-Generation Sequencing (NGS) and Genome-Wide Association Studies (GWAS), the volume, velocity, and variety of data being generated have skyrocketed. The high-resolution data obtained from these technologies is enabling a deeper understanding of complex biological systems.

Analyzing this colossal amount of data can unveil novel insights into disease mechanisms, drug discovery, and personalized medicine. The continuous influx of publications regarding big data in healthcare underscores the burgeoning interest and the myriad possibilities that big data holds in biomedical research.

Big Data from Omics Studies

The Omics revolution, characterized by genomics, transcriptomics, proteomics, and metabolomics, has further enriched the big data repository. Especially the advancements in NGS have drastically reduced the costs while exponentially increasing the volume of genomic data generated.

With the cost of whole genome sequencing plummeting, an estimated 100 million–2 billion human genomes could be sequenced by 2025. This deluge of genomic data, coupled with other omics data, is propelling the healthcare sector towards "individual, personalized, or precision healthcare." Analyzing omics data in conjunction with traditional healthcare data can significantly enhance treatment strategies, thus inching closer to the vision of personalized medicine (Ahmadi 2024).

The amalgamation of omics data with healthcare analytics heralds a new era in medicine. Although the integration of genomic data poses challenges due to its complexity and the myriad variables involved, the potential benefits are monumental. Commercial organizations are already leveraging human genome data to assist healthcare providers in making personalized medical decisions, indicating a promising trajectory towards a future where medicine and healthcare are tailored to individual genetic makeup.

The Approaching Horizon of Big Data in AI

The management and insightful analysis of healthcare big data are predicated on the continuous evolution of information technology. The potential to improve the quality, service efficiency, and cost-effectiveness of healthcare while minimizing medical errors is immense. As healthcare systems globally continue to embrace digital transformation, the promise of big data in ushering a new epoch of personalized medicine and improved health outcomes is on the horizon.

2.6 Challenges in AI for Healthcare Systems

The infusion of Artificial Intelligence (AI) into healthcare systems is reshaping patient care, administrative processes, and health outcomes. However, as AI becomes more pervasive, challenges centered on data privacy, ethical considerations, and practical implications become increasingly prominent. This section offers an in-depth analysis of these challenges, emphasizing the pressing need to address both ethical and practical gaps (Ajani et al. 2024). Table 2.1 presents summary of primarily challenges in AI for Healthcare Systems.

2.6.1 Data Privacy and Security

Ethical Concerns

1. Patient Autonomy: Every patient has the right to control who has access to their personal health information. AI systems, by their nature, aggregate and analyze vast amounts of data, often without explicit patient consent. This raises questions about patient autonomy and the right to privacy.
2. Informed Consent: When patients provide their data to healthcare providers, they often do so with the understanding that it will be used for their care. However, AI systems might utilize this data for research, analytics, or other purposes. Ensuring patients understand and consent to these uses is ethically paramount.

Practical Concerns

1. Data Aggregation Risks: As AI systems necessitate vast datasets to function optimally, data from various sources is often aggregated. This consolidation can inadvertently expose sensitive patient information, leading to potential misuse.
2. Interoperability Issues: Modern healthcare systems emphasize interoperability to ensure seamless patient care. However, this interconnectedness can sometimes result in unintended data sharing, posing significant privacy risks (Wang et al. 2024).

2.6.2 Bias and Fairness Ethical

Concerns

1. Representation: An AI system is only as good as the data it's trained on. If the training data lacks representation from certain demographics, the AI system can inadvertently marginalize these groups, leading to suboptimal or even harmful care.
2. Equity in Care: All patients, regardless of their background, deserve equitable healthcare. Biased AI systems can perpetuate existing healthcare disparities, undermining the fundamental principle of fairness in medical care.

Table 2.1 Challenges in AI for healthcare systems

Challenge	Description
Data privacy and security concerns	The sensitive nature of healthcare data raises concerns about privacy and security. Ensuring that patient information is adequately protected from unauthorized access or cyber threats is crucial. Striking a balance between utilizing data for AI applications and safeguarding patient confidentiality remains a complex challenge
Data standardization and interoperability	Healthcare data often resides in diverse formats and across various systems. The lack of standardized data formats and interoperability challenges hinder seamless integration of AI solutions across different healthcare platforms. Establishing universal standards for data representation and exchange is essential to enhance the effectiveness of AI applications and facilitate collaboration among healthcare systems
Ethical and regulatory compliance	Ethical considerations surrounding AI in healthcare, such as bias in algorithms, transparency, and accountability, pose significant challenges. Additionally, navigating complex regulatory frameworks and ensuring compliance with evolving healthcare laws is crucial. Establishing ethical guidelines, transparent practices, and comprehensive regulatory frameworks is essential for the responsible deployment of AI in healthcare
Integration with existing workflows	Incorporating AI seamlessly into existing healthcare workflows without causing disruption is a significant challenge. Resistance to change, workflow adaptations, and ensuring that AI systems complement human decision-making rather than hinder it are critical considerations. Striking a balance between the benefits of AI and the existing healthcare processes is essential for successful integration
Lack of standardization in AI models	The absence of standardized models and approaches in AI for healthcare complicates comparison, validation, and replication of results. Achieving consensus on best practices, model interpretability, and benchmarking standards is vital for building trust in AI applications and facilitating collaboration across healthcare institutions
Limited explainability of AI models	Many AI models, particularly deep learning algorithms, often function as "black boxes", making it challenging to explain their decisions. In healthcare, where interpretability is crucial for gaining trust from healthcare professionals and patients, addressing the lack of explainability remains a significant challenge. Developing interpretable AI models is essential for wider acceptance and adoption
Data quality and bias in AI algorithms	Biases present in healthcare data can be inadvertently perpetuated by AI algorithms, leading to disparities in diagnosis and treatment. Ensuring the quality and representativeness of training data, actively mitigating biases, and continually monitoring and refining AI models are essential to prevent the reinforcement of existing healthcare disparities. Addressing bias is critical for achieving fair and equitable healthcare outcomes

(continued)

Table 2.1 (continued)

Challenge	Description
Costs and resource allocation	Implementing AI solutions in healthcare requires significant financial investments, both in technology and staff training. Resource constraints, particularly in smaller healthcare facilities, can pose challenges in adopting and maintaining advanced AI systems. Balancing the costs with the potential benefits and ensuring equitable access to AI-driven technologies are crucial considerations for sustainable implementation
User acceptance and training	Healthcare professionals may face challenges in adapting to new AI technologies, impacting their acceptance and effective utilization. Providing comprehensive training programs, addressing user concerns, and actively involving healthcare professionals in the development and implementation processes are essential to fostering a positive attitude toward AI adoption within healthcare systems
Scalability and generalization	Developing AI solutions that are scalable and applicable across diverse healthcare settings is a challenge. AI models trained on data from specific populations or healthcare environments may not generalize well to others. Achieving scalability and generalization requires robust model architectures and continuous refinement to ensure effectiveness across diverse patient demographics and healthcare scenarios

Source Author

Practical Concerns

1. Dataset Limitations: Crafting a well-balanced and representative dataset is challenging. Often, data from marginalized groups is underrepresented, leading to biased AI models.
2. Transparency Challenges: The intricate architectures of certain AI models, especially deep learning models, make them opaque. This "black box" nature complicates the task of identifying and rectifying biases.

2.6.3 Reliability and Accountability

Ethical Concerns

1. Patient Safety: AI systems, when integrated into patient care, must be reliable. A misdiagnosis or inappropriate treatment recommendation can have dire consequences. Ensuring patient safety is thus an ethical imperative (Grzybowski et al. 2024).
2. Accountability: In case of errors or malfunctions, establishing accountability becomes crucial. Is the onus on the developers of the AI model, the healthcare providers, or the institutions using the technology?

Practical Concerns

1. Continuous Validation: AI models, especially in healthcare, require rigorous and continuous validation to ensure their reliability. As medical knowledge and patient profiles evolve, AI systems must adapt accordingly.
2. Regulatory Challenges: The dynamic landscape of AI necessitates robust regulatory frameworks. Crafting regulations that ensure patient safety without stifling innovation is a practical challenge that policymakers grapple with.

2.7 AI in Diagnostic Imaging: Transforming Radiology with Deep Learning

2.7.1 Introduction to AI in Diagnostic Imaging

The integration of Artificial Intelligence (AI) in diagnostic imaging, particularly in radiology, has marked a significant advancement in medical diagnostics. AI, especially deep learning algorithms, has shown remarkable proficiency in interpreting medical images, aiding radiologists in early and accurate disease detection.

2.7.2 The Role of AI in Radiology

Radiology has always been at the forefront of adopting new technologies. The use of AI in radiology primarily revolves around analyzing medical images, such as X-rays, CT scans, and MRIs, with greater precision and speed than traditional methods. This section explores a specific case where AI has been instrumental in diagnosing pulmonary diseases (Li et al. 2018).

2.7.3 Advanced Applications of AI in Radiology

1. Detection Diseases: AI systems are increasingly used to detect a range of conditions from cancerous tumors in oncology to neurological disorders in brain imaging.
2. Predictive Analysis: Some AI algorithms are capable of predicting the likelihood of disease progression or the risk of future medical conditions based on imaging data.
3. Personalized Treatment Planning: By analyzing imaging data, AI can assist in creating personalized treatment plans, considering the specific characteristics of a patient's condition.

2.7.4 Integration of AI in Radiological Workflows

1. Collaborative Models: AI systems are being integrated into radiological workflows as supportive tools, assisting radiologists in making more informed decisions.
2. Training and Adaptation: The successful integration of AI in radiology requires training radiologists to work alongside AI tools, understanding their capabilities, and interpreting their outputs effectively (Wenderott et al. 2024).

2.7.5 Addressing Challenges in AI-Driven Radiology

1. Data Quality and Diversity: Ensuring high-quality, diverse datasets for training AI models is crucial for their accuracy and reliability. This includes addressing potential biases in the data.
2. Regulatory and Ethical Concerns: Regulatory frameworks are evolving to address the ethical implications and ensure the responsible use of AI in radiology, focusing on patient safety and data privacy (Abbas).

2.8 Case Study: AI-Powered Detection of Pulmonary Diseases

1. Context: Pulmonary diseases, including lung cancer and tuberculosis, are among the leading causes of death worldwide. Early detection is crucial for successful treatment, yet it remains challenging due to the subtlety of early signs on scans.
2. AI Implementation: A leading hospital integrated a deep learning-based AI system to assist radiologists in detecting abnormal patterns in lung imaging. The system was trained on thousands of annotated images to identify various pulmonary conditions.
3. Technology Overview: The AI system utilized convolutional neural networks (CNNs), a class of deep learning algorithms particularly effective in analyzing visual imagery. These CNNs were trained to recognize patterns associated with specific pulmonary conditions (Gabrani et al. 2024).

Outcomes and Achievements

1. Enhanced Accuracy: The AI system demonstrated a significantly higher accuracy rate in detecting early-stage lung cancer and tuberculosis, compared to traditional diagnostic methods.
2. Reduced Diagnostic Time: The time taken to diagnose a patient is reduced considerably, enabling quicker decision-making for treatment plans.
3. Support to Radiologists: The AI system served as a second opinion, reducing the likelihood of misdiagnosis and overlooked anomalies.

Challenges and Solutions

1. Data Privacy and Security: Ensuring the confidentiality and security of patient data was a major concern. The hospital addressed this by implementing robust data encryption and access control measures.
2. Integration with Existing Systems: Seamlessly integrating the AI system with existing hospital infrastructure was challenging. This was overcome by customizing the AI application to be compatible with the hospital's existing digital systems.

2.9 Introduction to AI in Patient Monitoring

The realm of patient monitoring, a critical aspect of healthcare, is witnessing a significant transformation with the integration of Artificial Intelligence (AI). This paradigm shift is marked by the introduction of AI-driven technologies that enhance patient care through continuous, real-time monitoring and data analysis. This section delves into the role of AI in revolutionizing patient monitoring, particularly for chronic conditions and critical care settings (Feinstein et al. 2050). Table 2.2 shows the role of Artificial Intelligence (AI) in Modern Patient Monitoring.

AI's Role in Modern Patient Monitoring

Table 2.2 AI's role in modern patient monitoring

Aspect	Description
Patient monitoring contextualization	Traditionally, monitoring involves observing vital signs, but AI transforms this by using advanced algorithms to interpret and analyze large amounts of patient data in real time
Real-time insights empowerment	AI in patient monitoring offers healthcare professionals immediate insights into a patient's health. Through machine learning, it detects deviations from normal patterns, enabling early identification of potential health issues and prompt interventions
Continuous and remote monitoring	AI enables continuous and remote monitoring through wearable devices equipped with algorithms. This extends patient monitoring beyond traditional healthcare settings, enhancing comfort and enabling effective management of chronic conditions
Predictive analytics for prevention	AI's analytical capabilities predict health risks and identify patterns preceding adverse events. Predictive analytics assists in tailoring preventive care strategies, intervening before conditions worsen, thereby improving overall healthcare efficiency
Ethical considerations and data security	Integrating AI in patient monitoring prompts ethical considerations. Ensuring patient privacy, informed consent, and secure handling of health data are critical. A delicate balance between AI benefits and patient rights is essential for responsible deployment (Sood et al. 2024)

Source Author

1. Continuous and Real-Time Data Analysis: AI systems in patient monitoring are capable of analyzing vast streams of real-time data from various monitoring devices. This includes vital signs, ECG, blood glucose levels, and more, allowing for more nuanced and responsive patient care.
2. Predictive Analytics for Early Intervention: One of the key advantages of AI in patient monitoring is its ability to utilize predictive analytics. These systems can forecast potential health events or deterioration, enabling healthcare providers to intervene proactively, often before the patient or healthcare staff are aware of the emerging risk (Habbal et al. 2024).

Transforming Chronic Disease Management

1. Personalized Care Plans: For chronic diseases like diabetes, heart disease, and asthma, AI-enhanced monitoring systems can tailor care plans to individual patient needs based on their unique health data (Arkhipova-Jenkins and Rajupet 2024).
2. Improved Patient Engagement: These systems often come with user-friendly interfaces that encourage patients to actively engage in their health management, leading to better outcomes (Chen et al. 2024).

Enhancing Intensive Care Monitoring

1. Critical Care Applications: In ICUs, where patients require constant and meticulous monitoring, AI systems play a vital role in detecting subtle changes in a patient's condition, enabling timely interventions.
2. Data Integration and Analysis: AI in ICU settings can integrate data from various sources, providing a comprehensive picture of the patient's condition, which is crucial for making critical care decisions.

Overcoming Challenges in AI-Enhanced Monitoring

1. Data Privacy and Security: As with any healthcare technology that handles sensitive patient data, ensuring privacy and security is paramount. AI systems in patient monitoring must adhere to strict data protection protocols (SaberiKamarposhti 2024).
2. Interoperability with Healthcare Systems: Effective patient monitoring requires AI systems to seamlessly integrate with existing healthcare infrastructure. This interoperability is essential for the smooth functioning and utility of AI in patient monitoring (Kumari et al. 2024).

2.10 Case Study: AI for Enhanced Patient Monitoring and Care

1. Context: Diabetes management requires continuous monitoring and adjustment of treatment plans. AI can play a pivotal role in personalizing care for diabetic patients (Susnjak and Griffin 2024).

2. AI Implementation: A renowned clinic introduced an AI-powered system to assist in diabetes management. The system used machine learning algorithms to analyze patient data, including blood sugar levels, dietary intake, and lifestyle factors.
3. Technology Overview: The AI system employed predictive analytics to forecast blood sugar level fluctuations and provided recommendations for insulin dosage adjustments (Damre et al. 2024).

Outcomes and Achievements

1. Personalized Treatment Plans: The AI system enabled the creation of highly personalized treatment plans, improving patient adherence and satisfaction.
2. Proactive Health Management: Predictive insights allowed for early intervention, preventing severe blood sugar spikes or drops.
3. Efficiency in Healthcare Delivery: The system reduced the workload on healthcare professionals by automating routine monitoring tasks.

Challenges and Solutions

1. Data Accuracy and Reliability: Ensuring the accuracy of patient-provided data was crucial. The clinic introduced user-friendly mobile applications for easier and more accurate data entry.
2. Patient Privacy Concerns: The clinic ensured compliance with health data privacy regulations like HIPAA to protect patient information.

2.11 Introduction to AI in Drug Discovery

The field of drug discovery and pharmaceutical research is undergoing a revolutionary change with the integration of Artificial Intelligence (AI). This transformative shift is marked by AI's ability to drastically reduce the time and cost associated with the development of new drugs and therapies. In this section, we explore how AI is redefining the landscape of pharmaceutical research, from identifying potential drug candidates to predicting their efficacy and safety profiles (Singh et al. 2024). Figure 2.3 shows AI in drug discovery market size by component based upon the report published by market.us in Oct 2023 (Report ID: 99396).

2.11.1 AI's Impact on the Drug Discovery Process

1 Accelerating Compound Identification: AI algorithms, particularly those in machine learning and deep learning, are adept at analyzing complex biochemical data. They can rapidly identify compounds that may have therapeutic potential, a process that traditionally takes years.

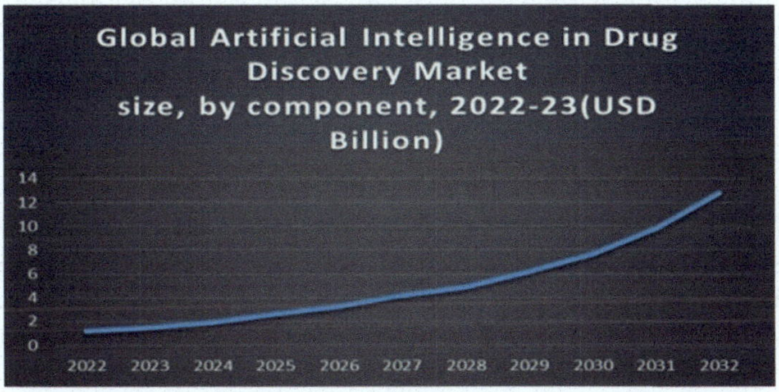

Fig. 2.3 AI in drug discovery market size by component. *Source* Artificial Intelligence in drug discovery market published date: Oct 2023. https://market.us/report/artificial-intelligence-in-drug-discovery-market/

2. Enhancing Predictive Modeling: AI's predictive modeling capabilities allow for the simulation of drug interactions and effects, helping researchers assess a drug's potential success before costly and time-consuming clinical trials.
3. Data-Driven Insights: With access to vast databases of medical and biological research, AI systems can uncover insights and connections that might be missed by traditional research methods, leading to novel therapeutic approaches (Hasselgren and Oprea 2024).

2.11.2 *The Role of AI in Personalized Medicine*

1. Targeted Therapy Development: AI's ability to analyze genetic, environmental, and lifestyle data is instrumental in the development of personalized medicine. It enables the creation of targeted therapies that are tailored to individual patient profiles, increasing the efficacy and reducing the side effects of treatments.
2. Molecular Characterization and Biomarker Identification: AI tools are being used to identify biomarkers and understand molecular characteristics of diseases, which is crucial for developing targeted therapies.

2.11.3 *Overcoming Challenges in Drug Discovery with AI*

1. Streamlining Clinical Trials: AI can help in designing more efficient clinical trials, predicting patient response to drugs, and identifying suitable candidates for trials. This not only accelerates the drug development process but also improves the likelihood of successful outcomes.
2. Addressing Data Quality and Ethical Concerns: Ensuring the quality and integrity of data used in AI-driven drug discovery is essential. Ethical considerations, such

as patient consent and data privacy, are also at the forefront of AI applications in this field (Hofmann et al. 2024).

2.11.4 AI Collaborations in Pharma

1. Partnerships Between Tech and Pharma: The rise of AI in drug discovery has led to significant collaborations between technology companies and pharmaceutical firms, combining expertise in AI with deep knowledge of biology and medicine.
2. Open Innovation Models: There is a growing trend towards open innovation in drug discovery, where AI-driven insights are shared across the industry to accelerate the development of new therapies.

Table 2.3 reflects the role of AI in the pharmaceutical domain.

2.12 Case Study: Accelerating Alzheimer's Drug Discovery

1. Context: Discovering drugs for neurodegenerative diseases like Alzheimer's is notoriously slow and expensive. AI offers a promising solution to expedite this process.
2. AI Implementation: A pharmaceutical company employed AI algorithms to analyze existing medical data and research papers to identify potential drug candidates for Alzheimers.
3. Technology Overview: The AI system used natural language processing to sift through vast amounts of research data and machine learning to identify compounds with potential therapeutic effects.

Outcomes and Achievements

1. Streamlined Drug Discovery Process: The AI system identified several promising compounds in a fraction of the time typically required.
2. Increased Success Rates in Clinical Trials: Early testing of these compounds showed higher efficacy and safety profiles, leading to more successful clinical trials.
3. Cost-Effective Research: The use of AI significantly reduced the overall research and development costs.

Challenges and Solutions

1. Ensuring Scientific Rigor: The company established protocols to rigorously validate AI-generated hypotheses through traditional experimental methods.
2. Collaboration Between AI Experts and Scientists: To maximize the potential of AI, the company fostered a collaborative environment where AI experts worked closely with pharmaceutical scientists.

Table 2.3 AI's role in medicine

Aspect	Description
Drug discovery and development	AI collaborations focus on expediting drug discovery and development processes. By leveraging advanced algorithms, companies aim to identify potential drug candidates, predict their efficacy, and optimize molecular structures, reducing time and costs in the early stages of R&D
Target identification and validation	AI is employed to identify and validate therapeutic targets by analyzing vast datasets. Pharmaceutical companies collaborate with AI firms to enhance their understanding of disease mechanisms, pinpoint potential targets, and increase the success rates of subsequent drug development phases
Clinical trial optimization	AI's predictive analytics capabilities are utilized to optimize clinical trials. Collaborations aim to improve patient recruitment, identify suitable trial designs, and enhance data analysis, ultimately accelerating the clinical development timeline and increasing the chances of successful trials
Real-world data analysis	Pharmaceutical companies collaborate with AI partners to analyze real-world data, such as electronic health records and patient data. This collaboration allows for better insights into disease patterns, treatment outcomes, and potential safety issues, contributing to more informed decision-making in drug development
Personalized medicine and biomarkers	AI collaborations play a crucial role in advancing personalized medicine. By analyzing patient data, including genetic information, collaborations seek to identify biomarkers for diseases, tailor treatment approaches, and develop more targeted therapies that consider individual variations in patient responses
Drug repurposing	AI is utilized in drug repurposing efforts, aiming to identify existing drugs with potential applications for new indications. Collaborations explore AI algorithms to analyze vast datasets and make connections between drugs and diseases, uncovering opportunities for the repurposing of existing compounds
Bioprocess optimization	Collaborations focus on optimizing bioprocessing parameters in pharmaceutical manufacturing. AI is employed to enhance efficiency, reduce costs, and improve the overall yield and quality of biopharmaceutical production, contributing to a more streamlined and effective manufacturing process
AI-powered imaging and diagnostics	AI collaborations in pharmaceuticals extend to medical imaging analysis. By partnering with AI companies, pharmaceutical firms aim to enhance diagnostic accuracy, particularly in areas like medical imaging for disease detection, providing more precise and efficient tools for patient diagnosis and monitoring (Lekadir et al. 2021)

(continued)

Table 2.3 (continued)

Aspect	Description
Drug safety and pharmacovigilance	Collaboration efforts focus on improving drug safety and pharmacovigilance through AI applications. By analyzing real-world data and adverse event reports, these collaborations aim to enhance the detection of potential safety issues, ensuring a more comprehensive understanding of a drug's safety profile throughout its lifecycle
Supply chain optimization	AI collaborations address supply chain challenges within the pharmaceutical industry. By leveraging AI-driven insights, companies aim to optimize supply chain processes, reduce lead times, minimize disruptions, and ensure the efficient and timely delivery of pharmaceutical products to meet global demand

Source Author

2.13 Ethical Debates and Perspectives in AI-Enhanced Healthcare

The Ethical Complexity of AI in Healthcare

The integration of Artificial Intelligence (AI) into healthcare is not only a technological evolution but also an ethical one. AI's ability to analyze vast datasets, predict outcomes, and suggest treatments brings about profound ethical implications. This section explores the ethical terrain of AI in healthcare, addressing key concerns like data privacy, patient consent, and the balance between AI efficiency and human oversight.

Data Privacy and Security in AI Healthcare

1. Core Concerns: In an era where data is invaluable, protecting patient data in AI-enhanced healthcare systems is paramount. AI systems often use sensitive personal health information, raising concerns about data breaches, misuse, and the ethical handling of this data.
2. Debating Data Usage: Ethical debates revolve around the extent and manner of data usage. Questions arise regarding data ownership, the boundaries of permissible data use, and safeguards against misuse.
3. Diverse Perspectives: Perspectives vary widely among stakeholders. Patients generally demand stringent data protection, whereas healthcare professionals emphasize the utility of data in improving healthcare outcomes. Policymakers grapple with creating regulations that balance these interests (Khan 2024).
4. Regulatory Responses: In response to these debates, various countries have implemented data protection regulations like the GDPR in Europe, emphasizing the principles of data minimization, purpose limitation, and consent.

Patient Consent in the Age of AI

1. Informed Consent Challenges: The traditional concept of informed consent is tested in the AI context. AI systems can use patient data in ways that extend beyond the initial scope of consent, making it challenging to ensure that consent is truly informed.
2. Ethical Dilemmas and Debates: The ethical dilemma lies in how to obtain genuine informed consent when the implications of data use are not fully predictable. Debates focus on balancing the need for comprehensive data usage in AI with respecting patient autonomy.
3. Innovative Consent Models: Emerging solutions include dynamic consent models, allowing patients to have ongoing control over their data. There's also a push towards more transparent and patient-friendly consent processes, ensuring patients understand the implications of their consent (Iserson 2024).

Balancing AI Efficiency with Human Oversight

1. The AI–Human Synergy: The efficiency and analytical prowess of AI in healthcare are undeniable, yet there's a critical need to maintain human oversight. The ethical concern is to prevent over-reliance on AI at the expense of human judgment and the nuances of patient care.
2. Navigating Ethical Waters: Central to this debate is the risk of algorithmic biases, the importance of human empathy in healthcare decisions, and the role of AI as a tool rather than a replacement for healthcare professionals.
3. Achieving Equilibrium: The ethical goal is to achieve a harmonious balance where AI supplements rather than supplants human expertise. This includes establishing protocols where AI's role is clearly defined, and its limitations understood, ensuring that healthcare professionals remain at the helm of patient care decisions (Younis et al. 2024).

Ethical Navigation in AI-Enhanced Healthcare

As AI becomes increasingly embedded in healthcare, the ethical landscape becomes more complex and critical to navigate. It requires a concerted effort from technologists, healthcare professionals, ethicists, and policymakers to address these ethical challenges. The goal is to harness the benefits of AI in healthcare while upholding the highest ethical standards and safeguarding patient trust and wellbeing (Bekbolatova et al. 2024; Jaber 2024).

Future Trends and Predictions in AI-Enhanced Healthcare

The healthcare sector is undergoing a transformative shift with the integration of Artificial Intelligence (AI) and Machine Learning (ML). These technologies are not only changing existing practices but also introducing innovative approaches to healthcare delivery and management (Abbas).

Increasing AI Investment and Efficiency

1. AI Spend in Healthcare: A Deloitte study indicated that 85% of healthcare business leaders planned to increase their AI spending before 2023, signaling a significant shift towards AI-driven healthcare models.

2. Economic Impact: According to Accenture, AI applications are anticipated to save the healthcare industry $150 billion annually by 2026, highlighting the economic efficiency AI brings to the sector.
3. Data Processing and Insights: AI's ability to transform large datasets into actionable insights is particularly crucial in healthcare, facilitating early disease detection and more accurate diagnostics (Bhambri and Rani 2024).

2.14 AI's Broad Impact Across Healthcare Sectors

1. Sector-Specific Adoption: AI and ML are making substantial inroads in various sectors, including biopharma, healthcare services and technology, life sciences tools, diagnostics, and medical technology. Morgan Stanley Research noted a projected increase in AI/ML budget allocation from 5.7% in 2022 to 10.5% in 2024.
2. Opportunities and Challenges: This trend represents both opportunities and challenges as healthcare organizations strive to harness AI's potential while navigating the complexities of its integration into existing systems and workflows (Ahmadi 2024).

Table 2.4 presents Summary of AI Applications in different areas of healthcare.

AI Advancements in Biopharma

1. Drug Discovery and Development: The biopharma industry is extensively using AI/ML in drug discovery, clinical development, manufacturing, and patient engagement (Nargund et al. 2024). More than 100 drug and biologic applications to the FDA included AI/ML components in 2021, a significant increase from 14 in 2020.
2. R&D Efficiency: AI/ML technologies are expected to reduce R&D spending, shorten development timelines for drugs, and increase the probability of successful patient outcomes (Alharbi et al. 2024).

Improving Healthcare Delivery with AI

1. Enhanced Patient Care: AI/ML tools are improving the speed and accuracy of disease detection, thereby allowing healthcare providers more time for patient care.
2. Operational Benefits: AI applications are streamlining patient access, diagnostics, risk coding, claims processing, and supply-chain management, thus enhancing overall care delivery efficiency.
3. Patient-Centric Solutions: On the patient side, AI is facilitating treatment access, optimizing insurance distribution channels, and enhancing telehealth services (Srivastava et al. 2024).

Table 2.4 Summary of AI application areas in healthcare

Application	Example	Key advancements
Drug discovery and design	Target identification	AI analyzes biological data to identify potential drug targets
	Drug design	Algorithms predict molecular structures for drug candidates
Drug repurposing	Identification of existing drugs for new uses	AI analyzes datasets to find connections between drugs and diseases
Predictive analytics	Success prediction of drug candidates	Models analyze data to predict the likelihood of drug candidate success
Clinical trial optimization	Patient population selection, trial design	AI optimizes clinical trial processes and designs
Bioprocess optimization	Manufacturing efficiency	AI optimizes parameters for efficient biopharmaceutical production
Personalized medicine	Tailoring treatments based on individual data	AI analyzes patient data to customize treatment approaches
Natural language processing (NLP)	Extraction of insights from scientific literature	NLP algorithms facilitate knowledge extraction from literature
Drug safety and adverse event prediction	Safety analysis	AI predicts potential safety issues and adverse events
Image analysis in drug development	Medical imaging data analysis	AI enhances the understanding of drug effects using imaging data
Supply chain optimization	Efficient pharmaceutical supply chain	AI optimizes supply chain processes for timely drug delivery
Collaboration and data sharing	Secure data sharing among researchers	AI facilitates collaboration by enabling secure data sharing

Source Author

Advanced Diagnostics Through AI

1. Diagnostic Tools and Data Integration: AI/ML tools are at the forefront of diagnostics, combining genomic data with patient health records, medical imaging, and other data sources. This integration is vital for developing personalized medicine approaches and improving patient care. Table 2.5 presents Diagnostics through AI.
2. AI in Imaging and Disease Detection: AI is particularly effective in examining imagery from MRIs and X-rays, offering diagnoses based on image qualities indicative of specific symptoms. This capability is critical for conditions ranging from colon cancer screenings to interventional radiology (Gutruf 2024). Artificial intelligence market for Healthcare applications in world (in millions) is shown in Fig. 2.4.

Table 2.5 Diagnostics through AI

Application	Example	Key advancements
Medical imaging	Breast cancer screening	Google health's AI outperformed radiologists in 2020
Pathology and histology (Klauschen 2024)	Skin cancer diagnosis	AI performed on par with dermatologists in 2018
Genomic data analysis	Cancer research and personalized medicine	Analyzing genetic data for patterns and mutations
Predictive analytics	Identifying health risks before symptoms	AI used for early detection and risk prediction
Global market trends (Ionescu et al. 2024)	–	Predicted CAGR of over 40% from 2020 to 2027
COVID-19 diagnostics	Chest X-ray and CT scan analysis	AI applied to diagnose COVID-19 from imaging data (Suba and Muthulakshmi 2023)

Source Author

Fig. 2.4 Artificial Intelligence market for healthcare applications in the world (in millions). *Source* Frost and Sullivan 2016 transforming healthcare through artificial intelligence system

In conclusion, this chapter has examined the complicated relationship among artificial intelligence (AI), healthcare, and the growing domain of big data on health. While big data is expanding at a rapid pace and has both great opportunities and challenges, artificial intelligence (AI) is emerging as a revolutionary force that promises never-before-seen benefits in patient care, operational efficiency, and predictive analytics. The study navigated this difficult terrain by closely examining the delicate balance that must be struck in order to improve AI applications while steadfastly maintaining patient data protection.

We conducted in-depth literature reviews, real-world case analyses, expert interviews, and an investigation of data breach instances in order to analyze the present frameworks, laws, and legislation controlling data privacy and security in AI-driven healthcare systems. Examining the broader societal implications was part of the inquiry, particularly in light of the crucial trust that forms the basis of doctor–patient relationships. The study looked at informed consent procedures, electronic health records, and the transformation of private patient data into de-identified research data, emphasizing the necessity for strategies to prevent confidentiality violations.

The paper also emphasized recent advancements in anonymization and encryption technology as potential safeguards against a loss of data security. The exhaustive review of existing and next-generation technologies for federated, secure, and privacy-preserving AI, with a special focus on medical imaging applications, provided a comprehensive understanding of the expanding privacy protection mechanisms.

However, the results demonstrated the glaring disparities between present policy frameworks and their practical applications, highlighting the urgent need for a dependable, standardized method that strikes a compromise between the conflicting objectives of utility and data protection. This paper aims to provide legislators, healthcare professionals, and AI developers with meaningful information to create a safer and more effective healthcare environment enhanced by AI.

In essence, the thorough research done in this study provides a roadmap for future projects. By giving data security and privacy first priority, we expect that future research efforts will be focused on a harmonious integration of AI in healthcare, delivering on the promise of technical advancements without compromising the fundamental principles of security and privacy.

References

Abbas A. AI in healthcare: applications, challenges, and future prospects

Abbas A. Radiology's radiance: shaping the future of emergency medical imaging

Adnan HS, Bankhead C, Perera R (2023) Implementation framework for AI deployment at scale in healthcare systems. Available SSRN 4465877

Ahmadi S (2024) A comprehensive study on integration of big data and AI in financial industry and its effect on present and future opportunities. Int J Curr Sci Res Rev 7(01)

Ajani SN, Khobragade P, Dhone M, Ganguly B, Shelke N, Parati N (2024) Advancements in computing: emerging trends in computational science with next-generation computing. Int J Intell Syst Appl Eng 12(7s):546–559

Alharbi HF, Bhupathyraaj M, Mohandoss K, Chacko L, Rani KRV (2024) An overview of artificial intelligence-driven pharmaceutical functionality. Artif Intell Pharm Sci 18–36

Arkhipova-Jenkins I, Rajupet SR (2024) population medicine, population health, and population health management: strategies that meet society's health needs. AJPM Focus 3(1)

Bai L, Wu Y, Li G, Zhang W, Zhang H, Su J (2024) AI-enabled organoids: construction, analysis, and application. Bioact Mater 31:525–548

Bekbolatova M, Mayer J, Ong CW, Toma M (2024) Transformative potential of AI in healthcare: definitions, applications, and navigating the ethical landscape and public perspectives. Healthcare 12(2):125

Bhambri P, Rani S (2024) Challenges, opportunities, and the future of industrial engineering with IoT and AI. Integr AI Based Manuf Ind Eng Syst Internet Things 1–18

Chen X, Duan R, Shen Y, Jiang H (2024) Design and evaluation of an intelligent physical examination system in improving the satisfaction of patients with chronic disease. Heliyon 10(1)

Chidambaram S et al (2024) An introduction to digital determinants of health. PLOS Digit Heal 3(1):e0000346

Dai T, Abràmoff MD (2023) Incorporating artificial intelligence into healthcare workflows: models and insights. In: Tutorials in operations research: advancing the frontiers of OR/MS: from methodologies to applications, INFORMS, pp 133–155

Damre SS, Shendkar BD, Kulkarni N, Chandre PR, Deshmukh S (2024) Smart healthcare wearable device for early disease detection using machine learning. Int J Intell Syst Appl Eng 12(4s):158–166

Dwivedi YK, Pandey N, Currie W, Micu A (2024) Leveraging ChatGPT and other generative artificial intelligence (AI)-based applications in the hospitality and tourism industry: practices, challenges and research agenda. Int J Contemp Hosp Manag 36(1):1–12

Ekambaram D, Ponnusamy V (2024) Real-time AI-assisted visual exercise pose correctness during rehabilitation training for musculoskeletal disorder. J Real-Time Image Process 21(1):2

Feinstein M, Katz D, Demaria S, Hofer IS (2024) Remote monitoring and artificial intelligence: outlook for 2050. Anesth Analg 138(2):350–357

Gabrani G, Gupta S, Vyas S, Arya P (2024) Revolutionizing healthcare: impact of artificial intelligence in disease diagnosis, treatment, and patient care. In: Handbook on augmenting telehealth services. CRC Press, pp 17–31

Ganapathy K (2023) Digital health in 2030: a peep into the future. CSI Trans ICT 11(1):103–109

Grzybowski A, Jin K, Wu H (2024) Challenges of artificial intelligence in medicine and dermatology. Clin Dermatol

Gutruf P (2024) Towards a digitally connected body for holistic and continuous health insight. Commun Mater 5(1):2

Habbal A, Ali MK, Abuzaraida MA (2024) Artificial intelligence trust, risk and security management (AI TRiSM): frameworks, applications, challenges and future research directions. Expert Syst Appl 240:122442

Hasselgren C, Oprea TI (2024) Artificial intelligence for drug discovery: are we there yet? Annu Rev Pharmacol Toxicol 64

Hofmann P, Lämmermann L, Urbach N (2024) Managing artificial intelligence applications in healthcare: promoting information processing among stakeholders. Int J Inf Manag 75:102728

Holley KL, Becker S (2021) AI-first healthcare. O'Reilly Media, Inc

Hunkenschroer AL, Luetge C (2022) Ethics of AI-enabled recruiting and selection: a review and research agenda. J Bus Ethics 178(4):977–1007

Ionescu Ș, Delcea C, Chirițua N, Nica I (2024) Exploring the use of artificial intelligence in agent-based modeling applications: a bibliometric study. Algorithms 17(1):21

Iserson KV (2024) Informed consent for artificial intelligence in emergency medicine: a practical guide. Am J Emerg Med 76:225–230

Iyke BN (2024) Climate change, energy security risk, and clean energy investment. Energy Econ 129:107225

Jaber W (2024) Future directions in AI and nanotechnology. In: Artificial intelligence in the age of nanotechnology. IGI Global, pp 62–75

Just J (2024) Natural language processing for innovation search—reviewing an emerging non-human innovation intermediary. Technovation 129:102883

Khan F (2024) Regulating the revolution: a legal roadmap to optimizing AI in healthcare. Minnesota J Law Sci Technol Spring

Khan IUKU, Ouaissa M, Ouaissa M, Abou El Houda Z, Ijaz MF (2024) Cyber security for next-generation computing technologies. CRC Press

Klauschen F et al (2024) Toward explainable artificial intelligence for precision pathology. Annu Rev Pathol Mech Dis 19

Kucirkova N, Leaton Gray S (2023) Beyond personalization: embracing democratic learning within artificially intelligent systems. Educ Theory 73(4):469–489

Kumari S, Chowdhry J, Garg MC (2024) AI-enhanced adsorption modeling: challenges, applications, and bibliographic analysis. J Environ Manag 351:119968

Lekadir K, Osuala R, Gallin C, Lazrak N, Kushibar K et al (2021) FUTURE-AI: guiding principles and consensus recommendations for trustworthy artificial intelligence in future medical imaging. arXiv Prepr. arXiv:2109.09658

Li Z, Zhang X, Müller H, Zhang S (2018) Large-scale retrieval for medical image analytics: a comprehensive review. Med Image Anal 43:66–84

Mamede HS, Santos A (2024) Creating learning organizations through digital transformation. IGI Global

McCarthy N et al (2021) Enterprise imaging and big data: a review from a medical physics perspective. Phys Medica 83:206–220

Meenakshi DU et al. Big data in disease diagnosis and healthcare. In: Big data in oncology: impact, challenges, and risk assessment. River Publishers, pp 145–176

Nargund S, Mauch K, Esswein S, Niebel B, Rafigh M, Pendse P (2024) Biopharma 4.0: digital technologies driving smart manufacturing. In: Biopharmaceutical manufacturing: progress, trends and challenges. Springer, pp 319–335

Nashwan AJ et al (2023) Harnessing artificial intelligence: strategies for mental health nurses in optimizing psychiatric patient care. Iss Ment Health Nurs 44(10):1020–1034

Nolan A (2024) Artificial intelligence in science: challenges, opportunities and the future of research

Panayides AS et al (2020) AI in medical imaging informatics: current challenges and future directions. IEEE J Biomed Heal Inform 24(7):1837–1857

SaberiKamarposhti M et al (2024) A comprehensive review of AI-enhanced smart grid integration for hydrogen energy: advances, challenges, and future prospects. Int J Hydrog Energy

Shah IA, Mishra S (2024) Artificial intelligence in advancing the occupational health and safety: an encapsulation of developments. J Occup Health uiad017

Singh S, Gupta H, Sharma P, Sahi S (2024) Advances in artificial intelligence (AI)-assisted approaches in drug screening. Artif Intell Chem 2(1):100039

Sood K, Grima S, Sharma G, Balusamy B (2024) The application of emerging technology and blockchain in the insurance industry. CRC Press

Srivastava M, Siddiqui AT, Srivastava V (2024) Application of artificial intelligence of medical things in remote healthcare delivery. In: Handbook of security and privacy of AI-enabled healthcare systems and internet of medical things. CRC Press, pp 169–190

Suba S, Muthulakshmi M (2023) A systematic review: chest radiography images (X-ray images) analysis and COVID-19 categorization diagnosis using artificial intelligence techniques. Netw Comput Neural Syst 34(1–2):26–64

Sufyan M, Shokat Z, Ashfaq UA (2023) Artificial intelligence in cancer diagnosis and therapy: Current status and future perspective. Comput Biol Med 107356

Susnjak T, Griffin E (2024) Towards clinical prediction with transparency: an explainable AI approach to survival modelling in residential aged care. medRxiv, pp 2001–2024

Tran K, Bøtker JP, Aframian A, Memarzadeh K (2020) Artificial intelligence for medical imaging. In: Artificial intelligence in healthcare. Elsevier, pp 143–162

Wang H (2024) The design and evaluation of intelligent computer-assisted language learning tools for beginner learners of Mandarin Chinese. Trinity College, Dublin

Wang B, Asan O, Zhang Y (2024) Shaping the future of chronic disease management: Insights into patient needs for AI-based homecare systems. Int J Med Inform 181:105301

Wenderott K, Krups J, Luetkens JA, Gambashidze N, Weigl M (2024) Prospective effects of an artificial intelligence-based computer-aided detection system for prostate imaging on routine workflow and radiologists' outcomes. Eur J Radiol 170:111252

Williamson SM, Prybutok V (2024) Balancing privacy and progress: a review of privacy challenges, systemic oversight, and patient perceptions in AI-driven healthcare. Appl Sci 14(2):675

Younis HA et al (2024) A systematic review and meta-analysis of artificial intelligence tools in medicine and healthcare: applications, considerations, limitations, motivation and challenges. Diagnostics 14(1):109

Chapter 3
Smart Healthcare: Paradigm Shift in Industry 5.0 Using AI

Hemant Yadav, Pooja Yadav, Nandkishor Joshi, and S. C. Sharma

Abstract An enormous revolution is happening within the healthcare industry in the twenty-first century with the development of Artificial Intelligence (AI). With the coming of artificial intelligence and its application in healthcare businesses, the chapter looks at the worldview move in smart healthcare. Having moved from Industry 4.0 to Industry 5.0, the healthcare industry has gone through a change that has given the industry an unused dimension and a sensational alter. This paradigm shift, known as Smart Healthcare, heralds a new era of personalized, proactive, and efficient healthcare delivery. Leveraging AI technologies, Smart Healthcare optimizes various aspects of healthcare operations, including personalized medicine, predictive analytics, remote patient monitoring, medical imaging, drug discovery, and virtual health assistants. This chapter explores the implications of AI in Smart Healthcare within the context of Industry 5.0, highlighting its potential to revolutionize healthcare delivery, improve patient outcomes, and address ethical considerations and data privacy concerns.

Keywords Artificial Intelligence · Smart Healthcare · Internet of Things · Industry 5.0 · Personalized medication

H. Yadav
Future Institute of Engineering and Technology, Bareilly, Uttar Pradesh, India

P. Yadav (✉)
Deptt. of CSIT, FET, MJP Rohilkhand University, Bareilly, Uttar Pradesh, India
e-mail: erpoojafet15@gmail.com; pooja.yadav@mjpru.ac.in

N. Joshi
Department of CSE, PIET, Parul University, Vadodara, India

S. C. Sharma
DPT, Indian Institute of Engineering and Technology, Roorkee, Uttarakhand, India

R. Arya et al. (eds.), *Recent Trends in Artificial Intelligence Towards a Smart World*, Frontiers of Artificial Intelligence, Ethics and Multidisciplinary Applications,
https://doi.org/10.1007/978-981-97-6790-8_3

3.1 Introduction

Smart Healthcare in Industry 5.0 recognizes that traditional healthcare strategies drop brief in assembly wants of an assorted understanding population, and the strategies are regularly reactive and give non-specific arrangements (Prasad and Srikanth 2015). Smart healthcare, on the other hand, looks to create a unified and personalized framework by combining human and machine endeavors and joining advanced innovation into mechanical processes. This approach adjusts consistently with the standards of Industry 5.0. Partners within the healthcare industry are endeavoring to go past constrained methods and adopt comprehensive practices that span the whole esteem chain. This includes moving forward networks and collaboration (Ali et al. 2020). Artificial Intelligence (AI) plays a crucial part in this change, acting as a catalyst with exceptional capabilities like information analysis, design recognition, and decision-making. AI has the potential to revolutionize the current standards within the healthcare industry by making processes more efficient and compelling. Smart Healthcare, powered by Artificial Intelligence (AI) in Industry 5.0, is not only a tech upgrade but also an essential change in how we approach and provide healthcare. It uses AI to create a sense of tremendous information, turning it into useful experiences for superior decision-making (Subasi et al. 2020). This makes healthcare more efficient, exact, and custom-made for each patient, moving from receptive strategies to a more proactive approach. Information is basic to this move since AI can analyze, comprehend, and estimate patterns in dialect. It is fundamental to utilize information to support personalized pharmaceutical, preventive care, and superior understanding results as the healthcare industry moves toward a value-based worldview.

AI exceeds expectations in diagnostics by quickly and dependably translating information from wearables, hereditary profiling, and progressed imaging (Vippalapalli and Ananthula 2016). This makes strides in exactness and speeds up the method, freeing medical staff individuals to concentrate on more complex highlights of quiet care. Smart Healthcare also computerizes regulatory obligations, counting arrangement planning, and charging (Ali et al. 2020). This dispenses with blunders and moves forward the proficiency of healthcare operations, in line with Industry 5.0's objective of an interconnected and collaborative environment. The association of patients is a significant objective, changing people who were already inactive beneficiaries into dynamic supporters to their well-being. AI-powered advances, such as chatbots and wearables, give real-time well-being observation and personalized treatment programs. The collaborative environment of Industry 5.0 extends these options (Haleem and Javaid 2019). However, moral concerns are basic. Protection, security, as well as avoiding inclination in AI decision-making are all issues that require consideration. The utilization of past data in AI frameworks might decline existing healthcare disparities. Adjusting advancement and moral considerations is basic for a feasible and impartial Smart Healthcare system in Industry 5.0. According to this worldview, robots outfitted with cutting-edge innovations like mechanical technology and artificial intelligence are great at exercises that call for accuracy, repeatability, and handling capacity. Human specialists also give components that robots are missing, such as innovative thinking, enthusiastic insights, and adaptability. This cooperative strategy not only increases total yield but also creates a dynamic work environment conducive to inventiveness. Industry 5.0 recognizes that the extreme potential of innovation rests in combining human creativity and innovative capability and highlights the significance of human gifts in coordinating, directing, and working with robots. To construct a business environment that's more balanced and productive, the objective is to set up workspaces where people discover delight in significant, inventive employments, whereas machines oversee ordinary and tedious capacities.

3.2 What Is Smart Healthcare?

Within the twenty-first century, smart healthcare has ended up a noteworthy drive, transforming restorative practices, persistent encounters, and healthcare organization. This paradigm move is recognized by the consolidation of cutting-edge innovations such as Manufactured Insights (AI), the Web of Things (IoT), huge information analytics, and telemedicine arrangements, all aimed at creating a more proficient, customized, and coordinated healthcare environment (Ali et al. 2020). At the center of smart healthcare is the utilization of AI, which is changing conclusions, treatment planning, and healthcare decision-making. Machine learning calculations, a sort of AI, have appeared as modern skills in assessing restorative pictures, outperforming human exactness, and speeding up the determination preparation. The repercussions are gigantic, conceivably clearing the way for prior ailment-distinguishing proof and more exact treatments, inevitably making a difference in patients. Figure 3.1 represents the digital transformation of healthcare (https://www.sap.com/industries/healthcare.html). Predictive analytics, driven by AI, is basic in moving from a reactive approach to a preventative healthcare technique. Predictive algorithms can recognize planned well-being risks by analyzing past patient information, permitting restorative experts to intervene early and alter preventative medicines to personal needs (Catarinucci et al. 2015). This move is steady with the common drift of pushing preventative strategies, minimizing the burden on healthcare frameworks, and advancing a comprehensive approach to public wellness. AI integration in analytics for prediction also makes it easier to identify high-risk patients for certain infections, allowing for more focus on medications and individualized healthcare regimens. Personalized pharmaceuticals are another trademark of smart healthcare within the twenty-first century, with AI playing a key part in personalizing treatment regimens based on one-of-a-kind patient characteristics and responses to past medicines (Vippalapalli and Ananthula 2016). This level of customization not as it moves progresses treatment success but too reduces potential negative impacts, in differentiation to conventional medicine's one-size-fits-all approach (Zhou et al. 2018). Personalized medication, empowered by AI, represents a paradigm change toward precision healthcare, in which treatments are perfectly balanced to everyone's special genetic composition and health profile.

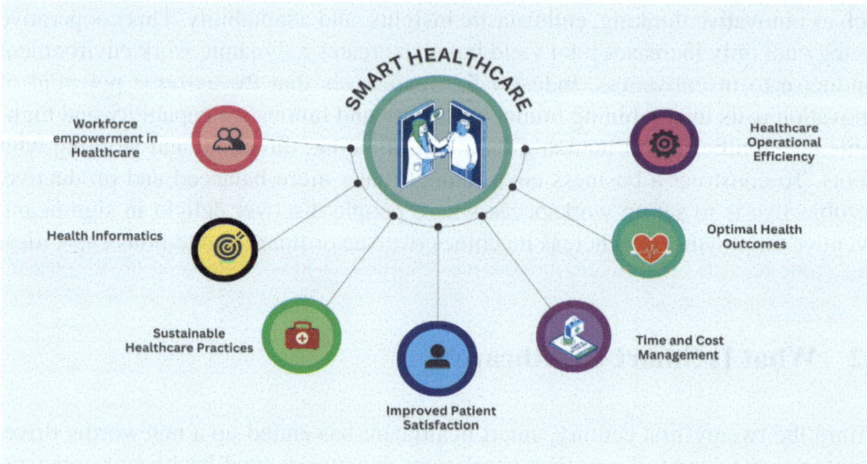

Fig. 3.1 Smart Healthcare. *Source* Author

The interconnecting of smart healthcare expands past AI, with the consolidation of the Internet of Things (IoT) as a significant component. IoT devices, which extend from wearable technology to smart restorative devices, generate real-time information that consistently coordinates with the broader healthcare environment. Wearable devices, for case, provide continuous tracking of crucial signs, action levels, and rest designs, engaging people to engage in their well-being effectively. Essentially, healthcare professionals utilize verifiable data, permitting for more broad and convenient understanding examinations (Vippalapalli and Ananthula 2016). The idea of a connected healthcare environment, supported by IoT, incorporates the advancement of smart healthcare teach and facilities (Selvarajan et al. 2022). These offices utilize connected medical devices and computerized frameworks to progress efficiency, care that prioritizes patients, and delivery of medical services. Huge information analytics may be an advanced fundamental perspective of smart healthcare, permitting the collection, examination, and extraction of important bits of knowledge from huge datasets made by the healthcare division (Udendhran and Yamini 2021). The plenitude of data, which incorporates electronic health records, symptomatic pictures, hereditary information, and quiet socioeconomics, makes a wealthy embroidered artwork for study. Huge information analytics instruments filter through this information to discover designs, relationships, and exceptions, giving valuable data for healthcare arrangements, budget allotment, and inquiries about endeavors (Rajan Jeyaraj and Nadar 2022). The capacity to assess population well-being information makes a difference in decision-making based on proof, public health initiatives, and far better information on epidemiological patterns.

Smart healthcare not as it were progresses clinical treatment but moreover has an impact on healthcare organizations and administration (Udendhran and Yamini 2021). AI-powered arrangements computerize authoritative assignments from invoicing and preparing claims to organizing arrangements and asset allotment. Schedule work automation not only brings down human mistakes but also ensures that assets are utilized effectively for superior quiet care. The interconnection of smart medical systems enables smooth communication and participation among partners, coming about in a coherent associated healthcare biological system. Telemedicine and remote patient tracking have become essential elements of smart healthcare, especially in an era of increasing digital connectivity. Telemedicine solutions allow healthcare providers to provide healthcare remotely, removing geographic limitations and improving access, especially for people living in rural and remote areas (Rajan Jeyaraj and Nadar 2022). Remote patient monitoring supported by IoT devices allows doctors to track patients' vital signs and health data in real time, enabling early intervention and personalized treatment programs. The global response to the COVID-19 pandemic has accelerated the adoption of telehealth services and highlighted the need for adaptive and resilient health systems. However, there are several obstacles and challenges to the implementation of smart healthcare. The growth of health data and the interconnectedness of health systems are raising privacy and security issues (Singh et al. 2022). Maintaining the confidentiality and authenticity of patient information is critical and requires strict cybersecurity measures and compliance with data protection regulations. Ethical issues such as the ethical use of AI to improve medical decision-making and correct algorithmic bias must be carefully considered to avoid unintended consequences and disparities in medical outcomes (Baker et al. 2017).

Implementing smart healthcare also requires significant investments in infrastructure, technology, and employee training. The transition from traditional healthcare models to smart healthcare ecosystems requires a coordinated effort by healthcare organizations, policymakers, and technology providers. Establishing interoperability standards and data exchange protocols is critical to allowing different systems to communicate seamlessly and facilitating information exchange between healthcare organizations. Bridging the digital divide is essential to ensure equal access to smart health technologies. Disparities in access to high-speed internet, digital literacy, and the availability of smart devices are likely to exacerbate existing health disparities. As smart healthcare continues to evolve, it is important to implement comprehensive strategies that address the needs of diverse populations and mitigate potential differences in technology adoption. Despite these challenges, the potential benefits of smart healthcare are vast and transformative. The convergence of AI, IoT, and big data analytics heralds a new era in healthcare delivery, marked by efficiency, personalization, and improved patient outcomes (Selvarajan et al. 2022). The shift from reactive to proactive healthcare, facilitated by predictive analytics and early intervention, has the potential to reduce the overall burden on healthcare systems and improve the quality of life for individuals. Moreover, smart healthcare stands as a beacon of innovation in the twenty-first century, revolutionizing the way healthcare is conceptualized, delivered, and managed (Sujith et al. 2022). The integration of AI, IoT, and big data analytics creates a dynamic and interconnected healthcare ecosystem that leverages technology to enhance efficiency, accessibility, and personalization. As the world continues to grapple with complex healthcare challenges, smart healthcare emerges as a transformative force, offering the promise of more resilient, responsive, and patient-centric healthcare systems. The journey toward smart healthcare requires a strategic and collaborative approach involving stakeholders from diverse sectors to navigate challenges, address ethical considerations, and unlock the full potential of technology in advancing global health.

3.3 Evolution of Industry 5.0

Figure 3.2 shows the evaluation of Healthcare 5.0. The evolution of Industry 5.0 represents a transformative journey that builds upon the foundations laid by its predecessors, marking a significant leap forward in industrial innovation. The technology integration in Industry 5.0, also known as the "Human-Centric Industrial Revolution," encapsulates a vision where humans and advanced technologies collaborate synergistically to enhance productivity, efficiency, and overall industrial capabilities (Sujith et al. 2022). This evolutionary process traces its roots back to the early stages of industrialization. The First Industrial Revolution, characterized by the mechanization of production processes through the introduction of water and steam power, laid the groundwork for the subsequent waves of the industrial revolution, which unfolded in the late eighteenth to early nineteenth century. This saw the emergence of textile mills, mechanized factories, and the mechanization of various industries (Maddikunta et al. 2022). A significant change in the manufacturing process was brought about by the change from manual labor to machine-driven procedures that marked a profound shift in the way goods were produced, and it set the stage for further advancements. The Second Industrial Revolution, occurring in the late nineteenth–early twentieth century, introduced significant technological innovations, including the adoption of electricity and the development of the assembly line in the widespread use of steel made the advancements led to increased industrialization, mass production, and the rise of large-scale manufacturing (Lu 2017). Moreover, the advent of the assembly line, famously implemented by Henry Ford in automotive production, revolutionized manufacturing processes and contributed to the standardization of products. The Third Industrial Revolution, or the Digital Revolution, unfolded in the mid-twentieth century with the advent of computerization and automation (Turner et al. 2022). The integration of computers, electronics, and information technology into industrial processes brought forth a new era of efficiency, precision, and interconnectedness (Tyagi 2022a). Moreover, automation in computer control systems streamlined production improved quality control and laid the groundwork for the digitalization of industries. This improved the quality and set the stage for turning industries into digital ones. The Fourth Industrial Revolution, often referred to as Industry 4.0, represents a pivotal moment in the convergence of physical and digital technologies. This era, which gained momentum in the late twentieth and the early twenty-first centuries, is characterized by the widespread adoption of cyber-physical systems, the Internet of Things (IoT), big data analytics, and artificial intelligence (Bigan 2022). Industry 4.0 gave momentum to the era of smart manufacturing. The

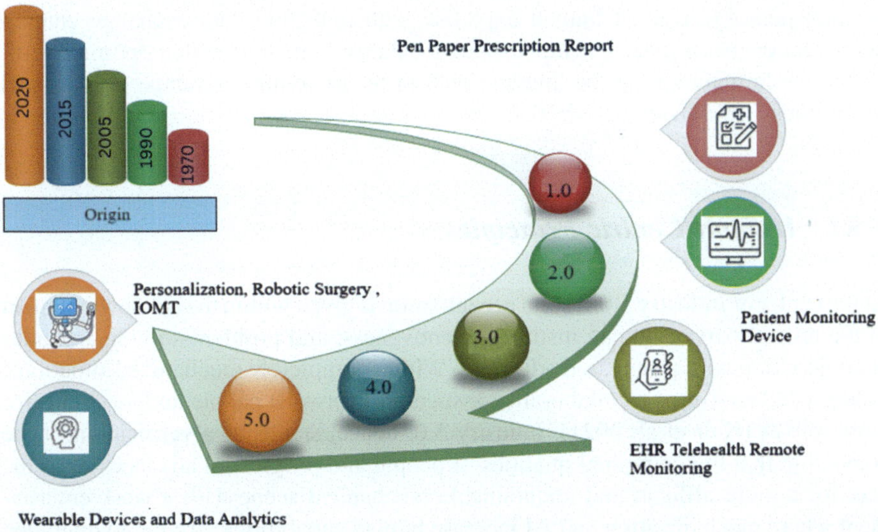

Fig. 3.2 Evaluation of Healthcare 5.0. *Source* Author

interconnected devices and systems communicated and collaborated in real time, enabling a more responsive and adaptive industrial ecosystem.

3.4 Industry 4.0 as a Precursor

Industry 4.0, the fourth industrial revolution, brought about a convergence of physical and digital technologies and the incorporation of cyber-physical systems. The cloud computing, big data analytics, and AI in manufacturing processes helped in a new era of connectivity and automation. Smart factories emerged, characterized by real-time data exchange between machines and systems, enabling intelligent decision-making and predictive maintenance (Tyagi 2022b). While Industry 4.0 sets up the basics for connected and automated manufacturing, Industry 5.0 brings in a more detailed and human-centered point of view.

3.5 Industry 5.0

Industry 5.0, termed the Human-Centric Industrial Revolution, breaks away from the exclusively digital and automated focus of Industry 4.0 (Adel 2022). Unlike Industry 4.0, the core distinction is prioritizing collaboration between humans and advanced technologies such as AI, robotics, and automation (Jagadeeswari et al. 2018). In Industry 5.0, technology is not a replacement but a collaborator; acknowledging the indispensable role of human expertise with real-time data exchange enables intelligent decision-making, emphasizing a balanced integration that optimizes efficiency while maintaining the human touch in the evolving landscape of industrial revolutions.

3.5.1 Human-Centric Principles

At the center of Industry 5.0, a solid accentuation is given within the acknowledgment of the crucial part of human instinct, inventiveness, and problem-solving aptitudes in conjunction with progressed advances. Within completely mechanized situations, Industry 5.0 envisions a collaborative association between people and machines for work moves (Nair et al. 2021). Industry 5.0, hence, stands as a verification of the conviction that the combined qualities of people and progressed advances clear the way for a more affluent and maintainable mechanical scene with a work environment where mechanization and AI increase human capabilities, driving to upgraded efficiency, proficiency, and advancement.

3.5.2 Cobots and Collaborative Robotics

One of the substantial signs of the human-centric standards in Industry 5.0 is the concept of collaborative robots or "cobots." These robots are planned to work near people, cultivating a collaborative and adaptable fabricating environment (Goyal and Tyagi 2020). Cobots are prepared with progressed sensors, machine learning calculations, and AI capabilities, empowering them to adjust to the energetic nature of human collaboration. This collaborative worldview points to an advantageous relationship where people and cobots complement each other's qualities, driving progressed general efficiency and security.

3.5.3 Immersive Technologies

The integration of augmented reality (AR) and virtual reality (VR) applications could be an essential viewpoint of Industry 5.0, contributing to both preparation and operational effectiveness (Pramod et al. 2022). AR overlays computerized data onto the physical world, giving real-time direction and data to specialists. VR, on the other hand, makes immersive recreated situations, encouraging virtual preparation, plan surveys, and situation testing (Mohanta et al. 2019). These immersive advances not only improve the skillsets of mechanical specialists but also contribute to expanded security, proficiency, and versatility in complex mechanical forms.

3.5.4 Lights-out Manufacturing with a Human Touch

Industry 5.0 rethinks the concept of "lights-out fabricating," which customarily alluded to completely mechanized industrial facilities working without human intercession (Saraswat et al. 2022). Within the Industry 5.0 setting, lights-out fabricating coexists with a human-centric approach. Whereas lights-out forms handle schedules and monotonous errands with tall effectiveness, human specialists center on more complex and value-added perspectives of generation (Tuppad and Patil 2022). This show optimizes proficiency in schedule operations, permitting human specialists to lock in higher-order errands that require imagination, basic consideration, and flexibility.

3.5.5 Edge Computing for Real-Time Decision-Making

The approach of edge computing could be a significant viewpoint of Industry 5.0, tending to the requirement for real-time information handling and decision-making (Mbunge and Muchemwa 2022). Edge computing includes preparing information closer to the source of the era, lessening inactivity, and empowering speedier reaction times. In mechanical settings where real-time experiences are vital, edge computing complements the broader Industry 5.0 system by encouraging fast and localized handling of information from IoT gadgets, sensors, and other sources.

3.5.6 The Role of Data

The role of data in Industry 5.0 is refined as a key resource, building upon the progressions of Industry 4.0. Progressed analytics, counting machine learning, and counterfeit insights infer significant experiences from tremendous datasets (Akundi et al. 2022). These experiences educate decision-making forms, optimize generation workflows, and contribute to a more versatile and cleverly mechanical environment. The dependable and moral utilize of information gets to be a basic thought in Industry 5.0, emphasizing security, security, and straightforwardness in data-driven operations.

3.5.7 Connectivity Through 5G Technology

5G innovation plays an essential part in Industry 5.0, giving high-speed, low-latency communication between gadgets and frameworks (Yadav et al. 2018). The capabilities of 5G systems empower consistent communication in mechanical settings where real-time responsiveness is foremost. The sending of 5G encourages quicker and more solid information exchange, supporting the integration of progressed innovations and the multiplication of IoT gadgets in mechanical situations.

3.6 Cybersecurity in Industry 5.0

With expanded networks and dependence on computerized advances, cybersecurity has become a fundamental concern within the Industry 5.0 scene. As mechanical frameworks get to be more interconnected, the defenselessness to cyber dangers increases. Industry 5.0 requires vigorous cybersecurity measures to protect basic foundations, touchy information, and the astuteness of mechanical operations (Mbunge and Muchemwa 2022). The execution of secure-by-design standards, encryption, and persistent observing are necessary components of a comprehensive cybersecurity technique within the Industry 5.0 period (Lu 2021).

3.6.1 Workforce Dynamics and Organizational Structures

The move to Industry 5.0 isn't exclusively a mechanical move; it requires a comparison of advancement in organizational structures and workforce flow (Madsen and Berg 2021). The rise of Industry 5.0 calls for a workforce with a mix of specialized capability, versatility, and basic aptitudes. Persistent learning and upskilling ended up basic as specialists lock in with advancing innovations and take on parts that require a combination of human and mechanical expertise (Özdemir and Hekim 2018). Collaborative approaches between industry, the scholarly community, and policymakers are basic to set up systems for long-lasting learning and ability improvement.

3.6.2 Societal Implications and Environmental Considerations

From a broader societal viewpoint, Industry 5.0 brings around a reevaluation of the relationship between industry and the environment. Economical and eco-friendly hones are necessary to the Industry 5.0 system, adjusting with worldwide endeavors toward natural preservation (Pathak et al. 2019). The accentuation on proficiency, optimization, and human–machine collaboration in Industry 5.0 contributes to diminishing squander, vitality utilization, and natural effect (Madsen and Berg 2021). This move reflects a broader mindfulness of the societal and natural suggestions of mechanical hones. The move to Industry 5.0 isn't exclusively innovative; it requires a comparison of advancement in organizational structures and workforce flow. The rise of Industry 5.0 calls for a workforce that has a mix of specialized capability, versatility, and basic considering abilities. Nonstop learning and upskilling are basic as laborers lock in with advancing innovations and take on parts that require a combination of human and mechanical mastery. Collaborative approaches between industry, the scholarly world, and policymakers are essential to set up systems for deep-rooted learning and aptitude improvement (Madsen and Berg 2021). From a broader societal point of view, Industry 5.0 brings around a reevaluation of the relationship between industry and the environment. Maintainable and eco-friendly homes are necessary to the industry.

3.7 Impact of AI in Healthcare

Artificial Intelligence (AI) has brought about transformative changes in the field of healthcare, revolutionizing the way medical professionals diagnose, treat, and manage patient care. This impact can be witnessed across various aspects of the healthcare ecosystem, ranging from diagnostics and personalized medicine to administrative tasks and patient engagement (Yadav and Sharma 2023). The integration of AI technologies in healthcare has not only improved efficiency and accuracy but also opened up new avenues for innovation and research. One of the most significant contributions of AI in healthcare is in the domain of diagnostics. AI algorithms, particularly machine learning models, have demonstrated remarkable capabilities in analyzing medical images such as X-rays, CT scans, and MRIs (Reischauer 2018). These algorithms can detect subtle patterns and anomalies that might be overlooked by human eyes, leading to earlier and more accurate diagnoses. For example, in radiology, AI systems have shown the ability to identify early signs of diseases like cancer, enabling timely interventions and improving patient outcomes.

Moreover, AI is playing a crucial role in genomics and personalized medicine. By analyzing large datasets of genomic information, AI algorithms can identify genetic markers associated with specific diseases or responses to treatments. This allows for the development of personalized treatment plans tailored to an individual's genetic makeup, maximizing the effectiveness of interventions and minimizing adverse effects (Yadav et al. 2023a). The integration of AI in genomics has accelerated the pace of genomic research, paving the way for more targeted and precise therapies. In addition to diagnostics and personalized medicine, AI has streamlined administrative tasks in healthcare settings. Natural Language Processing (NLP) algorithms extract relevant information from electronic health records (EHRs) and other medical documents, reducing the time and effort required for data entry and retrieval. AI-powered chatbots and virtual assistants are also deployed to handle routine inquiries, appointment scheduling, and medication reminders, freeing healthcare professionals to focus on more complex and patient-centric tasks. Another area where AI is making a significant impact is in drug discovery and development (Xu et al. 2021). The traditional drug discovery process is time-consuming and expensive, with a high rate of failure. AI, particularly machine learning models, is being employed to analyze vast datasets, including biological and chemical information, to identify potential drug candidates more efficiently (Sindhwani et al. 2022). This has the potential to accelerate the drug development pipeline, reduce costs, and increase the likelihood of discovering novel therapies for various diseases. Furthermore, AI is enhancing the capabilities of medical devices, making them more intelligent and adaptive. For example, AI algorithms integrated into monitoring devices can continuously analyze physiological data and detect subtle changes that may indicate the onset of a medical condition (Yadav et al. 2023a). This early detection can be crucial in preventing complications and improving patient outcomes. Additionally, AI is being used in the development of robotic-assisted surgeries, enabling surgeons to perform procedures with greater precision and control. AI technologies are also transforming patient engagement and healthcare delivery. Virtual health assistants and telemedicine platforms powered by AI enable remote consultations, monitoring, and follow-ups. This is particularly valuable for improving access to health services, especially in rural and underserved areas (Yadav et al. 2018). AI-driven mental health applications such as chatbots and virtual therapists can help address the growing challenges in mental healthcare by providing continuous support and monitoring. Despite its many benefits, the widespread adoption of AI in healthcare also raises ethical and privacy concerns. The use of sensitive patient data to train AI algorithms requires robust measures to ensure confidentiality and compliance with data protection regulations (Zhu et al. 2019). Additionally, understanding the rationale behind AI-generated recommendations is critical to gaining trust and acceptance among healthcare professionals and patients and, therefore, the interpretation of AI algorithms in healthcare decision-making. Possibilities have become challenges. In summary, the impact of AI in healthcare is wide-ranging, impacting diagnostics, personalized medicine, administrative tasks, drug development, medical devices, patient engagement, and healthcare delivery. The integration of AI has the potential to revolutionize the entire healthcare ecosystem, leading to more efficient, accurate, and personalized care. As technology continues to evolve, continued collaboration between medical professionals, researchers, and technology developers is critical to meeting challenges and ensuring the responsible and ethical use of AI in healthcare.

3.8 Paradigm Shift Using AI in Industry 5.0

The current revolution in manufacturing, known as Industry 5.0, is the result of the incorporation of advanced technology such as artificial intelligence (AI) (Iyengar et al. 2022). Industry 4.0, which popularized the ideas of smart manufacturing and digital transformation, set the groundwork for this new era. Industry 5.0 goes one step further by highlighting the cooperation between people and machines, appreciating their strengths, and utilizing AI to enhance human competencies. This paradigm change has significant effects on the manufacturing industry, changing workflows, employee relationships, and the way that production and innovation are approached in general. The idea of "cobotics", or human–machine cooperation, is the foundation of Industry 5.0. Unlike the dread of losing, one's job due to complete automation, Industry 5.0 sees a future in which humans and robots collaborate together, each using their talents to produce the best possible outcomes (Iyengar et al. 2022). AI is essential to this partnership because it gives computers sophisticated cognitive capacities and makes it possible for them to comprehend, learn from, and adapt to changing situations. Cobotics, which emphasizes the fusion of human innovative thinking, senses, and problem-solving abilities with the effectiveness, accuracy, and scalability of machines, is a paradigm change. Advanced technologies such as robots and artificial intelligence (AI) enable machines to do labor-intensive and repetitive jobs, freeing up human workers to concentrate on complicated decision-making, creativity, and tasks demanding emotional intelligence. With the help of this collaborative approach, workers may become more dynamic and adaptable as they monitor, guide, and work together with machines to improve output quality and productivity. In contrast to conventional production approaches, the symbiotic relationship that exists between humans and machines not only solves efficiency issues but also fosters innovation and creativity. Industry 5.0 aims to create a work atmosphere where humans and robots can collaborate harmoniously. As well as they utilize each other's unique strengths for mutual gain, rather than only focusing on technical advancements. Industry 5.0 represents a concept that goes beyond simple technical progress. In contrast to the worries expressed throughout previous industrial revolutions about the loss of jobs, Industry 5.0 sees a time when humans and robots collaborate to maximize efficiency, innovation, and production. In this paradigm, machines with cutting-edge technologies, such as AI and robotics, excel in tasks requiring precision, repetition, and computational power. Simultaneously, human workers contribute their creativity, critical thinking, emotional intelligence, and adaptability, aspects that machine inherently lack. This collaborative approach not only enhances overall productivity but also fosters a dynamic work culture where innovation thrives. Industry 5.0 emphasizes the value of human skills in guiding, supervising, and collaborating with machines, acknowledging that the true potential lies in the integration of human ingenuity with technological prowess. The vision is to create workplaces where humans find fulfillment in meaningful, creative tasks, and machines handle routine and repetitive functions, ultimately leading to a more balanced and productive industrial landscape. One of the key areas where AI is making a significant impact in Industry 5.0 is predictive maintenance. Traditional manufacturing systems often rely on scheduled maintenance routines, leading to unnecessary downtime and maintenance costs. AI, through the analysis of real-time sensor data and historical maintenance records, can predict when equipment will likely fail and schedule maintenance activities accordingly (Popov et al. 2140). This proactive approach not only minimizes downtime but also extends the lifespan of machinery, resulting in cost savings and increased overall efficiency. In Industry 5.0, Artificial Intelligence (AI) is making a substantial impact, particularly in predictive maintenance. This innovative approach leverages AI algorithms to anticipate equipment failures before they occur, optimizing maintenance schedules and minimizing downtime. AI-driven predictive maintenance harnesses the power of machine learning to analyze historical and real-time data from machinery and equipment.

By identifying patterns and anomalies, AI algorithms can forecast potential issues, enabling proactive maintenance interventions. This shift from traditional reactive maintenance to predictive strategies enhances overall operational efficiency, reduces unplanned downtime, and extends the lifespan of industrial equipment. The integration of sensors, IoT devices, and AI enables continuous monitoring of machinery conditions, facilitating a data-driven understanding of equipment health. Predictive maintenance not only enhances reliability but also reduces maintenance costs by ensuring that interventions are precisely timed, preventing unnecessary servicing or component replacements. In Industry 5.0, predictive maintenance contributes to a more streamlined and cost-effective industrial ecosystem. It epitomizes the collaborative synergy between humans and intelligent machines, allowing for preemptive decision-making and creating a more resilient and efficient manufacturing landscape. The predictive capabilities of AI in maintenance exemplify the transformative potential of Industry 5.0 in optimizing industrial processes. Furthermore, AI-driven optimization transforms production processes by fine-tuning parameters in real time (Yadav et al. 2023b). Machine learning algorithms can analyze vast amounts of data to identify the most efficient settings for equipment and production lines, leading to improved quality, reduced waste, and enhanced energy efficiency. This optimization level is challenging to achieve manually and highlights the potential of AI to unlock new levels of efficiency in manufacturing (Joshi and Jharia 2015; Joshi et al. 2023). In the context of product design and innovation, AI is playing a pivotal role in accelerating the development cycle. Generative design, a technique powered by AI, allows engineers and designers to input design parameters and constraints, after which the algorithm generates numerous design iterations. This not only speeds up the design process but also introduces innovative solutions that might not be immediately apparent to human designers. The synergy between human creativity and AI-driven design optimization represents a hallmark of Industry 5.0, where technology is a catalyst for innovation rather than a replacement for human ingenuity. Another significant aspect of Industry 5.0 is the rise of AI-powered digital twins. A digital twin is a virtual representation of a physical object or system, and AI enhances its capabilities by enabling real-time data analysis and simulation (Madsen and Berg 2021). In manufacturing, digital twins can be applied to model and simulate entire production processes, providing insights into performance, identifying potential bottlenecks, and facilitating continuous improvement. This level of digital representation allows for more informed decision-making and the ability to anticipate and address issues before they impact the physical production environment. In supply chain management, AI is instrumental in creating responsive and adaptive systems. Advanced analytics powered by AI can analyze historical data, current market conditions, and various external factors to predict demand more accurately (Popov et al. 2140). This not only optimizes inventory management but also enhances the overall efficiency of the supply chain. Additionally, AI enables the development of autonomous logistics, where self-driving vehicles and drones can navigate and transport goods within warehouses or across supply chain networks. The integration of AI in Industry 5.0 is also redefining the role of workers in the manufacturing sector. Rather than replacing human labor, AI is augmenting it. Human workers are increasingly collaborating with AI systems to perform tasks that require a combination of cognitive abilities, creativity, and emotional intelligence. This shift in the workforce dynamic necessitates focusing on upskilling and reskilling initiatives to ensure that workers are equipped with the necessary skills to collaborate effectively with AI technologies. One of the significant challenges in implementing Industry 5.0 is the need for a workforce with a diverse skill set that includes both technical and soft skills. Technical skills involve familiarity with AI technologies, data analysis, and digital literacy, while soft skills encompass problem-solving, communication, and adaptability (Özdemir and Hekim 2018). Educational institutions and training programs play a crucial role in preparing the workforce for this new era, and industry collaboration is essential to bridge the gap between academic curricula and the evolving demands of the manufacturing sector. Moreover, the ethical implications of AI in Industry 5.0 cannot be overlooked. As AI becomes more integrated into manufacturing processes, ethical considerations surrounding data privacy, algorithmic bias, and the potential misuse of AI technologies come to the forefront (Xu et al. 2021). Establishing ethical guidelines, regulatory frameworks, and industry standards is imperative to ensure that the adoption of AI in Industry 5.0 aligns with societal values and prioritizes the well-being of both workers and consumers. Industry 5.0 is not just about technological advancements; it represents a cultural shift in how organizations approach innovation and collaboration. The hierarchical structures of traditional manufacturing are giving way to more agile and collaborative frameworks, where cross-functional teams work together to solve complex problems (Sindhwani et al. 2022). AI facilitates this collaborative approach by providing tools for data-driven decision-making, fostering communication, and enabling organizations to adapt quickly to changing market conditions. The role of data in Industry 5.0 cannot be overstated. As AI relies on vast amounts of data for training and decision-making, the quality, accessibility, and security of data become critical considerations. Organizations must invest in robust data infrastructure, implement data governance practices, and ensure compliance with data protection regulations. Furthermore, the interoperability of systems and the ability to share data securely across the supply chain are essential components of a successful Industry 5.0 ecosystem. In conclusion, Industry 5.0 marks a paradigm shift in manufacturing, driven by the integration of AI and other advanced technologies. The collaborative relationship between humans and machines, the emphasis on human-centric innovation, and the transformative impact on various aspects of the manufacturing process define this new era. From predictive maintenance and production optimization to digital twins and workforce augmentation, AI is at the forefront of Industry 5.0, reshaping the manufacturing landscape and opening up new possibilities for efficiency, innovation, and sustainable growth. As organizations navigate this transformative journey, addressing ethical considerations, upskilling the workforce, and fostering a culture of collaboration will be crucial to realizing the full potential of Industry 5.0 in the manufacturing sector.

3.9 Comparative Study of Industry 4.0 and 5.0 in Healthcare

The move from Industry 4.0 to Healthcare 5.0 marks a critical advancement in the application of innovation inside the healthcare segment. Industry 4.0, characterized by the integration of advanced innovations into fabricating forms, emphasized robotization, connectivity, and data-driven decision-making. Within the healthcare setting, this deciphered to progressions such as telehealth (Iyengar et al. 2022). As the healthcare scene advanced, the confinements of a mechanized and data-centric approach became clear, driving the development of Healthcare 5.0. In Industry 4.0 healthcare applications, the essential center was leveraging computerized advances to upgrade operational productivity, streamline regulatory errands, and optimize supply chain administration. The utilization of the Web of Things (IoT) encouraged a network between therapeutic gadgets and frameworks, driving to made strides in information collection and examination (Maddikunta et al. 2022). Whereas Industry 4.0 brought approximately noteworthy enhancements in healthcare forms, it moreover raised concerns related to work relocation due to robotization, moral contemplations encompassing information security, and the require for vigorous cybersecurity measures to secure delicate healthcare data. Healthcare 5.0 speaks to a worldview move by moving past the mechanized and data-centric approach of Industry 4.0 (Akundi et al. 2022). The key highlight is the accentuation on human–machine collaboration, recognizing the interesting qualities of both people and machines within the healthcare environment. Progressed manufactured insights (AI) innovations, counting machine learning, and common dialect handling play a central part in Healthcare 5.0, expanding human capabilities and fostering collaboration between healthcare experts and brilliant frameworks. In terms of diagnostics, Healthcare 5.0 leverages AI to analyze restorative pictures with exceptional exactness. Machine learning calculations can identify inconspicuous designs and irregularities in symptomatic pictures, driving to early and exact locations of infections. This progressed symptomatic capability is instrumental in making strides in quiet results and empowering more compelling treatment plans. Additionally, Healthcare 5.0 places a more grounded center on personalized pharmaceuticals, utilizing AI to analyze endless datasets, count genomic data, and tailor treatment plans based on person persistent characteristics. This moves toward exactness in pharmaceutical upgrades helps viability and minimizes unfavorable impacts. The social move from Industry 4.0 to Healthcare 5.0 is obvious within the collaborative approach to healthcare conveyance. Whereas Industry 4.0 mechanized schedule regulatory errands and optimized forms, Healthcare 5.0 places human–machine collaboration at its center (Maddikunta et al. 2022). The healthcare workforce is viewed as dynamic collaborators, working near AI frameworks to supply more comprehensive and personalized care. This requires a differing ability set for the workforce, combining specialized skills with delicate abilities such as communication and versatility. Moral contemplations take on expanded noteworthiness in Healthcare 5.0. The capable utilization of AI, persistent security, and straightforward decision-making have gotten to be fundamental. Healthcare suppliers and technologists are careful of potential dangers related to progressed innovations, endeavoring to guarantee that their sending adjusts with moral benchmarks. This increased moral mindfulness reflects a commitment to prioritizing persistent well-being and keeping up beliefs within the healthcare framework. In conclusion, the move from Industry 4.0 to Healthcare 5.0 implies a transformative advancement in healthcare conveyance. Whereas Industry 4.0 laid the establishment for robotization and data-driven decision-making, Healthcare 5.0 speaks to an all-encompassing approach that prioritizes collaboration between people and machines (Nair et al. 2021). The integration of progressed AI advances in Healthcare 5.0 not as it were upgrades diagnostics and personalized pharmaceuticals but also cultivates a social move toward a more collaborative, patient-centric, and morally cognizant healthcare environment.

The above explanation is summarized in the form of Table 3.1.

3.10 Advantages and Disadvantages of Smart Healthcare in Industry 5.0

Figure 3.3 shows the graphical representation of the advantages, disadvantages, and challenges of Smart Healthcare in Industry 5.0.

3.10.1 Advantages of Smart Healthcare in Industry 5.0

Efficient Diagnostics and Personalized Medicine

Smart healthcare leverages AI calculations to analyze tremendous datasets of restorative data, empowering more precise and productive diagnostics. Models can distinguish modest designs in restorative pictures, driving to the early location of infections. Furthermore, AI plays an urgent part in genomics, permitting personalized medication by fitting treatment plans based on personal hereditary cosmetics.

Improved Patient Outcomes

The integration of AI in healthcare contributes to making strides in understanding results. Early location of maladies, personalized treatment plans, and nonstop observation through AI-powered gadgets result in more compelling intercessions (Lu 2017). Keen healthcare frameworks prioritize preventive measures, diminishing the by and large burden on the healthcare framework and improving the quality of persistent care.

Table 3.1 Industry 4.0 versus Industry 5.0

S. no.	Aspect	Industry 4.0 in healthcare	Industry 5.0 in healthcare
1	Focus	Integration of digital technologies in manufacturing	Synergy of AI, human expertise, and patient-centric care
2	Technological emphasis	IoT, big data, cloud computing, automation	AI, machine learning, human–machine collaboration
3	Data usage	Emphasis on data collection and connectivity	Advanced data analytics, AI-driven decision-making
4	Human–machine collaboration	Humans and machines work together	AI augments human skills, emphasizing collaboration
5	Diagnostics	Enhanced through IoT and data analytics	AI-driven diagnostics for accurate and early detection
6	Personalized medicine	Genomics and data-driven insights	AI-driven genomics, precision medicine, and tailored treatments
7	Administrative tasks	Automation of routine tasks, data management	AI-driven NLP for efficient data extraction administrative support
8	Drug discovery	Accelerated through data analytics and automation	AI-driven drug discovery, optimization, and novel therapies
9	Medical devices	Intelligent devices, IoT in remote monitoring	AI-enhanced medical devices, real-time monitoring, and early detection
10	Patient engagement	Remote patient monitoring, telehealth	Virtual health assistants, AI-driven patient engagement
11	Supply chain management	Smart logistics, real-time tracking	AI-enabled supply chain for efficient healthcare delivery
12	Workforce dynamics	Automation leading to concerns about job displacement	Human–machine collaboration, upskilling for synergy
13	Ethical considerations	Concerns around data privacy and security	Focus on ethical AI use, patient privacy, and responsible data handling
14	Cultural shift	Transition to smart factories and digital transformation	Emphasis on collaboration, patient-centric care, and data-driven decision-making
15	Interoperability	Integration of systems for streamlined processes	Interconnected systems with a focus on data sharing and interoperability
16	Educational emphasis	Need for technical skills for automation and data management	Emphasis on a diverse skill set, including technical and soft skills for collaboration
17	Patient-centric approach	Evolving toward personalized care	Patient centric model with a focus on individualized and holistic care
18	Overall goal	Increased efficiency, automation, and cost reduction	Enhanced patient outcomes, personalized care, and collaboration

Source Author

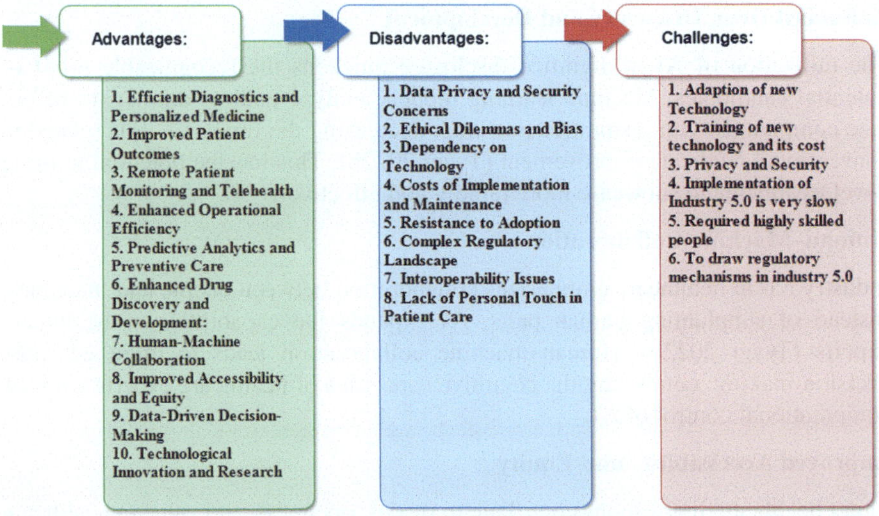

Fig. 3.3 Advantages, disadvantages, and challenges of Industries 5.0 in healthcare. *Source* Author

Remote Patient Monitoring and Telehealth

AI-driven innovations encourage inaccessible quiet checking and telehealth administration. Patients can be checked in real time, and healthcare suppliers can offer meetings and intercessions without the requirement for physical presence (Bigan 2022). This can be especially useful for people in farther or underserved ranges, progressing get to healthcare administrations and diminishing topographical boundaries.

Enhanced Operational Efficiency

Smart healthcare frameworks streamline authoritative assignments through robotization and AI-driven arrangements. From overseeing electronic well-being records (EHRs) to optimizing supply chain coordination, these efficiencies result in fetched investment funds, diminished mistakes, and more centered allotment of healthcare assets (Bigan 2022). AI-powered chatbots and virtual associates assist and contribute to making advances in regulatory forms.

Predictive Analytics and Preventive Care

AI empowers perceptive analytics by analyzing verifiable information and recognizing designs that can anticipate potential well-being issues. This permits healthcare suppliers to embrace a proactive approach to preventive care. By distinguishing people at the hazard of certain conditions, medications can be started early, anticipating the movement of illnesses, and lessening the general healthcare burden.

Enhanced Drug Discovery and Development

The utilization of AI in dignified disclosure quickens the recognizable proof of potential candidates. Machine learning models analyze endless datasets to recognize compounds with restorative potential, decreasing the time and costs related to conventional medicate improvement (Tyagi 2022b). This has the potential to bring novel treatments to showcase more rapidly and effectively.

Human–Machine Collaboration

Industry 5.0 in healthcare emphasizes collaboration between people and machines. Instead of supplanting human parts, AI expands the capabilities of healthcare experts (Tyagi 2022b). Human–machine collaboration leads to more educated decision-making, combining the cognitive capacities of healthcare experts with the computational control of AI.

Improved Accessibility and Equity

Smart healthcare innovations contribute to strides, openness, and value in healthcare administrations. Telehealth and virtual interviews break down geological boundaries, permitting people in inaccessible or rustic ranges to get therapeutic skills (Mohanta et al. 2019). This makes a difference in bridging healthcare of aberrations and guarantees a more evenhanded dissemination of healthcare assets.

Data-Driven Decision-Making

The riches of information produced by keen healthcare frameworks permit data-driven decision-making. Healthcare suppliers can utilize analytics and bits of knowledge from understanding information to tailor treatment plans, optimize operational forms, and make educated choices that upgrade general healthcare conveyance.

Technological Innovation and Research

The integration of AI in healthcare cultivates mechanical development and quickens inquiry about endeavors. AI-driven advances empower analysts to analyze complex datasets, distinguish unused designs, and pick up bits of knowledge that contribute to headways in restorative information, treatment modalities, and healthcare practices.

3.10.2 Disadvantages of Smart Healthcare in Industry 5.0

Data Privacy and Security Concerns

The expanded dependence on AI in healthcare leads to the era and utilization of enormous sums of touchy, quiet information. This raises concerns about information protection and security (Tyagi 2022b). Unauthorized get to, information breaches, or abuse of persistent data posture noteworthy dangers, and exacting measures are fundamental to guarantee the privacy and judgment of healthcare information.

Ethical Dilemmas and Bias

The utilization of AI calculations in decision-making forms presents moral problems. Issues such as algorithmic predisposition, reasonableness, and straightforwardness must be tended to guarantee that AI applications don't excessively affect certain populations or propagate existing healthcare incongruities (Jagadeeswari et al. 2018). Moral contemplations encompassing assent, responsibility, and the interpretability of AI choices are vital.

Dependency on Technology

The integration of shrewd healthcare advances may lead to a reliance on innovation, possibly lessening the dependence on conventional healthcare hones (Mohanta et al. 2019). Overreliance on AI and computerization may compromise the improvement of basic considering aptitudes among healthcare experts and make challenges when innovation breaks down or faces disturbances.

Costs of Implementation and Maintenance

The starting costs related to actualizing keen healthcare innovations, counting AI frameworks, can be considerable. Healthcare organizations have to contribute in the foundation, preparation, and continuous upkeep to guarantee the successful integration of these advances. Budgetary imperatives may pose challenges, particularly for smaller healthcare offices.

Resistance to Adoption

Healthcare experts and patients may show resistance to the appropriation of keen healthcare advances. Concerns almost work uprooting, a need to believe in AI-driven decision-making, and an inclination for conventional healthcare hones can ruin the broad acknowledgment and execution of these innovations.

Complex Regulatory Landscape

The quick advancement of savvy healthcare advances has outpaced the advancement of comprehensive administrative systems. Exploring the complex administrative scene postures challenges for healthcare organizations, driving to instabilities with respect to compliance, benchmarks, and lawful suggestions.

Interoperability Issues

The interoperability of diverse healthcare frameworks and gadgets remains a challenge. Irregularities in information groups, guidelines, and communication conventions can obstruct the consistent trade of data between diverse components of the healthcare environment, preventing the potential benefits of a completely coordinated keen healthcare framework.

Lack of Personal Touch in Patient Care

Whereas AI contributes to more proficient healthcare forms, there's a concern that an overemphasis on innovation may lead to a need for individual touch in quiet care

(Mohanta et al. 2019). The human component, counting sympathy and the capacity to get it nuanced understanding encounters, remains pivotal in healthcare and may be compromised with over-the-top dependence on AI.

Limited Access for Vulnerable Populations

In spite of the potential for made strides in openness, powerless populaces, such as those with constrained access to innovation or advanced proficiency, may confront challenges in profiting from savvy healthcare arrangements. This advanced isolate seems to worsen existing healthcare aberrations and ruin the objective of even-handed healthcare.

Potential Job Displacement

The mechanization and integration of AI innovations may lead to concerns almost work uprooting inside the healthcare workforce. Schedule and regulatory errands mechanized by AI may affect certain work parts, requiring workforce reskilling and a mindful approach to the advancing parts of healthcare experts. In conclusion, the points of interest and impediments of savvy healthcare in Industry 5.0 highlight the transformative potential of AI in moving forward healthcare conveyance whereas too emphasizing the requirement for cautious thought of moral, security, and execution challenges. Striking an adjustment between mechanical development and moral contemplations is fundamental to saddle the total potential of savvy healthcare while moderating potential dangers and downsides. The progressing improvement and selection of shrewd healthcare advances ought to be guided by a commitment to improving persistent results, advancing value, and keeping up the most noteworthy benchmarks of moral healthcare hones.

3.11 Applications of Smart Healthcare in Industry 5.0 Using AI

In the era of Industry 5.0, where the integration of advanced technologies is reshaping traditional industries, the healthcare sector stands at the forefront of innovation with the advent of Smart Healthcare powered by Artificial Intelligence (AI). This transformative combination is not merely a technological evolution, but a paradigm shift in the way healthcare is delivered, managed, and experienced. Few applications are mentioned in Fig. 3.4 Smart Healthcare in Industry 5.0 is characterized by the consistent integration of AI-driven arrangements over the complete healthcare environment. From understanding care to authoritative forms, AI is revolutionizing the industry, giving exceptional openings for productivity, precision, and personalized healthcare administrations. One of the key applications of AI in Healthcare is predictive analytics, where machine learning calculations analyze tremendous sums of information to figure out illness flare-ups, quiet confirmation rates, and treatment reactions, empowering proactive and targeted mediations. Within the domain of diagnostics, AI is playing a critical part in refining restorative imaging and pathology. Progressed picture acknowledgment calculations fueled by profound learning models are upgrading the precision of diagnostics, empowering the early location of maladies such as cancer and neurological clutters. AI-powered symptomatic devices are not as it was making strides in precision but to assisting the symptomatic handle, driving to opportune intercessions and superior understanding results. Moreover, the integration of AI in pathology is streamlining the investigation of tissue tests, diminishing manual blunders, and upgrading demonstrative exactness. Besides, AI is changing persistent care through the advancement of virtual well-being collaborators and chatbots, creating new benchmarks for healthcare systems. These expert frameworks give patients real-time well-being data, pharmaceutical updates, and way-of-life suggestions, advancing proactive healthcare administration. Additionally, AI-driven chatbots are upgrading the persistent involvement by advertising moment reactions to requests, arrangement planning, and personalized well-being counsel, contributing to forward quiet fulfillment and engagement of humans in healthcare systems. In Industry 5.0, the concept of the Web of Things (IoT) is profoundly interwoven with Perceptive Healthcare. Wearable gadgets prepared with sensors and AI capabilities are enabling people to screen their well-being in real time. These gadgets can track imperative signs of physical movement and indeed identify potential well-being issues, giving important information for preventive care (Charulatha and Sujatha 2020). Also, IoT-enabled restorative gadgets are upgrading further understanding observing, permitting healthcare suppliers to keep a nonstop check on patients' well-being status, diminishing healing center confirmations, and empowering convenient intercessions. Within the authoritative space, AI is optimizing healthcare operations by robotizing schedule errands, progressing productivity, and decreasing operational costs (Baker et al. 2017). AI-powered arrangements are streamlining charging forms, arrangement planning, and stock administration, permitting healthcare organizations to distribute assets more successfully. This not only improves operational proficiency but also contributes to fetched investment funds, eventually driving to more reasonable and open healthcare administrations. Another significant application of AI in Industry 5.0's Smart Healthcare is drug discovery and development (Pradhan and Chawla 2020). However, the traditional drug discovery process is time-consuming and costly, but AI is revolutionizing this by accelerating the identification of potential drug candidates. Machine learning calculations analyze natural information, foresee medicate intelligence, and optimize definitions lessening the time and assets required for medication improvements. This transformative approach holds the potential to bring unused and imaginative medicines to advertise speedier, tending to neglect restorative needs more proficiently. Within personalized pharmaceuticals, AI is reshaping treatment plans by analyzing person persistent information to tailor treatments based on the hereditary, way of life, and natural components. This approach upgrades treatment viability, minimizes unfavorable impacts, and makes strides by and large quiet results (Pathak et al. 2019). AI calculations can recognize designs and relationships inside expansive datasets, enabling healthcare experts to create more

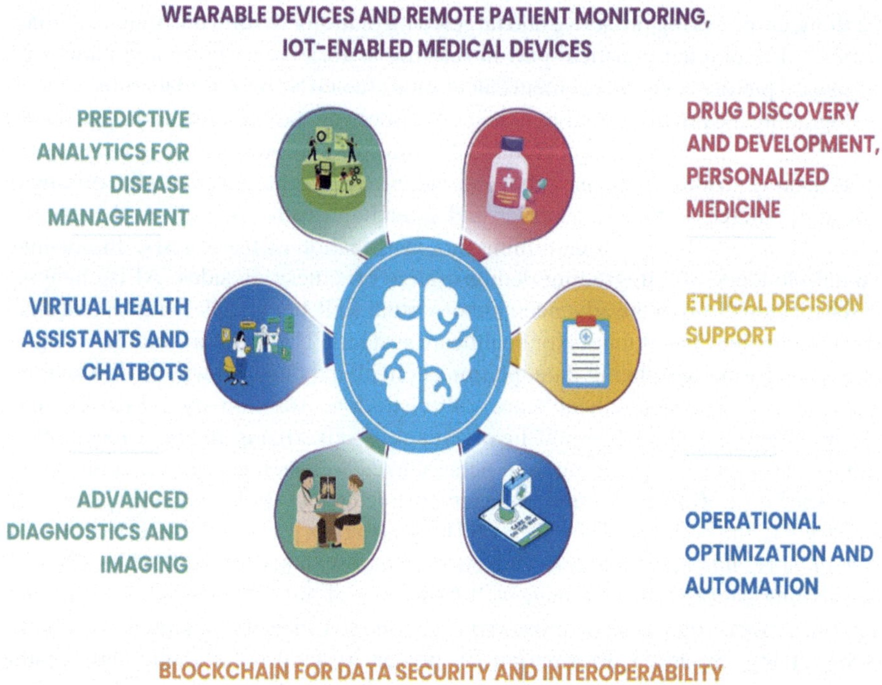

Fig. 3.4 Applications of Smart Healthcare. *Source* Author

educated choices approximately the foremost reasonable and personalized treatment strategies for each persistent.

3.12 Summary and Future Work

In times to come, Smart Healthcare in Industry 5.0 will be fortified by the nonstop progressions in Counterfeit Insights (AI), which holds tremendous potential for reshaping the healthcare scene. As we see, a few key points are likely to be the central focuses on driving the advancement of Smart Healthcare frameworks. One of the essential future avenues is the refinement and development of AI applications in diagnostics in the healthcare industry. To expect advanced improvements in therapeutic imaging investigation through the integration of progressed AI calculations. Moreover, these calculations are fueled by profound learning and neural systems, which will proceed to move forward the precision and proficiency of demonstrative forms. We anticipate AI to play a progressively basic part in distinguishing unpretentious designs and variations from the norm in restorative pictures, empowering the early location of illnesses with higher accuracy. The integration of multi-modal information, such as combining imaging information with hereditary data, will give a more comprehensive understanding of illnesses, clearing the way for more focused and personalized treatment methodologies. Besides, the development of AI applications in diagnostics will envelop a broader extend of restorative spaces, counting pathology, radiology, and genomics. The technology's capacity to analyze multifaceted information sets, such as therapeutic imaging and hereditary profiles, will result in a comprehensive and all-encompassing approach to illness location. This extension not only expands the capabilities of healthcare experts but also contributes to the democratization of progressed diagnostics, cultivating forward healthcare availability and results on a worldwide scale. As AI proceeds to refine and extend its demonstrative applications, it guarantees to be a transformative constraint in forming a long-standing time scene of healthcare. Within the domain of telemedicine and remote patient checking, the end of the holds the guarantee of indeed more modern and interconnected arrangements. AI-driven virtual well-being colleagues and chatbots are likely to advance into exceedingly natural and context-aware interfacing, giving not as it were restorative data but too sympathetic and candidly cleverly intuitive (Charulatha and Sujatha 2020). These progressed virtual associates may be able to analyze voice tones and facial expressions to measure understanding of well-being and enthusiastic states, contributing to a more all-encompassing approach to understanding care. Furthermore, the integration of augmented reality (AR) and virtual reality (VR) advances might assist in upgrading the telemedicine encounter, permitting healthcare suppliers to conduct virtual examinations and reenactments for more immersive and exact appraisals. Telemedicine stages will advance with AI-driven virtual collaborators able of nuanced, sympathetic, and intuitive, advertising a more human-like touch in further meetings. The integration of wearable gadgets and IoT sensors will empower nonstop and real-time checking of patients' imperative signs and well-being measurements, giving comprehensive information to healthcare suppliers. Moreover, these interconnected arrangements will encourage proactive mediations based on prescient analytics, anticipating potential well-being issues that, sometimes recently heightened. Patients will be involved in a more associated healthcare environment, with inaccessible observing gadgets consistently transmitting information to healthcare experts and AI algorithms giving noteworthy experiences. The merging of these technologies will not, as it were, upgrade healthcare openness but, moreover, contribute to more proficient and proactive healthcare administration. Patients will appreciate the benefits of personalized, inaccessible care that goes past the limits of conventional healthcare settings, checking a noteworthy jump toward a future where telemedicine and inaccessible understanding checking play essential parts in conveying patient-centric, tech-enabled healthcare. The long-standing time of wearables and IoT gadgets in Smart Healthcare will see a meeting of advances, driving to more consistent and coordinated arrangements. Wearable gadgets will advance past basic wellbeing trackers, joining more progressed sensors and AI capabilities. Prescient analytics will empower these gadgets to not as it were, screen current well-being measurements but, moreover, figure out potential well-being issues based on chronicled information (Zhu et al. 2019). The integration of 5G innovation will encourage speedier and more dependable communication between wearables and healthcare frameworks, empowering real-time information transmission and investigation. Besides, the advancement of bioelectronic gadgets, able to meddle specifically with the human anxious framework, seems to revolutionize the checking and administration of unremitting conditions. IoT gadgets will play a vital part in making a comprehensive healthcare environment. These gadgets will be interconnected to consistently collect, analyze, and transmit health-related information, cultivating an all-encompassing understanding of patients' well-being. This integration permits persistent farther observing, empowering early location of potential well-being issues, and encouraging opportune intercessions. Besides, wearables and IoT gadgets will use progressed Artificial Intelligence (AI) calculations to infer significant experiences from the collected information. Predictive analytics will be more refined, helping healthcare experts create personalized treatment plans and optimize preventive techniques. As these technologies evolve, they will not as it were, engage people to effectively oversee their well-being but empower healthcare suppliers to convey more exact and patient-centric care. The long run of wearables and IoT in Smart Healthcare envisions an associated environment where data-driven bits of knowledge contribute to strides in well-being results, preventive care, and a more productive and responsive healthcare system. AI's part in sedate revelation and advancement is balanced for significant development within the coming long time. The use of AI for a de novo sedate plan, where calculations create totally unused particles with craved restorative properties, could be a wilderness that holds noteworthy potential (Da Costa et al. 2018). AI models will progressively use tremendous datasets, counting genomics, proteomics, and clinical trial information, to distinguish novel medicate targets and foresee the adequacy and security of potential medicate candidates. The increasing speed of dignified improvement timelines through AI-driven reenactments and optimizations will not as it were, decrease costs but expedite the conveyance of innovative therapies to patients in require. Counterfeit Insights (AI) is revolutionizing medicate revelation and improvement, advertising exceptional speed, proficiency, and advancement within the pharmaceutical industry. In the future, AI's part in this preparation will be balanced to become more necessary. AI calculations analyze endless datasets, counting hereditary data, chemical properties, and clinical trial results to recognize potential medicate candidates with momentous exactness. Machine learning models foresee medicate intelligence, harmfulness, and adequacy, quickening the recognizable proof of promising compounds. AI-driven stages speed up the screening of enormous chemical libraries, lessening the time and fetched customarily related with medicate revelation. In addition, these calculations persistently learn from modern information, refining their forecasts and adjusting to developing patterns in biomedical inquiry. In medication improvement, AI facilitates personalized pharmaceuticals by analyzing persistent information to anticipate a person's reactions to medicines. This permits more focus on clinical trials, guaranteeing that drugs are developed and tried with particular quiet populaces in intellect. AI's capacity to reveal unobtrusive designs in organic information moreover helps within the distinguishing proof of novel medicate targets, contributing to the advancement of treatments for already challenging or rare illnesses. The long run of AI in medicate disclosure guarantees a worldview move, where the integration of progressed calculations leads to the fast development of inventive and personalized medicines, eventually making strides in understanding results and changing the scene of healthcare. The concept of explainable AI (XAI) will end up progressively pivotal within the healthcare space. As AI frameworks have gotten to be more complex and included in critical decision-making forms, there's a developing requirement for straightforwardness and interpretability. Future AI models in healthcare will be given clear clarifications of their thinking and choice pathways, empowering healthcare experts to believe and get the proposals and expectations made by these frameworks. This straightforwardness will not, as it were, upgrade the selection of AI in clinical settings but also contribute to the moral and dependable sending of these advances. The concept of Reasonable Counterfeit Insights (XAI) is set to end up progressively significant within the healthcare space. As AI calculations play a developing part in helping therapeutic choices, the requirement for straightforwardness and interpretability becomes fundamental. In healthcare, where choices straightforwardly affect quiet well-being, understanding how and why AI frameworks reach conclusions is basic for picking up beliefs and guaranteeing responsibility. Reasonable AI permits healthcare experts to comprehend the thinking behind AI-generated proposals, cultivating a collaborative relationship between people and machines. This transparency is particularly basic in delicate zones like diagnostics and treatment arranging, where the stakes are tall. Clinicians have to be approved AI proposals, and XAI gives the implies to do so by advertising clear bits of knowledge into the decision-making handle. Besides, administrative bodies progressively emphasize the significance of explainability in AI applications within healthcare. As security concerns and moral contemplations become more conspicuous, XAI has become an apparatus for addressing these issues. It empowers compliance with controls, guarantees moral AI hones, and eventually encourages the dependable integration of AI innovations into healthcare settings. Within the future, the far-reaching selection of Logical AI will not, as it were upgrade the unwavering quality of AI-assisted healthcare but also contribute to the moral and responsible advancement of innovation within the restorative field. The collaborative and interoperable nature of healthcare information will be a key center within the future advancement of Shrewd Healthcare. Blockchain innovation will play a central part in guaranteeing the security, astuteness, and interoperability of well-being information over distinctive healthcare suppliers. Decentralized and tamper-proof quiet records will encourage the consistent trade of data, empowering healthcare experts to get a comprehensive see of a patient's therapeutic history. This interoperability will progress care coordination, decrease excess tests and methods, and improve the general quality and efficiency of healthcare conveyance. Within the realm of personalized pharmaceuticals, long-standing time will witness an expanded integration of AI with genomics and other genomics information. Progressed AI calculations will analyze tremendous datasets comprising hereditary, epigenetic, and natural data to tailor treatment plans with phenomenal accuracy. This personalized approach will amplify past cancer medications to different helpful ranges, optimizing mediations for conditions extending from cardiovascular infections to neurodegenerative clutters. The integration of real-world information from electronic well-being records and wearable gadgets will advance and contribute to the refinement of personalized treatment methodologies. By consolidating AI, personalized pharmaceuticals will see progressions in quiet stratification, where AI calculations distinguish subpopulations with particular hereditary or biomarker profiles, directing more focus on viable intercessions. Machine learning models will contribute to the forecast of a person's reactions to medicines, optimizing medicate determination and measurement based on a person's interesting hereditary cosmetics. Besides, AI-driven stages will encourage the translation of complex hereditary varieties, empowering clinicians to distinguish illness susceptibilities and survey potential dangers more comprehensively. Real-time checking through wearable gadgets, coordinates with AI analytics will give ceaseless well-being information, permitting for energetic alterations in treatment plans based on the individual's changing well-being status. The expanded integration of AI in personalized medication not only enhances treatment exactness but also quickens the development of inventive treatments custom-made to particular quiet profiles. This collaboration between AI and personalized medication holds the guarantee of conveying more successful and patient-centric healthcare, introducing in an unused period where restorative mediations are finely tuned to the personal characteristics of each persistent. Within the realm of personalized pharmaceuticals, the long term will witness an expanded integration of AI with genomics and other genomics information. Progressed AI calculations will analyze tremendous datasets comprising hereditary, epigenetic, and natural data to tailor treatment plans with uncommon accuracy. This personalized approach will expand past cancer medications to different helpful ranges, optimizing mediations for conditions extending from cardiovascular maladies to neurodegenerative clutters. The integration of real-world information from electronic well-being records and wearable gadgets will advance and contribute to the refinement of personalized treatment methodologies. By joining AI, personalized pharmaceuticals will see progressions in persistent stratification, where AI calculations recognize subpopulations with hereditary or biomarker profiles, directing more focused on and successful intercessions. Machine learning models will contribute to the forecast of a person's reactions to medicines, optimizing sedate determination and dose based on a person's special hereditary cosmetics. Moreover, AI-driven stages will encourage the translation of complex hereditary varieties, empowering clinicians to recognize infection susceptibilities and evaluate potential dangers more comprehensively. Real-time observing through wearable gadgets coordinates with AI analytics, and will give ceaseless well-being information, permitting energetic alterations in treatment plans based on the individual's changing well-being status. The expanded integration of AI in personalized pharmaceuticals not as it were enhancing treatment exactness but also quickens the development of imaginative treatments custom-fitted to particular understanding profiles. This cooperative energy between AI and personalized medication holds the guarantee of conveying more viable and patient-centric healthcare, introduced in a modern period where restorative intercessions are finely tuned to the personal characteristics of each understanding. Moral contemplations and administrative systems will proceed to advance hand in hand with innovative progressions in Shrewd Healthcare. The mindful utilization of AI in healthcare settings requires clear rules and measures to address issues related to information security, understanding assent, and algorithmic predispositions. The improvement of vigorous moral systems and administrative approaches will be basic to guarantee that AI applications in healthcare follow standards of reasonableness, responsibility, and straight forwardness. In conclusion, the long-term work of Shrewd Healthcare in Industry 5.0 utilizing AI is balanced for groundbreaking advancements over different spaces. From refined diagnostics to progressed telemedicine, medicate revelation, and personalized medication, the integration of AI will proceed to drive advancement and reshape the healthcare scene. As we explore this energizing wilderness, it is pivotal to strike a adjustment between mechanical progressions and moral contemplations, guaranteeing that the transformative control of AI in healthcare is saddled dependably for the good thing about people and society as an entirety.

References

Adel A (2022) Future of Industry 5.0 in society: human-centric solutions, challenges and prospective research areas. J Cloud Comput 11(1):1–15

Akundi A, Euresti D, Luna S, Ankobiah W, Lopes A, Edinbarough I (2022) State of Industry 5.0—analysis and identification of current research trends. Appl Syst Innov 5(1):27

Ali F, El-Sappagh S, Islam SR, Kwak D, Ali A, Imran M, Kwak KS (2020) A smart healthcare monitoring system for heart disease prediction based on ensemble deep learning and feature fusion. Inf Fusion 63:208–222

Baker SB, Xiang W, Atkinson I (2017) Internet of things for smart healthcare: technologies, challenges, and opportunities. IEEE Access 5:26521–26544

Bigan C (2022) Trends in teaching artificial intelligence for Industry 5.0. Sustainability and innovation in manufacturing enterprises: indicators, models and assessment for Industry 5.0, pp 257–274

Catarinucci L, De Donno D, Mainetti L, Palano L, Patrono L, Stefanizzi ML, Tarricone L (2015) An IoT-aware architecture for smart healthcare systems. IEEE Internet Things J 2(6):515–526

Charulatha A, Sujatha R (2020) Smart healthcare use cases and applications. Internet of things use cases for the healthcare industry, pp 185–203

Da Costa CA, Pasluosta CF, Eskofier B, Da Silva DB, da Rosa Righi R (2018) Internet of health things: toward intelligent vital signs monitoring in hospital wards. Artif Intell Med 89:61–69

Goyal D, Tyagi AK (2020) ICT for competitive strategies. CRC Press, pp 379–396

Haleem A, Javaid M (2019) Industry 5.0 and its expected applications in medical field. Curr Med Res Pract 9(4):167–169

Iyengar KP, Pe EZ, Jalli J, Shashidhara MK, Jain VK, Vaish A, Vaishya R (2022) Industry 5.0 technology capabilities in trauma and orthopaedics. J Orthop 32:125–132

Jagadeeswari V, Subramaniyaswamy V, Logesh R, Vijayakumar V (2018) A study on medical internet of things and big data in personalized healthcare system. Health Inf Sci Syst 6:1–20

Joshi N, Jharia B (2015) Optimized fuzzy power control over fading channels in spectrum sharing cognitive radio using ANFIS. In: 2015 2nd International conference on signal processing and integrated networks (SPIN). IEEE, pp 329–333

Joshi N, Kumar A, Minenkov D, Kaplun D, Sharma S (2023) Optimized mac protocol using fuzzy-based framework for cognitive radio adhoc networks. IEEE Access 11:27506–27518

Lu Y (2017) Industry 4.0: a survey on technologies, applications and open research issues. J Ind Inf Integr 6:1–10

Lu Y (2021) The current status and developing trends of Industry 4.0: a review. Inf Syst Front 1–20

Maddikunta PKR, Pham QV, Prabadevi B, Deepa N, Dev K, Gadekallu TR, Ruby R, Liyanage M (2022) Industry 5.0: a survey on enabling technologies and potential applications. J Ind Inf Integr 26:100257

Madsen DØ, Berg T (2021) An exploratory bibliometric analysis of the birth and emergence of Industry 5.0. Appl Syst Innov 4(4):87
Mbunge E, Muchemwa B et al (2022) Towards emotive sensory web in virtual health care: trends, technologies, challenges and ethical issues. Sensors Int 3:100134
Mohanta B, Das P, Patnaik S (2019) Healthcare 5.0: a paradigm shift in digital health-care system using artificial intelligence, IOT and 5G communication. In: 2019 International conference on applied machine learning (ICAML). IEEE, pp 191–196
Nair MM, Tyagi AK, Sreenath N (2021) The future with Industry 4.0 at the core of society 5.0: open issues, future opportunities and challenges. In: 2021 International conference on computer communication and informatics (ICCCI). IEEE, pp 1–7
Özdemir V, Hekim N (2018) Birth of Industry 5.0: making sense of big data with artificial intelligence, "the internet of things" and next-generation technology policy. OMICS: J Integr Biol 22(1):65–76
Pathak P, Pal PR, Shrivastava M, Ora P (2019) Fifth revolution: applied AI & human intelligence with cyber physical systems. Int J Eng Adv Technol 8(3):23–27
Popov VV, Kudryavtseva EV, Kumar Katiyar N, Shishkin A, Stepanov SI, Goel S (2022) Industry 4.0 and digitalization in healthcare. Materials 15(6):2140
Pradhan K, Chawla P (2020) Medical internet of things using machine learning algorithms for lung cancer detection. J Manag Anal 7(4):591–623
Pramod A, Naicker HS, Tyagi AK (2022) Emerging innovations in the near future using deep learning techniques. Adv Anal Deep Learn Models 231–254
Prasad DH, Srikanth M (2015) Mobile healthcare monitoring system in mobile cloud computing. Int J Comput Technol Appl 6(1):43–46
Rajan Jeyaraj P, Nadar ERS (2022) Smart-monitor: patient monitoring system for IoT-based healthcare system using deep learning. IETE J Res 68(2):1435–1442
Reischauer G (2018) Industry 4.0 as policy-driven discourse to institutionalize innovation systems in manufacturing. Technol Forecast Soc Change 132:26–33
Saraswat D, Bhattacharya P, Verma A, Prasad VK, Tanwar S, Sharma G, Bokoro PN, Sharma R (2022) Explainable AI for Healthcare 5.0: opportunities and challenges. IEEE Access
Selvarajan S, Manoharan H, Hasanin T, Alsini R, Uddin M, Shorfuzzaman M, Alsufyani A (2022) Biomedical signals for healthcare using Hadoop infrastructure with artificial intelligence and fuzzy logic interpretation. Appl Sci 12(10):5097
Sindhwani R, Afridi S, Kumar A, Banaitis A, Luthra S, Singh PL (2022) Can Industry 5.0 revolutionize the wave of resilience and social value creation? A multi-criteria framework to analyze enablers. Technol Soc 68:101887
Singh PD, Dhiman G, Sharma R (2022) Internet of things for sustaining a smart and secure healthcare system. Sustain Comput: Inform Syst 33:100622
Subasi A, Khateeb K, Brahimi T, Sarirete A (2020) Innovation in health informatics. Elsevier, pp 123–144
Sujith A, Sajja GS, Mahalakshmi V, Nuhmani S, Prasanalakshmi B (2022) Systematic review of smart health monitoring using deep learning and artificial intelligence. Neurosci Inform 2(3):100028
The digital transformation of healthcare. https://www.sap.com/industries/healthcare.html
Tuppad A, Patil SD (2022) Society 5.0: smart future towards enhancing the quality of society. Springer, pp 209–227
Turner C, Oyekan J, Garn W, Duggan C, Abdou K (2022) Industry 5.0 and the circular economy: utilizing LCA with intelligent products. Sustainability 14(22):14847
Tyagi AK (2022a) Handbook of research on technical, privacy, and security challenges in a modern world. IGI Global
Tyagi AK (2022b) Using multimedia systems, tools, and technologies for smart healthcare services. IGI Global
Udendhran R, Yamini G (2021) The pivotal role of internet of things and ubiquitous computing in healthcare. Appl Ubiquitous Comput 3–12

Vippalapalli V, Ananthula S (2016) Internet of things (IoT) based smart health care system. In: 2016 International conference on signal processing, communication, power and embedded system (SCOPES). IEEE, pp 1229–1233

Xu X, Lu Y, Vogel-Heuser B, Wang L (2021) Industry 4.0 and Industry 5.0—inception, conception and perception. J Manuf Syst 61:530–535

Yadav P, Sharma S (2023) HFBO-KSELM: hybrid flash butterfly optimization-based kernel softplus extreme learning machine for classification of chronic kidney disease. J Supercomput 1–24

Yadav EP, Mittal EA, Yadav H (2018) IoT: challenges and issues in Indian perspective. In: 2018 3rd International conference on internet of things: smart innovation and usages (IoT-SIU). IEEE, pp 1–5

Yadav P, Sharma S, Mahadeva R, Patole SP (2023a) Exploring hyper-parameters and feature selection for predicting non-communicable chronic disease using stacking classifier. IEEE Access

Yadav P, Arora N, Sharma SC (2023b) Performance analysis of nature-inspired optimization algorithms for chronic disease prediction. In: 2023 International conference on device intelligence, computing and communication technologies (DICCT). IEEE, pp 1–6

Zhou B, Wu K, Lv P, Wang J, Chen G, Ji B, Liu S et al (2018) A new remote health-care system based on moving robot intended for the elderly at home. J Healthc Eng 2018

Zhu H, Wu CK, Koo CH, Tsang YT, Liu Y, Chi HR, Tsang KF (2019) Smart healthcare in the era of internet-of-things. IEEE Consum Electron Mag 8(5):26–30

Chapter 4
Navigating the Digital Age: Smart Manufacturing and Logistics

Dolly Sharma and Kitty Tripathi

Abstract This chapter provides a wide-ranging investigation of the transformative influence of smart manufacturing and logistics in the current industrial landscape. We have laid emphasis on the significance of Industry 4.0, IoT, AI, and automation. The historical framework presented here describes the evolution of manufacturing and logistics, underlining critical turning points that have led to the rise of smart practices. This work describes the core technologies such as IoT devices, sensors, big data analytics, and cloud computing with real-world examples explaining the benefits, including improved efficiency, cost savings, sustainability, and enhanced customer satisfaction. The chapter also addresses significant problems and issues associated with smart practice implementation. The inclusion of case studies demonstrates successful smart manufacturing and logistics system deployments, revealing specific techniques along with its outcomes. The incorporation of smart practices inside the bigger framework of Industry 4.0, notably the idea of the "smart factory," is methodically examined, with inferences for supply chain management. The paper also contemplates future developments, such as the effect of technologies like 5G, AI, and blockchain on the sector. Best practices and its application techniques are presented of the sectors which are implementing smart manufacturing and logistics. Ethical and regulatory issues are prioritized, with an emphasis on data protection and privacy rules. The chapter concludes by summarizing significant observations and highlighting the vital function of smart logistics and manufacturing in transforming industry's future operations.

Keywords Smart logistics · IoT · Machine learning · Smart manufacturing

D. Sharma (✉)
ABES Institute of Technology, Ghaziabad, UP, India
e-mail: dolly4friend@gmail.com

K. Tripathi
Babu Banarasi Das Northern India Institute of Technology, Lucknow, UP, India

R. Arya et al. (eds.), *Recent Trends in Artificial Intelligence Towards a Smart World*, Frontiers of Artificial Intelligence, Ethics and Multidisciplinary Applications,
https://doi.org/10.1007/978-981-97-6790-8_4

4.1 Introduction

4.1.1 Significance of Smart Manufacturing and Logistics in Today's Industrial Landscape

The modern industrial environment is greatly influenced by smart manufacturing and logistics, which also drive competitiveness, efficiency, sustainability, and innovation in a variety of other sectors and industries. Technology is predicted to become ever more significant as it develops, completely changing how companies function and provide value to their clients. Businesses can respond swiftly to shifting market conditions, disruptions, and unanticipated events like supply chain disruptions or natural disasters because of smart manufacturing and logistics. Businesses can detect possible hazards and opportunities using real-time data analytics and predictive capabilities, enabling them to act quickly and efficiently. The global industrial landscape is transformed by smart manufacturing and logistics, which is often referred to as Industry 4.0 by leveraging advanced technologies to improve sustainability, efficiency, and productivity. The terms and key concepts associated with this transformation include Industry 4.0, IoT, AI, and Automation as shown in Fig. 4.1.

In the digital age, industries are changing toward higher efficiency, flexibility, responsiveness, and competitiveness due to the terms and concepts' interconnectedness and synergy. Businesses can discover new avenues for innovation, expansion, and value creation by utilizing Industry 4.0 principles, IoT connection, AI-driven insights, and automation technologies. A paradigm shift in manufacturing and logistics is being brought about by the combination of technologies such as Industry 4.0, Internet of Things (IoT), Artificial Intelligence (AI), and automation, which are transforming entire industries. Below is a discussion of these words and important ideas:

- **Industry 4.0**: An architype changes in manufacturing and logistics that combines physical–cyber systems, the Internet of Things (IoT), cloud computation, cognitive computation, and artificial intelligence (AI) to design intelligent, capable of self-optimization, and interrelated production systems.

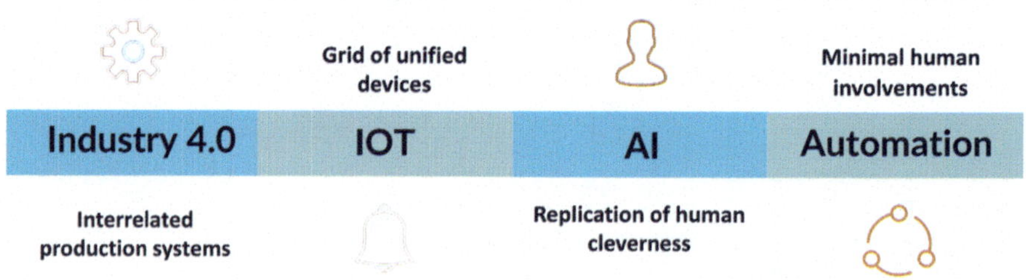

Fig. 4.1 Key concept associated with transformation in industry. *Source* Author

- **IoT (Internet of Things)**: A grid of unified devices that gather and exchange data to enhance progressions and improve decision-making.
- **AI (Artificial Intelligence)**: The replication of human cleverness in machines that act on data by learning from data.
- **Automation**: The usage of technology to accomplish errands with minimal human involvements.

The integrated smart structures in industrial logistics are thought as major chance to increase performance of logistics and diminution of logistics costs for both big corporations and minor and medium-sized initiatives.

The benefits of smart manufacturing and logistics include the following:

(i) **Efficiency improvement**: By incorporating automation and AI, smart systems can improve production processes, scale down waste, and increase throughput.
(ii) **Increased flexibility**: Rapid adaptation by smart systems is enable to response changing market demands and preferences of customers.
(iii) **Enhanced sustainability**: Smart manufacturing and logistics is capable of lessening energy consumption, waste and emissions thus can contribute for a more sustainable future.
(iv) **Increased safety**: Smart systems is capable of monitoring and analyzing production strategies in real time, and thus potential hazards can be identified dipping the risk of accidents.
(v) **Improved transparency**: Smart systems are capable of providing real-time data and perceptions into production processes that enable improved decision-making and supply chain management.

The combined structure of smart systems in industrial logistics is reinforced by a conceptual framework which contains decision-making support by IoT integration, supply chain alignment by SSI, smart system integration, transportation issues, and automation (Thales Group).

This framework supports to direct research and development in the field of smart manufacturing and logistics, confirming that application of these technologies will be in a way that benefits will be maximized, and their drawbacks will be minimized. The upcoming future of smart manufacturing and logistics is considered by continued modernization and the integration of new skills, such as virtual reality (VR) and augmented reality (AR), to generate wide immersive and interactive production environments. New opportunities for collaboration, innovation, and progress in the global industrial landscape will be enabled by continuous evolution of these technologies.

4.2 Industry 4.0

Industry 4.0 denotes the fourth industrial revolution, described by the inclusion of smart systems, such as the artificial intelligence (AI), automation, and Internet of Things (IoT) into manufacturing and logistics processes. This transformation focuses on to create extra flexible, sustainable, and efficient production systems.

The implementation of Industry 4.0 in manufacturing and logistics provides many benefits, including improved efficiency, enhanced flexibility, increased sustainability, improved safety, and increased transparency (Soori et al. 2023).

Advances in digital technologies, falling hardware and software prices, and the growing need for efficiency, flexibility, and creativity in the manufacturing and industrial sectors have all contributed to the emergence of Industry 4.0. Businesses stand to gain a great deal from the adoption of Industry 4.0 technology, but there are drawbacks as well, including issues with cybersecurity, workforce development, and legacy system integration. However, efforts and investments aimed at transforming the future of industry and manufacturing are still motivated by Industry 4.0's revolutionary potential.

The revolutionary effects of each industrial revolution (from Industry 1.0 to Industry 4.0) on economies, societies, and technological breakthroughs account for their historical significance as shown in Fig. 4.2.

4.2.1 The First Industrial Revolution (Industry 1.0—Late Eighteenth and Early Nineteenth Centuries)

Significance: During this time, economies transitioned from rural and craft based to industrialized, driven by steam power and mechanization. Important developments

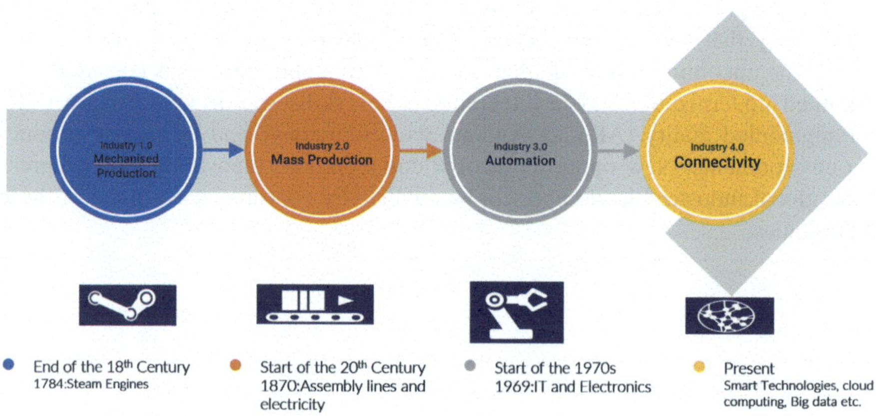

Fig. 4.2 Historical evolution of industry. *Source* Author

include the invention of the steam engine, the mechanization of the textile industry, and the construction of factories.

Impact: Caused new social classes to form, urbanization, and greater manufacturing efficiency. It changed the production and distribution of goods and established the groundwork for contemporary industrial economies.

4.2.2 Second Industrial Revolution (Industry 2.0—Late Nineteenth to Early Twentieth Centuries)

Significance: Distinguished by the extensive integration of electricity, large-scale manufacturing methodologies, and the emergence of dense industries. Important developments include the introduction of assembly lines, the electrification of factories, the expansion of railroads, and improvements in the manufacture of steel.

Impact: Accelerated urbanization, industrialization, and major advancements in communication, transportation, and living standards. It made it possible to produce items on a bigger scale and promoted the expansion of consumer markets.

4.2.3 Third Industrial Revolution (Industry 3.0—Late Twentieth Century)

Significance: Also referred to as the "Digital Revolution," this era witnessed the development of automation and information technology. Important developments include the advent of computers, the Internet, manufacturing process automation, and improvements in telecommunications.

Impact: Transformed industry, trade, and communication allowed for the globalization of markets, the digitalization of information, and the automation of repetitive tasks, which resulted in the development of new business models, service sectors, and knowledge-based economies.

4.2.4 Fourth Industrial Revolution (Industry 4.0—Present)

Significance: Distinguished by the combination of data analytics, physical systems, and digital technology to produce intelligent, networked systems. Important advancements include automation, big data analytics, IoT device integration, and artificial intelligence in manufacturing and industrial operations.

Impact: Using data-driven decision-making, automation, and enhanced connectivity to transform industries. Promises increased production, sustainability, customization, and efficiency. Resulting in the creation of digital supply chains, smart manufacturing, and new chances for economic expansion and innovation.

4.3 Internet of Things (IoT)

The Internet of Things (IoT) is network to optimize processes using a network of interconnected devices that collect and exchange data and improve decision-making. In the context of smart manufacturing and logistics, IoT plays a crucial role in enabling real-time data collection and analysis, which can be used to optimize production processes, reduce waste, and increase throughput. By integrating IoT with other smart systems such as artificial intelligence (AI) and automation, smart manufacturing and logistics can become more efficient, flexible, and sustainable. For example, IoT sensors can be cast-off to monitor and track inventory levels, equipment performance, and environmental situations, providing real-time data that can be used to improve logistics operations. Overall, IoT is a key enabler of Industry 4.0 and plays a critical role in the transformation of manufacturing and logistics processes.

Some examples of IoT devices used in smart logistics include the following:

- Real-time location systems (RTLS) for asset tracking inventory in warehouses and distribution centers.
- Sensors for temperature monitoring, humidity, and rest environmental conditions to guarantee proper storage and transportation of goods.
- For automated identification, RFID tags are used and also help in tracking of products during the supply chain.
- To monitor temperature, shock during transportation and humidity, smart containers and sensors equipped with pallets are used.
- IoT-based forklifts and other material handling equipment for optimization of warehouse operations and real-time monitoring.
- IoT-based fleet management systems for tracking and optimizing the vehicle's movement in transportation networks.
- IoT-enabled smart boxes for real-time monitoring of logistics processes and data analysis.
- IoT-based predictive maintenance systems for monitoring the condition of equipment and predicting failures to minimize downtime and maintenance costs.
- IoT-enabled smart warehouses for optimizing storage and retrieval processes, reducing energy consumption, and improving overall warehouse efficiency.
- IoT-based supply chain visibility platforms for real-time monitoring and optimization of supply chain operations.

IoT devices in smart logistics enable the following benefits:

Upgraded visibility: Real-time data is provided by IoT devices on the location, and it also includes condition and movement of goods during the supply chain thus enabling better decision-making and more clear logistics operations.

Improved reliability: IoT-enabled supply chains are less prone to disruptions and more reliable, as they can rapidly recognize and resolve issues at the source of inefficiencies and risks.

Increased agility: IoT-based supply chains are more reactive and agile, as they can adapt to changing requirements and market conditions.

Reduced costs: IoT-enabled supply chains can optimize processes, reduce waste, and improve efficiency and hence are more cost-effective.

Better quality: IoT devices can help to monitor and control production processes, ensuring that products meet quality standards and customer expectations.

In general, the Internet of Things (IoT) is a game-changer for efficiency and innovation in a variety of industries, empowering businesses to use data and connectivity to boost consumer experiences, streamline operations, and open up new business avenues as shown in Fig. 4.3.

The Internet of Things, or IoT, is a network of networked objects that can gather and share data via the Internet because they are embedded with sensors, software, and other technologies. Several industries, including manufacturing, retail, healthcare, security, surveillance, and transportation, will be significantly impacted by IoT.

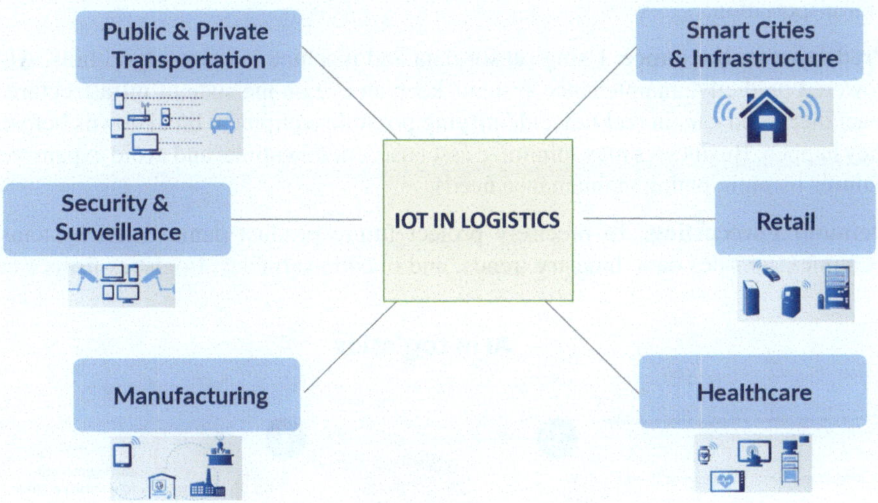

Fig. 4.3 Application of IoT in logistics. *Source* Author

4.4 Artificial Intelligence

Artificial intelligence (AI) refers to the simulation of human intelligence in machines that learn from and act on data. In the context of smart manufacturing and logistics, AI plays a crucial role in enabling real-time data analysis and decision-making. By leveraging AI algorithms, smart systems can optimize production processes, reduce waste, and increase throughput. For example, AI can be used to analyze data from IoT sensors to identify patterns and anomalies, enabling predictive maintenance and reducing downtime. AI can also be used to optimize logistics operations, such as route planning and inventory management, based on real-time data and demand forecasting.

Through the introduction of cutting-edge technology and capabilities that improve efficiency, visibility, and decision-making throughout the supply chain, artificial intelligence (AI) is completely transforming the logistics sector as shown in Fig. 4.4.

The following are some significant areas in which AI is influencing logistics:

Route Optimization: To optimize delivery routes, artificial intelligence (AI) systems examine past data, current traffic data, meteorological data, and other pertinent variables. AI can determine the most economical routes for trucks, ships, or drones by considering a variety of factors, including journey time, fuel consumption, and cost of transportation.

Predictive maintenance: Using sensor data and machine learning algorithms, AI-powered predictive maintenance systems keep an eye on the state of infrastructure, machinery, and cars in real time, identifying possible equipment breakdowns before they happen. Businesses may minimize asset use, cut downtime, and avoid expensive failures by anticipating maintenance needs.

Demand Forecasting: To precisely project future product demand, AI systems examine past sales data, industry trends, and outside variables. Logistics firms can

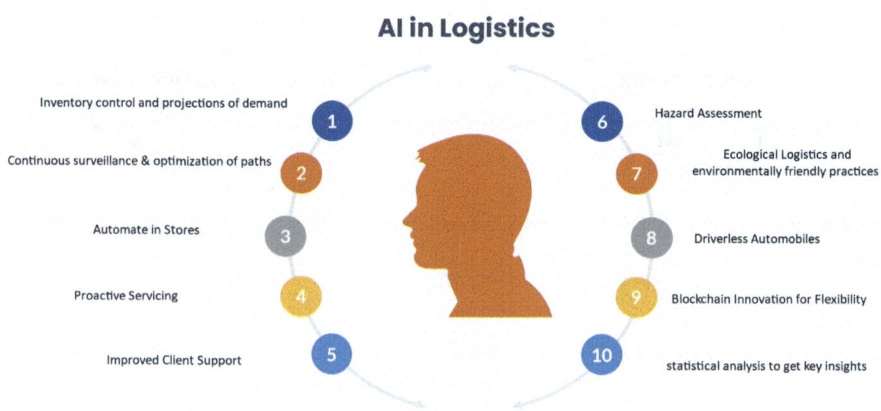

Fig. 4.4 Application of AI in logistics. *Source* Author

increase supply chain efficiency and customer satisfaction by optimizing inventory levels, minimizing stockouts, and reducing excess inventory carrying costs through more precise demand forecasting.

Warehouse Automation: By automating repetitive processes like picking, sorting, and inventory management, artificial intelligence (AI) technologies like robotic process automation (RPA), computer vision, and machine learning are revolutionizing warehouse operations. Robots and drones with AI capabilities can find objects quickly, navigate warehouses independently, and complete tasks quickly and accurately. This reduces labor costs and expedites order fulfillment.

Supply Chain Visibility: Artificial intelligence (AI)-driven supply chain visibility systems use information from several sources, like GPS trackers, RFID tags, and Internet of Things (IoT) sensors, to give real-time insights on the location, status, and condition of commodities along the supply chain. AI helps businesses discover possible bottlenecks, reduce risks, and improve inventory management and logistical operations by increasing visibility and transparency.

Dynamic Pricing and Yield Management: To optimize pricing and revenue management tactics dynamically, artificial intelligence (AI) algorithms examine market dynamics, rival pricing strategies, and customer behavior. AI-driven pricing solutions in logistics maximize profitability while preserving competitiveness by adjusting shipping prices and service levels in real time depending on variables including demand changes, capacity restrictions, and supply chain disruptions.

Customer Service and Experience: By offering immediate assistance, responding to questions, and helping with order tracking and logistics inquiries, chatbots and virtual assistants driven by artificial intelligence improve customer service and experience. Artificial intelligence (AI) improves responsiveness and overall customer satisfaction by automating routine customer contacts, freeing up human agents to concentrate on more complicated duties.

Risk management and fraud detection: To find irregularities, spot possible fraud, and reduce risks in logistics operations, AI systems examine transaction data, shipment trends, and other pertinent data. AI assists businesses with detecting new risks, averting losses, and guaranteeing that rules are followed by utilizing machine learning and predictive analytics.

With all factors considered, AI is revolutionizing the logistics sector by empowering businesses to streamline operations, enhance decision-making, and seize fresh chances for expansion and innovation. Logistics firms that use AI-driven solutions will have a competitive advantage in a world market that is becoming more dynamic and complicated as AI technologies advance.

4.5 Automation

Automation refers to making use of technology to accomplish tasks without human involvement. In the context of smart manufacturing and logistics, automation plays a crucial role in enabling real-time data analysis and decision-making. By automating production processes, smart systems can optimize production processes, reduce waste, and increase throughput. For example, automation can be used to control and monitor production lines, reducing the need for human intervention and improving efficiency. Automation can also be used to optimize logistics operations, such as route planning and inventory management, based on real-time data and demand forecasting.

The use of cutting-edge technology, including robotics, artificial intelligence (AI), the Internet of Things (IoT), and machine learning, to automate and optimize different processes in a manufacturing setting is known as automation in smart manufacturing. In smart manufacturing, automation is used in the following ways:

Robotic Automation: In smart manufacturing, robots are employed extensively to do jobs including material handling, welding, assembling, and packing. These robots can be trained to carry out repetitive jobs quickly, accurately, and reliably, which lowers the need for human labor and boosts productivity.

Autonomous Mobile Robots (AMRs) and Automated Guided Vehicles (AGVs): AMRs and AGVs are utilized in production facilities for material handling and transportation. These cars may move independently by either dynamically navigating in response to changing conditions or autonomously following predetermined routes thanks to the sensors and navigation systems installed in them.

Cobots: Collaborative robots or Cobots are robots that are made to work alongside humans to do jobs that call for human-like dexterity, flexibility, and interaction. Cobots, as opposed to conventional industrial robots, are outfitted with safety measures and sensors that provide safe human–robot collaboration, enabling more adaptive and flexible manufacturing processes.

Automated Inspection and Quality Control: In smart manufacturing, automated technologies like AI algorithms and machine vision systems are utilized for automated inspection and quality control. Real-time defect, deviation, and anomaly detection capabilities of these systems minimize the need for manual inspection while guaranteeing product quality and consistency.

Predictive Maintenance: Automation makes predictive maintenance tactics possible by employing Internet of Things (IoT) sensors to continuously monitor the state of machinery and equipment. By analyzing sensor data, machine learning algorithms can anticipate possible problems or maintenance requirements before they arise, enabling proactive maintenance scheduling and reducing unscheduled downtime.

Digital twins: These virtual copies of actual systems, assets, or processes allow for real-time analysis, optimization, and monitoring. Digital twins are used in smart manufacturing to anticipate product and equipment performance, find optimization opportunities, and simulate and visualize production processes.

Automated Data Collection and Analysis: By combining analytics platforms, data acquisition systems, and Internet of Things sensors, automation simplifies the procedures involved in gathering and analyzing data. To enhance decision-making, streamline manufacturing procedures, and support continuous improvement programs, real-time data from sensors and production systems is gathered, processed, and evaluated.

Supply Chain Automation: Demand forecasting, inventory control, and logistics are just a few of the supply chain management procedures that are automated. This technology goes beyond the manufacturing floor. Supply chains become more responsive and efficient when AI-powered algorithms automate replenishment procedures, manage inventory levels, and optimize transportation routes.

4.6 Historical Context

The foundation of smart logistics is current, advanced information and communication technology (ICT), which processes and analyzes data from all facets of logistics in real time to intelligently actualize the modern integrated logistics system. End-to-end visibility, enhanced distribution processing, warehousing, transportation, information services, and other logistics methods, as well as time and money savings, are all possible with smart logistics. Additionally, it might be able to lessen the environmental harm that logistics causes. However, there are still a lot of difficult problems to be solved before smart logistics can be implemented (Mentzer et al. 2001; Lee et al. 2016; Suma et al. 2017; Kawa 2012; Li et al. 2017).

The main challenges are enabling the complete interoperability of linked devices and enabling the smart logistics system's flexibility and autonomy to give it ever-increasing levels of intelligence. The Internet of Things, or IoT, is seen as one of the most significant areas of future technologies and is one of the major ICT technologies. IoT is gaining ground quickly in the context of contemporary wireless telecommunications, particularly with the quick development of wireless communication technologies (Li et al. 2017; Liu et al. 2019; Qiu et al. 2019).

Machine-to-machine (M2M) connections and applications were once the main focus of the definition of Internet of Things (IoT), but it has since expanded to include "ubiquitous aggregation" of data. That is, the Internet of Things has produced vast amounts of data, and with the aid of numerous technologies for mathematical analysis, it is possible to continuously investigate the intricate relationships between the transactions that these data represent. Without a doubt, IoT will be crucial to the implementation of smart logistics (Ashton 2009; Witkowski 2017), which will fundamentally alter the design of the logistics system and the mode of operation for logistics. Still, a lot of factors need to be taken into account in order to make IoT-based smart logistics a reality. These include relevant scenarios, current difficulties, and potential future directions.

The review by Ferreira et al. (2010) covered the key IoT technologies connected to automated logistics business process support. They introduce WSN and RFID among other smart goods. Then, with dynamic changes in business processes in mind, they concentrate on IoT-based support of design and runtime modifications. IoT is solely discussed in this survey in relation to wireless communication technologies and smart logistics information processing (such as business processes). Other pertinent uses, difficulties, and potential future directions of IoT in smart logistics are disregarded.

With the advent of the Industry IoT (IIoT), Barreto et al. (2017) introduced new issues in the logistics domain and addressed some reflections regarding the most crucial dimensions needed for the full implementation of the logistics 4.0 paradigm. The notion of smart logistics is put forth in this article along with an introduction to technology applications in the areas of information security, transportation, warehouse management, and resource planning.

Prasse et al. (2014) talked on the potential and new needs for Internet of Things (IoT)-based cyber–physical logistics systems (CPLSs). This article explains the notion of CPLS, enumerates the fundamental technological layers, and uses a distribution center as an example from everyday life to show how CPLS evolved. The poll does not specifically address the issues posed by IoT in smart logistics or the influence of emerging technologies on the field, despite providing thorough examples of IoT solutions in smart logistics coupled with real-world application scenarios.

In Liu and Gao (2014), the application of IoT in related sectors is introduced based on IoT theories. The impact of IoT on logistics information in the logistics service supply chain (LSSC) is analyzed, the architecture of LSSC is built on IoT, and the application prospects are forecasted. IoT applications in other facets of smart logistics and difficulties receive less attention than the impact of IoT on the logistics information issue, which includes fund flow, information flow, and logistics/service flow.

A survey of the literature on IoT technologies, such as RFID, WSN, and cloud computing, was conducted by Trappey et al. (2017). The patent roadmap visualization approach analyzes the development and use of several IoT key technologies in smart logistics.

To achieve data communication and information interchange in logistics, Lu and Teng (2012) examined the features of cloud computing and the Internet of Things and offered solutions based on these technologies.

Five IoT technologies—RFID, WSNN, cloud computing, etc.—that are necessary for the successful implementation of IoT-based goods and logistics services were presented by Lee and Lee (2015). The management and technical difficulties were examined concurrently.

A few computational technologies are employed in Taniguchi et al. (2015) to improve the planning and assessment of municipal logistics plans. This article discusses the impact of new cutting-edge manufacturing methods on urban logistics and describes how computational technologies are applied in depth; however, it doesn't go into enough detail about how new technologies are applied in all areas of logistics.

The fundamentals and evolution of smart cities, for instance, were covered by Song et al. (2017), who also addressed applications of smart cities in relation to connected vehicle (CV) and intelligent transportation systems (ITSs) and smart transportation/smart transportation. They also concentrated on the foundations and principles required for advancing the science, engineering, and technology of smart cities, including IoT.

There are other surveys, as those in articles (Song et al. 2017; Sun et al. 2016; Jeschke et al. 2017; Atzori et al. 2010; Al-Fuqaha et al. 2015), that primarily seek to introduce the IoT paradigm. These surveys introduce a variety of IoT applications across a range of industries, including smart cities, logistics, and transportation.

The use of IoT in smart logistics is introduced in Paper (Jiang and Hao 2011), which also analyzes the difficulties and prospects for IoT-based smart logistics in the areas of information processing and distribution logistics.

4.6.1 Family Histology in Smart Logistics

In the evolution of contemporary logistics, smart logistics is an unavoidable trend whose study has garnered significant interest from both academia and business. This section provides a quick overview of smart logistics, covering its concept, evolution, fundamental uses, and solutions.

Concept

Since the term "smart logistics" is introduced, academics have not been able to agree on what it means. The idea of smart products and services was initially put forth by Fleisch et al. (2005). This implies that people can assign certain tasks that require control to smart products and services. Uckelmann (2008) defines smart logistics in terms of smart products and smart services. Uckelmann goes into detail on the qualities of smart logistics, which are utilized as the criteria for defining smart logistics. According to Barretoa et al. (2017), smart logistics is a logistical system that can improve flexibility, allow for changes in the market, and bring a company in line with the requirements of its customers. According to Cullity (1972), logistics is the comprehensive planning, control, realization, and oversight of all material, part, and product flows both inside the organization and throughout the network throughout the entire value-added chain. The conceptual framework of smart logistics has evolved in tandem with the advancement of modern technologies since logistic performance is increasingly reliant on technology innovation.

According to McFarlane et al. (2016), the term "smart logistics" is frequently used to describe a variety of logistics operations (transport, inventory, order management, etc.) that are organized, managed, or regulated more intelligently than they would be if they were using traditional methods. Nonetheless, regardless of the researchers' precise definitions, we can discover that they all agree that smart logistics integrates

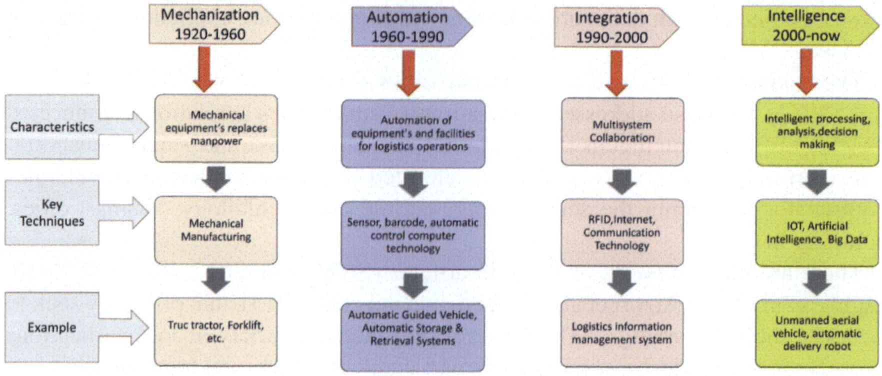

Fig. 4.5 Logistics' evolution. *Source* Author

cutting-edge communication and information technologies; integrates the logistics system; and optimizes it through thorough analysis, prompt processing, and self-adjustment to make the logistics system smarter.

Evolution

Technology development and logistical development are intimately intertwined. This chapter provides an overview of the growth of logistics from the standpoint of technical advancement. Logistics' evolution is depicted in Fig. 4.5. The fields of logistics, mechanization, automation, integration, and intelligence have all played major roles in the evolution of modern logistics. Logistics mechanization dates to the 1920s, when the CLARK Equipment Company produced the first truck tractor in 1917 (History 2019), which was used to transport cargo.

Initially, mechanical equipment replaces labor in logistical operations due to advancements in internal combustion engines, mechanical manufacturing, etc. The 1960s saw the steady transition of contemporary logistics from mechanization to automation with the introduction of sensors, bar codes, RFID technology, etc. Automated guided vehicles (AGVs) and automatic systems for storing and retrieving information (AS/RS) are two examples of representative equipment types. An AGV system divided into nonoverlapping, tandem single-vehicle loops was introduced by Bozer and Srinivasan (1991). A heuristic process was created by Hackman et al. (1990) to address the issue of the AS/RS's inability to store all things. In the 1990s and 2000s, as RFID, networks, and communication technologies advanced, logistics transitioned from automation to synergy.

The impact of information accessibility on logistics integration was examined by Gustin et al. (1995). The use of the Internet in managing the main elements of supply chains—such as buying goods, customer support, shipping, and so forth—was covered by Alancioni et al. (2000). The relationship among facts, the organizational framework, and the effective use of the integrated distribution idea is examined in Paper (Lisa et al. 1997).

To achieve the web-based incorporation of commercial operations, Leung et al. (2000) proposed a framework for an e-commerce community network that goes beyond conventional company-to-business e-commerce to e-commerce at the market level. The swift advancement of technology in the twenty-first century, such as big data, artificial intelligence, and the Internet of Things, has aided in the growth of smart logistics. To provide an intelligent production-logistics services control framework with multilayer dynamic flexibility, paper (Qu et al. 2016) develops a dynamic production-logistics synchronization system that strategically integrates cloud-based manufacturing and IoT infrastructures.

A framework explaining the process and mechanism of smart production-logistics systems was put forth by Zhang et al. (2018) to apply intelligent simulation of important manufacturing resources and look into self-organizing configuration processes. The smart linked logistic system, which makes use of all the most cutting-edge ideas, including multiagent cloud-based control, mobile robotic systems (MRSs), mobile automated platforms, and different IoT concepts, is the subject of paper (Gregor et al. 2017). A robot control system capable of autonomously sorting packages using a context-aware technique to generate information to direct a robot's movement was proposed by Shin et al. (2013). By merging the capabilities of different tracking systems, the study (Kim et al. 2015) creates an effective target-oriented smart integrated multiple tracking framework that searches for object location using information in real time and ensures the accuracy and dependability of logistical placement and handling of resources.

Fundamental uses

Figure 4.6 illustrates logistical scenarios as well as the fundamentals of smart logistics. Transportation, warehousing, loading/unloading, carrying, packing, distribution processing, distribution, and information processing are the eight scenarios that make up smart logistics.

Sensing, integration, intelligent analysis, optimized decision-making, system support, and rapid feedback for every logistical situation are the fundamental components of smart logistics.

Solutions

A lot of academics talk about smart logistics solutions from a technological development standpoint. Hofmann and Rüsch (2017), for instance, examined Industry 4.0's potential in the context of logistics management. They outline the essential elements of Industry 4.0, show off its possible effects on various logistics scenarios, and provide an implementation model for the technology that is focused on logistics. Witkowski (2017) addresses a few "smart" supply chain and logistics solutions based on Industry 4.0, big data, and IoT technological advancements.

Barretoa and colleagues (2017) provided an example of how Industry 4.0 advanced technologies are being applied to smart logistics, specifically in the areas of information security, intelligent transportation, and warehousing. The use of big data and decision support systems to improve the planning and assessment of city logistics plans is covered in Paper (Taniguchi et al. 2015). A few scholars examine how

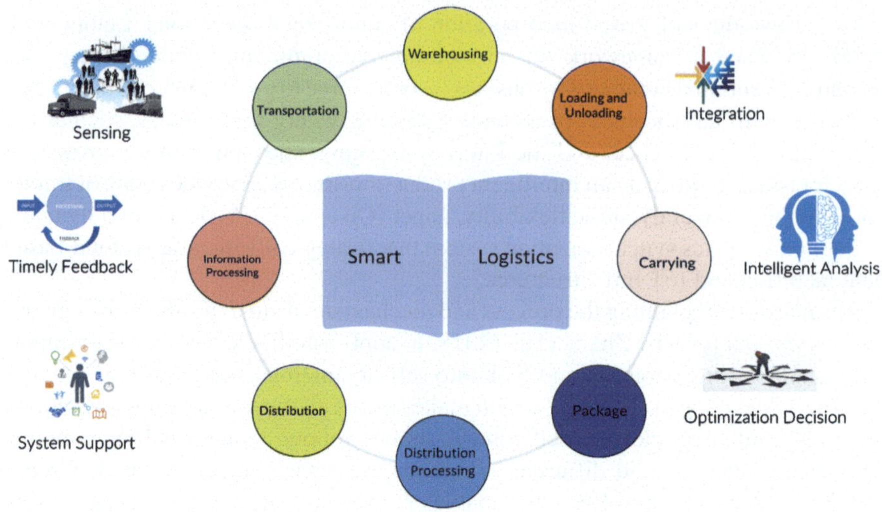

Fig. 4.6 Fundamentals of smart logistics

consumer behavior affects smart logistics systems and suggest ways to combine technological advancement with innovative solutions. For instance, McFarlane et al. (2016) enhanced the function of the client in logistics processes and put out a theoretical framework for client orientation in intelligent logistics.

4.7 Explore Fundamental Concepts and Principles of Smart Manufacturing and Logistics

A fundamental paradigm change, smart manufacturing, and logistics turn conventional production and delivery systems into intelligent ecosystems. An examination of the core ideas and precepts driving this shift is provided below:

Networking: The Internet of Things (IoT) Becomes the Main Event

Sensors and Devices: Real-time data on performance, resource consumption, and environmental variables are collected by sensors integrated in machines, equipment, and even products.

Machine-to-Machine Communication: This type of communication occurs naturally between devices, allowing data sharing and coordinated actions.

Integration with the cloud: Data is transmitted to the cloud for analyzing, storing, and visualizing.

Data-Driven Decision-Making: Transitioning from Feelings to Understanding

Big Data analytics: By processing enormous volumes of data, sophisticated analytics tools can reveal hidden patterns and trends.

Predictive maintenance: By using sensor data to anticipate equipment breakdowns, proactive maintenance can be carried out to minimize downtime.

Demand Forecasting: By predicting future demand using historical sales data and current market trends, production planning and inventory management are optimized.

Robotics and Automation: The Potential of Sensible Machines

Industrial robots: Increase productivity and safety by quickly and precisely completing repetitive jobs.

Autonomous Guided Vehicles (AGVs): These self-navigating vehicles move goods across factories and warehouses, optimizing logistics processes. Algorithms that use machine learning (ML) to automate processes like process optimization and quality control learn from data.

Visibility and Integration: An Operational Holistic Perspective

ERP systems: Combine data from manufacturing, inventory, and logistics to create a single, comprehensive picture of the supply chain.

Digital Twins: Processes can be simulated and optimized prior to being implemented in the real world through virtual copies of physical systems.

Supply Chain Visibility: Proactive modifications and faster delivery times are made possible by the real-time tracking of resources, products, and vehicles across the supply chain.

Sustainability: A Conscientious Approach to Production and Transportation

Energy Efficiency: By tracking and managing machinery functions and warehouse lighting, smart systems minimize energy usage.

Resource optimization: Reducing waste by using effective manufacturing techniques and planning the best possible routes for delivery.

Closed-Loop Manufacturing: Reducing environmental impact by implementing systems for material reuse and recycling.

Human–Machine Coordination: The Ideal Combination

Intelligent machines work in tandem with human skills to undertake monotonous jobs. Humans are more suited for making strategic decisions, coming up with new ideas, and solving problems.

Virtual Reality (VR) and Augmented Reality (AR)

It can help with difficult assembly processes, maintenance, and training for personnel. Together, these core ideas and precepts produce an environment for smart manufacturing and logistics that is:

Efficient: Processes that are optimized reduce waste, downtime, and needless resource usage.

Adaptable: The system can react instantly to shifts in market trends, demand, and interruptions.

Cost-effective: Significant cost savings are achieved through decreased waste, improved operations, and predictive maintenance.

Sustainable: Reducing environmental effect by using less energy and managing resources sensibly.

Four essential technologies are required as support to achieve smart logistics, that is, big data, AI, cloud computing, and IoT.

4.8 Use of IOT in Smart Manufacturing and Logistics

The development of smart logistics is based on IoT. The fundamental concept of the Internet of Things is that, thanks to special addressing schemes, different objects can communicate with one another and work together with adjacent objects to accomplish the primary objective of creating a computer sense of information without the assistance of humans. The smart logistics system can obtain information about cargoes, logistics vehicles, transportation routes, warehousing, etc. at any time and from any location using RFID tags, sensors, actuators, mobile phones, and other devices. It can also achieve end-to-end information interconnection through network communication technologies. The IoT platform serves as the foundation for the smart logistics system, which can evaluate and process vast volumes of logistics data and information. The Internet of Things requires a lot of technology to be enabled. In this section, we concentrate on several commonly used enabling technologies for the effective implementation of IoT-based goods and services in smart logistics.

4.8.1 RFID

RFID is widely employed in a variety of logistics settings and is crucial to smart logistics' ability to recognize and capture data. It automatically detects and tracks tags affixed to items using electromagnetic fields. RFID allows identification from a distance since, unlike bar codes, it does not need to be in the reader's line of sight. Compared to bar codes, RFID tags may handle a greater number of unique IDs and can also carry other information like the product kind, manufacturer, and even ambient temperature measurements. For various application items in smart logistics, there are four types of RFID tags based on varying frequency ranges: low frequency (LF), high frequency (HF), ultrahigh frequency (UHF), and ultrawideband (UWB).

4.8.2 WSN

It's critical to easily arrange and merge the numerous terminal sensor nodes that are present in smart logistics scenarios for applications. Because of their versatility in addressing issues related to smart logistics, such as tracking the current state of goods in smart storage and the transportation vehicle in smart transportation, WSN has thus become increasingly popular. WSN is an acronym for wireless sensor network, which uses wireless connectivity and spontaneous network formation to track, record, and organize acquisition data at a centralized point. It is composed of tens to thousands of spatially distributed and specially designated "sensor nodes."

4.8.3 Wireless Communication Technologies

These technologies are essential to the network field because they gather data from all sensor nodes and transmit it to the base station and the intended client.

Devices may now communicate with one another without having to be physically connected thanks to these technologies. There is a huge need for Internet of Things (IoT) applications in smart logistics, and wireless communication technologies are keeping up with the rise of cellular networks, radiofrequency (RF) technology, and other cutting-edge technologies.

4.9 Use of Cloud Computing in Smart Manufacturing and Logistics

The goal of logistics system integration is to address the issue of "information isolated island" in the supply chain process. On the other hand, the present logistics system is a big, dispersed, dynamic, heterogeneous system. Its drawbacks include low transmissibility, slow responsiveness, weak dynamic, expensive expansion, and maintenance. The industry consensus is that, as smart logistics technology advances further, large systems' logistics information resources should be integrated and shared to offer a wide range of on-demand logistical services to different customers via "cloud computing."

The concept of cloud computing allows for the widespread, easy, and instantaneous provisioning and releasing of a shared pool of reconfigurable computing resources (such as networks, servers, storage, apps, and services) with the least amount of management work or service provider interaction possible. The utilization of massive processing and storage resources under focused supervision is the primary goal of cloud computing. The following are its key features: quick elasticity, pooling of resources, wide network access, on-demand self-service, and measured service. Because of these features, cloud computing transparently distributes scalable elastic resources among users across an infinite network, making it more akin to both the brain of an individual and the hub of an intelligent logistical system.

4.9.1 Use of Big Data in Smart Manufacturing and Logistics

IoT technology can, as was previously indicated, recognize how items are connected in a logistics system and gather data from the nodes that are connected. Resource integration is made possible by the superior technological platform that cloud computing offers. Large-scale logistics data gathered by IoT in conjunction with cloud computing technology allows big data technology to extract new logistics business value, which will encourage the advancement of smart logistics.

Big data is a field of technology that deals with methods for methodically analyzing and extracting information from massive data volumes. Traditional data-processing application software cannot handle these datasets because they are too big or complicated. The phrase "big data" is rarely used to describe a specific amount of data collection these days; instead, it usually refers to the application of advanced data analysis techniques such as user behavior analysis, predictive analysis, and others to extract value from data. The term "big data" refers to a set of attributes that include large amounts of generated and stored data, a diverse range of data types and nature, real-time data-processing velocity, and high data quality and value.

4.9.2 Use of Artificial Intelligence in Smart Manufacturing and Logistics

Artificial intelligence (AI) is a significant technological advancement that enables a system to accurately understand external input, learn from that data, and use that learning to accomplish certain activities and goals through adaptable modification. Fuzzy logic, evolutionary computation, and artificial neural networks (ANNs) are the three main soft computing paradigms in AI technology. Researchers are focusing on artificial intelligence (AI) as a critical technology for smart logistics since it can help expedite the development of smart logistics.

4.10 Key Technologies

Smart manufacturing and logistics incorporate an extensive variety of technologies to boost productivity, efficacy, and overall performance. Cloud computing, artificial intelligence, Internet of Things (IoT), and other cutting-edge technologies and procedures are all essential to smart manufacturing and logistics (Thales Group; Telenor Group). Some of the key technologies used in smart manufacturing are mentioned below:

Internet of Things (IoT)

IoT devices are essential to smart manufacturing because they offer automation capabilities, real-time data, and predictive insights that boost productivity while cutting expenses (Soori et al. 2023; Ericsson 2018; Telenor Group; Vijayaraghavan and Rian Leevinson 2019). The process of improving the supply chain network's resilience, visibility, and performance is known as supply chain optimization. By offering real-time data and insights on inventory, demand, logistics, and delivery, IoT can facilitate supply chain optimization. IoT, for instance, can facilitate intelligent inventory management by monitoring the whereabouts; state; and accessibility of components, final goods, and raw materials. By streamlining operations, cutting expenses, and guaranteeing the prompt and secure delivery of goods, IoT may also facilitate smart logistics management.

Full visibility of assets, processes, resources, and products is made possible by IoT-enabled smart manufacturing, which also enables plant managers to automatically gather and analyze data to make more informed decisions (Garrido-Hidalgo et al. 2019). IoT technology facilitates data flow, allows for remote process monitoring and management, and allows for real-time production plan modification when necessary. It does this by utilizing both wired and wireless communication (Thales Group; Telenor Group). All manufacturing systems need to have security built in from the beginning to enable failsafe production and defence against cyber-threats.

Manufacturers can improve operational efficiency by automating additional operations, detecting abnormalities, reducing errors, and so on, by deploying IoT solutions. Industrial robots may now carry out operations like assembly on their own thanks to the Internet of Things. These robots can use sensors, cameras, wireless devices, and edge computing. IoT technologies facilitate the creation of manufacturing and commercial models that are more sustainable. Data contributes significantly to energy savings, lowers carbon footprint, and conserves water and other limited resources. Additionally, it can support the recycling and remanufacturing processes for products. Attracting top personnel, smart manufacturing may help create a safer and more productive work environment.

Smart Sensors

Smart sensors are just one of the many basic technologies that support smart manufacturing and logistics. These sensors, which offer real-time data and facilitate automation, are essential to several phases of the smart manufacturing process. Top sensors utilized in smart manufacturing include the following:

(i) Level sensors: Used to determine the fluid levels in storage and delivery containers.
(ii) Infrared sensors: Keep an eye on an object's infrared output, which can be used to remotely measure surface smoothness, reflectance, temperature, and gas composition.
(iii) Proximity sensors are widely employed in smart manufacturing applications where machines automate industrial actions. They detect the proximity of the sensor to an object.
(iv) Accelerometers: Found in many smart manufacturing applications, including machine dynamics, motor control, anti-theft, tilt, and tap detection.
(v) Temperature sensors are widely employed in the petrochemical, pharmaceutical, food, medical, and raw material manufacturing industries, among others, where certain temperatures must be reached to properly apply products.
(vi) Hall effect sensors: Usually used in counting applications, these sensors attach a magnet to a moving part of a machine. Among other things, these sensors make it possible to gather real-time data, which is crucial for streamlining production procedures and guaranteeing effective resource and product management all the way through the supply chain (Arrow Electronics n.d.).

In smart manufacturing and logistics, smart sensors provide several advantages, such as

Enhanced Operational Efficiency: Process automation, anomaly detection, and error reduction are all made possible by smart sensors, which raises operational efficiency.

Real-Time Monitoring: They provide preventive maintenance and improved decision-making by providing real-time data on a range of parameters, including temperature, speed, weight, and operational problems.

Improved Inventory Management: The use of smart sensors allows for more precise inventory control, demand forecasting, and asset location and presence tracking. These features eliminate excess inventory and enhance inventory management.

Energy Cost Control: Through the provision of energy usage statistics and the facilitation of energy-saving actions, they aid in the control of energy costs and the fulfillment of regulatory requirements.

Predictive maintenance is made possible by smart sensors by utilizing AI analytics and Internet of Things sensors (California Manufacturing Technology Consulting (CMTC) 2018; Deloitte 2022; Büchi et al. 2020).

Supply chain integration with smart sensors can reduce operational costs, boost asset efficiency, enhance demand planning, and offer vital insight into customer behavior. Organizations ought to start thinking about how to more effectively sensor-enable their supply chains from beginning to end as centralized platforms and communication networks for Internet of Things (IoT) devices continue to develop.

Big Data Analysis

Big data analytics is one of the key technologies that support smart manufacturing and logistics. Large data volumes, particularly real-time data that is challenging to evaluate using conventional techniques, may now be analyzed thanks to big data analytics. By offering unmatched visibility into every facet of the production process, it strengthens intelligent manufacturing systems and facilitates more sustainable and customized production as well as better decision-making, inventory control, and quality assurance. The utilization of automation, cutting-edge technologies, and real-time data can enhance the agility, efficiency, and resilience of the supply chain. Big data analytics has the potential to completely transform the supply chain by combining with other cutting-edge technologies like artificial intelligence (AI) and the Internet of Things (IoT) to create a more responsive and flexible network of production and distribution (Mittal et al. 2019; Lee et al. 2018).

Cloud Computing

The fundamental technology that powers smart manufacturing and logistics is cloud computing. Manufacturers can store and handle massive amounts of data thanks to cloud computing, which also makes scalable computing resources available over wireless channels like Wi-Fi and 5G and allows for real-time analytics.

Cloud connectivity makes system resources like IIoT data, analytics, and process automations available to manufacturers whenever they need them (SAP). Additionally, cloud computing makes it easier for enterprises to automate and standardize with one another, which improves supply chain visibility and collaboration.

Several advantages of cloud computing exist for smart manufacturing and logistics, such as

Scalability: Without having to invest in pricey hardware, cloud computing enables manufacturers to adjust the amount of processing power they have on hand in response to demand variations.

Savings: By removing the requirement for on-premises hardware and IT infrastructure, cloud computing can save capital expenses.

Enhanced agility: Cloud computing gives manufacturers the flexibility to quickly adapt their manufacturing processes to changing client demands and market conditions. Collaboration is enhanced because cloud computing makes it easier for manufacturers to share information and insights with their suppliers and partners along the supply chain.

Enhanced security: To safeguard data and guarantee adherence to industry rules, cloud computing providers use strong security measures.

Industry 4.0 relies heavily on cloud computing, which gives businesses the ability to use cutting-edge technologies like IoT, AI, and machine learning to enhance their processes and satisfy demands from the global market.

4.11 Benefits of Smart Manufacturing and Logistics

Enhanced customer happiness, cost savings, sustainability, and increased efficiency are just a few of the advantages and benefits that come with implementing smart manufacturing and logistics methods. Systems for smart factory logistics are engineered to adapt to various production configurations and manufacturing settings, guaranteeing optimal operational flexibility. Smart factory logistics systems instantly identify changes in manufacturing demand through the use of cutting-edge embedded sensor technology, giving the supply chain greater agility in response. Big data is analyzed by ARIMS application software to find significant trends that improve supply chain efficiency and predictability (Bossard Group n.d.). In addition to supply chain management, smart logistics solutions may help streamline transportation and warehousing, which can boost profitability and reduce costs while improving efficiency.

The time needed to collect and arrange goods as well as prepare and dispatch it from the warehouse can be decreased by automating some activities, which improves resource efficiency and cuts down on time. Additionally, lower operational risk, more control and accuracy, more storage space, and higher productivity are all provided by smart logistics facilities. On the other hand, establishing a smart logistics warehouse necessitates a substantial upfront investment in equipment and personnel development.

Through a variety of methods, smart manufacturing and logistics techniques can greatly increase sustainability. Among them are

Route optimization: Maximizing efficiency and minimizing environmental impact by optimizing delivery routes using cutting-edge technologies and route planning software.

Alternative fuel cars: Switching from conventional gasoline-powered cars to electric or hybrid cars, which have zero exhaust emissions and cause no air pollution, will lessen reliance on fossil fuels.

Green warehousing is the application of eco-friendly technologies, such as waste management systems, renewable energy sources, and energy-efficient lighting, in warehouses to cut down on resource usage and carbon emissions.

Modal shift: Adopting more environmentally friendly transportation options, such rail or waterways, to cut carbon emissions and boost productivity.

Packaging optimization: Cutting waste production and transportation costs by employing eco-friendly packaging materials and lowering package size.

Innovations in the last mile: Putting into practice cutting-edge strategies, such delivery drones and micro-fulfilment centers, to lessen the carbon footprint of last-mile deliveries.

Principles of the circular economy: Implementing a circular economy strategy, which seeks to reduce waste and pollution, maintain the useful life of goods and materials, and restore natural systems.

Sustainable Purchasing: Selecting suppliers who place a high priority on sustainability and utilizing renewable resources can help the supply chain have a more positive environmental impact by reducing waste.

Supply chain transparency involves tracking the origins of materials and goods using software and performing on-site inspections of vendor facilities. This helps businesses make sustainable decisions and guarantees that regulations are followed.

Creativity and cooperation: Promoting creativity and teamwork within the sector to propel the creation of novel technologies and solutions that enhance efficiency and sustainability.

These procedures not only lessen the negative effects of manufacturing and shipping on the environment, but they also save money, enhance the reputation of the industry, and strengthen the resilience of international supply chains (ZhenHub 2023; Oracle 2023).

The environmental effect is reduced using sustainable delivery practices. Businesses can cut down on air pollution, noise pollution, and greenhouse gas emissions by using energy-efficient cars and optimizing their routes. Using alternative fuels and switching to renewable energy sources can also help create a cleaner, healthier environment.

To reduce its environmental impact and encourage a better future, the logistics sector must embrace sustainable practices. Logistics companies can reap significant benefits by incorporating renewable supply chains, streamlining routes, utilizing alternative fuel vehicles, implementing green warehousing, transitioning to more environmentally friendly modes of transportation, optimizing packaging, utilizing last-mile innovations, embracing reverse logistics, and embracing the principles of the circular economy.

4.12 Challenges and Concerns

Several important issues are revealed when the difficulties and possible worries surrounding the application of smart manufacturing and logistics are examined, especially in light of data security, worker adaption, and infrastructure requirements.

Data Security: As smart manufacturing systems necessitate extensive communication between devices, processes, people, and organizations, cybersecurity risks surface. The attack surface grows when enterprise systems are connected to air-gapped plant networks. Risks can be reduced by updating technology and making sure a strategy to implementation is tested and phased in.

Workforce Adaptation: Workers could experience anxiety and fear about their job security and role changes. One of the HR problems facing enterprises implementing Industry 4.0 is attracting talent and retraining current workforce. Manufacturers need to make an investment in retraining current employees or hiring new ones with different capabilities.

Infrastructure Requirements: It's possible that older devices and systems can't exchange data when it's needed. It is possible to install new IIoT sensors and edge gateway devices on top of existing hardware, although this can be difficult. When determining the level of automation necessary for assembly operations, factors such as costs, labor availability, process conditions, and available floor space must be taken into account (Partner Content 2023).

Integration and Interoperability: Industry Integration In a plant, Industry 4.0 technology can leave networks and machinery vulnerable to cyberattacks or data breaches. Selecting the necessary technical standards and guaranteeing system interoperability can be difficult tasks. The adoption process may be slowed down if technology and business strategy are not linked.

Cost and Complexity of Implementation: The difficulty and expense of implementing these methods has been a major barrier to their wider adoption. It can be difficult to implement systems that have historically relied on system integrators with specific knowledge of private data. Upgrades can be made less risky and have less of an effect on the production line with a well-planned, staged, and proven deployment strategy (Ricadela 2023).

Supply Chain Management: Supply chain predicaments were revealed and made worse by the pandemic. Supply chain planning is becoming more agile with the emergence of digital forecasting and planning (Rockwell Automation and Plex Systems 2022).

Manufacturers embracing Industry 4.0 strategies frequently run across problems when putting automation technology into their factories. Costs might be prohibitive, particularly for small and mid-sized companies that can find it difficult to make the investment in new machinery, sensors, and software. Workers in plants might not be competent to manage cyber–physical production systems, operate portable computers, or modify procedures based on software suggestions. Additionally, manufacturers may need to hire software developers, engineers, and data scientists—roles for which there may not be a sufficient supply of skilled candidates. The difficulties go beyond finances and personnel: when Industry 4.0 technologies are integrated in a production, networks and machinery may become targets for cyberattacks or data breaches.

According to a 2020 McKinsey survey of more than 800 manufacturers worldwide, barriers to Industry 4.0 adoption include the high costs of scaling deployments; organizational challenges, like getting management buy-in for smart factory initiatives; and technology challenges, like selecting the necessary software and an implementation partner. Concerns about security (reported by 35% of respondents), worries about the capabilities and stability of the technology (indicated by 27%), and deployment costs (identified by 26% were the major obstacles to deploying IoT projects, according to a separate 2022 study of IT decision makers conducted by market research firm IDC (Oracle 2023).

Businesses tend to grow quite accustomed to their outdated procedures and infrastructure but to fully benefit from smart manufacturing approaches, it is critical to welcome innovation that simplifies supply chain and corporate collaboration processes. It is normal for the company to encounter resistance from some employees over revolutionary developments. Workers will be content with their current responsibilities and pleased with their accomplishments as they work to gradually enhance their departments. It is imperative to elucidate to the team the necessity of change to stay abreast of technological advancements, and the potential consequences of staying the same for the company's competitive future. Additionally, the management team needs to make it obvious how organizational and technological changes relate to the plan and how everyone will benefit from them.

People may be hesitant to share their knowledge and information across organizational borders if they have concerns about ownership and control of systems and procedures. In order to establish new business models and services, digital innovation forces an organization to take a different approach and bring people, processes, and technology together in novel ways. It is necessary to collaborate and innovate across previous departmental lines to challenge the legacy of clearly defined areas of responsibility.

Handling the changeover is not easy and the departmental boundaries and staff responsibilities may need to change to implement the transformative business changes. Sluggish and highly hierarchical old processes may prevent the manufacturing sector from taking full use of the speed and advantages offered by new smart manufacturing techniques. It is important to view the organizational structure as flexible to implement new operating models and reduce procedures. To expedite the integration of production and enterprise systems, for instance, several firms have combined the IT and industrial control teams. Some companies have removed a few tiers of management, giving the frontline staff more decision-making authority by providing them with improved real-time data that indicates non-routine events.

Workers could experience anxiety and fear about their job security and role changes. It is imperative to maintain transparency with employees regarding their evolving roles and the necessary training for new machinery and procedures. All phases of the implementation process should involve employee engagement. Older IT infrastructure may not work with more recent software for production data analysis, forcing manufacturers to update their systems, which takes time. Solution to this challenge is to install some IT infrastructure prior to constructing a smart factory or integrating Industry 4.0 technologies into an existing facility. It examine the status of your R&D, purchasing, production, and warehousing business management systems. It has been considered that the technological ramifications of Industry 4.0 initiate throughout all manufacturing locations, and make sure that IT department collaborates with other departments (Oracle 2023).

4.13 Case Studies

Smart Manufacturing and EV Production

Automotive firms can achieve extremely efficient production by utilizing innovations in supply chain, production, and product technology when they have a comprehensive digital twin. Siemens digital manufacturing solutions facilitate the development of a contemporary virtual factory to manufacture new products, the engineering and validation of the tools and processes needed for their assembly, and the utilization of data from the linked physical world to enhance and expedite supply chain and production management (Siemens 2022).

Another illustration is additive manufacturing, which has unique needs such as specialized machinery not commonly seen on conventional manufacturing shop floors. Additionally, during product design and early manufacturing planning, the carbon footprint of supply chains supporting these product improvements must be considered. Sustainability-related insights should be used for external cost and emission estimates as well as rating card management.

The first important feature of the industrial infrastructure to address will include a multidirectional architecture facilitated by autonomous transportation systems, reconfigurable modular line configurations for accommodating variations in demand, and sustainable manufacturing that uses minimal resources in terms of energy and materials. Furthermore, there will be more digitalization in factories. Intelligent robots with conditional awareness will be used to facilitate adaptable production situations, and cooperative robots, or co-bots, will be used to assist humans in manual tasks. It will become normal to support these complicated systems with digital tools like virtual reality, augmented reality, and simulation. Thereafter, it is needed to increase personalization for which the actual manufacturing processes will shift and become more focused on the needs of the consumer.

Engineers using VR can interact with the simulation and its components while fully submerged in the 3D scene. It is easier to recognize problems and record them for later investigation and resolution. The ability for several people to participate virtually and join from various physical locations greatly improves collaboration. Production scenarios like traffic control, obstacle avoidance, automation interlocks, and others can be tested and validated before being implemented on the production floor by directly connecting the digital twin of manufacturing to virtual models of the production centers and the fleet manager.

Engineers may easily conduct several trials to ensure their strategy and design which will fulfill production requirements by utilizing factory simulation. Models with various levels of detail can be created using the Tecno-matrix portfolio's plant simulation using data that is directly gathered from the shop floor. At any stage of the engineering lifecycle, these models can be used to address important concerns and are frequently employed to assess and optimize system architecture, material flow and logistics, and energy consumption. These insights may be expanded well into the vital logistics domain, such as transportation and warehousing, using supply chain suite, to produce a real end-to-end digital twin.

Amazon

Products are stored, inventory is managed, price is set, and logistics are all part of Amazon's supply chain operation. To maintain a seamless supply chain, this e-commerce business organization has effectively optimized all these components. Amazon gives customers options for fulfillments to optimize the supply of products. Amazon forecasts future demand across its vast product range using machine learning algorithms. Order planning and inventory optimization are made possible by this method. Robots are used extensively in Amazon's fulfillments facilities to automate tasks like picking, packing, and sorting to increase productivity. This enables quicker order processing and lowers personnel costs (Source Essay).

Throughout its logistics network, Amazon uses sophisticated optimization algorithms to determine the best delivery routes and truck loads which lowers gasoline expenses and mileage. Transparency across the supply chain is ensured by meticulous order tracking that allows for rerouting and dynamic modifications when necessary.

Amazon has a single logistics command center to continuously monitor data from the worldwide supply chain and make decisions in real time as needed. When inventory levels are low, machine learning helps forecast inventory demands and automatically generates restocking orders and reduces stock outs (AWS).

The key achievements using smart manufacturing and logistics include

Enhanced productivity: Costs have been reduced, profitability has increased, and productivity has improved because of clever production and logistics solutions.

Enhanced operations: Better and quicker decision-making, more competitiveness, and easier access to data are the outcomes of these solutions.

Logistics optimization: In the manufacturing industry, supply chain optimization increases productivity, reduces waste, and fosters sustainability.

Personalization and customization: A level of personalization and customization before unthinkable is made possible by smart manufacturing.

Improved inventory management: Demand forecasting and inventory control are made possible by real-time data and analytics.

Predictive maintenance: Predictive maintenance keeps manufacturing machinery operating at maximum efficiency and avoids unplanned downtime by utilizing IoT sensors and AI analytics.

Sustainability: Energy consumption, waste, and resource utilization can all be decreased with the aid of intelligent manufacturing and logistics systems.

4.14 Integration with Industry 4.0

Using the Internet of Things (IoT), cloud computing, big data, and cutting-edge technologies like artificial intelligence (AI) and machine learning, smart manufacturing builds digital facilities that are networked and integrated. Real-time data collecting, analysis, and decision-making are made possible by these technologies, which boost productivity, efficiency, and responsiveness to client needs. Additionally, predictive maintenance, self-optimization, and customized production—often referred to as "lot size of one"—are made possible by smart manufacturing (Amper; Impact Networking 2022; IBM 2023).

Smart factories are now a reality, or at least a step in that direction, thanks to recent technological advancements. Industry 4.0 and smart factories are comprised of a networked and integrated system where information flows between the physical infrastructure and the cyberspace are streamlined. The enhanced data management and analytics technologies are anticipated to help the system function at its best overall. Nevertheless, the benefits of the Industry 4.0 idea will not fully materialize unless and until the smart factory concept is transferred across the supply chain, i.e., smart supply chains. A growing number of small and large companies are moving toward smart manufacturing. These comprise companies in the automotive, electrical, pharmaceutical, and defence industries (Müller 2019).

The important step is to connect the data, and by identifying the flaw, the system became self-adaptive by implementing corrective actions when necessary. Ideally, though, this would necessitate ongoing investment in both the relationship and technical aspects of the problem. Furthermore, according to Haddud et al. (2017), this would necessitate investments in IoT devices for real-time information exchange among supply chain participants, RFID sensors for real-time automobile tracing, and centralized manufacturing execution systems powered by cloud computing, according to Barreto et al. (2017) and Almada-Lobo (2015).

It is critical to realize that Industry 4.0 intends to integrate smart technology into supply chain operations, and that this should not be viewed as the conclusion of the process. Instead, this was the beginning of a journey that would hopefully identify a significant number of interconnected areas that needed to be improved but would also necessitate recurring financial and time commitments in order for the ongoing experimentation to occur. Additionally, this could necessitate expanding the team's profile even more because they would need to keep moving forward to investigate the utilization of cutting-edge technologies even more (Ghadimi et al. 2019).

There is a close relationship between smart manufacturing and logistics, with logistics being essential to the overall efficacy and efficiency of the supply chain.

Logistics can enhance forecasting, transit routing, storage optimization, and environmental disruption planning by utilizing digital technologies. Additionally, logistics aids in matching the solution to the analytical requirements and degree of sophistication of the company (Penske Logistics).

A smart factory is a digitally connected facility that gathers, analyzes, and acts upon data via a network of computers, equipment, and cutting-edge technologies. This data-driven methodology facilitates improved decision-making, ongoing enhancement, and production process optimization. An ecosystem of developments in technology is created by smart factories' frequent connectivity with suppliers, logistical partners, third-party vendors, and distribution hubs.

Although there are many advantages to smart manufacturing and logistics, there are also issues that need to be resolved, like cybersecurity, data privacy, and the requirement for ongoing employee training and development. Nevertheless, as businesses adjust to the shifting business environment of Industry 4.0, these difficulties also offer chances for innovation and expansion (Impact Networking 2022; Amper).

The manufacturing sector is undergoing a transformation because of smart manufacturing and logistics, which are enabling more productive, individualized, and efficient production processes. Businesses may enhance supply chain management, cut expenses, and boost their competitiveness in the global market by utilizing digital technologies. However, in order to guarantee a seamless and effective transition to smart manufacturing and logistics, it is imperative that the issues raised by Industry 4.0 are addressed.

4.15 Best Practices

Investing in skills development, forming partnerships, and taking a gradual approach with pilot projects will help establish the technological and human capital basis for the transition of smart manufacturing (Davis et al. 2012; PCAST AMP Steering Committee Report–Accelerating U.S.). Some of the best practices in smart manufacturing are

Begin with a pilot project. Choose a small use case to adopt initially, such as a single product line or warehouse. This enables the development of the business case and solution testing prior to scale.

Concentrate on resolving a pain point: Determine the main operational pain issues, such as manufacturing bottlenecks and excessive transportation expenses, and begin by putting those into practice.

Utilize data analytics: Gather and examine logistical and production data to find areas for optimization and to enable predictive functions.

Start with gradual automation: Before advancing to more sophisticated automation, automate manual repetitive jobs using basic robots or software bots.

Skills development: Invest in the training of staff in digital skills such as robotics programming, AI/ML, and data analytics to strengthen internal capabilities.

Upgrade outdated systems: To enable smart manufacturing integration, evaluate the current infrastructure, and make plans to upgrade old equipment and IT systems.

Strategy: Develop a clear strategy that aligns with the organization's goals and objectives, involving all stakeholders in the development process.

Data Security: Ensure data security by adopting robust cybersecurity measures and educating employees about the importance of data protection.

This section concludes that, particularly in the domains of cybersecurity, cloud-based manufacturing services, supply chain integration, and data analytics, current manufacturing standards are inadequate to properly support smart manufacturing. The speed at which technology is developing is too fast for traditional standards development efforts, which are mostly concerned with making small enhancements to already-existing standards (PCAST AMP Steering Committee Report—Accelerating U.S.). New standards for smart manufacturing are being developed by industrial consortia and national manufacturing initiatives. The sources of new standard-related requirements for smart manufacturing were also covered in this section. These sources included manufacturing programs run by standard development organizations, Internet of Things initiatives, national and international manufacturing initiatives, and the rise of sustainable manufacturing requirements.

4.16 Popular Algorithms

This outline gives readers a thorough review of frequently used algorithms in smart manufacturing and logistics in an organized manner before diving into algorithmic techniques and applications. Because smart manufacturing and logistics involve complex processes and require high levels of efficiency, optimization is essential. Complex processes in smart manufacturing necessitate careful scheduling of labor, equipment, and resources to guarantee maximum output at the lowest possible cost. Algorithms for optimization are essential for production scheduling, inventory control, and smooth supply chain coordination. Similar to this, logistics depend on optimization for inventory control, load balance, and route planning in order to satisfy client requests quickly and efficiently. Manufacturing and logistics operations would be beset by inefficiencies, delays, and exorbitant costs in the absence of optimization, impeding competitiveness in the international market. Thus, in the smart manufacturing and logistics sectors, optimizing performance, optimizing usage, and attaining sustainable growth require the integration of optimization algorithms.

The various issues that smart manufacturing and logistics encounter can only be solved with the help of optimization algorithms. These algorithms are effective instruments for optimizing performance across a range of operations, reducing inefficiencies, and fine-tuning procedures. Optimal resource allocation, scheduling, and production planning are made possible in the intricate world of manufacturing by optimization algorithms, which maximize efficiency while reducing expenses. Like this, these algorithms in logistics enable efficient inventory control, route planning, and transportation scheduling, which lowers delivery times and raises customer satisfaction. Businesses can better manage the intricacies of contemporary supply chains, increase operational effectiveness, and obtain a competitive edge in today's fast-paced market by utilizing optimization algorithms. The commonly used algorithms in smart manufacturing and logistics are

- Machine learning algorithms.
- K-means clustering.
- Deep reinforcement learning.
- Dynamic programming.
- Simulated annealing.

4.16.1 Machine Learning Algorithms

In several domains, machine learning algorithms have become revolutionary instruments that are transforming data analysis, pattern recognition, and decision-making. Without explicit programming, these methods allow computers to learn from data and gradually improve their performance. Machine learning algorithms are driving innovations across industries, changing the way business' function, and improving our daily lives in areas such as image identification and predictive analytics (Sathasivam et al. 2022).

There are many useful machine learning algorithms for various applications, which can be categorized into four primary groups as shown in Fig. 4.7.

1. **Supervised Learning**: Supervised machine learning trains an algorithm to identify patterns and build the capacity to generate precise predictions for fresh data using human-labeled input and output data.
2. **Unsupervised Learning**: Algorithms used in unsupervised machine learning (ML) examine unlabeled data in order to find structures, correlations, or patterns without having been trained on any predetermined target outcomes.
3. **Semi-supervised Learning**: In semi-supervised machine learning, labeled and unlabeled data are combined to enhance model performance. Labeled data is used to inform the algorithm's interpretation of unlabeled inputs.

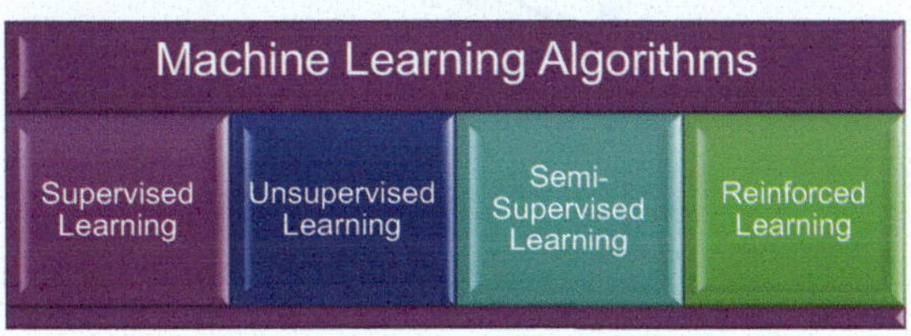

Fig. 4.7 Various machine learning algorithm. *Source* Author

4. **Reinforcement Learning**: ML algorithms that are placed in a regulated environment are trained to make successive decisions through the use of reinforcement learning. Probably the most famous example of a highly successful reinforcement learning project is OpenAI's well-known ChatGPT. In this instance, OpenAI combines human-readable, guided training with reward-based algorithms to provide continually improved outcomes through the use of reinforcement learning from human feedback (RLHF). Although this sector appears to be unrestricted, the algorithm is always guided by incentives or sanctions to build a comprehension of intent, rules, and even intricate reasoning. Classification, regression, grouping, and other typical learning problems are performed via reinforcement learning.

The following list of a few machine learning algorithms in manufacturing demonstrates how various ML techniques are applied for certain, highly specialized uses (Exploring 4 Popular Machine Learning Algorithms for Industrial Application n.d.). The machine learning algorithms listed below can all be classified into one of the four groups mentioned above.

Linear Regression (Supervised)

The relationship between a dependent variable and any number of independent variables can be modeled using linear regression. It is frequently used to forecast an event's chance of happening based on historical data as shown in Fig. 4.8.

Applications of linear regression could include forecasting health outcomes according to age, weight, and medical conditions, among other variables. Alternatively, projecting sales based on spending plan, rivalry, and other previously gathered information.

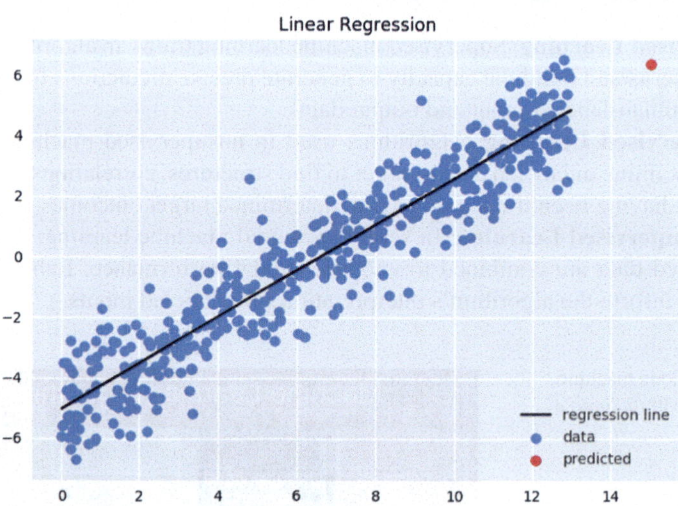

Fig. 4.8 Linear regression. *Source* Author

Logistic Regression (Supervised)

Binary classification is used in logistic regression to forecast the likelihood of a given event. This machine learning technique is utilized for probability-based classification. It can be applied in situations where forecasting binary outcomes is advantageous, such as when attempting to determine whether a fraudulent transaction might take place or when predicting whether a customer will respond favorably to an advertisement as shown in Fig. 4.9.

Artificial Neural Networks (ANN) (Reinforcement Learning)

The architecture of neural networks is intended to approximate the way the human brain functions. Data nodes function like the neural synapses in the brain, and units of data are structured in a network of interconnected datasets as depicted in Fig. 4.10.

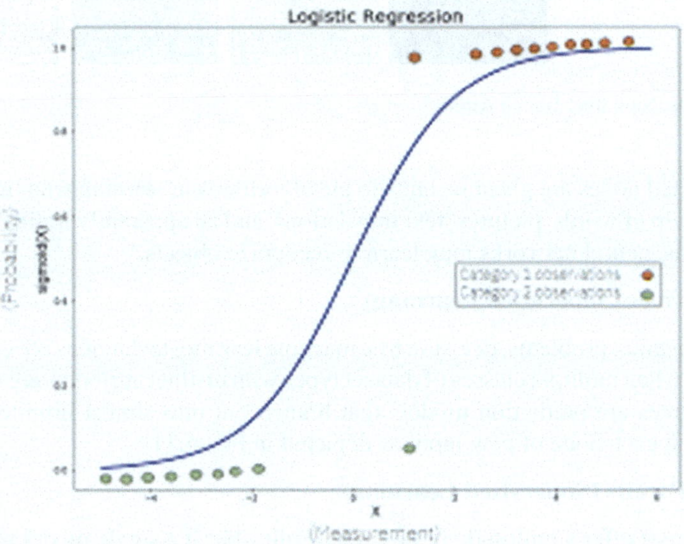

Fig. 4.9 Logistic regression. *Source* Author

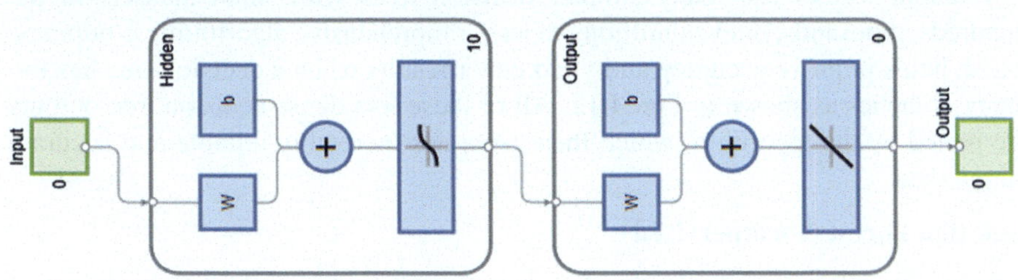

Fig. 4.10 ANN architecture. *Source* Author

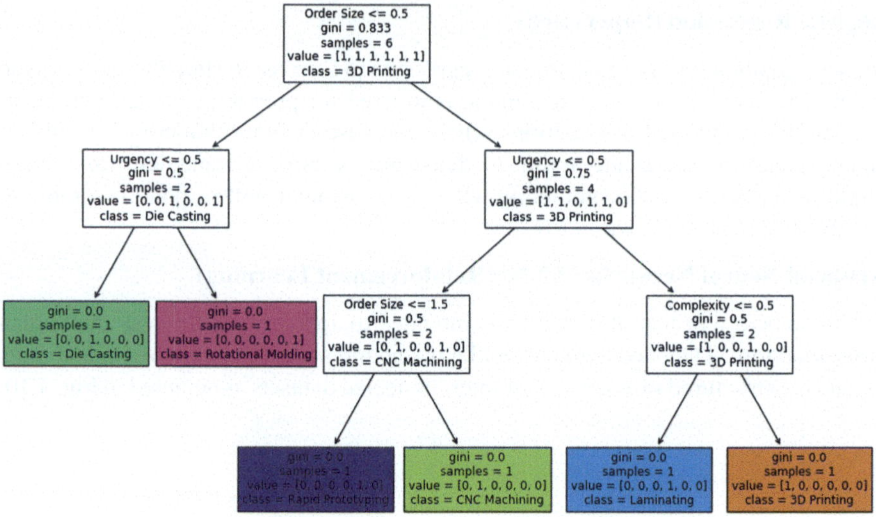

Fig. 4.11 Decision tree. *Source* Author

Connected nodes are given weights to aid algorithms in learning from input data. With the help of words, pictures, text translations, and an apparently limitless variety of scenarios, neural networks may learn to recognize objects.

Decision Trees (Supervised Learning)

For classification problems, decision tree machine learning techniques are employed, especially when multiple classes of dataset types with distinct attributes are available. Decision trees are prediction models that branch out into almost infinite possible outcomes at each node of new input as depicted in Fig. 4.11.

Random Forests (Supervised Learning)

Decision trees offer a multitude of possible results, but if a single model is run with an excessive number of branching outputs, it runs the risk of being unduly complex and challenging to understand.

Random forests test many simpler decision trees with small datasets in the hundreds, thousands, or even millions of less comprehensive algorithmic groupings, which helps improve accuracy and yield better results when a decision tree has too many branches as shown in Fig. 4.12. All of these less dense decision tree outputs are polled by the algorithm, which then generates incredibly reliable and accurate output data.

Isolation Forest (Unsupervised)

An algorithm for detecting anomalies is an isolation forest. Using a tree-based architecture in which a random feature is divided from random values in the data trees, this machine learning approach separates outlier datasets. An isolation forest

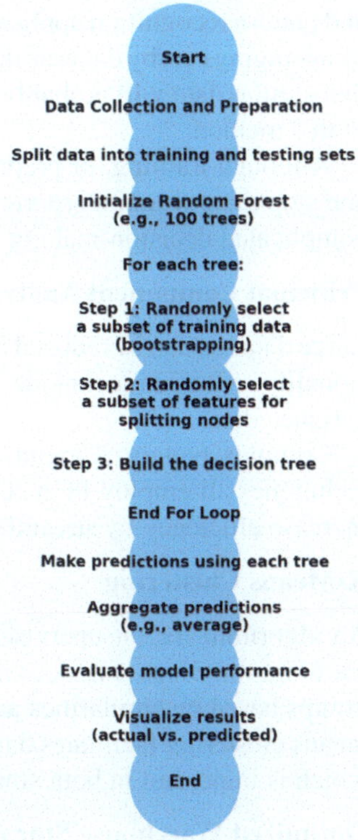

Fig. 4.12 Random forest.
Source Author

enables the discovery of unknown abnormalities as they emerge in the data, which is advantageous in situations like intricate fraud detection and network security.

Naïve Bayes Classifier Algorithm (Supervised)

Naïve Bayes is a classification technique that assigns each input value to an independent class, based on the Bayes theorem, a formula for calculating probability under various scenarios. This approach is distinct because it uses computer resources efficiently and yields precise, detailed results.

Support Vector Machine (SVM) (Supervised)

The SVM method is utilized for both classification and regression. In order to create new models, historical sample sets are utilized to extract the raw data for an infinite number of features or variables. SVMs are strong machine learning classifier algorithms because each value may be associated with a specific coordinate in the algorithm's output.

K-Nearest Neighbors (K-NN) (Supervised)

The K-nearest neighbors' algorithm is employed to approximate the membership of a data point in a certain group or classification. K-NN is frequently used in regression and pattern recognition applications. It works by assigning a label to a new data point by averaging nearby datasets that are comparable to it. The mathematical presumption that similar data will probably have the same label or values underlies the operation of this method.

Although training, or preprocessing, is required to keep K-NN models accurate and stop them from incorporating erroneous input, K-NNs are helpful for extremely complicated decision-making models.

Principal Component Analysis (PCA) (Unsupervised)

Large datasets can be reduced into a lower dimension representation using the dimensionality reduction technique PCA (see below), all the while preserving important variance data.

Complex pattern recognition, image processing, and other data preprocessing techniques all employ PCA. Using this strong machine learning approach, one can increase efficiency by streamlining unduly complicated calculations.

K-Means Clustering

An algorithm for unsupervised learning is k-means clustering. Unlike supervised learning, this clustering does not use labeled data. K-means divides the objects into groups based on similarities and differences between the objects in each cluster. K-means clustering facilitates data-driven decision-making for activities such as these, which is important in both smart manufacturing and logistics.

Optimized Warehouse Storage: K-means clustering can be used in a smart warehouse to group similar goods together by analyzing product data (size, weight, and demand). This makes it possible to allocate storage in an efficient manner, cutting down on picker trip time and optimizing the usage of warehouse space (Suma et al. 2017).

Better Demand Forecasting: Manufacturers can find trends in consumer demand for various product categories by employing K-means clustering to aggregate historical sales data. This makes it possible to plan production and manage inventories more effectively by improving the accuracy of future demand predictions. K-means clustering can be used to evaluate sensor data from factory floor machinery, which is useful for predictive maintenance. Manufacturers can reduce downtime and maintenance costs by proactively identifying probable equipment failures and scheduling maintenance before breakdowns occur by combining units with similar sensor values (temperature, vibration).

Logistics: K-means can cluster delivery locations according to order size, traffic patterns, and distance. As a result, delivery times and fuel usage are decreased for logistics businesses' trucks on optimized delivery routes.

Consumer Segmentation: To identify discrete consumer categories, K-means clustering can be applied to customer data, such as purchase history and demographics. This increases the efficacy of marketing by enabling businesses to target client groups with their product offerings and marketing activities.

K-means clustering, in general, helps find patterns and links within complicated information, making it a useful tool for smart manufacturing and logistics. This makes it possible to make data-driven decisions that can optimize operations, cut costs, and increase efficiency.

Dynamic Programming

The key to smart manufacturing and logistics is the optimization of intricate processes with dynamic variables. Rising to the occasion, dynamic programming provides an effective approach to these complex optimization issues. An optimizing method called dynamic programming divides larger issues into smaller, easier-to-manage subproblems. It functions by gradually creating answers to these subproblems and saving the best answers for later use. This removes the need for pointless computations and makes it possible to handle complicated issues with overlapping sub-structures effectively.

Dynamic programming finds numerous applications in smart logistics, particularly in areas where optimal routes and resource allocation are crucial.

Think of a delivery truck navigating a smart city as an example of shortest path finding. A single, fixed route becomes ineffective due to the frequent updating of real-time traffic data. Here, dynamic programming can take the lead. The algorithm creates a solution for the complete delivery route by breaking the city up into smaller grids and figuring out the best route via each grid based on current traffic conditions. The vehicle continues, considering the grids it has already crossed and using the previously saved best routes for the distance left to travel. This guarantees that the best path is chosen while considering real-time traffic updates.

Dynamic programming excels in situations requiring the best possible distribution of resources, such as delivery trucks or warehouse workers. Consider a scenario where a warehouse is inundated with orders of all different sizes and locations. The order data, warehouse layout, and worker capacities can all be analyzed by the program. By dividing the process of giving orders to employees into manageable chunks (assigning individual orders), it creates an ideal solution that reduces worker travel time and boosts productivity. In order to efficiently decide on the overall task, the ideal solutions for smaller subproblems (assigning specific orders) must be stored.

There are several benefits that dynamic programming offers to smart manufacturing and logistics.

Decision-Making: Dynamic programming produces data-driven, ideal decisions for complicated issues by considering all potential scenarios and their consequences.

Real-Time Optimization: As the environment changes, the capacity to adjust to new circumstances (traffic updates, order spikes) guarantees that solutions continue to be effective.

Decreased Costs: Fuel consumption, labor costs, and overall operating expenses are reduced by route optimization and resource allocation.

Enhanced Efficiency: Notable increases in efficiency can be attributed to expedited delivery, optimized warehousing procedures, and reduced idle time.

To sum up, dynamic programming provides an effective tool for intelligent manufacturing and transportation. Bite-sized solutions to intricate optimization challenges enable data-driven decision-making for effective and economical operations in a changing environment.

Regulatory and Ethical Considerations

A plethora of novel applications underpin the promise of smart manufacturing. The utilization of artificial intelligence (AI) in industrial environments has facilitated various benefits such as improved quality control (an engine manufacturer for an aircraft can examine turbofan blades in three dimensions with minuscule precision), demand-driven production, inventory optimization, lower energy and material costs, product design, improved safety, and environmental performance. Unique new uses are likely to arise when value chains are fully connected digitally to smart factories; the only thing limiting the possibilities appears to be entrepreneurial creativity.

Data has emerged as the essential resource for enterprises worldwide in an era characterized by the digital revolution. But there are now worries about data security, privacy, and ethical use due to the extraordinary rise in data collection and consumption. Governments and regulatory agencies have implemented strict data protection and compliance requirements in response to these worries. This article explores the world of industrial rules pertaining to data protection and compliance, emphasizing the importance of these standards, their essential elements, and the difficulties that organizations encounter in complying with them.

Privacy and Data Protection: It is very essential to make sure that sensitive personal information is not collected or handled by IoT devices and systems without the necessary authorization and security. There is also a need to respect privacy and data protection laws, such as the California Consumer Privacy Act (CCPA) and the General Data Protection Regulation (GDPR) (Sathasivam et al. 2022).

Cybersecurity: There is need of developing strong cybersecurity procedures in place to guard against data breaches and cyberattacks by ensuring that IoT systems and devices are safe, and that vulnerabilities be fixed quickly.

Product liability: The use of new technology and procedures in smart manufacturing and logistics systems may necessitate addressing product liability and recall issues.

Labor Practices: Human labor should not be completely replaced by automation. Its goal ought to be to upskill and enlarge the labor force. Retraining on the job and educational initiatives will be essential for affected personnel to shift into new positions.

AI Ethics and Algorithmic Bias: As AI is used more and more in fields like demand forecasting and predictive maintenance, it is imperative that AI systems be transparent and accountable. It is important to regularly assess AI algorithms and data to identify and address any prejudice or discrimination against protected groups.

Environmental Impact: Reduced carbon footprints can result from smart manufacturing technologies that optimize energy and resource utilization in facilities, such as industrial IoT and data analytics. AI-enabled logistics strategies like load consolidation and route optimization can save emissions by reducing distance. Yet, energy consumption is a major issue for technologies like blockchain and automation. To lessen this effect, renewable energy sources should be utilized. Implementing circular models, such as reusing and refurbishing items and components throughout the product lifespan, is made possible by smart supply chains. Supply chain traceability and transparency can facilitate advanced recycling, ethical sourcing, and sustainable raw materials.

Health and Safety: By lowering injuries, new technologies like exoskeletons, virtual/augmented reality, and collaborative robots can enhance worker health and safety. However, misusing technology can also raise the chance of mishaps and problems like technostress. Sufficient supervision, safety measures, and training are required.

Ethical Concerns: IoT and blockchain make it possible to track raw materials via intricate supply chains to confirm ethical and sustainable procurement. Having transparency into manufacturing outsourcing may guarantee ethical labor practices all the way down the supply chain.

Thus, to support sustainability, worker welfare, health, and safety, businesses must assess the ethical and environmental effects of the smart technology decisions they make.

4.17 Conclusion

In the concluding section of this chapter, we explored the complex relationship that artificial intelligence (AI) has with human cognition, emphasizing the significant influence that AI will have on society. Although the incorporation of AI into a variety of fields has already shown that it can improve human capabilities, it also poses important problems regarding the nature of intelligence, AI's place in society, and the moral issues that need to be resolved. The creation of AI systems that can learn, reason, and interact with humans in a more intuitive and natural way has been the main focus of the chapter's exploration of the current state of AI research. This work discussed about the potential advantages of AI, including better decision-making, more productivity, and the capacity to solve challenging issues that would be unsolvable in the absence of AI. We have, however, also recognized the difficulties that AI brings, such as the possibility of employment displacement; the necessity of responsible AI development; and the significance of guaranteeing that AI systems are open, equitable, and responsible.

In the long run, responsible innovation must serve as the compass for AI research and development. This entails making certain that AI systems are visible, explainable, and built in a way that minimizes possible harms—all while keeping human values in mind. Aside from tackling the ethical and sociological ramifications of these technologies, the area of artificial intelligence must also keep looking for fresh and creative approaches to incorporate AI systems into our everyday life. In order to do this, there are a few crucial areas that need more research:

Ethical AI: A dedication to moral values like accountability, openness, and fairness must direct the creation of AI systems. This involves making certain AI systems which are developed in a manner that respects human rights and values and that their potential damages are minimized.

Explainable AI: For consumers to comprehend how an artificial intelligence system makes decisions, it must be transparent and explicable in its design. This will guarantee that AI systems are used responsibly and contribute to the growth of public trust in them.

Collaboration between people and AI: AI systems should be created to work with humans, not in place of them. This is the philosophy that should drive the development of AI in the future. This will make it easier to make sure AI systems are used in a way that optimizes their potential advantages and minimizes their potential drawbacks.

AI education: A dedication to AI education is necessary to ensure that people have the information and abilities necessary to comprehend and utilize AI systems responsibly. This will lead the development of AI systems. This involves making certain that AI education is made available to everyone and that it is tailored to meet the needs of a wide variety of students.

AI policy: Governments and other stakeholders must collaborate to guarantee that AI systems are utilized responsibly, and this commitment should serve as a roadmap for the development of AI systems. This involves making certain that AI systems are utilized in a way that minimizes possible harms and that they are developed in a way that respects human rights and values.

In conclusion, a dedication to responsible innovation must serve as the foundation for the future of AI research and development. This entails making certain that AI systems are visible, explainable, and built in a way that minimizes possible harms—all while keeping human values in mind. We can make sure AI systems are employed in a way that optimizes their potential advantages while also reducing potential dangers by tackling these issues.

References

Alancioni R, Smith M, Oliva T (2000) The role of the Internet in supply chain management. Ind Mark Manag 29(1):45–56

Al-Fuqaha A, Guizani M, Mohammadi M, Aledhari M, Ayyash M (2015) Internet of things: a survey on enabling technologies, protocols, and applications. IEEE Commun Surv Tuts 17(4):2347–2376, 4th Quart

Almada-Lobo F (2015) The Industry 4.0 revolution and the future of manufacturing execution systems (MES). J Innov Manag 3(4):16–21

Amper. Industry 4.0: smart manufacturing explained. https://www.amper.xyz/post/industry-4-0-smart-manufacturing-explained. Accessed 28 Dec 2023

Amper. Industry 4.0: smart manufacturing explained. Amper. https://www.amper.xyz/post/industry-4-0-smart-manufacturing-explained. Accessed 21 Jan 2024

Arrow Electronics (n.d.) Top sensors used in smart manufacturing. https://www.arrow.com/en/research-and-events/articles/top-sensors-used-in-smart-manufacturing. Accessed 18 Jan 2024

Ashton K (2009) That 'Internet of Things' thing. RFID J 22(7):97–114

Atzori L, Iera A, Morabito G (2010) The internet of things: a survey. Comput Netw 54(14):2787–2805

AWS. How an old-fashioned doorstep delivery of bottled milk is making a comeback, powered by AI-driven supply chain. Amazon web services blog. https://aws.amazon.com/blogs/industries/how-an-old-fashioned-doorstep-delivery-of-bottled-milk-is-making-a-comeback-powered-by-ai-driven-supply-chain/. Accessed 28 Dec 2023

Barreto L, Amaral A, Pereira T (2017) Industry 4.0 implications in logistics: an overview. In: Proceedings of the international conference on manufacturing engineering society (MESIC 2017), vol 13, pp 1245–1252

Bossard Group (n.d.) Benefits of smart factory logistics. https://www.bossard.com/us-en/smart-factory-logistics/benefits/. Accessed 3 Feb 2024

Bozer Y, Srinivasan M (1991) Tandem configurations for automated guided vehicle systems and the analysis of single vehicle loops. IIETrans 23(1):72–82

Büchi G, Cugno M, Castagnoli R (2020) Smart factory performance and Industry 4.0. Technol Forecast Soc Change 150:119790. ISSN 0040-1625https://doi.org/10.1016/j.techfore.2019.119790

California Manufacturing Technology Consulting (CMTC) (2018) The new role of sensors in manufacturing. https://www.cmtc.com/blog/the-new-role-of-sensors-in-manufacturing. Accessed 3 Feb 2024

Cullity B (1972) Introduction to magnetic materials. Addison-Wesley, Reading, MA

Davis J, Edgar T, Porter J, Bernaden J, Sarli M (2012) Smart manufacturing, manufacturing intelligence and demand-dynamics performance. Comput Chem Eng 47:145–156

Deloitte (2022) Smart sensors and supply chain. https://www2.deloitte.com/us/en/pages/operations/articles/smart-sensors-and-supply-chain.html. Accessed 18 Jan 2024

Ericsson (2018) Realizing smart manufacturing with IoT. https://www.ericsson.com/en/reports-and-papers/mobility-report/articles/realizing-smart-manufact-iot. Accessed 28 Dec 2023

Exploring 4 Popular Machine Learning Algorithms for Industrial Applications (n.d.) Control.com technical articles. https://control.com/technical-articles/exploring-4-popular-machine-learning-algorithms-for-industrial-applications/

Ferreira P, Martinho R, Domingos D (2010) IoT-aware business processes for logistics: limitations of current approaches. In: Proceedings of the 16th annual conference on INFORUM, May 2010, pp 611–622

Fleisch E, Christ O, Dierkes M (2005) Die Betriebswirtschaftliche Vision des Internets der Dinge. Springer, Berlin

Garrido-Hidalgo C, Olivares T, Ramirez FJ, Roda-Sanchez L (2019) An end-to-end internet of things solution for reverse supply chain management in Industry 4.0. Comput Industry 112, Article 103127. https://doi.org/10.1016/j.compind.2019.103127

Ghadimi P, Wang C, Lim MK, Heavey C (2019) Intelligent sustainable supplier selection using multi-agent technology: theory and application for Industry 4.0 supply chains. Comput Ind Eng 127:588–600

Gregor T, Krajčovič M, Wiecek D (2017) Smart connected logistics. In: Proceedings of the international scientific conference on sustainable, modern and safe transport (TRANSCOM), vol 192, pp 265–270

Gustin C, Daugherty P, Stank T (1995) The effects of information availability on logistics integration. J Bus Logist 16(1):1–21

Hackman S, Rosenblatt M, Olin J (1990) Allocating items to an automated storage and retrieval system. IIE Trans 22(1):7–14

Haddud A, DeSouza A, Khare A, Lee H (2017) Examining potential benefits and challenges associated with the Internet of Things integration in supply chains. J Manuf Technol Manag 28(8):1055–1085

History, Clark Mater. Handling, Lexington, KY, USA, 2019. [Online]. Available: https://www.clarkmhc.com/Company/History

Hofmann E, Rüsch M (2017) Industry 4.0 and the current status as well as future prospects on logistics. Comput Ind 89:22–23

IBM. Industry 4.0. https://www.ibm.com/topics/industry-4-0. Accessed 28 Dec 2023

Impact Networking (2022) Defining the scope of smart manufacturing and Industry 4.0. Impact. https://www.impactmybiz.com/blog/defining-the-scope-of-smart-manufacturing-and-industry-4-0/. Accessed 7 Feb 2024

Jeschke S, Brecher C, Song H, Rawat D (2017) Industrial internet of things: cyber manufacturing systems. Springer, Cham

Jiang Y, Hao S (2011) Research on the development of intelligent logistics based on Internet of Things. In: Proceedings of the international conference on remote sensing, environment and transportation engineering, Jun 2011, pp 5254–5257

Kawa A (2012) SMART logistics chain. In: Proceedings of the Asian conference on intelligent information and database systems (ACIIDS), Mar 2012, pp 432–438.

Kim J, Lee H, Oh R (2015) Smart integrated multiple tracking system development for IoT based target-oriented logistics location and resource service. Int J Smart Home 9(5):195–204

Lee I, Lee K (2015) The internet of things (IoT): applications, investments, and challenges for enterprises. Bus Horiz 58(4):431–440

Lee S, Kang Y, Prabhu V (2016) Smart logistics: distributed control of green crowdsourced parcel services. Int J Prod Res 54(23):6956–6968

Lee CKM, Lv Y, Ng KKH, Ho W, Choy KL (2018) Design and application of internet of things-based warehouse management system for smart logistics. Int J Prod Res 56(8):2753–2768. https://doi.org/10.1080/00207543.2017.1394592

Leung L, Cheung W, Hai Y (2000) A framework for a logistics e-commerce community network: The Hong Kong air cargo industry. IEEE Trans Syst Man Cybern A Syst Humans 30(4):446–455

Li J, Yu FR, Deng G, Luo C, Ming Z, Yan Q (2017) Industrial internet: a survey on the enabling technologies, applications, and challenges. IEEE Commun Surv Tuts 19(3):1504–1526, 3rd Quart

Lisa W, Avril N, Dimples I, Terence F (1997) Logistics integration: the effect of information technology, team composition, and corporate competitive positioning. J Bus Logist 18(2):31–41

Liu W, Gao Z (2014) Study on IoT based architecture of logistics service supply chain. Int J Grid Distrib Comput 7(1):169–178

Liu M, Yu FR, Teng Y, Leung VCM, Song M (2019) Performance optimization for blockchain-enabled industrial Internet of Things (IIoT) systems: a deep reinforcement learning approach. IEEE Trans Ind Informat 15(6):3559–3570

Lu D, Teng Q (2012) A application of cloud computing and IoT in logistics. Int J Softw Eng Appl 5:204–207

McFarlane D, Giannikas V, Lu W (2016) Intelligent logistics: involving the customer. Comput Ind 81:105–115

Mentzer J, Flint D, Hult G (2001) Logistics service quality as a segment-customized process. J Mark 65(1):82–104

Mittal S, Khan MA, Romero D, Wuest T (2019) Smart manufacturing: characteristics, technologies and enabling factors. Proc Inst Mech Eng Part B: J Eng Manuf 233(5):1342–1361. https://doi.org/10.1177/0954405417736547

Müller JM (2019) Business model innovation in small-and medium-sized enterprises: strategies for Industry 4.0 providers and users. J Manuf Technol Manag 30(8):1127–1142

Oracle (2023) Improve supply chain sustainability. https://www.oracle.com/scm/sustainability/improve-supply-chain-sustainability/. Accessed 28 Jan 2023

Partner Content (2023) Solving EV challenges with smart manufacturing and logistics. Automotive logistics. https://www.automotivelogistics.media/partner-content/solving-ev-challenges-with-smart-manufacturing-and-logistics/44159.article. Accessed 7 Feb 2024
PCAST AMP Steering Committee Report—Accelerating U.S. Advanced manufacturing, 27 Oct 2014
Penske Logistics. Six ways to connect logistics with smart manufacturing. Penske Logistics. https://www.penskelogistics.com/industries/industrial-manufacturing/smart-manufacturing. Accessed 28 Dec 2023
Prasse C, Nettstraeter A, Hompel M (2014) How IoT will change the design and operation of logistics systems. In: Proceedings of the international conference on the internet of things (IoT), Cambridge, MA, USA, Oct. 2014, pp 55–60
Qiu C, Yu FR, Yao H, Jiang C, Xu F, Zhao C (2019) Blockchainbased software-defined industrial Internet of Things: a duelling deep Q-learning approach. IEEE Internet Things J 6(3):4627–4639
Qu T, Lei S, Wang Z, Nie D, Chen X, Huang G (2016) IoT-based real-time production logistics synchronization system under smart cloud manufacturing. Int J Adv Manuf Technol 84(1–4):147–164
Ricadela A (2023) Industry 4.0 challenges and risks. Oracle. https://www.oracle.com/industrial-manufacturing/industry-4-challenges/6. Accessed 7 Feb 2024
Rockwell Automation and Plex Systems (2022) 7th annual report, state of smart manufacturing report supply chain planning, 7th edn. https://www.plex.com/sites/default/files/2022-05/10292_7th_State-of-Smart-Manufacturing_Supply-Chain.pdf. Accessed 7 Feb 2024
SAP. Smart manufacturing in the cloud. https://www.sap.com/insights/smart-manufacturing-in-the-cloud.html. Accessed 3 Feb 2024
Sathasivam K, Rajesh AS, Prabhuswamy MS, Krishnasamy S (2022) Smart manufacturing through machine learning: a review, perspective, and future directions to the machining industry. J Eng (Hindawi) 2314–4904. https://doi.org/10.1155/2022/9735862
Shin M, Ko M, Ju Y, Jung Y, Lee B (2013) Implementation of context-aware based robot control system for automatic postal logistics. Stud Inform Control 22(1):71–80
Siemens (2022) Solving EV production challenges. Siemens digital industries software blog. https://blogs.sw.siemens.com/tecnomatix/solving-ev-production-challenges/. Accessed 21 Jan 2024
Song H, Srinivasan R, Sookoor T, Jeschke S (2017) Smart cities: foundations, principles, and applications. Wiley, Hoboken, NJ
Soori M, Arezoo B, Dastres R (2023) Internet of things for smart factories in Industry 4.0, a review. Internet of Things Cyber-Phys Syst 3:192–204. ISSN 2667-3452. https://doi.org/10.1016/j.iotcps.2023.04.006.
Source Essay. Amazon supply chain management case study. https://sourceessay.com/amazon-supply-chain-management-case-study/. Accessed 28 Dec 2023
Suma S, Mehmood R, Albugami N, Katib I, Albeshri A (2017) Enabling next generation logistics and planning for smarter societies. Procedia Comput Sci 440:1122–1127
Sun Y, Song H, Jara AJ, Bie R (2016) Internet of things and big data analytics for smart and connected communities. IEEE Access 4:766–773
Taniguchi E, Thompson R, Yamada T (2015) New opportunities and challenges for city logistics. In: Proceedings of the 9th international conference on city logistics Tenerife, Canary Islands, Spain, Jun 2015, pp 17–19
Telenor Group. Industry 4.0 and IoT in smart manufacturing. https://iot.telenor.com/industry-insights/industry4-iot-smart-manufacturing. Accessed 28 Dec 2023
Thales Group. Inspired smart manufacturing. https://www.thalesgroup.com/en/markets/digital-identity-and-security/iot/inspired/smart-manufacturing. Accessed 28 Dec 2023
Trappey A, Trappey C, Fan C, Hsu A, Li X, Lee I (2017) IoT patent roadmap for smart logistic service provision in the context of industry 4.0. J Chin Inst Eng 40(7):593–602
Tseng Y, Yue W (2005) The role of transportation in logistics chain. In: Proceedings of the Eastern Asia Society for transportation studies, vol 5, pp 1657–1672

Uckelmann D (2008) A definition approach to smart logistics. In: Proceedings of the 8th international conference on NEW2AN 1st Russian conference on smart spaces, Sep 2008, pp 273–284

Vijayaraghavan V, Rian Leevinson J (2019) Internet of things applications and use cases in the era of Industry 4.0. In: Mahmood Z (ed) The internet of things in the industrial sector. Computer communications and networks. Springer, Cham. https://doi.org/10.1007/978-3-030-24892-5_12

Witkowski K (2017) Internet of things, big data, industry 4.0—innovative solutions in logistics and supply chains management. In: Proceedings of the 7th international conference on engineering, project, and production management, vol 182, pp 763–769

Zhang Y, Guo Z, Lv J, Liu Y (2018) A framework for smart production-logistics systems based on CPS and industrial IoT. IEEE Trans Ind Informat 14(9):4019–4032

ZhenHub (2023) Sustainable logistics: a guide to reducing environmental impact. https://zhenhub.com/blog/sustainable-logistics/. Accessed 28 Jan 2023

Chapter 5
Industrial Automation Through AI-Powered Intelligent Machines—Enabling Real-Time Decision-Making

Neelam Yadav, Varuna Gupta, and Aakansha Garg

Abstract AI has transformed industrial automation, enabled real-time decision-making, and improved efficiency in many industries. This chapter discusses the importance of AI-powered machines in industrial automation, focusing on how they make operations more responsive and flexible in changing manufacturing environments. This chapter explores how industrial Internet of Things (IIOT) helps in performing various functions like remote monitoring and controlling, predictive maintenance, asset management, safety and compliances and supply chain integration. By analysing data, predicting challenges, optimizing processes and introducing robotics in manufacturing, AI technologies allow machines to operate with less human involvement. These systems can spot problems early on and prevent risks, resulting in less downtime and higher productivity. The chapter showcases case studies and success stories of AI solutions in various industries. It provides guidance for businesses wanting to capitalize on AI's potential to gain an edge in today's competitive market.

Keywords Industrial Internet of Things (IIOT) · AI · Smart manufacturing

---

N. Yadav
ABES Engineering College, Ghaziabad, UP, India

V. Gupta (✉)
Christ University, Bengaluru, India
e-mail: varunagupta.cs@gmail.com

A. Garg
ABES Institute of Technology, Ghaziabad, UP, India

R. Arya et al. (eds.), *Recent Trends in Artificial Intelligence Towards a Smart World*, Frontiers of Artificial Intelligence, Ethics and Multidisciplinary Applications,
https://doi.org/10.1007/978-981-97-6790-8_5

5.1 Introduction

5.1.1 Definition of Industrial Automation

Industrial Automation refers to the use of control systems such as computers or robots for handling different processes and machinery in an industry to replace human intervention. It involves the use of technologies like computers, programmable logic controllers (PLCs), sensors, and other advanced equipment to perform tasks with a high degree of precision, reliability, and efficiency.

5.1.2 Overview of Artificial Intelligence in Industrial Automation

To accurately comprehend the term 'Artificial Intelligence' in Industrial Automation first the Human intelligence must be understood (Jazdi et al. 2021). Human Intelligence refers to the cognitive capabilities and capacities that help individuals to acquire, reason, solve problems, realize multifaceted concepts, acclimatize to new situations and interact successfully with the environment. It includes a wide range of abilities:

Reasoning and Problem-Solving: The talent to evaluate information, draw conclusions, and solve the given problems logically.

Memory: The ability to store, encode and retrieve data from past experiences.

Creativity: The skill to produce unique and innovative ideas, theories and solutions.

Communication: The capacity to comprehend and produce spoken, written and nonverbal communication.

Perception: The process of interpreting sensory information from the environment, including vision, hearing, touch, taste and smell.

Emotional Intelligence: The capability to understand, perceive, manage and express emotions effectively, both in oneself and in others.

Social Skills: The ability for social interactions, create relationships and collaborate with others.

Adaptation: The talent to acquire new knowledge, skills and behaviours, and to adapt to varying circumstances.

Artificial Intelligence refers to the transformation of different aspects of human intelligence processes including perceiving, self-learning, decision making, analysing, reasoning and self-correction into a software. AI is the simulation of human intelligence by computer systems. AI machines are used to increase productivity, reduced the costs and freed the human user with repetitive and monotonous tasks. AI consists of several sub-fields including Machine Learning (ML), Modelling and Simulation, Natural Language Processing (NLP), Pattern Recognition, Deep learning though Artificial Neural Networks (ANN), Knowledge-based systems, Computer Vision (CV) and Robotics (Ribeiro et al. 2021). Due to the strong similarities between AI systems' features in all these sub-fields, the definition of a general AI framework for industrial automation systems (IAS) is feasible.

AI technologies are invading in the manufacturing industry and integrating the hydraulic and virtual worlds. AI enables the manufacturing industry smart and capable enough of addressing current challenges like automation, customizable requirements, and reduced time and effort and increasing the number of sensors and software bots used in modern equipment (Zheng et al. 2018). The use of automated robots with AI features allows for faster and easier manufacturing of varied products. AI methods (like pattern recognition, classification and data mining) have the ability of analysing big volumes of real-time data collected from different sensors.

Artificial Intelligence plays a key role in manufacturing industries by providing automated robots and monitor the safety of the human labour involved and provides safety measures to the employees. AI-driven predictive systems examine complex and huge data from different sensors placed in some areas and predict it. AI-powered robots help in reducing production costs and leverage the profits. AI cut down the production costs from 10 to 20% and this could lead to the saving of capitals of $100 billion to $1 trillion by 2025 (Ustundag and Cevikcan 2018). AI prevents cyber-attacks by its great security.

5.1.3 Significance of Combining AI and Industrial Automation

The digital world has transformed the strategy of different industry. It effects the business models, production, competitiveness, maintenance, sustainability, operations and logistics. Data, information and the Cyber-Physical Systems (physical machines) (Leitão et al. 2016) make the core of Industry 4.0 which further combines with communication, computational, communication and control capabilities with Artificial Intelligence (AI) in its various forms (Yao et al. 2017). Due to the cognitive capabilities of artificial intelligence (AI), it plays a progressively decisive role in the combined integration of machines, resources, automation and human beings (Lee et al. 2018). The integration of AI and industrial automation provides various benefits for automation of processes, increasing productivity, and refining decision-making in industrial sectors (Li et al. 2018). Following are numerous ways in how AI benefits after integration with industrial automation:

Predictive Maintenance: AI algorithms analyse data from various machinery and sensors to foresee equipment catastrophes, before they occur (Li et al. 2018). AI systems can minimize downtimes, reduce maintenance costs and schedule maintenance activities proactively by identifying outliers and varied patterns of sensor data.

Quality Control: AI-enabled computer vision systems examine products for defects with high accuracy and efficiency than old methods. Machine learning algorithms (classification and predictive algorithms) can ensure that only high-quality products reach the market by identifying subtle defects and deviations from well-defined quality standards.

Autonomous Robots: AI assists robots to perform tasks autonomously in industries. These robots free up human workers with monotonous and repetitive tasks such as assembling, packaging and material handling. It enables a human worker to focus on more innovative, complex and creative tasks. AI-enabled robots adapt to changing environments and can collaborate securely and sagely with humans.

Process Optimization: AI boosts industrial processes by analysing huge volumes of data from sensors, user interaction logs (Yadav and Panda 2024), production systems, inventory data and supply chains. Machine learning algorithms can detect inefficiencies, observe and enhance parameters in real-time, and can recommend certain actions to increase throughput, and resource utilization.

Supply Chain Management: AI improves the supply chain operations by forecasting demand, optimizing inventory levels, and streamlining logistics processes. AI algorithms analyse historical data, market trends, and external factors to make accurate predictions, reducing costs and improving efficiency throughout the supply chain. Adoption of AI (Artificial Intelligence) can improve the efficiency of food processing and distribution in food supply chain operations. AI robots are doing sensor-based packaging thereby increasing the marketing potential of food products after certifying the food quality and safety. Automatic sorting and retrieval system (AS/RS) is a warehouse automation technology specifically designed to store, buffer and show the products and inventory on demand (Henry 2024).

Energy Management: AI-based systems can easily monitor control and detect the timing in solar radiations and wind farms' energy generation. AI and machine learning (ML) algorithms are autonomously controlling energy sources, power supply and demand and decisive situations. By analysing data from smart meters and sensors, AI optimizes energy usage, identifies opportunities for energy savings, monitor and control energy consumption in industrial facilities. AI recommends tactics to minimize costs and environmental impact. AI and ML models help in feature selection, extraction, production, optimization of energy efficiency, infrastructure controllability, control of predictive maintenance, monitoring and operational performance, etc. Swarm intelligence, (FLC) fuzzy logic systems, genetic algorithms and expert systems of AI/ML are the most common algorithms that are used in energy management (Jain et al. 2023).

By combining AI and industrial automation, organizations can improve quality, efficiency, sustainability, and safety through their operations and can gain a viable edge in today's rapidly evolving digital market. However, it's essential to address challenges such as data quality, interoperability, and cyber security to realize the full potential of AI in industrial automation.

5.2 Foundations of Industrial Automation

5.2.1 Historical Evolution of Industrial Automation

Over several centuries, there have been major technological developments and paradigm shifts in manufacturing processes that have shaped the historical history of industrial automation. Below is a summary of significant turning points and advancements:

Pre-Industrial Revolution (before eighteenth century): Early forms of automation were rudimentary and primarily based on manual labour, with simple tools and machinery used to assist in production processes. Waterwheels and windmills were among the earliest examples of mechanization, providing mechanical power for tasks such as milling grain and pumping water.

First Industrial Revolution (late eighteenth- to early-nineteenth century): The advent of steam power and mechanized production techniques revolutionized manufacturing during the late eighteenth century. The expansion of steam engines, powered by coal, allowed the mechanization of textile production, transportation, and other industries. The factory system emerged, with centralized production facilities housing large-scale machinery and assembly lines.

Second Industrial Revolution (late nineteenth- to early-twentieth century): The Second Industrial Revolution brought significant advancements in technology, including steel production, electricity, and the internal combustion engine. The primary source of mechanical power in factories is electric motors instead of steam engines, leading to greater flexibility and productivity in production processes. With assembly line production and standardized parts, mass production techniques pioneered by innovators like Henry Ford transformed manufacturing.

Third Industrial Revolution (mid- to late-twentieth century): Digitization with computers in the mid-twentieth century marked the beginning of the Third Industrial Revolution, also known as the Digital Revolution. Programmable logic controllers (PLCs) were introduced in the 1960s. PLCs became a very reliable method for controlling industrial machinery and processes. Numerical control (NC) and computer numerical control (CNC) systems modernized machining and manufacturing processes with better precision and automation.

Fourth Industrial Revolution (late twentieth century to present): The Fourth Industrial Revolution, often referred to as Industry 4.0, builds upon the digital technologies of the previous era with a focus on connectivity, automation, and data-driven decision-making. This era utilizes the advancement of technologies including Artificial Intelligence (AI), block chain, Internet of Things (IoT), genetic engineering and 3D printing (Khalid et al. 2024a). Advancements in actuators, sensors, robotics, Internet of Things (IoT) and Artificial Intelligence (AI), are driving the integration of cyber-physical systems in manufacturing. Industry 4.0 technologies enable the creation of smart factories, where machines, products, and systems communicate and collaborate autonomously to optimize production processes. Concepts such as deep learning, natural language processing and big data analytics, machine learning and cloud computing are gradually applied to industrial automation, these technologies increase efficiency, productivity and innovation.

Industrial automation has developed throughout time from basic mechanization to complex cyber-physical systems that are changing the face of manufacturing. Every revolution has resulted in revolutionary shifts in economic structures, labor dynamics, and production techniques, opening the door for further advancements and innovation in the field of industrial automation. Technological developments in cyber-physical systems have opened new avenues for industrial automation innovation and progression.

5.2.2 Key Components and Technologies in Industrial Automation

Industrial automation relies on a variety of components and technologies to automate manufacturing processes efficiently and effectively. Here are some key components and technologies commonly used in industrial automation:

Sensors: Sensors are small devices used for sensing the changes in the environment and convert physical parameters (such as motion, pressure, temperature, pressure, or proximity) into electrical signals. These are self-controlled and self-triggered devices that help in reducing human interference. These sensors continuously collect real-time data and provide it to control systems thereby helping in monitoring and feedback mechanisms in industrial processes (Malik et al. 2021).

Actuators: Actuators are devices that convert electrical signals into mechanical motion or action. They are used to control the movement of valves, machinery, valves, motors, and other mechanical components in industrial automation systems (Goel and Gupta 2020).

Programmable Logic Controllers (PLCs): PLCs are industrial computers that consist of very powerful hardware devices including high speed processors, non-volatile memory up to 2 GB. These are designed to control manufacturing processes and machinery. They receive input signals from sensors, process data according to programmed logic, and generate output signals to control actuators and other devices. PLCs are widely used for monitoring, process control, monitoring, and automation in industrial applications (Kovalev et al. 2024).

Human–Machine Interface (HMI): HMIs provide a graphical interface for operators and engineers to monitor and interact with industrial automation systems. They display real-time data, status information, alarms, and control options, allowing users to monitor and control manufacturing processes effectively. HMIs are evolved into Human–Computer interaction where a human can query machines like Alexa and Siri (Janapati 2023).

Industrial Robots: Industrial robots are hydraulic and programmable machines specifically designed to perform tasks autonomously or semi-autonomously in industrial environments. They are used for repetitive tasks such as welding, assembly, painting, material handling, and inspection. These robots replace human labour and increase efficiency and productivity.

Machine Vision Systems: Machine vision systems use cameras, image processing algorithms, and artificial intelligence techniques like deep learning, face recognition mechanism to review and analyse visual information in industrial processes. They are used for recognition, inspections, process monitoring, optical gauging, quality control, alignment defect detection, measurement and other visual inspection tasks (Palanikumar et al. 2024).

Motion Control Systems: Motion control systems are utilized in industrial automation applications to regulate the movement of machinery and equipment. To regulate the speed, position, and acceleration of mechanical components, they consist of motors, drives, controllers and feedback devices (such encoders) that cooperate.

Industrial Communication Networks: In industrial automation contexts, industrial communication networks provide data interchange and communication between devices and systems. CAN bus, Ethernet, Profibus, Modbus and OPC-UA are examples of common communication protocols that help with automation system integration and interoperability.

5.3 Challenges Addressed by Industrial Automation

The goal of industrial automation is to increase productivity, safety, quality and efficiency by addressing several issues that the manufacturing and other industrial sectors confront. The following are some major issues that industrial automation aims to resolve:

Labor Shortages: By automating tedious, manual processes, decreasing the need for human labour and allowing businesses to continue producing at their current levels despite a lack of workers or skilled workers, industrial automation helps address the labour shortage.

Cost Reduction: For manufacturing and industrial processes, automation lowers labour costs, minimizes material waste and maximizes resource utilization, all of which add up to overall cost savings.

Increased Productivity: Automation increases throughput, shortens cycle times and streamlines procedures to increase production. Automated systems have the capacity to run at high rates constantly, which increases industrial productivity.

Quality Control: By introducing precise, repeatable procedures and integrating inspection and testing systems into production lines, automation improves quality control. As a result, there are fewer flaws, better-quality products, and less scrap or rework.

Safety Improvements: Automation improves workplace safety by replacing hazardous or strenuous tasks with automated processes and robotic systems. This reduces the risk of workplace accidents, injuries and exposure to hazardous materials.

Enhanced Flexibility: Systems for industrial automation are made to be adaptive and flexible in response to shifting demands for output. It is possible to reprogramme or reconfigure automated equipment to handle fluctuations in processes, manufacturing volumes or products.

Consistency and Reliability: Automation removes human error, variance, and fatigue-related problems to guarantee uniformity and dependability in production operations. Over time, automated systems consistently produce results by operating with accuracy and precision.

Compliance with Regulations: Automation employs standardized procedures, documentation, and traceability techniques to help guarantee adherence to industry laws, safety standards and quality requirements.

Inventory Management: By tracking supplies, keeping an eye on stock levels and applying lean manufacturing or just-in-time (JIT) techniques, automation systems improve inventory management. This lowers the cost of keeping inventory on hand, gets rid of extra inventory, and boosts supply chain effectiveness.

Data-Driven Decision-Making: Massive volumes of data are produced by sensors, machinery and production processes in industrial automation systems. Data-driven decision-making, optimization, and continual improvement are made possible by the advanced analytics and artificial intelligence used in this data analysis process.

Environmental Sustainability: Through waste reduction, energy optimization and environmental effect minimization, automation fosters environmental sustainability. Sustainable manufacturing methods can be enhanced by automated systems' ability to recycle materials, use resources more efficiently and apply energy-efficient techniques.

Overall, industrial automation helps businesses increase production, efficiency, quality, safety and sustainability while retaining their competitiveness in the fast-paced business world of today. It does this by addressing several issues that the manufacturing and industrial sectors face.

5.4 Intersection of AI and Industrial Automation

5.4.1 Integration of AI in Manufacturing Processes

The integration of Artificial Intelligence (AI) in manufacturing processes has the potential to transform the industry by optimizing operations, increasing productivity and permitting new levels of flexibility and innovation.

Here are several ways how AI is being integrated into manufacturing processes:

Predictive Maintenance: Artificial intelligence programs inspect sensor data from devices and machinery to anticipate any glitches before they happen. AI systems may schedule maintenance tasks proactively, decreasing downtime and lowering maintenance costs, by seeing trends and abnormalities in the data.

Quality Control and Defect Detection: Vision systems driven by AI can check products for flaws faster and more accurately than manual techniques. Machine learning algorithms examine pictures to find flaws, irregularities and departures from quality requirements, guaranteeing that only superior goods are released onto the market.

Process Optimization: AI analyses data from sensors, production systems, and supply networks to optimize manufacturing operations. To increase throughput, energy efficiency and resource utilization, machine learning algorithms find inefficiencies, optimize settings in real-time and make recommendations for action.

Supply Chain Management: Through demand forecasting, inventory optimization, and process simplification artificial intelligence (AI) improves supply chain operations. Artificial intelligence (AI) systems examine data from several sources to produce precise forecasts, lower expenses, and boost productivity across the supply chain.

Product Design and Development: AI algorithms are utilized to streamline the processes involved in product creation and design. With the aid of generative design algorithms, engineers may create design alternatives that maximize product performance while exploring novel ideas within predetermined parameters and goals.

Autonomous Robots and Manufacturing Systems: AI makes it possible to create manufacturing systems and autonomous robots that can complete tasks without the need for human interaction. Artificial intelligence (AI) algorithms are used by these systems to sense and interact with their surroundings, adjust to changing circumstances, and safely and effectively work alongside human workers.

Energy Management: Artificial intelligence (AI) systems keep an eye on and regulate manufacturing facilities' energy usage. Artificial Intelligence (AI) optimizes energy consumption, finds opportunities for energy savings, and suggests ways to lower costs and environmental effect by evaluating data from sensors and industrial systems.

Supply Chain Risk Management: By evaluating data from several sources to identify possible disruptions, weaknesses and opportunities, artificial intelligence (AI) helps mitigate supply chain risks. By evaluating risks and suggesting techniques for mitigation, machine learning algorithms help businesses make wise decisions and preserve supply chain resilience.

Demand Forecasting and Inventory Optimization: Demand forecasting, inventory optimization, and supply chain efficiency are all enhanced by AI algorithms. Artificial intelligence (AI) systems produce precise demand projections and suggest inventory strategies to reduce stock outs and excess inventory by evaluating past data, market trends and outside variables.

Customization and Personalization: AI analyses consumer preferences, market trends, and production capacities to enable mass customization and individualized manufacturing. Manufacturers can offer personalized items at scale by using machine learning algorithms to optimize production processes to match the needs of individual customers.

In today's dynamic market, businesses can gain a competitive edge and sustain growth by integrating artificial intelligence (AI) into their manufacturing processes to achieve higher levels of efficiency, flexibility and innovation.

5.4.2 AI Applications in Control Systems

AI applications in control systems offer innovative capabilities for improving performance, adaptability, and efficiency through various industries. Below are some key AI applications in control systems:

Model Predictive Control (MPC): MPC is a control approach that forecasts system behaviour and maximizes control actions over a future time horizon by using mathematical models. AI methods, such machine learning can handle complicated nonlinearities, increase model accuracy and adjust to shifting operating conditions to improve MPC.

Adaptive Control: Real-time parameter adjustments are made by adaptive control systems to account for variations in operating conditions or system dynamics. By learning system dynamics and optimizing control techniques, artificial intelligence (AI) algorithms like neural networks and reinforcement learning can help adaptive control systems respond to uncertainties and disruptions more skilfully.

Fuzzy Logic Control: Fuzzy logic control represents and rationalizes unclear or imprecise system behaviour using linguistic variables and fuzzy rules. Fuzzy logic control can be improved by artificial intelligence (AI) methods like fuzzy inference systems and genetic algorithms, which automatically adjust fuzzy rule sets and maximize control performance.

Neural Network Control: Neural network control systems use artificial neural networks to use complex system dynamics and learn control policies from data. Through the use of AI techniques like deep reinforcement learning, neural network controllers can learn the best control strategies through experience, which enhances their performance and flexibility. This can be particularly useful in domains where analytical models are difficult to formulate or incomplete (Prasanthi et al. 2024).

Genetic Algorithms: Genetic algorithms are optimization algorithms inspired by the principles of natural selection and evolution. AI applications of genetic algorithms in control systems include parameter optimization, controller tuning and system identification, allowing for the discovery of optimal control solutions in complex, high-dimensional search spaces (Khalid et al. 2024b).

Swarm Intelligence: Swarm intelligence algorithms, such as particle swarm optimization and ant colony optimization, model collective behaviour observed in natural systems to solve optimization problems. AI applications of swarm intelligence in control systems include optimization of control parameters, maintenance of autonomous functioning, coordination of multi-agent systems, and decentralized control strategies. Swarm intelligence algorithm increases the versatility and flexibility in conventional manufacturing systems (Chan et al. 2012).

Reinforcement Learning Control: Reinforcement learning is a machine learning paradigm where agents learn to make decisions by interacting with their environment and receiving feedback in the form of rewards or penalties (Liu et al. 2024).

5.4.3 Role of AI in Predictive Maintenance

The role of Artificial Intelligence (AI) in predictive maintenance is pivotal, offering proactive strategies for identifying and addressing potential equipment failures before they occur. Here's how AI contributes to predictive maintenance (Islam et al. 2024).

Data Analysis and Pattern Recognition: AI algorithms analyse historical and real-time data from sensors, actuators, equipment, and operational systems to identify patterns, trends, and anomalies that can further foresee equipment failures. By detecting subtle deviations in data patterns, AI systems can predict potential failures with high accuracy.

Condition Monitoring: AI-powered condition monitoring systems examine sensor data and other pertinent characteristics to continuously monitor the functionality and health of equipment. By using past data to create baseline performance measurements and identify anomalous behaviour, machine learning algorithms enable maintenance teams to act before problems get worse.

Fault Detection and Diagnostics: AI algorithms enable early fault detection and diagnosis of equipment faults by identifying outliers in sensor data for signs of degradation or malfunction. Machine learning techniques, such as anomaly detection and fault classification, identify abnormal conditions and locate the root causes of failures, enabling timely maintenance interventions.

Prognostics and Remaining Useful Life Prediction: AI-driven condition monitoring systems continuously check the operation and health of equipment by analysing sensor data and other relevant features. Machine learning techniques let maintenance teams act before issues worsen by leveraging historical data to establish baseline performance metrics and spot aberrant behaviour.

Optimized Maintenance Scheduling: Artificial intelligence (AI) algorithms maximize maintenance scheduling by considering a variety of variables, including corporate goals, operational restrictions, and equipment condition. Artificial intelligence (AI) solutions maximize equipment uptime and productivity by recommending the least disruptive and most cost-effective maintenance techniques through data analysis and simulation of various maintenance situations.

Integration with IoT and Edge Computing: Predictive maintenance systems with AI capabilities use edge computing and Internet of Things (IoT) devices to gather and process data at the source, allowing for real-time equipment health monitoring and analysis. Organizations can increase responsiveness, scalability, and latency in predictive maintenance systems by implementing AI algorithms at the edge.

5.5 Industrial Internet of Things (IIoT)

5.5.1 Overview of IIoT

The expansion and deployment of the Internet of Things (IoT) in industrial contexts and sectors is known as the Industrial Internet of Things (IIoT). While IoT usually refers to networks of interconnected devices and systems across a range of industries, including wearable technology, smart homes, and consumer electronics, IIoT focuses on the application of IoT technology in industrial environments, such as manufacturing, energy, transportation and healthcare. IIoT refers to the integration of sensors, actuators, and other intelligent devices into industrial machinery, infrastructure and equipment. These gadgets gather and send information about the operational parameters, equipment performance and physical surroundings. IIOT helps in performing the following functions as shown in Fig. 5.1 in industrial automation.

- Data Acquisition.
- Data Analysis.
- Remote Monitoring and controlling.
- Predictive maintenance.
- Asset Management.
- Supply Chain Integration.
- Safety and Compliance.

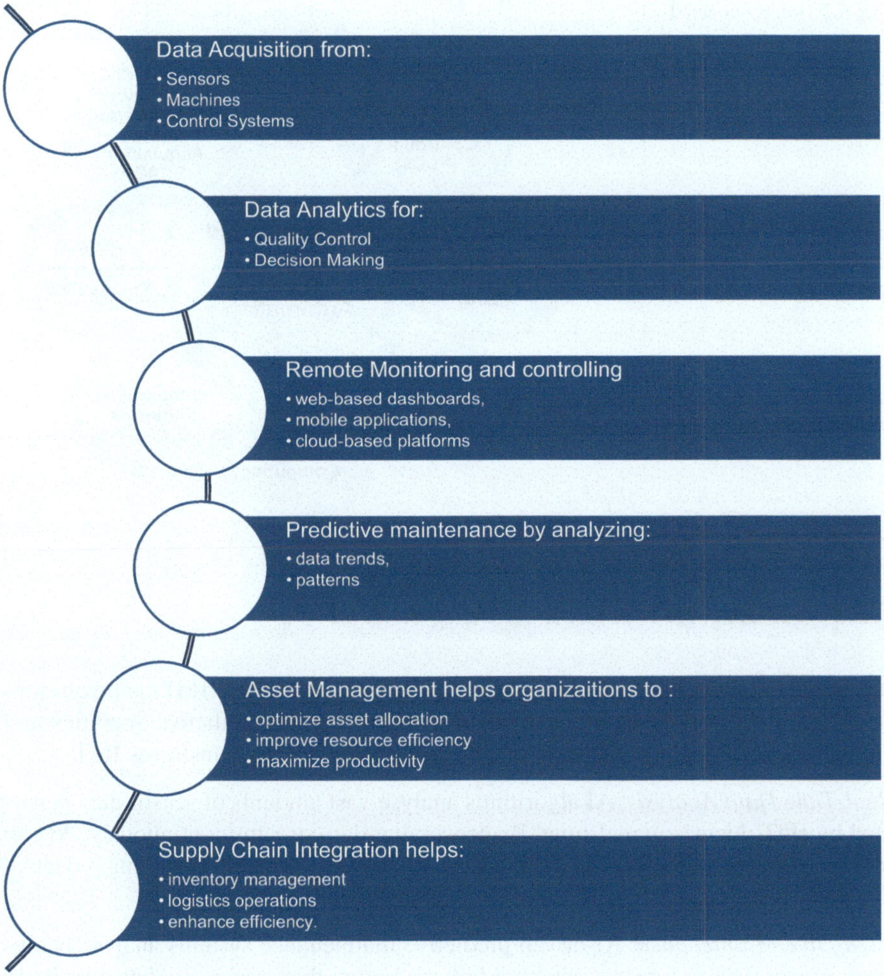

Fig. 5.1 IIOT characteristics and functions. *Source* Author

5.5.2 Interconnected Systems in Industrial Automation

Industrial automation relies heavily on interconnected systems since they facilitate smooth coordination and communication between different parts, apparatus and subsystems in a production setting. These networked systems make it easier to exchange, manage and synchronize data, which eventually improves productivity, flexibility and operational efficiency. Figure 5.2 shows some crucial elements of linked systems in industrial automation:

Fig. 5.2 Interconnected systems in industrial automation. *Source* Author

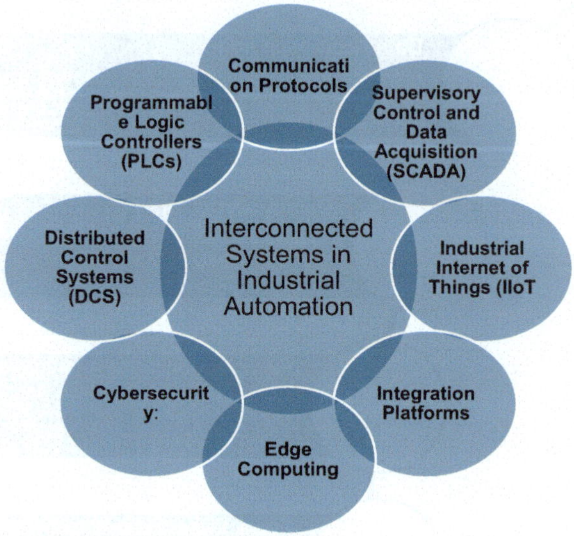

5.5.3 AI-Driven Decision-Making in IIoT

AI-driven decision-making in the Industrial Internet of Things (IIoT) is revolutionizing industrial processes by enabling real-time insights, predictive analytics and autonomous actions. Here's how AI-driven decision-making transforms IIoT:

Real-Time Data Analysis: AI algorithms analyse vast amounts of sensor data generated by IIoT devices in real-time. By processing data streams continuously, AI can identify patterns, anomalies and trends that humans may overlook, enabling proactive decision-making.

Predictive Maintenance: AI-driven predictive maintenance systems analyse equipment sensor data to forecast potential failures before they occur. By detecting early warning signs of equipment degradation or malfunctions, AI enables pre-emptive maintenance actions, reducing downtime and preventing costly breakdowns.

Optimized Operations: AI optimizes industrial operations by dynamically adjusting parameters such as temperature, pressure and speed to maximize efficiency and productivity. Machine learning algorithms learn from historical data and adapt operations in real-time to optimize resource utilization and minimize waste.

Quality Control and Defect Detection: AI-powered quality control systems inspect manufactured products for defects and deviations from specifications. Computer vision algorithms analyse images and sensor data to identify defects with high accuracy, ensuring consistent product quality and minimizing rework.

Supply Chain Optimization: AI optimizes supply chain management in IIoT by forecasting demand, optimizing inventory levels and identifying optimal transportation routes. AI-powered analytics provide insights into market trends, demand fluctuations and supply chain risks, enabling proactive decision-making and agile responses to changing conditions.

Energy Efficiency: AI-driven energy management systems optimize energy consumption in industrial facilities by analysing energy usage patterns and identifying opportunities for efficiency improvements. By optimizing equipment operation schedules and reducing energy waste, AI helps organizations achieve sustainability goals and reduce operational costs.

Autonomous Decision-Making: AI enables autonomous decision-making in IIoT by empowering devices and systems to make decisions and take actions independently. Autonomous systems equipped with AI algorithms can respond to changing conditions, adjust parameters and execute tasks without human intervention, improving operational efficiency and responsiveness.

Continuous Learning and Improvement: AI-driven decision-making in IIoT is characterized by continuous learning and improvement. Machine learning algorithms learn from new data and feedback to refine models, optimize algorithms, and enhance decision-making capabilities over time.

Overall, AI-driven decision-making in IIoT enhances operational efficiency, productivity and competitiveness by enabling real-time insights, predictive analytics and autonomous actions. By harnessing the power of AI, organizations can unlock new opportunities for optimization, innovation and growth in the digital age of industrial automation.

5.6 Data Analytics in Industrial Automation

5.6.1 Importance of Data in Automation

Data is essential to automation in many different businesses because it provides the basis for creative thinking, optimization and well-informed decision-making. Below is a summary of the role that data plays in automation:

- *Decision-making*: Organizations can use historical and real-time data (user interaction logs, sensor data) to take decisive actions in autonomous systems. Automation systems can find patterns, trends, and correlations in massive information that human operators can miss. As a result, decisions are made more quickly and accurately, which boosts operational effectiveness and efficiency.
- *Process Optimization*: Organizations may maximize productivity and efficiency by optimizing their operations with data-driven automation. Automation systems are able to pinpoint inefficiencies, bottlenecks and opportunities for improvement through the constant monitoring and analysis of operational data.

- *Predictive Maintenance*: Automation systems use machine learning algorithms and data analytics to anticipate equipment problems before they happen. These systems are able to detect possible problems early on and initiate preventive maintenance by evaluating sensor data and previous maintenance logs. This lessens unscheduled downtime, increases system longevity, and lowers maintenance expenses.
- *Quality Control*: Data-driven automation confirms reliable product quality by monitoring and analysing production data in real-time. By sensing deviations from predefined quality standards, automation systems can automatically adjust process parameters or alert operators to take corrective actions.
- *Resource Allocation*: Automation systems analyse production schedules, inventory levels, and demand projections to optimize resource allocation. These systems guarantee the best possible use of resources including personnel, raw materials and equipment by dynamically modifying production plans in response to shifting market conditions or operational limitations.
- *Customer Insights*: Automation systems record important consumer information from the point of sale to after-sale support throughout the product lifecycle. Organizations can learn a great deal about the preferences, actions and satisfaction levels of their customers by examining this data. This makes it possible for them to better customize goods and services to match the needs of their clients, which boosts client retention and loyalty.
- *Regulatory Compliance*: Organizations can guarantee adherence to industry standards and regulatory requirements with the use of data-driven automation. Automation systems can demonstrate compliance with safety, environmental, and quality laws by gathering and evaluating pertinent data. This lowers the possibility of fines for non-compliance, legal action and harm to one's reputation.
- *Innovation*: Automation powered by data encourages creativity by giving businesses insights into new trends, business prospects, and client demands. Organizations can identify new product or service offers, enter new markets, and maintain an advantage over competitors by evaluating market data, competitor performance and consumer feedback.

5.6.2 Role of Big Data Analytics

Big data analytics plays a crucial role in automation by enabling organizations to extract valuable insights from large and complex datasets (Allam 2022). Here's how big data analytics contributes to automation:

- *Data Collection*: Big data analytics collects large amount of structured and unstructured data from numerous sources, including sensors, user interface logs, customer interactions, process description, IoT devices, social media, and transaction records. This data serves as the raw material for analysis and decision-making in automation systems.

- *Data Integration*: Big data analytics unifies data from various sources and formats into a single dataset so that it can be analysed. Organizations are able to make more thorough and educated decisions thanks to this integration, which gives them a comprehensive perspective of their markets, customers and operations.
- *Data Processing*: Big data analytics processes huge volumes of data at high velocity. This data is distributed across computing clusters and can parallel processed by distributed computing frameworks such as Hadoop, Spark and Flink to analyse it quickly and efficiently.
- *Data Analysis*: Big data analytics uses various analytical techniques, including data mining, machine learning, natural language processing and statistical modelling. These techniques reveal patterns, trends, outliers, correlations and anomalies within the data, empowering organizations to take decisions.
- *Predictive Analytics*: Big data analytics empowers predictive modelling by classifying patterns and trends in historical data and using them to forecast future outcomes.
- *Prescriptive Analytics*: Big data analytics provide insights and recommendations. Prescriptive analytics proposes ideal courses of action to attain specific business objectives, such as maximizing revenue, reducing costs or enhancing resource allocation.
- *Performance Monitoring*: Big data analytics tracks metrics and key performance indicators (KPIs) in real-time to keep an eye on the effectiveness of automated systems and processes.
- *Quality Control*: By examining production data to find flaws, abnormalities and departures from quality standards, big data analytics helps quality control. Organizations can improve product quality and customer satisfaction by minimizing scrap, rework, and warranty claims by identifying quality concerns early in the production process and taking corrective action.
- *Continuous Improvement*: Continuous improvement is made possible by big data analytics, which offers feedback loops for iteratively improving automated procedures and algorithms. Organizations can find areas for improvement, innovation and optimization by examining user input and performance data. This helps to make sure that automated systems adapt to changing company goals and requirements.

5.6.3 Real-Time Data Processing and Analysis

The ability to manage and examine data streams as they are generated, without appreciable delay, is referred to as real-time data processing and analysis. This feature is crucial for many applications, particularly in sectors where quick decisions and insights are vital. Real-time Data processing and analysis helps in:

- Faster Response Time.
- Increased operational efficiency.
- Instant insights.

- Improved-Customer Experience.
- Fraud Detection and Security.
- Supply Chain Optimization.
- IoT and Sensor Networks.
- Healthcare monitoring and Patient Care.

5.7 Machine Learning in Industrial Automation

5.7.1 Basics of Machine Learning

A branch of artificial intelligence (AI) called "machine learning" is concerned with creating models and algorithms that let computers learn from data and make judgments or predictions (Carbonell et al. 1983).

5.7.1.1 Types of Machine Learning

Supervised Learning: Supervised Learning involves training the algorithm on labelled data, which is data that has been paired with the proper output. By predicting or making decisions based on fresh, unobserved data, the algorithm learns to map inputs to outputs (Rebala et al. 2019).

Unsupervised Learning: In unsupervised learning, the algorithm is trained using data that has not been labelled, i.e., without any pre-established output labels. Without explicit instructions, the algorithm picks up on relationships, patterns, and structures in the data.

Semi-supervised Learning: In semi-supervised learning, the algorithm is trained on a small amount of labelled data in addition to a larger amount of unlabelled data. This approach incorporates elements of both supervised and unsupervised learning (Jo 2021).

Reinforcement Learning: In this method, an algorithm gains the ability to interact with its surroundings by acting and getting feedback in the form of incentives or punishments. Finding a policy that optimizes cumulative reward over time is the aim.

5.7.1.2 Common Algorithms for Machine Learning

- *Linear Regression*: A supervised learning technique called linear regression is used to forecast continuous numerical values based on input data.

- *Logistic Regression*: A supervised learning approach called logistic regression is used for binary classification problems, in which a categorical variable with two possible outcomes is the output.
- *Decision Trees*: To generate predictions or classifications, decision trees are adaptable supervised learning algorithms that learn a hierarchy of decision rules.
- *Random Forests*: Several decision trees are combined in random forests, an ensemble learning technique, to enhance prediction accuracy and minimize over fitting.
- *Support Vector Machines (SVM)*: This supervised learning approach is applied to regression and classification problems. It determines which hyperplane optimally divides data points into distinct classes. Features: The variables or properties used to define the data as inputs are known as features. They may be text-based, categorized, or numerical (Rebala et al. 2019).
- *Neural Networks*: Inspired by the architecture and operations of the human brain, neural networks are a class of deep learning algorithms. They are made up of linked layers of neurons that can recognize intricate patterns and connections in data. Artificial Neural Network (ANN), Convolutional Neural Network (CNN) and Recurrent Neural Network (RNN) are the advanced techniques of neural networks.

5.7.2 Applications of Machine Learning in Manufacturing

Machine learning (ML) has numerous applications in manufacturing, as shown in Fig. 5.3 offering opportunities to enhance efficiency, quality, and productivity across various processes. Here are some key applications of machine learning in manufacturing.

5.7.3 Adaptive Learning and Continuous Improvement

In the context of industrial automation, adaptive learning and continuous improvement play crucial roles in enhancing operational efficiency, optimizing processes and driving innovation (Franco et al. 2021).

5.7.3.1 Adaptive Learning in Automation of Industry

- *Customized Training and Skill Development*: Using adaptive learning technologies, training curricula and skill-building projects can be made to specifically address the demands and skill levels of industrial workers.

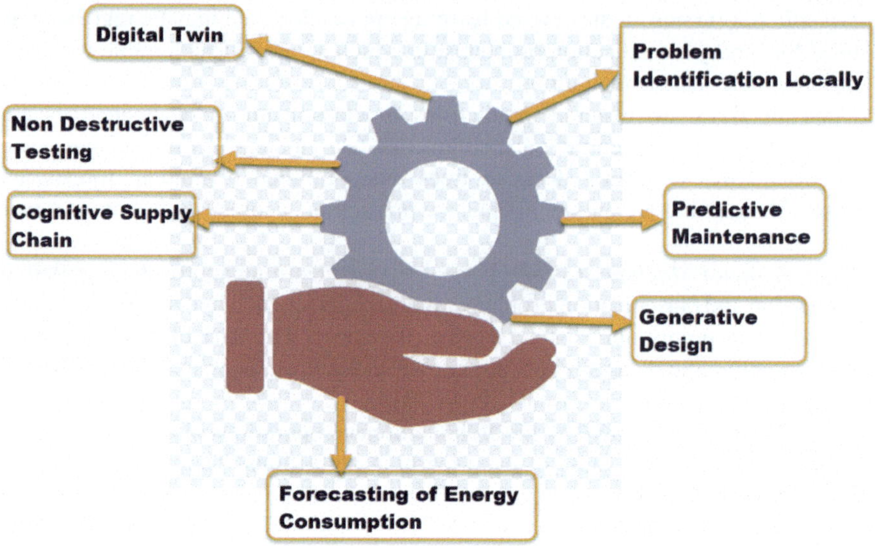

Fig. 5.3 Applications of machine learning in manufacturing. *Source* Author

- *Real-Time Feedback and Performance Monitoring*: In industrial settings, adaptive learning systems can give operators and technicians access to real-time feedback and performance monitoring.
- *Training for Predictive Maintenance*: Adaptive learning systems can assist technicians in gaining the knowledge necessary to properly maintain complicated industrial gear by offering realistic training scenarios.
- *Continuous Skills Development*: Lifelong learning and continuous skills development in industrial automation are made possible by adaptive learning. Adaptive learning platforms can provide workers with up-to-date training materials and resources to assist them stay up to date with industry trends and best practices when new challenges arise and technologies change.

5.7.3.2 Continuous Improvement in Industrial Automation

- *Process Optimization*: Lean manufacturing and Six Sigma are two examples of continuous improvement techniques that are frequently used in industrial automation to enhance workflows, cut waste, and optimize processes. Organizations can find areas for improvement and put corrective measures in place to increase efficiency and quality by evaluating production data and performance indicators.
- *Root Cause Analysis*: To find the underlying causes of quality problems, equipment malfunctions and process interruptions in industrial settings, continuous improvement approaches place a strong emphasis on root cause analysis.

- *Data-Driven Decision Making*: Organizations can acquire insights into process variability, performance trends, and opportunities for optimization by gathering and evaluating data from sensors, PLCs (Programmable Logic Controllers) and other automation systems. This allows for targeted interventions and well-informed decision-making (Elangovan et al. 2021).

5.8 Robotics in Smart Manufacturing

5.8.1 Role of Robotics in Automation

- Robotics is a key component of automation in many different industries, transforming production procedures, increasing productivity and opening new avenues. The following are some salient features of robotics' place in automation:
- Robotics automates labour-intensive, repetitive tasks that are unpleasant, unclean, or hazardous for human workers. This frees up human labourers to concentrate on higher-value duties by handling materials, assembling, welding, painting and packaging, among other things.
- Robots operate constantly and reliably, 24/7, without the need for breaks or rest, leading to increased productivity and efficiency in manufacturing operations. Robots reduce cycle times and increase throughput.
- Robots are skilled of performing tasks with very high accuracy ensuring high quality and helping in reducing defects in manufactured products.
- Modern AI-enabled robotic systems are highly flexible and adaptable, capable of being reprogrammed or reconfigured to perform different tasks or adapt to changes in production requirements.
- During operation, robotic systems produce enormous volumes of data, such as process data, sensor readings and performance indicators. It is possible to gather, examine and apply this data to enhance predictive maintenance, find areas for process optimization and optimize robotic operations.
- Robotics can be combined with other automation technologies such as artificial intelligence, Robotic Process Automation (RPA) (Yadav and Panda 2022), IoT, vision systems and machine learning.
- The long-term advantages of robotics include cost savings through higher productivity, lower labour expenses, better quality, and less waste, even though the initial investment may be substantial. Robotic automation can yield a significant return on investment (ROI) over time, especially in high-volume manufacturing settings.

5.8.2 AI-Enhanced Robotics

- Artificial intelligence (AI) technologies are being incorporated into robotic systems to improve their capabilities, autonomy and adaptability. This is known as AI-enhanced robotics. This is how robots benefits from AI:
- Robocops can see and understand their surroundings better because of artificial intelligence (AI) algorithms and sophisticated sensors including depth sensors, radar, LIDAR and cameras.
- Robots can securely interact with humans and other things in complicated situations by using machine learning algorithms to process sensor data and recognize objects, impediments and patterns.
- Reinforcement learning algorithms empower robots to learn from past experience and optimize their actions to achieve specific objectives, such as maximizing efficiency or minimizing energy consumption.
- With the use of artificial intelligence (AI), robots can adapt to changing conditions, unanticipated obstacles and new situations.
- AI-driven natural language processing (NLP) techniques allow robots to comprehend and react to human requests, questions, and commands.
- Robotic systems that have chatbots and virtual assistants embedded into them enable humans and robots to communicate in a natural and intuitive way, improving usability and cooperation across a range of applications.
- Robots can perceive and comprehend visual information, including gesture detection, object recognition, and scene understanding, thanks to AI algorithms.
- Robocops can now manipulate and interact with their surroundings more successfully because of the ability of deep learning models trained on massive datasets to reliably classify and identify items in real time.

5.8.3 Human–Robot Collaboration

The term "human–robot collaboration" (HRC) describes how employees who share a workspace with robotic technologies communicate and work together. Industrial automation is seeing a rise in the HRC trend, in which humans and robots collaborate to carry out activities that take advantage of each other's advantages. A wide range of sectors and applications, including manufacturing, logistics, healthcare and agriculture, use human–robot collaboration. Surgical robots, material handling, assembly, inspection and warehouse automation are a few examples of applications.

An outline of human–robot cooperation is provided below:

- Shared Workspace
- Safety
- Collaborative Robots
- Task Allocation
- Flexibility

- Skill Augmentation
- Training and Programming
- Real-time Communication.

5.9 Case Studies and Success Stories

5.9.1 Real-World Implementations

Here are some case studies and success stories as shown in Table 5.1. that highlight the successful implementation of industrial automation through AI.

Table 5.1 Real world implementations

Company name	Task	Solution	Outcome
Siemens (Kishorre Annanth et al. 2021)	Predictive maintenance in manufacturing	Siemens could predict potential failures and schedule maintenance proactively	Reduction in unplanned downtime, increased overall equipment effectiveness (OEE), and improved maintenance efficiency
Amazon (Laber et al. 2020)	Robotic automation in warehouses	Optimizing the movement of goods and streamlining the order-picking process	Increased the speed and accuracy of order processing, reducing delivery times and enhancing customer satisfaction
Tesla (Luckow et al. 2018)	AI in automotive manufacturing	AI-driven robots and automation systems in the production line, from assembly to quality control, contribute to efficient and high-quality manufacturing	Meeting high demand for electric vehicles and pushing the boundaries of automotive innovation
Bosch (Kalaycı et al. 2020)	AI for quality control in electronics manufacturing	AI-powered vision systems inspect electronic components, identifying defects with high precision	Improved product quality, reduced defects, and increased throughput in electronics manufacturing

Source Author

These case studies demonstrate the diverse applications of AI in industrial automation, showcasing how companies across different sectors have successfully leveraged artificial intelligence to enhance efficiency, reduce costs and improve overall operational performance.

5.9.2 Demonstrating Benefits and Outcomes

Demonstrating the benefits and outcomes of industrial automation involves showcasing how automation technologies improve efficiency, productivity, quality, safety and sustainability in manufacturing processes. Here's how you can demonstrate these benefits:

- *Efficiency Improvement*: Showcase how automation reduces cycle times, minimizes idle time, and optimizes resource utilization, leading to overall process efficiency gains. Provide data and metrics comparing production rates, throughput and lead times before and after implementing automation.
- *Productivity Enhancement*: Highlight how automation streamlines workflows, eliminates manual tasks, and increases output without requiring additional manpower. Present productivity metrics, such as units produced per hour or per shift, to demonstrate the impact of automation on manufacturing output.
- *Quality Enhancement*: Demonstrate how automation improves product quality by reducing defects, variability, and errors in manufacturing processes. Showcase before-and-after examples of product quality, highlighting reductions in defects, rework and scrap rates.
- *Safety Enhancement*: Illustrate how automation improves workplace safety by reducing exposure to hazardous conditions, repetitive tasks and ergonomic risks. Provide statistics on accident rates, near-misses, and safety incidents before and after automation implementation.
- *Sustainability Benefits*: Highlight how automation contributes to environmental sustainability by optimizing energy usage, reducing waste, and minimizing carbon footprint. Showcase reductions in energy consumption, material usage and emissions achieved through automation-enabled efficiency improvements.
- *Cost Savings*: Quantify cost savings achieved through automation, including reductions in labour costs, overhead expenses, and inventory holding costs. Present a cost–benefit analysis comparing upfront investment in automation technology with long-term savings and ROI.
- *Flexibility and Adaptability*: Highlight how automation enables greater flexibility and adaptability in manufacturing processes, allowing for rapid changeovers, customization, and scalability. Showcase examples of how automation facilitates quick reconfiguration of production lines or adaptation to changing market demands.
- *Competitive Advantage*: Illustrate how automation enhances competitiveness by enabling faster time-to-market, higher product quality, and greater agility in

responding to customer needs. Provide examples of how automation enables companies to differentiate themselves from competitors and capture market share.

- *Customer Satisfaction*: Demonstrate how automation enhances customer satisfaction by ensuring consistent product quality, on-time delivery and responsiveness to customer requirements. Share testimonials or feedback from customers highlighting the benefits of automation in meeting their needs and expectations.
- *Continuous Improvement*: Emphasize the role of automation in fostering a culture of continuous improvement, innovation, and learning within the organization. Showcase examples of how automation enables data-driven decision-making, process optimization, and iterative refinement of manufacturing operations.

By effectively demonstrating the benefits and outcomes of industrial automation, organizations can build a compelling case for investment in automation technologies and drive adoption across industries. Providing tangible evidence of how automation improves efficiency, productivity, quality, safety, sustainability and competitiveness is essential for gaining buy-in from stakeholders and maximizing the value of automation initiatives.

5.10 Challenges and Considerations

5.10.1 Ethical and Privacy Concerns

The incorporation of cutting-edge technology like artificial intelligence (AI), robotics, and the Internet of Things (IoT) into production processes is the main cause of ethical and privacy issues in industrial automation. These are some of the most important privacy and ethical issues with industrial automation.

- *Job Displacement and Worker Rights*: Human workers may lose their jobs due to automation, which would be concerning for worker rights, economic inequality, and unemployment. Safeguarding workers' rights in the face of automation-driven changes in employment patterns, offering retraining and reskilling opportunities and ensuring a reasonable transition for impacted workers are all ethical considerations.
- *Worker Safety*: There are safety concerns for human workers when robots and automated systems are used in industrial environments. These dangers include collisions, entanglement, and exposure to dangerous materials. Ensuring worker safety through appropriate risk assessment, training and the use of safety rules and standards to prevent accidents and injuries are the main ethical considerations.
- *Algorithmic Bias and Fairness*: Artificial intelligence (AI) algorithms employed in industrial automation may be biased or discriminatory, resulting in unjust treatment or decisions that are made. To ensure fairness and transparency in decision-making processes, bias in AI algorithms must be reduced. Additionally, issues with algorithmic accountability and responsibility must be addressed.

- *Privacy and Data Security*: Large volumes of data are produced by industrial automation from sensors, machinery, and manufacturing processes, which raises issues with data security and privacy. The gathering, storing and sharing of private information—such as personnel records, equipment performance data, and production metrics—as well as the possibility of data breaches, illegal access or misuse are among the privacy concerns.
- *Autonomy and Control*: Autonomy and control in production contexts are questioned by automation technologies like intelligent systems and autonomous robots. The delegation of decision-making authority to automated systems, maintaining human oversight and involvement when required, and resolving questions of accountability and culpability in the event of system faults or failures are the main ethical considerations.

5.10.2 Security in AI-Driven Industrial Automation

Because modern technologies like artificial intelligence (AI), machine learning (ML), robotics, and the Internet of Things (IoT) are being integrated into production processes, security is critical to AI-driven industrial automation. The following are important factors to consider when securing AI-driven industrial automation:

- *Encryption protocols*: These protocols should be used to safeguard private information when it is being sent between devices and kept in databases. Maintaining data confidentiality and integrity will stop unwanted access and manipulation.
- *Access control*: To limit access to sensitive information and systems, put strong access control measures in place. To confirm the identification of users and devices, utilize robust authentication techniques like multi-factor authentication.
- *Data governance*: To specify how data is gathered, handled and utilized inside the company, set up policies and processes. Verify adherence to industry standards and data protection laws. Create and put into place secure network architectures that divide enterprise networks and the internet from industrial control systems (ICS). Use network segmentation, firewalls, and intrusion detection systems (IDS) to thwart unwanted access and safeguard vital infrastructure.
- *Network monitoring*: Make use of tools for network monitoring to identify and address unusual activity or suspicious activity on the network. In order to spot possible security threats and breaches, keep an eye on system logs, network traffic and security events.
- *Secure software development*: To create and implement AI-driven software components and applications, adhere to secure coding standards and practices. To find and fix security issues, do vulnerability assessments, code reviews, and security testing on a regular basis. Application Programming Interfaces (APIs) should be implemented securely to integrate AI-driven applications with other platforms and systems. API endpoints can be secured by using encryption, authentication and authorization to stop illegal access and data leaks.

5.10.3 Workforce Adaptation and Training

For AI-driven industrial automation to be implemented and used successfully, workforce adaption and training are essential. Organizations may enable employees to embrace AI-driven industrial automation and effectively contribute to the success of the company in the digital age by prioritizing workforce adaptability and offering extensive training programs. To keep staff flexible, adaptive and resilient in the face of technological change, it's critical to promote a culture of ongoing learning and support their professional development. Here are some strategies that businesses can use to properly train employees and adjust their workforce:

- Assessing Current Skill Sets.
- Identifying Training Needs.
- Providing Technical Training.
- Promoting Digital Literacy.
- Emphasizing Soft Skills Development.
- Encouraging Continuous Learning.
- Providing Mentorship and Coaching.
- Evaluating Training Effectiveness.
- Measuring Impact on Business Performance.

5.11 Future Trends and Emerging Technologies

5.11.1 AI Innovations in Industrial Automation

Innovations in AI have had a significant impact on industrial automation, transforming production procedures, increasing productivity and opening up new possibilities. These advancements in AI are revolutionizing industrial automation and fostering productivity, efficiency, and creativity across a range of sectors. Organizations can seize new chances for cost savings, competitive advantage and optimization in the digital age by utilizing AI.

Here are a few noteworthy industrial automation AI innovations:

- *Quality Control and Inspection*: Artificial intelligence (AI)-driven predictive maintenance systems examine sensor data from equipment to forecast when equipment may break. These systems are capable of proactive maintenance scheduling, which minimizes downtime and lowers maintenance costs, by detecting trends and abnormalities in data.
- *Quality Control and Inspection*: Artificial intelligence (AI) systems examine photos and sensor data to find flaws and irregularities in manufactured goods. By spotting minute flaws that human inspectors would overlook, machine learning models help to ensure consistent product quality while cutting down on waste.

- *Process Optimization*: Large datasets are analysed by AI-driven process optimization tools to find inefficiencies and improve manufacturing procedures. Temperature, pressure and speed are just a few examples of the factors that machine learning algorithms may optimize to increase throughput and save energy.
- *Robotics and Automation*: Automation and robotics systems driven by AI are becoming more sophisticated and flexible. Artificial intelligence (AI) algorithms enable robots to learn from their surroundings, adjust to changing circumstances and carry out jobs more effectively and independently.
- *Supply Chain Management*: Supply chain operations are optimized through the application of AI technologies like machine learning and predictive analytics. Supply chain management systems driven by artificial intelligence (AI) examine demand projections, stock levels, and shipping routes to maximize inventory stockpiling, reduce lead times and enhance delivery dependability.
- *Digital Twins*: Digital twin technology powered by AI builds virtual equivalents of real-world assets, workflows, and systems. Through the application of AI algorithms, digital twins mimic and optimize performance, making scenario analysis, real-time monitoring and predictive maintenance possible (Gehrmann and Gunnarsson 2020).
- *Autonomous Vehicles and Drones*: Drones and autonomous cars with AI capabilities are being utilized more frequently in industrial settings for logistics, inventory control and material handling. By utilizing AI algorithms for navigation, obstacle avoidance and decision-making, these systems increase productivity and security.
- *Natural Language Processing (NLP)*: Natural language processing (NLP) technology driven by artificial intelligence (AI) facilitates human–machine communication via chatbots, virtual assistants and voice commands. NLP systems provide intuitive communication and control of automated systems by interpreting and responding to human requests (Zdravevski et al. 2019).
- *Augmented Reality (AR) and Virtual Reality (VR)*: AI-powered AR and VR technologies improve industrial automation maintenance, troubleshooting and training. AI algorithms are used by AR and VR systems to superimpose digital data on the real world, giving workers rich and engaging experiences.

5.11.2 Predictions for the Future of Smart Manufacturing

It is necessary to consider market dynamics, technology developments, and current trends to forecast the direction of smart manufacturing. Even though the future is unpredictable by nature, the following are some projections regarding smart manufacturing in the future:

- *Greater Adoption of Industrial IoT (IIoT)*: Industrial IoT (IIoT) technology will become more widely used, allowing for increased data collection, real-time monitoring and communication throughout production processes. IIoT platforms will easily interface with current hardware and software, delivering useful information and increasing operational effectiveness.

- *Expansion of AI and Machine Learning Applications*: Artificial intelligence (AI) and machine learning (ML) will become more and more important in smart manufacturing, enabling autonomous decision-making, process optimization, quality control and predictive maintenance. Manufacturers will be able to get more insight from big data and promote continuous improvement in every facet of the production process thanks to AI-driven analytics.
- *Advancements in Robotics and Automation*: Robotics and automation technology will keep developing, leading to increasingly intelligent, adaptable, and cooperative robots. Cobots, or collaborative robots, will complement human employees in shared workspaces to increase output, security and effectiveness.
- *Digital Twin Adoption*: Manufacturers will be able to generate virtual copies of real assets and processes for simulation, optimization, and predictive analytics as digital twin technology spreads. Real-time insights into equipment performance will be made possible by digital twins, allowing for pre-emptive maintenance and reduced downtime. Workflows in smart manufacturing will include AR and VR technology more and more, including remote help, augmented visualization for maintenance and immersive training experiences.
- *Integration of Augmented Reality (AR) and Virtual Reality (VR)*: Workflows in smart manufacturing will include AR and VR technology more and more, including remote help, augmented visualization for maintenance, and immersive training experiences. Smart glasses and headsets with augmented reality capabilities will provide employees with direction and contextual information, increasing efficiency and decreasing mistakes (Ma et al. 2011).
- *Focus on Sustainability and Resilience*: Sustainability and resilience will be given top priority in smart manufacturing, with an emphasis on waste minimization, resource efficiency and environmental impact. Manufacturers aim to reduce their carbon footprint and improve sustainability over the long run by implementing green technologies, renewable energy sources, and circular economy principles.
- *Customization and Personalization*: More personalization and customization of products to satisfy a range of consumer needs and preferences will be possible thanks to smart manufacturing. AI-driven insights, nimble supply networks and flexible production procedures will enable businesses to produce customized goods on a large scale. Manufacturers will be able to generate virtual copies of real assets and processes for simulation, optimization and predictive analytics as digital twin technology spreads.
- *Cybersecurity and Data Privacy*: The increasing connectivity and data-driven nature of smart manufacturing will make cyber security and data privacy critical issues. To defend sensitive data and prevent cyber-attacks, manufacturers will invest in strong cyber security systems, encryption procedures and staff training.

5.11.3 Potential Impacts on Global Industries

The adoption of smart manufacturing technologies is expected to have significant impacts on global industries across various sectors. Here are some potential impacts:

- *Increased Efficiency and Productivity*: Smart manufacturing technologies, such as AI, IoT, and automation, will enhance operational efficiency and productivity across industries. Streamlined processes, predictive maintenance and optimized resource allocation will lead to cost savings and improved competitiveness.
- *Supply Chain Optimization*: Smart manufacturing will optimize supply chain management, enabling real-time tracking, inventory management and demand forecasting. Agile supply chains will respond more effectively to changing market conditions and disruptions, improving resilience and reducing lead times.
- *Innovation and Customization*: Smart manufacturing will drive innovation and enable greater customization and personalization of products. Agile production processes, digital design tools and advanced analytics will empower manufacturers to develop new products and tailor offerings to meet diverse customer demands.
- *Workforce Transformation*: The adoption of smart manufacturing technologies will require a skilled workforce with expertise in areas such as data analytics, AI, robotics and cyber security. Workforce transformation initiatives, including training programs and up skilling efforts, will be essential to meet the evolving demands of smart manufacturing.
- *Global Competitiveness*: Smart manufacturing will enhance the global competitiveness of industries by enabling greater efficiency, innovation and agility. Countries and regions that invest in smart manufacturing initiatives and foster a supportive ecosystem for technology adoption will gain a competitive edge in the global marketplace.
- *Environmental Sustainability*: Smart manufacturing technologies will promote environmental sustainability by reducing waste, energy consumption and carbon emissions. Resource-efficient production processes, circular economy principles, and green technologies will contribute to a more sustainable future for industries worldwide.
- *Reshoring and Localization*: Smart manufacturing technologies may lead to reshoring and localization trends as companies seek to bring production closer to consumers and reduce supply chain risks. Proximity to markets, responsiveness to customer needs and flexibility in production will drive strategic decisions about manufacturing location.
- *Regulatory Compliance and Standards*: Smart manufacturing will require compliance with regulations and standards related to data privacy, cyber security, safety and environmental sustainability. Governments and regulatory bodies will play a crucial role in developing and enforcing policies to ensure responsible and ethical use of smart manufacturing technologies.
- *New Business Models and Opportunities*: Smart manufacturing will enable the emergence of new business models and opportunities, such as servitization,

subscription-based services and predictive maintenance contracts. Companies that embrace digital transformation and harness the power of smart manufacturing will unlock new revenue streams and growth opportunities.

- *Digital Divide and Inequality*: The adoption of smart manufacturing technologies may exacerbate the digital divide and inequality, as companies and regions with limited access to technology or resources may struggle to keep pace. Efforts to bridge the digital divide and promote inclusive growth will be essential to ensure that the benefits of smart manufacturing are shared equitably across society.

Overall, the adoption of smart manufacturing technologies has the potential to transform global industries, driving efficiency, innovation and sustainability while presenting new challenges and opportunities for businesses, governments and societies worldwide.

5.12 Conclusion

Envisioning a Smart World through AI-Driven Industrial Automation. The combination of artificial intelligence (AI) and automation technologies holds great promise for changing manufacturing processes and reshaping global industries. This is clear when picturing a smart world through AI-driven industrial automation. Beyond only increasing productivity, AI-driven industrial automation has the potential to revolutionize society by presenting never-before-seen chances for creativity, sustainability and prosperity.

Manufacturers may achieve unprecedented levels of efficiency, agility, and competitiveness by leveraging AI, machine learning, robots and the Internet of Things (IoT). Algorithms for predictive maintenance maximize the uptime of equipment while lowering maintenance expenses and downtime. Artificial intelligence (AI)-powered quality control solutions raise customer happiness and brand reputation by reducing faults and improving product uniformity. Autonomous robots operate in harmonious tandem with human workers, enhancing workforce productivity and guaranteeing security in communal work areas.

Furthermore, AI-powered industrial automation speeds up the shift to smart manufacturing ecosystems, which are defined by data-driven decision-making, flexible supply chains, and networked digital twins. Manufacturers can forecast market trends, allocate resources optimally, and react quickly to fluctuating demand thanks to real-time analytics. Capabilities for personalization and customization enable businesses to offer specialized goods and services, fostering client loyalty and differentiating themselves in the market.

But achieving the goal of an AI-driven smart world through industrial automation calls for coordinated efforts and cooperation from all relevant parties. Addressing issues with workforce adaption, cyber security, regulatory compliance, and ethical considerations will require collaboration between governments, business executives, academic institutions and researchers. It will be essential to fund education and training initiatives if we want to provide workers with the tools they need to prosper in the digital era. In a similar vein, putting strong cyber security safeguards and moral standards in place will guarantee the ethical and sustainable application of AI technologies.

To sum up, the transition to an AI-driven smart world through industrial automation signifies a fundamental change in the ways we produce, utilize and engage with technology. Through a combination of innovation, collaboration and human-centred ideals, we can fully utilize AI to build a more productive, sustainable and inclusive future for future generations.

References

Allam K (2022) Big data analytics in robotics: unleashing the potential for intelligent automation. EPH Int J Bus Manag Sci 8(4)

Carbonell JG, Michalski RS, Mitchell TM (1983) An overview of machine learning. In: Machine learning. Elsevier, pp 3–23. https://doi.org/10.1016/B978-0-08-051054-5.50005-4

Chan KY, Yiu CKF, Dillon TS, Nordholm S, Ling SH (2012) Enhancement of speech recognitions for control automation using an intelligent particle swarm optimization. IEEE Trans Ind Inf 8(4):869–879. https://doi.org/10.1109/TII.2012.2187910

Elangovan S, Jusoh MS, Muhd Yusuf DH, Ismail MS, Hj Din MS (2021) 8D problem solving methodology: continuous improvement in automation organization. J Phys Conf Ser 2129(1):012017. https://doi.org/10.1088/1742-6596/2129/1/012017

Franco N, Van HM, Dreiser M, Weiss G (2021) Towards a self-adaptive architecture for federated learning of industrial automation systems. In: 2021 International symposium on software engineering for adaptive and self-managing systems (SEAMS), May 2021. IEEE, Madrid, pp 210–216. https://doi.org/10.1109/SEAMS51251.2021.00035

Gehrmann C, Gunnarsson M (2020) A digital twin based industrial automation and control system security architecture. IEEE Trans Ind Inf 16(1):669–680. https://doi.org/10.1109/TII.2019.2938885

Goel R, Gupta P (2020) Robotics and industry 4.0. In: Nayyar A, Kumar A (eds) A roadmap to industry 4.0: smart production, sharp business and sustainable development. Advances in science, technology and innovation. Springer International Publishing, Cham, pp 157–169. https://doi.org/10.1007/978-3-030-14544-6_9

Henry L (2024) Impact of innovation tools in supply chain management and operations. Am Res J Contemp Iss 2(1):45–52. https://www.openjournals.ijaar.org/index.php/arjci/article/view/376

Islam MR, Begum S, Ahmed MU (2024) Artificial intelligence in predictive maintenance: a systematic literature review on review papers. In: Kumar U, Karim R, Galar D, Kour R (eds) International congress and workshop on industrial AI and emaintenance 2023. Lecture notes in mechanical engineering. Springer Nature Switzerland, Cham, pp 251–261. https://doi.org/10.1007/978-3-031-39619-9_18

Jain A, Sharma A, Jately V, Azzopardi B (2023) Sustainable energy solutions with artificial intelligence, blockchain technology, and internet of things, 1st edn. CRC Press, Boca Raton. https://doi.org/10.1201/9781003356639

Janapati R (ed) (2023) Human-machine interface technology advancements and applications, 1st edn. In: Materials, devices, and circuits: design and reliability. CRC Press, Boca Raton

Jazdi N, Ashtari Talkhestani B, Maschler B, Weyrich M (2021) Realization of AI-enhanced industrial automation systems using intelligent digital twins. Procedia CIRP 97:396–400. https://doi.org/10.1016/j.procir.2020.05.257

Jo T (2021) Machine learning foundations: supervised, unsupervised, and advanced learning. Springer International Publishing, Cham. https://doi.org/10.1007/978-3-030-65900-4

Kalaycı EG et al (2020) Semantic integration of Bosch manufacturing data using virtual knowledge graphs. In: Pan JZ, Tamma V, d'Amato C, Janowicz K, Fu B, Polleres A, Seneviratne O, Kagal L (eds) The semantic web—ISWC 2020. Lecture notes in computer science, vol 12507. Springer International Publishing, Cham, pp 464–481. https://doi.org/10.1007/978-3-030-62466-8_29

Khalid MY, Arif ZU, Tariq A, Hossain M, Ahmed Khan K, Umer R (2024a) 3D printing of magneto-active smart materials for advanced actuators and soft robotics applications. Eur Polym J 205:112718. https://doi.org/10.1016/j.eurpolymj.2023.112718

Khalid F, Aslam MN, Ghani MA, Ahmad N, Abdullah, Sattar K (2024b) Aging prediction in single based propellants using hybrid strategy of machine learning and genetic algorithm. Chemom Intell Lab Syst 245:105058. https://doi.org/10.1016/j.chemolab.2023.105058

Kishorre Annanth V, Abinash M, Rao LB (2021) Intelligent manufacturing in the context of industry 4.0: A case study of siemens industry. J Phys Conf Ser 1969(1):012019. https://doi.org/10.1088/1742-6596/1969/1/012019

Kovalev I, Losev V, Kovalev D, Voroshilova A (2024) Multi-level computer systems for automation of scientific research. ITM Web Conf 59:01020. https://doi.org/10.1051/itmconf/20245901020

Laber J, Thamma R, Daniel Kirby E (2020) The impact of warehouse automation in Amazon's success. IJISET Int J Innov Sci Eng Technol 7(8) [Online]. https://ijiset.com/vol7/v7s8/IJISET_V7_I8_07.pdf

Lee J, Davari H, Singh J, Pandhare V (2018) Industrial artificial intelligence for industry 4.0-based manufacturing systems. Manuf Lett 18:20–23. https://doi.org/10.1016/j.mfglet.2018.09.002

Leitão P, Colombo AW, Karnouskos S (2016) Industrial automation based on cyber-physical systems technologies: prototype implementations and challenges. Comput Ind 81:11–25. https://doi.org/10.1016/j.compind.2015.08.004

Li B, Chai X, Hou B, Zhang L, Zhou J, Liu Y (2018) New generation artificial intelligence-driven intelligent manufacturing (NGAIIM). In: 2018 IEEE SmartWorld, ubiquitous intelligence and computing, advanced and trusted computing, scalable computing and communications, cloud and big data computing, internet of people and smart city innovation (SmartWorld/SCALCOM/UIC/ATC/CBDCom/IOP/SCI). IEEE, Guangzhou, pp 1864–1869. https://doi.org/10.1109/SmartWorld.2018.00313

Liu C, Wang Y, Yang C, Gui W (2024) Multimodal data-driven reinforcement learning for operational decision-making in industrial processes. IEEE/CAA J Autom Sinica 11(1):252–254. https://doi.org/10.1109/JAS.2023.123741

Luckow A et al (2018) Artificial intelligence and deep learning applications for automotive manufacturing. In: 2018 IEEE International conference on big data (big data). IEEE, Seattle, WA, pp 3144–3152. https://doi.org/10.1109/BigData.2018.8622357

Ma D, Fan X, Gausemeier J, Grafe M (eds) (2011) Virtual reality and augmented reality in industry. Springer Berlin Heidelberg, Berlin, Heidelberg. https://doi.org/10.1007/978-3-642-17376-9

Malik PK et al (2021) Industrial internet of things and its applications in industry 4.0: state of the art. Comput Commun 166:125–139. https://doi.org/10.1016/j.comcom.2020.11.016

Palanikumar K, Natarajan E, Ponshanmugakumar A (2024) Application of machine vision technology in manufacturing industries—a study. In: Machine intelligence in mechanical engineering. Elsevier, pp 91–122. https://doi.org/10.1016/B978-0-443-18644-8.00018-6

Prasanthi YN, Ghali VS, Vesala GT, Suresh B (2024) Convolutional neural network for automatic defect detection in composites. Presented at the International conference on signal processing and communication engineering systems: spaces-2021, Andhra Pradesh, India, p 020045. https://doi.org/10.1063/5.0111836

Rebala G, Ravi A, Churiwala S (2019) An introduction to machine learning. Springer International Publishing, Cham. https://doi.org/10.1007/978-3-030-15729-6

Ribeiro J, Lima R, Eckhardt T, Paiva S (2021) Robotic process automation and artificial intelligence in industry 4.0—a literature review. Procedia Comput Sci 181:51–58. https://doi.org/10.1016/j.procs.2021.01.104

Ustundag A, Cevikcan E (2018) Industry 4.0: managing the digital transformation. In: Springer series in advanced manufacturing. Springer International Publishing, Cham. https://doi.org/10.1007/978-3-319-57870-5

Yadav N, Panda SP (2022) Robotic process automation: literature review, challenges and opportunities. In: 2nd International conference on research and development in science, technology and management, May 2022

Yadav N, Panda SP (2024) UI action logger to investigate potential robotic process automation routines. Tuijin Jishu/J Propuls Technol 45(01):4215. https://doi.org/10.52783/tjjpt.v45.i01.4215

Yao X, Zhou J, Zhang J, Boer CR (2017) From intelligent manufacturing to smart manufacturing for industry 4.0 driven by next generation artificial intelligence and further on. In: 2017 5th international conference on enterprise systems (ES). IEEE, Beijing, pp 311–318. https://doi.org/10.1109/ES.2017.58

Zdravevski E et al (2019) Automation in systematic, scoping and rapid reviews by an NLP toolkit: a case study in enhanced living environments. In: Ganchev I, Garcia NM, Dobre C, Mavromoustakis CX, Goleva R (eds) Enhanced living environments. Lecture notes in computer science, vol 11369. Springer International Publishing, Cham, pp 1–18. https://doi.org/10.1007/978-3-030-10752-9_1

Zheng P et al (2018) Smart manufacturing systems for industry 4.0: conceptual framework, scenarios, and future perspectives. Front Mech Eng 13(2):137–150. https://doi.org/10.1007/s11465-018-0499-5

Chapter 6
Artificial Intelligence and Machine Learning Technologies in Internet of Vehicles

Aakansha Garg, Sapna Katiyar, Varuna Gupta, Ajit Kumar Verma, and Rajeev Arya

Abstract With the increasing number of vehicular users, the driver and vehicular safety is a major concern. The integration of various technologies like AI, ML, etc., has enhanced the driver security by sensing and analysing various safety measures, i.e., termed as internet of vehicle. The fuel consumption optimization and regular monitoring of vehicle's health is one of the important features of Internet of Vehicle. These can be achieved by optimization. Various infrastructures like cloud server, fog server, roadside unit, etc., enhance the real-time capabilities of the vehicle. The security of Internet of Vehicles should be addressed as use of publicly available servers makes communication vulnerable.

Keywords Internet of vehicles · Artificial intelligence · Resource optimization · Security

A. Garg (✉)
ABES Institute of Technology, Ghaziabad, India
e-mail: aakansha1986@gmail.com

S. Katiyar
Impledge Technologies, Noida, India

V. Gupta
Christ University, Bengaluru, India

A. K. Verma
Faculty of Engineering and Natural Sciences, Western Norway University of Applied Sciences, Haugesund, Norway

R. Arya
Wireless Sensor Networks Lab, Department of Electronics and Communication Engineering, National Institute of Technology Patna, Patna 800005, Bihar, India

R. Arya et al. (eds.), *Recent Trends in Artificial Intelligence Towards a Smart World*, Frontiers of Artificial Intelligence, Ethics and Multidisciplinary Applications, https://doi.org/10.1007/978-981-97-6790-8_6

6.1 Introduction

With technological advancement and increasing user demands, the number of vehicles is increasing day-by-day. Although road developments have contributed a lot to avoid traffic congestions, accidents, etc. But the vehicles' efficiency and driver safety need to be addressed.

The integration of vehicle with artificial intelligence makes system more efficient (Xu et al. 2022). The various AI approaches help in optimal routing, resource and computing task optimization (Agbaje et al. 2022).

6.2 What Is the Internet of Vehicles (IoV)?

The Internet of Vehicles is a networking system with many users, thing, and sub-networks to control and manage vehicle connections. It includes vehicle-to-vehicle connection, Vehicle-to-human connection, Vehicle-to-things, etc. It connects humans, vehicles with smart onboard modules and various cyber systems while considering vehicle, sensors, and mobile device into the global networking system (Yang et al. 2014; Shirvani et al. 2024).

It has three basic components, depicted in Fig. 6.1:

- *Human* is not only related to people travelling in vehicle but include all the participants in services and applications of IoV. It can be anyone like cyclist, pedestrians, etc.
- *Vehicles* include all vehicles participating in services and applications of IoV.
- *Things* refer to anything other than vehicles and humans.
- The combination of human, vehicles and thing is known as environment.

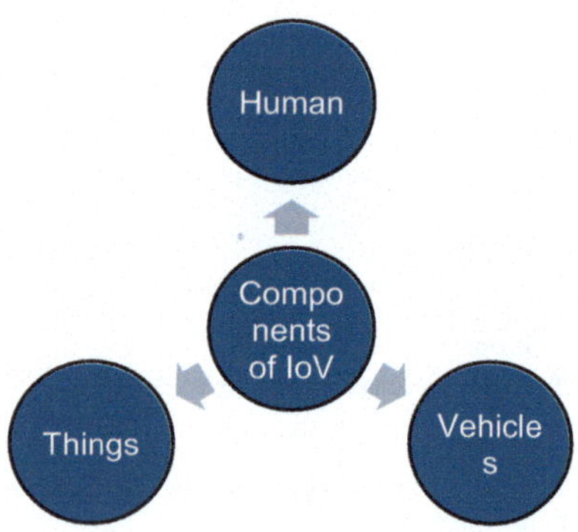

Fig. 6.1 Components of IoV. *Source* Author

6.3 What Is the Need of Internet of Vehicles (IoV)?

Some of the most desirable needs of IoV are as follows:

- To avoid accidents prone zones for secure and smart transportation.
- To reduce latency and energy consumption (Chaudhary and Kumar 2023).
- To ensure real-time data processing (Liu et al. 2023).
- To create an autonomous driving system (Pi et al. 2020).

6.3.1 How IoV Is Different from IoT?

Internet of thing is about connecting devices and establishing communication among them. Whereas in Internet of Vehicle devices are replaced by vehicles (Yang et al. 2014).

6.3.2 Vehicle Telematics

This feature of IoV ensures advancement to make communication easier and plays and important role in intelligent transportation system (Chang et al. 2019; Young et al. 2020).

6.3.3 How Does IoV Technology Works?

As we know that connectivity is the most important feature of IoV. So, to ensure it working a suitable hardware should be installed. This part includes:

- *Sources to connect within the network*: It includes vehicles, mobile phones, tablets, laptops, various IoT devices, etc.
- *Data collectors*: It includes vehicles, servers, other communicating nodes, etc.
- *Data storage*: Mainly servers have the capability to store the data collected from the network. But small information can be stored in cache memory of other devices for faster processing (Wu et al. 2023).
- *Data processing unit* to make decisions.

Apart from hardware manufacturing, other resources present in the network aid vehicle intelligent. These resources are roadside units, traffic lights, Units placed in parking area, public transport stations, etc.

6.4 IoV Architecture

IoV architecture consists of the three main layers, shown in Fig. 6.2:

Perception

In this layer, various physical structures like sensors, devices, vehicles of same network, vehicle telematics, mobiles, laptops, roadside units are included. This unit helps vehicle to collect and communicate data from these devices.

Networking

This layer ensures that physical devices or component mentioned in previous layer should be able to communicate to the other users present in the network. There are various existing technologies to ensure this communication:

- Wi-Fi (Su et al. 2024)
- Bluetooth
- 5G/6G
- Wireless local area network, etc.

Using these technologies the vehicles can manage traffic, avoid accidents, transfer information to another devices/vehicle.

Application

This layer is responsible for traffic and resource management. Some common usages are:

- Data collection from various sensors.
- Managing road traffic.
- Avoid accidents by pre-collision avoidance (Chang et al. 2021).
- Controlling various driving parameters to avoid accidents.

Figure 6.3 indicates the IoV architecture in detail. This contains three layers, i.e., perception layer, networking layer, application layer.

- Perception Layer: This layer includes all the physical units that participate in working of internet of vehicle like sensors, roadside units, smartphones, laptop, tablet, servers, etc.

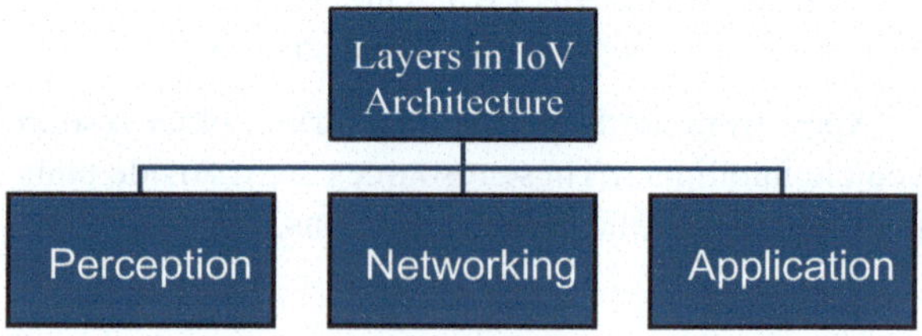

Fig. 6.2 Layout of IoV architecture. *Source* Author

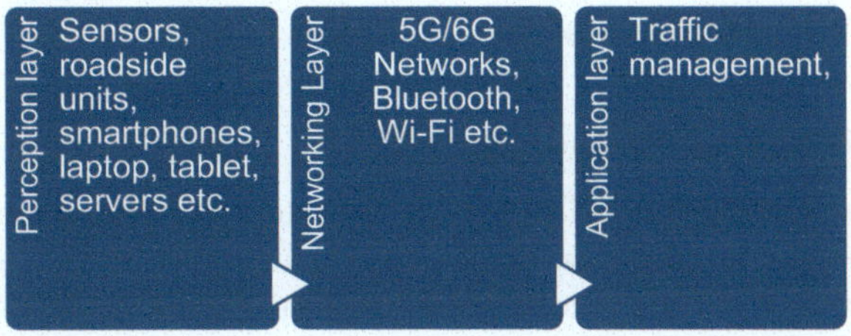

Fig. 6.3 IoV architecture in details. *Source* Author

- Networking Layer: This layer is responsible for communicating data to the users. It includes cellular networks, Bluetooth, wi-fi, etc.
- Application layer: This layer includes all the communication protocols and interactive methods.

6.5 Importance of IoV

In the smart city, inclusion of vehicles in the IoT infrastructure is an important part. It enhances the overall network efficiency. As the vehicle can offload/collect data to/from devices connected in the network. There are a few common areas in which IoV plays a crucial role (Tang et al. 2021):

- *Safety*: It can be ensured by getting low latency traffic information, complex processing, etc. This may lead to reroute precisely and avoid collisions, etc. Artificial intelligence and machine learning techniques have made it faster.
- *Efficiency and speed*: By mapping traffic the vehicles are routed optimally. It helps us to enhance efficiency and speed of the vehicle.
- *Environment*: By using AI intelligence routes and resources optimization the overall pollution in environment can be reduced.
- *Business benefits*: The Internet of Vehicle provides business to many people. You can get services from a company to maintain health and security of vehicle. Moreover, Driver safety can also be ensured using such vehicles.

6.6 IoV Networks

IoV can work using the following networks:

- *Ad-hoc Network*: IoV can use public internet for communication. It includes vehicle-to-vehicle communication in which another vehicle is considered as node.
- *Cellular Network*: IoV can use cellular channels for communication. This network can be used to provide in band and out band communication.

6.7 Benefits of IoV

There are following benefits of IoV:

- *Cost Optimization*: IoV smart system avoids accidents, optimize operational cost, etc. It reduces insurance claims and improves public health (Bagga et al. 2020).
- *Efficient Time*: IoV closely monitors the traffic conditions and makes effective use of drivers and riders' time.
- *Road Safety*: A proper communication among vehicles may avoid accidents.
- *Reduce Traffic Congestion*: The vehicle moving on the road are properly guided according to route traffic conditions.
- *Mitigate Pollution*: An optimized number of vehicles on one route avoids unnecessary waiting time which reduces fuel consumption hence pollution is also reduced (Agbaje et al. 2022).

6.7.1 What Is Needed to Maintain IoV?

To maintain IoV the following things are important:

- Delay tolerance
- Privacy maintenance
- Disaster management

6.8 IoV Participators

The vehicles are resource limited. The computational capability of vehicles can be improved by increasing computational resources of vehicle, but it leads to increase in cost. To enhance resources other expenditure like energy consumption, latency, etc. also increases along with cost of installation. Hence task offloading to the common resources is advisable. The various units that are used for task offloading are as follows:

- *Cloud Servers*: The cloud servers provide infinite computational capabilities. These servers are kept at some common centre which may be at a large distance from the user. The vehicle computing large task in low latency may choose cloud server to offload the task. The task offloading efficiency can be improved using various machine learning techniques for resource, power allocation, etc.
- *Fog Servers*: The fog servers are available nearer to the cloud server having finite computation capabilities the latency critical task can be offloaded to these servers.
- *Edge Computing Server*: These servers are generally kept within the cell network. Task requiring real-time processing and low energy consumption can be offloaded to these servers.

- *Roadside Unit:* As per the name these computation units are placed on the side of the road and provide low computational capability. Generally, these are used to communicate computational task to edge server, fog server, cloud server, etc.
- *Idle Vehicle Connected to the Network*: The parked vehicle or vehicles stuck in traffic may provide their resources for computation or communication.
- *Proximity Moving Vehicle Connected to the Network*: According to the age of information, i.e., vehicular movement path, the resources of proximity moving vehicles can be allocated for computation and communication.

6.9 Resource Optimization in IoV

6.9.1 Techniques for Optimization

To optimize resources for Internet of Vehicle communication various AI and ML techniques have been used. Some most used techniques are as follows:

- *Reinforcement Learning (RL)*: This unsupervised learning doesn't require any data for training instead it randomly tries multiple actions. Based on actions the system is rewarded or penalty is applied. This whole process enables us to make optimal decision.
- *Q-Learning*: The most used RL technique is Q-learning. It is basically a model-free learning and able to handle complex tasks with large number of states.
- *Deep Neural Network (DNN)*: The deep neural network consists of number of layers. Each layer has some neurons which can perform complex computations. The essential number of layers to perform computations is 3, i.e., input, output, and hidden layer. The neural network works in three phases, i.e., training, testing and validation.
- *Deep Reinforcement Learning (DRL)*: This technique is a combination of reinforcement learning and deep learning. This method is applied to make dynamic decisions. In deep learning, a large amount of training data is processed to make decisions whereas in deep reinforcement learning feedback is required by reinforcement learning to make decisions.
- *Double Deep Reinforcement Learning*: It is the advanced version of DRL. The DRL helps us to find the optimal action to obtain target region whereas double deep learning evaluates the action obtained from DRL.

The scope of techniques used is not limited to above-mentioned techniques. But these are the most used AI and ML techniques for resource optimization in IoV.

6.9.2 Optimization in IoV

- The task of offloading using parked vehicles and moving vehicles enhances resource utilization. The moving vehicle can offload the task to base station and base station further offloads it to the parked vehicle. The task is offloaded based on the duration of vehicle availability in the range of same base station. The resource allocation is allocated to reduce the path for communication (Fan et al. 2022).
- Deep deterministic policy gradient is used to identify the offloading strategy, optimizing the cost of computation in terms of energy consumption, latency and blockchain for secure computing (Qi et al. 2022).
- The vehicle can compute the task locally and offload the remaining part to roadside unit and cloud server respectively. Deep reinforcement learning techniques are used to reduce energy consumption while considering time constraint and selecting the appropriate resource, i.e., edge server or cloud to offload the task (Chen et al. 2022).
- The resource allocation while considering IEEE.802p standard for transmission is performed. The resources for task offloading to vehicular fog computing are optimized based on transmission delay, computation time, vehicle feature and roadside units, etc. The number of vehicles and task arrival rates are optimized (Wu et al. 2020a).
- Due to high computing requirement by various devices the tasks can be offloaded to vehicular edge computing system. Vehicle node selection and computing resource optimization reduce the latency of task computation (Xujie et al. 2023).
- A many-to-one approach can reduce the transmission time of the task to edge server. For the same idle vehicle present in the proximity works as a relay to offload the task. The increase in number of hops/vehicles reduces the overall computing latency (Chen et al. 2023).
- The deep Q-learning approach is used to optimize task offloading to idle vehicle or edge server. The task offloading is performed based on latency constraint and computing requirements to optimize energy consumption (Wu et al. 2022).
- A multiple MEC servers are used to adapt dynamically changing IoV requirements and resource availability. The task from vehicle is offloaded to roadside unit and this unit transmits it to edge server. Double deep Q learning optimizes task offloading for cost minimization (Wang et al. 2020).
- A vehicle-to-vehicle task offloading is established by resource allocation, i.e., based on the trust score. The trust score is calculated based on the computational capabilities and journey routes (Pratap et al. 2024).
- In fog computing the task is offloaded to several fog nodes. The task fragmentation optimization for offloading results in reduced energy consumption or latency (Tiwari et al. 2022).
- A transition probability is considered while offloading the task, i.e., if a vehicle having computational task moves out of the range, then it affects overall performance of the system. A vehicular fog and cloud computing is used to offload the task while considering vehicle movement (Wu et al. 2020b).

- The task offloading is optimized to improve quality of experience. The quality of experience is measured in terms of energy consumption. The task offloading modes used are vehicle-to-vehicle and vehicle-to-roadside units (He et al. 2021).
- A traffic light area may have a lot of idle vehicles that can be used to establish vehicle-to-vehicle communication. The vehicles' resources are allocated based on the age of information, i.e., the duration vehicle is present in urban area. The one-to-many approach is used to offload the task to meet latency requirements (Chen et al. 2020).
- The task offloading is performed by allocating proximity moving vehicles, parked vehicles, roadside unit, mobile edge computing server, cloud computing servers, etc. While allocating proximity resources consideration of vehicle state is very important. The multi-agent deep reinforcement learning is used to optimize energy consumption and latency (Alam and Jamalipour 2022).

6.10 Types of Communication and Challenges

Vehicle to cloud server

The vehicle's complete information can be stored in the cloud and can be reused whenever required. The vehicle-to-cloud server communication and challenges are as shown in Fig. 6.4. Moreover, cloud server resources can be used to compute complex tasks. The challenges in this communication are as follows:

- This communication is not suitable for real-time processing due to high latency.
- High energy consumption.
- Larger Noise.
- Requires more bandwidth.

Vehicle to fog

The vehicle-to-fog server communication and its challenges are shown in Fig. 6.5. The vehicle can use fog nodes for communication and computation. Although the path for communication has reduced still a lot of challenges are there:

- Latency: Although latency is lower than cloud server communication still it is not sufficient for real-time processing.
- High energy consumption.
- Larger noise.

Vehicle to roadside units

Figure 6.6 indicates the communication of vehicle to roadside unit, edge server and its challenges. The roadside units can act as relay for communicating vehicle task to server or may provide computation support. It faces the following challenges:

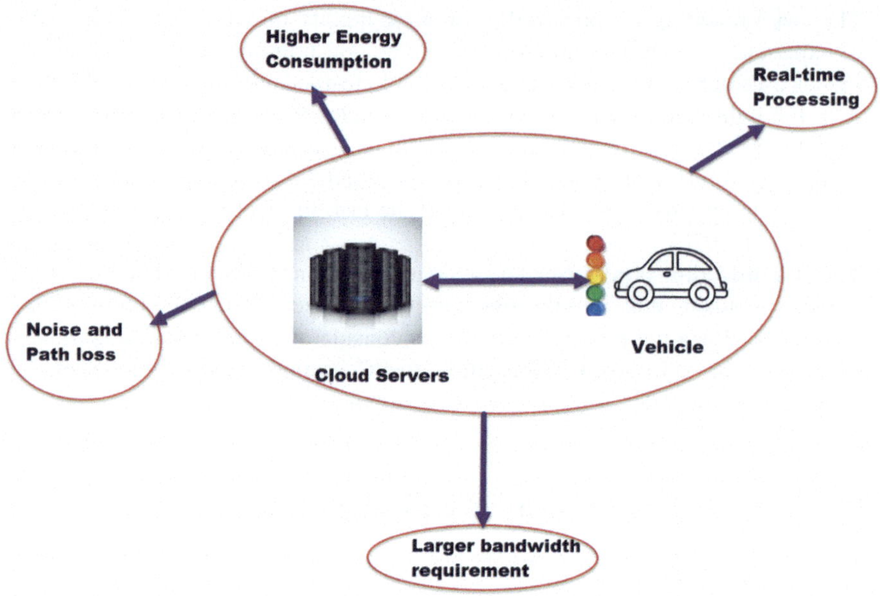

Fig. 6.4 Cloud server to vehicle communication and challenges. *Source* Author

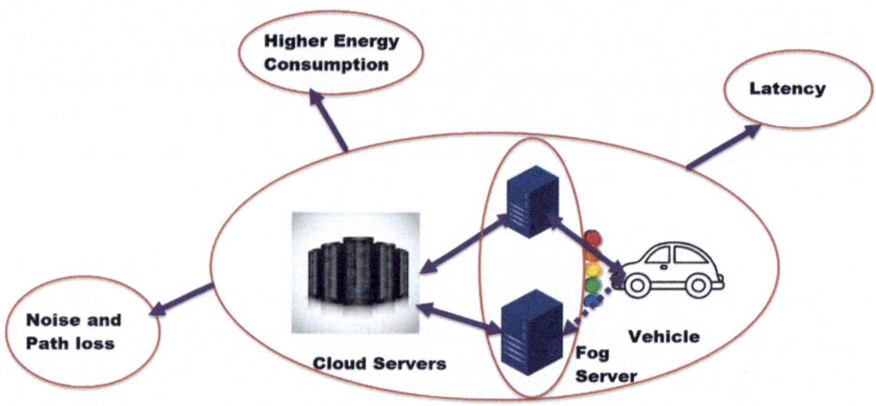

Fig. 6.5 Fog server to vehicle communication and challenges. *Source* Author

- *Limited amount of computation resources*: The roadside unit has limited storage and computation capacity. So, a large amount of task can't be processed by these units in small timeframe.
- *Vehicular movement*: The vehicle can move out of the network after offloading task to roadside unit. In this way the resources of roadside units are wasted.

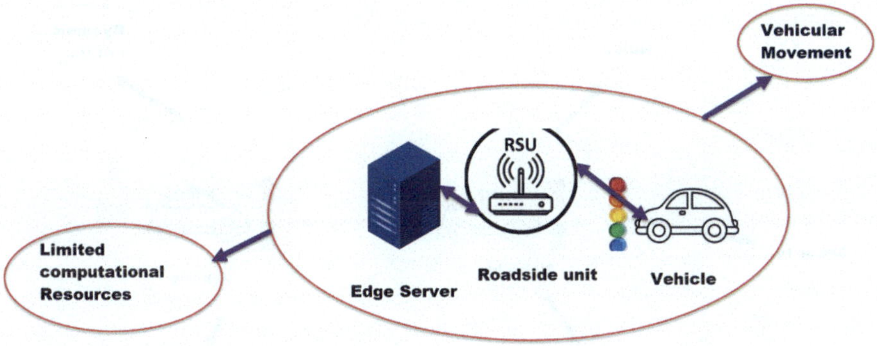

Fig. 6.6 Roadside unit to vehicle communication and challenges. *Source* Author

Vehicle to everything

Figure 6.7 shows that the vehicle can offload its task to nearby devices like computer, mobile, etc. The task can be offloaded to use node as a relay for communication and computation. The challenges for this offloading are:

- *Dynamic nature*: The vehicles and resources used in the network are mobile so resources allocation for seamless task execution is a challenge.
- *Security*: Resources sharing is possible among trusted users. One can have different criteria of trust like social networking, the devices state with respect to vehicle, etc.

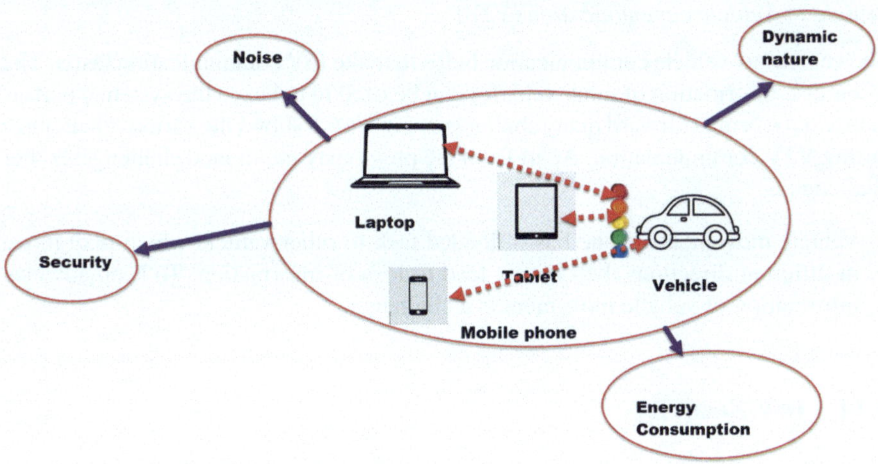

Fig. 6.7 Everything to vehicle communication and challenges. *Source* Author

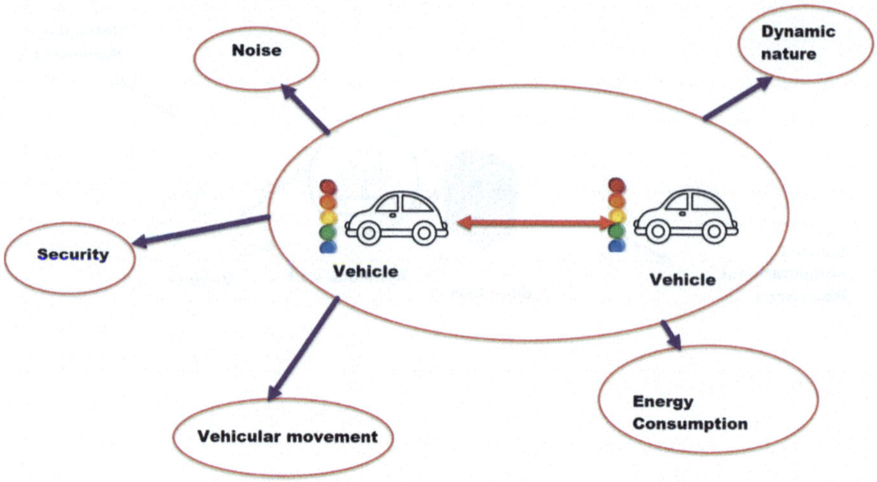

Fig. 6.8 Vehicle-to-vehicle communication and challenges. *Source* Author

- *Noise*: While using underlay communication, i.e., sharing the channels allocated for cellular communication or open channels noise increases. This noise is caused by proximity devices. To mitigate the effect of such noise is a challenge.
- *Energy consumption*: Although energy consumption during this communication is lower than other two communications mentioned above. Still, it should be optimized to obtain desired quality of service.

Vehicle-to-Vehicle communication (V2V)

The vehicle-to-vehicle communication helps to make IoV communication faster. The resources, information of other vehicles can be used to enhance the system's performance but it brings forward many challenges. Figure 6.8 shows the various challenges during V2V communication. Apart from the previously mentioned challenges, other challenge is:

- Vehicle movement: If one has offloaded task to other vehicle which may move in different directions then it may lead to loss of information. To keep advance information of vehicle movement is a challenge.

6.11 IoV Security

Components

The cost reduction in IoV has been achieved by sharing resources. But sharing resources has security concerns like:

- *Data breaches*: If the information exchanged is beyond the range of information shared.
- *Fault tolerance*: It is the measure of fault acceptability without affecting the overall performance of the system.
- *Accuracy*: It is the measure of closeness to the desired information.
- *Privacy*: It is measured as accessibility to the information that one wants to share.

Techniques

As per ISO 13335, guidelines have been issued to ensure IT security (Wang and Liu 2018). Still a secure communication and resource sharing can be established among vehicles in the following ways:

- *Decentralized IoV System*: *This* system enhances the capacity of IoV by dividing decisions into time-restricted, i.e., real-time and time-unrestricted, i.e., non-real time. The division of decisions enhances the efficient use of resources. Apart from its verification among vehicles is done by using blockchain technology (Yang et al. 2023). An authentication key from multi-server and key agreement protocol for ensuring system privacy also enhances security of the system (Wang et al. 2022). After establishing an authentication among communicating devices in IoV a session key establishment ensures a secure communication (Wazid et al. 2019; Saleem et al. 2020).
- *Social IoV*: Vehicles with common interests agree to behave ethically while sharing resources with each other. It minimizes the risk of data breaches and ensures privacy (Silva and Iqbal 2019).Knowledge about IoV components may keep attackers busy and help to find information of cyber threat. Implementation of such systems may increase the budget of Internet-enabled vehicle (Panda et al. 2022).
- *Blockchain-Enabled IoV*: The use of blockchain technology ensures trust, security, and reliability. The public/private key pair can be created among vehicles to confirm the vehicle's security (Xia et al. 2020). Some of the vehicles may use public channel for communication. To provide security to such communications blockchain-based decentralized techniques are helpful (Chattaraj et al. 2021). Figure 6.9 shows that secure communication is possible with the help of secret key. It shows that data is communicated to the roadside unit via a secret key. Then roadside unit sends it to the cloud servers. There the data is converted into blocks and then shared on cloud network. While using this technique the data is transferred in the following way:
- A tri-blockchain-based architecture ensures the security in IoV communication by ensuring permission. This architecture ensures storage and management of data dynamically (Qin et al. 2024).
- *Machine Learning in IoV*: The supervised machine learning techniques can be used to identify misbehaviour and its categories. This helps to identify the attacks (Sharma and Liu 2021).
- *Cognitive IoV*: The cognitive IoV provides security in the following ways (Qian et al. 2018):

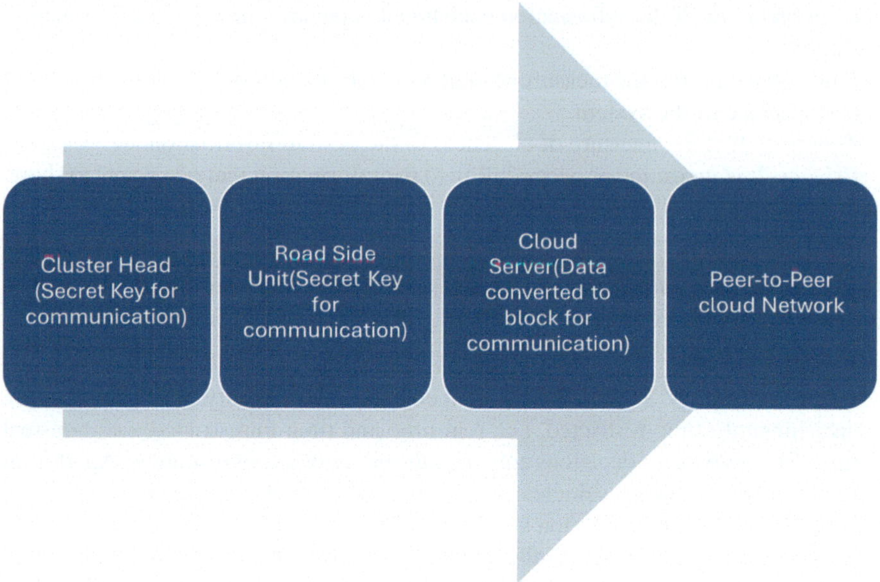

Fig. 6.9 Blockchain-based secure communication for devices using public channels. *Source* Author

- *Cognitive Engine*: The cognitive engine helps the physical layer in assessing the types of data to be collected from vehicle. Various advanced techniques like machine learning, data mining, artificial intelligence, etc., can be used to analyse the data.
- *Switches*: The switches used are openflow switches. Using software-defined networking the security policy can be deployed directly. The security policy can be updated as per the information received from the cognitive engine.

6.12 IoV Applications

Although IoV has a wide range of applications still there are few areas that are directly related to this.

- Intelligent Transport System
  The development of intelligent transport system has increased focus towards many challenges like enhancing data analysis like driver speed, fuel consumption, mostly used road conditions, enhancement in resource utilization, etc. Mostly the advancement in AI technologies has made such challenges easier (Wang et al. 2023).
- Safety

The various systems that make IoV secure are advance collision alert, identification of vehicle in proximity to get proper line of movement. Vehicle should be able to make internal decisions and external communication to ensure road safety for everyone (Li et al. 2021).

- Amenity
  There are many applications which work on voice-based command and provide comfortability to the driver. So, a proper connection established between human being to machine provides an efficient communication. So, the ability of nodes with different configuration and formats to interpolate enhances the overall system performance.
- Problem Extraction
  The intelligent transport system enables some features which may inform in advance. For example, if there is problem in internal part of the vehicle then one can get alert of different communication devices like information via mobile phone applications, mails, etc. The problem identification from remote area is also possible by establishing a proper internet connection to the vehicle (Xu et al. 2019).
- Infotainment
  This system provides facility of information and entertainment simultaneously. One could enjoy the travelling while using media resources. But the establishment of proper connection provides the desired location-based content and improves quality of experience (Duan et al. 2020).
- Efficient Resource Management
  The effective resource management improves the quality of experience for the user. The efficient use of energy resources results in enhanced battery life. Apart from it, the efficient brake system and speed management also ensure safety, etc. (Cao et al. 2022).
- Security and Privacy
  To trust a stranger for data offloading is difficult. The data authentication and privacy are very important to provide a seamless communication. Various methods adopted to ensure security and privacy have been explained in the previous section. These methods can be adapted with the proper connection establishment.
- Smart Cities
  The Internet of Vehicle provides resources for smart city applications like smart data gathering from various sensors, computation performance, etc. But each communicating object of IoV can perform various tasks like:

  Squint: Each device connected in the network can share resources. The resource in proximity helps to ensure connectivity and desired services.

  Resource Seeker: The vehicle in the network may demand resource from other connected users in the network. It improves the performance of vehicle.

  Relay: The vehicle in the network may collect data and transmit to the server for further processing.

Resource Splitting: Due to limited computation capability of the vehicle, the task is distributed among devices to get desired results.

6.13 IoV Users

Vehicles are the main users of IoV ecosystem. But the use of AI techniques has increased the horizon of users who can benefit by this:

- *Travellers*: These are the first users. The use of AI enhances their experiences in terms of traffic information, alert systems, neighbour vehicle information, etc. It also provides comfort to the travellers by voice command application, seamless connectivity for media, etc.
- *Public Sector Units and Government Organizations*: The government can use the traffic data for planning of roads (Spandonidis et al. 2022), traffic lights and others (Zhou et al. 2024). Moreover, researchers and educators may work with government for efficient planning. This planning mainly includes cost and resource optimization.
- *Businessman*: There are many companies who manages network and other resources using AI techniques. Moreover, insurance companies can also use the collected data to decide insurance premium for the vehicles. It can be decided by the usage of car, driver efficiency, risk of accidents, etc.
- *People*: The IoV connecting with people may make efficient resource utilization, low latency and improve quality of experience, etc. The vehicle to everything connection helps user to get various information via user device like mobile, laptop, tablet and other IoT devices. This information can increase the safety of road users and enhance confidence about the routes etc. The AI technology has made it possible by enabling real-time communications.
- *Prompt Helpers*: Accidents may be very risky for the life and health of the user. The users can keep connected with immediate helpers like paramedical staff and law persons for frequent actions. The AI technologies make the system efficient and reduce latency to provide information to helpers in real time.

6.14 Future of IoV

The advancement and continuous research in IoV technology creates many opportunities for the society:

- Driverless Cars
  It's a dream for people and includes lots of complex analysis. Although continuous research and development is taking place towards it. But the use of advanced AI features may make it to reality.
- Smart Green City

The various research is executed for smart cities still the interconnection of IoV leads to lower pollution and efficient use of resources. In the future, a smart city consisting of intelligent electric transport system can be proposed. The AI technologies will make this system smarter.

- Security
  The artificial intelligence-based network can make network connectivity more secure by finding relevant interest, trusted factors based on social relevance, etc.
- Automated Automobiles
  AI and seamless connectivity can lead to make automobiles not only driven but also self-repairable.

References

Agbaje P, Anjum A, Mitra A, Oseghale E, Bloom G, Olufowobi H (2022) Survey of interoperability challenges in the internet of vehicles. IEEE Trans Intell Transp Syst 23(12):22838–22861. https://doi.org/10.1109/TITS.2022.3194413

Alam MZ, Jamalipour A (2022) Multi-agent DRL-based Hungarian algorithm (MADRLHA) for task offloading in multi-access edge computing internet of vehicles (IoVs). IEEE Trans Wirel Commun 21(9):7641–7652. https://doi.org/10.1109/TWC.2022.3160099

Bagga P, Das AK, Wazid M, Rodrigues JJPC, Park Y (2020) Authentication protocols in internet of vehicles: taxonomy, analysis, and challenges. IEEE Access 8:54314–54344. https://doi.org/10.1109/ACCESS.2020.2981397

Cao H, Garg S, Kaddoum G, Singh S, Hossain MS (2022) Softwarized resource management and allocation with autonomous awareness for 6G-enabled cooperative intelligent transportation systems. IEEE Trans Intell Transp Syst 23(12):24662–24671. https://doi.org/10.1109/TITS.2022.3209899

Chang WJ, Chen LB, Su KY (2019) DeepCrash: a deep learning-based internet of vehicles system for head-on and single-vehicle accident detection with emergency notification. IEEE Access 7:148163–148175. https://doi.org/10.1109/ACCESS.2019.2946468

Chang CC, Ooi YM, Sieh BH (2021) IoV-based collision avoidance architecture using machine learning prediction. IEEE Access 9:115497–115505. https://doi.org/10.1109/ACCESS.2021.3105619

Chattaraj D, Bera B, Das AK, Saha S, Lorenz P, Park Y (2021) Block-CLAP: blockchain-assisted certificateless key agreement protocol for internet of vehicles in smart transportation. IEEE Trans Veh Technol 70(8):8092–8107. https://doi.org/10.1109/TVT.2021.3091163

Chaudhary R, Kumar N (2023) SecGreen: secrecy ensured power optimization scheme for software-defined connected IoV. IEEE Trans Mob Comput 22(4):2370–2386. https://doi.org/10.1109/TMC.2021.3116954

Chen C et al (2020) Delay-optimized V2V-based computation offloading in urban vehicular edge computing and networks. IEEE Access 8:18863–18873. https://doi.org/10.1109/ACCESS.2020.2968465

Chen C, Li H, Li H, Fu R, Liu Y, Wan S (2022) Efficiency and fairness oriented dynamic task offloading in internet of vehicles. IEEE Trans Green Commun Netw 6(3):1481–1493. https://doi.org/10.1109/TGCN.2022.3167643

Chen C, Zeng Y, Li H, Liu Y, Wan S (2023) A multihop task offloading decision model in MEC-enabled internet of vehicles. IEEE Internet Things J 10(4):3215–3230. https://doi.org/10.1109/JIOT.2022.3143529

Duan J, Li K, He Y, Zhang M, Yang X (2020) A bandwidth-aware video segments request strategy to optimize user's QoE in connected vehicle networks. IEEE Access 8:117493–117502. https://doi.org/10.1109/ACCESS.2020.3004228

Fan W, Liu J, Hua M, Wu F, Liu Y (2022) Joint task offloading and resource allocation for multi-access edge computing assisted by parked and moving vehicles. IEEE Trans Veh Technol 71(5):5314–5330. https://doi.org/10.1109/TVT.2022.3149937

He X, Lu H, Du M, Mao Y, Wang K (2021) QoE-based task offloading with deep reinforcement learning in edge-enabled internet of vehicles. IEEE Trans Intell Transp Syst 22(4):2252–2261. https://doi.org/10.1109/TITS.2020.3016002

Li H, Zhao G, Qin L, Aizeke H, Zhao X, Yang Y (2021) A survey of safety warnings under connected vehicle environments. IEEE Trans Intell Transp Syst 22(5):2572–2588. https://doi.org/10.1109/TITS.2020.3026309

Liu Y, Yang A, Zeng Q, Sun Y, Gao J, Lv Z (2023) Task scheduling of real-time traffic information processing based on digital twins. IEEE Trans Intell Transp Syst 24(11):13171–13179. https://doi.org/10.1109/TITS.2022.3196166

Panda S, Rass S, Moschoyiannis S, Liang K, Loukas G, Panaousis E (2022) HoneyCar: a framework to configure honeypot vulnerabilities on the internet of vehicles. IEEE Access 10(July):104671–104685. https://doi.org/10.1109/ACCESS.2022.3210117

Pi W et al (2020) Malicious user detection for cooperative mobility tracking in autonomous driving. IEEE Internet Things J 7(6):4922–4936. https://doi.org/10.1109/JIOT.2020.2973661

Pratap S, Dass P, Misra S (2024) CoTEV: trustworthy and cooperative task execution in internet of vehicles. IEEE Trans Mob Comput 23(4):2915–2926. https://doi.org/10.1109/TMC.2023.3267602

Qi J, Liu Y, Ling Y, Xu B, Dong Z, Sun Y (2022) Research on an intelligent computing offloading model for the internet of vehicles based on blockchain. IEEE Trans Netw Serv Manag 19(4):3908–3918. https://doi.org/10.1109/TNSM.2022.3210752

Qian Y, Chen M, Chen J, Hossain MS, Alamri A (2018) Secure enforcement in cognitive internet of vehicles. IEEE Internet Things J 5(2):1242–1250. https://doi.org/10.1109/JIOT.2018.2800035

Qin H, Tan Y, Chen Y, Ren W, Choo KKR (2024) TriBoDeS: a tri-blockchain-based detection and sharing scheme for dangerous road condition information in internet of vehicles. IEEE Internet Things J 11(2):3563–3577. https://doi.org/10.1109/JIOT.2023.3297259

Saleem MA, Mahmood K, Kumari S (2020) Comments on 'AKM-IoV: authenticated key management protocol in fog computing-based internet of vehicles deployment.' IEEE Internet Things J 7(5):4671–4675. https://doi.org/10.1109/JIOT.2020.2975207

Sharma P, Liu H (2021) A machine-learning-based data-centric misbehavior detection model for internet of vehicles. IEEE Internet Things J 8(6):4991–4999. https://doi.org/10.1109/JIOT.2020.3035035

Shirvani S, Baseri Y, Ghorbani A (2024) Evaluation framework for electric vehicle security risk assessment. IEEE Trans Intell Transp Syst 25(1):33–56. https://doi.org/10.1109/TITS.2023.3307660

Silva R, Iqbal R (2019) Ethical implications of social internet of vehicles systems. IEEE Internet Things J 6(1):517–531. https://doi.org/10.1109/JIOT.2018.2841969

Spandonidis C, Giannopoulos F, Sedikos E, Reppas D, Theodoropoulos P (2022) Development of a MEMS-based IoV system for augmenting road traffic survey. IEEE Trans Instrum Meas 71:1–8. https://doi.org/10.1109/TIM.2022.3198755

Su Y, Huang L, Liwang M (2024) Joint power control and time allocation for UAV-assisted IoV networks over licensed and unlicensed spectrum. IEEE Internet Things J 11(1):1522–1533. https://doi.org/10.1109/JIOT.2023.3291370

Tang F, Mao B, Kato N, Gui G (2021) Comprehensive survey on machine learning in vehicular network: technology, applications and challenges. IEEE Commun Surv Tutor 23(3):2027–2057. https://doi.org/10.1109/COMST.2021.3089688

Tiwari M, Maity I, Misra S (2022) FedServ: federated task service in fog-enabled internet of vehicles. IEEE Trans Intell Transp Syst 23(11):20943–20952. https://doi.org/10.1109/TITS.2022.3186401

Wang L, Liu X (2018) NOTSA: novel OBU with three-level security architecture for internet of vehicles. IEEE Internet Things J 5(5):3548–3558. https://doi.org/10.1109/JIOT.2018.2800281

Wang K, Wang X, Liu X, Jolfaei A (2020) Task offloading strategy based on reinforcement learning computing in edge computing architecture of internet of vehicles. IEEE Access 8:173779–173789. https://doi.org/10.1109/ACCESS.2020.3023939

Wang J, Wu L, Wang H, Choo KKR, Wang L, He D (2022) A secure and efficient multiserver authentication and key agreement protocol for internet of vehicles. IEEE Internet Things J 9(23):24398–24416. https://doi.org/10.1109/JIOT.2022.3188731

Wang FY et al (2023) Transportation 5.0: the DAO to safe, secure, and sustainable intelligent transportation systems. IEEE Trans Intell Transp Syst 24(10):10262–10278. https://doi.org/10.1109/TITS.2023.3305380

Wazid M, Bagga P, Das AK, Shetty S, Rodrigues JJPC, Park Y (2019) AKM-IoV: authenticated key management protocol in fog computing-based internet of vehicles deployment. IEEE Internet Things J 6(5):8804–8817. https://doi.org/10.1109/JIOT.2019.2923611

Wu Q, Liu H, Wang R, Fan P, Fan Q, Li Z (2020a) Delay-sensitive task offloading in the 802.11p-based vehicular fog computing systems. IEEE Internet Things J 7(1):773–785. https://doi.org/10.1109/JIOT.2019.2953047

Wu Q, Ge H, Liu H, Fan Q, Li Z, Wang Z (2020b) A task offloading scheme in vehicular fog and cloud computing system. IEEE Access 8:1173–1184. https://doi.org/10.1109/ACCESS.2019.2961802

Wu C, Huang Z, Zou Y (2022) Delay constrained hybrid task offloading of internet of vehicle: a deep reinforcement learning method. IEEE Access 10(September):102778–102788. https://doi.org/10.1109/ACCESS.2022.3206359

Wu H, Fan Y, Jin J, Ma H, Xing L (2023) Social-aware decentralized cooperative caching for internet of vehicles. IEEE Internet Things J 10(16):14834–14845. https://doi.org/10.1109/JIOT.2022.3229009

Xia S, Lin F, Chen Z, Tang C, Ma Y, Yu X (2020) A Bayesian game based vehicle-to-vehicle electricity trading scheme for blockchain-enabled internet of vehicles. IEEE Trans Veh Technol 69(7):6856–6868. https://doi.org/10.1109/TVT.2020.2990443

Xu J, Shu HB, Shao YM (2019) Modeling of driver behavior on trajectory-speed decision making in minor traffic roadways with complex features. IEEE Trans Intell Transp Syst 20(1):41–53. https://doi.org/10.1109/TITS.2018.2800086

Xu X, Li H, Xu W, Liu Z, Yao L, Dai F (2022) Artificial intelligence for edge service optimization in internet of vehicles: a survey. Tsinghua Sci Technol 27(2):270–287. https://doi.org/10.26599/TST.2020.9010025

Xujie L, Jing T, Yuan X, Ying S (2023) Mobility-aware multi-task migration and offloading scheme for internet of vehicles. Chin J Electron 32(6):1192–1202. https://doi.org/10.23919/cje.2022.00.333

Yang F, Wang S, Li J, Liu Z, Sun Q (2014) An overview of internet of vehicles. China Commun 11(10):1–15. https://doi.org/10.1109/CC.2014.6969789

Yang J, Ni Q, Luo G, Cheng Q, Oukhellou L, Han S (2023) A trustworthy internet of vehicles: the DAO to safe, secure, and collaborative autonomous driving. IEEE Trans Intell Veh 8(12):4678–4681. https://doi.org/10.1109/TIV.2023.3337345

Young R, Fallon S, Jacob P, O'Dwyer D (2020) Vehicle telematics and its role as a key enabler in the development of smart cities. IEEE Sens J 20(19):11713–11724. https://doi.org/10.1109/JSEN.2020.2997129

Zhou S, Chen J, Teng S, Zhang H, Wang FY (2024) Integrating sustainability in future traffic lighting: designing efficient light systems for vehicle, road, and traffic. IEEE Trans Intell Veh 9(1):65–68. https://doi.org/10.1109/TIV.2023.3331002

Chapter 7
Connecting the Dots: Unveiling the Power of Sensors in IoT

Vandana Mehndiratta, Varuna Gupta, and Aakansha Garg

Abstract The Internet of Things (IoT) has transformed how we interact with technology, and sensors are at the center of this transformation. This abstract investigates how sensors work as IoT's sensory organs, allowing for the capture of massive volumes of data from the actual world. Sensors are the silent observers who bridge the digital and physical worlds, measuring everything from temperature and humidity to motion and sound. The chapter highlights the critical role of sensors in enabling real-time monitoring, predictive maintenance, and improved decision-making in a variety of areas, including healthcare, agriculture, transportation, and smart cities. Organizations that use sensor data can obtain significant insights into operational efficiency, resource optimization, and consumer behavior. The chapter also discusses the problems and opportunities connected with sensor deployment in IoT ecosystems, which range from data privacy and security concerns to interoperability and scalability issues. This article, using case studies and industry insights, emphasizes sensors' revolutionary potential in determining the future of IoT and encouraging a more connected, intelligent, and responsive society.

Keywords IOT sensors · Data connection · Data security

7.1 Introduction

In today's increasingly connected world, the Internet of Things (IoT) has emerged as a transformative technology that is reshaping industries, improving our daily lives, and enabling more efficient and intelligent systems. At the heart of IoT are sensors, which play a pivotal role in collecting data from the physical world and transmitting

V. Mehndiratta · V. Gupta (✉)
Christ University, Bengaluru, India
e-mail: varunagupta.cs@gmail.com

A. Garg
ABES Institute of Technology, Ghaziabad, India

R. Arya et al. (eds.), *Recent Trends in Artificial Intelligence Towards a Smart World*,
Frontiers of Artificial Intelligence, Ethics and Multidisciplinary Applications,
https://doi.org/10.1007/978-981-97-6790-8_7

it to the digital realm. This chapter explores the fundamentals of sensors and their crucial role in powering the IoT revolution.

7.1.1 Overview of IoT's Impact

The Internet of Things (IoT) has ushered in a paradigm shift in the way we interact with technology and the physical world (Firozi et al. 2020). Its impact spans across various domains, reshaping industries, enhancing our daily lives, and offering unprecedented opportunities for innovation. In this section, we will delve into the profound impact of IoT on different aspects of our world.

7.1.2 Transforming Industries

- *Manufacturing*: IoT has revolutionized manufacturing processes through the implementation of sensors in production lines, enabling real-time monitoring, predictive maintenance, and increased efficiency.
- *Healthcare*: IoT applications in healthcare have resulted in remote patient monitoring, smart medical devices, and improved healthcare delivery, saving lives and reducing costs (Firouzi et al. 2018).
- *Agriculture*: Agriculture has embraced IoT for precision farming, crop monitoring, and livestock management, leading to increased productivity and sustainability (Ratnaparkhi et al. 2020).
- *Transportation*: In the transportation sector, IoT has facilitated vehicle tracking, traffic management, and the development of autonomous vehicles, paving the way for safer and more efficient transportation systems.

7.1.3 Enhancing Daily Life

- *Smart Homes*: IoT-connected smart homes offer convenience, security, and energy savings through devices like smart thermostats, voice assistants, and home automation systems (El-Azab 2021).
- *Wearables*: Wearable IoT devices, such as fitness trackers and smartwatches, have become integral in monitoring health, fitness, and lifestyle.
- *Smart Cities*: IoT is shaping the future of urban living, with smart city initiatives using sensors for traffic management, waste reduction, and improved public services.

7.1.4 Enabling New Possibilities

- *Data Analytics*: The massive volume of data generated by IoT sensors has opened doors for advanced data analytics and machine learning, providing insights that were previously inaccessible.
- *Environmental Monitoring*: IoT-enabled environmental sensors help us understand and combat climate change by collecting data on air quality, pollution levels, and natural disasters.
- *Retail and Customer Experience*: Retailers leverage IoT to optimize inventory management, personalize customer experiences, and streamline supply chains.

7.1.5 Challenges and Considerations

- *Privacy and Security*: As IoT spreads, worries about cybersecurity and data privacy have intensified, calling for strong solutions to safeguard private data (Touqeer et al. 2021).
- *Scalability and Interoperability*: IoT ecosystems are complex, thus standards and protocols that guarantee smooth interoperability and scalability are necessary.

7.2 Understanding Sensors

7.2.1 Decoding Sensors: Unveiling the Essence of Sensing

In their most basic form, sensors are digital representations of the analogue world. They enable the transformation of physical events into digital data by acting as the IoT systems' eyes, ears, and fingers (Patel et al. 2020). In this section, we dispel the mystery surrounding sensors by elucidating their basic function, parts, and mechanisms.

7.2.2 Importance of Sensors in Various Fields

- *Healthcare and Medical Sciences*
  Vital sign monitoring is made possible by sensors in medical equipment, which enable ongoing patient observation. For the remote diagnosis, management, and treatment of chronic illnesses, this data is essential.
- *Agriculture and Precision Farming*
  In agriculture, sensors keep an eye on weather patterns, crop health, and soil conditions. Farmers could maximize crop yields by using this information to optimize fertilization, irrigation, and insect management.

- *Energy Management*
  Energy use in factories, transportation networks, and buildings is tracked and managed using sensors. Cost reductions and energy efficiency result from this.
- *Safety and Security*
  By spotting intruders and keeping an eye on activity in both home and business settings, sensors like motion detectors and cameras improve security.
- *Wearable Technology*
  Wearable sensors track physiological data and give consumers insights into their fitness and health, like those found in fitness trackers and smartwatches.
- *Consumer Electronics and User Experience*
  The user experience is improved by features like gesture controls, touchscreens, and automated screen rotation that are made possible by sensors in gadgets like smartphones.
- *Predictive Maintenance in Industry*
  Industrial sensors help with predictive maintenance by keeping an ongoing eye on machines. By identifying possible problems before they result in equipment failure, this proactive method reduces maintenance expenses and downtime.
- *Data Collection and Measurement*
  As the main data collectors, sensors are essential to the Internet of Things (IoT). By gathering data on physical characteristics, they make it possible to monitor and manage linked systems and equipment.
- *Smart Homes and Consumer Electronics*
  Energy efficiency and convenience are improved by sensors in smart home appliances. Depending on user preferences, environmental factors, and occupancy, they can automate security, heating, and lighting systems.
- *Automation and Control System*
  Sensors are necessary in industrial and manufacturing settings to automate processes. They provide accurate control and optimization of industrial processes by providing real-time data on equipment performance.

7.2.3 An In-depth Exploration of Sensor Varieties

There are many types of sensors in the market (Sehrawat and Gill 2019). A few of them are listed below:

- ***Temperature Sensor***: It measures the variations in temperature.
- ***Motion Sensor***: It detects movement/acceleration. It is popularly used in security systems and gaming devices.
- ***Sound Sensors/Microphones***: It is used to convert sound waves into electrical signals. It is commonly used in communication devices and audio equipment.
- ***Biometric Sensors***: It captures biometric data for identification purposes like fingerprint or iris scanners.

- ***Light Sensors***: It captures variations in light intensity. It is used in cameras, automatic lighting systems, etc.
- ***Pressure Sensors***: It monitors changes in pressure. It is often used in industrial and automotive applications.
- ***Humidity Sensors***: It measures the moisture in the air.
- ***Gas Sensors***: It detects the presence and concentration of gases in the environment.
- ***Accelerometers and Gyroscopes***: It measures acceleration and rotational motion. It is commonly found in smart phones and navigation systems.
- ***Proximity Sensors***: It determines the presence and absence of any object in the given range.

7.3 Sensor Integration in IoT

Scope of Sensors in IoT: The IoT becomes smarter and intelligent when combined with sensors (Sharma et al. 2021).

- *Smart Home Applications*
  Smart houses with sensors improve user experiences and automation. They make elements like climate control, automated lighting, and security systems functional according on ambient circumstances, occupancy, and preferences.
- *Industrial IIoT*
  Sensors are essential for process optimization, predictive maintenance, and guaranteeing the smooth running of machinery in manufacturing and industrial environments. Applications for the Internet of Things (IIoT) use sensors to monitor machinery and production processes in real time.
- *Data Collection and Monitoring*
  As the eyes and ears of Internet of Things systems, sensors gather information on a wide range of physical characteristics, including motion, pressure, temperature, humidity, and more. Real-time insights into the environment are made possible by continuous monitoring, which makes it possible to react quickly to changes or anomalies.
- *Smart Cities and Urban Planning*
  By keeping an eye on traffic patterns, streamlining public transportation, controlling energy use, and boosting public safety, sensors help create smart cities. Sensor data is used in urban planning to enhance resource and infrastructure management.
- *Security and Surveillance*
  Security and surveillance applications benefit from the use of sensors, such as cameras and motion detectors. They make it possible to monitor sensitive areas, detect intrusions, and identify faces.
- *Data Analytics and Machine Learning*
  To extract valuable insights from the massive volume of data gathered by Internet of Things sensors, data analytics, and machine learning algorithms are employed. Making educated decisions, spotting patterns, and predicting trends are all made easier with the aid of predictive analytics.

- *Logistics and Supply Chain Management*
  IoT sensors enhance supply chain efficiency and logistics by enabling real-time tracking and monitoring of items in transit. Applications include vehicle predictive maintenance, asset tracking, and temperature monitoring for perishable commodities.
- *Consumer Electronics and Smart Devices*
  Numerous sensors are used in smartphones, smartwatches, and other consumer devices to provide functions like GPS, gyroscopes, accelerometers, and touch-screens. These sensors improve user experience and open new possibilities for communication, navigation, and entertainment applications.
- *Environmental Monitoring*
  IoT sensors are used to measure air and water quality, monitor biodiversity, monitor the environment, and evaluate the effects of climate change. Sustainable resource management is facilitated, and environmental conservation efforts are supported by this data.
- *Agriculture and Precision Farming*
  Sensors are used in agricultural IoT applications to track weather patterns, crop health, and soil conditions. Precision farming techniques are informed by this data, which maximizes fertilization and irrigation.
  Precision farming methods are made possible by sensors, which further advances smart agriculture.

7.4 Sensor Network

A sensor is an electrical device that senses external stimuli and transforms raw data into a format that can be read by computers or people. In essence, sensors are devices that are able to recognize and react to optical or electrical signals. It transforms observed physical properties into quantifiable electrical signals (Sharma et al. 2021). A sensor network is an assembly of geographically dispersed sensors connected to one another so they can measure, monitor, and react to environmental changes together. These networks play a critical role in the larger Internet of Things (IoT) space by facilitating the smooth integration of sensors for a wide range of applications.

7.4.1 Key Aspects of Sensor Network

- *Wireless Communication*: Wireless communication allows sensors in a network to exchange information, plan tasks, and send data to other network nodes or the central processing unit.
- Wi-Fi, Bluetooth, Zigbee, LoRa, and other wireless communication technologies are available, contingent upon the needs of the application.

- *Distributed Sensing*: Sensor networks enable broad coverage of a region or environment by utilizing many geographically dispersed sensors.
- Together, these sensors gather information on a range of physical characteristics, including motion, pressure, temperature, humidity, and more.
- *Collaborative Sensing*: In a network, sensor nodes frequently work together to accomplish a similar objective. This cooperation could entail exchanging data, compiling information, or working together to react to changes in the environment.

The sensor network's overall dependability and efficiency are increased by collaborative sensing.

7.4.2 Research Area and Advancements:

- *Wireless Sensor Network (WSN) Protocols*: The goal of ongoing research is to create effective communication protocols for WSNs that will decrease energy usage and increase data reliability (Brida et al. 2021).
- *Edge Computing*: Edge computing is being used by sensor networks more and more to analyze data closer to the source, which lowers latency and improves real-time capabilities.

7.4.3 Application of Sensors

- *Healthcare*: Wireless sensor networks are employed for patient monitoring, tracking medical equipment, and managing healthcare facilities (Formica and Schena 2021).
- *Industrial IIoT*: In industrial applications, sensor networks are essential for real-time equipment monitoring, predictive maintenance, and process optimization.
- *Environmental Monitoring*: Sensor networks are used to monitor and collect data on environmental conditions, including air and water quality, weather patterns, and biodiversity.
- *Smart Agriculture*: IN precision farming, sensor networks help monitor soil moisture, temperature, and crop health, optimizing agricultural practices.

7.5 Advantages and Disadvantages of Sensor Network

Sensor network dominates the entire world because of its benefits over other technologies, which are stated below:

- Provide the remote monitoring of physical characteristics, hence eliminating the necessity for physical presence and enabling real-time data collecting.

- Less expensive to install than conventional wired systems, particularly for large-scale applications (Tiwari et al. 2015).
- Rapid deployment capabilities of wireless sensor networks make them appropriate for time-sensitive applications such as environmental monitoring and emergency response scenarios.
- Achieve high data accuracy through redundant measurements and data validation by placing multiple sensors in a given region.
- Energy-efficient protocols are incorporated into many sensor networks, enabling longer sensor operation times, particularly in low-power applications.

Monitor environmental conditions in real time and react quickly to events and changes. Sensor networks can be used in a wide range of situations and contexts, from industrial settings to medical and agricultural settings.

Every technology comes with a few shortcomings. A few of the shortcomings of the sensor network is given below:

- Due to the restricted range of wireless transmission in sensor networks, larger areas will require more infrastructure and precise sensor placement.
- Many sensors in a network operate on batteries, and managing power consumption is a constant challenge. This limitation affects the lifespan of the sensors.
- Security issues arise when data is transmitted wirelessly, and sensor networks are open to illegal access and eavesdropping. Strong security measures must be put in place.
- Interference and signal loss are common in wireless sensor networks, which can result in inaccurate data or poor communication (Tiwari et al. 2015).
- Long-term cost-effectiveness of sensor networks may be questionable, but upfront deployment expenses, such as those associated with sensor hardware and network infrastructure, may be high.

7.6 Wireless Communication

The transfer of data or information between devices without the use of physical connections or wires is referred to as wireless communication. It is a basic technology that has completely changed how we exchange information and communicate across a range of industries.

7.6.1 Protocols and Standards

In the realm of technology and communication, protocols and standards are essential components because they offer norms and principles that guarantee smooth communication and interoperability amongst systems, networks, and devices. These are a few well-known protocols and standards from various fields:

Network Communication Protocol

- *TCP/IP (Transmission Control Protocol/Internet Protocol)*
  The foundation of the internet, TCP/IP defines how data is transmitted and received across networks. It consists of multiple protocols, including HTTP, FTP, and SMTP.
- *HTTP/HTTPS (Hypertext Transfer Protocol/Secure)*
  HTTP is a protocol used for online browsing and data transmission on the Worldwide online; HTTPS provides an additional layer of security by encrypting data.
- *FTP (File Transfer Protocol)*
  File transfers between computers connected to a network are done via FTP. It specifies the proper upload and download procedures for files.
- *DNS (Domain Name System)*
  Users may access websites with names that are legible by humans thanks to DNS, which converts domain names into IP addresses.
- *UDP (User Datagram Protocol)*
  Faster communication is possible with UDP since it lacks TCP's error-checking and correction capabilities.
- *SMTP/POP/IMAP (Simple Mail Transfer Protocol/Internet Message Access Protocol)*
  Protocols for sending, receiving, and storing email messages.
- *VoIP (Voice over Internet Protocol)*
  VoIP protocols make it possible to communicate via voice over the internet, which makes services like video conferencing and internet telephony possible.

7.6.2 Wireless Communication Protocol

- *WiFi (IEEE 802.11)*
  A group of wireless local area network (LAN) communication standards that enable devices to connect to the internet without the need for physical connections.
- *Bluetooth*
  A standard for short-range wireless communication that can be used to link accessories, headphones, and smartphones.
- *Zigbee (IEEE 802.15.4)*
  Zigbee is a popular low-power, low-data-rate wireless communication technology for home automation and Internet of Things applications.
- *NFC (Near Field Communication)*
  NFC makes it possible for contactless data exchange across short distances, which is useful for mobile payments and identity.
- *LoRa (Long Range)*
  Extended coverage is provided using LoRa, a low-power, long-range wireless communication protocol intended for Internet of Things applications.

7.6.3 Internet Security Standards

- *SSL/TLS (Secure Socket Layer/Transport Layer Security)*
- Protocols that ensure secure data transmission over the internet are commonly used in HTTPS for secure web browsing.
- *IPsec (Internet Protocol Security)*
- IPsec offers a set of protocols that encrypt and authenticate every data packet to secure internet protocol interactions.
- *WPA/WPA2/WPA3 (Wi-Fi Protected Access)*
- Wi-Fi network security standards that offer authentication and encryption techniques to protect wireless communication.

7.6.4 IoT Protocols

- MQTT (Message Queuing Telemetry Transport)
  A simple, effective messaging protocol that is frequently used in the Internet of Things and is intended for networks with low capacity, high latency, or instability.
- CoAP (Constrained Application Protocol)
  CoAP is used for low-power, basic devices in Internet of Things applications. It is designed for devices and networks with little resources.
- DDS (Data Distribution Service)
  A standard for real-time, scalable, and interoperable data sharing between networked devices.

7.6.5 Data Exchange and Representation Standards

- JSON (JavaScript Object Notation)
  A lightweight data interchange format is used for data exchange between a server and a web application.
- XML (eXtensible Markup Language)
  A markup language for encoding documents in a format that is both human-readable and machine-readable.
- CSV (Comma-Separated Values)
  A simple file format is used for tabular data, with each line of the file representing a data record.
- HL7 (Health Level Seven)
  A set of standards for the exchange, integration, sharing, and retrieval of electronic health information.

7.6.6 Power Efficiency

Power efficiency is an important factor to consider when designing sensor networks, particularly when many sensors are used in difficult or remote locations where it may not be feasible to repair or recharge the batteries (Akende et al. 2022). These are some methods to improve sensor network power efficiency:

- Low-Power Sensor Design
- Energy-Efficient Components

Choose sensors that are designed for low power consumption. This includes using energy-efficient transducers and components to reduce the overall power requirements.

7.6.7 Low-Power Microcontrollers

Employ microcontrollers with low-power modes and capabilities. This allows sensors to operate in low-power states when not actively collecting or transmitting data.

7.6.8 Duty Cycling and Sleep Modes

- *Duty Cycling*
  Implement duty cycling strategies where sensors periodically wake up, collect data, and transmit it, and then enter sleep modes to conserve power between active periods.
- *Sleep Modes and Power Gating*
  Utilize sleep modes or power gating to turn off components or even entire sensors when not in use. This can significantly reduce power consumption during idle times.

7.6.9 Data Compression and Aggregation

- *Data Compression*
  Implement data compression techniques to reduce the amount of data that needs to be transmitted. This not only conserves energy but also minimizes the load on communication channels.
- *Data Aggregation*
  Aggregate data at the sensor node level before transmission. This reduces the number of transmissions and, consequently, lowers the energy consumption associated with radio communication.

7.6.10 Optimized Communication Protocols

Use of Low-Power Wireless Protocols

Choose wireless communication protocols that are designed for low power, such as Zigbee or LoRa. These protocols typically offer longer range and lower power consumption compared to traditional Wi-Fi or cellular communication.

Shorter Transmission Ranges

Limit the transmission range between sensor nodes to minimize the power required for communication. Adjusting transmission power based on the distance between nodes can be an effective strategy.

Energy Harvesting

Solar, Vibration, or Thermal Harvesting

Integrate energy harvesting solutions, such as solar panels, vibration harvesters, or thermoelectric generators, to harness ambient energy and supplement or replace battery power.

Adaptive Sensing and Sampling

Adaptive Sampling Rates

Implement adaptive sensing techniques that adjust the sampling rates based on the dynamics of the monitored environment. This prevents unnecessary energy consumption during stable conditions.

Event-Driven Sensing

Use event-driven sensing where the sensor is triggered to collect and transmit data only when specific events or thresholds are met, reducing unnecessary data transmission.

Power-Aware Routing

Energy-Efficient Routing Protocols

Utilize routing protocols that consider the energy levels of individual nodes when determining communication paths. This helps balance energy consumption across the network.

Over-the-Air (OTA) Firmware Updates

Efficient Firmware Updates

When updating sensor node firmware, implement efficient OTA updates to minimize the power required for the update process.

Predictive Maintenance

Predictive Algorithms

Implement predictive maintenance algorithms that analyze sensor data to anticipate when a sensor or component is likely to fail. This allows for proactive maintenance, reducing downtime and unnecessary power consumption.

Sleep Scheduling

Synchronized Sleep Schedules

Implement synchronized sleep schedules for nodes in the network. This coordination allows multiple nodes to enter sleep modes simultaneously, reducing the overall power consumption.

7.7 Sensor Fusion

The term "sensor fusion" describes a computational approach that combines data from several sensors to provide a more comprehensive picture of the system under study than any one sensor could by itself. Sensor fusion is a major aspect of contemporary civilization and finds applications in a wide range of daily activities (Fung et al. 2017). It is utilized, for instance, in autonomous vehicles to understand traffic scenes, in robotics for navigation and localization, in aerial photography and delivery to control drones, and in biomedical engineering to analyze bio signals.

Sensor fusion systems share the common denominator and primary goal of combining measurements from several sensors to estimate or infer one or more quantities of interest (Yeong et al. 2021). For instance, we can determine the location and potentially even the velocity of an autonomous vehicle or drone by utilizing several sensors. In summary, this pertains to three primary elements and their delivery, as well as biosignal analysis in the field of biomedical engineering (Fig. 7.1):

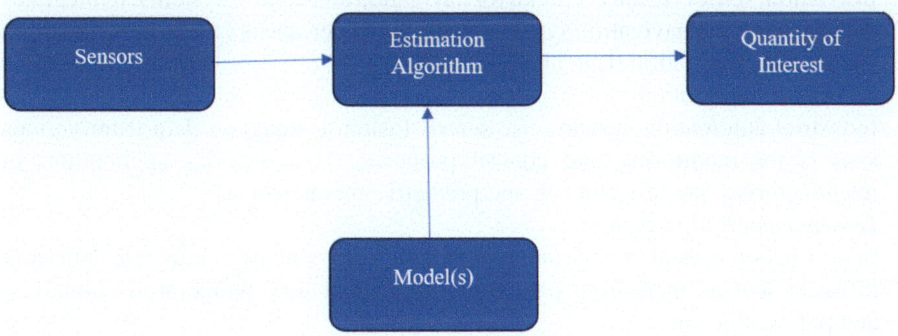

Fig. 7.1 Components of sensor fusion system. *Source* Author

- More than one *sensor* that measures an observable quantity.
- *Model(s)* that relate the observed quantity to the quality of interest, and
- An *estimation algorithm* that estimates the quantity of interest by combining the model and the measured data.

7.7.1 Applications of Sensor Fusion

Sensor fusion finds applications in various fields where accurate and reliable information is crucial. Here are some common applications:

- *Autonomous Vehicles*
  Sensor fusion is used in autonomous vehicles to integrate data from cameras, LiDAR, radar, and other sensors. This provides a comprehensive perception of the vehicle's surroundings for navigation and obstacle avoidance.
- *Robotics*
  Robots use sensor fusion to integrate data from vision sensors, inertial sensors, and other environmental sensors (Luo and Yih 2002). This helps in tasks such as mapping, localization, and object recognition.
- *Augmented Reality (AR) and Virtual Reality (VR)*
  In AR and VR applications, sensor fusion is employed to combine data from accelerometers, gyroscopes, and vision sensors to provide accurate and responsive user experiences.
- *Health Monitoring and Wearables*
  Wearable devices often use sensor fusion to combine data from accelerometers, heart rate monitors, and other sensors to provide accurate health-related information, such as activity tracking and sleep monitoring.
- *Smartphones*
  Smartphones use sensor fusion for applications like navigation (combining GPS, accelerometer, and gyroscope data), gesture recognition, and augmented reality (Luo and Yih 2002).
- *Aerospace and Aviation*
  In aviation, sensor fusion is crucial for navigation and control systems. It integrates data from inertial navigation systems, GPS, and other sensors for accurate position and attitude estimation (Luo and Yih 2002).
- *Industrial Automation*
  Industrial automation systems use sensor fusion to integrate data from various sensors for monitoring and control purposes. This includes applications in manufacturing, process control, and predictive maintenance.
- *Environmental Monitoring*
  Sensor fusion is used in environmental monitoring systems to integrate data from different sensors measuring parameters like air quality, temperature, humidity, and pollutant levels.
- *Security and Surveillance*

Surveillance systems use sensor fusion to combine data from cameras, motion detectors, and other sensors for effective monitoring and threat detection.

- *Medical Imaging*
  In medical imaging, sensor fusion combines data from different imaging modalities (e.g., MRI, CT, PET) to create a more comprehensive and accurate representation for diagnostic purposes.

Sensor fusion plays a pivotal role in enhancing the capabilities of systems and devices across various domains, contributing to improved accuracy, reliability, and overall performance.

7.7.2 Types of Sensor Fusion

When you combine data from many sensors at once, it means that this method needs fewer sensors than when using just one sensor for audible reasons; just as multiple people watching an incident give a better idea than a single observer. An illustration of the many types of sensor fusions can be seen in Fig. 7.2.

Data Fusion: At the raw data level, this kind of sensor fusion integrates information from several sensors. By merging data from several sources, the aim is to increase the data's precision and accuracy.

Feature Fusion: At the feature level, this kind of sensor fusion integrates information from several sensors. To build a more complete picture of the environment, the objective is to extract pertinent data from each sensor and combine them.

Decision Fusion: This kind of sensor fusion integrates the judgments or findings from various sensors. By considering several information sources, the overall decision-making process is intended to be improved.

Multi-modal Sensor Algorithm: This kind of sensor fusion blends information from several sensors measuring various physical events. For instance, it can combine

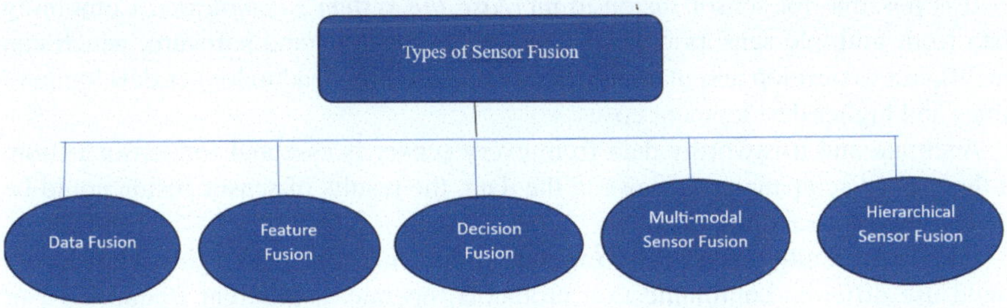

Fig. 7.2 Types of sensor fusion. *Source* Author

information from a lidar sensor with a camera to get a more comprehensive picture of the surroundings.

Hierarchical Fusion: Combining data from several sensors at several system levels, such as the sensor, feature, and decision levels, is known as this kind of sensor fusion.

7.7.3 The Coign of Vantage of Sensor Fusion

Combining data from several sensors can significantly boost the *accuracy* of the information (Hostettler and Sarkka 2020). For example, an automobile equipped with lidar, radar, and cameras may view the world from various angles thanks to these sensors. Combining these data can give the car a more accurate view of its surroundings.

The system is more *resilient* to a single sensor failing when multiple sensors are used. Even if one sensor fails, the system will still be able to operate thanks to the data from the other sensors.

Redundancy is provided by sensor fusion, which is crucial for applications that need to be safe. If one sensor fails, the information gathered from the other sensors can serve as a fallback source.

When the system integrates data from multiple sensors, it can make more *intelligent decisions* (Kumar et al. 2020). For example, an autonomous car's system can make greater use of data from lidar, radar, and cameras to ascertain the vehicle's direction, speed, and overall behavior.

Sensor fusion can help *improve one's awareness* of their surroundings. By combining data from several sensors, the system may obtain a more comprehensive image of the surroundings and recognize objects that may not be visible to individual sensors.

Sometimes it's more *cost-effective* to use multiple sensors than just one expensive sensor. The system can use multiple less expensive sensors to provide the same or greater performance at a lower cost.

The hindrance to implementing sensor fusion is given below:

It is possible for sensor fusion to *increase the system's complexity*. Combining data from multiple sensors requires complex algorithms and software, which can be difficult to develop and maintain. This intricacy may lead to longer development times and higher development costs.

Accurate and trustworthy data from every sensor is essential for sensor fusion. If there are discrepancies or flaws in the data, the results of sensor fusion could be *misleading or erroneous*.

Integrating multiple sensors into a single system might be challenging. The sensors could use different communication protocols, operate at different frequencies, or offer varying levels of precision. *Integration problems* can lead to delays and higher development costs.

Although sensor fusion can sometimes save money, it can sometimes be *expensive*. High-end sensors can be pricey, and using multiple sensors might increase the system's overall cost.

The functionality of the system may be compromised if one or more of the *sensors fail*. The accuracy and effectiveness of the system may be compromised by sensor failures that go unnoticed, leading to inaccurate or incomplete data.

Using a lot of sensors could raise the system's *power consumption*, which could be an issue for devices that run on batteries. Larger batteries may be required as a result, which could increase the device's weight and size or shorten its battery life.

7.7.4 Sensor Fusion Algorithms

7.7.4.1 Kalman Filter

A recursive method called the Kalman Filter uses a sequence of noisy observations to estimate the state of a dynamic system (Kim and Bang 2018; Li et al. 2015). Sensor fusion is a common usage for it in applications including control systems, tracking, and navigation. Kalman filtering uses measurements taken over time to estimate certain unknown variables. Kalman filters have proven to be beneficial in a variety of applications. Kalman filters are low-complexity and low-processor-load algorithms. Still, understanding and using the Kalman filters remains difficult for those unfamiliar with estimate theory.

The Kalman Filter is based on a mathematical model that describes the evolution of a system over time and the relationship between the system's state, observations, and control inputs (Li et al. 2015). The following is a simplified mathematical representation of the Kalman Filter for a linear, discrete-time system.

Mathematical Model

State Transition Model

The state transition model describes how the system's state evolves from one time step to the next in the absence of control inputs and measurements. It is typically represented by the equation:

$$x_k = F \cdot x_{k-1} + B \cdot u_k + w_k$$

where,

x_k State vector at time k
F State transition matrix
B Control input matrix
u_k Control input at time (k)
w_k Process noise (assumed to be zero-mean Gaussian noise)

Observation Model

The observation model relates the system's state to the measurements obtained from sensors. It is expressed by the equation:

$$z_k = H \cdot x_k + v_k$$

where,

z_k Measurement vector at time k
H Observation matrix x-KxK-predicted state estimate at time K
v_k Measurement noise (assumed to be zero-mean Gaussian noise)

State Prediction

The state prediction step estimates the next state based on the previous state and control inputs. It involves predicting the state and updating the covariance matrix associated with the predicted state. The equations for the prediction step are:

$$x_k^- = F \cdot x^{k-1} + B \cdot uk$$
$$P_k^- = F \cdot P_{k-1} \cdot F^T + Q$$

x_k^- Predicted state estimate at time k
P_k^- Predicted error covariance matrix at time k
Q Covariance matrix associated with the process noise

Measurement Update

The measurement update step corrects the predicted state estimate based on the actual measurements. It involves updating the state estimate and the associated error covariance matrix. The equations for the update step are:

$$Kk = Pk - \cdot HT \cdot (H \cdot Pk - \cdot HT + R) - 1$$

$$x^k = x^k - +Kk \cdot (zk - H \cdot x^k -)$$

$$Pk = (I - Kk \cdot H) \cdot Pk-$$

where,

Kk Kalman Gain at time k
x^k Corrected state estimate at time k
Pk Corrected error covariance matrix at time k
R Covariance matrix associated with the measurement noise.

Initialization

The filter is initialized with an initial state estimate (x^k0) and an initial error covariance matrix (P_0). The initial state estimate represents the best estimate of the system's state before any measurements are available.

Iteration

The prediction and measurement update steps are iteratively applied as new measurements become available. The Kalman Filter continually refines its estimate of the system's state based on the evolving measurements and the dynamics of the system.

Summary

The Kalman Filter's mathematical model combines the system's dynamics, control inputs, measurements, and associated uncertainties to provide an optimal estimate of the system's state. The effectiveness of the filter lies in its ability to adaptively balance predictions and measurements, considering the inherent uncertainties in both the system and the measurements.

Steps in Kalman Filter

- *Initialization*: An initial estimate of the state and covariance matrices is used by the procedure to get started.
- *Prediction*: The Kalman Filter predicts the next state and covariance matrices based on the system model.
- *Measurement Update*: Measurements are used to update the anticipated state, and the covariance matrices are modified in accordance with the uncertainties.
- *Iterative Process*: As additional measurements become available, the prediction and measurement update stages are performed recursively, continuously improving the state estimate.

Advantages of Kalman Filter

- *Optimal estimation*: The Kalman Filter provides an optimal estimate in the sense that it minimizes the mean squared error of the estimated state.
- *Adaptability*: The filter is condition-adaptive because it constantly modifies the weights allocated to measurement and prediction in response to shifting uncertainty.
- *Efficiency*: The Kalman Filter is a popular choice for systems that need fast and precise state estimates since it is computationally economical and suitable for real-time applications.

Applications of the Kalman Filter

- *Navigation Systems*
  Used for estimating the position, velocity, and orientation of vehicles or objects in navigation systems, such as GPS-aided navigation.
- *Control Systems*

Applied in control systems to estimate the state of a dynamic system and provide feedback for control actions.

- *Signal Processing*
  Utilized in signal processing for tracking and filtering applications, where accurate estimation of a signal is required.
- *Robotics*
  Employed in robotics for localization and mapping, allowing robots to estimate their position and orientation in an environment.
- *Aerospace*
  Used in aerospace applications for guidance, navigation, and control of aircraft and spacecraft.
- *Financial Modelling*
  Applied in financial modelling for estimating hidden states and predicting future values based on uncertain measurements.
- *Medical Imaging*
  Utilized in medical imaging for motion correction and tracking, where it helps estimate and correct for patient movement during imaging procedures.

The Kalman Filter's versatility and effectiveness make it a fundamental tool in various fields where accurate and dynamic state estimation is essential. Its ability to handle noise and uncertainties in measurements makes it a robust choice for real-world applications.

7.7.4.2 Extended Kalman Filter (EKF) Algorithm

An expansion of the classic Kalman filter that can handle data and models of non-linear systems is the Extended Kalman Filter (EKF). The main distinction is in the linearization stage, where the EKF uses first-order Taylor series expansion to linearize the non-linear equations (Xu et al. 2022). The Extended Kalman Filter mathematical model for a discrete-time non-linear system is shown below.

The **Extended Kalman Filter (EKF)** is an extension of the traditional Kalman Filter that accommodates non-linear system models and measurements. The primary difference lies in the linearization step, where the EKF linearizes the non-linear equations using first-order Taylor series expansion. Below is the mathematical model of the Extended Kalman Filter for a discrete-time, non-linear system.

State Transition Model

The state transition model describes how the system's state evolves over time. In the Extended Kalman Filter, this is a non-linear function:

$$x_k = f(x_{k-1}, u_k) + w_k$$

where,

x_k State vector at time k

f Non-linear state transition function
u_k Control input at time k
w_k Process noise (assumed to be zero-mean Gaussian noise)

Observation Model

The observation model relates the system's state to the measurements obtained from sensors. Again, this is a non-linear function:

$$zk = h(xk) + vk$$

where,

zk Measurement vector at time k
h Non-linear observation function
vk Measurement noise (assumed to be zero-mean Gaussian noise)

State Prediction

The state prediction step involves predicting the next state based on the non-linear state transition function and updating the error covariance matrix:

$$x^k - = f(x^k - 1, uk)$$

$$Pk- = Ak \cdot Pk - 1 \cdot AkT + Qk$$

where,

x^k- Predicted state estimate at time k
$Pk-$ Predicted error covariance matrix at time k
Ak Jacobian matrix of the state transition function with respect to the state variables
Qk Covariance matrix associated with the process noise

Measurement Update

The measurement update step corrects the predicted state estimate based on the actual measurements and updates the error covariance matrix:

$$Kk = Pk - \cdot HkT \cdot (Hk \cdot Pk - \cdot HkT + Rk) - 1$$

$$x^k = x^k - +Kk \cdot (zk - h(x^k -))$$

$$Pk = (I - Kk \cdot Hk) \cdot Pk-$$

where,

Kk Kalman Gain at time k
x^k Corrected state estimate at time k
Pk Corrected error covariance matrix at time k
Hk Jacobian matrix of the observation function with respect to the state variables
Rk Covariance matrix associated with the measurement noise

Initialization

The filter is initialized with an initial state estimate (x^0), an initial error covariance matrix (P_0), and the appropriate process noise and measurement noise covariance matrices.

Iteration

The prediction and measurement update steps are iteratively applied as new measurements become available. The non-linear state transition and observation functions are linearized using Jacobian matrices to update the state estimate and error covariance matrix.

Summary

The Extended Kalman Filter allows for the estimation of non-linear systems by linearizing the system equations during each iteration. The success of the EKF depends on the accuracy of the linearization, and it is particularly effective in situations where the system's dynamics or sensor measurements are inherently non-linear.

7.7.4.3 Complimentary Filter Algorithm

To produce a more precise and reliable estimation of orientation or angular displacement, data from various sensors—typically an accelerometer and a gyroscope—is combined using the straightforward and efficient Complementary Filter sensor fusion algorithm. Applications like orientation tracking in smartphones, drones, and other inertial measurement units (IMUs) frequently use this technique (Yadav et al. 2023). The Complementary Filter is renowned for its ease of use, cheap computational cost, and capacity to offer a responsiveness and accuracy balance that is good. An outline of the Complementary Filter algorithm can be seen below:

The Complementary Filter is a device that estimates an object's orientation by combining the outputs of two devices: an accelerometer (a_{acc}) and a gyroscope (w_{gyro}). The main idea is to employ the gyroscope for high-frequency components (angular velocity) and the accelerometer for low-frequency components (gravity or linear acceleration). The filter's name refers to the way it enhances the data from the accelerometer and gyroscope (Zhaihe et al. 2018).

Read Sensor Data

- Accelerometer Data (a_{acc}): Provides information about the acceleration experienced by the device, including the influence of gravity.
- Gyroscope Data (w_{gyro}): Provides information about the rate of angular rotation.

Calculate Pitch and Roll Angles

- Pitch (θ_{acc}): Calculate the pitch angle using the arctangent of the ratio of the accelerometer's measured acceleration components along the x and z axes.

$$\theta acc = atan2(a_{accx}, \sqrt{a^2}_{accy} + a^2_{accz})$$

- Roll (φ_{acc}): Calculate the roll angle using the arctangent of the ratio of the accelerometer's measured acceleration components along the (y) and (z) axes.

$$\varphi_{acc} = atan2(a_{accx}, \sqrt{a^2}_{accy} + a^2_{accz})$$

Integrate Gyroscope Data for Angular Rate

- Angular Rate (Ω_{gyro}): Integrate the gyroscope data to obtain the angular rate over time.

$\Omega_{gyro} = \Omega_{gyro}.dt$

Complementary Filter Equation

- Combine the accelerometer and gyroscope data using a weighted average to obtain the final orientation estimate.

$$\theta = \alpha \cdot \left(\theta_{gyro} + \Omega_{gyro}\right) + (1 - \alpha) \cdot \theta_{acc}$$
$$\varphi = \alpha \cdot \left(\varphi_{gyro} + \Omega_{gyro}\right) + (1 - \alpha) \cdot \varphi_{acc}$$

Here, (α) is a tuning parameter that determines the trade-off between the gyroscope and accelerometer data. A typical value is around 0.98.

Update Gyroscope Integration Variables

Update the gyroscope integration variables for the next iteration.

$$\theta_{gyro} = \theta$$
$$\varphi_{gyro} = \varphi$$

Advantages

- Simple and computationally efficient.
- Provides good performance for applications where slow drift over time is acceptable.

Limitations

- Susceptible to noise, especially during rapid movements.
- May exhibit slow response to sudden changes due to reliance on accelerometer data.

Applications

- Inertial measurement and orientation tracking in devices such as drones, smartphones, and wearable devices.

The Complementary Filter is a practical solution for applications that require a balance between accuracy and real-time responsiveness, making it well-suited for many orientation tracking scenarios.

7.7.4.4 Particle Filter Algorithm

Particle Filter is a statistical technique used for recursive Bayesian filtering, also referred to as Sequential Monte Carlo (SMC) methods. It is especially helpful in non-linear and non-Gaussian systems for sensor fusion and state estimation, where the Kalman or Extended Kalman Filter may perform less well. With a set of weighted particles, each representing a hypothesis about the current state, the Particle Filter expresses the belief about the system state (Elfring et al. 2021; Yang et al. 2021).

Particle Filter Algorithm

1. Initialization:
   - Generate an initial set of particles representing possible states of the system.
   - Assign equal weights to each particle.
   - These particles can be randomly sampled from the initial state distribution.
2. Prediction:
   - Propagate each particle forward in time using the system's dynamic model.
     $x_t{}^{(i)} = f(x^{(i)}{}_{t-1}, u_t) + \epsilon_t{}^{(i)}$
     where,
     $x_t{}^{(i)}$ is the new state of particle i at time t.
     f is the system's dynamic model
     u_t is the control unit.
     $\epsilon_t{}^{(i)}$ is the process noise.
3. Update (Correction):

   Incorporate measurements from sensors to adjust the weights of particles.
   $wt^{(i)} \propto p(z_t | xt^{(i)})$
   where,
   z_t is the measurement
   $p(z_t | xt^{(i)})$ is the likelihood of the measurement given the state of particle i
   $wt^{(i)}$ is the weight of particle i at time t.

4. Resampling:
   - Resample particles based on their weights to create a new set of particles.
   - Particles with higher weights are more likely to be replicated, while particles with lower weights may be discarded.
   - This step prevents particle degeneracy, ensuring that particles represent the most probable states.
5. State Estimate:
   - Estimate the system state based on the weighted sum of the particles.

$$x^t = \Sigma i = 1Nwt(i) \quad \cdot xt(i)$$

6. Advantages:
   - Suitable for non-linear and non-Gaussian systems.
   - Handles multi-modal distributions effectively.
   - Can model complex and highly dynamic systems.
7. Limitations:
   - Sensitive to the number of particles (computational cost).
   - May require tuning of parameters, such as the number of particles and process noise.
8. Applications:
   - Robotics: Localization and mapping in environments with non-linearities.
   - Sensor Fusion: Combining data from different sensors in complex systems.
   - Tracking: Object tracking in computer vision and surveillance.

In many different applications, particle filters are effective instruments for managing complexity and ambiguity. They are especially useful in situations when typical linear models are inadequate, such as in dynamic and non-linear real-world events. Accuracy and computing efficiency must be balanced, though, as their computational cost rises with the number of particles.

7.8 Case Study: Smart Building Management with IoT Sensors

The use of sensors to construct an Internet of Things-based solution for smart building management is examined in this case study. To maximize space utilization, increase passenger comfort, and improve energy efficiency, a variety of sensors must be integrated during deployment.

Objectives

1. Energy Efficiency: Reduce energy consumption and enhance sustainability.
2. Space Utilization: Optimize the use of office spaces based on occupancy.
3. Occupant Comfort: Improve the indoor environment for enhanced well-being.

Implementation

1. Sensor Deployment
   - Occupancy Sensors: Installed in offices, meeting rooms, and common areas to detect the presence of occupants.
   - Temperature and Humidity Sensors: Placed throughout the building to monitor and control climate conditions.
   - Lighting Control Sensors: Integrated with smart lighting systems to adjust lighting based on occupancy and natural light levels.
   - Energy Meters: Installed on electrical panels to monitor energy consumption.
2. Connectivity and Data Aggregation:
   - IoT Gateway: Acts as a central hub to collect data from sensors.
   - Wireless Connectivity: Sensors communicate wirelessly with the IoT gateway using protocols like MQTT or CoAP.
   - Cloud Platform: Data is transmitted to a cloud-based platform for storage, analysis, and visualization.
3. Building Management System (BMS):
   - Data Analytics: The cloud platform employs machine learning algorithms to analyze sensor data and identify patterns.
   - Energy Consumption Monitoring: Real-time monitoring of energy consumption helps identify areas for optimization.
   - Predictive Maintenance: Machine learning models predict potential equipment failures, allowing for proactive maintenance.
4. Automated Controls:
   - HVAC System: Connected to temperature and occupancy sensors, the HVAC system adjusts heating and cooling based on real-time data.
   - Lighting System: Automated lighting control ensures that lights are only active in occupied areas, reducing unnecessary energy use.
   - Space Reservation System: Occupancy data is integrated with a space reservation system, allowing employees to book meeting rooms based on availability.
5. User Interface:
   - Occupant App: Employees have access to a mobile app that provides real-time information on environmental conditions, room availability, and energy consumption.
   - Dashboard: Facility managers utilize a dashboard for an overview of building performance, energy usage trends, and alerts for maintenance issues.

Results and Benefits

1. Energy Efficiency:
   - Energy Savings: The implementation resulted in a 20% reduction in overall energy consumption.
   - Cost Reduction: Lower energy bills contribute to operational cost savings.
2. Space Utilization:
   - Optimized Spaces: The occupancy data helps facility managers optimize office layouts and allocate resources more efficiently.
   - Cost-Efficient Planning: Improved space utilization reduces the need for additional office space.
3. Occupant Comfort:
   - Personalized Comfort: Employees experience a more comfortable working environment with tailored climate control.
   - Employee Satisfaction: Enhanced indoor conditions contribute to higher employee satisfaction and well-being.
4. Predictive Maintenance:
   - Reduced Downtime: Predictive maintenance reduces equipment downtime by addressing issues before they become critical.
   - Extended Equipment Lifespan: Proactive maintenance practices contribute to prolonging the lifespan of HVAC systems and other equipment.

The installation of Internet of Things sensors for smart building management has made the building a more economical, user-friendly, and energy-efficient space. In addition to lowering operating expenses, the data-driven strategy helps create a sustainable and cozy work environment for employees. This case study serves as an excellent illustration of how IoT solutions can enhance the sustainability and operational effectiveness of contemporary buildings.

7.9 Conclusion

Recap of the Importance of Sensors

In today's environment, sensors are essential since they act as the eyes and ears of technology systems for a wide range of uses. These tools are essential for gathering data because they convert physical occurrences into knowledge that can be used. Numerous technologies rely on their capacity to measure and track factors like motion, pressure, temperature, and environmental conditions. Sensors provide real-time insights that promote efficiency, sustainability, and an enhanced quality of life in a variety of applications, including the automation of industrial processes, the development of smart cities, and the widespread use of wearable health devices.

Sensors are the key that binds the digital and physical worlds together in the Internet of Things (IoT) era. Sensors are essential parts of the infrastructure that support intelligent decision-making and smooth device-to-device communication (Patel et al. 2020). Sensors are the unsung heroes that propel innovation and advancement, whether they are used to improve security through surveillance systems, ensure precision agriculture for sustainable food production, or optimize traffic flow in urban areas. Beyond just gathering data, sensors are key players in the development of revolutionary technologies that change the way we work, live, and engage with the world.

Potential for Further Advancements in IoT and Sensors

The Internet of Things (IoT) and sensor technology have enormous room to grow and might completely transform how we use technology, collect data, and make choices. The ongoing improvement and downsizing of sensor technologies is one field with a lot of promise. Sensors that are more compact and energy-efficient will be able to be integrated into a greater variety of devices, which will help the Internet of Things spread to additional consumer and industrial applications. The process of miniaturization has the potential to result in the creation of wearable sensors, which can be easily integrated into apparel or accessories to offer individualized support, activity tracking, and ongoing health monitoring.

The development of edge computing capabilities and sensor networks presents another opportunity for progress. Improvements in communication protocols, like 5G, will make data transport faster and more dependable, which will make it easier to integrate sensors into industrial processes, smart cities, and driverless cars. By integrating edge computing, data processing may be done closer to the source, which lowers latency and speeds up reaction times. This will enable sensors to gather data as well as analyze and draw relevant insights in real time, resulting in more autonomous and efficient systems. It will also combine advances in artificial intelligence and machine learning algorithms.

In conclusion, there will be significant advancements in sensors and IoT in the future. We can expect developments that improve the functionality, dependability, and security of sensors as technology progresses, opening up new avenues for a networked and intelligent society. IoT and sensor technologies working together could change entire industries, boost productivity, and improve our everyday lives in ways we can't even begin to comprehend.

References

Akende SS, Ahaneku MA, Nwawelu UN, Amazue UC, Amoke DA (2022) Improving energy efficiency of wireless sensor networksthrough topology optimization. Int J Emerg Technol Adv Eng. https://doi.org/10.46338/ijetae1222_12

Brida P, Krejcar O, Selamat A, Kertesz A (2021) Smart sensor technologies for IoT, sensors. MDPI. https://doi.org/10.3390/s21175890

El-Azab R (2021) Smart homes: potential and challenges. Clean Energy 5(2). https://doi.org/10.1093/ce/zkab010

Elfring J, Torta E, van de Molengraft R (2021) Particle filters: a hands-on tutorial. MDPI. https://doi.org/10.3390/s21020438

Firouzi F et al (2018) Keynote paper: from EDA to IoT eHealth: promises, challenges, and solutions. IEEE Trans Comput Aided Des Integr Circuits Syst 37(12):2965–2978

Firozi F, Farahani B, Weinberger M, DePace G, Aliee FS (2020) IoT fundamentals: definitions, architecture, challenges and promises. In: Intelligent internet of things

Formica D, Schena E (2021) Smart sensors for healthcare and medical applications, sensors. MDPI. https://doi.org/10.3390/s21020543

Fung ML, Chen MZQ, Chen YH (2017) Sensor fusion: a review of method and applications. In: 2017 29th Chinese control and decision conference (CCDC). IEEE

Hostettler R, Sarkka S (2020) Basics of sensor fusion. Uppsala University, Sweden; Aalto University, Finland

Kim Y, Bang H (2018) Introduction to Kalman filter and its applications. In: Kalman filter. InTechOpen

Kumar A, Stephen K, Sai Sabitha A (2020) A systematic review on sensor fusion technology in autonomous vehicles. In: ICESC 2020

Li Q, Ranyang L, Ji K, Dai W (2015) Kalman filters and its applications. ICINIS. https://doi.org/10.1109/ICINIS.2015.35

Luo RC, Yih C-C (2002) Multisensor fusion and integration: approaches, applications, and future research directions. IEEE Sens J

Patel BC, Sinha GR, Goel N (2020) Introduction to sensors. In: Advances in modern sensors.https://doi.org/10.1088/978-0-7503-2707-7ch1

Ratnaparkhi S, Khan S, Arya C, Khapre S, Singh P, Diwakar M, Shankar A (2020) Smart agriculture sensors in IOT: a review. Mater Today Proc

Sehrawat D, Gill NS (2019) Smart sensors: analysis of different types of IoT sensors. In: 3rd International conference on trends in electronics and informatics (ICOEI). IEEE. https://doi.org/10.1109/ICOEI.2019.8862778

Sharma A, Sharma S, Gupta D (2021) A review of sensors and their application in internet of things (IOT). Int J Comput Appl 174

Tiwari P, Saxena VP, Mishra RG, Bhavsar D (2015) Wireless sensor networks: introduction, advantages, applications and research challenges. HCTL Open Int J Technol Innov Res (IJTIR)

Touqeer H, Zaman S, Amin R, Hussain M, Al-Turjman F, Bilal M (2021) Smart home security: challenges, issues and solutions at different IoT layers. J Supercomput 77:14053–14089

Xu F, Zhang X, Lu Z, Wang S (2022) Design of extended Kalman filtering neural network control system based on particle swarm identification of nonlinear U-model. J Control Meas Electron Comput Commun 63(3)

Yadav P, Gera J, Kaur H (2023) Enhancing the accuracy of collaborative filtering based recommender system with novel similarity measure. Multimed Tools Appl

Yang J, Cui X, Li J, Li S, Liu J, Chen H (2021) Particle Filter algorithm optimized by genetic algorithm combined with particle swarm optimization. Procedia Comput Scic (Elsevier) 187:206–211

Yeong DJ, Velasco-Hernandez G, Barry J, Walsh J (2021) Sensor and sensor fusion technology inautonomous vehicles: a review. https://doi.org/10.20944/preprints202102.0459.v1

Zhaihe Z, Fu J, Lv J, Zhang Q (2018) An improved complementary filter algorithm in the application of the mobile robot attitude estimation. Int J Online Eng

Chapter 8
A Complex Intersection and Sustainable Solution of Smart Cities and Smart Homes: Building a Connected Habitat

Yash Thakur, Varuna Gupta, and Bosco Paul Alapatt

Abstract The ongoing surge in urbanization underscores the critical synergy between smart cities and smart homes as a sustainable solution to contemporary urban challenges. This chapter delves into the complex interplay between these two domains, focusing on the creation of a connected urban habitat. With urban populations on the rise, ensuring liveable conditions within cities has become increasingly intricate. In response, smart cities have emerged, leveraging advanced technology and digital planning to enhance urban liveability and foster sustainability. Central to this vision is the integration of smart homes. Smart homes, equipped with cutting-edge technologies and digital devices, seek to enhance safety, convenience, energy efficiency and sustainability within residential settings. By seamlessly integrating smart homes into the broader framework of smart cities, a holistic approach to urban development can be achieved. This chapter explores the nuances of this integration, examining how smart homes contribute to the overall well-being and quality of life in urban environments. It addresses the challenges and opportunities inherent in building a connected urban habitat, emphasizing the imperative for sustainable urban development practices. By embracing the potential synergies between smart cities and smart homes, we can pave the way for a more connected, efficient and sustainable urban future.

Keywords Urbanization · Smart cities · Smart homes · Sustainable solution

8.1 Introduction

Smart cities are defined by their use of new technology and data-driven decision-making processes, with the objective of improving urban living by promoting efficiency, sustainability and an enhanced quality of life. Meanwhile, smart homes

Y. Thakur · V. Gupta (✉) · B. P. Alapatt
Christ University, Bengaluru, India
e-mail: varunagupta.cs@gmail.com

R. Arya et al. (eds.), *Recent Trends in Artificial Intelligence Towards a Smart World*, Frontiers of Artificial Intelligence, Ethics and Multidisciplinary Applications,
https://doi.org/10.1007/978-981-97-6790-8_8

harness the power of automation, the Internet of Things (IoT), and artificial intelligence to create living spaces that are safer, more energy-efficient and intuitively responsive to residents' needs.

By delving into the foundations of smart cities and smart homes, we uncover the key components and technologies that underpin their functionality. From IoT sensors to big data analytics, from renewable energy integration to AI-driven automation, each element contributes to the vision of a seamlessly connected urban ecosystem.

This chapter examines the ways in which smart homes integrate with the broader smart city framework, offering solutions for resource optimization, environmental monitoring, and enhanced citizen engagement. Real-world examples and case studies illustrate how data from smart homes can inform urban planning, improve public services and create more sustainable and resilient cities.

But along with the promise of a future where everything is linked, there are also difficulties and ethical questions. These include worries about data privacy, security and digital equality. We look at these problems and suggest ways to reduce risks and get the most out of the smart city-smart home relationship.

Ultimately, the intersection of smart cities and smart homes represents a transformative force that has the potential to redefine urban living. As cities continue to evolve and homes become more intelligent, the vision of a connected future emerges—a future where our living spaces seamlessly interact with the urban environment, enhancing our quality of life, conserving resources and fostering sustainability.

Join us on this journey as we explore the intricate tapestry of technologies, innovations, and possibilities at the crossroads of smart cities and smart homes—a journey that is shaping the way we live, work, and thrive in the cities of tomorrow.

8.2 Smart Cities

8.2.1 Understanding Smart Cities

Smart cities are urban areas that use technology, information and communications technology (ICT) and various physical devices connected to the Internet of Things network to improve city services and improve the quality of life of citizens. The basic principles of the smart city are:

1. Connectivity: Seamless communication and exchange of information through strong ICT infrastructure.
2. Sustainability: Efficient use of resources, reducing environmental impact, and ensuring long-term sustainability.
3. Efficiency: Improve city services by analysing data and smart devices to improve quality of life.

8.2.2 Benefits of Smart Cities

Smart cities represent a revolutionary vision for urban development that uses new technologies to improve residents' quality of life and stimulate long-term growth. The benefits of smart cities are many and can solve some of the most pressing challenges facing urban areas today.

Reduce Traffic Congestion: Smart cities use intelligent transportation systems to integrate information from multiple sources to improve traffic flow. Real-time traffic management and signal changes will reduce congestion and shorten working hours, making cities more convenient and less crowded (Advantages and disadvantages of smart cities—Trilliant company).

Improving Air Quality: Smart cities can reduce emissions by using smart grids and encouraging the use of electric vehicles. Sensors monitor air quality, providing valuable information that can be used to develop policies to reduce pollution and improve public health.

Improve Public Safety: Create IoT devices (such as surveillance cameras and emergency systems) and urban security. Data analysis helps police prevent crime and promote faster response time in emergencies.

Economic Growth: Smart cities attract businesses and investment capital by providing a strong framework that supports innovation and entrepreneurship. Efficient use of resources and improvements in public services create a favourable environment for the business world.

Citizen Participation: Smart management ensures citizens' participation in decisions. Digital tools can provide transparency and support collaboration between city government and residents (Thinking about becoming a smart city? 10 benefits of smart cities | Our Insights | Plante Moran).

At its core, the smart city is not about integrating technology into the urban fabric. They aim to redesign the future of urban living to be more efficient, safe and inclusive for everyone.

8.2.3 Applications of IoT in Smart Cities

The smart city concept has become a powerful force that causes rapid changes in cities, and the Internet of Things (IoT) is indispensable for this change. The integration of IoT technology and urban development has changed the operational landscape of the city, promoting sustainability, efficiency and improving the quality of life of citizens.

In the field of smart infrastructure, the smart city principle, and the Internet of Things play an important role (Milosevic et al. 2021). The application of IoT is being considered in the creation of smart grids that support real-time monitoring of energy consumption, integration of renewable energy and optimization of energy distribution. This not only improves energy efficiency but also supports the stability of the city. Additionally, smart buildings use IoT to improve energy management, security, and maintenance. Sensors and actuators in buildings collect information about occupancy, lighting and temperature, enabling control, reducing energy waste and restoring safety.

Urban transportation is undergoing a transformation with the integration of the Internet of Things. Connected vehicles equipped with IoT devices can communicate with infrastructure, alter traffic flow, reduce accidents, and improve safety. Smart parking solutions using IoT sensors direct drivers to parking spaces, reducing traffic and emissions. Public transport increases efficiency and reliability by utilizing real-time tracking and predictive maintenance, making cities flexible and easy to move around (Hudson-Smith et al. 2021).

In the field of public safety and surveillance, IoT increases the security of smart cities through the connection of cameras and sensors. These systems monitor public spaces in real time, detect anomalies, identify patterns, and provide vital information to law enforcement and emergency responders. In emergency management, IoT devices provide real-time data at multiple scales to assist authorities with resource allocation, evacuation planning and response strategies (Tsai et al. 2021).

Effective waste management is important in city planning and IoT makes a great contribution in this field. Sensor-mediated smart equipment optimizes waste management by increasing extraction time, reducing operating costs and improving hygiene and safety (Bashir et al. 2022; Shafi et al. 2022). Additionally, IoT helps make decisions about recycling and reducing waste by promoting environmental sustainability.

Environmental monitoring, which takes advantage of instantaneous data provided by IoT sensors that measure air and water quality, is another important aspect of smart cities. Using this information leads to timely interventions to solve environmental problems and reduce their impact on public health (Karkuzhali and Senthilkumar 2022). Climate control implemented by IoT improves energy efficiency by adjusting heating, ventilation, and air conditioning, thus reducing energy consumption and the environmental footprint of the city.

In healthcare, IoT facilitates remote monitoring of patients and sensors through wearable devices. This not only improves patient care, but also reduces the burden on medical facilities, especially in crowded cities (Bovenizer and Chetthamrongchai 2023). During an epidemic or public health crisis, IoT can help prevent disease tracking and control, provide instant information for countermeasures and improve overall health assessment.

Smart agriculture is a new application of the Internet of Things in urban planning that uses sensors to monitor soil, crop health and weather (Friha 2021). A data-driven approach can increase agricultural productivity, improve resource utilization and increase overall profitability. Integrating smart agriculture into urban planning can help increase local food production, reduce the environmental impact of food transportation and improve food security.

The Internet of Things facilitates urban management and efficiency by tracking assets, allowing cities to better manage vehicles, equipment and construction. Lighting is another application of IoT in urban management, where lighting can adjust its brightness according to instant conditions, improving energy efficiency and safety throughout the city.

Public participation, enhanced by IoT applications that facilitate communication between citizens and governments, is the foundation of smart city development (Gil-Garcia et al. 2020). Smart public services such as mobile stations, public transport information and community engagement are using IoT to improve the overall city experience, supporting greater communication and citizens' participation in improving their environment.

Commerce and hospitality sectors also benefit from smart city IoT technology. Location-based services, personalized recommendations and city discussion guides create a harmonious and comfortable experience for visitors, helping not only the business to grow but also the development of the entire city (Liu et al. 2019).

8.3 Digital Urbanization: IoT Solutions for Smart and Sustainable Cities

8.3.1 Traffic Control Mechanism Using IoT in Smart Cities

Traffic congestion is a major urban problem that affects transportation performance and citizens' quality of life. In the smart city era, the Internet of Things (IoT) has become a powerful tool that will change the traffic management process. Using IoT technology, cities can use smart and powerful solutions to improve traffic flow, reduce congestion and improve mobility (Geda and Motade 2022). This article explores how IoT is revolutionizing smart city traffic management and the various benefits and challenges associated with its implementation.

The use of the Internet of Things (IoT) in vehicle management has introduced many new solutions to increase efficiency and reduce constraints. First, the integration of IoT functionality into the railway signal allows changes to be made according to the timing of traffic. This connection allows signals to be prioritized for specific flows, improving response time, and reducing downtime, thus improving overall traffic flow.

Secondly, IoT-driven smart parking solutions use sensors placed in parking spaces to transmit real-time information about available spaces. Drivers can access this information from their mobile phones, ensuring more efficient and time-saving parking. This will not only improve driving but also help reduce traffic congestion in the city.

In addition, IoT plays an important role in the development of smart vehicle management by integrating various data such as vehicle cameras, sensors and GPS into the central system. Real-time monitoring data allows traffic management agencies to identify congestion points, manage traffic flow and intervene immediately to resolve problems (Elkin and Vyatkin 2020).

In addition, the connection between vehicles and infrastructure is facilitated by the Internet of Things. Cars can communicate with traffic signals, road signs and other devices to create a shared experience. This connectivity provides the best driver support, traffic prediction and rapid recovery, ultimately increasing the efficiency of the road and reducing restrictions.

Additionally, static road signs will be converted into IoT connection signs (Humayun et al. 2022). These signs can display real-time information about traffic, incidents, closures and other methods. The benign nature of these signs helps increase the efficiency and ease of traffic control strategies by increasing driver awareness. Therefore, using IoT in traffic management can help create a more responsive, flexible, and convenient urban transportation system.

8.3.2 Effective Construction Site Monitoring Using AI

Effective construction site monitoring using artificial intelligence (AI) and the Internet of Things (IoT) has transformed the construction industry by improving safety, efficiency and project management. Artificial Intelligence and IoT technologies work together to create a comprehensive system that constantly collects and analyses data from various parts of the construction site.

IoT devices such as sensors, cameras and wearables are being placed all over the construction site. These tools collect real-time data on parameters such as equipment usage (Popov et al. 2017), employee performance, environment, and project performance. The connection between these devices forms the backbone of smart infrastructure, facilitating communication and information exchange.

Artificial Intelligence algorithms process large amounts of data from products created by IoT devices to get recommendations. For example, AI can analyse video from onboard cameras to monitor worker safety, identify hazards and enforce safety procedures. It also reduces the risk of downtime by predicting maintenance equipment needs based on usage patterns.

An important application is predictive analysis of business planning and resource allocation. AI algorithms can analyse historical data and current events to predict potential delays, allowing project managers to make informed decisions quickly. This best approach will help prevent outages and improve resource utilization.

Additionally, artificial intelligence-supported monitoring systems can increase security by detecting unauthorized access or unusual activities at the construction site. This not only protects valuable equipment but also ensures the safety of employees.

The integration of artificial intelligence and IoT in construction site monitoring has changed the way construction is done. Now the information gained from these technologies helps improve security, resource management and overall project success. As the construction industry embraces the era of smart technology, the synergy of artificial intelligence and the Internet of Things continues to drive innovation and excellence in space management.

8.3.3 *Smart Healthcare in Smart Cities (Emerging Trends, Application and Challenges)*

Smart healthcare in smart cities is a topic that deals with the use of Internet of Things (IoT) devices and systems to improve the quality and efficiency of health services and outcomes in urban areas. IoT enables the collection, processing and sharing of data from various sources, such as sensors, wearables, medical devices and mobile applications, to support the diagnosis, treatment, and prevention of diseases, as well as the management of chronic conditions, aging and wellness (Poongodi et al. 2021). In the field of smart healthcare, many developments, and applications in the Internet of Things (IoT) are changing the landscape. One important application is remote patient monitoring (Casaccia et al. 2016), where IoT devices are used to track patients' vital signs, symptoms and activities at home or elsewhere. The collected data will be sent to doctors or supervisors for timely intervention and advice.

In addition, the integration of IoT devices into smart hospitals is optimized in terms of operations and management. These tools track the location and status of medical equipment, staff, and patients, improving the use of resources, reducing errors and contamination, and ultimately increasing patient safety and satisfaction.

Another important application is smart health education. IoT devices facilitate education and training for healthcare professionals and students by providing interactive and hands-on experiments, virtual experiences and usable real and personal advice.

In smart health monitoring, IoT devices generate a wealth of data that can be analysed using artificial intelligence and big data. This analysis provides insights and insights into healthcare decision-making, including areas such as diagnosis, prognosis, treatment and prevention. The growth of IoT applications in smart healthcare reflects the evolution of technology to improve patient care, hospital operations education and awareness, and decision-making in a healthy ecosystem.

8.3.4 *Smart Waste Management System in Smart Cities—Smart Bin*

As smart cities continue to use new technologies, the field of waste management has changed significantly. Thanks to the integration of the Internet of Things (IoT), traditional waste management processes are being transformed into smart, efficient and effective solutions (Sosunova and Porras 2022). An important development in this field is the use of IoT-oriented smart devices. This article explores the role and benefits of smart devices in smart cities and how IoT technology can revolutionize waste management.

The concept of smart garbage is the essence of smart waste management. These bins are equipped with IoT sensors and communication devices that help instantly monitor and manage waste. This integrated technology represents a transition from traditional waste management methods to efficient online waste management.

The operation of the smart trash can includes the following main steps. First, the base is equipped with a variety of sensors, including ultrasonic, weight and level sensors, to constantly monitor the status of the waste inside. The collected data, including fill level, weight and waste type, is then sent to central control using the IoT communication protocol (Ali et al. 2020). The central hub processes incoming data, provides insight into citywide waste, and uses analytics to optimize waste collection and planning. Additionally, smart devices generate automatic alerts or notifications when they reach pre-filled levels, allowing the waste management team to regulate collection times and avoid overtaking, reducing the risk of environmental damage.

The benefits of smart garbage brought by IoT support are many. First, they improve waste collection methods by providing real-time information to waste management agencies. This identifies bins that require immediate attention and improves the collection process, reducing fuel consumption and operating costs. Information generated by smart devices helps allocate resources efficiently, enabling waste management teams to prioritize high-volume products and maximize resource use. In addition, timely alerts from smart devices help prevent water leaks, reduce the risk of waste and improve the cleanliness of the urban environment. This not only beautifies the urban landscape, but also promotes more sustainable waste management. In terms of environmental impact, improving waste management and reducing operating costs is compatible with the green waste management goals of smart cities and helps reduce fuel consumption and greenhouse gases. Data boxes created by smart cities support informed decision-making by analysing big data. Waste management officials can identify trends, predict future waste, and implement effective strategies to solve emerging problems. These optimizations can deliver cost savings and support financial stability for waste management organizations. In addition, the integration of smart devices with social networks increases social awareness by providing information about waste habits, recycling processes and interventions in the environment. This increases public accountability and promotes sustainable waste management practices, in line with the broader goals of smart cities and a healthy environment.

8.3.5 Cybersecurity in Smart Cities

For smart cities using the Internet of Things (IoT), the cybersecurity environment is an important issue that addresses challenges and solutions related to protecting digital and physical infrastructure. Integration of IoT into the urban environment connects various devices, sensors, networks, and systems, enabling the collection, processing and distribution of data across functions such as transportation, electricity, healthcare, public safety and governance (Almeida 2023). While IoT improves efficiency and urban services, it also introduces cybersecurity risks that can compromise data integrity, privacy, public safety and operations throughout the city.

Many of the significant cyber threats facing the smart city using the Internet of Things involve the proliferation and growth of interconnected content. The diversity of IoT devices creates many easy access points for cyber-attacks, posing a threat to city services and critical systems. Additionally, since smart city ecosystems depend on the way ICT equipment is connected, they introduce risks associated with different levels of cybersecurity across different suppliers and service providers. This difference can expose smart cities to criminal activities.

In addition, big data generated by the Internet of Things requires strong data protection and encryption measures. While encryption is important to ensure data confidentiality and integrity, issues such as performance, scalability, and interoperability also need to be addressed. As smart cities continue to use IoT technology, it is important to address these cybersecurity issues to ensure the security and resilience of urban environments.

8.3.6 Smart City Green Monitoring System

Smart city green monitoring systems using the Internet of Things (IoT) represent solutions for sustainable urban development. Addressing the urgent need for environmental awareness and resource development, the system integrates advanced technology, instant data collection and cloud-based analytics to create a platform for monitoring and managing green areas in the city.

At the heart of the system are strategically placed sensors that measure various environmental factors to assess the health of green spaces (Almalki et al. 2023). Sensors include air quality sensors, humidity sensors, temperature and humidity sensors and noise sensors. These sensors are distributed in parks, streets, public spaces and even public transportation, constantly collecting data to create a powerful network (Ramakrishna et al. 2020).

Data collection using efficient and secure IoT communication protocols. In this case, the data is subjected to complex analysis by advanced analysis algorithms. The cloud-based platform acts as the brain, processing a lot of data to provide better information about the state of the city environment.

The user interface is designed as an intuitive control panel that can be used by city authorities, environment lists and individuals. This dashboard visually presents statistical data, providing a clear and detailed overview of the city's green areas (Bibri et al. 2023). It becomes a powerful tool for decision makers to understand the current environment, analyse situations, and make informed choices about resource allocation, management strategies, and security plans.

The benefits of this smart green city monitoring system are diverse. In addition to providing real-time information about air quality, soil health and the general environment, it also helps take important steps towards improving green spaces. As decision makers can prioritize areas that need attention, resource allocation becomes more efficient, thus increasing the efficiency of resource use. City residents benefit from an increased quality of life, and the entire city moves towards a better, more productive future. Essentially, this IoT-powered system becomes the core of the smart city landscape, promoting environmental protection and better living conditions for residents.

8.3.7 Smart Agriculture and Farming

Using the Internet of Things (IoT), smart agriculture is changing traditional agriculture, bringing better results, sustainability and success to the agricultural sector. This new approach involves the integration of electronic technology, data analysis and connectivity to optimize all aspects of agriculture.

Deploy IoT-enabled devices such as sensors and actuators on farms to monitor and collect real-time data on agriculture (Friha 2021). key parameter. Soil moisture sensors, weather stations and crop health sensors provide excellent insight into the environment. This information is then sent to a central location using the IoT communication protocol.

In smart farming, precision agriculture is used to maximize profits. Automatic irrigation systems reduce water waste and increase crop yield by delivering water exactly when and where it is needed, based on data obtained from soil moisture sensors. Drones equipped with sensors and cameras can scan the air and provide farmers with detailed information about the health of crops, pests and the entire region.

Use advanced analytics tools to process and analyse data collected from various IoT devices. Predictive analytics can predict the best planting time, identify crop diseases, and recommend fertilization plans. The decision of this information increases efficiency and reduces resource use, helping to implement permaculture.

In addition, smart agriculture allows remote monitoring. Farmers can control water flow, monitor animal health, and receive real-time alerts from their smartphones or computers. This connection makes it easier to react quickly to changes, intervene in a timely manner and improve the overall management of agriculture.

In summary, smart agriculture using IoT technology has made agriculture data-driven, efficient, and sustainable. By leveraging the power of real-time data and technology, farmers can improve resource use, increase productivity, and contribute to a stable and sustainable agricultural economy.

8.4 Implementation Challenges of IoT for Smart and Sustainable Cities

The use of the Internet of Things (IoT) in smart cities presents challenges that need to be carefully considered to ensure integration and sustainability. The biggest challenge is interoperability, as various IoT devices often run on different models and protocols, causing communication and data exchange between devices to gain and platforms to work hard. Security concerns are important because a large parking area is spread across many connected devices. Preventing cyber threats and ensuring data privacy is the key to smart city installation.

Confidentiality and ethical considerations are also important. The large amounts of data generated by IoT devices often contain sensitive data (Janssen et al. 2019), raising questions about how data is collected, stored and used. Clear and ethical management practices are essential to addressing individual concerns and building public trust. The scalability of IoT infrastructure poses another challenge that must be carefully planned to accommodate more devices and data as cities grow.

High initial cost is the main problem and requires significant investment for the installation of sensors, communication networks and analysis platforms. Regulatory issues, including a lack of regulatory requirements, increase the complexity of implementing IoT. Providing public participation and support for IoT projects is important, as is ensuring transparent communication about the benefits and risks associated with the technology. In addition, energy efficiency considerations, infrastructure planning and data quality management and analysis present additional challenges that smart cities must address to reap the benefits of IoT technology for urban development.

8.5 Smart Homes

8.5.1 Understanding Smart Homes

A smart home is the perfect place to live in a home with connected devices and systems designed to improve comfort, security, energy efficiency and overall quality of life. Unlike traditional homes, smart homes use technologies such as home automation, Internet of Things (IoT), and artificial intelligence (AI) to create an intelligent, connected ecosystem.

Home automation is an important project for the implementation of smart home. Every family. It involves the use of technology to perform and manage a variety of tasks at home and at work. This can include thermostats, lighting, automatic door locks and other devices that can often be monitored and controlled remotely from a central hub or mobile app (Touqeer et al. 2021).

Internet of Things devices in smart buildings because they are interconnected through a network to enable communication and data exchange. These devices include smart thermostats, security cameras, smart appliances and more. The integration of IoT enables the interaction of devices, creating an integrated and responsive environment.

Artificial intelligence further improves the intelligence of smart homes. Artificial intelligence algorithms analyse data from various devices to understand customer preferences, predict patterns and optimize the performance of smart devices. This can include temperature control, personalized lighting, and even equipment monitoring (Ghayvat et al. 2015a, Taiwo and Ezugwu 2021).

Smart homes give residents more control and customization over their living spaces than traditional homes. Residents can manage and monitor their homes remotely, create automated tasks, and receive instant updates on security and energy efficiency. The integration of these technologies not only provides convenience, but also leads to energy savings, increased security, and a more resilient and resilient environment.

8.5.2 Key Components of Smart Homes

Smart homes combine various materials and technologies to create smart living spaces that increase comfort, security and energy efficiency. Key features include smart devices, security connections, electronic controls and voice assistants.

Smart Home Devices

Smart home devices are equipped with sensors, connectivity features and often IoT features. These include refrigerators, stoves, washing machines and more. Remote access via mobile applications allows users to monitor and control these devices from anywhere. For example, a smart oven can preheat the aisle, or a smart refrigerator can provide fresh produce. This level of control makes household chores easier to manage and saves time and energy (Kelly et ai. 2013).

Interconnected Security Systems

Interconnected security systems play an important role in protecting your home security. Smart cameras, sound sensors and smart locks are the main features of the product. These systems provide immediate monitoring and immediate warning in case of abnormal operation. The remote control allows users to lock or unlock doors, monitor access points and receive notifications on their mobile devices. The result is a greater sense of security as residents can monitor and control the security of their home even when they are away.

Energy Management

Energy management tools contribute to the energy efficiency of smart buildings. For example, a smart air conditioner can learn customer preferences and adjust heating or cooling based on occupancy and external conditions. This optimization reduces energy consumption without compromising comfort. Similarly, smart lighting uses sensors to adjust brightness based on occupancy and lighting levels, reducing energy consumption. With real-time monitoring and data analysis, homeowners can make informed decisions about energy use, promoting sustainability and cost savings.

Voice Assistant

Assistive Assistants such as Amazon Alexa, Google Assistant or Apple's Siri form the basis of smart home management. They allow users to interact with various devices using commands. Voice control automation makes work easier by allowing users to operate multiple devices simultaneously. For example, you can adjust the temperature, dim the lights and play music with a simple voice command. Voice helps simplify the user experience, making it easier to understand and understand.

8.5.3 Benefits of Smart Home

Convenience

Smart homes offer unparalleled convenience thanks to remote access and automation. Residents can control devices, set preferences, and control home functions via smartphones or voice speakers. Automation allows creating scenes and routines, such as waking up in a preheated house or arriving in a well-lit interior.

Enhanced Security

An integrated security system provides instant monitoring, alerts and remote control to enhance home security. Residents can monitor access points, receive alerts about suspicious activity, and control access through smart locks. These features help promote a sense of security and peace of mind (Lundgren and Padyab 2022, Nag and Mukhopadhyay 2015).

Energy Efficiency

Energy management devices optimize resource use and reduce energy consumption without compromising comfort. Smart heating and lighting improves safety by adapting to the user's behaviour and the environment. The ability to monitor current energy usage allows users to make informed decisions that save costs and reduce environmental impact.

Maximize Value

Integration of smart home devices can increase the overall value of the property. Home buyers are increasingly looking for homes with features such as modern appliances that add to the appeal and functionality of the property.

Daily Life Experience

Smart home provides daily life experience and connectivity. Seamless integration of technology creates an environment where tools work harmoniously and respond to user needs and preferences. This modern lifestyle follows the changing expectations of people living in a technological world.

Sustainable Development

The energy-saving features of smart buildings contribute to sustainable development. Smart buildings are aligned with environmental goals by increasing energy efficiency, reducing waste and participating in environmental practices. Focusing on sustainability is becoming more important as people look for ways to reduce their carbon footprint.

8.6 IoT Devices and Privacy Concerns: Safeguarding the Connected Home

- *Privacy issues*
  Smart devices collect and process information to provide personal information. Privacy issues arise when this information is misused or unauthorized access occurs (Pirbhulal et al. 2017). To address these issues, developers need to prioritize strong privacy policies, documentation, and user agreements.
- *Network security risks*
  The connection of smart homes increases the risk of network security (Suryadevara et al. 2015; Suryadevara and Mukhopadhyay 2013) . Vulnerabilities in a device or network can be exploited and, as a result, unauthorized or controlled. Strong encryption, regular software updates and secure network configuration are crucial to mitigating these risks.
- *Data security*
  The data produced by smart homes (including personal preferences and usage patterns) is important. Ensuring that this information is stored and transmitted securely is important to prevent unauthorized access or misuse.
- *Standardization and regulation*
  The lack of standard security protocols across devices and platforms creates problems. Compliance with industry-wide industry standards and strong regulatory frameworks can help ensure that smart home devices comply with high security standards.

In summary, while the smart home provides significant benefits in terms of energy savings, security, comfort and accessibility, concerns about privacy and cybersecurity are also important. Business stakeholders, including manufacturers and regulators, play an important role in developing and maintaining security systems to provide confidence and support for the use of smart home devices.

8.7 Complex Intersection of Smart Cities and Smart Homes

8.7.1 Interconnected Technologies: The Rise of the Internet of Things (IoT)

Smart buildings can be integrated into a wider smart city and help create a connected, smart city. The key to this integration is information sharing and collaboration (Khatib et al. 2023).

8.7.2 Data Sharing

Smart homes generate large amounts of data on energy consumption, living arrangements and user preferences. Valuable insights can be gained by sharing this information with the larger smart city. For example, data collected by smart buildings can inform city planners about peak energy usage times, helping to improve energy efficiency and reduce overall consumption. Information sharing now enables cities to respond to events such as environmental or emergencies.

8.7.3 Interoperability

Interoperability is an important factor for creating a unified smart home and smart city ecosystem. It involves ensuring that different devices and systems can communicate and work together seamlessly. A good way to communicate protocol and data input is important. For example, smart home heating systems should interact with the city's electrical grid, allowing them to adapt to citywide energy needs.

8.7.4 Grid Optimization

Smart buildings can contribute to the optimization of city planning. Smart homes can help balance energy supply and demand by sharing information about energy consumption patterns and responding to demand. This optimization not only increases energy efficiency but also supports the city's sustainability goals.

8.7.5 *Traffic and Transportation Management*

Data obtained from smart buildings, such as housing models and transportation preferences, can be used for better traffic and traffic management transportation. Integrated systems can provide instant information about traffic conditions, improve public transport and improve overall mobility in the city.

8.7.6 *Environmental Monitoring*

Smart buildings can play a role in environmental monitoring by sharing information on air quality, temperature and other parameters. Environmental information from various smart buildings can help better understand the city's environment and enable timely intervention to solve pollution or air problems.

8.8 Case Study

Smart buildings play an important role in fast tracking of smart cities' goals such as energy saving, waste management and emergency response. The following case study in Table 8.1 shows how a smart home can affect these areas.

This case study shows that smart city and smart home technology can work together to create an efficient, safe, and connected urban environment.

8.8.1 *Implementation Challenges and Considerations*

Data Privacy

The integration of smart homes and smart cities raises serious concerns about data privacy. The widespread collection of personal information, from routine activities to preferences, raises questions about how this information is stored, shared and used.

Vulnerabilities

The interaction of smart buildings has vulnerabilities that can be exploited by cybercriminals. Security breaches can lead to unauthorized access to sensitive data or control of smart home devices.

Digital Divide

The use of technology at home is likely to widen the digital divide because not everyone has the same level or knowledge of this technology. This will create a gap between benefits and opportunities.

Table 8.1 Case study of impact of smart city and smart home in different areas

Company	Country	Smart city initiatives	Smart home initiatives
Songdo International Business District	South Korea	Songdo is a planned smart city with advanced technology for efficient energy management, waste treatment and transportation (Discover Songdo, the $35 billion South Korean city built to banish cars—interesting engineering)	Residents of the building have access to a smart home with lighting, heating and security features connected to the entire city system
Amsterdam	Netherlands	This includes smart parking, waste management and energy efficiency	The entire system of the city, such as lighting, heating and security, is interconnected
Singapore	–	Integrating traffic management, public safety and environmental protection	Combine smart home features with energy-efficient lighting, smart home security, and integration with public transportation
Dubai	UAE	First-of-its-kind smart transportation, city-wide Wi-Fi and blockchain services (https://www.weforum.org/agenda/2021/04/how-blockchain-can-empower-smart-cities-gtgs21/) Residential developments in Dubai often feature	Smart home technology for climate control, lighting and security improves overall city living
Copenhagen	Denmark	Focus on becoming a carbon neutral city with smart solutions for waste management, efficient public transport and green spaces	–
Barcelona	Spain	Most smart cities have smart parking, waste management and city Wi-Fi	Many areas of Barcelona are using smart home technology to improve energy efficiency, home security and seamless connections to city services (https://www.digitaltrends.com/home/barcelona-smart-city-technology/)

Thinking about justice

- *Data Privacy*
  Protecting personal privacy is critical to maintaining trust in the smart city.
- *Security*
  Smart home security is crucial to prevent privacy breaches and unauthorized access.
- *Digitization*

Achieving unity and addressing the digital divide is crucial to prevent further conflict.

- *Privacy Policy*
  Clarify and enforce the right to privacy. Smart cities need to clearly state that data is collected, processed, and shared and obtain consent from users.

Strong Security Measures

Implement strong cybersecurity measures, including regular access and software updates, to protect the smart home from its ability to weatherize. Regular audits and compliance checks are necessary to ensure ongoing security.

Inclusive Access

Promote inclusion by ensuring smart city plans are designed to be accessible to all economic groups. Use programs to provide training and support to individuals who may have difficulty using smart home devices.

Data Anonymization and Collection

Advanced data anonymization and collection technologies to reduce the risk of personal privacy leaks. Aggregate, anonymous data can also provide insights into urban planning without compromising privacy.

Community Engagement

Involve the community in decision-making. Make recommendations, solve problems, and communicate with residents under the guidance of smart city leaders. This partnership promotes understanding among members and ensures that the benefits of technology are shared equally.

8.8.2 Urban Planning and Residential Design

The integration of smart technologies is changing urban planning and housing construction and leading to the development of smart cities and smart buildings.

Incorporating Smart Technologies in City Planning

Smart city planning uses technology to improve quality of life, sustainability and resilience while encouraging innovation and collaboration. Integration of Internet of Things (IoT) devices can collect data instantly, increasing the speed and ability to quickly mobilize, repair and adapt. This includes monitoring and managing traffic and transport, electricity and water, waste management, information systems, schools, libraries and hospitals. The European Union (EU) has identified eight key elements that define smart cities: smart management, smart energy, smart building, smart mobility, smart construction, technology, medical smart and public smart.

Architectural Considerations for Smart Homes

Smart home design requires attention to the connection between technology and important functions such as security and energy efficiency. Home automation is an important part of building a smart home and involves using technology to perform and manage various tasks in the home. IoT devices are connected through networks to enable communication and data exchange, creating an integrated and responsive environment. These devices include smart thermostats, security cameras, smart appliances and more.

Community-Wide Smart Initiatives

Smart ideas in society are reshaping the urban landscape, creating a smarter, safer and more liveable city. For example, nine independent electricity, heating and water companies in Jutland, Denmark, collaborated to create a common database that allows experts to use big data to improve operations and maintenance. This new material allows electricity, heating, and water connections to be operated with as little expense as possible. It also improves infrastructure.

In short, the integration of smart technology in urban planning and housing construction paves the way for the development of smart cities and smart buildings, improves the quality of life of urban residents and promotes the development of cities.

8.9 Conclusion

This chapter highlights the evolution of smart cities and smart buildings in shaping the future of urban living. Using technologies such as the Internet of Things (IoT), data analysis and artificial intelligence, innovations need to increase efficiency, sustainability and deliver a better life for people. Smart infrastructure, urban transportation, public safety, waste management and health are considered as the main areas to benefit from increases at this level.

The need for collaboration between government agencies, industry stakeholders and the public to unlock the full potential of smart technology is a recurring theme. Transparency, inclusivity, and protection of privacy are important in the design and implementation of these solutions. This chapter emphasizes that inclusivity is necessary to ensure that smart city projects are fair, safe, and meet the needs of different communities in the city.

When we look to the future, the future of smart cities and smart homes will be more integrated, more independent from artificial intelligence and stability oriented. As technology continues to evolve, continued collaboration and ethical engagement will be critical to navigating changing urban development patterns and enabling technology. This technology improves life in the city.

References

Advantages and disadvantages of smart cities—Trilliant company. primestone.com

Ali T, Irfan M, Alwadie AS et al (2020) IoT-based smart waste bin monitoring and municipal solid waste management system for smart cities. Arab J Sci Eng 45:10185–10198

Almalki FA, Alsamhi SH, Sahal R et al (2023) Green IoT for eco-friendly and sustainable smart cities: future directions and opportunities. Mobile Netw Appl 28:178–202

Almeida F (2023) Prospects of cybersecurity in smart cities. Future Internet 15:285

Bashir MR, Gill AQ, Beydoun G (2022) A reference architecture for IoT-enabled smart buildings. SN Comput Sci 3:493

Bibri SE, Alexandre A, Sharifi A et al (2023) Environmentally sustainable smart cities and their converging AI, IoT, and big data technologies and solutions: an integrated approach to an extensive literature review. Energy Inform 6:9

Bovenizer W, Chetthamrongchai P (2023) A comprehensive systematic and bibliometric review of the IoT-based healthcare systems. Cluster Comput 26:3291–3317. https://doi.org/10.1007/s10586-023-04047-1

Casaccia S, Pietroni F, Calvaresi A, Revel GM, Scalise L (2016) Smart monitoring of user's health at home: performance evaluation and signal processing of a wearable sensor for the measurement of heart rate and breathing rate. https://doi.org/10.5220/0005694901750182

Discover Songdo, the $35 billion South Korean city built to banish cars—interesting engineering

El Khatib M, Ahmed G, Alshurideh M, Al-Nakeeb A (2023) Interdependencies and integration of smart buildings and smart cities: a case of Dubai. In: Alshurideh M, Al Kurdi BH, Masa'deh R, Alzoubi HM, Salloum S (eds) The effect of information technology on business and marketing intelligence systems. Studies in computational intelligence, vol 1056. Springer, Cham

Elkin D, Vyatkin V (2020) IoT in traffic management: review of existing methods of road traffic regulation. In: Silhavy R (ed) Applied informatics and cybernetics in intelligent systems. CSOC 2020. Advances in intelligent systems and computing, vol 1226. Springer, Cham

Friha O, Ferrag MA, Shu L, Maglaras L, Wang X (2021) Internet of things for the future of smart agriculture: a comprehensive survey of emerging technologies. IEEE/CAA J Autom Sinica 8(4):718–752. https://doi.org/10.1109/JAS.2021.1003925

Geda P, Motade S (2022) Traffic management system using AI and IoT. In: Chakravarthy VVSSS, Flores-Fuentes W, Bhateja V, Biswal B (eds) Advances in micro-electronics, embedded systems and IoT. Lecture notes in electrical engineering, vol 838. Springer, Singapore

Ghayvat H, Liu J, Mukhopadhyay SC, Gui X (2015a) Wellness sensor networks: a proposal and implementation for smart home for assisted living. IEEE Sens J 15:7341–7348

Ghayvat H, Liu J, Alahi MEE, Mukhopadhyay SC, Gui X (2015b) Internet of things for smart homes and buildings: opportunities and challenges. Aust J Telecommun Digit Econ 3:33–47

Gil-Garcia JR, Pardo TA, Gasco-Hernandez M (2020) Internet of things and the public sector. In: Gil-Garcia JR, Pardo TA, Gasco-Hernandez M (eds) Beyond smart and connected governments. Public administration and information technology, vol 30. Springer, Cham. https://doi.org/10.1007/978-3-030-37464-8_1

https://www.digitaltrends.com/home/barcelona-smart-city-technology/

https://www.weforum.org/agenda/2021/04/how-blockchain-can-empower-smart-cities-gtgs21/

Hudson-Smith A, Wilson D, Gray S, Dawkins O (2021) Urban IoT: advances, challenges, and opportunities for mass data collection, analysis, and visualization. In: Shi W, Goodchild MF, Batty M, Kwan MP, Zhang A (eds) Urban informatics. The urban book series. Springer, Singapore. https://doi.org/10.1007/978-981-15-8983-6_38

Humayun M, Afsar S, Almufareh MF, Jhanjhi NZ, AlSuwailem M (2022) Smart traffic management system for metropolitan cities of kingdom using cutting edge technologies. J Adv Transp 2022, Article ID 4687319, 13

Janssen M, Luthra S, Mangla S, Rana NP, Dwivedi YK (2019) Challenges for adopting and implementing IoT in smart cities: an integrated MICMAC-ISM approach. Internet Res 29(6):1589–1616. https://doi.org/10.1108/INTR-06-2018-0252

Karkuzhali S, Senthilkumar S (2022) Role of artificial intelligence and IoT in environmental monitoring—a survey. In: Paul PK, Choudhury A, Biswas A, Singh BK (eds) Environmental informatics. Springer, Singapore. https://doi.org/10.1007/978-981-19-2083-7_8

Kelly SDT, Suryadevara NK, Mukhopadhyay SC (2013) Towards the implementation of IoT for environmental condition monitoring in homes. IEEE Sens J 13:3846–3853

Liu C, Balestrini M, Vilaza GN (2019) From social to civic: public engagement with IoT in places and communities. In: Soro A, Brereton M, Roe P (eds) Social internet of things. Internet of Things. Springer, Cham. https://doi.org/10.1007/978-3-319-94659-7_10

Lundgren M, Padyab A (2022) Security and privacy of smart homes: issues and solutions. In: Security and privacy in the internet of things: architectures, techniques, and applications. IEEE, pp 235–260. https://doi.org/10.1002/9781119607755.ch9

Milosevic D, Milošević M, Simjanović DJ (2021) A comparative study of FAHP with type-1 and interval type-2 fuzzy sets for ICT implementation in smart cities. https://doi.org/10.1007/978-3-030-85577-2_97

Nag A, Mukhopadhyay SC (2015) Occupancy detection at smart home using real time dynamic thresholding of flexiforce sensor. IEEE Sens J 15:4457–4463

Pandya S, Ghayvat H, Kotecha K, Awais M, Akbarzadeh S, Gope P, Mukhopadhyay SC, Chen W (2018) Smart home anti-theft system: a novel approach for near real-time monitoring and smart home security for wellness protocol. Appl Syst Innov 1:42

Pirbhulal S, Zhang H, EAlahi ME, Ghayvat H, Mukhopadhyay SC, Zhang YT, Wu W (2017) A novel secure IoT-based smart home automation system using a wireless sensor network. Sensors 17:69

Poongodi M, Sharma A, Hamdi M et al (2021) Smart healthcare in smart cities: wireless patient monitoring system using IoT. J Supercomput 77:12230–12255

Popov M, Fedorovsky O, Stankevich S, Filipovich V, Khyzhniak A, Piestova I, Lubskyi MS, Svideniuk M (2017) Remote sensing technologies and geospatial modelling hierarchy for smart city support. https://doi.org/10.5194/isprs-annals-iv-5-w1-51-2017

Ramakrishna VA, Chamoli U, Rajan G, Mukhopadhyay SC, Prusty BG, Diwan AD (2020) Smart orthopaedic implants: a targeted approach for continuous postoperative evaluation in the spine. J Biomech 104:109690

Shafi Q, Elkamel A, Shareefdeen Z (2022) Application of internet of things (IoT) in waste management. In: Shareefdeen Z (ed) Hazardous waste management. Springer, Cham. https://doi.org/10.1007/978-3-030-95262-4_12

Sosunova I, Porras J (2022) IoT-enabled smart waste management systems for smart cities: a systematic review. IEEE Access 10:73326–73363. https://doi.org/10.1109/ACCESS.2022.3188308

Suryadevara NK, Mukhopadhyay SC, Wang R, Rayudu RK (2013) Forecasting the behavior of an elderly using wireless sensors data in a smart home. Eng Appl Artif Intell 26:2641–2652

Suryadevara NK, Mukhopadhyay SC, Kelly SDT, Gill SPS (2015) WSN-based smart sensors and actuator for power management in intelligent buildings. IEEE Trans Mechatron 20:564–571

Taiwo O, Ezugwu AE (2021) Internet of things-based intelligent smart home control system. Secur Commun Netw 2021, Article ID 9928254, 17

Thinking about becoming a smart city? 10 benefits of smart cities | Our Insights | Plante Moran

Touqeer H, Zaman S, Amin R et al (2021) Smart home security: challenges, issues and solutions at different IoT layers. J Supercomput 77:14053–14089

Tsai S-B, Gupta BB, Agrawal DP, Wu W, Liu A (2021) Recent advances in intelligent transportation systems for cloud-enabled smart cities. J Adv Transp 2021, Article ID 9792543, 2. https://doi.org/10.1155/2021/9792543

Chapter 9
Customized CNN-Based Condition Monitoring of Road Traffic for Intelligent Transportation Routing

U. Penchalaiah, Suman Mishra, B. Hari Krishna, G. Udaya Sree, and N. Soumya

Abstract This study wants to make road traffic monitoring better by using a complete way that includes many necessary tasks. The study begins by carefully fixing the images to improve the quality of the seen information. Sophisticated deep learning methods are then used to spot helmets using computer vision. This makes road safety better by finding people wearing helmets. The study also investigates getting car license plates. It uses a mix of image processing and advanced ways to read letters and numbers in images to get correct identification. Counting cars, a key part of studying traffic movement is done using advanced computer vision techniques. These methods use hard algorithms to dependably find and count cars in images. The research not only numbers but also uses machine learning to sort cars into different types. This helps us understand more about the make-up of traffic. Hidden Markov Models (HMMs) are used in time study to get features from video data. This helps us find and study patterns in a row, and changes. This makes understanding how a car moves over time better. To make road traffic sorting better, a new type of Custom Hierarchical Convolutional Neural Network (HCNN) is suggested. This HCNN uses the good parts of 1D and 2D CNNs. It can get important features from

U. Penchalaiah (✉)
Geetanjali Institute of Science and Technology, Nellore, Andhra Pradesh, India
e-mail: penchal.upr@gmail.com; upenchalaiah@gist.edu.in

S. Mishra
CMR Engineering College, Hyderabad, Telangana, India
e-mail: emailssuman@gmail.com

B. Hari Krishna · G. Udaya Sree · N. Soumya
St. Martins Engineering College, Kompally, Hyderabad, Telangana, India
e-mail: drhariece@smec.ac.in

G. Udaya Sree
e-mail: gudayasreeece@smec.ac.in

N. Soumya
e-mail: nsoumyaece@smec.ac.in

R. Arya et al. (eds.), *Recent Trends in Artificial Intelligence Towards a Smart World*,
Frontiers of Artificial Intelligence, Ethics and Multidisciplinary Applications,
https://doi.org/10.1007/978-981-97-6790-8_9

both image and video data in a big way. The use of HCNN helps make the identification of vehicle types better, which leads to smarter study of road traffic situations. This study's findings are very important for smart transport systems, city planning and traffic control.

Keywords Convolutional neural network · Traffic condition monitoring · Intelligent transportation routing · Smart cities · Machine learning · Traffic flow optimization

9.1 Introduction

Advances in managing road traffic conditions for intelligent transport modes are closely linked to improvements in transportation infrastructure and embedded technologies to improve efficiency and improve safety are beginning to be explored as much as possible using lean (Ranyal et al. 2022; Rajput et al. 2022). More with traffic signal control technologies Management of junctions was enhanced by enabling dynamic and responsive control. Advances in information technology in the 1980s led to the integration of sensors and cameras into traffic systems. This provided authorities with real-time information on road conditions (Jahan et al. 2022).

The growth of the Internet in the 1990s and the widespread use of digital technologies caused smart transportation systems to quickly advance. As the power to gather and handle data got better, traffic control systems became more complex. Using things like sensors and monitoring tools, we can now watch stuff like traffic jams, how fast cars go, and how crowded roads are. This has made the idea of knowing what's happening more noticeable. In the twenty-first century, smart transport systems have grown quickly. Many mobile apps and other sources of information are now easy to join. This helps us get a better idea of what's happening on the roads. Now, condition monitoring has grown to use guessing systems which help leaders see accidents ahead, find possible problems and quickly change traffic paths (Hijji et al. 2023; Kohm et al. 2023). Today, checking road traffic conditions for smart travel options is a tricky thing. It involves using current information from many places to make clear and quick directions for people. The increase in smart cities comes from a strong promise to use creativity to make transport systems better (Ramesh et al. 2022; Singh et al. 2021a). The goal is to make a safe, fast and green city transportation system. This dedication to the history of this tech is clear. In this paper, there are several impressive things done. They are as follows: The study gives a complete way to combine monitoring helmets, automatic number plate recognition (ALPR), counting and classifying cars to better guess how busy the roads are.

Precise image preparation methods are used to improve the quality of data, resulting in more accurate results in the following tasks.

- The work uses HMMs to extract features from video data, effectively capturing the temporal dynamics and sequential patterns in vehicle movement.

- A HCNN is proposed, combining the advantages of both 1D and 2D CNNs to improve the precision of vehicle categorization and provide a more detailed examination of traffic composition.
- The study goes beyond basic vehicle counting and explores vehicle categorization, which enhances the analysis of road traffic situations and assists in making educated decisions for urban planning and traffic management.
- The use of helmet detection enhances road safety by recognizing persons who are wearing helmets, providing vital information for programmes focused on improving general road safety.

9.2 Literature Survey

Kuo and others (2022) developed a robust mathematical framework for quality control of wind turbines. Their method incorporates several features, providing comprehensive and immediate analysis to improve the operational reliability of wind power systems. This method plays an important role in the optimization of renewable energy production. But wind turbine blades have problems in predicting and understanding accurately and understanding complex and ever-changing conditions. Bachechi et al. (2022) present sophisticated methods of big data analysis and visualization specially optimized for traffic management applications available bae. The advantage is the ability to extract important patterns from broad data sets, while there are technical challenges in analysing large traffic data in real time.

Anjaia and others (2022) developed an ALPR system specifically designed to detect helmetless motorcyclists. Their approach using machine learning algorithms enhances road safety by accurately detecting violations and facilitating timely enforcement. The benefits of the algorithms depend on how effective they are better at detecting violations but may have potential drawbacks when used in challenging traffic conditions in the real world. Charran and Dubey (2022) developed a singular computerized ticketing system especially tailor-made to address traffic offences by-wheeler motors inside the context of Indian avenue conditions. Their approach combines advanced transport generation and computer vision to offer efficient and automatic ticketing. While striving to improve the enforcement of traffic policies, there are difficulties in ensuring that the gadget can take care of a big variety of users and minimising the prevalence of incorrect detections with a purpose to maintain the machine's dependability. Liu (2023) created a utility and completed an intensive technical study with a selected emphasis on monitoring the extent to which riders adhere to helmet-sporting requirements. The system's goal is to enhance safety by way of ensuring ordinary compliance with helmet regulations. Nevertheless, there are problems that arise whilst setting the system into practice in the actual world, namely in making certain the precision and dependability of the tracking device underneath numerous environmental situations and traffic conditions.

Kumar et al. (2023a) evolved a system that could identify motorcyclists who are not wearing helmets and retrieve the licence plate numbers. Their method is to improve avenue safety via the enforcement of helmet legal guidelines and the implementation of licence plate recognition technology. Nevertheless, problems occur in precisely detecting hid licence plates and guaranteeing the machine's immediate practicality. Singh et al. (2022b) finished research on helmet and ALPR with the use of deep studying, offering a comparative evaluation. Their method is to enhance the general management of traffic and enforcement of legal guidelines. The gain lies in the thorough observe, but the model is designed to accommodate. Waris et al. (2022) created a CNN version to pick out instances of helmet infringement in motorcyclists, subsequently enhancing sensible transportation structures. The gadget improves avenue safety through successfully detecting and punishing times of helmet non-compliance. The demanding situations encompass the optimization of the model for real-global conditions and the resolution of possible times of wrong high-quality identifications.

Premmaran and Sathishkumar (2022) supplied a method that makes use of gadget learning to become aware of motorcyclists who are not wearing helmets and to execute ALPR. The approach enhances road protection and permits automated law enforcement. Nevertheless, there are questions about the precision, mainly in destructive weather and illumination instances. Aswini and Hegde (2023) designed an actual time traffic monitoring machine using You Only Look at Once (YOLO)-V5 model. Their method utilizes modern-day deep gaining knowledge of methods to enhance accuracy and enable real-time application. The machine's efficiency is its principal benefit, but there are boundaries in adjusting the model to various traffics' occasions and ensuring scalability. Sreeja et al. (2023) advanced a traffic violation detection and caution machine for motorcycles with the use of YOLO-V3, a deep learning approach. Nevertheless, the device's capability to handle difficult traffic' conditions and assure on the spot reaction.

Choudhari et al. (2023) evolved a machine for detecting traffic rule violations using the Detectron2 and YOLO-V7 frameworks. Their method consists of state-of-the-art item identity algorithms to provide unique and brief detection of violations. Nevertheless, the gadget is designed to evolve to convert traffic' circumstances and offer prompt processing of records. Kishore et al. (2023) used artificial intelligence to identify traffic' infractions devoted by using motorcycles. Their technique complements the implementation of automatic regulation enforcement and enhances street safety. Nevertheless, the version's capacity to address various traffic occasions and substantial moral worries. Gomathy et al. (2023) advanced an artificial intelligence-based technique to realize helmets on-wheelers and generate consequences. Their method is the implementation of helmet laws and the imposition of consequences for non-adherence. Tippannavar and Yashwanth (2023) carried out an evaluation of methodologies used for real-time vehicle identity to enhance traffic control systems. Their thorough analysis gives valuable views on exclusive identity strategies and their suitability. One of the demanding situations is to combine several figuring out systems right into a unified gadget to provide efficient traffic management.

Ghadekar et al. (2022) enhanced the accuracy and applicability of a helmet detection model by using YOLO-V5. Their methodology contributes to more reliable helmet detection for improved road safety. Challenges involve optimizing the model for real-world scenarios and addressing potential false positives. Pujar and Kulkarni (2022) explored ALPR using machine learning. Their approach aims to enhance vehicle identification and contribute to automated law enforcement. However, the system is for diverse environmental conditions and ensuring accuracy in license plate recognition. Chythanya et al. (2022) developed a deep learning and Internet of Things (IoT)-based system for driver helmet detection and bike ignition check updates. Their methodology integrates IoT for real-time updates on helmet compliance. Challenges include ensuring the seamless integration of IoT components and addressing potential communication delays.

Ghosh et al. (2023) proposed a smart helmet detection system with e-challan issuance for traffic fines using deep learning. Their approach contributes to automated penalty enforcement for traffic violations. However, potential false positives and ensuring the system's reliability in real-world scenarios. Chen et al. (2022) focused on helmet-wearing detection of motorcycle drivers using a deep learning network with residual transformer-spatial attention. Their methodology aims to improve accuracy in detecting helmet compliance. However, the model for real-world scenarios and addressing potential false negatives. Arshad and Kumar (2022) implemented a system for the detection of two-wheeler traffic rule violations using deep learning. Their methodology aims to enhance traffic monitoring and contribute to improved law enforcement. However, the model for various traffic scenarios and ensuring real-time applicability. Bouhayane et al. (2023) developed a Swin Transformer-based system for motorcycle helmet detection, contributing to advanced object detection techniques. The advantage lies in the model's potential for accurate and efficient helmet detection. Challenges involve adapting the system to diverse environmental conditions and ensuring scalability.

Arshad and Prasanthi focused on the detection and identification of non-helmet riders and their license plate numbers. Their approach contributes to comprehensive traffic monitoring and law enforcement. However, potential inaccuracies in license plate recognition and optimizing the model for real-world scenarios. Wei et al. (2023) proposed a fast helmet and license plate detection system based on the lightweight YOLO-V5. Their methodology aims to improve the speed and efficiency of detection while maintaining accuracy. However, the model for real-world scenarios addresses potential trade-offs between speed and accuracy. Devi et al. (2022) explored license plate detection of motorcyclists without helmets. Their approach aims to contribute to law enforcement and road safety. However, accuracy concerns, especially in challenging weather and lighting conditions. Anoop et al. (2022) created a system for monitoring traffic and identifying criminals by using image processing techniques and deep learning algorithms. Their approach incorporates cutting-edge technology to achieve thorough traffic surveillance and criminal identification. Nevertheless, the technology is designed to handle real-world situations and tackle any ethical concerns. Kumar et al. (2023b) developed an ALPR system using Artificial Intelligence. Their methodology aids in improving vehicle identification and law enforcement. Nevertheless, the technology is designed to accommodate various climatic circumstances and guarantee precision in licence plate identification.

Gupta et al. (2023) concentrated on identifying number plates in automobiles by using a deep learning-based image labeler model. Their technique is to enhance the automation of law enforcement and traffic management. Nevertheless, there were possible discrepancies in licence plate identification and the need to optimize the model for real-world situations. Saini et al. (2022) investigated the detection of helmets worn by motorcyclists and seat belts used by drivers of four-wheelers. Their methodology enhances the scope of traffic surveillance and enforcement of regulations. Nevertheless, there were possible discrepancies in object detection and the need to optimize the model for real-world situations. Paul et al. (2022) used deep learning techniques to do image analysis for a sophisticated traffic management system. Their methodology incorporates cutting-edge technology to enhance traffic control and law enforcement. Nevertheless, the technology is designed to handle real-world situations and tackle possible ethical concerns. Mercado Reyna et al. (2023) used a CNN to identify whether motorbike drivers had been wearing helmets. An inherent technological challenge turned into the model's susceptibility to overall performance fluctuations when uncovered to specific lights and weather conditions, which affected its capability to characteristic reliably in actual international conditions. Peña Cáceres et al. (2022) devised a way of the usage of YOLO to pick out motorcyclists who aren't sporting a safety helmet. A significant challenge of the model was its susceptibility to noise or fake positives, necessitating meticulous adjustment to minimize those instances and improve precision.

Shambharkar et al. (2023) added an automated gadget for ALPR using Optical Character Recognition (OCR) and deep mastering. An inherent technological impediment turned into the gadget's ability to accurately technique licence plates that were deformed or hidden, as a result affecting its dependability in real-existence situations. Parikh et al. (2022) developed an automatic helmet detection technique with the usage of YOLO-V3. Bhavsar et al. (2023) performed a visual analysis of road traffic and infractions using footage captured by unmanned aerial vehicles (UAVs). An issue that might arise is the precision of the vision-based system in accurately detecting and recognizing individual traffic offences. This would need further adjustments to ensure accurate analysis. Lee et al. (2022) investigated the patterns in smart helmets equipped with several sensing capabilities to monitor health and ensure safety. However, the integration and synchronization of diverse sensors, ensuring real-time data processing and system responsiveness. Nijim et al. (2023) proposed an advanced traffic management system for smart cities. However, the scalability of the system and its adaptability to dynamic urban environments necessitate careful consideration of deployment scenarios.

Tiwari et al. (2023) developed a real-time traffic surveillance and detection system using deep learning and computer vision. However, the system's performance in handling occlusions or complex traffic scenarios, impacting its overall reliability. Teja et al. (2023) conducted a comparative analysis of optimizers and transfer learning methods for headgear detection using CNN. A technical challenge was the generalization of the model across diverse headgear types, requiring robust feature extraction for accurate detection. Akinsemoyin et al. (2023) explored unmanned aerial systems and deep learning for safety and health activity monitoring on construction sites. However, the integration of aerial systems with deep learning models, ensuring accurate monitoring in dynamic construction environments.

9.2.1 Research Motivation

The motivation behind this research stems from the pressing need to address the escalating challenges associated with urban transportation. As cities worldwide grapple with increasing population density and expanding vehicular traffic, traditional transportation systems are strained, leading to congestion, delays, and environmental concerns. Recognizing the transformative potential of intelligent transportation systems, our research seeks to contribute to the ongoing efforts to optimize traffic flow and enhance urban mobility.

The motivation is further fuelled by the evolution of information and communication technologies, which offer unprecedented opportunities for real-time data collection and analysis. The integration of sensors, global position system (GPS), and communication networks provides a wealth of information about road conditions, traffic patterns, and user behavior. Utilizing this data to create an intelligent transportation routing system has the potential to not only mitigate traffic congestion, but also enhance overall road safety and minimize environmental harm.

Moreover, the rising frequency of smart cities and the expanding interconnection of urban infrastructure provide an ideal setting for the adoption of inventive mobility solutions. The rationale behind this study is to apply a cutting-edge era to set up a transport community that is prompter and more flexible. Our goal is to create a reliable condition monitoring gadget to help with the implementation of smart transport structures. These systems were capable of adapting routing in real-time, offering a sustainable and green option to the complicated issues confronted with the aid of urban mobility these days. In essence, our examination is inspired through the choice to sell progress that has a beneficial effect on the standard of living in metropolitan regions, by way of growing transit structures which was extra green, steady and eco-friendly.

9.2.2 Problem Statement

The proliferation of urbanization and the continuous surge in vehicle traffic has caused a pressing problem in contemporary cities: the ineffectiveness and gridlock of conventional transportation systems. Urban growth exacerbates the pressure on infrastructure, ensuring in elevated travel durations, elevated environmental contamination, and weakened road security. The insufficiency of present-day technologies to adjust to fluctuating traffic instances worsens those problems. The undertaking of our observation addresses is the pressing need for an innovative approach to urban mobility. This approach utilizes wise technology to actively reveal and manage traffic situations.

The existing transport structures are not sufficiently flexible to address the unpredictable nature of town traffic, leading to much less-than-ideal direction selections and longer adventure intervals. Furthermore, the environmental effects of congestion, inclusive of increased carbon emissions and worse air first-class, emphasize the need for a more effective and sustainable solution. This work seeks to deal with those demanding situations through presenting a groundbreaking technique that includes up-to-the-minute facts from several assets, taking into consideration the creation of a flexible and adaptive clever transportation routing device.

9.2.3 Research Gaps

Our work intends to resolve enormous study gaps in clever transportation systems, no matter the promising enhancements made in this area. Currently, there is an absence of thorough surveys inside the literature that consolidate numerous tactics and eras used for situation monitoring in intelligent transportation routing. We propose to slender these divides by way of a complete examination, pinpointing great styles, and setting up the muse for an extra complete comprehension of the challenge.

Furthermore, there is a deficiency within the development of current techniques that correctly integrate diverse statistical assets to analyse traffic in actual time. Several modern studies give attention to certain factors, which include sensor information or GPS information, without investigating the potential blessings that are probably obtained by way of integrating these resources. The objective of our recommended approach is to cope with this hole with the aid of introducing an innovative technique that optimizes the use of numerous facts inputs to enhance the precision and efficiency of shrewd transportation routing systems.

Moreover, there is a big disparity within the use of predictive analytics to forecast traffic situations and pre-emptively redirect vehicles. Although numerous research briefly discusses predictive modelling, there is a need for extra state-of-the-art techniques that use device studying and statistics analytics to correctly anticipate traffic' styles. To fill these problems, this work integrates predictive analytics into the proposed machine, imparting a proactive issue to situation monitoring and routing choices.

9.3 Proposed Methodology

When it comes to the field of monitoring the circumstances of road traffic, a comprehensive research attempt involves several important steps that are aimed at strengthening both safety and efficiency. Using both image and video data, the investigation covers a wide variety of topics, including the identification of helmets, ALPR,

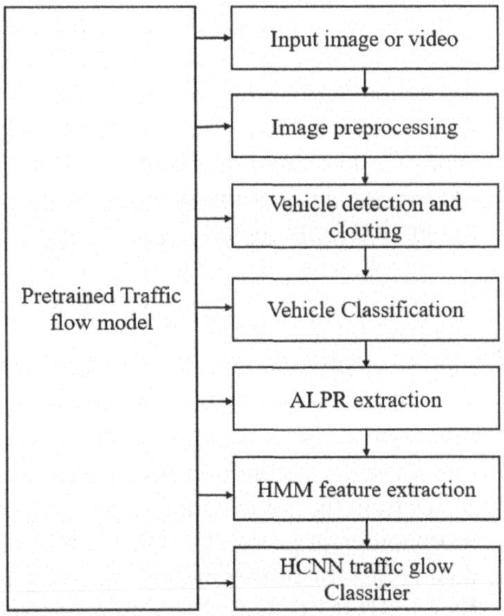

Fig. 9.1 Proposed methodology. *Source* Author

counting of vehicles, and classification. Figure 9.1 is a depiction of the suggested system in the form of a schematic. The next section provides a detailed explanation of the sequential process that this research endeavour demonstrates:

- Step 1: In the early stage of our research, we pay attention to how we get ready and prepare the images. This is called preprocessing of images. To make the data better for future study, these need to improve its quality and how much it matters. We need to get images of different traffic situations. Think about things like light, viewpoints, and quality of images. To make things equal, we use ways like making them smaller, changing numbers the same and taking out noise from images. We also use methods like histogram equalization and contrast fixes to make sure the image quality stays the same, no matter what settings are used.
- Step 2: Detection of helmets: We need to find the helmets used by motorcycle riders next. For making roads safer, knowing about helmets is very important. Our company uses special object detection algorithms like YOLO. These are made possible by advanced technology found in programs called deep learning frameworks. The algorithms are taught to find and spot helmets in images accurately by using our prepared dataset. This helps them to recognize and point out those helmets correctly. Then, the results of checking are looked at and fixed to be sure they're right in finding out if people wear helmets. This is needed to follow rules about safe driving.
- Step 3: Counting Cars: The counting of cars is an important part of keeping an eye on road traffic. It gives important details about the movement of cars and how many there are. In this step, methods like image processing and object tracking are used. They help count how many cars are in a specific image. The aim of this task

is to create a strong system that can manage changing amounts of traffic, all kinds of vehicle sizes and complicated traffic situations. Counting cars is important to know how traffic flows and gets stuck. This helps control traffic better.

- Step 4: Vehicle Class: Our study looks at how to sort cars into groups based on their types. To put cars into different groups, like cars, trucks, motorbikes and more we use special learning ways with things called CNNs. The traffic monitoring system has better details because of this grouping. It gives useful information to the people who plan for traffic and law enforcement. To make sure we correctly label many types of cars, the way we classify them is made using a set of data that has all kinds of vehicles in it.
- Step 5: ALPR: After successfully identifying helmets, the next step in our research is to obtain license plate numbers using images. ALPR uses image segmentation techniques to accurately identify the area containing the number plate. In this phase, it is common practice to accurately identify and extract the license plates from the vehicle images by using techniques such as contour detection and morphological processes. The number plates that were gathered serve as crucial data points for further operations, such as identifying and tracking vehicles.
- Step 6: HMM Feature Extraction: We successfully capture the temporal correlations and patterns in traffic data with HMMs. Its characteristics like the temporal aspects of vehicle movement in films are possible to extract from sequential data. The HMMs measure the latent structure that is present in the vehicles' trajectories, so we can accurately forecast and analyse the temporal traffic patterns. Over the course of time, this step enhances the grasp of the conditions around road traffic, which in turn enables more accurate predictions and assessments.
- Step 7: HCNN Classifier: The CNNs can retrieve spatial features, but this model uses HMMs' temporal insights to create a synergistic experience. A combination of images and videos, along with the temporal patterns gathered by the HMM, was used to train the HCNN. This hybrid technique's goal is to create a comprehensive, robust road traffic condition monitoring system that integrates geographical and temporal data to facilitate precise analysis and decision-making.

9.3.1 Image Preprocessing

The traffic images underwent several changes during the information augmentation process to enhance the dataset. At first, the image was flipped both horizontally and vertically after which circled in a random way. Afterwards, a center cropping method was used, ensuring in a discount of the resolution from 512 by 512 to 224 through 224 pixels. The augmentation approach turned into iterated three instances to enhance the diversity of the dataset. The Retinex theory was used to enhance traffic image processing. The use of the Multi-Scale Retinex (MSR) enhancement technique aimed to boost contrast and improve the visibility of features in the images. The MSR approach entails the application of Gaussian blur to every scale of the image, thereafter, doing cumulative calculations to ascertain the maximum and lowest values for each scale. Subsequently, the obtained values are quantized in a linear manner. The R_{MSR_i} value for the ith spectral component is determined by using the following formula:

$$R_{\mathrm{MSR}_i} = \sum_{n=1}^{N} \omega_n R_{n_i} = \sum_{n=1}^{N} \omega_n \left[\log I_i(x, y) - \log F_n(x, y)^* I_i(x, y) \right] \quad (9.1)$$

Here, $I_i(x, y)$ represents the image distribution in the ith spectral band, $F_n(x, y)^*$ is the surround function, N is the number of scales, R_{n_i} is the ith component of the nth scale, ω_n denotes the weight associated with the nth scale, * signifies the convolution operation, and ω_n is the weight associated with the nth scale. However, since MSR images often exhibit artifacts such as "halo" and low contrast, a preprocessing step was undertaken. The Traffic images were converted from RGB to grayscale to reduce processing requirements. To further enhance contrast and prevent the loss of image features, the Contrast Limited Adaptive Histogram Equalization (CLAHE) procedure was employed. The CLAHE proved more effective than traditional histogram equalization, mitigating issues like enlarged noise regions and improving road area extraction.

9.3.2 Helmet Detection

Figure 9.2 displays the counseled block diagram for helmet detection, used for figuring out folks who are motorcycle riders and are carrying helmets. The YOLO version is a widely used approach for real-time object identification, specially designed to understand items in images or motion images. The YOLO model makes use of a dataset consisting of labelled images of people to train the algorithm for character identification. The YOLO version operates through partitioning the entered image right into a grid of cells and making predictions for each cellular, inclusive of bounding box coordinates and probabilities for specific training. The YOLO version employs a pre-skilled CNN to extract exceptional traits from the image for the reason of human identification. After the YOLO version makes predictions for the bounding box and sophistication possibilities of every cell, a submit-processing method is executed to mix overlapping bounding boxes and do away with incorrect high-quality detections. The output consists of a collection of bounding boxes and corresponding class probabilities for every individual detected in the provided image.

- Step 1: Image testing. Begin by acquiring the image that will undergo analysis. The image was obtained via a surveillance camera, an image, or any other relevant source.
- Step 2. Image Preprocessing: Prior to executing YOLO-V3 for the purpose of detecting individuals and helmets, do preprocessing on the image to improve the accuracy of detection. Typical preparation procedures are adjusting the image

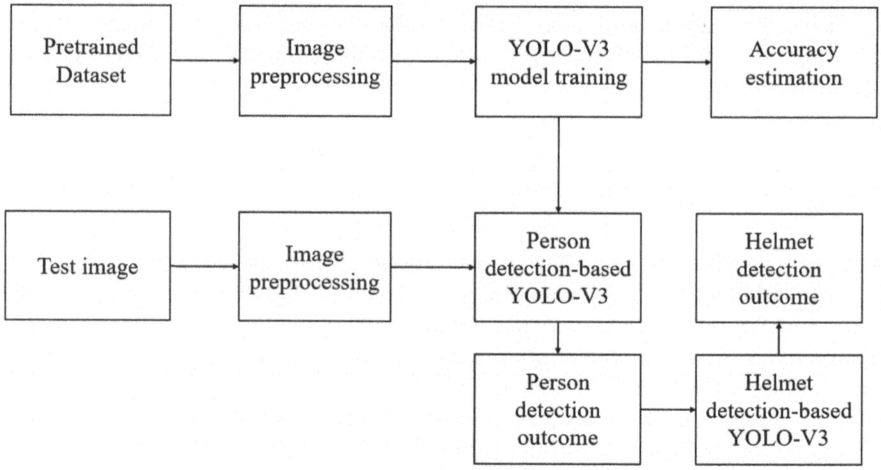

Fig. 9.2 Proposed helmet detection methodology. *Source* Author

size to match the desired input size for YOLO-V3, standardizing pixel values, and managing colour channels (such as converting from BGR to RGB).

- Step 3. Person Detection using YOLO-V3: Employ a pre-trained YOLO-V3 model for object detection. Pre-trained weights and configurations for YOLO-V3 were sourced from resources such as the Darknet website or other deep learning libraries. Load the YOLO-V3 model into the working environment. Input the Preprocessed image into the YOLO-V3 model. Extract the detection results, including bounding boxes around detected persons, their confidence scores, and class labels (e.g., "person"). Apply filtering to retain only high confidence bounding boxes on test image.
- Step 4. Helmet Detection using YOLO-V3: Analogously, use a pre-trained YOLO-V3 model specialized in helmet detection. This model should be trained specifically to recognize helmets. Load the helmet detection YOLO-V3 model into the working environment. Input the same pre-processed image into the helmet detection YOLO-V3 model. Extract the detection results, which encompass bounding boxes around detected helmets, their confidence scores, and class labels (e.g., "helmet").
- Step 5. Output: Combine the person and helmet detection results to identify individuals wearing helmets. Visualize the results by drawing bounding boxes around persons and helmets in the original image for clarity and interpretation.

9.3.3 *Vehicle Detection and Counting*

Vehicle counting and classification begin with the acquisition of real-time video streams as the primary input source, typically sourced from surveillance cameras

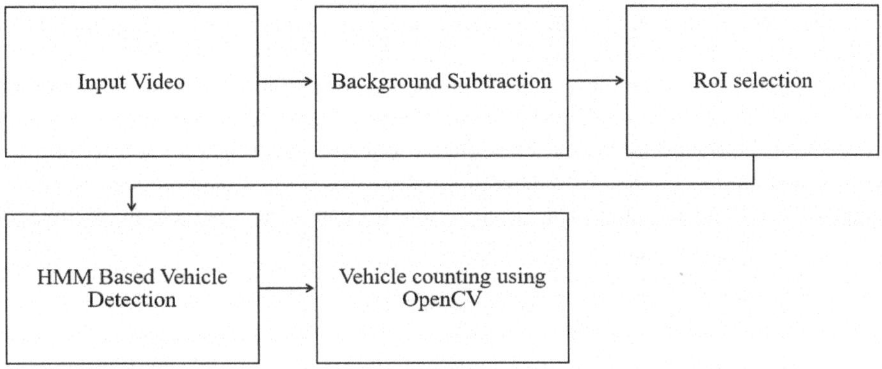

Fig. 9.3 Proposed vehicle detection methodology. *Source* Author

or traffic monitoring systems. Figure 9.3 shows the vehicle detection and counting system block diagram. The first module, background subtraction and Region of Interest (ROI) plays a crucial role in isolating moving objects, i.e., vehicles, from the stationary background. This is achieved using advanced algorithms to create an ROI that narrows down the area for subsequent analysis, reducing computational load and minimizing false positives. The heart of the system lies in the vehicle detection and tracking module, which employs the YOLO deep learning model. YOLO excels at real-time object detection and tracking, enabling the system to identify vehicles within the defined ROI and track their movements across frames, allowing for continuous monitoring.

Upon implementing the foreground extraction module, accurate contours are obtained. These contours possess distinctive features, such as the centroid. The vehicles are classified based on the extraction of aspect ratio, area, size, and solidity. This module has three sequential steps: background removal, frame enhancement and foreground extraction. The backdrop is eliminated to enhance the visibility of the foreground items. Typically, this is achieved by converting the static pixels of static objects into binary 0. Following the process of background removal, frame-enhancing methods such as noise filtering, dilation, and erosion are used to accurately outline the foreground items. The outcome derived from this module is at the forefront.

Moreover, the suggested system operates on a video stream, and this module specifically pulls the frames from it to get knowledge about the backdrop. When a traffic scene is recorded using a stationary camera positioned on the side of the road, the items that are in motion may be regarded as the foreground, while the objects that are not moving are considered as the backdrop. The approach is used to get knowledge about the backdrop via the utilization of image processing techniques.

In the first frame of the video, establish an ROI by delineating a precise line on the frame. The objective is to identify the ROI in a subsequent frame; however, the ROI does not stand out as a prominent vehicle. It is a component of a vehicle that can change shape, rotate move in a straight line, and may not be completely visible inside the frame.

A method for detecting vehicles using an image context was suggested. This method uses an HMM framework to capture the vehicle by sequentially selecting search windows based on top-down attention. The system has successfully obtained adequate results on the vehicle detection benchmark by iteratively improving the accuracy of the bounding boxes. Presented a sequential search approach for identifying visual cars in photos. The detection model was trained using a deep learning framework to determine the appropriate action for capturing a vehicle in an image.

The Vehicle Counting module will accurately count the observed cars and continuously update the count depending on vehicle detection. The results will be shown in real-time on the streaming video using OpenCV.

9.4 Vehicle Classification

The subsequent phase entails the use of the vehicle Classification module, which is driven by the DarkNet architecture. This module categorizes the identified vehicles into several classifications, such as automobiles, trucks, or motorbikes. Subsequently, the Counting and Analytics module precisely measures the movements of vehicles, including counting, measuring speed and other pertinent analytics. This module yields beneficial statistics for the purposes of traffic management and observation. Ultimately, the device produces a video output that superimposes analysed information onto the preliminary video circulation, providing an easily understandable visible depiction of the vehicle counting and class consequences. This makes it a flexible device suitable for a range of packages in traffic surveillance, city development, and transportation evaluation. Figure 9.4 depicts the recommended version of vehicle classification. The operation was defined in elements as follows:

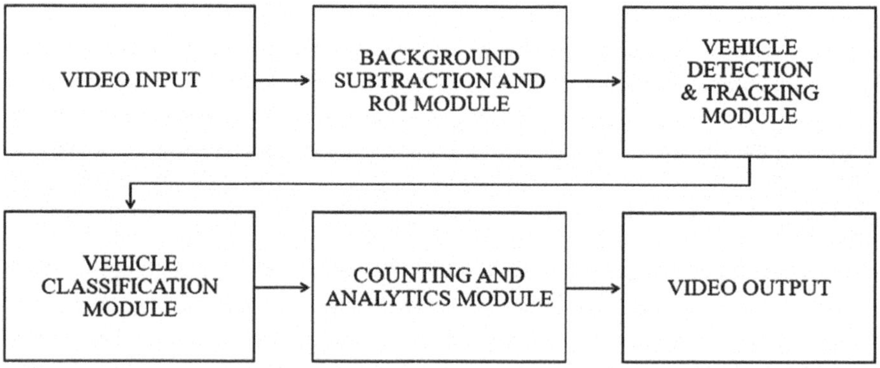

Fig. 9.4 Proposed vehicle detection and classification methodology. *Source* Author

- Step 1: Obtain live video feeds and enter information for the device. The video feeds may additionally originate from safety cameras, traffic cameras, or any other device that data car movements.
- Step 2: Background subtraction is an important technique for separating shifting gadgets (along with vehicles) from the motionless background. Use algorithms and methodologies to become aware of the background and set up a ROI, where vehicle detection will take place. This process aids in reducing noise and directing interest onto the pertinent place.
- Step 3: Employ YOLO, a deep getting to know-primarily based version for object identification, specifically for detecting motors. The YOLO algorithm can appropriately and unexpectedly identify and pinpoint gadgets internal video frames in real time. The system recognises the automobiles positioned inside the ROI and may screen their actions among frames, enabling us to track the vehicle as they traverse the film.
- Step 4: Once the vehicle has been detected and tracked, proceed to analyse, and categorize them with the Darknet framework. Darknet is a foremost neural network structure for issues related to categorization. The gadget can categorize motors into many classifications, along with cars, trucks, motorbikes and other pertinent classes.
- Step 5: In this stage, enumerate and compare the diagnosed and categorized automobiles. We have the capability to screen and report the number of vehicles that traverse certain places or ROI, determine the velocity at which the automobiles are traveling, and collect other pertinent statistics for evaluation. This information was valuable for the purposes of traffic management, and monitoring.
- Step 6: Ultimately, the system gives you a visual output that superimposes the processed information over the authentic video enter. The output may additionally encompass the number of vehicles detected, their categorizations, and another pertinent facts. Users may additionally use the system to visually see and realize the results of the automobile counting and categorization approach.

9.5 HMM Feature Extraction

The HMM classifier was properly regarded in numerous applications because of its intrinsic hyperlink to the technique of producing function vectors. The connection has shown to be very beneficial in duties like figuring out isolating traits, which has significantly contributed to its contemporary achievement. The HMM is a computational model that uses a first-order Markov chain with hidden states to predict destiny occurrences. Every kingdom is connected to a stochastic system that determines the sequence of observations, taking images of the temporal sample of the records inside the version. The HMM postulates the presence of a latent Markov chain that generates the observed sequence. The model's parameters, including the number of states (K), starting state probabilities (π_i), and transition probabilities (a_{ij}), are often estimated using the Maximum Likelihood approach. Mathematically, for a given state sequence (s_1, ..., s_T), the probability of the observable data is calculated using the formula:

$$p(x_1, s_1 \ldots, X_T, S_T) = \pi_{s_1} b_{s_1}(x_1) a_{s_1,s_2} b_2(X_2) \ldots a_{s_T-1,S_t} b_{S_T}(X_T)$$
$$= \pi_{s_1} b_{s_1}(X_1) \prod_{t=2}^{T} a_{S_{t-1}} b_{s_t}(X_t) \quad (9.2)$$

Here, $p(x_1, s_1 \ldots, X_T, S_T)$ represents the density of observations in the ith state $\pi_{s_1} b_{s_1}$, which was discrete or continuous, often a combination of Gaussian densities. Since the actual state sequence is usually unknown, determining the probability of a specific data sequence involves summation over all potential state sequences:

$$b_i(X_t) \equiv P(X \,|\, S_t = i) \quad (9.3)$$

To facilitate efficient computation, techniques like forward and backward recursion algorithms are employed. During training, the HMM's parameters are adjusted using the Expectation–Maximization procedure to optimize for the highest probability value. However, challenges arise in the design of the HMM classifier's structure, particularly in relation to its training and topology assumptions. In traffic pattern identification, the conventional left-to-right topology is not suitable, as traffic patterns, like pauses, do not adhere to a specific temporal order. A fully connected HMM topology waste captures the diverse nature of traffic features. So, HMMs have demonstrated comparable accuracy in traffic pattern identification tasks, outperforming human classification in specific datasets.

9.6 HCNN Classifier

In road traffic condition classification, the concept of Transfer Learning, particularly as implemented through Cross-Domain Learning (CDL), proves valuable. Instead of constructing a neural network from scratch, CDL involves repurposing an existing network pretrained on one task to address a new problem. This method leverages the knowledge acquired during the initial training, allowing for the application of previously gained insights to previously unsolved challenges. For example, a neural network trained for object identification was adapted for diagnosing traffic-related issues.

In the research on classifying road traffic conditions, various types of pre-trained neural networks are employed. These networks are typically designed for tasks such as image recognition but were repurposed for traffic feature extraction (TFI) fault diagnostics. Adjustments are made in the advanced layers of the networks, particularly focusing on the fully connected layers that learn new weights. For road traffic condition classification, the adaptation involves swapping out the original fully connected layer with a new one suited for the task, often with a different number

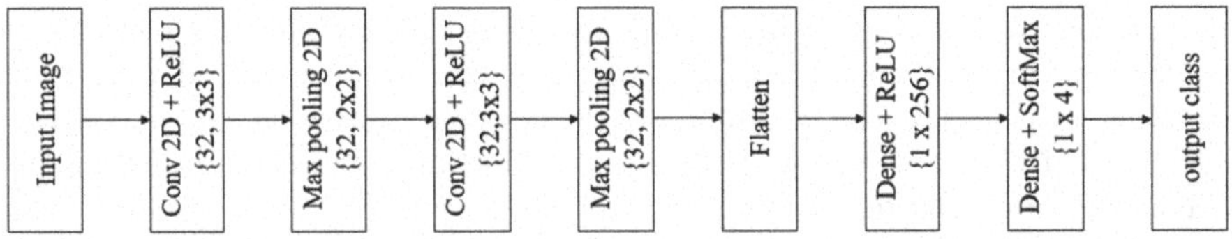

Fig. 9.5 Proposed HCNN classifier methodology. *Source* Author

of outputs representing traffic conditions. One specific architecture explored is the HCNN as shown in Fig. 9.5. In the traditional CNN, widely used in image recognition, the superior feature extraction capabilities are repurposed for TFI analysis. To adapt to one-dimensional fault signal data, a 1D-CNN is considered, but it suffers from limited receptive fields. An alternative is to reshape the fault data signal into a matrix and feed it into a 2D-CNN. However, this approach sacrifices spatial correlation in the original sequence. HCNN is proposed as a solution, combining the strengths of both 1D and 2D CNNs. Feature vectors extracted from each network are concatenated in the fully connected layer to form the HCNN's fault function vectors, facilitating greater strong avenue traffic situation classification.

The technique of constructing the community includes the use of Fast Fourier Transform (FFT) to technique the statistics, and then making use of the acquired outputs as inputs for both 1D-CNN and 2D-CNN. The networks are constructed from convolutional and pooling layers to extract capabilities, which can then be integrated into the related layer. The SoftMax classifier is then used to categorize the road traffic situations. During the studying segment, the move-entropy loss function is used because the training target, includes disorder characteristics.

The equation for this function contains variables representing training samples, fault categories, and weight factors, making certain that the community adjusts successfully to the intricacies of avenue traffic' situations. The optimization approach involves enhancing weight parameters with the aid of gradient descent, with a predetermined studying fee, with the principal objective of minimizing the pass-entropy loss for the street traffic categorization process.

$$J(\omega) = -\frac{1}{m}\left[\sum_{i=1}^{m}\sum_{j=1}^{n} I\overline{y_i} = j\log\frac{\exp\left(x_i^T w_j\right)}{\sum_{j=1}^{k}\exp\left(x_i^T w_j\right)}\right] \quad (9.4)$$

Equation (9.4) represents the cross-entropy loss function used in the training of the neural network. In this equation, $I\overline{y_i}$ is the indicator function, and $\left(\exp\left(x_i^T w_j\right)\right)$ represents a training sample, where m is the total number of training samples, and n is the total number of fault categories. The goal of this loss function is to measure how well the predicted outputs of the model match the true labels.

Here, $\overline{y_i}$ is the true label of the i-th training sample. The x_i^T is the transpose of the feature vector of the i-th training sample. The w_j represents the weight parameter corresponding to the j-th fault category. The numerator $\exp\left(x_i^T w_j\right)$ computes the exponentiated dot product of the feature vector and the weight vector for the *j*-th category. The denominator $\exp(x_i^T w_j)$ sums up the exponentiated dot products overall fault categories. The logarithm and the negative sign are applied to penalize large errors. The partial derivatives of this loss function with respect to the weight parameters are crucial for updating the weights during the training process. The weight parameters (w) are modified on a layer-by-layer basis using the gradient descent optimization algorithm. The updates are computed using the formulas:

$$\omega' = \omega - \eta \frac{\partial J}{\partial \omega} \tag{9.5}$$

$$b' = b - \eta \frac{\partial J}{\partial b} \tag{9.6}$$

Here, ω' and b' represent the modified weight and bias parameters, while ω and b are the current parameters being applied to the data. The learning rate (η) determines the step size of the weight updates, ensuring a balance between convergence speed and stability during training. The primary objective during training is to minimize the cross-entropy loss (J), emphasizing a reduction in this loss as the central focus.

9.7 Advantages of Proposed System

The study presents an integrated architecture for road traffic monitoring that provides numerous significant benefits. To begin with, the careful use of sophisticated image preprocessing methods guarantees improved data quality, establishing a basis for more precise and dependable outcomes in succeeding activities.

Moreover, the usage of helmet detection in the research complements efforts to promote street safety. They have a look at contributes to the promotion of more secure conduct through identifying people who put on helmets. The framework offers complete and insightful expertise on avenue traffic' conditions by integrating sophisticated image processing, temporal dynamics evaluation, and hybrid neural community methodologies. These technological improvements can provide treasured data for city planning and traffic management methods, in the end main to safer networks.

The versatility of actual-time automobile counting and category systems makes them valuable in numerous fields because they offer unique and set-off information on traffic styles and automobile categorization. Real-time automobile counting and categorization structures are vital for the powerful control of traffic. They facilitate the surveillance of traffic congestion, identification of regions of congestion, and implementation of adaptive traffic management measures via traffic authorities. These structures decorate the efficiency of traffic signal timing, lane management, and the distribution of traffic resources to enhance common traffic go with the flow, and minimize congestion.

Ensuring the protection of roads and stopping accidents: These technologies are critical for enhancing avenue protection. Through ongoing traffic surveillance and detection of perilous occasions, along with immoderate pace or unpredictable driving conduct, these structures may additionally right away alert government and set off fast moves to avert injuries. The received information may also be used to analyse coincidence traits and follow precise safety measures. Accurate and immediate vehicle enumeration and categorization are important for the functioning of automated toll-amassing structures. Toll cubicles ready with this technology have the capability to precisely calculate toll costs by way of thinking about the car categories and the space protected. This enhances the efficacy of toll collection and minimizes congestion at toll plazas.

Efficient parking control is a sizable issue in metropolitan settings. These systems assist manage parking centres by using tracking occupancy and supplying real-time records to drivers about to have parking spaces. This minimizes the time devoted to parking search, decreases emissions, and improves the entire parking revel. Public Transportation Planning: Understanding traffic patterns and vehicle sorts is vital for public transportation planning. These systems offer facts that facilitate authorities optimize public transportation routes, schedules, and potential to better meet the needs of commuters. This ends in more efficient and sustainable public transit structures.

Real-time automobile counting and class enable exams of the environmental impact of various forms of automobiles. By categorizing automobiles by means of emissions, those structures help environmental guidelines aimed toward lowering pollution and promoting cleanser transportation alternatives. Law Enforcement: Law enforcement organizations make use of this generation to put in force traffic legal guidelines and guidelines. ALPR structures, often incorporated with real-time car counting and category, assist in identifying and apprehending automobiles concerned with crook activities.

Intelligent Transportation Systems (ITS): These systems are a fundamental issue of ITS. ITS integrates information from real-time automobile counting and category structures with other technology which includes traffic signals, variable message symptoms, and traffic cameras to create responsive and adaptive transportation networks. Urban Planning and Development: Urban planners use traffic records to tell choices approximately avenue enlargement, infrastructure improvement, and metropolis planning. Real-time statistics allow examine the impact of recent traits on traffic glide and ensure that city planning aligns with future transportation needs.

Research and Data Analysis: Researchers in transportation and concrete studies depend on real-time car facts for an extensive variety of studies, such as traffic modelling, urban improvement studies, and transportation policy evaluation. The availability of extraordinary, real-time facts complements the accuracy and reliability of the study's findings.

9.8 Results and Discussion

The proposed road traffic monitoring architecture was assessed using a uniform dataset to guarantee equitable and comparable outcomes. A wide range of performance criteria, including accuracy, precision, and recall, were considered to conduct a thorough evaluation. The findings demonstrated the efficacy of the integrated methodology, exhibiting greater proficiency in helmet detection, ALPR and vehicle classification in comparison to conventional techniques. The dataset's consistency allowed a dependable comparison, highlighting the strength and dependability of the suggested framework.

9.8.1 Traffic Flow Monitoring Dataset

The dataset compilation comprises three separate datasets, each specifically designed to tackle certain issues in computer vision applications.

ALPR Dataset: The collection consists of 4,500 well-annotated images, which together include more than 30,000 characters from licence plates. These images are obtained from 150 automobiles that were recorded in real-world situations, creating a dynamic effect where both the vehicle being studied and the camera collecting the images (which is situated inside another vehicle) are in motion. The images are encoded in the PNG format and have a resolution of 1,920 $\times$ 1,080 pixels. The data collecting endeavour included taking a total of 1,500 images using each camera. The distribution of images was as follows: There are 900 images showing automobiles with grey licence plates, 300 images displaying vehicles with red license plates, and another 300 images presenting motorbikes with grey licence plates. Every image is accompanied through a textual content file that includes complete annotations, which include records of the camera used, the location of the car, and particular parameters consisting of its type (car or bike), and version. Moreover, the dataset consists of annotations for the detection and site of the licence plate, as well as the precise coordinates of its characters. This properly organised dataset serves as a terrific asset for growing research on licence plate reputation and item detection in dynamic, real-global environments.

Roboflow Helmet Detection Dataset: This dataset includes a compilation of 1,371 images of people wearing and not sporting motorbike helmets. This dataset is supplied under the public license, promoting accessibility and usage for many purposes. Every image in the collection goes via preprocessing, which includes automatic orientation adjustment and scaling, resulting in a standardized resolution of 416 $\times$ 416 pixels. Prior to importing, augmentations which include Bounding Box Blur (as much as 10px) are finished to decorate the form of the dataset. The schooling method entails using the COCO Checkpoint in Public Models and employing switch studying strategies on Roboflow. The dataset was up to date to Version 2 (v2), with an increase within the range of images such as 735, while preserving the same preprocessing criteria. Further upgrades are being applied, inclusive of a broader variety of adjustments. Each schooling example now produces three outputs, including rotations spanning from −30° to 30°, horizontal and vertical shearing of ±15°, blur up to 1.5 pixels, and using the mosaic method. These upgrades add to an extra complete and numerous datasets, as it should be representing actual-existence situations. Both variations offer an extraordinary aid for tasks that contain detecting helmets and serve as a foundation for building machine learning methods. The dataset can be accessed from: https://universe.roboflow.com/bike-helmets/bike-helmet-detection-2vdjo.

Kaggle Vehicle Classification Dataset: The most important intention of the category is to categorize images that depict exceptional varieties of cars, including automobiles, bicycles, trucks, ambulances, like 17 separate categories. It is a key and enduring endeavour within the domain of system studying, performing as a foundational element for look at since the emergence of deep neural networks. The dataset used is received from the complete open access dataset, that's well-known for its annotation of more than 9 million images. The dataset can be accessed from: https://www.kaggle.com/datasets/vivek603/vehicle-detection-sample-and-output-videos.

9.8.2 Prediction Results

Figure 9.6a was processed using YOLO-V3, an extensively used method for item identification. YOLO-V3 has effectively recognized and delineated someone within the image by means of drawing a bounding box round them. Furthermore, this detection is observed with an accuracy rating of 99%. The model's high accuracy rating suggests that it's miles positive in its dedication that a human is present within the image, with little room for mistake. Figure 9.6b depicts a distinct situation wherein YOLO-V3 was used on an image, although it has not become aware of a helmet. The result indicates that YOLO-V3 did not locate a helmet in the image, maybe because of variables together with the helmet's absence, confined visibility, or difficult angles. Figure 9.7a is much like Fig. 9.6 as it illustrates a success detection of someone by way of YOLO-V3, followed by means of the detecting of a bounding box around the located person. The number one difference lies within the accuracy score, that's in addition elevated to 89%. This demonstrates a heightened diploma of reality within the version's potential too as it should be hit upon a person within the image with totally little risk of creating mistakes. Figure 9.7b suggests the identification of a helmet with the aid of YOLO-V3 in an image. The model has detected the presence of a helmet with a precision score of 99.00%. The excessive accuracy rating suggests a sturdy degree of truth inside the model's potential to appropriately discover a helmet within the image, with a minimal opportunity of mistake, confined to a 1% margin.

(a) (b)

Fig. 9.6 Prediction outcomes. **a** Person detected with bounding box. **b** Helmet not detected. *Source* Author. The figure was generated by python simulations on authenticated dataset

(a) (b)

Fig. 9.7 Prediction outcomes. **a** Person detected with bounding box. (b) Helmet detected with ALPR. *Source* Author. The figure was generated by python simulations on authenticated dataset

9.8.3 Traffic Flow Analysis

Figure 9.8 depicts a personal frame extracted from a video. Within this frame, automobiles have been identified: a bus and a vehicle. The item detection version has correctly detected a vehicle within the body, and it has offered a high self-belief stage to this classification, suggesting a 97% accuracy in classifying it as a vehicle. Similarly, the model has also detected a bus in the image, but with a touch decrease

Fig. 9.8 Frame with bus and car vehicle classification. *Source* Author. The figure was generated by python simulations on authenticated dataset

self-assurance rating, suggesting a sixty-one. The 74% accuracy in classifying it as a bus.

Figure 9.9 is the next frame extracted from the equal film. Within this frame, matters were diagnosed: someone and a bike. The object detection algorithm has efficaciously detected someone in the frame and has provided a high confidence rating to this type, suggesting a 94% accuracy in recognizing it as a human. Similarly, the version has additionally detected a motorcycle in the body, but with a truly decreased self-belief rating, suggesting a 64% accuracy in classifying it as a bike.

Figure 9.10 depicts an additional frame extracted from the same video. Within this frame, different objects were diagnosed, consisting of individuals, motors, and buses. The item detection version has correctly detected individuals inside the body with an excessive self-belief rating, suggesting 94% accuracy in classifying them as people. The model has effectively recognized automobiles within the frame with an excessive degree of self-assurance, boasting 96% accuracy in classifying them as vehicles. In addition, the model has correctly identified buses inside the frame with a confidence rating that is very excessive, suggesting 99% accuracy in classifying them as buses.

Table 9.1 is an overall performance contrast table that presents the accuracy chances of several tactics used for person and helmet identity. The modern Support Vector Machine (SVM) method typically obtains a detection accuracy of 95.47% for identifying individuals. The current Random Forest Classifier (RFC) approach attains a precision of 92.00% for human identification. The unspecified advised technique affords an extensively higher accuracy of 88% for character detection. This suggests that the advised method surpasses both the modern SVM and RFC techniques in reliably figuring out people.

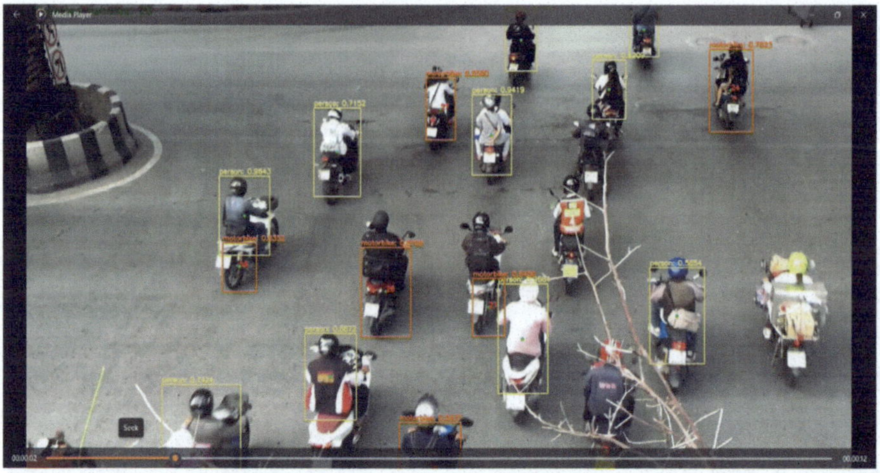

Fig. 9.9 Video frame with classification of both person and motor bike. *Source* Author. The figure was generated by python simulations on authenticated dataset

Fig. 9.10 Video frame with classification of persons, vehicle and buses. *Source* Author. The figure was generated by python simulations on authenticated dataset

Table 9.1 Performance comparison

Method	Existing SVM (Bhavsar et al. 2023)	Existing RFC (Nijim et al. 2023)	Proposed method
Person detection accuracy (%)	95.47	92.00	99.88
Helmet detection accuracy (%)	93.13	96.48	99.00
Vehicle detection accuracy (%)	79.58	95.97	98.29
Vehicle classification accuracy (%)	84.85	97.68	99.64
License plate extraction accuracy (%)	87.95	96.93	99.26

Source Author

9.9 Conclusion

This study offers a comprehensive and inventive approach to road traffic monitoring. Advanced image preprocessing techniques guarantee the input data's quality, which lays the groundwork for accurate and reliable outcomes. A method that incorporates a dynamic component in the analysis is using HMMs to extract temporal characteristics from video data. As a result, periodic patterns in the movement of cars over time were identified. The introduction of HCNN is a significant advancement because it improves vehicle classification accuracy by using the combined power of one-dimensional and two-dimensional CNNs. To gain a more comprehensive understanding of the composition of traffic, the study goes beyond the conventional methods of counting vehicles and emphasizes the importance of categorizing vehicles. The identification of helmets is a way to improve road safety by encouraging people to wear helmets. Intelligent transportation systems, urban planning and traffic management are all affected by the results of this study. This research provides a comprehensive framework for studying traffic, which will help planners improve road safety, optimize traffic flow and help build more efficient and safe urban transportation networks.

References

Akinsemoyin A et al (2023) Unmanned aerial systems and deep learning for safety and health activity monitoring on construction sites. Sensors 23(15):6690

Anjaiah A et al (2022) Automatic number plate detection for motorcyclists riding without helmet. J Algebr Stat 13(3):2158–2165

Anoop A et al (2022) Traffic surveillance system and criminal detection using image processing and deep learning. In: 2022 International conference on innovations in science and technology for sustainable development (ICISTSD). IEEE

Arshad M, Kumar P (2022) Detection of two-wheeler traffic rule violation using deep learning. In: 2022 IEEE World conference on applied intelligence and computing (AIC). IEEE
Arshad S, Prasanthi B. Detection and identification of non-helmet riders and their license plate numbers
Aswini N, Hegde R (2023) Real time traffic monitoring using YOLO V5. In: 2023 5th International conference on inventive research in computing applications (ICIRCA). IEEE
Bachechi C, Po L, Rollo F (2022) Big data analytics and visualization in traffic monitoring. Big Data Res 27:100292
Bhavsar YM et al (2023) Vision-based investigation of road traffic and violations at urban roundabout in India using UAV video: a case study. Transp Eng 14:100207
Bouhayane A et al (2023) A swin transformer-based system for motorcycle helmet detection. IEEE Access
Charran RS, Dubey RK (2022) Two-wheeler vehicle traffic violations detection and automated ticketing for Indian road scenario. IEEE Trans Intell Transp Syst 23(11):22002–22007
Chen S et al (2022) Helmet wearing detection of motorcycle drivers using deep learning network with residual transformer-spatial attention. Drones 6(12):415
Choudhari R et al (2023) Traffic rule violation detection using Detectron2 and Yolov7. In: 2023 World conference on communication and computing (WCONF). IEEE
Chythanya KR et al (2023) Deep learning and IoT-based driver helmet detection and bike ignition check for updates. In: Proceedings of the 2nd international conference on cognitive and intelligent computing: ICCIC 2022, 27–28 December, Hyderabad, India, vol 2. Springer Nature
Devi SKC et al (2022) License plate detection of motorcyclists without helmets. In: Computational intelligence and data analytics: proceedings of ICCIDA 2022. Springer Nature Singapore, Singapore, pp 295–301
Ghadekar P et al (2023) Improved helmet detection model using YOLOv5. In: Intelligent computing and networking: proceedings of IC-ICN 2022. Springer Nature Singapore, Singapore, pp 35–44
Ghosh R et al (2023) A deep learning-based smart helmet detection and notification with e-challan issuance for traffic fines. In: 2023 IEEE 4th annual flagship India Council international subsections conference (INDISCON). IEEE
Gomathy B, Niranjana S, Vignesh K (2023) Helmet detection on two wheelers and penalty generation using artificial intelligence. In: 2023 7th International conference on trends in electronics and informatics (ICOEI). IEEE
Gupta SK et al (2023) Detection of number plate in vehicles using deep learning based image labeler model. In: 2023 International conference on recent trends in electronics and communication (ICRTEC). IEEE
Hijji M et al (2023) 6G connected vehicle framework to support intelligent road maintenance using deep learning data fusion. IEEE Trans Intell Transp Syst
Jahan IA et al (2022) Accident detection and road condition monitoring using blackbox module. In: 2022 Thirteenth international conference on ubiquitous and future networks (ICUFN). IEEE
Kishore MB et al (2023) Artificial intelligence (AI) based detection of traffic violations by two-wheeler vehicles. In: 2023 7th International conference on intelligent computing and control systems (ICICCS). IEEE
Kohm M, Stempniewski L, Stark A (2023) Influence of vehicle traffic on modal-based bridge monitoring. J Civ Struct Heal Monit 13(1):219–234
Kumar KA, Sekhar C, Manikanta SD (2023a) Detection of non helmet riders and extraction of licence plate number. In: 2023 International conference on innovations in engineering and technology (ICIET). IEEE
Kumar B et al (2023b) An implementation of automatic number plate detection and recognition using AI. In: 2023 International conference on advances in computing, communication and applied informatics (ACCAI). IEEE
Kuo J-Y et al (2022) Constructing condition monitoring model of wind turbine blades. Mathematics 10(6):972

Lee P et al (2022) Trends in smart helmets with multimodal sensing for health and safety: scoping review. JMIR mHealth uHealth 10(11):e40797

Liu J (2023) Application development and technical analysis of rider helmet wearing monitoring system. In: Third international conference on advanced algorithms and signal image processing (AASIP 2023), vol 12799, SPIE

Mercado Reyna J et al (2023) Detection of helmet use in motorcycle drivers using convolutional neural network. Appl Sci 13(10):5882

Nijim M et al (2023) Advanced traffic management system for smart cities. In: International conference on advances in computing research. Springer Nature Switzerland, Cham

Parikh V et al (2022) Automatic helmet detection and gate opening using YOLO-V3. Grenze Int J Eng Technol (GIJET) 8(2)

Paul S et al (2022) Image analysis using deep learning for a smart traffic control system. In: Proceedings of the 2nd international conference on computing advancements

Peña Cáceres OJM et al (2022) Detection of motorcyclists without a safety helmet through YOLO: Support for road safety. In: International conference on technologies and innovation. Springer International Publishing, Cham

Premmaran G, Sathishkumar P (2022) Detection of helmetless riders and automatic number plate recognition using machine learning. In: 2022 International conference on applied artificial intelligence and computing (ICAAIC). IEEE

Pujar AM, Kulkarni PB (2023) Automatic number plate recognition using machine learning. In: International conference on applications of machine intelligence and data analytics (ICAMIDA 2022). Atlantis Press

Rajput P, Chaturvedi M, Patel V (2022) Road condition monitoring using unsupervised learning-based bus trajectory processing. Multimodal Transp 1(4):100041

Ramesh A et al (2022) Cloud-based collaborative road-damage monitoring with deep learning and smartphones. Sustainability 14(14):8682

Ranyal E, Sadhu A, Jain K (2022) Road condition monitoring using smart sensing and artificial intelligence: a review. Sensors 22(8):3044

Saini D et al (2022) Identification of helmets on motorcyclists and seatbelt on four-wheeler drivers. In: Recent advances in artificial intelligence and data engineering: select proceedings of AIDE 2020. Springer Singapore

Shambharkar Y et al (2023) An automatic framework for number plate detection using OCR and deep learning approach. Int J Adv Comput Sci Appl 14(4)

Singh P et al (2022a) Road surface quality monitoring using machine learning algorithm. In: Intelligent manufacturing and energy sustainability: proceedings of ICIMES 2021. Springer Singapore

Singh A et al (2022b) Helmet and number plate detection using deep learning and its comparative analysis. Available at SSRN 4149145

Sreeja GG et al (2023) Traffic infraction and alert system for two-wheelers using deep learning and YOLO v3. In: 2023 9th International conference on advanced computing and communication systems (ICACCS), vol 1. IEEE

Teja SS et al (2023) Comparative analysis of optimizers and transfer learning methods for headgear detection using convolutional neural network. In: 2023 International conference on network, multimedia and information technology (NMITCON). IEEE

Tippannavar SS, Yashwanth SD (2023) Real-time vehicle identification for improving the traffic management system—a review. J Trends Comput Sci Smart Technol 5(3):323–342

Tiwari R, Rumaney AH, Saravanan M (2023) Real-time traffic surveillance and detection using deep learning and computer vision techniques. In: 2023 2nd International conference on vision towards emerging trends in communication and networking technologies (ViTECoN). IEEE

Waris T et al (2022) CNN-based automatic helmet violation detection of motorcyclists for an intelligent transportation system. Math Probl Eng 2022

Wei C et al (2023) Fast helmet and license plate detection based on lightweight YOLOv5. Sensors 23(9):4335

Chapter 10
Remote Monitoring and Control Systems in Agriculture and Farming

Varuna Gupta, Aditi Garg, and Swati Agrawal

Abstract This chapter explores the transformative role of remote monitoring and control management systems in revolutionizing agricultural practices to achieve enhanced efficiency and sustainability. With the increasing demand for food production amidst growing environmental challenges, adopting advanced technologies becomes imperative to optimize resource utilization and mitigate risks. Remote monitoring and control systems offer a holistic approach to farm management by enabling real-time monitoring, data-driven decision-making, and automated control of critical agricultural operations. The chapter begins with an overview of the key components and functionalities of remote monitoring and control systems, including sensor networks, communication protocols, and data analytics platforms. Moreover, the chapter elucidates the significance of data analytics and machine learning algorithms. By leveraging predictive analytics, farmers can anticipate crop stress, pest infestations, and irrigation requirements, enabling proactive management strategies and optimizing resource allocation. Furthermore, the chapter explores the applications of remote monitoring and control systems in digital agriculture and decision, fertilization, sustainable water management, soil health preservation, and ecosystem resilience, thereby minimizing manual intervention, reducing labour costs, and enhancing operational efficiency. Case studies and real-world examples demonstrate the successful implementation of remote monitoring and control systems across diverse agricultural systems. Additionally, the chapter discussed also addresses the challenges and barriers to adoption. In conclusion, the chapter underscores the transformative potential of remote monitoring and control management systems. By empowering farmers with actionable insights and automated control capabilities, these technologies pave the way toward a more efficient, productive, and sustainable agricultural future.

Keywords IOT · Machine learning · Smart agriculture

V. Gupta (✉) · S. Agrawal
Christ University, Bengaluru, India
e-mail: varunagupta.cs@gmail.com

A. Garg
J.C. Bose University of Science and Technology, YMCA, Faridabad, India

R. Arya et al. (eds.), *Recent Trends in Artificial Intelligence Towards a Smart World*, Frontiers of Artificial Intelligence, Ethics and Multidisciplinary Applications, https://doi.org/10.1007/978-981-97-6790-8_10

10.1 Introduction

10.1.1 Overview of Remote Monitoring and Control Systems

Remote monitoring and control systems have revolutionized agriculture and farming by providing real-time insights into crop conditions, environmental factors, and farm operations, ultimately enhancing productivity, sustainability, and efficiency. These systems typically consist of sensors deployed across fields to collect data on soil moisture, temperature, humidity, and crop health, which is then transmitted to a central monitoring platform via communication networks such as cellular, satellite, or LoRaWAN. Gateways and communication equipment play a crucial role in aggregating data from sensors, translating protocols for interoperability, and ensuring secure communication channels across remote farm locations. Once collected, this data is processed and analysed using advanced analytics and machine learning algorithms to generate actionable insights and recommendations for farmers. Research in this field, such as the paper "Wireless Sensor Networks for Agriculture: The State-of-the-Art in Practice and Future Challenges" by Suryadevara et al., highlights the practical implementation and challenges of remote monitoring systems in agriculture, underscoring the importance of scalable and interoperable solutions to address the unique needs of farming operations. Overall, remote monitoring and control systems offer unprecedented capabilities for farmers to optimize resource usage, mitigate risks, and make data-driven decisions, thereby driving innovation and sustainability in agriculture (Kumar et al. 2022).

10.2 Importance of Technology in Enhancing Agricultural Efficiency and Sustainability

Precision Agriculture

Precision agriculture utilizes technologies such as GPS, sensors, drones, and data analytics to optimize farming practices. By precisely monitoring soil conditions, crop health, and weather patterns, farmers can make informed decisions regarding planting, irrigation, fertilization, and pest management. Precision agriculture minimizes input wastage, maximizes yield, and reduces environmental impacts associated with excessive pesticide and fertilizer use.

Mechanization and Automation

Mechanization and automation technologies such as tractors, harvesters, and robotic systems streamline agricultural tasks, saving time and labour. Automated systems improve efficiency and accuracy in planting, harvesting, and post-harvest handling, resulting in higher productivity and reduced labor costs. Furthermore, robotic systems enable selective harvesting and weed control, minimizing damage to crops and reducing the need for chemical inputs.

Sustainable Water Management

Technology plays a crucial role in sustainable water management through innovations in irrigation systems and water-saving techniques. Drip irrigation, precision irrigation, and soil moisture sensors help optimize water usage by delivering the right amount of water directly to the roots of plants. Additionally, technologies such as rainwater harvesting, wastewater recycling, and desalination contribute to water conservation and resilience against droughts.

Digital Agriculture and Decision Support Systems

Digital agriculture platforms and decision support systems integrate data from various sources to provide farmers with real-time insights and recommendations. By analysing data on weather forecasts, soil conditions, crop performance, and market trends, farmers can make timely and informed decisions to optimize productivity and profitability. Digital agriculture empowers farmers to adopt evidence-based practices, enhance resource efficiency, and mitigate risks associated with climate variability and market fluctuations.

Conservation Agriculture

Conservation agriculture practices such as minimal tillage, cover cropping, and crop rotation help preserve soil health and biodiversity. Technological innovations such as no-till planters, cover crop rollers, and precision seekers facilitate the adoption of conservation agriculture by farmers. Conservation agriculture reduces soil erosion, enhances water retention, and promotes carbon sequestration, contributing to long-term agricultural sustainability.

Climate-Smart Agriculture

Climate-smart agriculture integrates climate-resilient practices and technologies to mitigate the impacts of climate change on agriculture. Technologies such as drought-resistant crop varieties, weather-resistant shelters, and greenhouse gas monitoring systems help farmers adapt to changing climatic conditions. Climate-smart agriculture enhances resilience, reduces greenhouse gas emissions, and promotes sustainable intensification, ensuring food security in the face of climate uncertainty.

Sustainable Livestock Farming

Technology plays a crucial role in promoting sustainable livestock farming through improved animal health, welfare, and efficiency. Innovations such as precision feeding systems, remote monitoring devices, and biogas digesters help optimize feed utilization, reduce emissions, and manage waste. Sustainable livestock farming practices mitigate environmental impacts, enhance animal productivity, and improve livelihoods for farmers, contributing to overall agricultural sustainability (Suryadevara et al. 2017).

10.3 Components of Remote Monitoring Systems

10.3.1 Sensor Networks

Sensor networks in remote monitoring systems refer to interconnected sensors deployed in remote or distributed locations to collect data on various physical phenomena. These networks are a fundamental component of remote monitoring systems and are crucial in capturing real-time information from the environment.

Deployment: Sensors are strategically deployed in the field or at remote locations where monitoring is required. They may be stationary or mobile, depending on the application.

Types of Sensors: Sensor networks can comprise various sensors depending on the parameters being monitored. Common types of sensors include temperature sensors, humidity sensors, pressure sensors, motion sensors, gas sensors, proximity sensors, and many others.

Interconnection: Sensors within a network are interconnected through wired or wireless communication protocols. Wired connections may include Ethernet or serial connections, while wireless connections could involve Wi-Fi, cellular, satellite, or Low-Power Wide-Area Network (LPWAN) technologies such as LoRa or NB-IoT.

Data Collection: Sensors continuously collect data from the environment according to their specific measurement capabilities. This data can include environmental conditions, machine status, energy consumption, and more.

Data Aggregation: In sensor networks, data from individual sensors are often aggregated at intermediate points, such as gateways, before being transmitted to the central monitoring system. Aggregation helps reduce the volume of data transmitted and can also involve preprocessing tasks such as data filtering and compression.

10.3.2 Communication Protocols

Communication protocols serve as the backbone of remote monitoring systems, facilitating the seamless transmission of data between remote sensors, devices, and the central monitoring station. These protocols define the rules and formats for data exchange, ensuring compatibility and reliability across various components of the system. Common communication protocols used in remote monitoring systems include Internet Protocol (IP), Wireless protocol and Cellular Networks (Kurniawan et al. 2015).

10.3.3 Data Acquisition and Processing Platforms

Data acquisition and processing platforms form the core of remote monitoring systems, collecting, analysing, and visualizing data from remote sensors and devices. These platforms integrate hardware and software components to ensure efficient data collection, storage, and interpretation.

Key features of data acquisition and processing platforms include:

Sensor Integration: The platform should support a wide range of sensors and devices, allowing seamless integration of data from various sources. This includes environmental sensors, IoT devices, SCADA systems, and industrial equipment.

Real-Time Data Processing: Advanced algorithms and analytics capabilities enable real-time processing of streaming data, allowing for immediate insights and actionable intelligence. This involves data filtering, aggregation, anomaly detection, and predictive analytics.

Data Visualization and Reporting: User-friendly dashboards, charts, and reports provide stakeholders with intuitive access to monitored data and key performance indicators (KPIs). Visualization tools enable trend analysis, historical data comparison, and performance optimization.

Integration with External Systems: The platform should support integration with external systems such as ERP (Enterprise Resource Planning) software, CRM (Customer Relationship Management) systems, and third-party APIs, enabling seamless data exchange and workflow automation.

Scalability and Flexibility: Scalable architecture and modular design allow the platform to accommodate growing data volumes and evolving requirements. Cloud-based platforms offer scalability, while on-premises solutions provide flexibility and data sovereignty (Yan et al. 2014).

10.3.4 Communication Equipment and Gateways

Various gateways can be used in agriculture monitoring, like Cellular Gateways, Satellite Gateways, LoRaWAN Gateways, Wi-Fi Gateways, and Ethernet Gateways.

10.4 Functions of Gateways in Agricultural Monitoring

10.4.1 Aggregating Data from Sensors and Devices

Aggregating data from sensors and devices is a critical function within remote monitoring systems, especially in agricultural contexts. This process involves collecting and consolidating data generated by various sensors deployed across farms, including soil moisture sensors, weather stations, and crop health monitors. By aggregating this diverse range of data streams, farmers and agricultural professionals can gain a comprehensive understanding of environmental conditions, crop health, and resource usage in their fields.

10.4.2 Translating Protocols to Ensure Interoperability

Translating protocols to ensure interoperability is a vital aspect of remote monitoring systems, particularly in agricultural settings where various sensors and devices may use different communication standards and protocols. This process involves converting data formats and communication protocols to facilitate seamless interaction and data exchange between different components of the monitoring system.

10.4.3 Providing Secure Communication Channels

Providing secure communication channels is essential for ensuring the integrity and confidentiality of data transmitted within remote monitoring systems, especially in agricultural contexts where sensitive information about crop yields, environmental conditions, and farm operations is exchanged. Secure communication channels employ encryption techniques and authentication protocols to safeguard data against unauthorized access, interception, or tampering (Suryadevara et al. 2017; Wenz 1999).

10.4.4 Managing Connectivity Across Remote Farm Locations

Managing connectivity across remote farm locations is crucial for ensuring the reliability and effectiveness of remote monitoring systems in agriculture. Remote farms often face challenges such as limited internet access, unstable network coverage, and geographic isolation, which can hinder data transmission and communication between sensors, gateways, and central servers. Effective management of connectivity involves deploying robust communication infrastructure, such as cellular networks, satellite internet, or long-range wireless technologies like LoRaWAN, to overcome geographical barriers and ensure seamless data transmission from remote areas (Bobitan et al. 2023; Brower-Toland et al. 2024).

10.5 Sensor Technologies for Remote Monitoring

Sensor technologies for remote monitoring involve the use of various sensors to collect data from remote or inaccessible locations and transmit it wirelessly or via networks for monitoring, analysis, and decision-making. These sensors can measure a wide range of parameters such as temperature, humidity, pressure, soil moisture, air quality, water quality, motion, sound, and light intensity, among others (Al-Mutairi et al. 2021; Raju and Varma 2017).

Agricultural choices are significantly impacted using soil moisture sensors, which play an important role in remote monitoring. Farmers can make informed judgements regarding their crops and seeds in advance if they have a comprehensive understanding of the soil situation during the growing season.

There are several types of sensors commonly used in agriculture and farming to collect data from remote or inaccessible locations. These sensors help farmers monitor various parameters such as soil moisture, temperature, humidity, crop health, weather conditions, and more. Here are some examples.

10.5.1 Soil Moisture Sensors

Soil moisture sensors are used to gauge the amount of moisture in the soil, helping farmers schedule irrigation more efficiently and avoid over or underwatering their crops. They can be placed at various depths to track moisture levels across the soil profile.

10.5.2 Weather Stations Sensors

Weather stations sensors contain a range of sensors that measure temperature, humidity, wind speed, wind direction, rainfall, and solar radiation. This data is essential for making decisions about crop management, pest control, and disease prevention.

10.5.3 Crop Health Sensors

Crop health sensors like multispectral or hyperspectral cameras, are attached to drones or satellites to keep an eye on crop health by taking pictures of fields and studying vegetation indices. These sensors can identify nutrient shortages, pest attacks, and diseases in their beginning stages, giving farmers the opportunity to make necessary adjustments.

10.5.4 GPS Trackers

GPS trackers are employed to oversee the movement of farming tools and animals. They are useful in streamlining field activities, locating machinery, and deterring theft.

10.5.5 Remote Cameras

Farmers can install remote cameras or surveillance systems in their fields or barns to monitor crops, livestock, and infrastructure from a distance. These cameras offer real-time visual information, assisting in identifying issues like trespassing, theft, or unusual animal behaviour.

10.5.6 Water Quality Sensors

Farmers with water sources on their farms, like ponds or streams, can use water quality sensors to monitor pH levels, dissolved oxygen, conductivity, and turbidity. These sensors help ensure that the water used for irrigation or livestock is safe and clean from any pollutants.

10.5.7 Drone Technology

Drones come with sensors like cameras, LiDAR, and thermal imaging to gather data across vast areas in a fast and efficient way. They are employed in tasks like monitoring crops, creating maps, and surveying difficult or vast landscapes.

10.5.8 Satellite Imagery

Remote sensing platforms based on satellites offer important data on crop health, soil moisture, and land use patterns over large areas. They provide regular and reliable monitoring, making them perfect for precision agriculture applications.

10.6 Data Analytics in Agricultural Remote Monitoring

Data analytics significantly transforms conventional farming into smart agriculture by providing insights that help farmers make informed decisions. Farmers and agricultural businesses can improve productivity, efficiency, and sustainability by leveraging various data sources and advanced analytical techniques. Here are key ways in which data analytics is used in smart agriculture:

Precision Farming

- *Soil Analysis*: Analysing soil data helps determine the optimal planting times and the right types of crops for maximizing yield.
- *Yield Prediction*: Data from past crop yields alongside current data from sensors can help predict future crop performance and yields.

Crop Monitoring

- Satellite Imagery and Drones: Remote sensing technology provides high-resolution images that can be used to assess crop health, identify pests and diseases, and measure the effects of environmental factors.
- Sensor Data: IoT sensors in the field capture real-time data about soil moisture, temperature, and nutrient levels, enabling precise irrigation and fertilization.

Livestock Management

Monitoring animal health through wearable sensors can provide data on movement, consumption patterns, and other well-being indicators, allowing for early intervention.

Weather Forecasting and Analysis

Weather data analytics can help farmers make proactive decisions to mitigate the impact of adverse weather conditions on crops and livestock.

Resource Management

Water usage can be optimized through analytics, ensuring crops receive the right amount of water at the right time.

Energy consumption in various agricultural processes can be tracked and reduced.

Supply Chain Optimization

Analytics can forecast demand for crops and agricultural products, leading to better supply chain management from production to market.

Sustainability

By analysing data on crop yields, resource usage, and environmental conditions, farmers can adopt practices that reduce their environmental footprint.

Disease Prediction and Pest Control

Data analytics can identify patterns that signal the outbreak of diseases or infestation by pests, enabling pre-emptive actions.

Machine Learning and Predictive Analytics

Advanced algorithms can learn from data to predict future outcomes, such as which crop rotations will be the most beneficial or when to harvest for optimal quality and quantity.

Market Analysis

Farmers can use market trends, pricing data, and consumer behaviour analytics to decide what to plant and when to sell.

Integrating these data-driven approaches into agriculture requires sophisticated data collection tools like drones, satellites, IoT sensors, and farm management software. Furthermore, the implementation of big data infrastructure and analytics tools is necessary to process and analyse vast amounts (McFadden et al. 2023; Monteiro et al. 2021).

10.6.1 Predictive Analytics

Predictive analytics in smart agriculture and farming is an effective instrument for improving decision-making, resource allocation, and overall agricultural outcomes. Using data, algorithms, and machine learning, predictive analytics may give useful insights for precision agriculture, allowing farmers to make educated decisions based on accurate data evaluation. Using past and current data, predictive analytics can help farms optimize their operations, leading to better practices and results. By incorporating field sensors and other technology, this method can enable precision farming. This approach enhances productivity and quality by accurately forecasting and supplying the right amounts of agricultural inputs (https://www.taylorfrancis.com/books/edit/10.1201/9781003391302/predictive-analytics-smart-agriculture-saravanan-krishnan-jose-anand-narayanan-prasanth-sam-goundar-christo-ananth).

10.6.2 Machine Learning Algorithms

Machine learning algorithms play a crucial role in smart agriculture and farming, offering innovative solutions to enhance agricultural practices.

10.7 Applications of Remote Monitoring Systems in Agriculture

Remote Monitoring Systems in Agriculture leverage various IoT technologies to offer diverse applications. These systems empower farmers with valuable insights into their production, enabling them to enhance operations remotely without needing physical presence.

10.7.1 Soil Health Monitoring

Optimizing soil quality in agricultural fields leads to improved production outcomes. Various IoT devices, including those monitoring soil moisture, pH levels, temperature, and nutrient content, are deployed in the field for this purpose. This information equips farmers with insights to determine appropriate irrigation levels and the optimal application of chemicals and fertilizers, thereby enhancing overall production efficiency (Hundal et al. 2023; Javaid et al. 2022; Datta and Taghvaeian 2023).

10.7.2 Crop Health Monitoring

Utilizing multispectral sensors and optical sensing systems, farmers can capture high-resolution field images to evaluate crop health and identify diseases and pests. This advanced technology streamlines harvesting, minimizing farmers' time and labour demands (Walter et al. 2017).

10.7.3 Environmental Parameter Monitoring

Deploying IoT sensors to forecast various environmental factors such as temperature, humidity, wind speed, light intensity, pressure, carbon dioxide levels, and sunlight intensity within farms empowers farmers to make informed decisions regarding planting and harvesting timelines. Additionally, these sensors aid in crop protection measures, enhancing overall agricultural efficiency (Punithavathi et al. 2023).

10.7.4 Automated Irrigation Systems

Advanced irrigation systems driven by technology enable farmers to precisely determine the timing and volume of water required for their fields. Soil moisture sensors provide vital data, guiding the irrigation process to ensure soil moisture reaches optimal levels. This approach not only boosts production efficiency but also prevents crop damage resulting from excessive water supply (Vellidis et al. 2016; Shaikh et al. 2022).

10.7.5 Precision Fertilization

In agricultural scenarios, smart sensors are deployed to gather various soil parameters, including temperature, humidity, nutrient levels, and pH values. Analysis of this data enables the determination of optimal fertilization levels. Subsequently, personalized fertilizer recommendations based on these analyses can be provided to farmers, aiding them in determining the precise number of fertilizers required for their fields (Vernunft et al. 2023).

10.8 Case Studies and Success Stories

In this chapter, a total of 5 cases have been discussed of different companies like CropX, Sensaphone, DroneDeploy, The Climate Corporation, Teralytic. First case is talking about precision irrigation that helps farmers to use soil monitors and online tracking to get information about temperature, moisture levels, and other important things. The second case is about watching cattle, which offers ways for livestock facilities to be monitored from afar. In barns or pens, their devices have monitors that check the temperature, humidity, and other environmental factors. The third case is about crop health monitoring which offers drone-based imaging and mapping solutions for agriculture. Whereas the fourth case is about Weather Monitoring and Forecasting and the fifth case is focusing on Soil Health Management which offers soil monitoring solutions. Table 10.1 depicts the detailed case studies of different companies in the field of Agriculture and Farming.

Table 10.1 Case studies of different companies on agriculture and farming

Cases	Company name	Description
Precision irrigation	CropX	Combines soil sensors with remote monitoring technology to collect data on soil moisture levels, temperature, and other relevant factors (Scherer 2009)
Livestock monitoring	Sensaphone	Provides remote monitoring solutions for livestock facilities. Their systems include sensors for monitoring temperature, humidity, and other environmental factors in barns or pens
Crop health monitoring	DroneDeploy	Offers drone-based imaging and mapping solutions for agriculture. Farmers can use drones equipped with cameras and sensors to capture high-resolution aerial imagery of their fields (Dandois and Leite 2016)
Weather monitoring and forecasting	The Climate Corporation	A subsidiary of Bayer, offers digital agriculture tools for farmers. Their FieldView platform provides access to weather data, forecasts, and field-specific insights (Amir et al. 2018)
Soil health management	Teralytic	Teralytic offers soil monitoring solutions that utilize wireless sensors to collect data on soil moisture, temperature, pH, and nutrient levels (Schulte et al. 2020)

10.9 Challenges and Barriers to Adoption

Although smart farming holds the potential to enhance efficiency and sustainability in agriculture, it encounters various obstacles and barriers that hinder its widespread adoption (Bhat and Huang 2021; Hundal et al. 2023).

10.9.1 Technical and Operational Challenges

- *Cost*
  Buying sensors, software, and equipment for smart farming can be expensive, especially for small farms.
- *Connectivity*
  Ensuring seamless data interoperability among various sensors, software, and equipment is crucial for the effective implementation of smart farming practices.
- *Data interoperability*
  Interconnecting and matching up different technologies and platforms used in smart farming is difficult. Making sure that different systems can share data and work together easily is still a complex technical problem.

10.9.2 Social and Economic Challenges

- *Knowledge skill*
  Smart farming requires technical knowledge and digital skills. Older farmers or those with less education may not have these skills, which can make it hard for them to use smart farming technology effectively.
- *Data security and privacy*
  Smart farming involves gathering and studying a huge amount of important data, such as crop output, soil quality, and animal well-being. Protecting this data from online risks and unauthorized access is very important for farmers and others involved in the agriculture sector.
- *Limited access to financing and support*
  Farmers, especially small-scale ones, face challenges in accessing financial resources and support needed to invest in smart farming technologies.

10.10 Future Trends and Innovations

Automated agricultural machines: The future of agriculture looks bright with the continued advancement of autonomous tractors, drones, and robotic systems. These technologies promise to revolutionize farmwork by enabling tasks like planting, spraying, and harvesting to be done with minimal human involvement, leading to increased efficiency and potentially lower labor costs (Kefyalew et al. 2021).

Internet of Things (IoT) Integration: Smart farm helpers, called "IoT sensors", will get better and cheaper, letting farmers see in real-time how healthy their crops are, what the soil needs, and even what the weather will be like. This information will help farmers make more intelligent choices about what to do and use less water, fertilizer, and other resources (Qin et al. 2020).

Artificial Intelligence and Machine Learning: Artificial Intelligence will analyse all the information collected from farms to help farmers understand how their crops are doing, control pests and diseases, and grow the most significant harvest possible. Machine Learning models will keep getting better and better at making predictions and giving helpful advice (Mohanty et al. 2016).

Precision Livestock Farming: Just like in farming, where smart technology helps grow healthy crops, similar tools can be used for animals. Sensors and computers can keep track of how animals are feeling, acting, and staying healthy. This helps farmers take better care of their animals and get even better results (Wathes et al. 2016).

Remote Sensing and Satellite Imagery: Farmers can now use special tools like satellites to see their entire farm from way up high. These tools can tell them how healthy their crops are, how much water the soil has, and even how different plants are growing across the whole farm. This information helps farmers make smarter decisions about what to do and where to put their resources (Wardlow and Egbert 2008).

Biotechnology and Genetic Engineering: Ongoing progress in biotechnology and genetic engineering will result in the creation of crop strains possessing enhanced resistance to pests, diseases, and environmental challenges. This fosters sustainable agricultural practices and bolsters food security (Godfray et al. 2010).

Smart Irrigation Systems: Smart irrigation systems, outfitted with sensors and actuators, will finely tune water distribution to crops, adjusting to their requirements and the prevailing environmental factors. This efficient management conserves water resources and minimizes irrigation expenses (Ahmadi et al. 2018).

Vertical Farming and Controlled Environment Agriculture: Amid mounting worries regarding food security and urban expansion, vertical farming and Controlled Environment Agriculture (CEA) techniques will rise in prominence. These approaches enable year-round cultivation within regulated settings, requiring less water and land compared to conventional farming methods (Zou et al. 2020).

Cooperative Platforms and Agricultural Market Networks: Online platforms and marketplaces are poised to facilitate collaboration among farmers, agribusinesses, and technology providers, allowing for the exchange of knowledge, resources, and best practices in smart farming (Galloway et al. 2017).

References

Ahmadi M, Balasundram SK, Talib JBA, Abbaspour-Gilandeh Y (2018) Smart irrigation technologies for sustainable water use in agriculture: a review. Comput Electron Agric 144:354–374

Al-Mutairi AW, Al-Aubidy KM, Alhalaiqa FN (2021) IoT-based real-time monitoring system for epidemic diseases patients: design and evaluation. Int J Online Biomed Eng 17(1):63–82. https://doi.org/10.3991/ijoe.v17i01.18849

Amir M et al (2018) Using weather data for crop yield prediction: a review. Comput Electron Agric

Bhat SA, Huang N-F (2021) Big data and AI revolution in precision agriculture: survey and challenges. IEEE Access 9:110209–110222

Bobitan N, Dumitrescu D, Burca V (2023) Agriculture's efficiency in the context of sustainable agriculture—a benchmarking analysis of financial performance with data envelopment analysis and malmquist index. Sustainability 15(16):12169

Brower-Toland B et al (2024) A crucial role for technology in sustainable agriculture. ACS Agric Sci Technol

Dandois JP, Leite F (2016) Assessment of the potential of unmanned aerial systems for monitoring oilseed rape (Brassica napus L.) development. Remote Sens

Datta S, Taghvaeian S (2023) Soil water sensors for irrigation scheduling in the United States: a systematic review of literature. Agric Water Manag 278:108148

Galloway PR, Davidson BN, Burton RJF (2017) Agri-environmental collaboration and the emergence of 'sustainable' agri-food governance in the UK. J Rural Stud 50:35–47

Godfray HCJ, Beddington JR, Crute IR, Haddad L, Lawrence D, Muir JF, Toulmin C (2010) Food security: the challenge of feeding 9 billion people. Science 327(5967):812–818

https://www.sciencedirect.com/science/article/abs/pii/B9780323910682000059

https://www.taylorfrancis.com/books/edit/10.1201/9781003391302/predictive-analytics-smart-agriculture-saravanan-krishnan-jose-anand-narayanan-prasanth-sam-goundar-christo-ananth

Hundal GS, Laux CM, Buckmaster D, Sutton MJ, Langemeier M (2023) Exploring barriers to the adoption of internet of things-based precision agriculture practices. Agriculture 13:163

Javaid M, Haleem A, Singh RP, Suman R (2022) Enhancing smart farming through the applications of agriculture 4.0 technologies. Int J Intell Netw 3:150–164
Kefyalew T, Alene AD, Ge L (2021) Design and implementation of an autonomous farming robot for weeding, planting, and spraying tasks. Comput Electron Agric 184:106007
Kumar A et al (2022) Drone technology in sustainable agriculture: the future of farming is precision agriculture and mapping. Agriculture, livestock production and aquaculture: advances for smallholder farming systems, vol 2. Springer International Publishing, Cham, pp 3–12
Kurniawan E et al (2015) A survey on communication protocols for internet of things. Procedia Comput Sci
McFadden J, Njuki E, Griffin T (2023) Precision agriculture in the digital era: recent adoption on U.S. farms. US Department of Agriculture, Economic Research Service 248. https://www.ers.usda.gov. Accessed 2 March 2023
Mohanty SP, Hughes DP, Salathé M (2016) Using deep learning for image-based plant disease detection. Front Plant Sci 7:1419
Monteiro A, Santos S, Gonçalves P (2021) Precision agriculture for crop and livestock farming—brief review. Animals 11:2345
Punithavathi R, Rani ADC, Sughashini KR, Kurangi C, Nirmala M, Ahmed HFT, Balamurugan SP (2023) Computer vision and deep learning-enabled weed detection model for precision agriculture. Comput Syst Sci Eng 44:2759–2774
Qin C, Yu M, Han S, Song L, Wang Z, Wang D, Zhang J (2020) Data-driven decision support for smart agriculture: literature review, trends, and challenges. Comput Electron Agric 176:105657
Raju KRSR, Varma GHK (2017) Knowledge based real time monitoring system for aquaculture using IoT. In: 2017 IEEE 7th International advance computing conference (IACC), pp 318–321. https://doi.org/10.1109/IACC.2017.0075
Scherer TF (2009) Precision irrigation management with soil water sensors—an update. Irrigation Sci
Schulte RPO et al (2020) Assessing soil health and quality: current status and opportunities for transformational change. Front Environ Sci
Shaikh TA, Rasool T, Lone FR (2022) Towards leveraging the role of machine learning and artificial intelligence in precision agriculture and smart farming. Comput Electron Agric 198:107119
Suryadevara NK et al (2017) Wireless sensor networks for agriculture: the state-of-the-art in practice and future challenges. Comput Electron Agric
Vellidis G, Liakos V, Porter W, Tucker M, Liang X (2016) A dynamic variable rate irrigation control system. International Society of Precision Agriculture, Monticello, IL
Vernunft A, Eggert A, Brüssow K-P (2023) Ultrasonographic monitoring of fetal growth and fetal weight calculation in sows during gestation. Agriculture 13(1):16. https://doi.org/10.3390/agriculture13010016
Walter A, Finger R, Huber R, Buchmann N (2017) Opinion: smart farming is key to developing sustainable agriculture. Proc Natl Acad Sci USA 114:6148–6150
Wardlow BD, Egbert SL (2008) Large-area crop mapping using time-series MODIS 250 m NDVI data: an assessment for the U.S. Central Great Plains. Remote Sens Environ 112(3):1096–1116
Wathes CM, Kristensen HH, Aerts JM, Berckmans D, Ismayilova G (2016) Precision livestock farming: a perspective on the future of monitoring and control of pig and poultry production. Animal 10(1):120–127
Wenz PS (1999) Pragmatism in practice: the efficiency of sustainable agriculture. Environ Ethics 21(4):391–410
Yan Z et al (2014) A survey on internet of things: architecture, enabling technologies, security and privacy, and applications. IEEE Internet Things J
Zou X, Ali S, Yan Z (2020) Vertical farming and sustainable urban agriculture: the future of food production. J Hortic Sci Biotechnol 95(2):129–135

Chapter 11
Enhanced Deep Learning Model for Road Transportation Safety with Accident Detection and Traffic Flow Analysis

P. Santosh Kumar Patra, B. Hari Krishna, Janapati Chaitanya Krishna, M. Krishna Satya Varma, and V. Bharath Simha Reddy

Abstract Intelligent road traffic monitoring necessitates the development of efficient systems capable of handling the substantial data volumes continuously generated by traffic surveillance cameras. Automated solutions are essential since manual data analysis is both labour-intensive and impractical. The goal of our deep learning-based method is to build a traffic detection system that is both quick and accurate, with no human involvement required. The study focuses on two critical aspects of intelligent traffic monitoring: accident detection and traffic flow analysis. The goal of this project is to improve future intelligent transportation systems by using TrafficNet technology. The TrafficNet system performs multiple activities, including data splitting, data analysis, deep learning convolutional neural network (DLCNN) model training, traffic forecasting, and performance evaluation. Following that, DLCNN model for diverse traffic scenarios was developed. The TrafficNet system eventually anticipates numerous categories, such as heavy traffic, light traffic, accidents, and fires. The proposed TrafficNet demonstrates its accuracy and versatility by effectively identifying regions in a wide range of applications.

P. Santosh Kumar Patra (✉) · B. Hari Krishna
St. Martins Engineering College, Kompally, Hyderabad, Telangana, India
e-mail: drpskpatra@gmail.com

B. Hari Krishna
e-mail: drhariece@smec.ac.in

J. C. Krishna
Vardhaman College of Engineering, Hyderabad, Telangana, India
e-mail: janapatikrishnachaithanya@gmail.com

M. Krishna Satya Varma
SRKR Engineering College, Bhimavaram, Andhra Pradesh, India

V. Bharath Simha Reddy
Malla Reddy Engineering College and Management Sciences, Medchal, Hyderabad, Telangana, India
e-mail: bharath@mrem.ac.in

R. Arya et al. (eds.), *Recent Trends in Artificial Intelligence Towards a Smart World*, Frontiers of Artificial Intelligence, Ethics and Multidisciplinary Applications, https://doi.org/10.1007/978-981-97-6790-8_11

Keywords Accident detection · Automated solutions · Convolutional neural networks · Traffic flow analysis · Traffic monitoring

11.1 Introduction

Improving traffic management, decreasing congestion, and raising road safety all depend on intelligent road traffic monitoring systems (Mehrannia et al. 2023; Sharma and Singh 2023). These systems rely on cutting-edge tech and data analytics to accomplish their goals. The purpose of installing a system of sensors and cameras along roads is to detect accidents and other traffic issues in real time (Bharadiya 2023). These sensors detect accidents or other dangers by picking up on abrupt changes in speed, pauses in traffic, or strange patterns. The technology potentially notifies relevant authorities, such as traffic control centres and emergency services, in a flash when certain circumstances are recognized (Zhao et al. 2023a), allowing for a rapid reaction and perhaps averting fatalities.

In addition, these systems anticipate potentially dangerous locations by analysing past accident data using machine learning algorithms (Fang et al. 2023). Traffic flow analysis, on the other hand, is an attempt to comprehend and improve traffic movement. This method entails collecting and analysing large volumes of data from several sources, including sensors in vehicles (Fang et al. 2023), global position system devices (Hassan et al. 2023), and traffic cameras (Gaber et al. 2023). After collecting this data, traffic management systems use it to provide drivers with the most recent information via digital signs (Oladimeji et al. 2023), mobile applications or navigation systems to reduce traffic congestion. Transportation authority's get advantages from traffic flow research as it provides guidance for their choices pertaining to road design, infrastructure enhancements, and optimization of traffic signals. These judgments are based on insights derived from data analysis.

Typical features of intelligent traffic monitoring systems for roads include the ability to identify accidents and analyse traffic flows simultaneously. A more complete image of traffic conditions was obtained via this integration, which in turn allows for better traffic management. Automatically adjusting traffic lights, rerouting traffic, or providing other routes to reduce delays was done, for instance, when an accident is detected (Zhang et al. 2023). By automatically removing traffic lanes, it also speeds up the arrival of rescue workers. Intelligent road traffic monitoring systems use data analysis and technology to improve traffic flow, decrease congestion, and prevent accidents, making these two components crucial. These technologies are essential for better transportation efficiency and commuter quality of life because they make traffic operations run more smoothly and respond to road problems faster. The novel contribution of this work is as follows:

- Introduction of a TrafficNet dataset for training a DLCNN for traffic status prediction including dense traffic, low traffic, accidents, and fires.

- Incorporation of dataset and image preprocessing to ensure consistency and efficiency in the training process.
- Demonstration of the DLCNN's efficiency through high accuracy in a case study, affirming its potential for large-scale traffic surveillance applications.
- A promising approach with potential applications in intelligent transport systems for future traffic surveillance enhancements.

11.2 Literature Survey

The exponential growth in the number of vehicles on the roads, largely driven by rapid industrialization, has led to a significant increase in road accidents, resulting in substantial economic losses and human casualties by Micheale (2017). According to the World Health Organization, more than 1.25 million lives are lost annually in road traffic accidents, with an additional 20 to 50 million people suffering injuries according to Bahiru et al. (2018). These statistics underscore the global challenge of road accidents, making it a leading cause of fatalities and injuries. In recent years, there has been a heightened focus in the fields of traffic science and intelligent vehicle research on how to prevent and predict automobile collisions. The extent of damage in traffic accidents is often correlated with the severity of the collisions, influenced by various factors. Research in this area has uncovered a wealth of information, exploring different variables and aspects.

Lu et al. (2015) assessed the positioning of vehicles in road segments and examined factors like road safety grade, road surface conditions, visual conditions, vehicle conditions, and driver states, developing an accuracy model with an 86.67% prediction accuracy. Alkheder et al. (2017) utilized artificial neural networks to predict traffic accident severity based on 16 variables and four injury levels. Akanbi et al. (2009) identified primary human factors contributing to road accidents and species extinction, including old age, overtaking, speeding, religious beliefs, poor braking, and faulty tires. Environmental factors, such as weather and accident situations, were found to influence highway traffic behaviour by Caleffi et al. (2016). An et al. (2019) used a fuzzy convolutional neural network to forecast traffic flow amid uncertain information on accidents.

Multiobjective genetic algorithms have demonstrated success in predicting accident severity based on consumer preferences, as noted in Hashmienejad's research (Hashmienejad and Hasheminejad 2017). Ren et al. (2017) applied deep learning to develop a short-term traffic accident risk prediction model, considering previous accidents, traffic flow, meteorological conditions, and air pollution levels. The spatio-temporal correlation of road accidents was also explored for urban accident risk prediction (Ren et al. 2018). Huang et al. (2019) introduced a temporal aggregation neural network layer to forecast traffic accidents by capturing correlations in the temporal dimension. According to Kumeda et al. (2019), lighting conditions, road class, and the number of automobiles all have a role in producing accidents. Using spatial and temporal correlations, Bao et al. (2020) developed a model that explicitly discussed accident prediction. Murphy et al. (2020) did, however, use data mining methods to analyse driving behaviour.

Yaman et al. (2022) studied the effects of age, sex, seat belt use, alcohol, and drug use on injury severity in motor vehicle accidents by simple data mining methods for random forest roads have gained popularity in many algorithms used for accident prediction and prevention. It shows promise in reducing traffic accidents and has applications in other fields such as meteorology according to Ding et al. (2023), statistics by Schonlau and Zou (2020), and medicine by Iwendi et al. (2020). Zhao et al. (2022) used random forest with deep diffraction neural networks to predict accident risk, while Yan and Shen (2022) used random forest and Bayesian optimization to select the most efficient variables and materials interpolation by Chen and Chen (2020) was used to analyses the samples.

In Koma et al. (2017) authors used a random forest to investigate cognitive distractions based on eye movements. Wang et al. (2021) examined traffic effects and preventive measures on congested roads, considering characteristics such as time, road gradient, waveguide, proximity to infrastructure, and accident-prone areas. Zhang et al. (2022) introduced a generalized random forest model to predict treatment outcomes and to enhance road safety research.

Regarding traffic accident severity prediction, Gan et al. (2020) proposed an alternative approach using the deep forest algorithm, which leverages machine learning methods to forecast accident severity based on various characteristics. Sinha et al. (2023) developed a machine learning method to prevent traffic accidents by studying and predicting accident-prone situations, emphasizing the importance of reliable data and efficient models.

Wang (2023) introduced a risk detection approach that considers traffic conflicts to ensure road traffic safety. Li et al. (2023) created a model for forecasting the severity of traffic accidents on mountain highways, considering real-time environmental data. Zhao et al. (2023b) suggested an approach for predicting the likelihood of traffic accidents on highways by incorporating temporal correlation features. Zhang et al. conducted a social network analysis-based risk assessment for urban road tunnels' safe operation.

Demir (2023) focused on road problem diagnosis using multi-agent systems in traffic management. Lastly, Karthikeyan et al. (2023) developed an Internet of Things (IoT)-based system for accident detection and prevention, relying on IoT technologies for identifying and avoiding mishaps. The effectiveness of this system depends on IoT sensor coverage and reliability. Working with data analysis made possible by machine learning, Pourroostaei Ardakani et al. (2023) attempted to forecast road automobile accidents. Predicting accidents using data analysis is the main emphasis of their technique. Prediction accuracy was impacted by factors such as the variety and quality of data sources, the machine learning models used, and so on. An IoT smart city traffic control system and an intelligent transportation system supported by the cloud were investigated by Liu and Ke (2023). To achieve intelligent traffic control, their method combines cloud computing with the IoT. The dependability of cloud services and the IoT infrastructure determines the system's success. Using the

IoT, Babu et al. (2023) developed a smart system for detecting and alerting accidents. Their system is designed to identify accidents and provide alarms using IoT technology. Timely warning generation, comprehensive IoT sensor coverage, and the efficacy of the system are critical.

11.2.1 Research Motivation

Detecting accidents and analysing traffic flows for intelligent road traffic monitoring is important because we need to find solutions to the growing problems caused by urbanization, population growth, and traffic congestion in today's cities and regions. The potential for this field of study to completely alter our approaches to transportation system optimization and management has made it an issue of paramount importance. Research in this area is crucial for several important reasons. To begin, the enormous human and monetary losses, as well as the destruction of property, caused by traffic accidents remain a pressing worldwide issue. A greater chance of saving lives and limiting injuries was achieved via the development of improved accident detection systems, which can significantly decrease reaction times for emergency services. Reduce the frequency and severity of accidents by proactively identifying locations prone to them and adopting preventative measures like better road design or optimizing traffic signals. This would contribute to greater road safety.

Second, urban regions are notorious for their traffic problems, which cause people to lose time, use more gas, and pollute the environment. By giving commuters access to real-time data, effective traffic flow analysis helps reduce congestion by letting them plan their routes and travel times more wisely. Reduced congestion and more effective transportation networks are the end goals of this study, which also educate politicians and urban planners on how to improve road infrastructure, install intelligent transportation systems, and optimize traffic management. Intelligent road traffic monitoring systems that are both strong and flexible are in high demand, especially as transportation networks and cities rely more and more on data-driven technology. These systems need to be able to process massive volumes of data produced by different devices and sensors and then provide insights that are used in real-time. To construct robust and extensible traffic monitoring systems, it is crucial to fund research into the development of state-of-the-art algorithms, machine learning models, and data analytics approaches.

The enormous socio-economic value of this research cannot be denied. In addition to saving lives through reduced healthcare costs, better traffic management and avoidance of accidents, increased efficiency through shorter travel times and lower fuel costs energy consumption and greenhouse gases reducing emissions are both ways that improved transportation planning contributes to long-term economic growth. Given the complexity of road safety, traffic congestion, and transportation system optimization, research on accident monitoring and traffic analysis is essential to build intelligent monitoring systems road Scientists use data and state-of-the-art technology to create smarter and safer transportation systems.

11.2.2 Problem Statement

The main research topic of intelligent road traffic monitoring and accident management is the complex challenges faced by modern urban transportation systems. Motor vehicle accidents are on the rise, resulting in serious bodily injuries, fatalities, and extensive property damage. This highlights an important road safety problem. To reduce response times, the case statement highlights the need for accident detection technology that can quickly identify issues and call emergency responders. Conducting data analysis to identify places with a high incidence of incidents is critical for proactive safety measures.

Congestion in urban areas is a chronic problem, resulting in enormous economic expenditures, time waste, and environmental deterioration. As stated in the issue description, doing traffic flow analysis is critical to reduce congestion. Using real-time traffic information, commuters improve their journey plans, while intelligent traffic management systems optimize traffic signal timing and minimize congestion.

Data Overload: We must effectively gather, process, and analyses huge amounts of data generated by the ubiquitous use of sensors, cameras, and networked vehicles. To effectively handle this overwhelming amount of data, as mentioned in the problem statement, and to extract valuable insights from it, state-of-the-art algorithms and data analytics techniques are necessary.

Intelligent road traffic monitoring systems consist of several technologies and devices, but their interoperability is not always guaranteed. The description of the issue emphasizes the need of conducting research into developing comprehensive and effective traffic management systems by integrating different components smoothly and guaranteeing their compatibility.

Traffic monitoring systems need to be resilient and scalable so they can handle the growing amount of data generated by more urban populations and adjust to new traffic patterns. The issue statement stresses the need of developing systems that can endure cyberattacks or technological breakdowns to guarantee the consistent and dependable functioning of traffic monitoring infrastructure.

Economic and Social Effects: The issue statement concludes by drawing attention to the larger social and economic consequences of these problems. It highlights how better transportation efficiency, less traffic, and safer roads are saving lives, increasing productivity, and promoting sustainability.

11.3 Applications

There is great promise for intelligent road traffic monitoring to revolutionize transportation system management and user experience via the use of accident detection and traffic flow analysis. Some important uses are described in detail here:

Systems for detecting accidents and analysing traffic flows provide real-time insights into traffic conditions, allowing for better traffic management. With this data, traffic management agencies redirect cars, manage lane closures, and dynamically change traffic signals to keep traffic flowing smoothly and reduce congestion. Commuters cut down on journey time and fuel usage using this software.

Among the most important uses are the provision of emergency services and the rapid reaction to incidents. Automated accident detection, localization, and quick notification to emergency services are all capabilities of these systems. This results in quicker reaction times, which lessens the severity of injuries and saves lives.

Analytics for the Future

These technologies can foretell locations prone to accidents and congestion by examining past traffic data. Using this tool, traffic management authorities optimize road designs, deploy more resources to high-risk areas, and alter traffic patterns to prevent accidents.

To assist commuters in circumventing traffic congestion and potential collisions, navigation software enhances route planning by including up-to-the-minute traffic information. This program enhances the entire travel experience by minimizing travel time and reducing the frustration caused by traffic congestion. Examining traffic patterns enables public transportation networks to more effectively schedule bus and train services based on real-time traffic needs. This ensures that even during peak hours, public transportation remains a viable and pragmatic option.

Data received from these devices is crucial for making decisions on road designs, infrastructure expenditures, and traffic signal optimizations. This data is used by city planners and politicians in urban planning and infrastructure development. It contributes to sustainable urban development by mitigating pollutants, minimizing energy consumption, and avoiding needless road infrastructure.

The program facilitates sustainable urban growth by optimizing traffic flow, resulting in decreased air pollution and greenhouse gas emissions. Urban areas aiming to achieve sustainability and environmental goals should give priority to this method. Data from these systems contributes to transportation research, allowing the examination of traffic patterns, driver behaviour, and the impacts of various interventions on traffic flow and safety. This type of research leads to improved transportation regulations and technology.

Logistics

With the use of real-time traffic data, commercial transportation firms streamline their routes, cut down on fuel usage, and speed up delivery times. Customers will be more satisfied, and costs will go down thanks to this software. Law enforcement and transportation authority use accident data and traffic flow patterns to perform safety audits and guarantee regulatory compliance. This application helps find places where stricter enforcement or improved safety measures could benefit.

11.4 Proposed Methodology

Figure 11.1 displays a block diagram outlining the method used for forecasting traffic conditions using DLCNN on the TrafficNet dataset. The detailed operation is given as follows

- Step 1: Data splitting: The TrafficNet dataset comprises a diverse collection of images and data samples connected to traffic. The dataset is partitioned into two equal subsets: one for training and the other for testing. For demonstration purposes, we assign 20% of the dataset for testing and allot 80% for training. This division enables the model to acquire knowledge from a certain dataset while simultaneously assessing its performance on a separate dataset.
- Step 2: Image preprocessing: Prior to inputting the data into the neural network, preprocessing techniques are used to prepare it for the purposes of training and testing. We will mostly examine the preprocessing technique of normalization. Usually, this process entails rescaling the data to guarantee that it is confined inside a uniform range of values. This facilitates training by mitigating problems arising from features with very disparate scales.
- Step 3: Image resizes: it is essential when the dataset includes images. To ensure uniformity, all the images are resized to identical dimensions. This ensures that the neural network can properly analyse the images while maintaining a constant input scale.
- Step 4: DLCNN is used to predict traffic patterns. DLCNN forms the basis of our approach to traffic condition forecasting. These neurons exhibit exceptional abilities in imaging and extracting appropriate features. DLCNN uses enhanced training data to learn patterns and features related to various traffic situations, such as heavy traffic, light traffic, accidents, and fires.
- Step 5: Vehicle State Prediction: After DLCNN training, the next objective is to predict the vehicle state of the test samples. During the training process, the samples were not matched to 20% of the data sets specifically isolated for testing

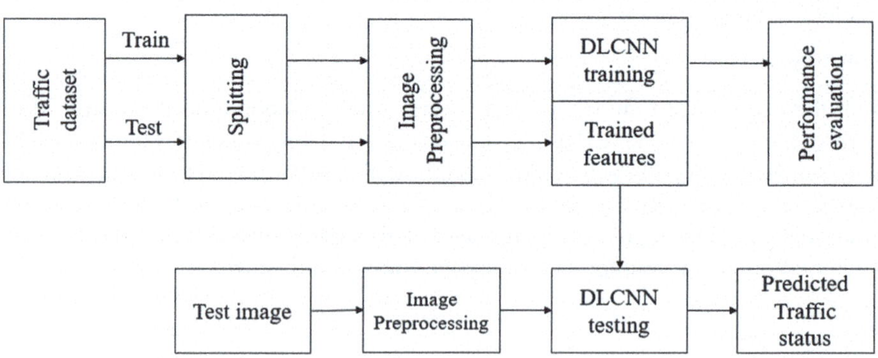

Fig. 11.1 Proposed methodology. *Source* Author

reasons. DLCNN receives pre-processed test images and uses them to predict traffic conditions such as heavy traffic, light traffic, accidents, or fires.

- Step 6: Evaluation: The final step is to evaluate the effectiveness of our proposed method. Using additional data, this study investigates the predictive ability of the DLCNN model on traffic conditions. To measure the model's capacity to recognize various types of traffic situations, standard performance metrics such as recall, accuracy, precision, $F1$ score, and confusion matrices are utilized.

11.4.1 Image Preprocessing

Image preprocessing is critical in computer vision and image analysis. The approach involves several steps to prepare raw images for algorithmic or neural network processing. Figure 11.2 shows a representation of the organization of an image processing pipeline. This paper gives a full description of each stage in the image processing process.

Step 1: Initially, image preprocessing work is to get an unprocessed image from a source. There are several image formats accessible, including JPEG, PNG, BMP, and many more. The libraries or functions of the chosen programming environment or framework are utilized to read images. This step results in a programmatically manipulable digital duplicate of the image.

Step 2: Resize the images: This is a typical preprocessing step, particularly when dealing with deep neural networks or machine learning models. It entails adjusting the image's proportions (width and height). Several factors need resizing:

- Maintaining consistent input size: Many ML models, notably CNNs, need input images with consistent dimensions. By resizing, we standardize the sizes of the inputs.
- Lowering computational complexity: Training and inference times were improved with smaller images since fewer calculations are needed.
- Handling memory limitations: Sometimes, images must be resized to fit into the allotted capacity.

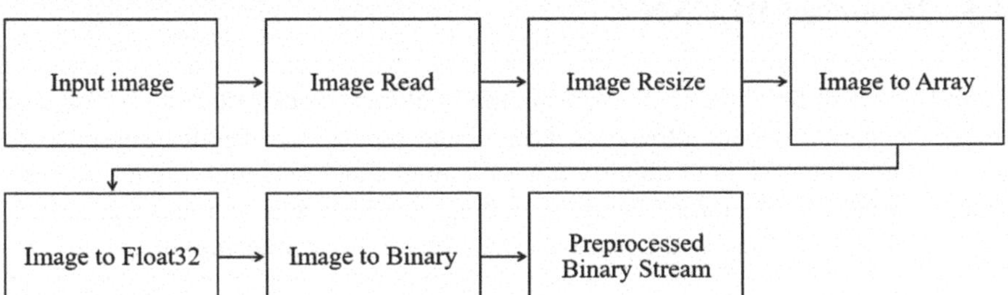

Fig. 11.2 Image preprocessing operational flow. *Source* Author

- It is critical to maintain the aspect ratio while resizing to avoid distorting the image. We can usually find easy image resizing routines in libraries like OpenCV or Pillow.

Step 3: Image to Array Conversion: Currently, the image is transformed into a numerical tensor or multidimensional array. An array value is associated with each image pixel. The array is usually structured with dimensions representing height, width, and color channels (if applicable). For grayscale images, the array is 2D, with each element representing the intensity of a pixel. For color images, it's a 3D or 4D array, with dimensions for height, width, color channels (e.g., Red, Green, Blue), and potentially batch size (if processing multiple images simultaneously). The conversion from an image to an array allows for numerical manipulation and analysis, making it compatible with various data processing libraries and deep learning frameworks like NumPy or TensorFlow.

Step 4: Convert the image to a float32 format, which is the default for most algorithms used in computer vision and machine learning. By changing the image array to float32, the pixel values now reflect a much wider range of intensities than before, often between -1.0 and 1.0 (or 0.0 for black and 1.0 for white, depending on the normalization method). To ensure data type consistency and enable interoperability with different machine learning frameworks and libraries, this step is necessary. To scale the pixel values to the [0.0, 1.0] range, it is common practice to divide them by the highest intensity value (for example, 255 for an 8-bit image).

Step 5: Convert Image to Binary: By using a predetermined threshold, grayscale images were "binarized" into binary images where each pixel is assigned a value of either 0 (black) or 1 (white). When we wish to isolate objects from their backgrounds, like in image segmentation, we often resort to binarization. First, a threshold value is established. Then, for every grayscale image pixel, if the pixel value is equal to or higher than the threshold, it is set to 1. Else, it is set to 0. For tasks like character identification or object tracking, where we need to isolate certain areas of interest, binarization was a lifesaver since it streamlines the image and extracts the most important details.

11.5 Proposed DLCNN

The utilization of DLCNN components in the intelligent road traffic monitoring and accident detection system allows for the efficient processing of traffic surveillance data, enabling the system to identify critical patterns and make informed decisions related to road transportation safety, including accident detection and traffic flow analysis. Figure 11.3 shows the proposed DLCNN layer architecture diagram.

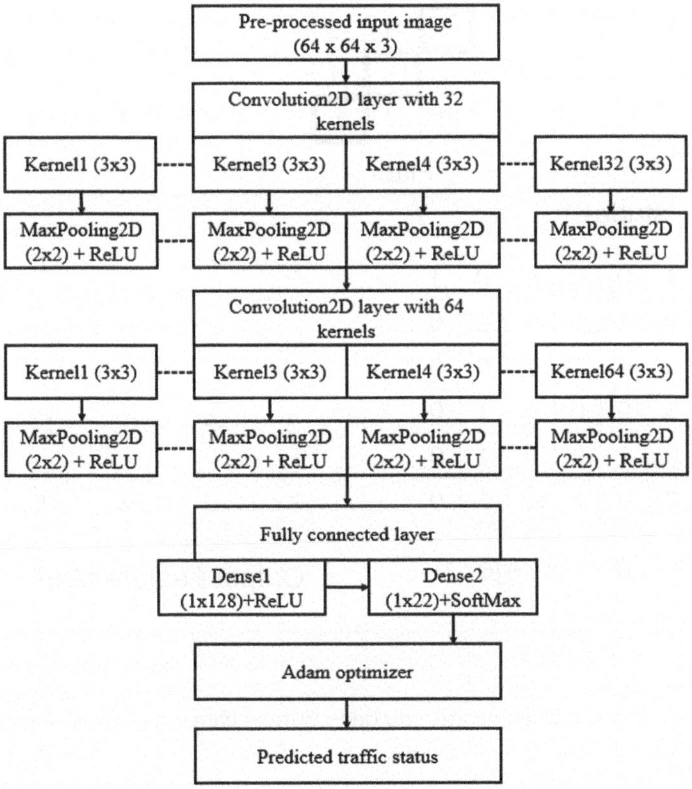

Fig. 11.3 Proposed DLCNN block diagram. *Source* Author

Convolution Layer

In the traffic monitoring system, the convolution layer plays a crucial role in processing input data, like the way it analyses the pre-processed image in transportation applications. Figure 11.4 shows the operational flow of convolutional layer with example. Here, the convolution layer processes traffic surveillance data and traffic flow images, using receptive fields and common weights to identify variations in the visual material. It detects key features and patterns in the road traffic scenarios, such as congestion, accident locations, and traffic density. This layer plays a pivotal role in identifying these critical regions within the traffic images.

ReLU Activation Function

The Rectified Linear Unit (ReLU) activation function, as applied in the intelligent traffic monitoring system, enhances the network's ability to identify meaningful features in the data as shown in Fig. 11.5. Just as it selects positive values from the input data, it helps accentuate significant aspects of the traffic scenarios. The ReLU activation function aids in making the system more robust in recognizing patterns

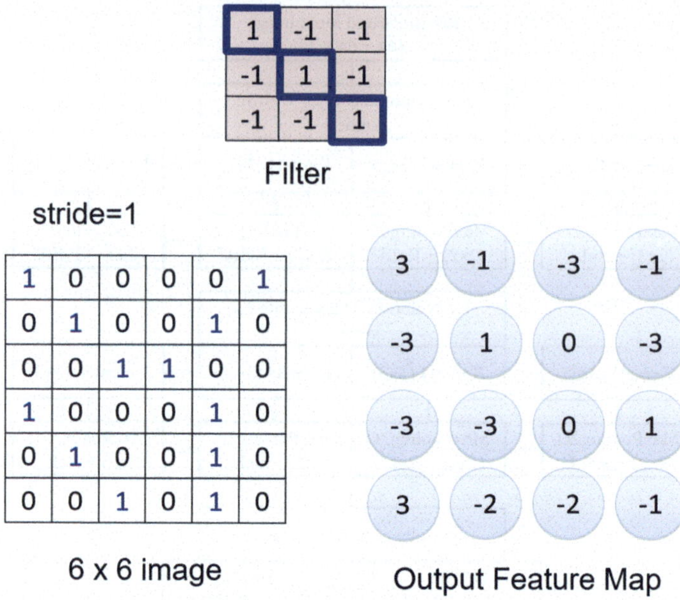

Fig. 11.4 Convolution layer operation. *Source* Author

related to accidents, traffic density, and other critical elements in road transportation safety.

Pooling Layer

The pooling layer, as in the case of image processing, is employed to reduce the dimensions and complexity of the data while retaining essential information. Figure 11.6 shows the examples of Max Pooling layer operation, which reduces the samples by half of size based on 2 × 2 kernel. In traffic monitoring, a pooling

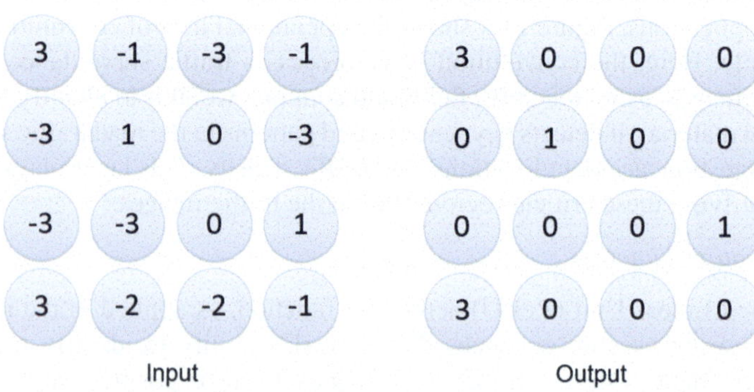

Fig. 11.5 ReLU operation process. *Source* Author

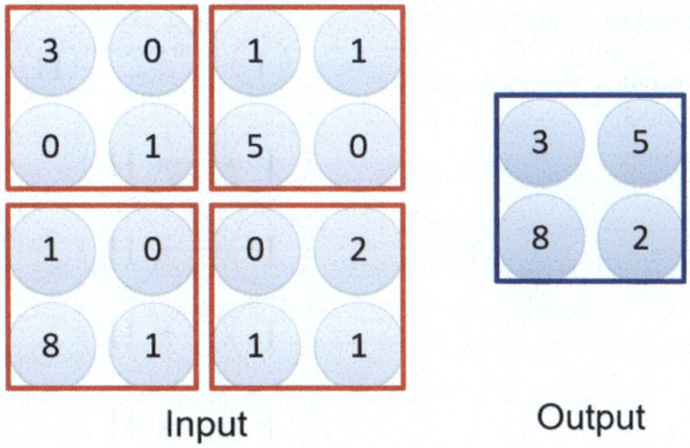

Fig. 11.6 Pooling layer operation process. *Source* Author

layer can be utilized to down sample the data, capturing key characteristics of the traffic flow, much like it captures the maximum values in the activation map of a pre-processed image. By prioritizing significant parts of the traffic data, it optimizes the allocation of computing resources and mitigates overfitting, hence enhancing the overall efficacy of the system.

Fully Connected Layer

The last phase in the data processing pipeline from the preceding phases encompasses the fully connected layer as shown in Fig. 11.7, which is a vital element within the DLCNN framework of a traffic monitoring system. It aggregates data from multiple sources across the network to provide an accurate image of traffic conditions. This level of processing is crucial in the identification and analysis of specific traffic situations, such as accidents or traffic accidents, and in making informed decisions based on processed data This choice ultimately leads to prediction and classification of the last of these.

The traffic management algorithm uses the SoftMax classifier, which is well suited for classifying different traffic characteristics. This combination improves road safety decision-making by calculating accident locations, traffic congestion probabilities, and appropriate solutions to real-time traffic situations.

11.6 Advantages of Proposed TrafficNet

There are several notable advantages of using TrafficNet dataset with DLCNN for traffic condition forecasting.

Accuracy and Accuracy: DLCNNs excel in classifying complex traffic accidents due to their well-known ability to extract detailed patterns and discriminatory features from images. This provides highly accurate and precise traffic forecasts, enabling

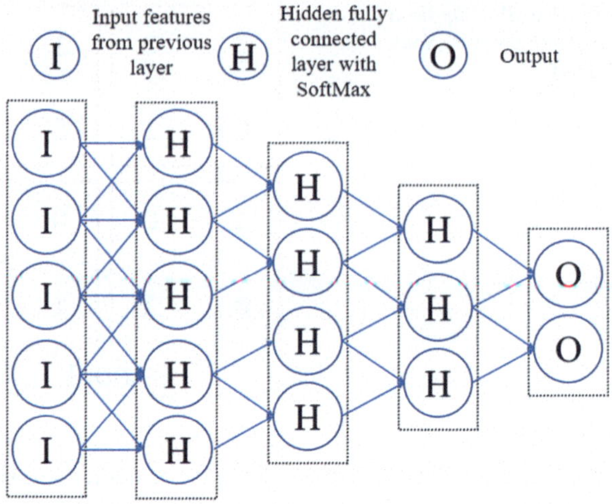

Fig. 11.7 Fully connected layer with SoftMax classifier operation process. *Source* Author

reliable traffic management and safety assessments. It automates the process of forecasting traffic conditions, eliminating the need for human monitoring and analysis. This automation is especially useful in densely populated cities because it saves drivers time and money by providing real-time accurate traffic information.

Scalability Flexibility: Deep learning models such as DLCNNs can handle large data sets efficiently. Prediction accuracy continues to increase as more traffic data is collected due to the system's ability to efficiently handle large data sets without significantly increasing operational complexity. The ability of long-term and short-term active memory to respond quickly to new or changing traffic conditions ensures that predictions remain current and even accurate even when traffic plans change due to factors such as weather, accidents, and special events.

Enhanced Safety: Accurate prediction of traffic conditions is essential to enhance road safety. In the event of a car accident or fire, immediately notifying emergency personnel can save lives and prevent injuries, with significant benefits to emergency response and public safety. Statistical analysis is used to obtain useful information about web traffic. City planners and transportation professionals can learn a lot about traffic, accident scenes, and crowded places.

11.7 Results and Discussion

The "Results and Discussion" section presents the results and analysis of the study. Using the same data for all methods ensures uniformity of the experimental design and allows for better comparability. Different performance indicators are analysed to study the effectiveness of each technique in forecasting traffic conditions and optimizing accident detection. Recall, accuracy, precision, $F1$ score, and confusion matrix are among the metrics used. Using these parameters, the accuracy of models in classifying different traffic crash scenarios is examined, revealing their individual strengths and weaknesses. Based on the observations and findings, this section presents a comprehensive review of the model's types that provide capabilities and implications for traffic management and intelligent safety.

11.7.1 Traffic Condition Dataset

The information we use includes many groups from the Internet. Each class is associated with an output class. The algorithm trains and validates using 900 images, and they are equally distributed among four folders: "sparse traffic", "dense traffic," "fire", and "accident". In Fig. 11.8, sample example images for each category or subfolder. The dataset was open access Kaggle dataset, which can be accessed with link: https://www.kaggle.com/datasets/umairshahpirzada/traffic-net.

Class Labels: Class Labels: The dataset assigns a unique class label to each data sample (or image) that denotes the kind of traffic circumstance to which it belongs. Sporadic traffic, heavy traffic, fire, and accident are the four separate category names here. To forecast the current traffic situation from the given data, classification tasks make use of these class labels.

Training and Validation: There seems to be a further division in the dataset into a training set and a validation set. Normally, machine learning models are trained using training sets, and any necessary adjustments are made using validation sets to evaluate the model's performance during training. The model's ability to generalize to new data depends on its training and validation sets being distinct.

11.7.2 Prediction Results

We provide the findings of the simulations run in a "python environment" and explain them in depth. Additionally, the suggested method's performance is contrasted with that of previous approaches that have been tested on the same dataset. Figure 11.9 indicates that the classifier has made a prediction, and the outcome of that prediction is "low traffic." In other words, when the classifier was presented with a specific input or data instance, it classified the traffic condition associated with that instance as "low traffic".

Figure 11.10 shows an alternative result of the prediction. Here, the classifier has predicted "heavy traffic". The classifier has concluded that the traffic situation was marked by significant traffic flow or congestion based on the characteristics or attributes of the input data. Indicates that the content of Fig. 11.11 is connected to the predictions provided by a classifier. The classifier has produced the prediction

(a)

(b)

Fig. 11.8 Sample image from traffic condition dataset. **a** Dense traffic. **b** Sparse traffic. **c** Fire. **d** Accident. *Source* Author. The figure was generated by python simulations on authenticated dataset

that a "fire accident occurred" using the characteristics and data that were supplied to it. What this means is that the classifier has determined that the incident is a traffic-related fire accident based on certain patterns or traits in the data.

Another outcome of the predictions is shown in Fig. 11.12. This time around, the classifier has predicted that an "accident occurred". This means that the classifier identified certain signs or patterns in the input data that caused it to label the traffic situation as an accident.

Figure 11.13 contains the information about the accuracy and loss estimation for the proposed method during its training. This indicates that the figure will display two key metrics: accuracy and loss. Accuracy typically measures the proportion of

(c)

(d)

Fig. 11.8 (continued)

correctly classified instances, while loss reflects how well or poorly the model is performing during training. This suggests that the training process was conducted for a total of 10 epochs. An epoch represents one complete pass through the entire training dataset. Training a model for multiple epochs allows it to learn and adjust its parameters over time. The graph specifies the colours used in the chart or graph to represent the accuracy and loss values. The accuracy values are typically plotted using a green line, while the loss values are represented with a red line. These lines will show how accuracy and loss change over the course of the 10 training epochs.

Table 11.1 compares the performance of different methods, specifically the Naive Bayes Classifier (NBC), Support Vector Machine (SVM), and the proposed DLCNN. The comparison is based on accuracy, measured in percentages. Figure 11.14 shows the accuracy metric performance comparison. Accuracy is a common performance metric in classification tasks and represents the proportion of correctly predicted instances out of the total instances in the dataset.

Fig. 11.9 Predicted outcome as low traffic. *Source* Author. The figure was generated by python simulations on authenticated dataset

Fig. 11.10 Predicted outcome as heavy traffic detected. *Source* Author. The figure was generated by python simulations on authenticated dataset

Figure 11.15 shows the loss metric performance comparison. The NBC achieved an accuracy of 89.5%. This means that, when applied to the dataset or task under consideration, the NBC correctly predicted the class labels for 89.5% of the instances. The SVM achieved an accuracy of 92.48%. This indicates that the SVM performed

Fig. 11.11 Predicted outcome as fire accident occurred. *Source* Author. The figure was generated by python simulations on authenticated dataset

Fig. 11.12 Predicted outcome as accident occurred. *Source* Author. The figure was generated by python simulations on authenticated dataset

slightly better than the NBC, with an accuracy rate of 92.48%. The proposed DLCNN achieved an impressive accuracy of 99.3%. This suggests that the DLCNN outperformed both NBC and SVM, achieving the highest accuracy rate among the methods compared.

Table 11.2 shows the performance comparison for the proposed DLCNN method against other models, including NBC (Lu et al. 2015) and SVM (An et al. 2019), across various metrics. Figure 11.16 shows the precision metric performance comparison over methods. The proposed DLCNN achieves the highest precision at 99.983%, surpassing NBC (Lu et al. 2015) by 2.13% and SVM (An et al. 2019) by 1.243%,

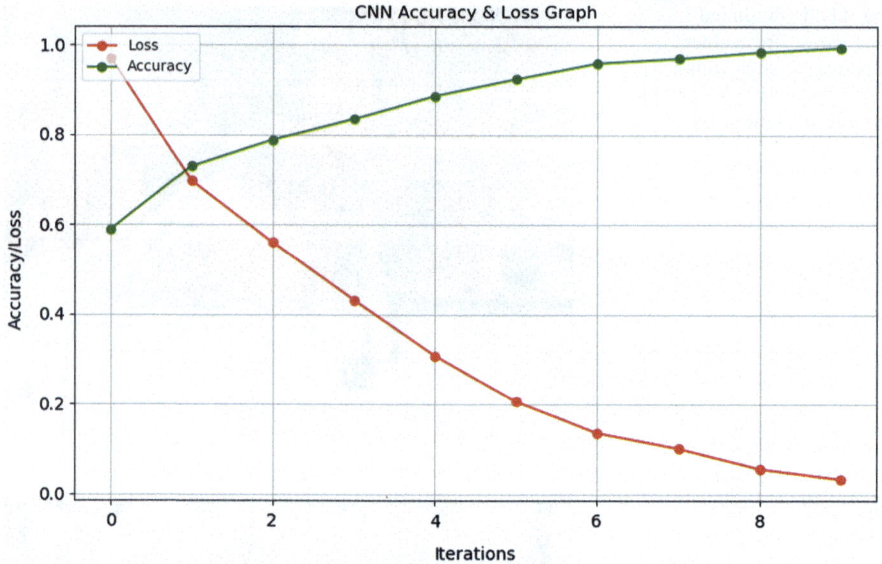

Fig. 11.13 Accuracy and loss comparison graph for multiple epochs. *Source* Author. The figure was originally simulated using python software

Table 11.1 Accuracy and loss comparison

Method	NBC (Lu et al. 2015)	SVM (An et al. 2019)	Proposed DLCNN
Accuracy (%)	89.5	92.48	99.3
Loss	0.748	0.37	0.183

Source Author

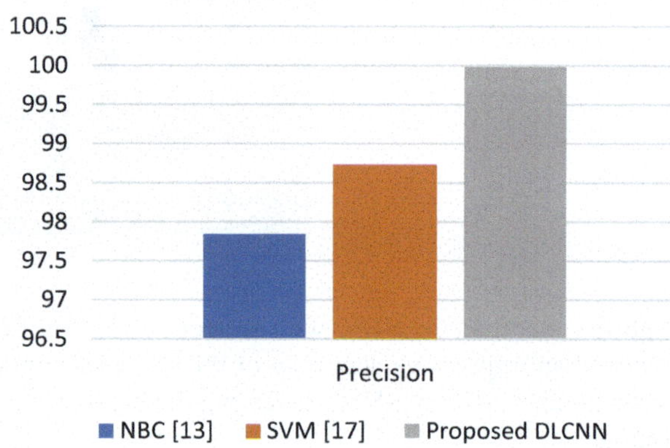

Fig. 11.14 Accuracy metric performance estimation. *Source* Author

Fig. 11.15 Loss metric performance estimation. *Source* Author

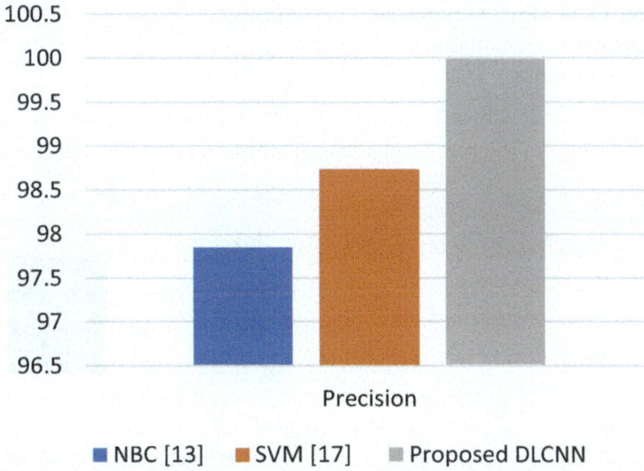

indicating its strong capability to correctly classify positive instances. Figure 11.17 shows the recall metric performance comparison over methods. In terms of recall, the DLCNN outperforms both NBC (Lu et al. 2015) and SVM (An et al. 2019) with a recall of 99.013%, exceeding NBC (Lu et al. 2015) by 2.156% and SVM (An et al. 2019) by 1.469%, demonstrating its ability to capture true positive instances. Figure 11.18 shows the $F1$-score metric performance comparison over methods. The $F1$-Score for the Proposed DLCNN is 99.74%, significantly higher than NBC (Lu et al. 2015) by 4.056% and SVM (An et al. 2019) by 2.9%, reflecting the excellent balance between precision and recall.

Figure 11.19 shows the sensitivity metric performance comparison over methods. The DLCNN exhibits a sensitivity of 99.463%, surpassing NBC (Lu et al. 2015) by 1.818% and SVM (An et al. 2019) by 1.506%, indicating its exceptional ability to identify true positive instances. Figure 11.20 shows the specificity metric performance comparison over methods. The specificity of DLCNN is 99.624%, higher than NBC (Lu et al. 2015) by 3.38% and SVM (An et al. 2019) by 1.05%, highlighting its proficiency in correctly classifying negative instances.

Table 11.2 Performance comparison

Method	NBC (Lu et al. 2015)	SVM (An et al. 2019)	Proposed DLCNN
Precision	97.85	98.740	99.983
Recall	96.857	97.544	99.013
$F1$-score	95.684	96.84	99.74
Sensitivity	97.645	97.957	99.463
Specificity	96.24	98.574	99.624

Source Author

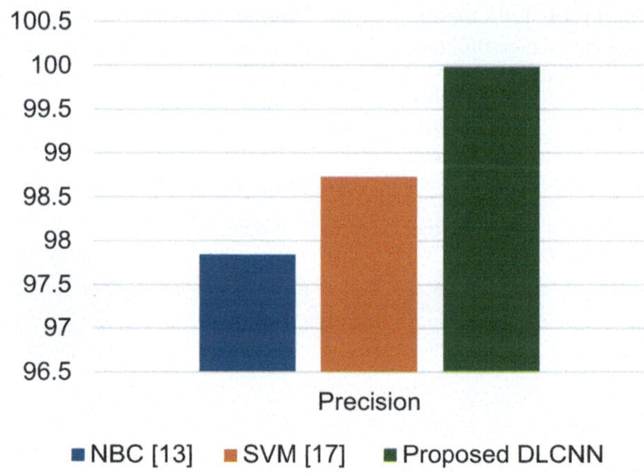

Fig. 11.16 Precision metric performance estimation. *Source* Author

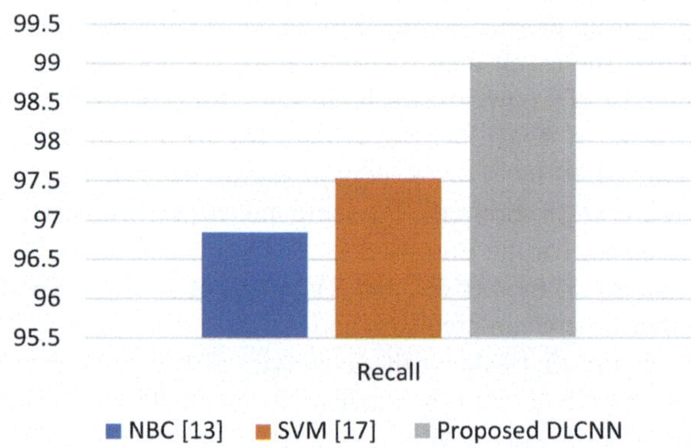

Fig. 11.17 Recall metric performance estimation. *Source* Author

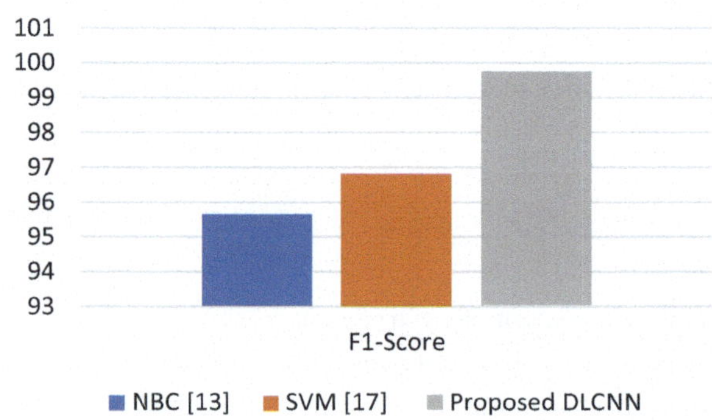

Fig. 11.18 $F1$-score metric performance estimation. *Source* Author

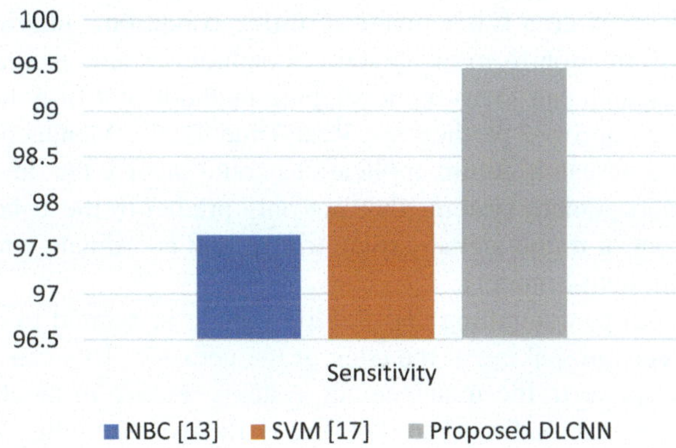

Fig. 11.19 Sensitivity metric performance estimation. *Source* Author

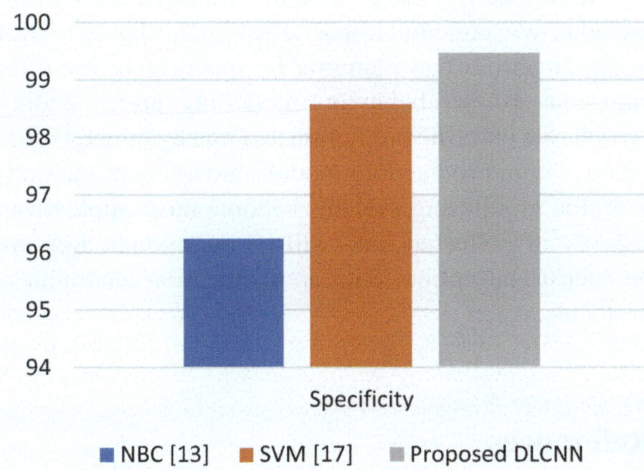

Fig. 11.20 Specificity metric performance estimation. *Source* Author

11.8 Conclusion

Automated, scalable, and monitored in real time, this TrafficNet approach uses deep learning to correctly categorize traffic situations. TrafficNet helps make transportation systems more efficient, decreases congestion, and improves road safety by giving accurate insights into traffic dynamics. Because of its flexibility and room for refinement, the model was used to tackle the ever-changing problems of urban transportation. These technologies provide a way towards safer and smarter urban transportation, which is crucial as cities keep expanding and traffic becomes more complicated.

Several promising avenues will be explored in the future of this study. Using state-of-the-art deep learning architectures, deep learning is a dynamic and ever-changing area. To further improve the accuracy of traffic predictions and to capture temporal relationships in traffic data, future research investigates more sophisticated neural network topologies, such as transformers and recurrent neural networks (RNNs).

To provide a fuller image of traffic conditions, multimodal data fusion combines information from many sources including social media, video, and sensors. Future research can focus on developing methods that fuse these multimodal data sources for improved predictions. Real-Time Traffic Management Systems, building upon this research, future applications could involve the development of real-time traffic management systems that not only predict traffic conditions but also dynamically control traffic signals, route traffic, and coordinate emergency responses based on predictive models.

Edge computing and the IoT can be integrated to enable faster processing and decision-making at the edge of the network. This can lead to more responsive and adaptive traffic management systems. Future research could extend the scope to address broader urban mobility challenges, including intelligent public transportation systems, smart parking solutions, and the integration of autonomous vehicles into urban traffic. Environmental Impact Assessment, Expanding the analysis to include environmental impact assessments based on traffic conditions can contribute to sustainable urban planning by quantifying the effects of traffic congestion and emissions. Human behaviour modelling, understanding driver behaviour can play a pivotal role in traffic prediction and management. Future studies explore the incorporation of human behaviour models into traffic prediction models. Privacy and security, as traffic monitoring systems become more sophisticated, ensuring the privacy and security of collected data will be paramount. Research in this area should focus on robust encryption, data anonymization techniques, and secure communication protocols.

References

Akanbi G, Charles-Owaba OE, Oluleye AE (2009) Human factors in traffic accidents in Lagos, Nigeria. Disaster Prev Manag 18(4):397–409

Alkheder S, Taamneh M, Taamneh S (2017) Severity prediction of traffic accident using an artificial neural network. J Forecast 36(1):100–108

An J, Fu L, Hu M, Chen W, Zhan J (2019) A novel fuzzy-based convolutional neural network method to traffic flow prediction with uncertain traffic accident information. IEEE Access 7:20708–20722

Babu, CVS, Akshayah NS, Janapriyan R (2023) IoT-based smart accident detection and alert system. In: Handbook of research on deep learning techniques for cloud-based industrial IoT. IGI Global, pp 322–337

Bahiru TK, Singh DK, Tessfaw EA (2018) Comparative study on data mining classification algorithms for predicting road traffic accident severity. In: Proceedings of the 2018 second international conference on inventive communication and computational technologies (ICICCT). IEEE, Coimbatore

Bao W, Qi Y, Kong Y (2020) Uncertainty-based traffic accident anticipation with spatio-temporal relational learning. In: Proceedings of the 28th ACM international conference on multimedia, Seattle, WA, USA, October 2020

Bharadiya J (2023) Artificial intelligence in transportation systems a critical review. Am J Comput Eng 6(1):34–45

Caleffi F, Lucchesi ST, Anzanello MJ, Cybis HBB (2016) Influência das condições climáticas e de acidentes na caracterização do comportamento do tráfego em rodovias. Transport 24(4):57–63
Chen M-M, Chen M-C (2020) Modeling road accident severity with comparisons of logistic regression, decision tree and random forest. Information 11(5)
Demir M (2023) Road problem diagnosis with multi-agent systems in traffic. Intell Methods Eng Sci 2(1):35–41
Ding J, Dai Q, Fan W et al (2023) Impacts of meteorology and precursor emission change on O_3 variation in Tianjin, China from 2015 to 2021. J Environ Sci 126:506–516
Fang J et al (2023) Vision-based traffic accident detection and anticipation: a survey. IEEE Trans Circuits Syst Video Technol
Gaber M et al (2023) Analysis and modeling of rural roads traffic safety data. Sohag Eng J 3(1):57–67
Gan J, Li L, Zhang D, Yi Z, Xiang Q (2020) An alternative method for traffic accident severity prediction: using deep forests algorithm. J Adv Transp 2020, Article ID 1257627, 13
Hashmienejad SHA, Hasheminejad SMH (2017) Traffic accident severity prediction using a novel multi-objective genetic algorithm. Int J Crashworthiness 22(4):425–440
Hassan MA et al (2023) Intelligent transportation systems in smart city: a systematic survey. In: 2023 International conference on robotics and automation in industry (ICRAI). IEEE
Huang C, Zhang C, Dai P, Bo L (2019) Deep dynamic fusion network for traffic accident forecasting. In: Proceedings of the 28th ACM international conference on information and knowledge management, Beijing, China, November 2019
Iwendi C, Bashir AK, Peshkar A et al (2020) COVID-19 patient health prediction using boosted random forest algorithm. Front Public Health 8
Karthikeyan S et al (2023) Design and implementation of IoT based accident detection and prevention system. In: 2023 7th International conference on trends in electronics and informatics (ICOEI). IEEE
Koma H, Harada T, Yoshizawa A, Iwasaki H (2017) Detecting cognitive distraction using random forest by considering eye movement type. Int J Cognit Inform Nat Intell 11(1):16–28
Kumeda B, Zhang F, Zhou F, Hussain S, Almasri A, Assefa M (2019) Classification of road traffic accident data using machine learning algorithms. In: Proceedings of the 2019 IEEE 11th international conference on communication software and networks (ICCSN). IEEE, Chongqing, pp 682–687
Li J et al (2023) Predicting the severity of traffic accidents on mountain freeways with dynamic traffic and weather data. Transp Saf Environ tdad001
Liu C, Ke L (2023) Cloud assisted internet of things intelligent transportation system and the traffic control system in the smart city. J Control Decis 10(2):174–187
Lu T, Dunyao ZHU, Lixin Y, Pan Z (2015) The traffic accident hotspot prediction: based on the logistic regression method. In: Proceedings of the 2015 international conference on transportation information and safety (ICTIS). IEEE, Wuhan
Mehrannia P et al (2023) Deep representation of imbalanced spatio-temporal traffic flow data for traffic accident detection. IET Intell Transp Syst 17(3):606–619
Micheale KG (2017) Road traffic accident: human security perspective. Int J Peace Dev Stud 8(2):15–24
Murphey YL, Wang K, Molnar LJ et al (2020) Development of data mining methodologies to advance knowledge of driver behaviors in naturalistic driving. SAE Int J Transp Saf 8(2):77–94
Oladimeji D et al (2023) Smart transportation: an overview of technologies and applications. Sensors 23(8):3880
Pourroostaei Ardakani S et al (2023) Road car accident prediction using a machine-learning-enabled data analysis. Sustainability 15(7):5939
Ren H, Song Y, Wang J, Hu Y, Lei J (2017) A deep learning approach to the prediction of short-term traffic accident risk. https://arxiv.org/abs/1710.09543
Ren H, Song Y, Wang J, Hu Y, Lei J (2018) A deep learning approach to the citywide traffic accident risk prediction. In: Proceedings of the 2018 21st international conference on intelligent transportation systems (ITSC). IEEE, Maui, HI

Schonlau M, Zou RY (2020) The random forest algorithm for statistical learning. STATA J 20(1):3–29

Sharma SN, Singh D (2023) Understanding mid-block traffic analysis: a crucial tool for road safety. Think India J 26(3):5–9

Sinha A et al (2023) Traffic road accident prevention using machine learning. Available at SSRN 4387789

Wang H (2023) A risk identification method of road traffic operation safety considering traffic conflict. Adv Transp Stud

Wang L, Wu J, Li R et al (2021) A weight assignment algorithm for incomplete traffic information road based on fuzzy random forest method. Symmetry 13(9)

Yaman TT, Bilgic E, Fevzi Esen M (2022) Analysis of traffic accidents with fuzzy and crisp data mining techniques to identify factors affecting injury severity. J Intell Fuzzy Syst 42(1):575–592

Yan M, Shen Y (2022) Traffic accident severity prediction based on random forest. Sustainability 14(3)

Zhang C, Hu H, Xue J. Risk analysis for urban road tunnel operation safety based on social network analysis. Available at SSRN 4488166

Zhang Y, Li H, Ren G (2022) Estimating heterogeneous treatment effects in road safety analysis using generalized random forests. Accid Anal Prev 165, Article ID 106507

Zhang Q et al (2023) Causal analysis of coach and bus accidents in China based on road alignments. Heliyon 9(4)

Zhao H, Li X, Cheng H, Zhang J, Wang Q, Zhu H (2022) Deep learning-based prediction of traffic accidents risk for Internet of vehicles. China Commun 19(2):214–224

Zhao C et al (2023a) Unsupervised anomaly detection based method of risk evaluation for road traffic accident Appl Intell 53(1):369–384

Zhao L et al (2023b) Highway traffic crash risk prediction method considering temporal correlation characteristics. J Adv Transp 2023

Chapter 12
Unmanned Aerial Networks—UAVs and AI

Neha Jain, Ankit Gambhir, and Medhavi Pandey

Abstract This chapter provides an in-depth exploration of Unmanned Aerial Networks (UANs), which are characterized by the integration of aerial robotics, artificial intelligence (AI), and wireless communications. UANs have the capacity to revolutionize various industries and societal operations by enabling tasks such as environmental monitoring and delivery services through interconnected unmanned aerial vehicles (UAVs). The discussion in this chapter covers the conceptualization, development, applications, and challenges associated with UANs, emphasizing the importance of addressing regulatory, privacy, ethical, and technical concerns through ongoing research and collaboration among stakeholders. Responsible integration of UANs is highlighted as crucial for maximizing benefits and ensuring sustainability in the technological landscape. Looking ahead, the growth of UANs is contingent upon continuous innovations in drone technology, AI algorithms, and communication infrastructures. The convergence of AI and UAVs holds promise for profound impacts on industries and society, shaping the future of automation and connectivity. In summary, this chapter offers a comprehensive perspective on UANs, underscoring their transformative potential and the necessity of responsible integration to navigate challenges and realize benefits in a rapidly evolving technological era.

Keywords Unmanned Aerial Networks (UANs) · Unmanned Aerial Vehicle (UAV) · Aerial robotics · AI-powered UAVs · Technological innovation

---

N. Jain · A. Gambhir (✉)
Delhi Technical Campus, Greater Noida, India
e-mail: er.ankit.gambhir@gmail.com

N. Jain
e-mail: nehajain312@gmail.com

M. Pandey
Galgotias College of Engineering and Technology, Greater Noida, India
e-mail: medhaviipandey@gmail.com

R. Arya et al. (eds.), *Recent Trends in Artificial Intelligence Towards a Smart World*, Frontiers of Artificial Intelligence, Ethics and Multidisciplinary Applications,
https://doi.org/10.1007/978-981-97-6790-8_12

12.1 Introduction to Unmanned Aerial Networks

The advent of Unmanned Aerial Networks (UANs) represents a significant leap in the evolution of aerial surveillance, delivery systems, and communication infrastructures. This chapter delves into the foundational aspects of UANs, exploring their conceptualization, development, applications, and the challenges they present. As a multidisciplinary field, UANs incorporate principles from robotics, wireless communication, and artificial intelligence (AI) to create networks of unmanned aerial vehicles (UAVs) that can operate autonomously or be remotely controlled to perform a variety of tasks (Austin 2010). Unmanned Aerial Networks consist of multiple UAVs, commonly known as drones, which are interconnected through wireless communication to form a cohesive network. These networks can operate independently or integrate with ground-based and satellite communication systems to perform complex tasks ranging from environmental monitoring to delivering internet connectivity in remote areas (Završnik 2016).

12.2 Components of a UAN

A UAN is composed of several key components, including the UAVs themselves, communication systems, control systems, and the payload or sensors carried by the UAVs. Each component plays a critical role in the functionality and efficiency of the network. Figure 12.1 presents UAN architecture block diagram.

- Unmanned Aerial Vehicles (UAVs): These are the network's mobile nodes, capable of flying autonomously or being remotely piloted. They vary in size, shape, and capabilities depending on their intended application (Valavanis and Vachtsevanos 2015).
- Communication Systems: Essential for the coordination and control of UAVs within the network. This includes intra-network communication between UAVs and communication with ground control stations (Sekander et al. 2019).

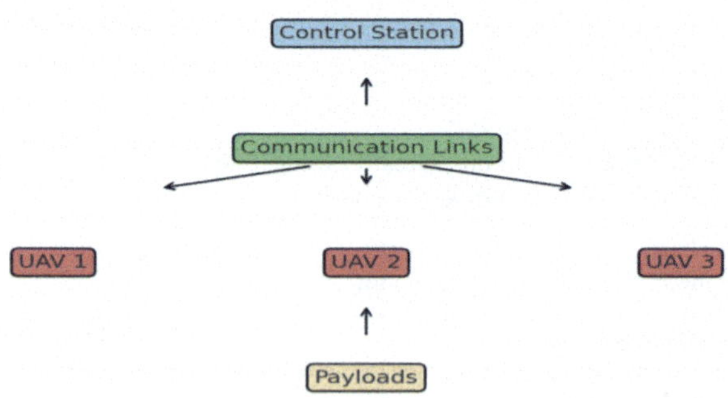

Fig. 12.1 UAN architecture block diagram. *Source* Author

- Control Systems: These systems enable the autonomous operation of UAVs. They include software algorithms that process data from the UAV's sensors to make real-time decisions about navigation, obstacle avoidance, and task execution (Gilbert and Kirksey 2019).
- Payload/Sensors: The equipment carried by UAVs to fulfil their mission. This can range from high-resolution cameras and environmental sensors to packages for delivery.

12.3 Applications of UANs

UANs have a wide range of applications across various sectors. UANs have transcended the capabilities of individual drones by leveraging the power of connectivity and advanced coordination (Kaminski 2017). These networks find applications across various sectors, demonstrating remarkable versatility and efficiency. Figure 12.2 reflects major sector of applications of UAV.

Environmental Monitoring

Disaster Management and Response: UANs are deployed to monitor natural disasters in real-time, such as wildfires, floods, and hurricanes, offering critical data for emergency response teams and aiding in damage assessment and recovery planning.

Climate Research and Atmospheric Studies: By collecting data on air quality, temperature, humidity, and other atmospheric parameters, UANs contribute valuable insights into climate change and environmental health.

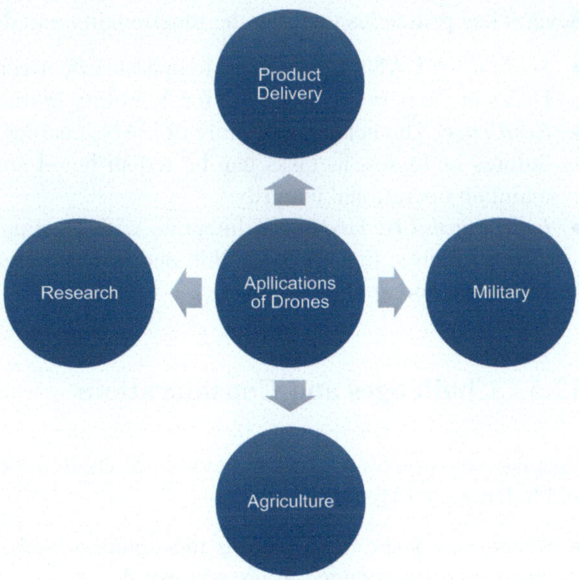

Fig. 12.2 Applications of UAV. *Source* Author

Agriculture

Precision Farming: UANs enhance agricultural practices by providing detailed imagery and data for crop health monitoring, soil analysis, and irrigation optimization, allowing for targeted interventions and improved crop yields.

Security and Surveillance

Border Control and Maritime Surveillance: UANs offer a cost-effective solution for monitoring vast stretches of land and sea borders, detecting unauthorized entries, and aiding in search and rescue operations.

Public Safety: In urban environments, UANs can enhance public safety by monitoring crowds, traffic conditions, and critical infrastructure, providing real-time data to law enforcement and emergency services.

Infrastructure Inspection

Energy Sector: UANs are instrumental in inspecting and maintaining energy infrastructure, including pipelines, power lines, wind turbines, and solar panels, enabling early detection of potential issues and reducing downtime.

Civil Infrastructure: Roads, bridges, and buildings can be regularly inspected with UANs for structural integrity, contributing to safer and more resilient urban and rural infrastructure (Saad et al. 2020).

12.4 Key Principles

Several key principles underlie the functionality and design of UANs:

- *Scalability*: UANs are designed to operate effectively regardless of the number of UAVs in the network, allowing for flexibility in mission scope and complexity.
- *Resilience*: The networked nature of UANs enables them to withstand individual failures or losses, as tasks can be redistributed among the remaining UAVs to maintain operational integrity.
- *Interoperability*: UANs can integrate with existing communication and control infrastructures, including satellite and ground-based networks, enhancing their versatility and application range.

12.5 Challenges and Considerations

Despite their potential, UANs face several challenges few of them are (Capozzoli and Sabatini 2014):

- *Regulatory Issues*: Navigating the complex web of airspace regulations and ensuring privacy concerns are addressed.

- *Technical Challenges*: Including battery life limitations, reliable communication in diverse environments, and ensuring robustness against failures or attacks.
- *Ethical and Privacy Concerns*: Balancing the benefits of UANs with the potential for invasive surveillance and data collection (Justice and Pack 2018).

Unmanned Aerial Networks represent a frontier in the application of UAV technology, offering promising solutions to a variety of modern challenges. As these networks evolve, they will undoubtedly play an increasingly significant role in shaping our approach to logistics, communication, and environmental monitoring. The continued development of UANs will require interdisciplinary collaboration to overcome the technical, regulatory, and ethical challenges that lie ahead.

12.6 Potential Future Uses of UANs

The potential future applications of UANs promise to further revolutionize industries and societal functions by harnessing advancements in drone technology, AI, and communication systems (Capozzoli and Sabatini 2014; Justice and Pack 2018).

- *Advanced Delivery Systems*
  Integrated Urban Delivery Networks: UANs could be at the forefront of creating highly efficient, automated delivery systems within urban areas, reducing traffic congestion and pollution associated with traditional delivery methods.
- *Enhanced Internet Connectivity*
  Remote Area Connectivity: UANs could serve as airborne internet access points, providing high-speed internet to remote and underserved areas, bridging the digital divide.
- *Autonomous Transportation Networks*
  Air Taxis and Urban Air Mobility (UAM): The evolution of UANs could lead to the development of autonomous air taxis and cargo drones, offering new modes of transportation and logistics solutions in congested urban environments.
- *Environmental Conservation*
  Habitat Restoration and Monitoring: UANs could play a crucial role in large-scale environmental conservation efforts, including reforestation projects, wildlife protection, and monitoring of protected areas to prevent illegal activities.
- *Disaster Resilience and Recovery*
  Automated Disaster Response: Future UANs could autonomously respond to disasters, from initial assessment to delivering supplies and aiding in search and rescue operations, significantly improving disaster resilience and recovery times.
- *Smart City Integration*
  Comprehensive Urban Management: UANs could be integrated into smart city frameworks, contributing to traffic management, environmental monitoring, and public services, enhancing the quality of life and sustainability of urban areas (Ansell et al. 2016).

12.7 Brief History and Evolution of Drone Technology

The history and evolution of drone technology span several decades, tracing back to the early twentieth century. Initially developed for military purposes, drone technology has undergone significant transformation, evolving into a versatile tool used across various civilian and commercial sectors. This narrative outlines key milestones and technological advancements that have shaped the development of drone technology (Filali and Abu-Dayya 2017).

Early Beginnings

1910s–1940s: The concept of unmanned aerial vehicles (UAVs) emerged during World War I and II, with various countries experimenting with remote-controlled aircraft for military applications, such as target practice and reconnaissance missions. One of the earliest recorded uses was the development of radio-controlled planes, like the Kettering Bug in the United States during World War I, designed for delivering explosives to enemy targets (Filali and Abu-Dayya 2017).

Cold War Era

1950s–1980s: The Cold War accelerated the development of UAVs for espionage and reconnaissance. The U.S. and the Soviet Union invested heavily in developing UAVs capable of overflying enemy territory to gather intelligence without risking human pilots. During this period, UAVs like the Ryan Firebee and the Lockheed D-21 were developed, showcasing advancements in range, endurance, and payload capacity.

Technological Advancements

1990s: The Gulf War marked a turning point for drone technology, demonstrating its utility in modern warfare for surveillance, intelligence gathering, and later, for direct attack missions. The use of UAVs like the Predator drone highlighted the strategic value of drones in conflict zones, leading to increased investment in UAV research and development.

Commercial and Civilian Adoption

2000s–Present: Advances in technology, including miniaturization, improved battery life, and enhanced control systems, have facilitated the expansion of drone applications beyond military use. The reduction in costs and the availability of consumer-friendly drones have led to widespread adoption in various fields such as (Liu et al. 2018).

12.8 Regulatory Framework

The proliferation of drones has necessitated the development of regulatory frameworks to ensure safe airspace integration and address privacy concerns. Organizations like the Federal Aviation Administration (FAA) in the United States and the European Aviation Safety Agency (EASA) in Europe have established guidelines for drone operations, marking a significant step towards standardizing drone usage globally.

Introduction to UAVs

Unmanned Aerial Vehicles (UAVs), often colloquially referred to as drones, have emerged as transformative tools with applications spanning diverse sectors, from military and surveillance to agriculture, environmental monitoring, and beyond. This section provides a comprehensive introduction to UAVs, exploring their fundamental characteristics, historical development, and the various terms used to describe these unmanned flying machines (Feron 2012; Knupp et al. 2016; Kovar 2015; Guerrero-Bonilla et al. 2017). UAVs are aerial vehicles that operate without a human pilot on board. They are remotely controlled or, in more advanced cases, operate autonomously through pre-programmed flight plans or real-time decision-making capabilities powered by Artificial Intelligence. The absence of a human pilot allows UAVs to navigate through challenging environments, collect data, and perform tasks that may be too hazardous or impractical for manned aircraft (Bekhti and Sebbane 2018).

The concept of UAVs is not new; they have been used in various capacities for decades, primarily in military applications. However, the notion of networking these UAVs to form a UAN is a relatively recent development. This evolution is largely attributed to advancements in technology, including improvements in battery life, miniaturization of sensors, and the proliferation of high-speed wireless communication networks.

Historical Development of UAVs

The roots of UAVs can be traced back to the early twentieth century, with the advent of radio-controlled aircraft. However, it was during the mid-twentieth century that UAVs began to gain prominence, primarily for military reconnaissance purposes. The United States, for instance, employed UAVs such as the Radio plane OQ-2 during World War II for target practice and aerial surveillance (Beard and McLain 2012).

The Cold War era witnessed further advancements in UAV technology, with a focus on developing reconnaissance drones for intelligence gathering. These early UAVs were often primitive compared to contemporary models, lacking the sophistication and capabilities seen today. However, they laid the groundwork for the rapid evolution that followed.

The late twentieth century and the early twenty-first century witnessed a paradigm shift in UAV development. Technological advancements, particularly in miniaturization, sensor capabilities, and communication systems, led to the creation of more versatile and efficient UAVs. The Predator and Reaper drones, widely used by the military, exemplify this evolution, featuring long-endurance flights and the ability to carry various payloads.

Simultaneously, the commercial and civilian applications of UAVs expanded rapidly. Small consumer drones became widely available, revolutionizing industries such as photography, filmmaking, and recreational activities. The technology's democratization led to a diverse range of UAV applications beyond their military origins.

The history and development of UAVs present a fascinating journey from their early inception to their status as indispensable tools across both military and civilian spheres. This evolution is marked by significant technological advancements and expanding applications that have propelled UAVs from the fringes of experimentation to the forefront of modern technology (Vitzilaios and Singhose 2017).

The roots of UAV technology can be traced back to the early twentieth century, when the potential for using unmanned platforms for military purposes first emerged. Initially, these systems were simple, remotely controlled aircraft used for target practice, providing a safer and more cost-effective means for military personnel to hone their skills. The concept of using these vehicles for reconnaissance was realized during World War I and II, albeit in a very primitive form. These early UAVs were rudimentary and limited in capability, primarily due to the technological constraints of the time.

The Vietnam War era marked a significant turning point for UAV development. It was during this period that UAVs began to be used more extensively for surveillance and reconnaissance missions. The hostile and complex environment of the Vietnam conflict necessitated innovations in remote sensing and control technologies, leading to the development of more sophisticated UAV systems. These advancements allowed for the real-time transmission of battlefield imagery and data, providing a strategic advantage that was previously unattainable.

The subsequent decades saw continued innovation and expansion of UAV roles, particularly during the Gulf War and the conflicts in the Balkans, where their utility in providing intelligence, surveillance, and reconnaissance (ISR) capabilities became unequivocally clear. The success of UAVs in these conflicts underscored their value in modern warfare, leading to increased investment and development in UAV technology.

However, the most transformative period for UAV development occurred in the late 1990s and early 2000s. This era was characterized by significant technological leaps in miniaturization, cost reduction in sensors and communications, and advances in computing power. These developments made UAVs smaller, cheaper, and more capable, allowing for a broad range of applications beyond military operations. The integration of advanced navigation systems, such as GPS, and improvements in battery technology further expanded the potential uses of UAVs, making them accessible for commercial, scientific, and recreational purposes.

The commercial sector quickly recognized the benefits of UAV technology, adopting drones for a variety of applications, including aerial photography, agriculture, infrastructure inspection, and delivery services. In the scientific community,

UAVs became valuable tools for environmental monitoring, wildlife research, and climate studies, offering a new perspective on data collection that was previously challenging or impossible to obtain.

Recreational use of UAVs also surged during this period, with the availability of affordable and easy-to-operate drones opening the skies to hobbyists and enthusiasts. This democratization of UAV technology has not only spurred innovation and creativity but has also raised important questions regarding privacy, safety, and regulation.

In summary, the history and development of UAVs reflect a remarkable trajectory of technological advancement and expanding utility. From their humble beginnings as remote-controlled targets to their status as versatile and sophisticated platforms, UAVs have profoundly impacted military operations, commercial enterprises, scientific research, and recreational activities. As technology continues to advance, the future of UAVs promises even greater possibilities, further cementing their role as a pivotal technology of the twenty-first century.

12.9 Different Names for UAVs

The terminology used to describe UAVs reflects the multifaceted nature of these aerial vehicles. While the term "drone" is widely recognized and often used in everyday language, it doesn't encompass the full spectrum of UAV classifications (D'Andrea 2014).

Drones: This is the most common and colloquial term for UAVs. It has its roots in military contexts but has become a catch-all phrase for any unmanned aerial vehicle, regardless of its size or purpose. Consumer drones have contributed to the widespread use of this term.

UAVs (Unmanned Aerial Vehicles): This is a more formal and precise term used in both military and civilian contexts. It emphasizes the vehicle's unmanned nature, providing a broad and inclusive umbrella term for all types of flying unmanned systems.

UAS (Unmanned Aerial Systems): This term expands the scope to include not only the aircraft (UAV) but also the entire system, including ground control stations, communication links, and any other components associated with the unmanned aerial operation. UAS is often used in a more technical or regulatory context.

RPAS (Remotely Piloted Aircraft Systems): Like UAS, RPAS emphasizes the remote-control aspect, underlining the role of human operators in guiding the UAV's flight.

Each of these terms carries its own nuances and is employed in specific contexts based on the intended emphasis—be it the vehicle itself, the broader operational system, or the method of control (Griffiths 2015).

In short, UAVs represent a dynamic and evolving technology that has come a long way from its rudimentary beginnings. From military reconnaissance to commercial applications and scientific research, UAVs continue to redefine the possibilities of aerial operations. The subsequent sections will delve deeper into the specific roles, technologies, and societal impacts of UAVs in various domains.

12.10 Types of UAVs

The landscape of Unmanned Aerial Vehicles (UAVs) is diverse, encompassing a wide array of designs, sizes, and configurations. This section provides an in-depth exploration of the various categories of UAVs, including fixed-wing, rotary-wing, and hybrid designs. Additionally, it delves into the spectrum of sizes, ranging from nano and micro-UAVs to larger, more sophisticated models.

12.10.1 Fixed-Wing UAVs

Fixed-wing UAVs, resembling traditional airplanes, are characterized by wings that generate lift as the UAV moves forward. These UAVs offer distinct advantages, particularly in terms of endurance and speed. They are well-suited for applications requiring long-range surveillance, mapping, and data collection.

- *Applications*: Fixed-wing UAVs find extensive use in military reconnaissance, border patrol, and aerial mapping. Their ability to cover large distances efficiently makes them ideal for monitoring expansive areas.
- *Design Characteristics*: These UAVs have a streamlined design with wings that remain fixed in position, hence the name "fixed wing". They are powered by traditional propellers or jet engines (Mozaffari et al. 2019a).
- *Advantages*: Longer flight times, higher speeds, and greater endurance are key advantages of fixed-wing UAVs. Their design allows for stable, efficient flight over extended periods.

12.10.2 Rotary-Wing UAVs: Versatile Hoverers

Rotary-wing UAVs, commonly known as drones with propellers, distinguish themselves by their ability to hover and take off vertically. This unique feature enables them to operate in confined spaces and perform tasks that demand a high degree of manoeuvrability.

- *Applications*: Rotary-wing UAVs are extensively used in surveillance, filmmaking, search and rescue operations, and precision agriculture. Their versatility makes them suitable for scenarios where vertical take-off and landing (VTOL) are essential (How and Schumacher 2013).

- *Design Characteristics*: Characterized by rotating blades or rotors, these UAVs can vary in size and configuration. Quadcopters, hex copters, and octocopters are common examples.
- *Advantages*: The ability to hover, take off vertically, and manoeuvre in tight spaces are distinct advantages of rotary-wing UAVs. They are often chosen for tasks that demand agility and close-quarters operation.

12.10.3 Hybrid Designs: Bridging the Divide

Hybrid UAVs combine features of both fixed-wing and rotary-wing designs, offering a flexible solution that bridges the gap between endurance and manoeuvrability. These UAVs often feature the capacity for vertical take-off and landing (VTOL) while also providing the efficiency of fixed-wing flight.

- Applications: Hybrid UAVs are utilized in applications where the benefits of both fixed-wing and rotary-wing designs are required. This includes surveillance, environmental monitoring, and certain military operations.
- Design Characteristics: The hybrid design incorporates elements of both fixed-wing and rotary-wing configurations. Some models have rotating wings or tilt-rotors, allowing for a seamless transition between hovering and forward flight (Baillieul and Antsaklis 2007).
- Advantages: Hybrid UAVs provide a compromise between the endurance of fixed-wing models and the manoeuvrability of rotary-wing ones. This versatility makes them adaptable to a broader range of missions.

12.11 Size Spectrum: From Nano to Large-Scale

UAVs come in a range of sizes, each catering to specific applications based on their payload capacity, endurance, and manoeuvrability.

Nano and Micro UAVs: These compact UAVs, often weighing less than a few kilograms, are designed for tasks that require agility and accessibility. Examples include indoor surveillance, environmental monitoring, and even entertainment drones used for light shows.

Small and Medium UAVs: With increased payload capacities and endurance, small and medium UAVs find applications in agriculture, aerial mapping, and infrastructure inspection. They strike a balance between versatility and operational capability.

This column graph illustrates the advancements in UAV technology over the years from 2015 to 2022, focusing on three key metrics: battery life (in hours), communication range (in 100 km), and payload capacity (in kg). The graph shows a steady increase in each of these areas, highlighting the technological progress made within the UAV industry. Battery life, communication range, and payload capacity

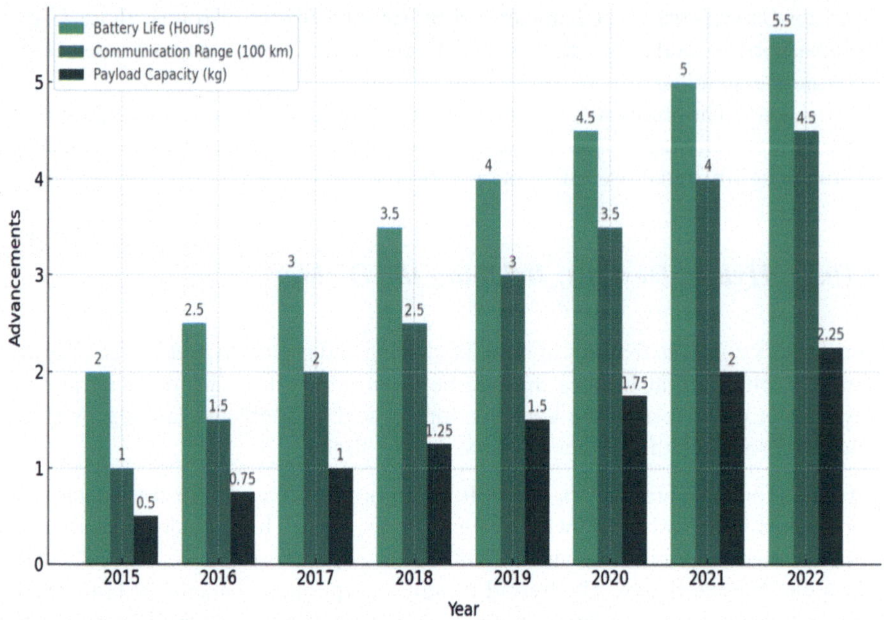

Fig. 12.3 Advancements in UAV Technology over years. *Source* Author

have all seen significant improvements, demonstrating the rapid development and enhancement of UAV capabilities over the specified period.

Large and Heavy UAVs: These UAVs, with substantial payload capacities and extended flight times, are employed in military reconnaissance, surveillance, and cargo delivery. Their robust designs allow for the integration of advanced sensor systems and sophisticated technologies.

The diversity in size and design within the realm of UAVs underscores their adaptability to a myriad of tasks across various industries. The subsequent sections will delve into specific applications of these UAV types, exploring how their unique characteristics are harnessed to meet the demands of modern technology and innovation (Kovacina and Martin 2016). Advancements in UAV Technology over the years are shown in Fig. 12.3.

12.12 Defining AI in UAVs: An Overview

Artificial Intelligence (AI) refers to the simulation of human intelligence in machines that are programmed to think and learn like humans. The integration of AI into UAV technology has been a game-changer, enabling drones to perform complex tasks autonomously. AI empowers UAVs with capabilities such as real-time data processing, environmental understanding, object detection, and adaptive decision-making, which are crucial for navigating and operating in diverse and unpredictable environments. This autonomy is particularly vital for missions that are too dangerous, dull, or dirty for human involvement, allowing UAVs to go further and do more than ever before.

In recent years, the synergy between AI and UAVs has propelled technological advancements to unprecedented heights. The fusion of AI and UAVs has not only revolutionized the capabilities of these aerial systems but has also opened new frontiers in various industries, from military operations to agriculture, environmental monitoring, and beyond (Michael et al. 2010). This section provides a comprehensive exploration of the defining characteristics of AI in UAVs, traces the historical trajectory of their integration, and underscores the significance of this technological marriage.

The relevance of AI to UAVs extends beyond autonomy. It enhances data analysis capabilities, enabling the processing of vast amounts of information captured by UAV sensors rapidly. This capability is invaluable across a wide spectrum of applications, from precision agriculture, where drones monitor crop health and irrigation needs, to search and rescue missions, where they identify survivors in disaster-stricken areas. Moreover, AI-driven UAVs contribute significantly to the advancement of research in areas such as climate change, wildlife conservation, and urban planning, by providing detailed, accurate data that was previously unattainable.

In sum, the integration of AI into UAVs represents a pivotal shift in the potential applications and capabilities of these versatile machines. It not only amplifies their operational effectiveness but also opens new avenues for innovation across various sectors of society. As we stand on the brink of this technological revolution, it is essential to understand the historical journey of UAVs development and the transformative role of AI in shaping the future of unmanned flight.

At its core, AI in the context of UAVs refers to the incorporation of intelligent algorithms and computational systems that empower these unmanned vehicles to perform tasks without explicit human guidance. Unlike traditional UAVs that operate under rigid pre-programmed instructions, AI-equipped UAVs possess the ability to adapt, learn, and make decisions based on real-time data. The integration of AI extends beyond mere automation; it endows UAVs with a level of autonomy that transforms them from passive tools to intelligent collaborators in various applications (Johnson and Humbert 2012).

AI in UAVs encompasses a spectrum of technologies, including machine learning, computer vision, natural language processing, and decision-making algorithms. These technologies collectively enable UAVs to process vast amounts of data, identify patterns, and execute complex tasks that were once solely within the realm of human expertise.

12.13 Historical Perspective: The Gradual Integration of AI into UAV Technology

The marriage of AI and UAVs did not happen overnight; instead, it represents a progressive evolution that has spanned several decades. In the early stages, UAVs were primarily controlled through manual remote operation, limiting their versatility and applications. The introduction of basic automation in the form of pre-programmed flight paths marked the first steps towards autonomy (Jordan and Mitchell 2015).

As computational capabilities surged and AI algorithms matured, UAVs began to exhibit enhanced cognitive functions. Machine learning algorithms allowed UAVs to recognize and adapt to changing environments, paving the way for more sophisticated applications. The military sector played a pivotal role in driving the integration of AI into UAVs, seeking to augment reconnaissance capabilities and minimize human risk in hazardous missions.

The turning point came with the development of advanced sensor technologies and the rise of powerful on-board processors. These technological leaps facilitated real-time data analysis, enabling UAVs to process information autonomously. Computer vision, a branch of AI, allows UAVs to interpret visual data, identify objects, and navigate dynamically in response to their surroundings. The historical integration of AI into UAVs has thus been a journey from basic automation to true autonomy, shaping the landscape of modern unmanned aerial systems.

Beyond military applications, AI-driven UAVs are transforming industries like agriculture. Equipped with advanced sensors and machine learning algorithms, these UAVs can analyze crop health, optimize irrigation, and facilitate precision agriculture. The environmental monitoring sector benefits from AI-enabled UAVs for tasks such as wildlife tracking, deforestation analysis, and climate research (Duffy 2018).

In essence, the significance of AI in UAVs lies in its capacity to elevate these aerial systems from mere tools to intelligent partners, capable of adapting to diverse scenarios, learning from experiences, and contributing meaningfully across a spectrum of applications. The subsequent sections of this exploration will delve deeper into specific applications, technologies, and the future trajectory of this symbiotic relationship between AI and UAVs.

12.13.1 AI-Powered Autonomy

The marriage of AI and UAVs brings forth a new era of autonomy, where UAVs operate not as mere extensions of human control but as intelligent entities capable of making decisions, navigating complex environments, and learning from their experiences. This section delves into the fundamental aspects of AI-powered autonomy in UAVs, exploring how AI enables basic autonomy, facilitates precise navigation and collision avoidance, and incorporates adaptive learning mechanisms.

Basic Autonomy: Making Decisions Without Human Intervention

At the heart of AI-powered autonomy in UAVs lies the ability to operate independently, making decisions in real-time without direct human intervention. Traditional UAVs were bound by pre-programmed flight paths, limiting their flexibility and adaptability to dynamic situations. AI changes this paradigm by endowing UAVs with decision-making capabilities based on the analysis of sensory data.

Through advanced algorithms, AI-equipped UAVs can assess their surroundings, interpret data from various sensors, and dynamically adjust their flight paths or operational parameters. This level of autonomy is particularly crucial in scenarios where human response times may be insufficient, such as in military reconnaissance or emergency response missions (Tang and Glässer 2014).

The integration of basic autonomy in UAVs is not merely about automation but about responsiveness to the environment. For example, a surveillance UAV with basic autonomy can autonomously follow a moving target, adapt to changes in weather conditions, or re-route its course to avoid potential obstacles. This newfound independence amplifies the operational scope of UAVs, making them versatile tools in a myriad of applications.

Navigation and Collision Avoidance: AI Algorithms for Precision Flight

Precise navigation is a cornerstone of effective UAV operations. AI algorithms play a pivotal role in enhancing the navigation capabilities of UAVs, ensuring they can traverse complex environments with accuracy and efficiency. Traditional navigation systems relied on GPS coordinates and pre-programmed routes, but AI introduced a dynamic and adaptive approach.

AI-powered navigation involves real-time analysis of sensory data, including data from GPS, inertial sensors, and visual inputs. Machine learning algorithms process this information, allowing UAVs to calculate optimal routes, adjust flight altitudes, and respond to changes in the environment. This is particularly crucial in scenarios where GPS signals might be compromised, such as in urban canyons or densely forested areas (Zeng et al. 2019).

Collision avoidance is another critical aspect of AI-enhanced navigation. Through computer vision and sensor fusion, AI-equipped UAVs can detect obstacles in their path and autonomously adjust their trajectory to avoid collisions. This capability is especially vital in applications like package delivery, where UAVs need to navigate through urban landscapes filled with buildings, trees, and other potential obstructions.

In military contexts, AI-powered collision avoidance ensures the stealth and safety of UAV missions. These vehicles can autonomously navigate complex terrains, evade enemy radar, and adapt their flight patterns to minimize the risk of detection or interception.

Adaptive Learning: UAVs That Learn from Experience

One of the most transformative aspects of AI in UAVs is adaptive learning, where these aerial systems can evolve and improve their performance over time based on their experiences. This is achieved through machine learning algorithms that enable UAVs to analyse data, identify patterns, and adjust their behaviour accordingly.

In practical terms, adaptive learning allows UAVs to refine their navigation strategies, optimize energy consumption, and enhance their decision-making processes based on the outcomes of previous missions. For example, a UAV involved in agricultural monitoring can learn to recognize specific crop diseases or patterns of plant health, improving the accuracy of its assessments with each mission.

The adaptive learning capabilities of AI in UAVs extend beyond individual vehicles. UAV swarms, consisting of multiple coordinated units, can share knowledge and experiences, enabling the entire swarm to collectively learn and adapt to changing conditions. This collaborative learning approach holds immense potential in scenarios where a group of UAVs needs to accomplish complex tasks collectively, such as environmental monitoring or search and rescue operations (Broughton and Valavanis 2020).

In conclusion, the integration of AI-powered autonomy in UAVs marks a paradigm shift in their capabilities. These vehicles are no longer limited by static instructions but can dynamically respond to their surroundings, navigate with precision, and continuously improve through adaptive learning. The subsequent sections will delve deeper into specific applications where these autonomous features redefine the potential and impact of UAVs across diverse industries.

12.14 The Evolution and Impact of AI on Unmanned Aerial Vehicles

The introduction of UAVs or drones, into the modern lexicon represents a significant leap forward in technology and operational capability, marking a new era in both military and civilian domains. Initially conceived for military purposes, these sophisticated machines have rapidly evolved, transcending their initial scope to become versatile tools that cater to a wide range of applications across various sectors. This remarkable journey from rudimentary remote-controlled aircraft to highly sophisticated systems capable of autonomous operation highlights a dynamic field that is at the forefront of technological innovation (Chung et al. 2018).

The genesis of UAV technology can be traced back to the early twentieth century, primarily designed to serve as target practice for training military personnel. However, it wasn't long before the potential of these vehicles was recognized for reconnaissance missions, providing a safer alternative to manned aircraft in hostile environments. Over the decades, the military utility of UAVs expanded significantly, encompassing surveillance, target acquisition, and even direct attack missions. This military heritage laid the groundwork for the technological advancements that would later allow UAVs to break into the civilian sector.

The transition of UAVs from exclusively military assets to valuable civilian tools has been driven by rapid advancements in technology. Key among these advancements is the development of artificial intelligence (AI) and machine learning algorithms, which have dramatically expanded the capabilities of UAVs. AI has enabled these machines to process vast amounts of data in real-time, make autonomous decisions, and perform complex tasks with minimal human intervention. This leap in capability has not only enhanced the efficiency and effectiveness of UAVs in traditional roles but has also opened new possibilities for their application (Erdelj et al. 2017).

Today, UAVs are employed in a wide array of civilian and commercial functions that were once thought impossible. In agriculture, drones equipped with advanced sensors and AI algorithms are used for precision farming practices, such as monitoring crop health, optimizing water usage, and managing pests and diseases. This not only increases crop yields but also reduces the environmental impact of farming by minimizing the use of water, fertilizers, and pesticides.

In the realm of public safety and emergency response, UAVs have become indispensable tools for search and rescue operations. Equipped with thermal imaging and high-resolution cameras, drones can quickly cover large areas, providing real-time information to rescue teams and significantly improving the chances of finding survivors in disaster-stricken areas. Similarly, in environmental monitoring, UAVs are used to track changes in ecosystems, monitor wildlife populations, and assess the impact of climate change, providing valuable data that can inform conservation efforts and policy decisions (Stöcker et al. 2017).

Moreover, the commercial sector has embraced UAV technology for a variety of applications, from aerial photography and film production to infrastructure inspection and delivery services. This broad spectrum of applications underscores the versatility and utility of UAVs, transforming industries and opening new avenues for innovation and entrepreneurship (Torres-Sánchez et al. 2018).

In conclusion, the evolution of UAVs from military tools to multipurpose platforms for civilian and commercial use is a testament to the profound impact of technological advancements, particularly in AI and machine learning. As these technologies continue to advance, the potential applications for UAVs are bound to expand further, offering exciting possibilities for the future. This transition not only highlights the technological capabilities of UAVs but also raises important considerations regarding their ethical use, regulatory challenges, and the societal implications of widespread drone deployment (Sparrow 2016).

12.15 Enhancing UAV Capabilities with AI

The integration of AI into UAVs has significantly expanded their capabilities, enabling them to undertake complex missions with higher autonomy, manage payloads more efficiently, and communicate more effectively. This section delves into the transformative impact of AI on enhancing the operational capabilities of UAVs.

- *Autonomy*
  AI has been pivotal in advancing the autonomy of UAVs, allowing them to perform a wide range of tasks without direct human intervention. Through the incorporation of sophisticated AI algorithms, UAVs can now navigate complex environments, make real-time decisions, and execute missions under challenging conditions (Scott and Scott 2017).
- *Navigation*
  AI enables UAVs to understand and interact with their environment, facilitating autonomous flight paths and dynamic adjustment to unforeseen obstacles. By processing data from various sensors in real-time, such as cameras, LiDAR, and GPS, UAVs can map their surroundings, identify safe flight corridors, and adapt to changes in the terrain or unexpected obstacles.
- *Obstacle Avoidance*
  AI systems equipped with machine vision and sensor fusion capabilities allow UAVs to detect and avoid obstacles. These systems analyse the sensory information to identify potential hazards and dynamically alter the UAV's flight path to ensure safety without compromising the mission objectives.
- *Decision-Making*
  AI enhances UAVs' decision-making capabilities in dynamic environments. Whether it's adjusting to weather conditions, responding to moving objects, or optimizing mission parameters on the fly, AI algorithms enable UAVs to make informed decisions based on the analysis of real-time data, ensuring mission success under varying conditions.
- *Payload Management*
  The effective management of payloads, including sensors, cameras, and operational equipment, is crucial for the success of UAV missions. AI plays a critical role in optimizing payload utilization to enhance mission effectiveness (Mozaffari et al. 2019b).
- *Sensor Optimization*
  AI algorithms analyse data from onboard sensors to optimize their operation, ensuring that the UAV collects the highest quality data possible. This is particularly important in applications like environmental monitoring and precision agriculture, where data accuracy is paramount.
- *Adaptive Payload Control*
  AI enables dynamic control over payloads based on the mission's requirements. For instance, in surveillance operations, AI can direct cameras to focus on specific areas of interest or adjust sensor settings in response to environmental conditions, ensuring optimal data collection.
- *Communication and Networking*
  AI-driven improvements in UAV communication systems have revolutionized how UAVs interact with each other and with ground control stations, enabling advanced swarming capabilities and networked operations.

- *Swarming Capabilities*
  AI enables multiple UAVs to operate in coordination, simulating the behaviour of a swarm. This allows for complex, distributed missions to be performed with a high degree of efficiency and resilience. Swarming UAVs can cover larger areas, provide redundant coverage, and adapt to mission changes collectively.
- *Networked Operations*
  Enhanced communication protocols driven by AI facilitate seamless data sharing and coordination among UAVs and control systems. This networked approach improves situational awareness, enables collaborative mission execution, and supports dynamic re-tasking of assets based on real-time information.

12.16 Applications Transformed by AI-Driven UAVs

From agriculture to search and rescue, surveillance, and environmental monitoring, AI-driven UAVs are revolutionizing the way tasks are performed, enhancing efficiency, accuracy, and outcomes (Kapoor et al. 2020).

Agriculture

In the agricultural sector, AI-driven UAVs are at the forefront of pioneering precision agriculture practices (Kapoor et al. 2020). These practices include:

Crop Monitoring

UAVs equipped with AI-powered sensors and imaging technology can monitor crop health across vast areas, identifying issues like nutrient deficiencies, water stress, and disease before they become visible to the human eye. This allows for timely intervention, reducing the risk of crop failure.

Pest Control

AI algorithms analyse images captured by UAVs to detect pest infestations, enabling targeted pest control measures. This not only improves the effectiveness of pest management strategies but also reduces the environmental impact by minimizing the use of pesticides.

Yield Optimization

By analysing data collected on crop conditions, soil health, and environmental factors, AI-driven UAVs can provide recommendations for optimizing planting densities, irrigation schedules, and fertilization plans, leading to improved yields and resource efficiency.

Search and Rescue

AI-enhanced UAVs have become invaluable assets in search and rescue operations, significantly improving efficiency and outcomes (Nex and Remondino 2014):

- Advanced Pattern Recognition: AI-driven image analysis enables UAVs to quickly identify individuals in distress over large and inaccessible areas, even in challenging conditions such as at night or in dense forests.
- Environmental Analysis: AI algorithms process environmental data to optimize search patterns and identify likely locations of missing persons based on terrain, weather, and other factors, improving the speed and success rate of search and rescue missions.

Surveillance and Security

In the realm of surveillance and security, AI has greatly enhanced the capabilities of UAVs for military, border control, and urban security applications:

- Military Surveillance: AI-driven UAVs can autonomously patrol areas of interest, detecting and tracking suspicious activities or threats, and providing real-time intelligence without putting human lives at risk.
- Border Control: UAVs equipped with AI can monitor borders more efficiently, detecting illegal crossings, trafficking activities, and other security breaches with high precision and over extensive areas.
- Urban Security: AI-enabled UAVs support law enforcement by providing aerial surveillance during large public events, traffic monitoring, and crime scene analysis, enhancing public safety and situational awareness.

Environmental Monitoring

AI-driven UAVs play a critical role in environmental conservation efforts, including climate change research, wildlife conservation, and pollution tracking:

- *Climate Change Research*: By collecting and analysing environmental data, UAVs can monitor changes in ecosystems, glacier movements, and sea-level rises, contributing valuable insights to climate change studies (Gong et al. 2020).
- *Wildlife Conservation*: UAVs equipped with AI can monitor wildlife populations, track migration patterns, and detect poaching activities, providing crucial data for conservation efforts without disturbing the animals.
- *Pollution Tracking*: AI-driven UAVs are used to monitor air and water quality, identify sources of pollution, and assess the environmental impact of industrial activities, facilitating more effective environmental protection measures.

12.17 Applications of AI-Powered UAVs

The integration of AI into UAVs has unlocked a plethora of possibilities across various sectors. This section explores the transformative impact of AI in UAV applications, ranging from military operations and agriculture to search and rescue missions and the burgeoning field of delivery services (Motlagh et al. 2017).

Military Applications

Military UAVs have witnessed a paradigm shift with the infusion of AI technologies. These enhancements not only bolster surveillance and reconnaissance capabilities but also extend into combat scenarios, creating more agile and responsive unmanned platforms.

Surveillance and Reconnaissance

AI-powered UAVs excel in collecting and processing vast amounts of data. Computer vision algorithms enable real-time object detection, tracking, and identification, significantly improving the efficiency of surveillance missions. UAVs equipped with AI can autonomously scan large areas, identify potential threats, and relay critical information to military operators.

Target Identification and Tracking

Machine learning algorithms, integrated into military UAV systems, enhance the accuracy of target identification. AI-driven target tracking enables continuous monitoring and updates on the movements of potential threats, providing invaluable intelligence to military decision-makers.

Autonomous Decision-Making

In combat scenarios, AI enables UAVs to make rapid decisions based on real-time data analysis. These decisions may include adjusting flight paths, evading threats, or even collaborating with other AI-enabled assets for coordinated operations. This autonomy reduces the cognitive load on human operators and enhances the responsiveness of military UAVs.

Stealth Operations

AI contributes to the development of stealthy UAVs capable of evading enemy detection. Adaptive learning algorithms allow these UAVs to analyse and learn from past missions, optimizing their flight patterns and minimizing the risk of detection by enemy radar systems.

The incorporation of AI in military UAVs transforms these unmanned platforms into intelligent, adaptive assets that play a crucial role in modern warfare, providing strategic advantages in surveillance, reconnaissance, and combat scenarios.

Agricultural Drones

AI has emerged as a game-changer in agriculture, with UAVs equipped with advanced sensors and machine learning algorithms transforming farming practices. These agricultural drones offer unprecedented precision, enabling farmers to monitor and manage their fields with unparalleled efficiency (Williams 2017).

Crop Monitoring

AI-powered UAVs equipped with high-resolution cameras and sensors can analyze crop health, identify diseases, and assess the overall condition of crops. Machine learning algorithms process this visual data, providing farmers with actionable insights into the state of their fields. This real-time monitoring allows for early detection of issues, optimizing crop yield.

Pest Control

AI facilitates the identification of pest infestations through image recognition and data analysis. Drones can autonomously survey fields, detect signs of pest damage, and deliver targeted interventions, reducing the need for broad-spectrum pesticides. This precision in pest control contributes to sustainable and environmentally friendly farming practices.

Precision Agriculture

AI-driven UAVs enable precision agriculture by creating detailed maps of fields, indicating variations in soil composition, moisture levels, and crop health. Farmers can then make data-driven decisions, optimizing irrigation, fertilization, and other inputs. This not only enhances crop yields but also promotes resource efficiency.

Automated Crop Spraying

AI enables drones to autonomously navigate fields and apply fertilizers or pesticides precisely where needed. This targeted approach minimizes waste, reduces environmental impact, and ensures that crops receive the necessary treatments for optimal growth.

The application of AI in agricultural drones marks a revolution in precision farming, empowering farmers with data-driven insights and sustainable practices.

Search and Rescue Operations: Aiding in Critical Missions

AI-equipped UAVs play a pivotal role in search and rescue operations, where time is often of the essence. These unmanned systems leverage AI to enhance efficiency, provide real-time information, and assist in locating missing persons or responding to disaster-stricken areas.

Autonomous Surveying: In search and rescue scenarios, time is critical. AI enables UAVs to autonomously survey vast areas, scanning for signs of distress or survivors. Computer vision algorithms can detect human shapes, identify signals, and relay this information to rescue teams, expediting the search process.

Mapping and Navigation: AI enhances UAVs' mapping capabilities, allowing them to create detailed maps of disaster-stricken areas. This assists rescue teams in planning routes, identifying hazards, and optimizing their response. AI-driven navigation systems enable drones to navigate complex and dynamic environments, such as collapsed buildings or rugged terrains.

Communication Relay: AI-enabled UAVs can serve as communication relays in areas where traditional communication infrastructure is compromised. Equipped with AI-driven communication systems, these drones ensure that rescue teams maintain connectivity, facilitating coordination and information exchange in challenging environments.

Victim Detection: AI algorithms, integrated with sensors and cameras on UAVs, enable the detection of signs of life in disaster-stricken areas. Thermal imaging, for instance, allows drones to identify body heat, helping locate survivors who may be difficult to find through traditional means.

In search and rescue operations, the synergy between AI and UAVs enhances the capabilities of response teams, increasing the chances of locating and rescuing individuals in distress (Gupta et al. 2016).

Delivery Drones: Redefining Logistics with AI Precision

The advent of delivery drones has ushered in a new era of logistics, and AI plays a central role in ensuring the efficiency, safety, and reliability of these autonomous delivery systems.

Route Optimization: AI algorithms analyze real-time data, including weather conditions, traffic patterns, and terrain, to optimize delivery routes. This not only ensures the fastest delivery times but also minimizes energy consumption and operational costs.

Obstacle Avoidance: AI-powered UAVs incorporate obstacle avoidance systems, utilizing sensors and computer vision to detect and navigate around obstacles during flight. This technology ensures the safe delivery of packages in dynamic urban environments or areas with challenging terrain (Bazi et al. 2018).

Weather Adaptability: AI enhances the ability of delivery drones to adapt to changing weather conditions. Drones equipped with AI algorithms can adjust their flight paths, speeds, and altitudes in response to weather changes, ensuring the safety of both the drone and the delivered goods.

Security Measures: AI contributes to the implementation of robust security measures in delivery drones. This includes features such as biometric authentication for package recipients, tamper-evident packaging, and real-time monitoring of the delivery process to prevent theft or unauthorized access.

The integration of AI in delivery drones not only streamlines the logistics of package delivery but also sets the stage for innovations in last-mile delivery services, particularly in urban areas.

In conclusion, the applications of AI in UAVs transcend traditional boundaries, revolutionizing industries and reshaping the possibilities of unmanned aerial systems. From military operations and agriculture to search and rescue missions and the future of delivery services, AI-powered UAVs stand at the forefront of technological innovation, providing solutions to complex challenges across diverse domains.

12.18 Challenges and Ethical Considerations in AI-Powered UAVs

The integration of AI and UAVs brings about transformative capabilities, but it also raises significant challenges and ethical considerations. This section explores two critical aspects: security concerns, focusing on potential vulnerabilities and the importance of cybersecurity, and ethical considerations, addressing issues related to privacy, surveillance, and the potential misuse of AI in UAV technology (Vas et al. 2015).

The widespread adoption of AI-driven UAVs across various sectors brings with it a host of challenges and ethical considerations. While these technologies offer significant benefits, they also raise concerns related to privacy, regulatory compliance, and the ethical implications of their deployment.

Privacy Concerns

One of the most pressing issues associated with UAV surveillance is the potential infringement on individual privacy rights. UAVs, especially those equipped with sophisticated AI-enabled cameras and sensors, can collect detailed information over private and public spaces, often without the explicit consent of the individuals being monitored. This capability poses significant questions about:

- Surveillance and Consent: The balance between leveraging UAVs for legitimate purposes such as security and law enforcement and ensuring that individuals' privacy rights are not violated.
- Data Management: The ethical handling, storage, and destruction of data collected by UAVs. Ensuring that this data is protected against unauthorized access and misuse is paramount to maintaining public trust.

Regulatory Challenges

The rapid development of UAV technology, coupled with the integration of AI, presents substantial regulatory challenges. These challenges include ensuring safety, managing airspace, and establishing international norms for UAV operations (Shraim et al. 2019):

- Safety Regulations: As UAVs become more common in urban and rural areas, ensuring their safe operation to prevent accidents with other aircraft, wildlife, and humans is critical. This involves developing comprehensive guidelines for UAV design, testing, and maintenance.
- Airspace Integration: The integration of UAVs into existing airspace systems requires sophisticated traffic management solutions to prevent collisions and ensure the smooth flow of all air traffic.
- International Norms: With UAVs capable of long-range operations, establishing international norms and agreements is essential to manage cross-border flights, surveillance, and data collection activities in a way that respects the sovereignty and legal frameworks of different countries.

Ethical Implications

The deployment of autonomous UAVs, particularly in sensitive sectors such as military and employment, raises several ethical questions:

- Accountability in Military Use: The use of AI-driven UAVs in military operations, including targeted strikes, introduces complex ethical and legal challenges. Determining accountability for actions taken by autonomous systems, particularly in cases of collateral damage or wrongful deaths, is a significant concern.
- Impacts on Employment: The automation and efficiency offered by UAVs could lead to job displacement in sectors such as agriculture, surveying, and logistics. While they create opportunities for new types of jobs, the net impact on employment and the economy raises ethical considerations about the equitable distribution of benefits and the responsibility of governments and corporations to support affected workers.

Security Concerns: Navigating Potential Vulnerabilities

As AI becomes an integral part of UAV technology, it introduces a new set of security challenges that need to be carefully navigated. AI-powered UAVs, like any other technology, are susceptible to vulnerabilities that, if exploited, could have serious consequences.

- Cybersecurity Risks: One of the primary security concerns revolves around the cybersecurity of AI-powered UAVs. As these systems rely on interconnected networks, they become potential targets for cyber-attacks. Malicious actors could exploit vulnerabilities in the software, manipulate data, or even take control of the UAV, posing risks to both the vehicle itself and the data it collects.
- Data Integrity and Privacy: AI-equipped UAVs gather and process vast amounts of data, often sensitive or personal in nature. Ensuring the integrity and privacy of this data is crucial. Breaches in data security not only compromise individual privacy but may also have broader implications, especially in applications like military surveillance or law enforcement.
- Counter-AI Measures: The use of AI in UAVs opens the door to potential countermeasures by adversaries. As AI algorithms become more sophisticated, so do the methods to deceive or disrupt them. Adversarial attacks, where subtle modifications are made to inputs to mislead AI systems, pose a significant challenge in the context of UAVs, potentially leading to erroneous decisions or compromised mission outcomes.
- Dependency on AI Decision-Making: Overreliance on AI for decision-making in UAVs can be a vulnerability. If the AI system encounters an unexpected situation or a scenario it hasn't been explicitly trained for, it may struggle to make accurate decisions. Human oversight and intervention become critical to mitigate the risks associated with the limitations of AI (Siebert and Teizer 2014).
- Addressing these security concerns requires a multi-faceted approach, including robust cybersecurity protocols, regular software updates, and ongoing research into AI resilience against adversarial attacks.

- Ethical Considerations: Balancing Progress with Responsibility
  The ethical considerations surrounding AI-powered UAVs are intertwined with broader societal concerns related to privacy, surveillance, and the responsible use of advanced technologies. Striking a balance between technological progress and ethical responsibility is imperative to ensure that AI in UAVs benefits society without compromising fundamental values (Siebert and Teizer 2014).
- Privacy Concerns: The extensive data collection capabilities of AI-powered UAVs raise concerns about individual privacy. In applications like surveillance or urban monitoring, where UAVs may capture images or videos of people without their explicit consent, there's a risk of infringing on personal privacy rights. Clear regulations and guidelines must be established to govern the collection, storage, and use of data obtained by UAVs.
- Surveillance and Civil Liberties: The increased use of UAVs for surveillance purposes raises questions about civil liberties and the potential for unwarranted intrusion into private lives. Striking a balance between the legitimate use of UAVs for public safety and respecting individual freedoms is a delicate ethical consideration that requires careful legislation and oversight.
- Misuse of AI Technology: The powerful capabilities of AI in UAVs can be misused for malicious purposes, such as unauthorized surveillance, stalking, or even acts of terrorism. Ethical considerations extend to ensuring that regulations are in place to prevent the misuse of UAV technology and that the responsible authorities have the means to detect and respond to such activities.
- Bias and Fairness: The algorithms powering AI systems, including those in UAVs, are not immune to biases. If training data contains biases, AI models can perpetuate and even exacerbate these biases in their decision-making processes. This raises concerns about fairness, particularly in applications like law enforcement where AI may be used to identify individuals or assess potential threats.
- Transparency and Accountability: The opacity of AI decision-making processes poses ethical challenges. Ensuring transparency in how AI algorithms operate, particularly in critical applications, is essential for accountability. This includes understanding the factors influencing AI decisions and having mechanisms in place for auditing and challenging those decisions when necessary.
- The ethical considerations surrounding AI-powered UAVs underscore the need for a holistic approach that involves regulatory frameworks, public discourse, and continuous ethical evaluations to ensure that these technologies align with societal values and norms.

In nutshell, the integration of AI into UAVs presents a dual challenge: addressing security concerns to protect the technology from exploitation and navigating ethical considerations to ensure responsible and fair use. As AI-powered UAVs continue to evolve, an ongoing dialogue between technologists, policymakers, and the public becomes paramount to foster a collective understanding of the risks and benefits associated with this transformative technology. Balancing innovation with ethical responsibility will be instrumental in shaping the future trajectory of AI-powered UAVs.

12.19 Conclusion

Unmanned Aerial Networks (UANs) represent a frontier in the evolution of autonomous systems, merging advancements in aerial robotics, artificial intelligence, and wireless communications to address complex challenges across various domains. From enhancing agricultural productivity and environmental monitoring to revolutionizing delivery services and emergency response, UANs demonstrate the potential to significantly impact societal norms, economic models, and environmental strategies. The integration of UANs into daily operations and strategic initiatives reflects a broader shift towards automation and smart technology solutions. However, the deployment and expansion of UANs are not without challenges. Regulatory frameworks, privacy concerns, ethical implications, and technical hurdles such as battery life, navigation precision, and data security remain critical areas for ongoing research and development.

As we look to the future, the role of UANs is poised for exponential growth, driven by continuous innovation in drone technology, AI algorithms, and communication infrastructures. The collaborative efforts of researchers, industry stakeholders, and policymakers will be paramount in navigating the complexities of integrating UANs into an increasingly digital and interconnected world. Ensuring the responsible and ethical use of UANs while maximizing their benefits will be a delicate balance to achieve but is essential for fostering a sustainable and technologically advanced society.

In conclusion, Unmanned Aerial Networks hold the promise of transforming numerous aspects of our lives, from enhancing the efficiency of industries to contributing to the safeguarding of our planet. The journey ahead for UANs is filled with potential and pitfalls alike, necessitating a concerted effort to harness their capabilities for the greater good while mitigating the risks associated with their deployment. As we venture further into this era of innovation, the evolution of UANs will undoubtedly continue to be a key area of focus, symbolizing a significant step forward in the march towards an automated, interconnected, and smarter world.

The intersection of AI and UAVs is poised for significant advancements, promising to reshape industries, society, and the very fabric of human-technology interaction. The future of AI and UAVs is likely to be characterized by groundbreaking technological innovations, expansion into new applications, and profound societal impacts.

Technological Advances

Future developments in AI and UAV technology are expected to focus on enhancing performance, expanding capabilities, and reducing environmental impacts. Key areas of innovation include:

- Energy Efficiency: Advances in battery technology and energy harvesting techniques will extend UAV flight times and reduce the environmental footprint of these devices. Innovations such as solar-powered UAVs or those using hydrogen fuel cells could revolutionize long-duration missions.

- AI Algorithms: The evolution of AI algorithms will enhance UAV autonomy, enabling more complex decision-making processes and adaptive learning capabilities. This will allow UAVs to perform increasingly sophisticated tasks with minimal human oversight, including dynamic problem-solving in unpredictable environments.
- Materials Science: Breakthroughs in lightweight and durable materials will improve UAV performance and durability. Advanced composites or nanomaterials could offer new possibilities for UAV design, ranging from enhanced aerodynamics to self-healing structures (Williams 2017).

Expanding Applications

As technology progresses, UAVs are set to impact a broader array of industries and sectors, some of which are only beginning to explore the potential of these devices:

- Space Exploration: UAVs, particularly those equipped with advanced AI, could play a critical role in exploring other planets and moons. Drones like NASA's Ingenuity, already testing flight in Mars' atmosphere, pave the way for more sophisticated missions that could explore hard-to-reach locations or even search for signs of extra-terrestrial life.
- Deep-Sea Research: AI-driven UAVs could dive into the depths of the oceans, exploring uncharted territories, monitoring marine biodiversity, and investigating the impacts of climate change on underwater ecosystems, where human access is limited or impossible.
- Urban Planning: UAVs will increasingly assist in urban planning and smart city development, from 3D mapping and infrastructure inspection to traffic management and disaster response planning, offering insights and data analytics to build more resilient and efficient urban environments.

Societal Impact

The advancements in AI-driven UAV technology will have wide-ranging implications for society, influencing warfare, privacy, and human-AI interaction:

- Changes in Warfare: The use of AI-driven UAVs in military operations is likely to change the nature of warfare, making it more automated and potentially altering the strategic balance between nations. This raises ethical and security concerns about autonomous weapon systems and the need for international agreements to regulate their use.
- Privacy Dynamics: As UAVs become more integrated into daily life, navigating the balance between beneficial applications and individual privacy rights will become increasingly complex. Society will need to address the implications of pervasive surveillance and develop safeguards to protect privacy.
- Human-AI Interaction: The integration of AI-driven UAVs into various sectors will change how humans interact with machines. As UAVs take on more roles traditionally performed by humans, adapting to this new relationship will require adjustments in education, workforce development, and societal norms.

The synergy between AI and UAVs is set to unlock unprecedented advancements, with significant ripples across economic sectors, societal structures, and ecological conservation efforts. These developments forecast a surge in efficiency for traditional industries and open avenues for exploration in realms once thought inaccessible.

References

Ansell D, Egglestone P, Lochrie M (2016) UAV applications in civilian space. Technol Innov Manag Rev. Explores civilian applications of UAV technology

Austin R (2010) Unmanned aircraft systems: UAVS design, development and deployment. Wiley. This book covers the fundamentals of UAS design and operation

Baillieul J, Antsaklis PJ (2007) Control and communication challenges in networked real-time systems. Proc IEEE. Relates to challenges in UAN communication

Bazi Y, Al Rahhal MM, AlHichri H, Alajlan N (2018) Unmanned aerial vehicles (UAVs) for crowd sensing: opportunities, challenges, and applications. IEEE Access 6:67917–67937

Beard R, McLain TW (2012) Small unmanned aircraft: theory and practice. Princeton University Press. Provides a foundational text on UAV design and control

Bekhti A, Sebbane YB (2018) Planning and decision making for aerial robots. Springer. Covers planning and decision-making processes for UAVs

Broughton G, Valavanis KP (2020) Machine learning approaches for path planning of autonomous UAVs. J Intell Rob Syst 99(3–4):557–582

Capozzoli V, Sabatini AM (2014) UAVs and UAV swarms for civilian applications: communications and image processing in the SCI framework. J Intell Robot Syst. Discusses civilian applications of UAVs

Chung SJ, Paranjape AA, Dames P, Shen S, Kumar V (2018) A survey on aerial swarm robotics. IEEE Trans Rob 34(4):837–855

D'Andrea R (2014) Guest editorial: special issue on the 2013 international symposium on robotics research. Int J Robot Res. Highlights innovative UAV research

Duffy VD (2018) Handbook of human factors for UAVs and drones. CRC Press. Discusses human factors in UAV operations

Erdelj M, Król M, Natalizio E (2017) UAV-assisted disaster management: applications and open issues. In: International conference on computing, networking and communications (ICNC), pp 1–5

Feron E (2012) Drones for peace: design, control, and applications of unmanned aerial vehicles for humanitarian missions. Peace Technol

Filali F, Abu-Dayya A (2017) Autonomous UAVs for disaster management and rescue operations. Wirel Commun Mob Comput

Gilbert M, Kirksey H (2019). Artificial intelligence for autonomous networks. CRC Press. Offers insights into AI's role in network autonomy, relevant for UAN management

Gong X, Jiang T, Gunduz D (2020) A survey of energy-efficient wireless communications with unmanned aerial vehicles. J Commun Netw 22(2):157–171

Griffiths H (2015) Radar technology for unmanned aerial vehicles. IEEE Aerosp Electron Syst Mag

Guerrero-Bonilla LE, Kumar V, Tokekar P (2017) Formations for resilient robot teams. IEEE Robot Autom Mag. Explores formations and strategies for UAV teams

Gupta L, Jain R, Vaszkun G (2016) Survey of important issues in UAV communication networks. IEEE Commun Surv Tutor 18(2):1123–1152

How JP, Schumacher B (2013) Unmanned aerial vehicle systems for disaster relief: Tornado Alley Aerial Reconn. AIAA Infotech@Aerospace conference

Johnson E, Humbert S (2012) Autonomy in UAVs for tactical missions: technology and applications. UAV technology and applications

Jordan MI, Mitchell TM (2015) Machine learning for UAV-based data collection: a review. Mach Learn J

Justice IG, Pack DJ (2018) Design, control and applications of autonomous drone systems. Robot Autom Eng J. Covers design and control aspects of autonomous drones

Kaminski ME (2017) Civilian drones and privacy: a primer. Priv Mod Age. It addresses privacy concerns around civilian drone use

Kapoor R, Ojha A, Patel N (2020) A comprehensive review on technological advancements in UAVs. Unmanned Syst 8(3):195–224

Knupp KH et al (2016) Meteorological applications of unmanned aerial vehicles. Meteorological applications. Discusses UAVs in weather monitoring and research

Kovacina MA, Martin DP (2016) Autonomous UAV path planning and estimation. IEEE Robot Autom Mag

Kovar D (2015) UAVs for search and rescue: a field guide. Search and rescue magazine. Offers practical guidance on using UAVs in SAR operations

Liu Y, Qin Z, Elkashlan M, Gao Y (2018) Non-orthogonal multiple access for 5G and beyond. Proc IEEE. Discusses NOMA technology in UAV communications

Michael N, Mellinger D, Lindsey Q, Kumar V (2010) The GRASP multiple UAV testbed: design and experiments. Int J Robot Res

Motlagh NH, Taleb T, Arouk O (2017) Low-Altitude unmanned aerial vehicles-based internet of things services: comprehensive survey and future perspectives. IEEE Internet Things J 3(6):899–922

Mozaffari M, Saad W, Bennis M, Nam Y, Debbah M (2019a) A tutorial on UAVs for wireless networks: applications, challenges, and open problems. IEEE Commun Surv Tutor

Mozaffari M, Saad W, Bennis M, Debbah M (2019b) Mobile unmanned aerial vehicles (UAVs) for energy-efficient internet of things communications. IEEE Trans Wirel Commun 18(11):5120–5135

Nex F, Remondino F (2014) UAV for 3D mapping applications: a review. Appl Geomat 6(1):1–15

Saad W, Bennis M, Mozaffari M (2020) Wireless communications and networking for unmanned aerial vehicles. Wiley. Focuses on UAV-specific communication and networking challenges

Scott J, Scott C (2017) Drone delivery models for healthcare. In: Proceedings of the 50th Hawaii international conference on system sciences

Sekander S, Tabassum H, Hossain E (2019) Networking for autonomous UAVs: protocols, practices, and future directions. Wiley, This book discusses networking aspects crucial for UAV operations

Shraim H, Khattab A, Shraim N (2019) Path planning for autonomous UAVs: a survey. Prog Aerosp Sci 107:1–23

Siebert S, Teizer J (2014) Mobile 3D mapping for surveying earthwork projects using an unmanned aerial vehicle (UAV) system. Autom Constr 41:1–14

Sparrow R (2016) Robots and respect: assessing the case against autonomous weapon systems. Ethics Int Aff 30(1):93–116

Stöcker C, Bennett R, Nex F, Gerke M, Zevenbergen J (2017) Review of the current state of UAV regulations. Remote Sens 9(5):459

Tang Z, Glässer U (2014) Formal methods for dynamic information flow analysis in UAV operating systems. J Aerosp Inf Syst

Torres-Sánchez J, López-Granados F, De Castro AI (2018) Multi-temporal mapping of the vegetation fraction in early-season wheat fields using images from UAV. Comput Electron Agric 144:111–121

Valavanis KP, Vachtsevanos GJ (eds) (2015) Handbook of unmanned aerial vehicles. Springer. A comprehensive resource on UAV technologies and applications

Vas E, Lescroël A, Duriez O, Boguszewski G, Grémillet D (2015) Approaching birds with drones: first experiments and ethical guidelines. Biol Lett 11(2):20140754

Vitzilaios N, Singhose W (2017) Unmanned aerial vehicle design and control: challenges and opportunities. Control Eng Pract

Williams KW (2017) Safety risk management for unmanned aircraft systems (UAS). J Air Transp Manag 62:182–191

Završnik A (ed) (2016) Drones and unmanned aerial systems: legal and social implications for security and surveillance. Springer. It explores the societal and legal dimensions of UAS use

Zeng Y, Lyu J, Zhang R (2019) Cellular-connected UAV: potential, challenges, and promising technologies. IEEE Wirel Commun 26(1):120–127

Chapter 13
Internet of Drones

Dilip Mandloi, Rajeev Arya, and Ajit Kumar Verma

Abstract The integration of unmanned aerial vehicle (UAV) technology with interconnected networks has ushered in the era of the Internet of Drones (IoD), marking a profound shift with far-reaching implications across industries. This chapter offers a comprehensive exploration of IoD, delving into its myriad aspects including applications, key components, challenges, future trends, and industrial evolution. Initially, the chapter surveys the extensive applications enabled by IoD across various industries, showcasing how interconnected drones are revolutionizing operations in agriculture, emergency response, surveillance, logistics, and beyond. Subsequently, it delves into the core components of IoD networks, encompassing the drone structure, sensing units, communication capabilities, and processing units. Additionally, the chapter addresses critical considerations such as security, privacy, interoperability, and regulatory frameworks, offering insights into navigating the evolving landscape of IoD. Moreover, it offers a proactive outlook on the future potential of IoD, projecting its development in response to fast-paced technical breakthroughs and changing social demands. Furthermore, the chapter explores the industrial evolution of IoD, highlighting its transformative impact on traditional sectors through increased efficiency, innovative partnerships, and job creation in emerging fields. Through this comprehensive analysis, individuals gain valuable insights on effectively utilizing the revolutionary capabilities of IoD technology in the current digital era.

Keywords Internet of Drones (IoD) · Unmanned aerial vehicle · IoD applications · IoD challenges · IoD components

---

D. Mandloi (✉)
Shri Vaishnav Vidyapeeth Vishwavidyalaya, Indore 452001, MP, India
e-mail: mandloidilip@gmail.com

R. Arya
Wireless Sensor Networks Lab, Department of Electronics and Communication Engineering, National Institute of Technology Patna, Patna, Bihar, India

A. K. Verma
Faculty of Engineering and Natural Sciences, Western Norway University of Applied Sciences, Haugesund, Norway

R. Arya et al. (eds.), *Recent Trends in Artificial Intelligence Towards a Smart World*, Frontiers of Artificial Intelligence, Ethics and Multidisciplinary Applications,
https://doi.org/10.1007/978-981-97-6790-8_13

13.1 Introduction

Recently, unmanned aerial vehicles (UAVs), commonly referred to as drones, have become increasingly popular due to advantages like mobility, easy deployment, load transport capabilities, real-time monitoring, and accessibility to remote areas (Abualigah et al. 2021). The drones have been widely embraced across numerous sectors for their versatility in tasks such as traffic and wildlife surveillance, disaster management, on-demand package delivery, environmental monitoring, mapping and surveying, aerial photography, and agricultural operations (Alsamhi et al. 2019). Drones can also navigate and operate in locations that are challenging for humans to access, thereby bolstering network connectivity, coverage, and capacity, particularly when integrated with other wireless or wired network architectures (Dahiya 2023). Each of these applications demands precise navigation, network connectivity, and airspace management to ensure smooth and successful execution. The fusion of drone technology with the internet has introduced an innovative concept called the Internet of Drones (IoD) (Yang et al. 2022). This convergence has unlocked a new realm of possibilities, enabling seamless integration and communication between drones and Internet of Things (IoT) connectivity. This synergy, establishes enhanced data collection, real-time analysis, and efficient communication channels, thereby streamlining operations and enhancing effectiveness across various domains (Heidari et al. 2023).

The effective operation of drone missions in the IoD ecosystem depends on the efficient management of extensive data volumes. Timely and precise decision-making is critical for mission success, and any errors or delays could lead to significant consequences (Nguyen et al. 2023). Artificial intelligence (AI) plays a pivotal role in managing this complexity by enabling machines to mimic human cognitive functions such as learning from data, recognizing patterns, and making informed decisions (Bera et al. 2021). The concept of the IoD encompasses the interconnected network of technologies and sensors that facilitate communication and data exchange within the network (Gharibi et al. 2016). This network serves as the foundation for gathering data from various sources, including onboard sensors, weather forecasting systems, traffic surveillance cameras, satellite feeds, and more. Real-time analysis of this diverse data is essential for identifying patterns, detecting anomalies, and facilitating informed decision-making (LNC Prakash et al. 2023).

The concept of the IoD is emerging, facing legal hurdles and operational costs. Unlike traditional internet frameworks, IoD must navigate jurisdictional complexities due to drones' border-crossing capabilities. IoD functions as a network of machines, sensors, and data storage, akin to a mobile IoT or Internet of Drone Things (IoDT) (Heidari et al. 2023). Operational costs are significant, especially with mobile end nodes, and energy constraints pose challenges for drone-based networks. However, IoD offers adaptability and benefits across sectors like agriculture, manufacturing, government operations, and smart cities. Figure 13.1 illustrates the organization of the chapter.

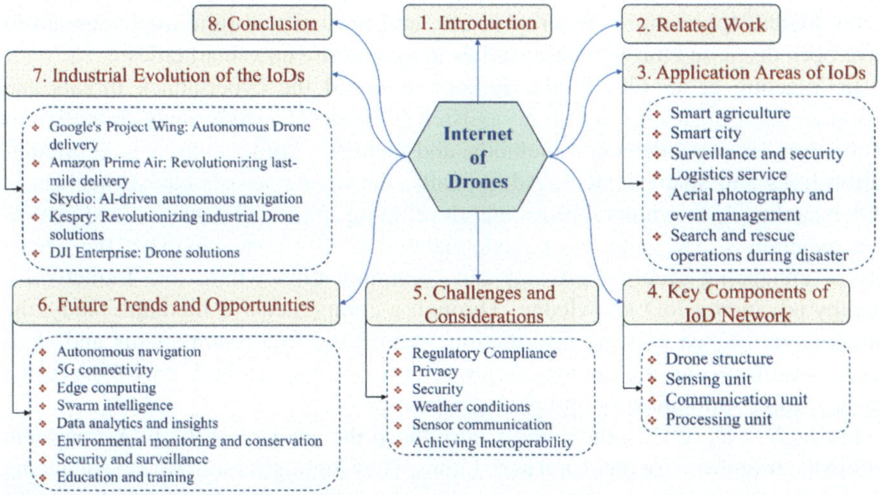

Fig. 13.1 Organization of the chapter. *Source* Author

13.1.1 Related Work

Numerous survey studies have been conducted to explore the potential solutions and applications of the IoD. These surveys offer valuable insights into the current state of research, existing challenges, and future directions within the IoD domain. This section provides a summary of selected survey studies, highlighting their key findings and contributions.

In Abualigah et al. (2021), the authors present a comprehensive survey of the IoD, a burgeoning research area with wide-ranging applications in fields like aerial photography, civilian, and military sectors. The survey covers IoD applications including smart cities surveillance, cloud and fog frameworks, unmanned aerial vehicles, wireless sensor networks, mobile computing, and business paradigms. Additionally, it explores integration aspects such as privacy protection, security authentication, neural networks, blockchain, and optimization-based methods. In Yang et al. (2022), the authors provide a comprehensive analysis of security challenges and solutions in the IoD network. They highlight the limited coverage of IoD security in existing literature and offer detailed insights into authentication techniques and blockchain-powered schemes. The authors also discussed the challenges facing these solutions and presents promising research directions for strengthening IoD protection. In Yahuza et al. (2021), the authors investigated security and privacy challenges in IoD networks. Authors explore the integration of security features into IoD architecture, classify drones based on vulnerability levels, outline attacks on IoD networks, and discuss mitigation techniques. In Nayyar et al. (2020), the authors introduce the concept of the IoDT as the future integration of drones with IoT, smart computer vision, cloud computing, and advanced wireless communication. The IoDT's related technologies, applications, security issues, and present real-time implementations have been discussed through case studies in agriculture and smart cities.

In Yaacoub et al. (2020), the authors reviewed the cyber-attack threats and propose countermeasures in a drone-assisted network. The study analyses malicious drone uses, assesses detection methods, and identifies vulnerabilities in communication links and smart devices. Additionally, the review assists ethical hackers in understanding UAV vulnerabilities and developing improved detection and protection techniques. The authors of Abdelmaboud (2021) conceptualized the necessity of enhancing security, privacy, and communication within IoD frameworks, thereby advancing IoD knowledge. Through a comprehensive literature study, the authors synthesized existing information, identifying IoD requirements and challenges. Additionally, the authors reviewed cutting-edge research on IoD security, privacy, and communication, proposing remedies.

In Singh et al. (2022), the authors introduced the concept of the IoD ecosystem within the framework of precision agriculture. They highlight IoD's role in enhancing agricultural productivity and discuss challenges, solutions, and research opportunities in this domain. In Alsamhi et al. (2019), the authors studied collaborative drones and IoT applications in smart cities, offering a comprehensive overview of the field. The study synthesized existing research contributions, addressed gaps in the literature, and provided insights into applications, challenges, and opportunities. Additionally, the potential of drones to enhance IoT services in smart cities, emphasizing their role in urban development and improving quality of life, is also highlighted. In Nguyen et al. (2023), the authors studied the feasibility of an IoD system integrating blockchain and artificial intelligence at the edge to enhance QoS in search and rescue operations. An advanced IoD system architecture is proposed to introduce edge-based AI for automating search operations and discuss strategies to improve energy efficiency. Additionally, public and private blockchain technologies has been investigated for providing secure healthcare platforms.

In Tilburg (2017), the authors identified and highlighted the valuable role of drones in search and rescue missions, demonstrating their effectiveness in confirming fatalities, clearing terrain, and providing visual data. Through a comprehensive literature review, authors synthesized existing knowledge on drone applications, contributing to the advancement of discourse in this field. The authors of Kim et al. (2018) investigate the use of drones for entertainment, notably using augmented and virtual reality technology. The authors of Rejeb et al. (2023) reviewed the drones' potential and challenges in supply chain management and logistics. The authors highlight drones' strengths, such as supporting humanitarian logistics, reducing delivery time and cost, enhancing flexibility, and promoting sustainability. Additionally, they categorize challenges into technical, organizational, safety-related, and regulatory issues, providing insights into real-life drone deployments and setting a future research agenda.

13.2 Application Areas of IoD

This section presents a variety of applications enabled by IoD technology. In recent years, the proliferation of IoD devices has driven innovation and efficiency across various sectors, such as healthcare, logistics, agriculture, disaster management (Savkin and Huang 2020), manufacturing smart cities, and industrial automation (Abualigah et al. 2021). By seamlessly integrating sensors, actuators, and intelligent algorithms, IoD systems empower organizations and individuals to make more informed decisions, optimize processes, and enhance experiences. IoD is considered cost-effective mobile sensing platforms, particularly valuable in scenarios such as disaster response and hazardous environments where human intervention may be risky (Banafaa et al. 2024). Figure 13.2 illustrates the application areas and key components of the IoD network.

Smart Agriculture

The integration of IoD technologies with smart agriculture, a contemporary agricultural technique that uses technology to maximize crop productivity and efficiency, is expected to produce considerable benefits. IoD devices equipped with a range of sensors, including thermal, hyperspectral, and multispectral cameras, collect copious amounts of data on crop health, soil properties, and environmental factors. To extract useful insights, this data is subjected to in-depth analysis using AI algorithms and machine learning models. IoD provides farmers with quantitative evaluations of plant health by producing indices like NDVI and NDRE, which allow for the early diagnosis of illnesses, nutritional deficits, and insect infestations (Singh et al. 2022).

Additionally, IoD with GPS and precision positioning systems enables the creation of detailed yield maps, aiding in the identification of spatial yield variations and the refinement of management practices. The precise application of inputs such as

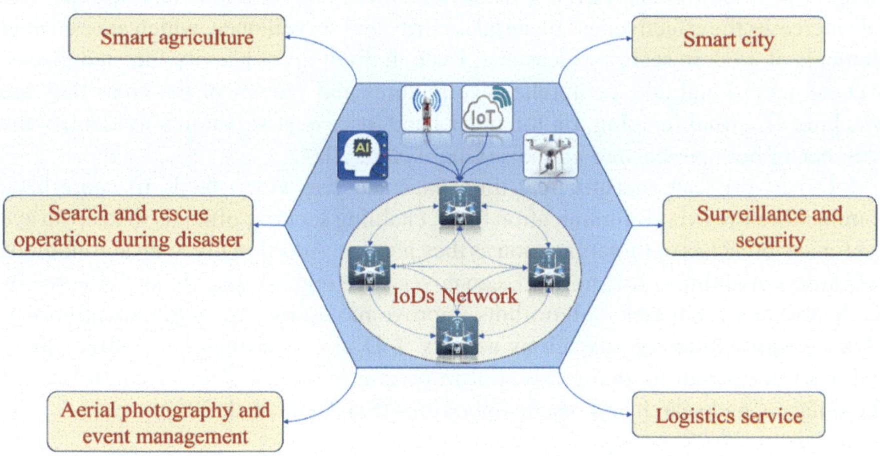

Fig. 13.2 Illustration of the application areas and key components of IoD network. *Source* Author

fertilizers, pesticides, and irrigation water is facilitated by accurately mapping field conditions, reducing resource usage while maximizing productivity. In managing irrigation, drones monitor soil moisture levels and pinpoint areas experiencing water stress, allowing farmers to adjust irrigation schedules and conserve water efficiently (Boursianis et al. 2022).

Smart City

The IoD ecosystem is critical to the development of smart cities, allowing a network of interconnected physical devices outfitted with sensors and software to collect and share data via the internet. IoD is widely used in smart city programs across a variety of sectors. In transportation and mobility management, IoD devices monitor traffic flow, optimize signals, and direct cars to available parking spaces, lowering congestion and pollution. Energy management benefits from IoD-enabled smart meters and automated systems that limit use in real time, increasing efficiency (Hoque et al. 2022).

Environmental monitoring uses IoD sensors to detect air quality, noise levels, and water contamination, allowing for preventative steps in public health and disaster management. IoD-enabled monitoring systems and emergency response mechanisms enhance public safety by providing quick action in the event of an accident or crisis. Waste management uses IoD sensors in bins to optimize collection routes and encourage recycling. IoD also transforms healthcare by enabling wearable devices for remote patient monitoring and early identification of health concerns. Furthermore, IoD insights on population dynamics and citizen engagement platforms assist urban planning and governance by promoting data-driven decision-making and community involvement (Alsamhi et al. 2019).

Surveillance and Security

The onboard integration of a variety of sensors, such as thermal imaging cameras, radar, light detection and ranging (LiDAR), and high-resolution cameras, over the IoD increases the effectiveness of aerial security and surveillance, which are essential elements of modern security measures. Even in dimly lit or heavily forested places, IoD can record and take comprehensive pictures and movies of the areas they are watching. Thermal imaging, on the other hand, uses heat signatures to identify the presence of both people and animals (Gilani et al. 2024).

IoD network can transmit real-time data and live video feeds to centralized command centres via communication links, enabling security officials to keep an eye out for any breaches or threats as soon as they happen. Additionally, with autonomous patrolling capabilities, IoD network can cover large regions quickly and effectively, while artificial intelligence algorithms improve monitoring by automatically identifying abnormalities or suspicious activity. IoD also contributes to public safety and asset protection by being essential in perimeter security, crowd control, event surveillance, and search and rescue operations (Sai Theja et al. 2022).

Logistics Services

The IoD can revolutionize delivery services by making it possible to transport deliveries, medical supplies, and other commodities more quickly, efficiently, and affordably. The IoD is especially good at last-mile delivery, delivering straight to clients' doorsteps while avoiding traffic jams and other physical barriers. They facilitate the delivery of vital supplies to disaster-affected communities, supporting emergency response operations by granting access to inaccessible or isolated places (Chen et al. 2022).

Additionally, IoD can be customized as delivery drones for specific requirements such as temperature-controlled compartments, offering personalized delivery options based on customer preferences and location. As delivery companies, e-commerce retailers, and logistics providers invest in drone delivery programs, the future of delivery services lies in the continued integration of IoD technologies, shaping the landscape of logistics and supply chain management (Edwards et al. 2023).

Aerial Photography and Event Management

The IoD opens a world of creative possibilities in entertainment and events, improving the experience for both audiences and participants. IoD equipped with high-resolution cameras captures stunning aerial photography and videography, providing unique perspectives and angles for event coverage. Furthermore, IoD equipped with programmable arrays and LED lights provides captivating light displays and exhibitions that enhance the ambiance of gatherings via coordinated airborne acts (Mohamadi et al. 2022).

From artistic installations to interactive experiences, IoD serve as a tool for creative expression and audience engagement, fostering connections and leaving lasting impressions. However, to guarantee the safe and responsible usage of drones in entertainment contexts, event organizers, drone operators, and regulatory agencies must work closely together in order to establish safety standards and regulatory compliance. IoD, taken as a whole, provides a dynamic and immersive element to the events and entertainment sector, pushing the limits of technology and innovation while improving the entire experience for customers (Serafinelli and O'Hagan).

Search and Rescue Operations During a Disaster

The IoD, equipped with a variety of advanced sensors and operated by artificial intelligence algorithms, plays a crucial role as an essential resource during the disaster management process. During the initiation of disasters, IoT technologies serve as first responders, using their real-time monitoring capabilities to identify initial indicators and promptly evaluate developing circumstances. This enables authorities to promptly issue warnings, establish evacuation plans, and strategically deploy resources. Adopting this preventive strategy not only guarantees the preservation of life but also reduces the extent of harm to infrastructure and property (Mukherjee et al. 2023).

Following disasters, IoD systems consistently demonstrate their abilities by enabling prompt and effective response operations. IoD, equipped with sophisticated imaging technology and object identification algorithms driven by artificial intelligence, plays a crucial role in search and rescue operations by efficiently finding survivors, detecting potential dangers, and evaluating the extent of structural damage (Krupakar et al. 2024).

13.3 Key Components of IoD Network

As illustrated in Fig. 13.2, the IoD encompasses a networked ecosystem where drones interact with each other and with ground control stations through high-speed internet connectivity. The IoD has four distinct units, namely the drone structure, sensing unit, communication unit, and processing unit.

Drone Structure

The frame serves as the foundation of the drone structure, providing structural support and housing for internal components. Constructed from lightweight and durable materials like carbon fiber or aluminium, the frame's design optimizes strength, rigidity, and weight reduction to enhance flight performance. IoD systems often feature a modular design, enabling flexibility, scalability, and customization to accommodate various types of drones, including fixed-wing, multirotor, and hybrid configurations. These drones serve different purposes such as surveillance, reconnaissance, mapping, and environmental monitoring (Anush Lakshman and Ebenezer 2021).

Communication and networking equipment integration is facilitated through mounting points, antennas, and enclosures, allowing drones to establish communication links within the IoD ecosystem. Payload mounting and integration are supported with mounting points, payload bays, or compartments for specialized applications. Power and battery management components ensure uninterrupted operation and optimal power efficiency. Environmental protection measures safeguard internal components from environmental factors, while flight control systems and fail-safe mechanisms ensure stability, precision, and safety during autonomous flight and mission execution (Sharma and Mehra 2023).

Sensing Unit

In an IoD system, the sensing unit, also known as the payload, is the primary component responsible for gathering data from the surrounding environment. This data includes a wide range of information, from visual aspects such as images and videos to environmental measurements like temperature, humidity, and air quality. IoD systems use a wide range of sensor types adapted to particular purposes. Cameras are the key sensory input for drones, allowing them to collect photographs and videos using RGB cameras for colour vision and high-resolution cameras for thorough investigations.

Furthermore, hyperspectral or multispectral sensors improve capabilities, allowing for sophisticated analysis in agricultural and ecological contexts (Chen 2021).

Another important category is LiDAR sensors, which use laser pulses to estimate the period of reflection from surrounding objects. This technique provides exact 3D mapping and terrain modelling, which is very useful in urban planning, infrastructure evaluation, and disaster management. The integration of LiDAR data with camera video allows for the creation of complete point clouds, which help in precise analysis and measurement. Inertial Measurement Units (IMUs) are built into IoD, monitoring acceleration, angular velocity, and magnetic field strength to provide critical orientation, velocity, and position information. Accelerometers, gyroscopes, magnetometers, and altimeters are critical components for flight stabilization, control, and correct attitude estimates, as well as collision risk mitigation and terrain tracking (Chen et al. 2022; Bruce Ralphin Rose et al. 2023).

Additionally, GPS receivers are critical for identifying exact drone location and navigation during flight, which is required for autonomous flight, waypoint navigation, and georeferencing data. Furthermore, specialized sensors, such as thermal cameras for detecting heat signatures, gas sensors for environmental monitoring, radiation detectors for nuclear safety inspections, and echo sounders for underwater surveys, meet specific application requirements, increasing the versatility and utility of IoD systems.

Communication Unit

The communication unit plays a crucial role in facilitating seamless communication among drones, ground stations, and other relevant entities within the network of an IoD system. Its design and functionality are crucial for ensuring efficient operation, safety, and reliability of drone operations. Drones typically rely on wireless communication protocols to establish connections with each other and with ground stations. Common protocols include Wi-Fi, Bluetooth, Zigbee, and cellular networks such as 4G and 5G. These protocols facilitate data exchange for command and control, telemetry, video streaming, and sensor data (Sharma and Mehra 2023).

Furthermore, it enables the establishment of mesh networking, which allows drones to create linked networks. This feature improves the resilience of communication and expands the range of drones by facilitating direct message relaying. The use of ad hoc networking methods allows drones to autonomously construct temporary networks, which is crucial in remote or disaster-affected regions that lack conventional infrastructure.

Processing Unit

The processing unit of an IoD system is responsible for managing and executing essential computational tasks for drone operations. Equipped with onboard computing power, including processors, memory, and storage, it handles tasks such as sensor data processing, autonomous navigation, and decision-making. By analysing real-time sensor data from GPS, cameras, LiDAR, and IMUs, the processing unit enables drones to determine their position, detect obstacles, and plan safe flight paths autonomously. Utilizing computer vision and object recognition algorithms, drones identify objects in their surroundings, facilitating tasks like inspection and surveillance (Garima Kulshreshtha and Maurya 2022).

Additionally, through data fusion techniques, the processing unit integrates information from multiple sensors to create a comprehensive understanding of the environment. Real-time decision-making algorithms prioritize safety and efficiency, enabling drones to adapt dynamically to changing conditions. Moreover, the processing unit manages communication and networking protocols for collaborative tasks within IoD systems, such as swarm intelligence and distributed sensing. Efficiency measures like energy-efficient algorithms optimize resource usage, prolonging flight endurance. In essence, the processing unit empowers drones to navigate autonomously, perceive their environment, and execute complex tasks efficiently and safely across various applications within the IoD ecosystem (Bruce Ralphin Rose et al. 2023).

13.4 Challenges and Considerations

The IoD has enormous potential for revolutionizing numerous industries and sectors by utilizing autonomous aerial capabilities. However, as with any developing technology, we must address significant challenges and considerations to ensure the widespread adoption and successful integration of IoD systems. Here are some important issues and considerations:

Regulatory Compliance

The IoD ecosystem faces significant regulatory compliance challenges due to the complex and constantly changing laws governing drone deployment and operation. Regulations addressing drone height limitations, flight patterns, and authorization procedures aim to ensure safe integration with manned aircraft. Remote identification and tracking legislation may necessitate the implementation of electronic identification modules and tracking systems to enhance accountability and security (Huang et al. 2021).

Environmental regulations may also restrict drone operations to minimize ecological and wildlife damage. Collaboration among regulators, industry stakeholders, and policymakers is crucial to establishing clear, consistent, and adaptive regulations that strike a balance between fostering innovation and addressing safety, privacy, and environmental concerns. Such regulatory frameworks are essential for enabling IoD systems to operate effectively and responsibly across various domains (Ahmed and Sheltami 2023).

Privacy

The multidimensional nature of privacy problems in Internet of Drone (IoD) systems arises from several facets of drone operations and data management. The deployment of drones with sensors and cameras raises concerns about data privacy and surveillance since they record visual media in both residential and public domains. The secure handling of data gathered by drones is crucial to mitigate any dangers associated with its storage and preservation. Mishandling this data could lead to privacy violations and unauthorized monitoring, compromising individuals' rights (Banafaa et al. 2024).

The act of transmitting data from drones to ground control stations presents potential privacy hazards, hence requiring the implementation of secure communication protocols in order to mitigate the possibility of unauthorized interception. Moreover, the use of position tracking and identification technology in drones gives rise to apprehensions over the acquisition and utilization of geospatial and personally identifiable data without the explicit agreement of persons. To overcome privacy problems and sustain public trust in IoD systems, it is crucial to adhere to privacy legislation, get consent for data gathering, and provide openness and accountability in drone operations (Tedeschi et al. 2024).

Security

Ensuring the security of IoD ecosystems is paramount to mitigate various threats that can compromise system components like IoD devices, networks, and communication links. These threats can lead to significant losses in terms of resources, trust, and availability. Attackers often target IoD systems to gain access to sensitive information through tactics such as traffic analysis, interception, and data capturing (Wang et al. 2022). These attacks can compromise the privacy of IoD systems by revealing sensitive information shared between IoD devices and ground control systems. Maintaining data integrity is crucial, and attacks such as substitution or alteration of information, access-control modification, and man-in-the-middle attacks pose significant risks. Protecting confidentiality involves thwarting identity spoofing, unauthorized access, replay attacks, and eavesdropping (Pauner et al. 2015).

Moreover, ensuring availability is essential, and attacks such as physical attacks, denial-of-service (DoS) and distributed denial-of-service (DDoS) attacks, GPS spoofing, channel jamming, and routing attacks can disrupt IoD operations. Trust is also critical, and threats like the use of falsified IoD, keyloggers, third-party violations, and firmware replacement attacks undermine trust relationships in IoD systems. Therefore, implementing robust security measures and maintaining continuous vigilance is necessary to mitigate risks and ensure the security and reliability of IoD systems (Choudhary et al. 2018).

Weather Conditions

Weather and environmental conditions pose significant challenges to the operation of drones within an IoD system. Adverse weather such as high winds, rainfall, snowfall, and extreme temperatures can impair visibility, affect flight stability, and decrease battery efficiency, potentially leading to loss of control or crashes. Additionally, electromagnetic interference from power lines and electronic devices can disrupt communication signals, posing safety risks during flight. Flight planning and risk assessment processes must carefully consider real-time weather data and forecasts to determine suitable flight windows and avoid hazardous conditions (Yahuza et al. 2021).

Moreover, operational restrictions may be imposed during adverse weather events to ensure compliance with regulations and maintain safety standards. Robust fail-safe mechanisms and emergency protocols are essential for the safe recovery of drones in unforeseen weather conditions. By leveraging advancements in weather forecasting, sensor technology, and drone resilience, operators can enhance the safety, efficiency, and reliability of drone operations in diverse environmental conditions within IoD systems (Liao et al. 2021).

Sensor Communication

Sensor communication in IoD systems faces several challenges that impact the reliability and efficiency of data exchange. Bandwidth limitations, especially in remote or congested areas, can hinder the transmission of large sensor datasets, leading to delays or packet loss. Latency issues can affect real-time decision-making and autonomous control, crucial for tasks like obstacle avoidance. Additionally, environmental factors such as electromagnetic interference and signal obstructions pose threats to communication reliability.

Energy efficiency is vital to extend drone mission duration, necessitating optimization of communication protocols and transmission power. Scalability concerns arise as IoD systems grow, requiring scalable architectures and congestion management solutions. Security measures must also be implemented to protect sensitive sensor data from cyber threats. Addressing these challenges demands advancements in communication technologies, network optimization, and cybersecurity protocols to ensure the robustness and effectiveness of sensor communication within IoD systems.

Achieving Interoperability

Interoperability plays a crucial role in facilitating uninterrupted communication and collaboration among drones, ground control systems, and other devices within the IoD ecosystem, irrespective of their respective manufacturers or operational protocols. Nevertheless, the attainment of interoperability presents several obstacles. The use of distinct communication protocols and data formats between drones and ground control systems frequently creates challenges to the efficient sharing of data. Ensuring compatibility and facilitating interoperability requires the standardization of communication protocols and data formats.

Moreover, the process of incorporating hardware components and software modules from several suppliers might present challenges on account of compatibility concerns and the use of proprietary interfaces. To handle the increasing number of drones and devices in IoD systems while ensuring interoperability, it is necessary to have scalable architectures and adaptable communication frameworks. To solve these issues and build interoperable IoD systems that can operate quickly and securely in different applications and settings, it is crucial to have collaborative efforts from stakeholders (Lee et al. 2021).

13.5 Future Trends and Opportunities

The prospects of the IoD are highly promising, as technological breakthroughs continue to open up new opportunities for innovation and change across a variety of sectors. From self-contained operations to improved connectivity, the landscape of IoD systems has the potential for tremendous expansion and innovation. In this section, the important trends and possibilities influencing the future of IoD, emphasizing their potential influence on industry, society, and the environment is presented. These trends represent the confluence of cutting-edge technology, legislative advancements, and industrial alliances, resulting in the formation of a more connected, efficient, and sustainable drone ecosystem.

Autonomous Navigation: AI and ML are advancing at a rapid pace, pushing the development of drones equipped with increasingly autonomous capabilities. The drones can see their surroundings, making judgments, and carrying out tasks without the need for direct human direction.

- Logistic services: Drones can transfer things from one point to another autonomously, which enables delivery services to be implemented more quickly and effectively.
- Infrastructure inspection: Autonomous drones can inspect critical infrastructure such as bridges, power lines, and pipelines, identifying potential issues and hazards.
- Surveillance and security: Autonomous drones can patrol designated areas, monitor for security threats, and alert human operators when anomalies are detected.

5G Connectivity: The deployment of 5G networks provides drones with high-speed, low-latency connectivity, enabling real-time communication and data transmission.

- Live video streaming: Drones equipped with high-definition cameras can stream live video feeds to operators or remote viewers for real-time situational awareness.
- Remote piloting: 5G connectivity enables operators to remotely control drones from anywhere with minimal latency, expanding the range and flexibility of drone operations.
- Collaborative missions: Drones can communicate with each other and share data in real-time over 5G networks, enabling collaborative missions such as search and rescue operations.

Edge Computing: Edge computing brings data processing and analysis closer to the source of data generation, reducing latency and bandwidth requirements.

- Real-time data analysis: Edge computing allows drones to analyse sensor data and make decisions locally, without relying on centralized servers or cloud infrastructure.

- Object detection and recognition: Drones can use edge computing to process images and videos in real time, enabling tasks such as object detection, tracking, and recognition.
- Onboard intelligence: Edge computing enables drones to have onboard intelligence, making them more responsive and capable of autonomous operation in dynamic environments.

Swarm Intelligence: Drone swarms consist of multiple drones that collaborate and communicate with each other to achieve common goals.

- Scalability: Drone swarms can scale to accommodate a large number of drones, enabling them to cover vast areas and perform complex tasks more efficiently.
- Redundancy and resilience: Drone swarms are inherently redundant, meaning that if one drone fails, the rest of the swarm can continue the mission. This resilience makes drone swarms well-suited for applications such as search and rescue operations.
- Task distribution: Drone swarms can distribute tasks among individual drones based on their capabilities and proximity to targets, optimizing resource utilization and mission efficiency.

Data Analytics and Insights: Data collected by drones provides valuable insights that can be used to optimize operations, improve decision-making, and drive innovation.

- Data analysis services: Companies can offer data analysis services to extract actionable insights from drone-collected data, such as crop health assessments, infrastructure condition monitoring, and traffic flow analysis.
- Predictive analytics: By analysing historical data collected by drones, companies can develop predictive models and algorithms to anticipate future events and trends, enabling proactive decision-making and resource allocation.
- AI-powered insights: AI and ML algorithms can analyse drone-collected data to identify patterns, trends, and anomalies that may not be apparent to human operators, unlocking new opportunities for optimization and innovation.

Environmental Monitoring and Conservation: Drones play a significant role in environmental monitoring and conservation efforts, providing valuable data on ecosystems, wildlife populations, and environmental changes.

- Environmental monitoring services: Companies can offer drone-based environmental monitoring services to governments, conservation organizations, and research institutions, providing valuable data on biodiversity, habitat health, and ecosystem dynamics.
- Wildlife conservation: Drones can be used to monitor endangered species, track wildlife populations, and detect illegal activities such as poaching and deforestation, enabling more effective conservation efforts and wildlife protection.
- Environmental impact assessments: Drones can conduct aerial surveys and assessments to evaluate the environmental impact of human activities such as mining, logging, and urban development, helping stakeholders make informed decisions and mitigate negative impacts.

Security and Surveillance: Drones equipped with cameras and sensors are increasingly used for security and surveillance applications, such as perimeter monitoring, crowd control, and event security.

- Security solutions: Companies can develop drone-based security solutions for various applications, including critical infrastructure protection, event security, and border surveillance, providing enhanced situational awareness and threat detection capabilities.
- Surveillance services: Security agencies and private companies can offer drone-based surveillance services to monitor large areas, detect suspicious activities, and respond to security incidents more effectively than traditional methods.
- Privacy protection: Companies can develop technologies and solutions to address privacy concerns associated with drone-based surveillance, such as encryption, anonymization, and compliance with data protection regulations, ensuring that privacy rights are respected while maintaining security.

Education and Training: With the growing demand for drone operators and technicians, there are opportunities for companies to provide education and training services for drone operation, maintenance, and repair.

- Drone pilot training: Companies can offer training programs and certification courses to individuals interested in becoming certified drone pilots, covering topics such as flight operations, airspace regulations, and safety procedures.
- Technical training: Companies can provide technical training for drone maintenance and repair, equipping technicians with the skills and knowledge to troubleshoot and repair drone hardware and software components.
- Industry-specific training: Companies can develop specialized training programs tailored to specific industries and applications, such as agriculture, construction, and public safety, providing hands-on experience and practical knowledge relevant to each sector.

13.6 Industrial Evolution of the IoD

The Industrial Evolution of the IoD represents a significant paradigm shift in establishing an interconnected drone ecosystem aimed at streamlining operations, boosting efficiency, and unleashing novel capabilities. This evolution is driven by the convergence of cutting-edge technologies such as artificial intelligence, advanced sensors, robust communication networks, and scalable computing infrastructure Prominent industry frontrunners, like Google, Amazon, Skydio, DJI enterprise, Kespry, and Facebook, have acknowledged the extensive prospects inherent in the IoD and have initiated ambitious projects to capitalize on its potential.

Google's Project Wing: Autonomous Drone Delivery

Traditional methods of delivery face significant challenges, including traffic congestion, high operational costs, and environmental impact due to their reliance on fossil fuel-powered vehicles. In response to these challenges, Project Wing, an initiative by Alphabet Inc., was launched in 2014. The Project Wing integrates Internet connectivity and advancements in robotics, artificial intelligence, and aviation technology to develop autonomous delivery drones. The primary goal of Project Wing is to revolutionize goods transportation, particularly in areas with challenging terrains or limited infrastructure. Project Wing offers a scalable, sustainable alternative, making deliveries more efficient, accessible, and eco-friendly in diverse environments, ultimately fostering socio-economic development.

Project Wing used cutting-edge technology to produce autonomous drones for accurate navigation and safe delivery. Furthermore, powerful sensors and computer vision systems were combined for precise sensing, machine learning assured adaptable performance, and updated algorithms permitted autonomous flying. The technology was verified in a successful 2014 experiment in rural Australia, cementing Project Wing's position as a pioneer in autonomous drone delivery and sparking more ideas for a sustainable delivery ecosystem (X.company).

Amazon Prime Air: Revolutionizing Last-Mile Delivery

Amazon Prime Air, introduced by Amazon in 2013, aims to revolutionize last-mile delivery via Drones. Increasing demand for faster delivery times and better customer service prompted the idea. Amazon has invested much in Prime Air technology R&D since its founding. Drone design, flying algorithms, sense-and-avoid systems, and cargo capacity have improved. Drones with advanced sensors and GPS can travel independently and deliver things precisely. However, airspace rules, collision avoidance issues, and technological limits like battery life and cargo capacity have made implementation difficult (AWS).

Amazon has run numerous pilot programmes and test flights to assess Prime Air's safety and practicality in real life despite these challenges. Tests have shown operational issues and regulatory compliance, directing technological development and refinement. Amazon is determined to overcome these hurdles and maximize Prime Air's potential to provide consumers quicker, more efficient, and environmentally friendly delivery choices. Prime Air has the potential to revolutionize logistics and e-commerce delivery as technology and regulations change (Singireddy and Daim 2018).

Skydio: AI-Driven Autonomous Navigation

Historically, the operational capabilities of drones have been limited by several variables, including lighting conditions, impediments, and the proficiency of the operator. To overcome these challenges, Skydio drones provide a complete solution. Skydio drones use sophisticated autonomy, predictive AI algorithms, and night-time navigation capabilities to enable users to achieve greater distances, enhanced safety, and improved performance, regardless of the time of day. The drones' capacity to mitigate blind spots and autonomously navigate around obstacles guarantees secure and certain flying, even in the most demanding surroundings. The use of superior AI and sensor technologies by Skydio drones has brought about a significant transformation in autonomous flying. Skydio drones are equipped with advanced AI algorithms and cutting-edge sensors that emulate the capabilities of a proficient pilot. The drones are equipped with NVIDIA Jetson Orin GPUs, which allow for real-time navigation and decision-making by providing the required computational capability (Consumer Technology Association 2021).

The use of Skydio drones has yielded remarkable results for businesses across many industries. One notable application is the use of Skydio drones for industrial inspections. For instance, a power plant seeking to do infrastructure inspections for maintenance purposes may now use Skydio drones, which possess a notable level of accuracy, measuring centimetres. The enhanced autonomy of unmanned aerial vehicles (UAVs) allows them to navigate through restricted interior spaces and areas with inadequate lighting, therefore obtaining data with exceptional accuracy and effectiveness. Autonomous targeted inspections have the capacity to reduce the temporal and resource requirements associated with manual inspections. Furthermore, the drones' ability to rapidly create 2D and 3D models at the site enhances their data collection capabilities, so enabling more informed decision-making (Bachrach 2021).

Kespry: Revolutionizing Industrial Drone Solutions

The aerial intelligence platform developed by Kespry has significantly transformed several sectors, including aggregate mining, pulp and paper, and waste management services. Kespry's drones utilize sophisticated sensors and AI-powered analytics to provide accurate and practical insights, enabling businesses to optimize their resources and make well-informed decisions. These drones operate autonomously, performing inspections of mining locations and acquiring detailed aerial images and multi-dimensional data with remarkable precision and effectiveness. The implementation of Kespry's drone solutions has produced notable outcomes, such as higher precision in stockpile assessments, increased operational effectiveness, improved safety measures, and significant financial savings.

Furthermore, Kespry has lately implemented innovative functionalities on its platform, hence augmenting its potential. These include cutting-edge LiDAR technology for enhanced accuracy in mapping topography and enhanced thermal imaging capabilities for detecting safety threats and monitoring the environment. These latest innovations reaffirm Kespry's position as a pioneering entity in providing comprehensive aerial intelligence solutions to industries worldwide. By prioritizing regulatory adherence alongside technological innovation, Kespry empowers its clients to achieve their productivity, profitability, and sustainability objectives (Kespry).

DJI Enterprise Drone Solutions

DJI serves the distinct requirements of business entities that extend beyond the limits of recreation and photography. Recognizing the increased need for drones in agriculture, construction, public safety, and infrastructure inspection, DJI set out to answer particular difficulties encountered by businesses and organizations. The difficulties encompassed a wide variety of areas, including precision farming, construction site monitoring, public safety response, and infrastructure inspection. Each of these issues need customized solutions to ensure effective data collecting, analysis, and decision-making processes. The DJI Enterprise solutions were carefully designed to address these requirements, providing a wide array of goods and services that are customized to match the demands of various industries.

For instance, in the agricultural sector, the utilization of DJI Agras drones has helped the precise application of sprays and the monitoring of crops. Similarly, in the building industry, DJI Matrice drones have played a crucial role in enabling accurate site surveys and progress tracking. In the context of public safety, DJI Mavic drones offered aerial reconnaissance capabilities in emergency situations, while DJI Phantom drones facilitated secure and effective inspections of vital assets for infrastructure assessment. The aforementioned results highlight the significant influence of DJI's technology in facilitating novel opportunities for innovation and enhanced productivity across many sectors (DJI Enterprise).

13.7 Conclusion

The incorporation of Drones into the AI-enabled IoT framework offers a wide range of potential advantages and obstacles. Drones possess the potential to significantly transform several sectors, such as agriculture, construction, logistics, and emergency services, by virtue of their ability to link to the internet and other electronic devices. These technologies include advanced data collecting, real-time monitoring, and automation functionalities that have the potential to boost efficiency, safety, and productivity.

Nevertheless, the extensive integration of drones into the AI-enabled IoT infrastructure also gives rise to concerns surrounding privacy, security, and adherence to legal requirements. Ensuring the appropriate and successful deployment of drone technology requires addressing crucial factors such as safeguarding data transfer, securing sensitive information, and complying with airspace rules. However, the continuous progress in technology and the cooperation among many parties involved have the potential to significantly transform industries, foster innovation, and generate fresh prospects for economic expansion and societal progress through IoD ecosystem.

References

Abdelmaboud A (2021) The internet of drones: requirements, taxonomy, recent advances, and challenges of research trends. Sensors 21(17). https://doi.org/10.3390/s21175718

Abualigah L, Diabat A, Sumari P, Gandomi AH (2021) Applications, deployments, and integration of internet of drones (IoD): a review. IEEE Sens J 21(22):25532–25546. https://doi.org/10.1109/JSEN.2021.3114266

Ahmed G, Sheltami TR (2023) A safety system for maximizing operated UAVs capacity under regulation constraints. IEEE Access 11:139069–139081. https://doi.org/10.1109/ACCESS.2023.3338377

Alsamhi SH, Ma O, Ansari MS, Almalki FA (2019) Survey on collaborative smart drones and internet of things for improving smartness of smart cities. IEEE Access 7:128125–128152. https://doi.org/10.1109/ACCESS.2019.2934998

Anush Lakshman S, Ebenezer D (2021) Integration of internet of things and drones and its future applications. Mater Today: Proc 47:944–949. https://doi.org/10.1016/j.matpr.2021.05.039

AWS. Amazon Prime Air's drone takes flight with AWS and Siemens. https://aws.amazon.com/partners/success/prime-air-siemens/

Bachrach A (2021) Skydio autonomy engine: enabling the next generation of autonomous flight. In: 2021 IEEE hot chips 33 symposium (HCS). IEEE Computer Society, Los Alamitos, CA, pp 1–43. https://doi.org/10.1109/HCS52781.2021.9567400

Banafaa MK et al (2024) A comprehensive survey on 5G-and-beyond networks with UAVs: applications, emerging technologies, regulatory aspects, research trends and challenges. IEEE Access 12:7786–7826. https://doi.org/10.1109/ACCESS.2023.3349208

Bera B, Wazid M, Das AK, Rodrigues JJPC (2021) Securing internet of drones networks using AI-envisioned smart-contract-based blockchain. IEEE Internet Things Mag 4(4):68–73. https://doi.org/10.1109/IOTM.001.2100044

Boursianis AD et al (2022) Internet of things (IoT) and agricultural unmanned aerial vehicles (UAVs) in smart farming: a comprehensive review. Internet Things 18:100187. https://doi.org/10.1016/j.iot.2020.100187

Bruce Ralphin Rose JVBBJ, Arulmozhinathan T, Gopinathan VT (2023) Internet of drones: applications, challenges, opportunities. In: Internet of drones, 1st edn

Chen CW (2021) Drones as internet of video things front-end sensors: challenges and opportunities. Discov Internet Things 1(1):13. https://doi.org/10.1007/s43926-021-00014-7

Chen K-W, Xie M-R, Chen Y-M, Chu T-T, Lin Y-B (2022) DroneTalk: an internet-of-things-based drone system for last-mile drone delivery. IEEE Trans Intell Transp Syst 23(9):15204–15217. https://doi.org/10.1109/TITS.2021.3138432

Choudhary G, Sharma V, Gupta T, Kim J, You I (2018) Internet of drones (IoD): threats, vulnerability, and security perspectives. In: Research briefs on information and communication technology evolution, vol 4, no SE-Articles, pp 64–77, Aug 2018. https://doi.org/10.56801/rebicte.v4i.67

Consumer Technology Association (2021) Skydio: the age of AI-driven, true autonomous drones. https://www.ces.tech/articles/2021/february/skydio-the-age-of-ai-driven,-true-autonomous-dron.aspx

Dahiya P (2023) Internet of drone things. In: Machine intelligence, big data analytics, and IoT in image processing. Wiley, pp 269–304. https://doi.org/10.1002/9781119865513.ch11

DJI Enterprise. Architecture, engineering, and construction (AEC). https://enterprise.dji.com/surveying/aec

Edwards D, Subramanian N, Chaudhuri A, Morlacchi P, Zeng W (2023) Use of delivery drones for humanitarian operations: analysis of adoption barriers among logistics service providers from the technology acceptance model perspective. Ann Oper Res. https://doi.org/10.1007/s10479-023-05307-4

Garima Kulshreshtha S-LP, Maurya AK (2022) The internet of things (IoT) architectures and protocols for drone communications. In: The internet of drones, 1st edn. Apple Academic Press, p 20

Gharibi M, Boutaba R, Waslander SL (2016) Internet of drones. IEEE Access 4:1148–1162. https://doi.org/10.1109/ACCESS.2016.2537208

Gilani SM, Anjum A, Khan A, Syed MH, Moqurrab SA, Srivastava G (2024) A robust internet of drones security surveillance communication network based on IOTA. Internet Things 25:101066. https://doi.org/10.1016/j.iot.2024.101066

Heidari A, Jafari Navimipour N, Unal M, Zhang G (2023) Machine learning applications in internet-of-drones: systematic review, recent deployments, and open issues. ACM Comput Surv 55(12). https://doi.org/10.1145/3571728

Hoque MA, Hossain M, Noor S, Islam SMR, Hasan R (2022) IoTaaS: drone-based internet of things as a service framework for smart cities. IEEE Internet Things J 9(14):12425–12439. https://doi.org/10.1109/JIOT.2021.3137362

Huang C, Chen Y-C, Harris J (2021) Regulatory compliance and socio-demographic analyses of civil unmanned aircraft systems users. Technol Soc 65:101578. https://doi.org/10.1016/j.techsoc.2021.101578

Kespry. Drone-based aerial intelligence. https://kespry.com/

Kim SJ, Jeong Y, Park S, Ryu K, Oh G (2018) A survey of drone use for entertainment and AVR (augmented and virtual reality). In: Jung T, tom Dieck MC (eds) Augmented reality and virtual reality: empowering human, place and business. Augmented and virtual reality. Springer International Publishing, Cham, pp 339–352. https://doi.org/10.1007/978-3-319-64027-3_23

Krupakar D, Sankeerth C, Akash M, Velamala D, Valiveti HB (2024) Design and analysis of dual mobility drone-rover system for disaster management scenarios. In: 2024 Fourth international conference on advances in electrical, computing, communication and sustainable technologies (ICAECT), pp 1–6. https://doi.org/10.1109/ICAECT60202.2024.10468829

Lee E, Seo Y-D, Oh S-R, Kim Y-G (2021) A survey on standards for interoperability and security in the internet of things. IEEE Commun Surv Tutor 23(2):1020–1047. https://doi.org/10.1109/COMST.2021.3067354

Liao S, Wu J, Li J, Bashir AK, Yang W (2021) Securing collaborative environment monitoring in smart cities using blockchain enabled software-defined internet of drones. IEEE Internet Things Mag 4(1):12–18. https://doi.org/10.1109/IOTM.0011.2000045

LNC Prakash K, Ravva SK, Rathnamma MV, Suryanarayana G (2023) AI applications of drones. Drone Technol 153–182. https://doi.org/10.1002/9781394168002.ch7

Mohamadi HE, Kara N, Lagha M (2022) Heuristic-driven strategy for boosting aerial photography with multi-UAV-aided internet-of-things platforms. Eng Appl Artif Intell 112:104854. https://doi.org/10.1016/j.engappai.2022.104854

Mukherjee A, De D, Dey N, Crespo RG, Herrera-Viedma E (2023) DisastDrone: a disaster aware consumer internet of drone things system in ultra-low latent 6G network. IEEE Trans Consum Electron 69(1):38–48. https://doi.org/10.1109/TCE.2022.3214568

Nayyar A, Nguyen B-L, Nguyen NG (2020) The internet of drone things (IoDT): future envision of smart drones. In: Luhach AK, Kosa JA, Poonia RC, Gao X-Z, Singh D (eds) First international conference on sustainable technologies for computational intelligence. Springer Singapore, Singapore, pp 563–580

Nguyen T, Katila R, Gia TN (2023) An advanced internet-of-drones system with blockchain for improving quality of service of search and rescue: a feasibility study. Futur Gener Comput Syst 140:36–52. https://doi.org/10.1016/j.future.2022.10.002

Pauner C, Kamara I, Viguri J (2015) Drones. Current challenges and standardisation solutions in the field of privacy and data protection. In: 2015 ITU kaleidoscope: trust in the information society (K-2015), pp 1–7. https://doi.org/10.1109/Kaleidoscope.2015.7383633

Rejeb A, Rejeb K, Simske SJ, Treiblmaier H (2023) Drones for supply chain management and logistics: a review and research agenda. Int J Log Res Appl 26(6):708–731. https://doi.org/10.1080/13675567.2021.1981273

Sai Theja GU, Murari MS, Singha MF, Patgiri R, Choudhury A (2022) A survey on surveillance using drones. In: Proceedings of the 2022 fourteenth international conference on contemporary computing, IC3-2022. Association for Computing Machinery, New York, NY, pp 250–257. https://doi.org/10.1145/3549206.3549253

Savkin AV, Huang H (2020) Navigation of a network of aerial drones for monitoring a frontier of a moving environmental disaster area. IEEE Syst J 14(4):4746–4749. https://doi.org/10.1109/JSYST.2020.2966779

Serafinelli E, O'Hagan LA. Drone views: a multimodal ethnographic perspective. Vis Commun 14703572211065092. https://doi.org/10.1177/14703572211065093

Sharma J, Mehra PS (2023) Secure communication in IOT-based UAV networks: a systematic survey. Internet Things 23:100883. https://doi.org/10.1016/j.iot.2023.100883

Singh C, Mishra R, Gupta HP, Kumari P (2022) The internet of drones in precision agriculture: challenges, solutions, and research opportunities. IEEE Internet Things Mag 5(1):180–184. https://doi.org/10.1109/IOTM.006.2100100

Singireddy SRR, Daim TU (2018) Technology roadmap: drone delivery—Amazon Prime Air. In: Daim TU, Chan L, Estep J (eds) Infrastructure and technology management: contributions from the energy, healthcare and transportation sectors. Springer International Publishing, Cham, pp 387–412. https://doi.org/10.1007/978-3-319-68987-6_13

Tedeschi P, Al Nuaimi FA, Awad AI, Natalizio E (2024) Privacy-aware remote identification for unmanned aerial vehicles: current solutions, potential threats, and future directions. IEEE Trans Ind Inform 20(2):1069–1080. https://doi.org/10.1109/TII.2023.3280325

Van Tilburg C (2017) First report of using portable unmanned aircraft systems (drones) for search and rescue. Wilderness Environ Med 28(2):116–118. https://doi.org/10.1016/j.wem.2016.12.010

Wang J et al (2022) Physical layer security for UAV communications: a comprehensive survey. China Commun 19(9):77–115. https://doi.org/10.23919/JCC.2022.09.007

X.company. Wing. https://x.company/projects/wing/

Yaacoub J-P, Noura H, Salman O, Chehab A (2020) Security analysis of drones systems: attacks, limitations, and recommendations. Internet of Things 11:100218. https://doi.org/10.1016/j.iot.2020.100218

Yahuza M et al (2021) Internet of drones security and privacy issues: taxonomy and open challenges. IEEE Access 9:57243–57270. https://doi.org/10.1109/ACCESS.2021.3072030

Yang W, Wang S, Yin X, Wang X, Hu J (2022) A review on security issues and solutions of the internet of drones. IEEE Open J Comput Soc 3(01):96–110. https://doi.org/10.1109/OJCS.2022.3183003

Chapter 14
Advancements in Traffic Sign Detection and Recognition for Adverse Image and Motion Artifacts in Transportation Systems

B. Hari Krishna, P. Santosh Kumar Patra, Ganga Rama Koteswara Rao, K. Satyanarayana Raju, and Dara Eshwar

Abstract Traffic sign detection and recognition (TSDR) contributes to the development of autonomous vehicle technology and driver assistance systems. The development of a TSDR that not only demonstrates high accuracy but also demonstrates robustness and reliability in a wide range of real-world scenarios is a critical prerequisite for the safe and widespread adoption of this technology. Nonetheless, the difficulty lies in the significant variability existing among traffic signs that must be identified, as well as the less-than-ideal quality of traffic images obtained in uncontrolled conditions, often obscured by bad image and motion artifacts. So, this research focuses on improving TSDR-Net, a traffic sign recognition system for autonomous driverless vehicles that work in harsh image conditions. The method uses multiple steps. It starts with hazy traffic sign images and uses deep learning techniques, particularly Deep Learning Convolutional Neural Network (DLCNN), to remove haze. The TSDR-Net begins by gathering hazy traffic sign images that have been affected by bad image; using deep learning for haze removal to improve visibility; using a DLCNN to detect traffic signs; and evaluating model performance through accuracy and loss

B. Hari Krishna (✉) · P. Santosh Kumar Patra
St. Martins Engineering College, Kompally, Hyderabad, Telangana, India
e-mail: drhariece@smec.ac.in

P. Santosh Kumar Patra
e-mail: drpskpatra@gmail.com

G. R. K. Rao
Koneru Lakshmaiah Education Foundation, Vaddeswaram, Guntur, Andhra Pradesh, India
e-mail: drgrrao@kluniversity.in

K. Satyanarayana Raju · D. Eshwar
SRKR Engineering College, Bhimavaram, Andhra Pradesh, India
e-mail: ksnraju@srkrec.ac.in

D. Eshwar
e-mail: dreshwar@kpritech.ac.in

R. Arya et al. (eds.), *Recent Trends in Artificial Intelligence Towards a Smart World*, Frontiers of Artificial Intelligence, Ethics and Multidisciplinary Applications,
https://doi.org/10.1007/978-981-97-6790-8_14

calculations. By addressing the crucial task of traffic sign recognition in harsh image conditions, this research improves the safety and efficiency of autonomous driving systems.

Keywords Adverse image conditions · Autonomous vehicle technology · Challenging conditions · Convolutional neural network · Driver assistance systems · Traffic sign detection

14.1 Introduction

TSDR helps self-driving cars go safely and make smart driving choices (Gharaibeh et al. 2017). TSDR systems feel and understand traffic signs and signals to tell the car's control system. These systems use computer vision, machine learning, and deep neural networks to process camera and sensor data onboard. Cameras take images of what's happening around the car, like road signs, traffic lights, and other stuff about driving. Fancy image checking systems can understand and sort out traffic signs like speed limits, stop signs, give way signs, and so on. For better sign visibility in various light and image situations, this identification method usually uses big image preparation. When identifying a traffic sign, the TSDR system tells the car's control system. For example, seeing a speed limit sign lets the car change how fast it is going to follow traffic rules and safety needs (Bai et al. 2023). The TSDR helps to identify stop signs and traffic lights, letting cars stop safely at crossings.

The TSDR systems use machine learning to make things more precise and stronger. Training machines with lots of images from different traffic signs in all kinds of situations helps them adjust to the real world better (Li et al. 2023). Improving the TSDR system speed and accuracy, hardware upgrades include better cameras, quicker graphical processor units, and artificial intelligence (AI) processors (Megalingam et al. 2023). TSDR makes driverless cars better at understanding and following road rules. This keeps passengers safe along with pedestrians and other people using the roads. As cars that can drive themselves become more normal, TSDR systems will get better. This will help make transportation without a driver possible.

The smart traffic control system in Fig. 14.1 uses a smart camera for TSDR. This system uses lots of tech to make traffic control and safety better. This system optimizes traffic control. Monitoring and optimizing traffic flow need sophisticated technology like AI. This AI-equipped camera captures real-time traffic images and videos. AI-powered cameras detect, recognize, and analyse objects. Traffic sign recognition is the AI camera's main function. Traffic management relies on this to comprehend and react to traffic indicators including speed restrictions, stop signs, yield signs, and more. The AI camera probably employs object detection algorithms to find items in its range of vision. Detecting traffic indicators is its emphasis. Traffic sign detection activates the AI camera's recognition. It specifies traffic sign type and meaning. It knows whether a sign is a speed limit sign, a no-entry sign, or another sort.

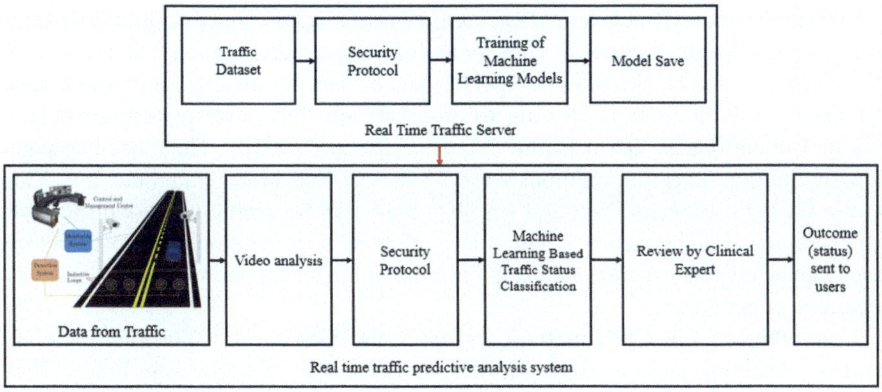

Fig. 14.1 Smart traffic management system. *Source* Author

Real-time processing of AI camera data, including traffic sign detection, is likely. This data processing stage is essential for traffic management choices and actions. The system utilizes its data to optimize traffic flow. It activates traffic lights, shows warnings on electronic road signs, or connect with other smart traffic management system components to regulate traffic.

The following are new contributions to this work:

- Primary objective is to improve the recognition of traffic signs for autonomous driverless vehicles, especially in harsh image.
- A new approach to haze removal is the use of deep learning techniques. It solves the problem of obscured visibility due to bad image.
- A DLCNN-based model for traffic sign detection, it helps to make autonomous driving safer. The model is designed to recognize a variety of traffic sign types, such as stop signs, yield signs, speed limits, and more. This makes it versatile for real-world situations.

14.2 Literature Survey

Mannan et al. (2019) developed a unique and adaptive Gaussian mixture model-based method to recognize traffic signs in degraded environments. Their technique uses automated split-and-merge. For sign content identification, they recommended a multiscale convolutional neural network with dimensionality reduction. After collecting images of partially degraded traffic signs, the scientists found that their method outperformed others. Jin et al. (2020) developed MF-SSD, a Multi Frame Single Shot Detector, to recognize traffic signs. They combined low-level and high-level features, adjusted feature channels, and performed well on the German Traffic Sign Recognition Benchmark (GTSRB) dataset to recognize small signs.

Gámez Serna and Ruichek (2018) classified traffic signs using over 80,000 images from six European countries. They examined class heterogeneity and convolutional neural network classification performance. Varytimidis et al. employed Joint Attention for Autonomous Driving to automatically recognize pedestrian behaviors and intentions in urban traffic (Varytimidis et al. 2018). Their head orientation and motion detection methods were 72 and 85% accurate. Bangquan and Xiao Xiong (2019) presented ENet and EmdNet networks for traffic sign identification, which achieved great accuracy with a large reduction in the number of parameters. They enhanced performance using data mining, multiscale operation, and depthwise separable convolution.

Using the Mask R-CNN method, Tabernik and Skočaj (2020) tackled the challenge of detecting and identifying a diverse assortment of traffic sign kinds. They suggested improvements that increased performance, even for difficult traffic sign categories, achieving error rates of less than 3%. An algorithm for the detection and identification of traffic signals was created by Cao and colleagues (2019), with a primary emphasis on exact segmentation, network model upgrades, and the use of the GTSRB for experimental purposes. With their method, they were able to obtain a high percentage of accurate identification (99.75%) and a short processing time. Wali and colleagues (2019) conducted a thorough investigation on the detection, tracking, and classification of traffic signs, reviewing the opportunities and problems given by driver assistance systems, as well as presenting methods and methodologies. The authors Liu et al. (2018) presented a new framework for transfer learning that integrated additional boosting and cascaded ConvNet for efficient object detection, with a particular emphasis on the recognition of traffic signs.

Zhang et al. (2019) introduced an original approach to evaluate the visual recognizability of traffic signs placed on highways, considering visibility and recognizability in 3D space, overcoming a disadvantage of prior approaches that relied on perspectives from just two dimensions. Malarvizhi et al. (2022) concentrated their efforts on the autonomous detection and identification of traffic signs in real time, most likely using computer vision techniques, including CNNs. Research on the identification and categorization of traffic signs using data augmentation was carried out by Yao and colleagues (Yao et al. 2023). Data augmentation methods are often used to enhance the overall performance of machine learning models by increasing the variety of training data. Khan et al. (2023) presented a lightweight CNN design for traffic sign identification in metropolitan road networks. Lightweight CNN architectures aim to be computationally economical while retaining a high level of accuracy.

Saxena et al. (2023) conducted research on the recognition of traffic signs in unconstrained situations using an upgraded version of the YOLO-V4 model, focusing on the real-time object identification capabilities of YOLO. Baruah et al. (2023) investigated the use of neural networks for TSDR in automated transportation systems. To make driving easier and less stressful, Aguilar and Recario (2023) designed "HINAY," a smartphone software that recognizes traffic signs in real time. Purwar and Chaudhry (2023) extensively studied ITS traffic sign detection. "TSDRDL," developed by Tumuluru et al. (2023), uses deep learning to identify traffic signs. Rashid et al. (2023) employed CNNs to identify traffic signals and stressed architecture, training data quality, and hyperparameter selection.

Shanmugavel et al. (2023) developed an ensemble-based CNN traffic sign detection model to prevent overfitting and increase accuracy. Puli et al. (2023) created a deep learning-based traffic sign detection system that works effectively in bad image. Chaudhary et al. (2022) investigated vision use cases and traffic situations relevant to visually impaired individuals, using computer vision and recognition software to aid in navigating various types of traffic settings. Younes et al. (2023) conducted research on automated TSDR systems, examining a wide variety of applications, datasets, and techniques. Using Raspberry Pi, Kavitha et al. (2023) built a system that recognizes traffic signs and is triggered by speech to provide driving assistance. Machine learning was used by Biswas et al. (2023) to research the identification of infractions of traffic rules, contributing to improved traffic safety and law enforcement. Saber et al. (2023) examined driver behavior detection in time series data over a period of ten years, reviewing and analysing the development in the field of machine learning for the study of driver behavior.

Triki et al. (2023) presented a solution for the identification of real-time traffic signs using an attention-based deep CNN for intelligent cars, aiming to increase recognition accuracy in real time. Hasanujjaman et al. (2023) collaborated on developing a traffic surveillance camera system that incorporates sensor fusion for autonomous cars, combining data from various sensors to improve precision and reliability. The TSDR-YOLO, presented by Song and Suandi (2023), is a Chinese TSDR system for autonomous cars operating in challenging environments. Zhang et al. (2023) offered a solution for TSDR using a storage-efficient SNN–CNN hybrid network with RRAM-implemented weights. Sato et al. (2023) presented an infrared laser reflection attack that was used against TSDR systems, focusing on potential vulnerabilities and system security. Naranjo and colleagues (2023) developed an object detection-based approach for identifying traffic signs on drone-captured images, taking advantage of the drone's elevated vantage point for monitoring, and locating traffic signs. Maletzky et al. (2023) contributed to the Austrian Highway Traffic Sign Data Set by working on the detection and categorization of traffic signs.

Taşyurek (2023) presented ODRP, a novel method for detecting spatial street signs using EXIF data, focusing on accurate detection for navigation and mapping. Khalid et al. (2023) created a traffic sign-detecting system for intelligent cars based on hybrid characteristics with low complexity, improving detection performance. Someswari et al. (2023) used deep learning methods for identifying traffic signs, emphasizing the deployment of a variety of deep learning architectures and models to handle complex patterns in image data effectively. Nguyen et al. (2023) proposed an effective method for the detection, categorization, and location of traffic signs for use in autonomous intelligent cars, addressing critical tasks for the safety and decision-making of autonomous vehicles. Atif et al. (2023) presented a method using robust image classifiers to withstand failures of the visual camera, an essential aspect for autonomous cars that heavily rely on visual cameras for perception. Kim et al. (2023) used deep learning methods to develop a real-time traffic sign identification system for urban areas, addressing the unique challenges of urban contexts. Additional works

(Purwar and Chaudhry 2023) jointly contribute to the development of sophisticated TSDR systems and technologies, playing a significant role in increasing road safety and enabling intelligent transportation systems.

14.2.1 Research Motivation

Researching TSDR in autonomous driverless cars seeks safer, more efficient, and greener transportation solutions. Many strong reasons need substantial study and development in this field. First, road traffic accidents continue to kill and damage property worldwide. Human mistake, such as misinterpreting traffic signals or violating traffic laws, causes many of these incidents. TSDR technology in autonomous cars reduces such mistakes by adding vigilance and enforcing traffic laws. Accident reduction and road safety are the main goals of this study. Next, driverless cars could change how we travel in cities and make traffic better. These cars need good TSDR systems to work safely and well on shared roads.

Self-driving cars use these systems to change the speed to match speed limits, handle tricky turns, and quickly respond to signs on the road that change from time to time. So, TSDR research helps to reduce traffic and emissions in the city. Also, the increasing demand for environmentally friendly travel pushes TSDR research. Self-driving cars use less fuel and make driving better. TSDR makes things faster and gives road details to reach these goals and support green driving. The use of self-driving cars across the world causes problems with rules and standards. Countries, styles, colors, and meanings differ in traffic signs. TSDR research wants to make smart systems that can see and understand many traffic signs in different areas. This will help bring together self-driving car technology all around the world. In the end, tech, machine learning, and computer vision give chances to make TSDR systems better. By using these improvements to make things more accurate, strong, and fast, TSDR can keep up with traffic situations. The cause for TSDR in self-driving cars is manyfold. TSDR tries to make roads safer, cut down on traffic problems, push for green living, manage rules, and use tech to make TSDR systems better and more trusted. TSDR research is very important to realize the full potential of self-driving cars in future transportation settings.

14.2.2 Problem Statement

The issue for TSDR in self-driving cars is to make sure they go safe and fast through hard and changing traffic. Fast robot car technology needs strong and trustworthy TSDR systems to handle many big issues. The main problem with road networks is their built-in complexity. Signs and lights on roads give drivers important information they need while driving. Making TSDR systems that can find, sort, and understand these signs quickly without any changes in light or image is hard. Not doing this causes traffic violations, accidents, and danger for road users.

As road signs change from place to place, TSDR systems need to manage different types and layouts of traffic signs. In different areas, the types of signs can vary in shape, color, size, and sometimes use unusual or short-term signs. This requires flexible and widespread TSDR systems.

Learning and getting better all the time is also needed for solving problems. TSDR systems must follow changing traffic rules and road signs. Putting together big groups of data with different kinds of signs, changes, and situations needs good computer learning methods and often changing the system. Making self-driving cars safe is important, and TSDR is key. Not noticing and doing something about traffic signs can lead to crashes and legal problems. The problem statement shows why TSDR systems must be very precise and work well to keep travelers, walkers, and other people using roads safely.

Lastly, the problem summary talks about integrating TSDR into the self-driving car world. TSDR should easily give sign info to the car's control system. This helps change speed, give way, or stop at crossroads. Making things work well together is a big problem. So, TSDR in self-driving cars needs strong computer vision and smart learning methods to see and understand many traffic signs in different situations. Adaptability to regional sign variances, constant learning and updates, and seamless interaction with the vehicle's control system are also required, along with safety and traffic compliance. Addressing these issues is crucial to deploying autonomous cars on our roads.

14.2.3 Applications

The TSDR in self-sufficient driverless automobiles has numerous sensible makes use of that enhance safety, efficiency, and functionality in various traffic eventualities. Details on TSDR programs:

TSDR's main use is to enhance self-sufficient automobile and occupant safety. TSDR structures efficiently recognize stop symptoms, yield symptoms, and speed regulations to ensure the vehicle follows traffic guidelines. This reduces human-brought injuries because the auto can react quickly to those cues, ensuring secure navigation. TSDR Speed Control lets self-sufficient motors modify their velocity relying on speed restrict signs and symptoms in real time. This application optimizes pace for road conditions to conform with pace limits and shop gasoline and pollution. In intersection management, TSDR is important to safety. Autonomous vehicles additionally stop at junctions and move when safe by way of detecting visitor alerts and forestalling signs and symptoms. This software is important for junction protection and traffic movement.

TSDR structures understand and interpret temporary street signals including creation area alerts and diversion markers. This allows autonomous automobiles to adapt to changing road conditions, improving construction and street upkeep safety.

School area safety, TSDR can apprehend school quarter symptoms and restrict automobile speed to protect youngsters for the duration of pick out-up and drop-off. It enables school buses to apprehend forestall signs and forestall while wanted.

TSDR facilitates comply with local and municipal traffic legal guidelines. TSDR structures adapt to local signs and norms, permitting self-sufficient vehicles to travel among countries. For pedestrian protection, TSDR can pick out pedestrian crossing symptoms, making automobiles greater cautious at crosswalks. This app reduces independent car accidents, improving pedestrian safety. For Traffic Jam Assistance, TSDR can also apprehend variable message symptoms (VMS) that supply actual-time traffic conditions and trade routes. Automatic motors also use this information to make judgments at some stage in traffic congestion, lowering journey time and fuel utilization. Enhanced Emergency Response, TSDR can understand and react to emergency automobile indicators like yielding to ambulances or following evacuation instructions. This guarantees self-sufficient motors work with emergency services for safety and speed.

Data Collection and Analytics, TSDR structures can song street signs and symptoms, visitors, and compliance. Traffic management, city planning, and transportation infrastructure optimization additionally utilize these statistics. Thus, TSDR in autonomous driverless automobiles has numerous makes use of. It improves avenue protection, visitor glide, regulatory compliance, electricity performance, and records-pushed decision-making. As self-reliant vehicles enhance and become increasingly more incorporated into our transportation networks, TSDR will help them reach their full capability.

14.3 Proposed Methodology

This technique improves TSDR for autonomous driverless cars in bad image. It starts with foggy traffic sign images, then haze reduction, DLCNN-based sign detection, and performance assessment using loss and accuracy estimations. The objective is to create a reliable system that can detect and interpret traffic signs in tough environments to improve autonomous driving safety and efficiency. The suggested TSDR-Net model is shown in Fig. 14.2. Details of the operation:

- Step 1: Hazy traffic sign images: Starting with foggy or deteriorated traffic sign images. Image conditions like fog, rain, or haze conceal traffic signs in these images.
- Step 2: Use deep learning to remove haze from traffic sign images: DLCNNs or similar deep learning architectures reduce haze to improve traffic sign visibility in images.
- Step 3: Detect DLCNN Traffic Signs: TSDR's fundamental mission follows haze removal. This stage detected and recognized traffic signs in processed images using a DLCNN model.

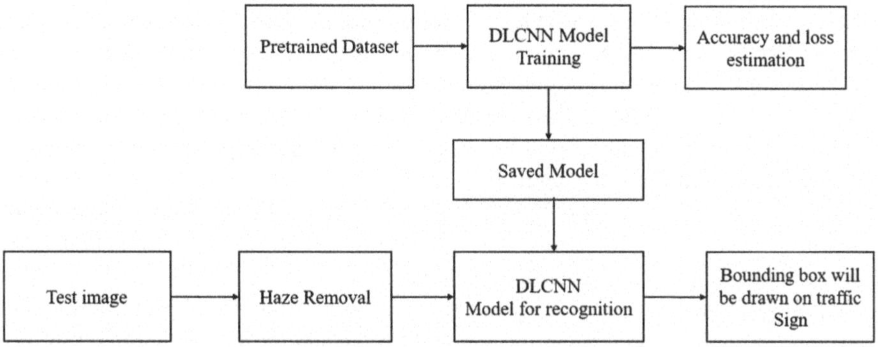

Fig. 14.2 Block diagram of proposed TSDR-Net. *Source* Author

- Step 4: Estimating accuracy and loss: Calculate performance metrics during DLCNN model training to assess performance. The loss function compares anticipated traffic sign labels to ground truth labels.

14.3.1 Haze Removal Model Deployment

A significant difficulty in image processing and computer vision is hazy or clouded images. This study develops a deep learning-based solution to improve image clarity. Figure 14.3 depicts the haze removal model deployment architecture using the hazy image dataset. Then, creates the learned model using multi-level gradient division training.

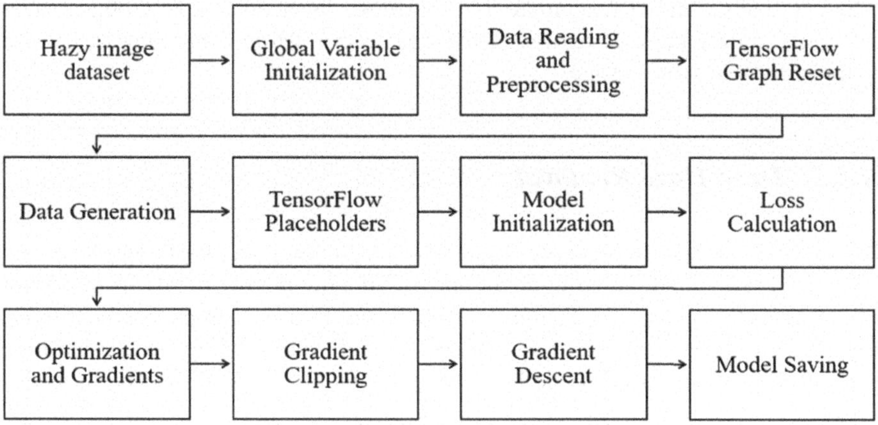

Fig. 14.3 Haze removal model building of TSDR-Net. *Source* Author

- Step 1: Initialize global variables: Declared global variables are dehaze_model, saver, RGB, and MAX. Storage and management of deep learning model components depend on these characteristics.
- Step 2: Reading and Preprocessing Data: Begin by collecting "clear" and "haze." images. For training and testing the model, these images typically show clear and fuzzy versions of the same scenes.
- Step 3: TensorFlow Graph Reset: We utilize TensorFlow, a prominent deep-learning framework. Resetting the TensorFlow graph allows new calculations to be defined and executed without intervention.
- Step 4: Data Generation: Preprocessed and arranged data for model training and assessment. This process comprises scaling, standardizing, and separating the dataset into training and testing subsets.
- Step 5 introduces RGB and MAX TensorFlow placeholders: These placeholders feed the deep learning model symbolically. RGB probably symbolizes input fuzzy images, whereas MAX indicates desired clean images.
- Step 6: Building and initializing a deep learning model, dehaze_model, which is the main task. This model presumably uses an image dehazing-specific encoder-decoder architecture.
- Step 7: Calculate Loss: A loss function measures model performance. Mean squared error (training loss) is the loss statistic. It quantifies the difference between model-predicted dehazed images and clear ones.
- Step 8: An Adam optimizer, a typical deep learning optimization technique, optimizes the model's parameters. We calculate loss gradients about trainable model parameters.
- Step 9: Gradient clipping ensures steady training. This method prevents gradients from getting excessively big and unstable during optimization.
- Step 10: Gradient Descent: The calculated and clipped gradients update the model parameters to minimize loss. This step is crucial to teaching the model dehazing.
- Step 11: Save Model Instantiate a TensorFlow Saver object. This object saves learned model parameters to disk. This step is essential for maintaining the learned model for real-world usage.

14.3.2 Deep Haze Removal

This study shows how to use a pre-trained deep learning model for image dehazing. It requires loading and preparing input images, running them through the model for inference, post-processing the output, storing it, and visually comparing the original hazy image to the improved, haze-cleared image. In Fig. 14.4, the suggested haze removal block diagram takes the hazy image as input and produces the haze-free output.

- Step 1: Model Restoration: The code initiates by restoring a pre-trained deep learning model. This model has previously been trained on a dataset to perform a

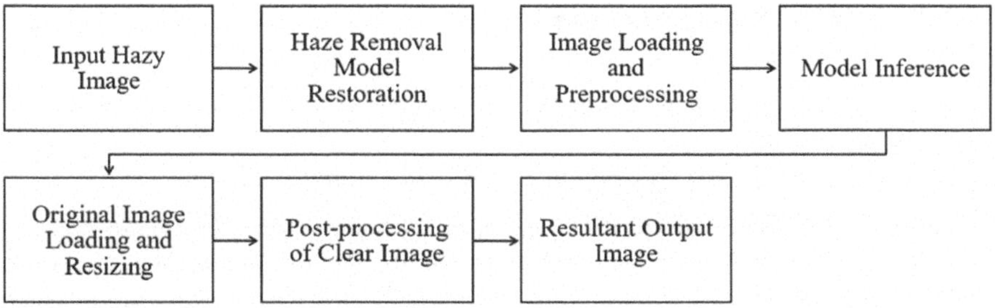

Fig. 14.4 Proposed haze removal block diagram. *Source* Author

specific task, likely image dehazing. The saver.restore function loads the model's pre-trained parameters from a saved checkpoint file, allowing us to use the learned knowledge for further tasks.

- Step 2: Image Loading and Preprocessing: An image file (filename) is loaded for processing. This image is assumed to be a hazy or degraded image. It is essential to prepare the image for the deep learning model's input. This involves resizing the image to match the expected dimensions of the model (in this case, 640 × 480 pixels). Additionally, the pixel values are normalized to a range between 0 and 1 by dividing by 255.0.

- Step 3: Model Inference: The preprocessed image is passed through the restored deep learning model (dehaze_model) using a TensorFlow session (session.run). This step is known as inference or forward pass. The model leverages its learned parameters to process the input image and produce an output.
- Step 4: Original Image Loading and Resizing: Another image, referred to as the "original" image, is loaded. This image is likely the original hazy image before any processing. The image is resized to dimensions 400 × 364, possibly for visualization purposes. This step doesn't modify the original image data but changes its display size.
- Step 5: Post-processing of Clear Image: The output of the model, referred to as clear_Image, represents the image with the haze removed. To make it visually compatible and interpretable:
  The pixel values are scaled back to the 8-bit range [0, 255] by multiplying by 255.
  The image is resized to dimensions 480 × 364.
  A color space transformation is applied to convert the image from BGR to RGB, which is a common format for displaying images.
- Step 6: Image Saving: The processed clear image (clear_Image) is saved as 'test.png'. This step preserves the result of the dehazing process for future reference or analysis.
- Step 7: Displaying Images: A visual comparison of the original hazy image (orig) and the dehazed image (dehaze) is presented using a matplotlib figure. The figure is divided into two subplots arranged side by side, each with a title. The left subplot displays the original hazy image, and the right subplot displays the dehazed image.

14.3.3 Traffic Sign Detection

Figure 14.5 shows the DLCNN architecture, which is used to perform the classification of different traffic signs.

The layers operation of DLCNN in TSDR is illustrated as follows:

Convolutional Layer: The TSDR's convolutional layer extracts key characteristics from input data, notably for traffic sign detection. It uses several convolution kernels with learnable parameters. Figure 14.6 illustrates 3 × 3 kernal convolution layer. Kernels are 1 × 1, 3 × 3, 5 × 5, or 7 × 7 matrices used to build feature maps. Convolution between input feature maps and convolution kernels creates these feature maps. The output feature map size is determined by the convolution kernel size (k), input size (i), padding (p), and strides (s). The equation for the output feature map size (o) is as follows:

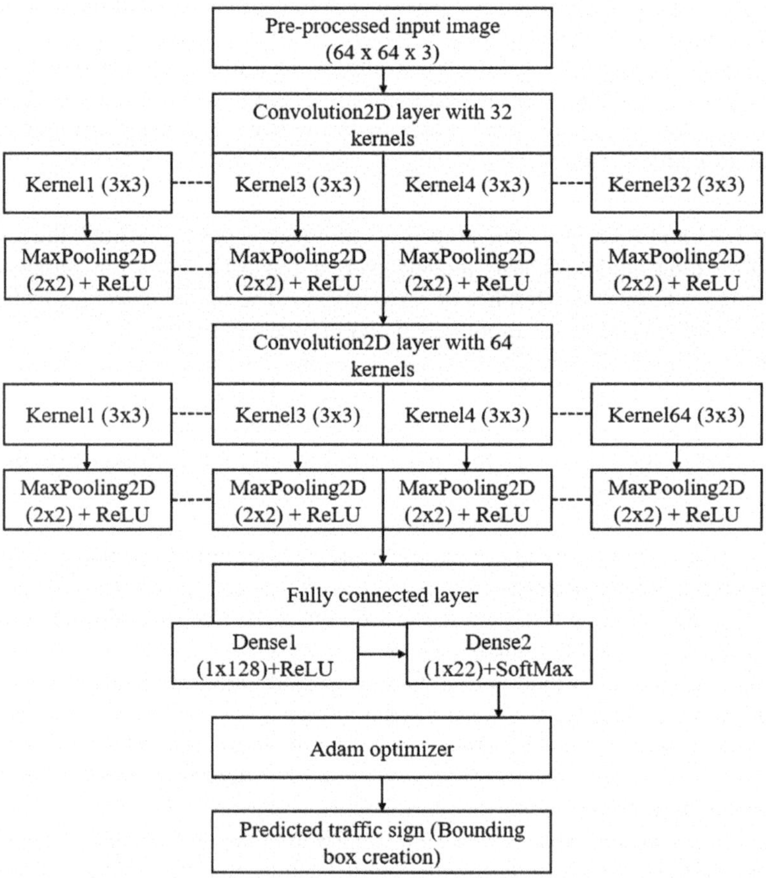

Fig. 14.5 Representation of DLCNN model. *Source* Author

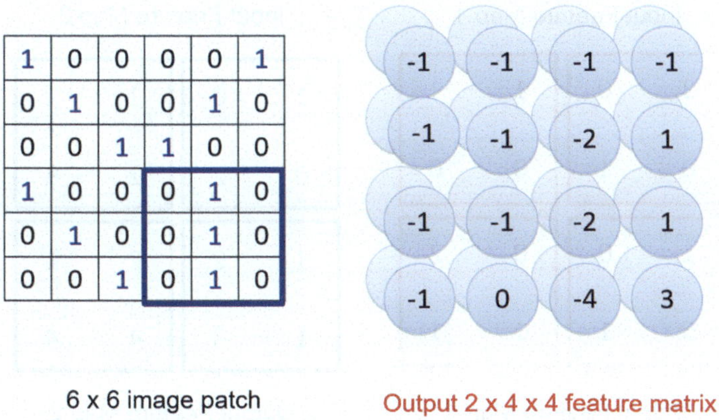

Fig. 14.6 Convolution layer example for 3 × 3 kernel. *Source* Author

$$o = \left[\frac{(i + 2p - k)}{s} \right] + 1 \tag{14.1}$$

The TSDR emphasizes convolution kernel weight parameters, which aid learning. Sharing parameters makes the method computationally efficient and reduces overfitting.

MaxPooling Layer: The TSDR uses MaxPooling after the convolutional layer. It down samples and reduces dimensionality to simplify the network. This layer maintains input data translation, scale, and rotation invariance. Figure 14.7 shows how it improves the output feature map by eliminating mistakes and distortions. The output feature map size (o) equation is:

$$o = \left[\left(\frac{(i - k)}{s} \right) \right] + 1 \tag{14.2}$$

Nonlinear ReLU Activation Function: The use of ReLU is essential in TSDR to improve. The ReLU activation function helps establish a functional relationship between input and output, introducing nonlinearity into the network. Figure 14.8 shows the ReLU operational process, which selects only positive numbers. ReLU is preferred for its speed compared to other activation functions like tanh.

Fully Connected (FC) Layer: In TSDR, the FC Layer follows the convolution and pooling layers. The number of categories is equal to the number of neurons at the output end. The FC layer is used as a classifier, and its output is evaluated to determine the category to which the data belongs. During training, the output of the network is often normalized using SoftMax, and gradient backpropagation updates the FC layer's parameters. Figure 14.9 shows the FC layer with cross-entropy loss optimization process for reducing the losses in the training process. Dropout and

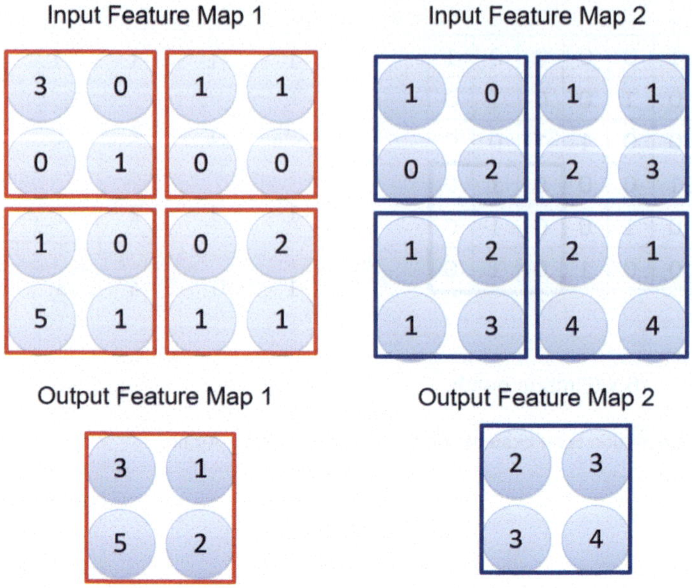

Fig. 14.7 Max Pooling layer example for 2 × 2 kernel. *Source* Author

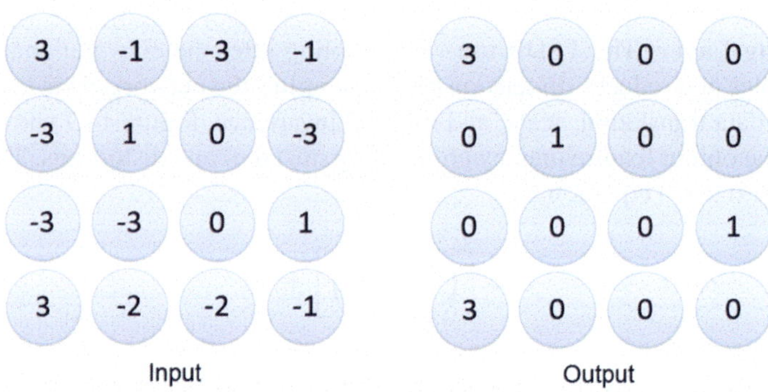

Fig. 14.8 ReLU example. *Source* Author

L2 regularization were used to prevent overfitting, especially when training a large model on a smaller dataset. The traditional TSDR approach relies on ReLU with a SoftMax classifier and has been successful in achieving positive classification results.

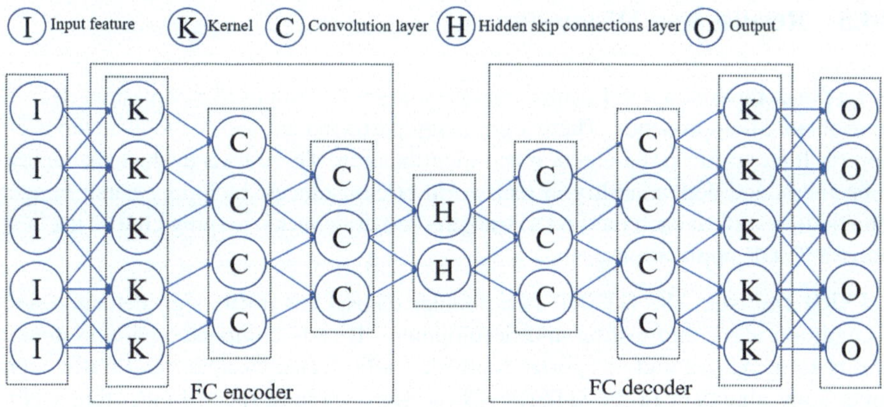

Fig. 14.9 FC layer with cross entropy loss optimization. *Source* Author

14.4 Advantages

The DLCNNs can learn complicated image patterns and features with high accuracy. CNNs can accurately recognize and categorize traffic signs in diverse lighting and image situations. Accuracy is essential for autonomous vehicles and driver safety. Their parallel processing allows speedy video stream analysis and low-latency traffic sign identification. Traffic signs vary in design, size, and orientation. The DLCNNs are resilient to appearance, scale, and rotation because they automatically learn and extract key characteristics. This versatility facilitates traffic sign detection under various settings.

Easily scalable, DLCNN-based visitors sign detection structures can manage numerous areas or international locations with wonderful traffic signal designs and laws. Training the version on a huge dataset we could generalize to distinctive signage designs and languages. The DLCNN-based systems decrease guide annotation and rule-based total programming. After education, the version can apprehend and categorize traffic signs and symptoms without human intervention, decreasing mistakes.

Advanced driving force assistance structures (ADAS) and driverless automobiles need effective site visitors signal reputation. The DLCNNs help cars understand and obey traffic indicators which includes pace limits, prevent symptoms, and caution signs, making roads more secure. The DLCNNs can discover traffic symptoms in rain, fog, and snow. This flexibility makes site visitors sign identification reliable even in bad conditions, improving autonomous vehicle dependability. Once adopted, cost efficiency blessings mass-market cars and transportation infrastructure.

14.5 Results and Discussion

For a fair comparison, the Results and Discussions section used a consistent dataset to evaluate all approaches. There were many performance metrics to evaluate each approach for traffic sign detection and identification. These tests evaluate accuracy, robustness, and dependability in real-world circumstances, including harsh image. The findings reveal each method's strengths and drawbacks, helping choose the best one for TSDR applications.

GTSRB Dataset: The GTSRB is a popular dataset for traffic sign detection and recognition algorithm testing and development. It tests computer vision systems' ability to recognize and categorize roadside traffic signs. German road traffic sign images are abundant in the GTSRB. These signs include speed limit, stop, yield, no-entry, and others. For realistic simulations, the dataset includes image, lighting, and views. GTSRB has approximately 50,000 traffic sign images. Sample traffic sign images from dataset are shown in Fig. 14.10. Each image class represents a traffic sign type. The dataset has several images per class for robust model training and assessment. The dataset can be accessed from: https://www.kaggle.com/datasets/meowmeowmeowmeowmeow/gtsrb-german-traffic-sign.

14.5.1 Subjective Performance

Figure 14.11 provides a visual demonstration of the performance of a dehazing model. It consists of two images side by side. The first image is an "image-affected" image, which is hazy, cloudy, rainy, or captured in poor lighting conditions. This image is typically challenging to interpret due to the image-related issues. The second image is the "clean" image, which serves as a reference or ground truth. It represents what the image should ideally look like without any image-induced degradation. In Fig. 14.12, the focus is on traffic sign detection using a DLCNN model. It likely shows an image

Fig. 14.10 Sample traffic sign images from GTSRB dataset. *Source* Author

with detected traffic signs, and bounding boxes were drawn around them to indicate their locations. This figure demonstrates the successful application of the DLCNN model for TSDR.

Figure 14.13 represents a line plot or a graph that visualizes the performance of the proposed TSDR-Net model over the course of training. Here, the green line shows the model's accuracy on the training and validation datasets over the course of 10 training epochs. This helps assess how well the model is learning to recognize traffic signs. Then, the blue line shows the model's loss (e.g., cross-entropy loss) on the training and validation datasets across the 10 epochs. This helps monitor how well the model is converging during training and whether it's overfitting or underfitting.

In Table 14.1, performance metrics are compared across three different models: the "Existing SVM" model, the "Existing RFC" (Random Forest Classifier) model,

Fig. 14.11 Dehazed performance. **a** Sample image 1. **b** Sample image 2. *Source* Author

Fig. 14.12 Traffic sign detected image. **a** Sample image 1. **b** Sample image 2. *Source* Author

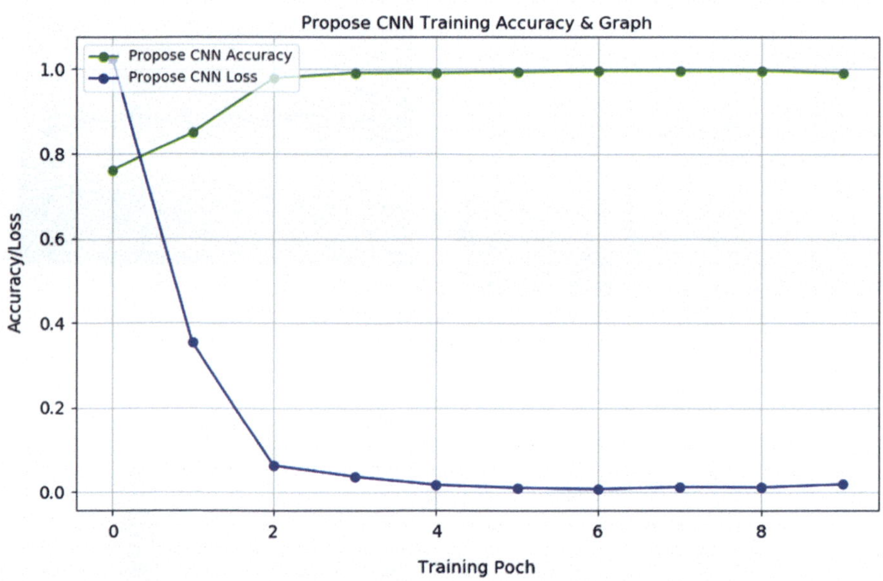

Fig. 14.13 Proposed TSDR-Net accuracy and loss for 10 epochs. *Source* Author

and the "Proposed DLCNN" model. Figure 14.14 shows the accuracy performance graph of various methods and Fig. 14.15 shows the loss performance graph.

Existing SVM: The "Existing SVM" model achieves an accuracy of 96.91%. This means that the SVM model correctly classifies approximately 96.91% of the test data samples, indicating a high level of accuracy. The loss for the "Existing SVM" model

Table 14.1 Accuracy and loss performance comparison

Metric	Existing SVM	Existing RFC	Proposed CNN
Accuracy (%)	96.91	98.85	100
Loss	0.142	0.0846	0.0584

Source Author

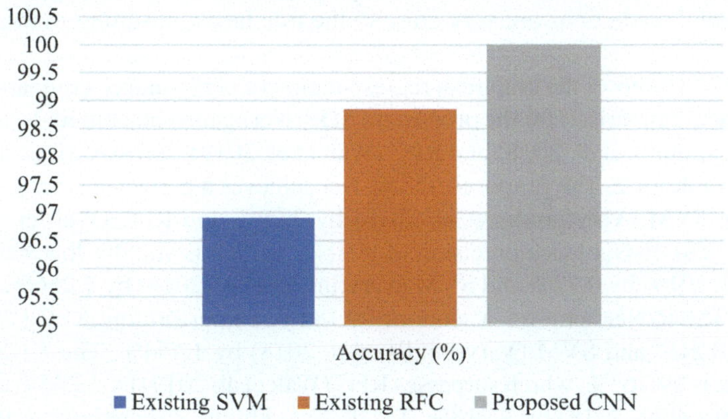

Fig. 14.14 Accuracy performance comparison of various methods. *Source* Author

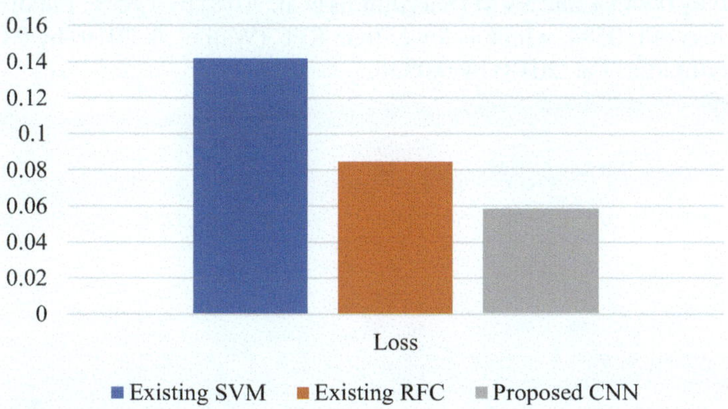

Fig. 14.15 Loss performance comparison of various methods. *Source* Author

is 0.142. The loss is a measure of how well the model's predictions align with the true labels. A lower loss value indicates better alignment.

Existing RFC: The "Existing RFC" model achieves a higher accuracy of 98.85% compared to the SVM model. It correctly classifies approximately 98.85% of the test data samples, demonstrating improved accuracy over the SVM. The loss for the "Existing RFC" model is 0.0846, which is lower than that of the SVM model. This indicates that the RFC model's predictions are closer to the true labels, resulting in a lower loss.

Proposed CNN: The "Proposed CNN" model attains a perfect accuracy of 100%. This implies that the CNN model correctly classifies all the test data samples, indicating a flawless performance in terms of accuracy. The loss for the "Proposed CNN" model is 0.0584, which is the lowest among the three models. This suggests that the CNN model's predictions are very close to the true labels, resulting in the smallest loss.

Figure 14.16 shows the graphical representation of performance comparison. The performance comparison for the proposed TSDR-Net against other models, including SVM (Varytimidis et al. 2018) and RFC (Wali et al. 2019), across various metrics is shown in Table 14.2. The proposed TSDR-Net achieves a perfect accuracy of 100%, surpassing SVM (Varytimidis et al. 2018) by 3.09% and RFC (Wali et al. 2019) by 1.15%. TSDR-Net has a precision of 99.04%, which is slightly lower than RFC (Wali et al. 2019) by 0.72% and SVM (Varytimidis et al. 2018) by 1.256%. In terms of recall, TSDR-Net achieves a score of 99.184%, outperforming RFC (Wali et al. 2019) by 0.21% and SVM (Varytimidis et al. 2018) by 1.454%. The $F1$-Score for TSDR-Net is 99.763%, which surpasses RFC (Wali et al. 2019) by 1.203% and SVM (Varytimidis et al. 2018) by 2.918%. TSDR-Net exhibits a sensitivity of 99.567%, exceeding RFC (Wali et al. 2019) by 1.437% and SVM (Varytimidis et al. 2018) by 3.533%. The specificity of TSDR-Net is 99.743%, which is higher than RFC (Wali et al. 2019) by 0.843% and SVM (Varytimidis et al. 2018) by 1.85%. Finally, TSDR-Net has a loss of 0.0584, which is lower than RFC (Wali et al. 2019) by 0.0262 and SVM (Varytimidis et al. 2018) by 0.0836.

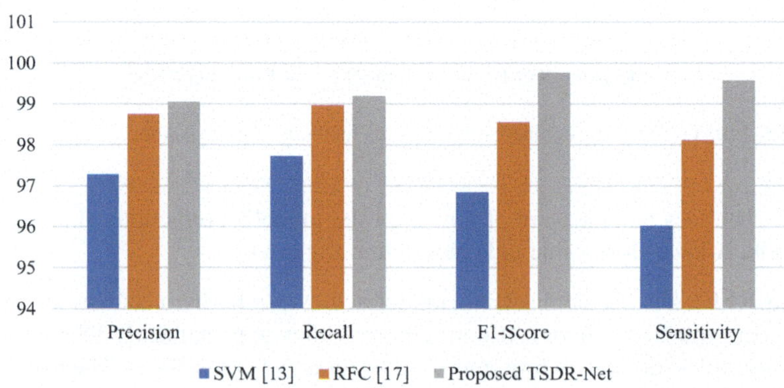

Fig. 14.16 Proposed TSDR-Net performance comparison graph. *Source* Author

Table 14.2 Performance comparison

Metric (%)	SVM (Varytimidis et al. 2018)	RFC (Wali et al. 2019)	Proposed TSDR-Net
Precision	97.283	98.76	99.04
Recall	97.73	98.974	99.184
$F1$-score	96.845	98.56	99.763
Sensitivity	96.037	98.13	99.567
Specificity	97.89	98.90	99.743

Source Author

14.6 Conclusion

In conclusion, TSDR-Net traffic sign detection revolutionizes computer vision and autonomous transportation systems. DLCNNs provide several benefits, including unmatched accuracy in identifying and classifying traffic signs, resilience in varied environmental circumstances and sign variances, and real-time processing for road safety. These solutions minimize human interaction, mistakes, and autonomous vehicle adaptation to varied geographies and signpost types. They also enhance road safety and traffic management by ensuring cars correctly comprehend and react to traffic signals. As autonomous vehicle technology advances, DLCNN-based traffic sign detection systems will help make roadways safer and more efficient.

Traffic monitoring and control, especially with deep learning and AI, has a bright future. As technology advances, we anticipate fascinating innovations. First, real-time data from traffic cameras, sensors, and linked cars will be better integrated. This will allow more advanced and adaptive traffic management systems that react to changing circumstances. The suggested TSDR-Net model shows that deep learning will likely develop. Another exciting development is autonomous automobiles. Future traffic management systems will require intelligence algorithms to forecast and regulate traffic flow from human-driven and autonomous vehicles. Sustainability and environmental concerns will also increase. Traffic monitoring systems use emissions and environmental data to improve traffic patterns for lower pollution and energy use.

References

Aguilar DPM, Recario RNC (2023) HINAY: a mobile application for real-time traffic sign detection. In: Science and information conference. Springer Nature Switzerland, Cham

Atif M et al (2023) Tolerate failures of the visual camera with robust image classifiers. IEEE Access 11:5132–5143

Bai W, Zhao J, Dai C, Zhang H, Zhao L, Ji Z, Ganchev I (2023) Two novel models for traffic sign detection based on YOLOv5s. Axioms 12(2):160

Bangquan X, Xiao Xiong W (2019) Real-time embedded traffic sign recognition using efficient convolutional neural network. IEEE Access 7:53330–53346. https://doi.org/10.1109/ACCESS.2019.2912311

Baruah A, Kumar R, Gupta M (2023) Analysis of traffic sign recognition for automated transportation systems using neural networks. In: 2023 IEEE 8th International conference for convergence in technology (I2CT). IEEE

Biswas K et al (2023) Detection of traffic rule violations using machine learning: an analytical review. Malays J Sci Adv Technol 37–47

Cao J, Song C, Peng S, Xiao F, Song S (2019) Improved traffic sign detection and recognition algorithm for intelligent vehicles. Sensors 19(18):4021

Chaudhary B et al (2023) Traffic scenarios and vision used cases for the visually impaired clients. In: Micro-electronics and telecommunication engineering: proceedings of 6th ICMETE 2022. Springer Nature Singapore, Singapore, pp 49–59

Gámez Serna C, Ruichek Y (2018) Classification of traffic signs: the European dataset. IEEE Access 6:78136–78148. https://doi.org/10.1109/ACCESS.2018.2884826

Gharaibeh, A, Salahuddin MA, Hussini SJ, Khreishah A, Khalil I, Guizani M, Al-Fuqaha A (2017) Smart cities: a survey on data management, security, and enabling technologies. IEEE Commun Surv Tutor 19(4):2456–2501

Hasanujjaman M, Chowdhury MZ, Jang YM (2023) Sensor fusion in autonomous vehicle with traffic surveillance camera system: detection, localization, and AI networking. Sensors 23(6):3335

Jin Y, Fu Y, Wang W, Guo J, Ren C, Xiang X (2020) Multi-feature fusion and enhancement single shot detector for traffic sign recognition. IEEE Access 8:38931–38940. https://doi.org/10.1109/ACCESS.2020.2975828

Kavitha C et al (2023) Traffic sign recognition and voice-activated driving assistance using Raspberry Pi. In: 2023 Eighth international conference on science technology engineering and mathematics (ICONSTEM). IEEE

Khalid S et al (2023) Traffic sign detection with low complexity for intelligent vehicles based on hybrid features. Comput Mater Continua 76(1)

Khan MA, Park H, Chae J (2023) A lightweight convolutional neural network (CNN) architecture for traffic sign recognition in urban road networks. Electronics 12(8):1802

Kim C et al (2023) Deep learning-based real-time traffic sign recognition system for urban environments. Infrastructures 8(2):20

Li Y, Li J, Meng P (2023) Attention-YOLOV4: a real-time and high-accurate traffic sign detection algorithm. Multimed Tools Appl 82(5):7567–7582

Liu C, Li S, Chang F, Dong W (2018) Supplemental boosting and cascaded ConvNet based transfer learning structure for fast traffic sign detection in unknown application scenes. Sensors 18(7):2386

Malarvizhi N et al (2023) Autonomous traffic sign detection and recognition in real time. In: Proceedings of 3rd international conference on recent trends in machine learning, IoT, smart cities and applications: ICMISC 2022. Springer Nature Singapore, Singapore

Maletzky A et al (2023) Traffic sign detection and classification on the Austrian highway traffic sign data set. Data 8(1):16

Mannan A, Javed K, Ur Rehman A, Babri HA, Noon SK (2019) Classification of degraded traffic signs using flexible mixture model and transfer learning. IEEE Access 7:148800–148813. https://doi.org/10.1109/ACCESS.2019.2947069

Megalingam RK et al (2023) Indian traffic sign detection and recognition using deep learning. Int J Transp Sci Technol 12(3):683–699

Naranjo M et al (2023) Object detection-based system for traffic signs on drone-captured images. Drones 7(2):112

Nguyen HX et al (2023) An efficient approach for traffic sign detection, classification, and localization applied for autonomous intelligent vehicles. Mod Phys Lett B 37(17):2340011

Puli S et al (2023) Deep learning-based framework for robust traffic sign detection under challenging image conditions. J Surv Fish Sci 2650–2657

Purwar S, Chaudhry R (2023) A comprehensive study on traffic sign detection in ITS. In: 2023 International conference on disruptive technologies (ICDT). IEEE

Rashid MM, Siddique SMT, Chakraborty NR (2023) A proposed approach to detect traffic signs by using convolutional neural network. In: 2023 8th international conference on communication and electronics systems (ICCES). IEEE

Saber RG, Ghoniemy S, Al-Qutt MM (2023) Driver behavior detection in time series decade review. Int J Intell Comput Inf Sci 23(3):114–140

Sato T et al (2023) WIP: infrared laser reflection attack against traffic sign recognition systems. In: Proceedings inaugural international symposium on vehicle security and privacy. Internet Society, San Diego, CA

Saxena S et al (2023) Traffic sign detection in unconstrained environment using improved YOLOv4. Expert Syst Appl 121836

Shanmugavel AB et al (2023) A novel ensemble based reduced overfitting model with convolutional neural network for traffic sign recognition system. Electronics 12(4):926

Someswari P, Cristin R, Daniya T (2023) Traffic sign detection using deep learning techniques. In: 2023 Third international conference on advances in electrical, computing, communication and sustainable technologies (ICAECT). IEEE

Song W, Suandi SA (2023) TSDR-yolo: a Chinese traffic sign recognition algorithm for intelligent vehicles in complex scenes. Sensors 23(2):749

Tabernik D, Skočaj D (2020) Deep learning for large-scale traffic-sign detection and recognition. IEEE Trans Intell Transp Syst 21(4):1427–1440. https://doi.org/10.1109/TITS.2019.2913588

Taşyürek M (2023) ODRP: a new approach for spatial street sign detection from EXIF using deep learning-based object detection, distance estimation, rotation and projection system. Vis Comput 1–21

Triki N, Karray M, Ksantini M (2023) A real-time traffic sign recognition method using a new attention-based deep convolutional neural network for smart vehicles. Appl Sci 13(8):4793

Tumuluru P et al (2023) TSDRDL: traffic sign detection and recognition using deep learning techniques. In: 2023 IEEE International conference on contemporary computing and communications (InC4), vol 1. IEEE

Varytimidis D, Alonso-Fernandez F, Duran B, Englund C (2018) Action and intention recognition of pedestrians in urban traffic. In: 2018 14th International conference on signal-image technology & internet-based systems (SITIS), pp 676–682. https://doi.org/10.1109/SITIS.2018.00109

Wali SB, Abdullah MA, Hannan MA, Hussain A, Samad SA, Ker PJ, Mansor MB (2019) Vision-based traffic sign detection and recognition systems: current trends and challenges. Sensors 19(9):2093

Yao J et al (2023) Research on detection and classification of traffic signs with data augmentation. Multimed Tools Appl 1–25

Younes Z, Ayoub E (2023) A review of automatic road sign recognition systems. In: 2023 3rd International conference on innovative research in applied science, engineering and technology (IRASET). IEEE

Zhang S, Wang C, Lin L, Wen C, Yang C, Zhang Z, Li J (2019) Automated visual recognizability evaluation of traffic sign based on 3D LiDAR point clouds. Remote Sens 11(12):1453

Zhang Y et al (2023) A storage-efficient SNN–CNN hybrid network with RRAM-implemented weights for traffic signs recognition. Eng Appl Artif Intell 123:106232

Chapter 15
Building Smart Campuses: Integrating AI in Higher Education

Swati Tyagi, Varuna Gupta, and Vandana Mehndiratta

Abstract This chapter explores the transformative integration of artificial intelligence (AI) in higher education to build smart campuses that enhance both the learning experience and administrative efficiency. The foundation of smart campuses is laid out, emphasizing the role of technology in shaping the future of education. Various AI technologies, including machine learning, natural language processing, and predictive analytics, are examined in the context of personalized learning and student support. The chapter explores the ways in which AI improves teaching and learning, highlighting examples such as intelligent tutoring systems and gamification. Automated operations, such as enrollment and security, are utilized to address administrative efficiency and campus administration, resulting in the optimization of resource allocation. Real-life case studies showcase effective AI deployments in various educational institutions, providing valuable insights and knowledge gained. However, the integration of AI in higher education poses challenges, from ethical considerations to concerns about job displacement. The chapter addresses these issues and emphasizes the need for ethical AI practices, inclusivity, and privacy considerations. Future trends and innovations in AI for education are discussed, offering a glimpse into the evolving landscape of smart campuses. The concluding section summarizes key takeaways, highlighting the potential of AI to revolutionize higher education. Implementation strategies are outlined, encouraging collaboration between academia and industry to create a supportive infrastructure for AI integration. The chapter provides a comprehensive overview of the current state and future possibilities of building smart campuses through the integration of AI.

Keywords AI · Traditional education · Smart education

S. Tyagi
Dronacharya Group of Institutions, Greater Noida, India

V. Gupta (✉) · V. Mehndiratta
Christ University, Bengaluru, India
e-mail: varunagupta.cs@gmail.com

R. Arya et al. (eds.), *Recent Trends in Artificial Intelligence Towards a Smart World*,
Frontiers of Artificial Intelligence, Ethics and Multidisciplinary Applications,
https://doi.org/10.1007/978-981-97-6790-8_15

15.1 Introduction

Since human evolution, the need for the advancement of scientific knowledge has been witnessed. Technology has developed quickly throughout its history, with new advancements appearing practically every day. With the new advancement and development of these technologies, varieties of changes have been faced by every human being in day-to-day life. All these new technologies have the power to upgrade our working style, transform our world, and look at working areas with different perspectives. However, every new or ongoing technology always comes along with a question of how effectively it can be used in an area and what kind of result it will show. One area that has seen significant investment in recent years is education, with virtual reality, augmented reality, metaverse, blockchain, simulation, mobile technologies, robotics and automation, and online learning environments all being implemented (Talan and Kalinkara 2023). Merely there will be a working area that is untouched by Artificial Intelligence. One such area where AI has a remarkable impact is education. Educational and academic practices have been exposed to significant and far-reaching technological advancements in recent times, no better exemplified by the recent intervention of Artificial Intelligence (Tuomi 2019).

AI inception opened up new opportunities to enhance the functionality of different fields. AI primarily focuses to mimic human intelligence and to expand intelligence of machines to receive most benefits from them. With increasing integration of Artificial Intelligence, varieties of improvement and benefits can be seen in different areas. One of such areas that is being influenced by AI is Higher education with various aspects. AI is transforming education by modifying the way the institute operates, teaches, and supports students. The potential use of AI in education, its contribution to education, and its impact on education are still subjects of debate, with numerous predictions and considerations (Talan and Kalinkara 2023). With various convincing opportunities during AI development for the education sector, few budding threats also occur. Threats and opportunities being offered by AI need to be evaluated carefully before implementing or utilizing AI further.

AI primarily focuses to mimic human intelligence and to expand intelligence of machines to receive the most benefits from them.

15.2 Current State of Higher Education

There are a large variety of methodologies, contexts, and perspectives that have been used to evaluate the use of technology in education (Lai and Bower 2019). Keeping an eye on the state of higher education in today's era one thing can be concluded different technology usage, new learning methodologies, and globalization of education have changed today's education perspective. Disruptive educational innovation replaces existing methodologies and modes of knowledge transmission by opening new alternatives for learning (García-Morales et al. 2021).

Several factors are responsible to change the higher education from what it was in past decades. On strict analysis, it is being seen that advancement of technologies, adaptivity, research, and practical-oriented study demand are few important aspects that differentiate our education model from past to present. Majorly important factors that upholding our education system in the present era are:

Technological Integration

Technology has modified the way we live today from chalk and duster to digital boards in classrooms demonstrating the way our education system has adapted such technological advancement so normally. The adoption of digital technologies continues to be a major trend in higher education. There are different motivations for integrating technology into learning, for instance, to improve student learning outcomes, improve access to learning, and enhance learner motivation (Li et al. 2022).

Integration of new trends and technology in higher education institutions promoting new teaching methodology, with a growing emphasis on online learning, digital resources, and the use of educational technology tools. Online learning platforms, virtual classrooms, and digital collaboration tools have become essential components of the educational experience.

On close look, one may find that even though technology is serving us in a far better way and helping us to become more efficient and productive, many resistances and challenges can be seen to adapting new technology in higher education. Utilizing and adapting technology less usually by instructors or teachers can be seen. This could be because of fear of job snatching, resistance to learning and changing their old methodology, and many more.

Few findings state that lack of technological knowledge by the teacher or partial knowledge of ongoing technology creates barriers for introducing technological usage among themselves. Many students are knowledgeable about technological tools that will benefit them but due to lack of guidance and correct usage students either misuse these tools or ignore them.

With great advancement of technology, replacement of many traditional technologies like classroom teaching has been overtaken by upcoming and ongoing technologies. But one question still arises in today's time: can we replace everything with technology? Technology can be a great aid to the learning experience, it cannot act as a complete substitute, particularly for STEM fields that require hands-on training in laboratories or operation rooms (Yigitcanlar and Limb 2023).

Adaptive Learning and Globalization of Education

Two major trends that can change the face of education and open up fresh prospects for students everywhere are adaptive learning and globalization. Learning platforms leading today are gaining popularity due to adaptive learning and personalization. These platforms are working with the power of AI while using various algorithms and data analytics to customize or tailor content and progress speed as per individual. Leading platforms like Udemy, Coursera, and many more are fully utilizing AI for betterment of their as well as students. By adapting to the specific requirements of each student, adaptive learning promotes effective and efficient learning, maximizes engagement, and enhances educational outcomes (Gligorea et al. 2023). Immediate feedback system data-driven decision making helping them to improvise students as well as their performance. On the other hand, global partnerships of such platforms with eminent international universities attract diverse student groups. This was made possible once more by the advent of remote online learning environments, content delivery networks, and assessment tools that eliminated all geographic barriers. Cross-cultural collaboration, forum discussions, knowledge sharing sessions are prominent features that attract knowledge seekers to update themselves with global knowledge and updates. In concise, adaptive learning and globalization are capable to create best individualized, tailor-ready and globalized education with technological integration.

Focus on Skills Development and Shifts in Pedagogy

Since the beginning of the twenty-first century skill development has integrated along disciplinary contents. This need was realized when industry started transforming them into faster peace. Any organization demands an employee who is not only a good scholar but must possess practical hands-on experience to face real-life scenarios. Emphasis increased over time on practical skill development in parallel with syllabus-based knowledge. Numerous institutes adapted learning through doing approach, which is known as experiential learning, internships, and even started collaborating with several industries for more exposure to learn and adapt workforce culture.

One of the major shifts in education one can see is traditional lecture delivery to pedagogical approach that has enhanced learning ability. Adding technology in this approach, like project-oriented learning, audio–video tools, and other interesting innovative teaching methodology promoted pedagogy much higher. For instance, simply teaching to a child in manner like 'A' for Apple teacher initiated to show real apple, later teachers adapted audio–video tools to teach them about more with sound, pictures, and videos. Such an approach actually enhanced the analytical skills of students which are actually needed for any work.

Concerns About Student Well-Being

The competitive world and updated technology have stressed students somewhere which is a concern to be focused on. Academic Institutions recognized the importance of students' mental well-being and started services to support them. Hiring counselors, creating a positive campus environment, and organizing events for stress release are a few steps towards this well-being catering. Many researchers are even focusing on this field to generate models to predict mental health, consequences and suggest remedies to overcome it.

Evolving Human Ecology

The entire human ecology is on change, now a day's age is not a bar to retain for education. People who are in jobs, older or even younger desire to obtain knowledge from their benefits. The increasing number of non-traditional students, adults or grown-up people are again fore step for education. Also, a diverse population of students demands for change in teaching strategies and tools.

Research and Innovation

Research and innovation is always a demand for developed or developing countries. Higher education institutions are always dedicated to playing a significant role in research and development. Collaboration among industry and academia is on the boom to impart the best knowledge to look forward to technology enhancement and innovations. Faculties and students are indulged in research projects. Collaborations and interdisciplinary studies are raising this research and innovation environment in academia.

15.3 The Necessity of Integrating New Technologies into Education

Integration of technological development with education system is a major concern which is affected by numerous parameters, moreover such development in technology playing significant role in transforming overall experience of learning. The following are some main arguments in favor of technology's importance in education.

15.3.1 Information Accessibility

While utilizing technologies an abundance of knowledge is easily and readily available. Students and teachers can access a multitude of materials through the internet, digital libraries, and online databases, which promotes self-directed learning and research. This information not only enhances their knowledge but also provides a base to carry out numerous researches and projects. For instance, if one is carrying out research on some syndrome's identification than datasets and existing information become necessary which cannot be collected in traditional ways in huge amount and effectiveness.

15.3.2 Connection Around the Globe

In today's era accessing knowledge from the entire world is not just a dream. New technologies cater to this need for connectivity around the globe. Peers' connection for meeting or discussion, experts talk, webinars from different countries are being possible with usage of technology in current working culture. Students are not deprived of renowned professors teaching; they can access their recorded or live lectures through internet. 24 * 7 assistance is available even without the presence of human. These global connections and accessibility facilitate cross-cultural understanding, collaboration, and the exchange of ideas.

15.3.3 Personalized Learning

Since decades a traditional give and take relation has been followed in higher education also. Faculties or teachers are burdened to create course content, assessment grading and such for all irrespective of different needs as course content is designed to fit all learners in one size. Using technologies, many such software can tailor curriculum to fit individual demands with style and pace in accordance to their need. This adaptive learning approach enhances learning efficiency and effectiveness. Also helps educators to manage and design content as per individual needs within the same premises.

15.3.4 Engaging Learning Environments

Visual appeal is necessary to cater to the audience's attention. Also, the study proves that learning by seeing is faster to grasp rather than with just verbal or written content. In this changing era, students learning capability and concentration have been shifted to new ways so integration of technologies was a must. So as a result we could witness various Interactive technologies, multimedia content, and educational games make learning more engaging and interactive. Incorporating these elements into lessons can enhance student motivation and make complex concepts more accessible.

15.3.5 Efficiency and Productivity

In the education system, educators are not only responsible to impart knowledge and to teach but also burdened with some administrative tasks like tracking attendance, grading, creating lesson plans and several tests. This sometime reduces the productivity and efficiency of educators if done on the traditional basis approach. But educational technologies like automatic attendance tracker and others are streamlining such tasks. This technological integration allows educators to allocate maximum time to student interaction, individual attention, and self-professional development. This enhances one's productivity and efficiency.

15.3.6 Preparation for the Digital Economy

As most countries are moving towards digital economies, it has become mandatory for students to inculcate technology-based education to develop and enhance digital literacy and technical skills. Such education and exposure will make students comfortable to work with digital tools and platforms to use in the workforce.

15.3.7 Flexibility and Accessibility

Flexibility enhances the interest of students as it allows them to access any course as per their accordance. In this context, online courses or distance education is focused. These education schemes make flexibility in course accessibility even if in job or residing at remote area. Diversity of schedules, geographical locations and individual circumstances are overcome with technologies in terms of education.

15.3.8 Real-World Applications

Theoretical knowledge is of no worth until an individual doesn't know how and where to apply that knowledge and understanding. To enhance knowledge and make it practical and implementation-oriented, educators included several labs, collaboration, training, and such more activities in their curriculum. Here technology played a significant role as it allows students to apply their concept read during classes to real-world situations through labs, simulations, virtual platforms, and others. These practical experiments and learning prepare students for future ready.

15.3.9 Innovation in Teaching Methods

With the introduction and enhancement in technology, teaching is becoming interesting. Technologies create a door to look for new innovative teaching methodology, utilizing visual and other tools like augmented reality-based cameras and others. Inclusion of flipped classrooms, project-based learning, smart boards, etc. generated more interest in teachers for delivering part. Such approaches not only cater to different needs and learning styles but also promote critical thinking and problem-solving skills.

15.3.9.1 Data-Driven Decision Making

By gathering and analyzing data on student performance, educational technology enables teachers to decide on the best ways to teach, pinpoint areas that need work, and offer focused interventions.

15.3.9.2 Lifelong Learning Opportunities

During past decades geographical distance and age were a barrier to ongoing or lifelong learning process. But with the availability of technologies it has made it easier. Webinars, Online courses, and e-learning platforms offer opportunities for continuous learning throughout one's life. Technologies are making individuals learn from the comfort of home.

Even though there are many advantages to technology in education, there are also drawbacks. These include privacy issues, the digital divide, and the requirement for continuous professional development for teachers to successfully incorporate technology into the classroom.

15.4 The Role of AI in Transforming Traditional Learning Environments

AI empowers every field among which education is the important one. With time AI's impression and importance are growing rapidly and stronger. It is envisaged that universities and other comparable organizations would be involved in creating and executing infrastructures for technological communication that will provide them access to the right channels for learning their viewers. Additionally, these technologies ought to give students and teachers the resources. To fulfill the teaching and learning objective, they must encourage their contact (Howard 2019). AI applications in education area is transforming the methodology used by educators or teachers to propagate knowledge, content. Other stakeholders like students also interact with more interest and easiness with upgraded educational tools. Integrating AI with Education can support interested and immediate stakeholders and decision makers to come up with new educated decisions.

AI and technological merger with education has brought a paradigm shift from traditional to smart education. Even though historically, this kind of technology has mostly taken place in the classroom, it is clear that it no longer just occurs in this location and that it may now happen practically anywhere and at any time (Li et al. 2022). Changes started from transforming old pedagogy to new then adapting various AI-based tools by every stakeholder of education. Following are the education system components which have changed from traditional to smart while using AI technology.

15.4.1 Physical Classrooms

Nowadays to adapt knowledge and gain learning, physical presence is not a bar. Creating a virtual classroom while adopting new technologies like Microsoft teams, Google meet, and others one can create virtual classroom space where a student can join from anywhere over the globe. Also, such classrooms are equipped with automatic attendance system, changing of class environment, utilizing whiteboard on screen, and other tools that create interactive and effective learning environments.

15.4.2 Hard Book or Traditional Books

Decades ago acquiring knowledge was a tough task as either books or teachers were the source of delivering knowledge. But as technology enhanced it brought various resources and repositories to gain knowledge online. Even various content generative tools like chatGPT, perplexity is available to gather more content and discussion about a particular topic.

15.4.2.1 Define Time Slots Teaching

Traditional teaching which binds individuals to be available in the class at time slots was mandatory to collect knowledge about a particular subject. Like in accordance with the timetable. But with changing technology and AI assistance learners can access their tutorials, classes, contents and even impart knowledge at any moment of time. If a person is working and receives time for learning at midnight even though he has a scope to join AI-based tutorial classes, Adaptive and flexible learning platforms are in trend for the same reasons.

15.4.3 Content and Syllabus Design

In the past education system designing course content and syllabus was generally to cater to the needs of the group or mass. This methodology affects those learners which didn't fall into such a category where this content is applicable. Due to this, many scholars left their learning in between. But with AI-based systems educators are free from such administrative tasks and the system will generate tailor-ready content and syllabus according to individual needs. Such a system uses various machine learning algorithms that make it possible to suggest and predict the needs of individuals.

15.4.4 Lecture Delivery Tools

With the change of time and advancement of technology past tools of education have been upgraded. For instance, normal black and green boards are replaced by smart boards that even work according to gestures also. Notion is a multifaceted AI tool that allows a student or educator to make digital note making, project management, and collaboration can be used for notetaking, project management, and collaboration, making it a valuable resource for students and teachers.

15.4.5 Manual Attendance

AI-empowered the teachers with the facilities of marking attendance of students inside the class automatically. AI has several ways to do this among which facial recognition is best that can capture images, recognize faces, and mark attendance accordingly. This system makes marking attendance more efficient and accurate. Marking proxy chances become almost zero with such systems. Figure 15.1 depicts the shift in education from traditional to technological education system.

15.5 The Foundations of Smart Campuses

Increasing demand for university education is putting pressure on campuses to make better use of their real-estate resources (Sutjarittham et al. 2019).

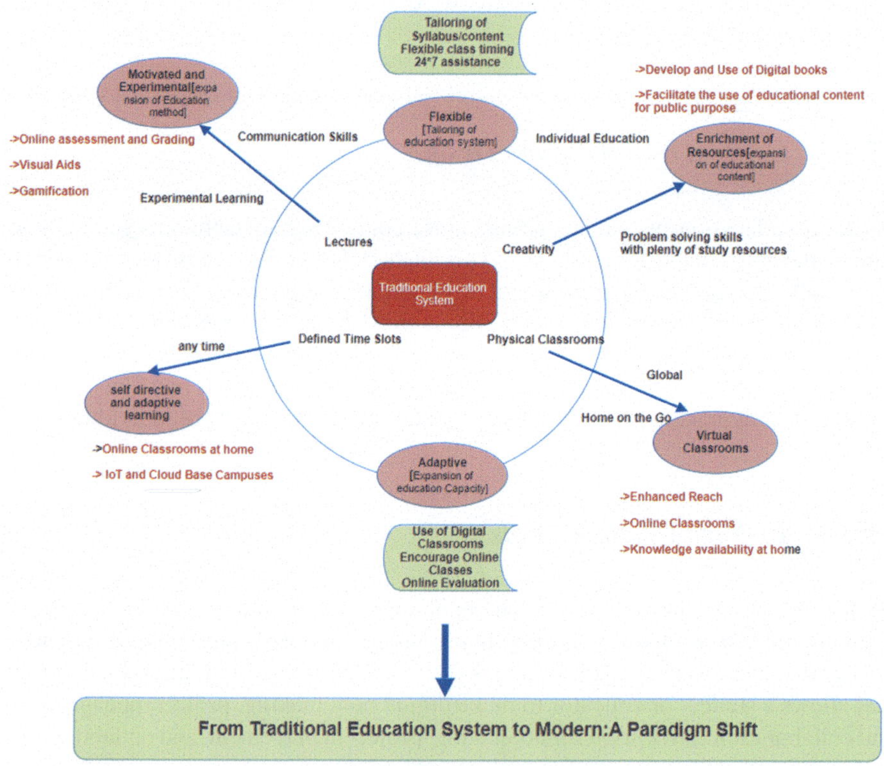

Fig. 15.1 Traditional education system to modern. *Source* Author

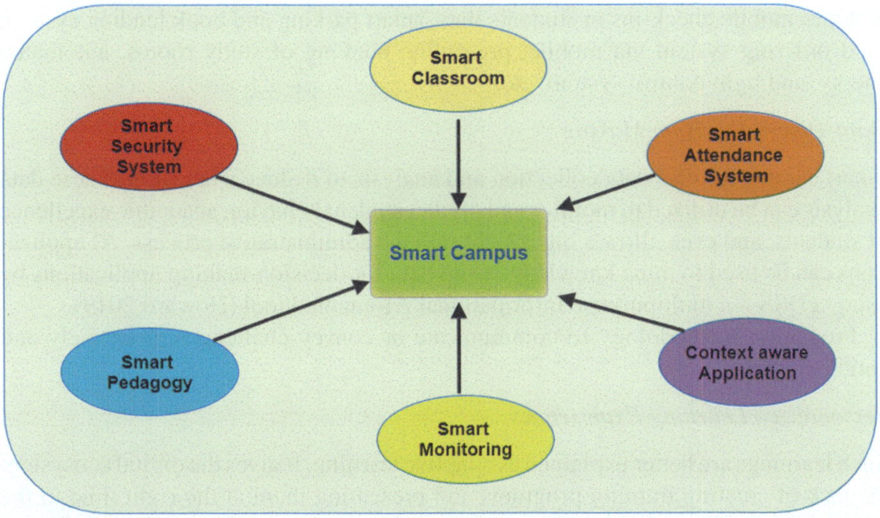

Fig. 15.2 Components related to smart campus. *Source* Author

15.5.1 Definition and Characteristics of Smart Campuses

Definition

Smart campuses are academic establishments that leverage cutting-edge technologies to improve student experience, boost operational effectiveness, and offer accessible learning. Smart campus is an emerging concept enabled by digital transformation opportunities in higher education. Smart campuses are often perceived as miniature replicas of smart cities and serve as living labs for smart technology research, development, and adoption, along with their traditional teaching, learning, and research functions (Yigitcanlar and Limb 2023). These campuses grip numerous technologies to generate instinctive, smooth, and touch-free environments for all stakeholders of campus. The aim of smart campus is to establish an educational ecosystem with various technologies to create a more intelligent, adaptive, and user-centric system of education. This ecosystem integrates various territories like economy, society, and the environment. Figure 15.2 is depicting the components of smart campus where various components like smart classroom, smart monitoring, smart attendance system, etc., have been discussed.

15.5.2 Characteristics of Smart Campuses

Integration of IoT devices: Smart campuses integrate IoT (Internet of Things) devices and sensors to build networks of interconnected devices. Incorporation of these range includes mobile check-ins in students flats, smart parking and book lending system, food ordering system via mobile, pre-online booking of study rooms, automated energy, and light control system, etc.

Data-Driven Decision Making

Smart campuses offer data collection and analysis to deduce a decision. These data analysis can be utilized to monitor and predict student behavior, academic excellence of students, and even allow a big insight into the administrative process. AI applications can be used to mine knowledge from data for decision-making applications by using a DSS—a multipurpose informational AI-enabled tool (Howard 2019).

Prediction methodology to communicate or convey challenges proactively and anticipate those.

Personalized Learning Experiences

Such learnings are better explained as adaptive learning. It gives the digital ecosystem the task of creating training programs and presenting them at the right time to the right person (Palanivel 2020). Adopting such platforms that fabricate academic and educational content as per individual needs with adaptive and flexible learning.

Integrating AI tools and machine learning algorithms for personalized monitoring, tutoring, and feedback systems.

Advanced Security Systems

Smart surveillance system, Strong smart security system enabled with live face recognition system for campuses.

Access control through smart systems like behaviometric, biometrics, voice recognition system, smart cards, and others.

Efficient Administrative Processes

Replacing traditional administrative processes with automated ones like data collection, registration and enrollment, grading and assessment, creation of quizzes or tests.

Blending AI-driven chatbots to entertain students queries and for support.

Sustainability Initiatives

Optimization of resources and waste reduction with smart management implementation.

Choosing sustainable habits and green technologies like smart light systems to reduce environmental footprints.

Technology-Enhanced Classrooms

Fusing Technological tools like smart boards, projectors, virtual reality, and other tools during classroom teaching.

Augmented reality-oriented applications for mesmerizing experience of learning.

Real-Time Communication

Real-time-based information and alert-based mobile apps for immediate communication.

Delivering updates and announcements through digital media.

Collaborative Spaces

Usage of technological tools for generating collaborative space for group work.

Remote and online learning with virtual platforms in relation to collaboration.

Innovation Hubs

Adapting trending technologies for research and development.

Generating a group or hub with collaboration to look forward to innovations.

A smart campus uses technology to build a connected, data-driven, and sustainable educational environment that improves learning outcomes and operational efficiency. The specific qualities may differ depending on the institution's objectives, resources, and technological infrastructure.

15.6 The Importance of Integrating Technology into Higher Education

Technological advancement creates remarkable opportunities to improvise educating and learning techniques in higher education. In today's era technological adaptation in higher education has a two-way opinion over the potency of such an approach and dimensions up to which technology should seize in education. Several studies demonstrate that technology in higher education can considerably boost student learning when properly linked with teaching objectives and thoroughly integrated into a program. With the onset of computers in education, it has become easier for teachers to impart knowledge and for students to acquire it. The use of technology has made the process of teaching and learning all the more enjoyable (Raja and Nagasubramani 2018).

Integration of technology into higher education becomes important due to several reasons. Few among those can be listed as below.

15.6.1 Tailor Ready Content

Instead of creating curriculum for mass technology empowers facilitators to generate content and curriculum to cater individual needs.

15.6.2 Fostering Collaboration and Communication

Higher education is far away from mere theoretical knowledge; it requires learning through collaboration, experience, and practicality. technology bridges this gap which was there in past decades.

15.6.3 Administrative Efficiency and Cost Savings

Manual administrative task by educators, administrative task not only consumes most of the productive time but also incur lots of cost. By automating several processes like attendance and monitoring systems, institutes can grow exponentially and focus on the actual needs of students and time.

15.6.4 Skill Development

The twenty-first century is full of competition where the fittest of all survives. To stand by this a student should be competent in various skills like analytical, technical, communication, creativity, and others. Technology enhances such skills while using various technological tools like virtual labs, Communication improvises platforms, and others.

15.6.5 Comfortable and Effective Learning

Technology utilization during lecture delivery in higher education makes it easy for learners to adapt what is being taught to them. Also, technological tools like smart boards, smart projectors, and smart classrooms create a comfortable environment for students.

15.7 Overview of the Benefits of Creating Smart Campuses Using AI

Smart Campuses with integration of AI and other technology is not a dream. Many of the universities across the globe are adopting AI to create "Smart Campuses". These Campuses are utilizing technologies to enhance all stakeholders' experiences, efficiency, and outcomes. After an IOT, AI is the one technology that is the attention of all. Education is one among which is influenced by AI and integrating it in all possible areas specially to transform educational institutes into smart campuses. Different perspectives suggest different benefits of integrating AI technology among smart campuses along with other technologies. Following are a few among those.

15.7.1 Customized Educational Experiences

AI-based algorithms provide analysis and monitoring methods for student's performance, learning habits, and preferences.

- Accessibility to customized educational resources and personalized academic assistance.
- AI-driven personalized learning methodology and pathways.
- Adaptive and flexible learning ways.
- Caters diverse learning needs of individual.

15.7.2 Improvised Campus Safety

- Supreme importance of any campus or institute is safety. AI is playing a vital role to ensure safety and security in campuses.
- Integration of AI with surveillance systems for monitoring unusual activities in real time.
- Advanced algorithms being used to work on live feeds to detect safety hazards in real time and generate alerts.
- Handling of critical situations with AI-enabled emergence systems with quick and effective communication methods.

15.7.3 Streamlined Administrative Processes

- AI helps to streamline manual administrative tasks with AI-driven tools to enhance efficiency and productivity.
- AI supports round-the-clock assistants and support through various mechanisms like chatbots.
- Optimization of resources allocation and utilization, scheduling, and others are possible through AI integration.

15.7.4 Sustainable and Efficient Campus Management

- Intelligent water management systems, heating and lighting systems are forwarding campuses towards sustainability.
- AI offers help with predictive maintenance of campus buildings, recognizing possible problems before they become serious, lowering downtime and repair costs.

15.7.5 Enhanced Campus Engagement and Community Building

- AI-based apps recommend clubs, events, activities, and such relevant activities to students in accordance with their interest.
- Social platforms integrated with AI connecting students with peers, alumni, researchers, and others with similar academic goals or interests.
- Analysis of Engagement patterns is possible through AI to understand and improve student involvement.

Mentioned benefits are few in accordance to education with AI. Integration of AI into smart campuses and Higher education is presently a reality that is continuously evolving. The entire educational world is undergoing transformation with AI. One can recommend that AI is important to behave important in the education system in the upcoming future also while making campuses and education smarter and more attuned to the requirement of students.

15.8 AI Technologies in Higher Education

Artificial intelligence (AI) holds significant implications for higher education (Bearman et al. 2023). Role and support of Artificial intelligence in higher education is not negligible. Many authors have worked in this field to identify the areas where AI is transforming the education system. Four areas of AIEd applications in academic support services, and institutional and administrative services: 1. profiling and prediction, 2. assessment and evaluation, 3. adaptive systems and personalization, and 4. intelligent tutoring systems (Zawacki-Richter et al. 2019).

15.8.1 Machine Learning in Adaptive Learning Systems

Machine learning made it possible to have adaptive learning systems in today's time. ML enables this system to personalized learning experience in accordance with individuals' needs and characteristics. Adaptive learning systems use various ML algorithms for its success rate. Machine learning has been used for a variety of reasons, ranging from learning a model of the environment of a system during operation to filtering large sets of possible configurations before analyzing them (Gheibi et al. 2021). Few of the ML implementation in adaptive learning are as:

- *Recommendation Systems*: One of the most popular systems among ML is the recommender system. Clustering models, user-based k-nearest neighbors, matrix factorization, and Bayesian networks, help to capture learners' perception and recommend content and courses accordingly.
- *Assessment Analytics*: Multilinear Regression. Logistic Regression. Decision Tree. SVM. KNN are a few popular algorithms to analyze students' responses in real-time, identification of strong and weak areas, and generate instant feedback
- *Performance prediction*: Clustering of data and using predictive algorithms like decision tree, SVM, and others helps to analyze current performance and predict future one to anticipate future degradation.
- *Cognitive Modeling*: To recognize and simulate individual cognitive processes, machine learning models can be trained which may result in more precise predictions of learning styles and preferences.
- *Data-Driven Decision Making*: Machine learning algorithms process massive amounts of data to derive useful insights into student learning patterns, enabling educators to make data-driven decisions that improve the overall efficacy of the learning environment.

15.8.2 Natural Language Processing (NLP) for Personalized Education

The power of understanding and interpreting human language in AI is being offered by NLP. This powerful tool of AI unfolds many aspects in the higher education system. Advances in Natural Language Processing (NLP) have yielded significant advances in the language assessment field (Aluthman 2016).

- Intelligent tutoring system: NLP helps to collect students' text and responses in their language and process them to facilitate them with answers or solutions.
- Chatbots: Mostly educational institutes encompass AI-based chatbots either through web-based system or app-based to support students and handle their grievance 24 * 7. Chatbots are mainly based on NLP.
- Feedback system: While collecting data from real-time activities of students and monitoring their text, replies and activities, AI-based systems generate immediate feedback where NLP plays a crucial role.
- Assistance for question answer: On posing a query by students question answer-based systems identify precise portions of text out of all collected documents based on NLP.

15.8.3 *Predictive Analytics for Student Success and Retention*

For educators, it is equally important to detect early students with a lack of academic motivation as it is to detect those with a high level of academic motivation (Babić 2017). Machine learning is full of predictive algorithms including supervised and unsupervised ones. With the usage of ML algorithms like gradient booster, KNN, and others it is easy to train a model and then test it for future prediction. This functionality is used by higher educational institutes to observe the learning pattern and behavior of students to predict their future performance and rate of success. This strategy may involve series of assessment, real-time performance observation, and others.

Also, with the usage of ML retention rate of students to any content or learning platform can be predicted. Such retention helps facilitator to rate their products and contents. Also, it helps to identify areas of interest of individuals and enforce the use of recommender systems.

15.8.4 *Virtual Assistants and Chatbots for Student Support*

AI and ML-enabled virtual assistants and chatbots are gaining popularity due to 24 * 7 availability, global reach of contents and facilitator, access to repository of knowledge, and problem-solving support. Widely popular such platforms are Winston.ai, Brainly, ScribeSense, Dr. Ivy. Such platforms are not only popular among students but also trusted by parents.

15.9 Enhancing Teaching and Learning

Technology like AI and others enhance Teaching and learning experiences. The findings show that social media, gamification, blended learning, E-books, remote learning, and self-directed professional development are the technological trends used in post-graduate classes of Education faculty (Wali and Popal 2020).

15.9.1 *AI-Powered Personalized Learning Experiences*

AI supports individualized learning experience by facilitating through various tools. These tools are not only supporting students but facilitating instructors also. List of such tools is long but few powerful and useful tools are as:

- Got Feedback: This artificial intelligence application automates the feedback process on student essays, allowing teachers to deliver individualized feedback that closely corresponds with their grading criteria.
- Grammarly: This is an AI-powered assistant for writing skills. This tool helps to enhance English writing skills by providing correction, suggestions, and real-time feedback.
- Tutor.ai: tutoring-based platform for personalized assistance with assignments and questions to students.
- ChatGPT: An AI-empowered tool to generate content and also answers queries of teacher or student in form of text or images.
- Lumen5: A video creator tool that helps to create video content for teachers for lecture delivery.
- Bing Chat: AI-enabled chatbot to aid students with their problems, questions or browsing web content.

15.9.2 Intelligent Tutoring Systems

Intelligent tutoring systems have been used in corporate training contexts as well as in a variety of educational settings, from kindergarten to higher education. Their capacity to provide tailored, adaptable, and interactive learning experiences makes them ideal tools for improving education and promoting specific learning paths. The aim of implementing AI in education is not to replace tutors, but to assist them in understanding the potential and limitations of each student individually (Jupalli et al. 2022).

Intelligent tutoring system is designed to imitate the real world on one tutoring system through individualized instructions, support, and feedback. One of the components of an ITS is a learning assistant, which can enable students to seek assistance as and when they need it, wherever they are (Mathew et al. 2021). Popularity of such a system is not restricted to students but among teachers also even especially in higher education due to several features it offers. Tailored content, instant feedback, cognitive modeling, conversational interfaces, skill and knowledge assessments are few features of the Intelligent tutoring system equipped with. Some of such popular systems are:

iTalk2Learn, third space learning, Duolingo chatbot, thinkster math, Edtech foundry are globally recognized Intelligent tutoring systems designed to solve different purposes.

15.9.3 Gamification and AI in Educational Content Development

The new education system stepped out from boundaries as it modified traditional classroom learning to E-learning. These learning methods serve knowledge hunger of individual from anywhere throughout the globe. To motivate learners, to seek their attention and concentration, and to engage them more several pedagogical practices have implemented in e-learning environment. Emerging technologies and techniques, such as Artificial Intelligence (AI) and gamification, are constantly informing educational innovations and interventions, with the aim of optimizing teaching and learning (Bezzina et al. 2022). This field not only engages the learner but also motivate them for learning through game-like activity through several gaming elements in non-gaming environment. Some examples to support this are gamified quiz with badges as rewards, game-like quiz, product knowledge quiz and lot more.

Parallelly, AI enforcing its usage for educational content development. Basic computerized tools like Microsoft PowerPoint are also integrating AI tools to create more appealing visual aids. Various editor, design apps and content create sites are available in market which generate deliverable content with high visual and understanding impact. Canva, Lumen5 are such tools available in the market.

15.10 Administrative Efficiency and Campus Management

One key advantage of an AI-centered smart university is its potential to lower costs while enhancing efficiency and accessibility (Goulart et al. 2021). AI systems can handle admissions, enrollment, and course scheduling, thus reducing the workload for administrative staff. This decrease in variable costs, combined with the potential for tailored curriculum offerings, augments accessibility (George and Wooden 2023).

15.10.1 AI for Streamlining Administrative Processes

- AI integration is always seen from the perspective of learners or educators in higher education. On the other side of the coin smart campuses with AI integration will be successful if it upgrade and automate all aspects and educational institutes. Among these sides, administrative processes like student enrollment, admission process, and lots more are required to be automated and streamlined with AI.
- Integration of chatbots on institution websites, AI-driven student registration systems, AI-powered employee onboard process are examples of AI implementation for streamlining administrative process.

15.10.2 Automated Student Enrollment and Registration

- Students are the foundation of any educational institute. This reason requires great attention to students enrollment and registration at institutes for different courses. But monotonous manual administrative process for enrollment and registration slows down efficiency and speed of work.
- AI-based tools or processes fire up this ongoing process of enrollment and registration.

15.10.2.1 Automated Registration Solutions

AI-powered solutions streamline the registration process for students, enabling them to select classes, make timetables, and better manage their academic obligations.

15.10.2.2 Application Processing

AI systems are capable of dealing with vast amounts of admission applications, evaluating the requirements for admission, verifying the accuracy of the documents, and even spotting possible fraud or inconsistencies.

15.10.3 AI-Driven Campus Security and Surveillance

Security is one of the challenges in any campus that requires 24 * 7 attention. Campuses offering AI-enabled video surveillance that works on live feeds and on detecting any malicious and suspicious activity, generate an alert proactively. incorporating new artificial intelligence (AI) and deep learning technologies is increasing the real-time capabilities of video surveillance to provide early warning of a possible security threat as it enters a campus (Ogunode et al. 2023). Some of the areas of security and surveillance are:

- Real-Time Threat Detection: Real-time threat detection is a major demand of higher education institutes and AI made it possible. Several algorithms are available in AI that allow to analyze of live video streaming to identify potential threats or suspicious behavior like unauthorized individual accessibility in campus, loitering in unauthorized or restricted areas.
- Facial Recognition and Access Control: These features can control access measures to authorized personnel like students, admin staff students or other enrolled people on campus. On the other side, it may be used to identify intruders or individuals with history of violence to generate proactive reactions.
- Behavioral Analysis for Early Intervention: Bullying, ragging, stress, anxiety are such problems that every campus finds among their students. Early detection

of such behaviors empowers campuses to provide necessary action and support. This is being possible via AI-powered video analytics to foster a more inclusive learning environment.
- Weapon Detection and Prevention: Any of the security systems finds it difficult to identify firearms or another weapon present with an individual or group. The same concern can be addressed by AI in educational campuses along with metal detectors to detect such unwanted and harmful things. These early measures may slow down hazardous effects on life.

15.11 Optimizing Resource Allocation Through AI

Smart technologies have become increasingly prevalent in various industries due to their potential for energy cost reduction, productivity gains, and sustainability (Ahmed et al. 2023). AI and machine learning are playing as game changer technology. It not only saddled automation to enhance efficiency and speed but along it offers optimization in fields wherever it is applicable. Resources and their proper utilization are the backbone of any educational institute specially in higher education where students are being ready to serve industry. Various technologies of AI that offer optimizations are listed here.

- Staffing optimization: AI has the capability to analyze historical data of students and workforce and predict the right amount of teacher and student ratio for optimization.
- Space utilization: Several algorithms are being offered by AI for data analysis, which is beautifully applicable to look at the usage of classrooms, laboratories, and other infrastructure. Identification of peak utilization time helps to optimize resources.
- Predictive Maintenance: Predictive analysis feature which can be applied on-campus building to forecast about maintenance of equipment, building or other resources.
- Energy efficiency: Smart campuses are enabled with several sensors and AI-enabled algorithms to detect patterns for adjustment of heating, light requirement, and cooling in an environment which reduces wastage of energy.

15.12 Challenges and Considerations

Every innovation comes with two faces of coin, like if it serves benefits then may pose some challenges and drawbacks. Artificial intelligence certainly has the potential to make our lives better. It is in fact already happening, but as the adoption of any new technology, the welcoming of artificial intelligence into our lives is not without challenges and obstacles along the way (Perc et al. 2019). AI-technology in demand has a great impact on our higher education system but merging AI with education system has landed with challenges and ethical concerns.

15.12.1 Ethical Considerations in AI Implementation

AI has changed the way people learn. However, its adoption in the educational sector has been saddled with challenges and ethical issues (Tahiru 2021). Ethical consideration that requires consideration while adopting AI in higher education can be listed as below.

15.12.2 Bias and Discrimination

Biases may occur due to algorithmic biases which may be inherited through biased data sets for training. This may lead to unfair outcomes and inequality. Also, AI may benefit certain groups in accordance with demographic data or existing educational disparities.

15.12.3 Data Security and Privacy

AI has the potential to advance the capabilities of learning anaaccessibilitiesn the other hand, such systems require huge amounts of data, including confidential information about students and faculty, which raises serious issues of privacy and data protection (Zawacki-Richter et al. 2019). To facilitate learners and educators AI-enabled educational tools ask several information accessibility while seeking permission for accessing academic performance, behavior, biometric, and biometric data, This may impose risk to data security and protection rights majorly in terms of usage of data for commercialization or advertisement purpose.

15.12.4 Responsibility and Accountability

Question for accountancy and responsibility of content design, development, and deployment may be raised through the AI system with its impact on education. This affects the role and duties of different actors attached to the AI ecosystem.

15.12.5 Explainability

Lack of this feature in AI tools and models may generate a gap in adoption of AI by different stakeholders of education. They may resist cherishing the adoption of AI if they don't understand how decisions are being made.

15.13 Addressing Concerns About Job Displacement

We are on the edge of technological revolution and with any new technology resistance from the audience always occurs. Such resistance could be due to several reasons like problems in learning new things, non-adaptive attitude, fear of domination by technology, and most importantly fear of a job.

Mostly people from non-tech backgrounds always fear to learn, adapt new technology as they are burdened by several myths like in promoting technologies humans will be replaced with machines and will be jobless. But the implication is different. With the rapid growth of technologies and integration of AI more positive impacts on the working area, environment, and individuals have been reported.

Rapid growth in AI and its integration has captivated the world, which is creating excitement and alarm both. The integration of artificial intelligence (AI) and machine learning (ML) in various industries has been increasing rapidly in recent years. As a result, there is a growing concern about the potential impact of these technologies on employment opportunities and job displacement (Tiwari 2023). Various job areas are affected by AI like routine jobs like data collection and summarization, clerical work, and similar. The Net effect is difficult to portray, as it ripples through the economy in complex ways. But still, we can foresee two distinct paths this technological revolution could go for. A proactive approach to AI and its implications for the future of work require occupational safety and health professionals to develop strategic foresight to better anticipate and prepare for the possibilities and challenges of AI-enabled technologies on worker safety, health, and well-being (Howard 2019).

15.13.1 Automation

With this pathway, AI's role is to perform traditional processes in an automatic manner like human or better than that. Many leading countries like the US follow this domination. This negative impact of job loss along the automation path is easy to calculate or predict contrary to robotics or other prior technological waves.

15.13.2 Creation of New Tasks or Jobs

This path is readily visible and available to us. Throughout history, technological advancements have led to the displacement of certain jobs while creating new employment opportunities in other areas (Tiwari 2023). AI creates new functionalities or jobs along with more capabilities among humans instead of forcing them out. Data Scientist, analytics are a few examples of creating new opportunities for job and the workforce.

15.13.3 Legal and Privacy Implications

Considering its multifaceted character, artificial intelligence inherently touches upon a full spectrum of legal fields, from legal philosophy, human rights, contract law, tort law, labor law, criminal law, tax law, procedural law, etc. (Perc et al. 2019). Legal and privacy implications require careful consideration as AI is expanding all its arms approaching every field. Some of the major concerns are highlighted here:

- Data Privacy and Security: Consent of information gathering and processing should be mandated. Also, focus on collecting intended data instead of all personal information.
- Intellectual Property: Ownership of AI-oriented outcomes should be clear and defined and addressed. Also, need to take care of patients as this debate still persists that AI-generated patents should be given to machines or humans.
- Legal Responsibility: On harmful impact generated by AI, who will be answerable for such legal aspects.
- Cybersecurity Threats and Security Breach: AI systems are susceptible to cybersecurity threats, and data leaks could jeopardize privacy. To prevent unwanted access and data breaches, strong security procedures and processes must be implemented.

15.14 Case Studies and Future Trends

Smart campuses are not a new theme or idea of this decade, it started since long back and reached popularity because of IOT and the enabling use of sensors to gather data and process it to generate real-time action. But with the involvement of AI, this plan could raise it heights in implementation standards and popularity. As we have seen AI facilitates and education system in numerous ways starting from smart building to making smart teaching pedagogy. All over the globe academic institutions are adopting AI-enabled technologies wherever best applicable to come as best in all. Over the years, AI technologies have evolved and taken various forms. Despite the fact that AI research has a long history, these systems have now become an essential part of human life thanks to the investments made over the years and the widespread use of technological tools such as the internet and smart devices (Talan and Kalinkara 2023).

Several such examples exist that show real-world implementation of smart campuses using is not a dream anymore.

15.14.1 Implementation of AI-Based Smart Campuses in the Real World

- Telkom University, Indonesia: it was determined that Telkom University has adopted nine components that reflect a digital-based smart campus. Among the 9 components examined, three have shown to be successful on this campus [ahmad qurtubi].
- Universal AI University, Mumbai: India's first AI university equipped with innovative technological solution. They are focused on imparting AI-based education with all experiments.
- Northern Arizona University, Flagstaff, arizona: This university officially announced AI-based smart campus in April 2022. They are incorporating all working areas, stakeholders' interest to be binder by AI. They had declaration of focusing and encompassing upcoming 10 years. This university is a great example of complete implementation of AI-based smart campuses.

15.14.2 Diverse Examples from Various Educational Institutions

Improvements in technology appear to provide an unprecedented opportunity to improve learning and teaching within the higher education system (Turney et al. 2009). As all universities and educational institutes can't be turned easily into AI-based smart campuses. Though they adopted various AI tools and technologies to make AI-based workforce culture. Diverse examples stated below from various institutes prove that AI integration is shifting educational policy and methodology from traditional to modern.

- Stanford University (United States): This University incorporates AI to implement virtual Labs. Virtual labs and simulators integrated with AI provide real-world experience while performing experiments. Such technology provides pleasant and interactive understanding in the field of science and engineering.
- Technological University Dublin (Ireland): Implementation of trending predictive analysis empowered by AI is another example in series. These people are using it for sensing and identifying students who are at risk of dropping out. Early warnings through this analysis help academic advisors to support and assist struggling students.

- Imperial College London (United Kingdom): They have incorporated AI-enabled chatbots in the student support system to support students while providing needed information and support. It helps to boost admission-related query, academics, and others.
- National University of Singapore (Singapore): Integration of AI-based language learning platform is the facility they are famous for. These platforms follow NLP and speech recognition systems for enhancing personalized language instruction and feedback to learners.

15.15 Emerging Technologies in AI for Education

Technology is advancing rapidly, bringing new concepts and innovations to various aspects of our lives. Among these concepts, AI technology has become increasingly prevalent in recent years, thanks to extensive research and development efforts (Talan and Kalinkara 2023). Various stakeholders of higher education systems are benefitted by AI with a variety of tools and systems. AI supports Learners, Teachers as well as Institutes in various aspects. Such technology support is shown in Fig. 15.3.

15.15.1 Predictions for the Future of Smart Campuses

While looking at the trend being followed by various educational institutes over the globe, demand and implementation of Smart campuses are going to increase.

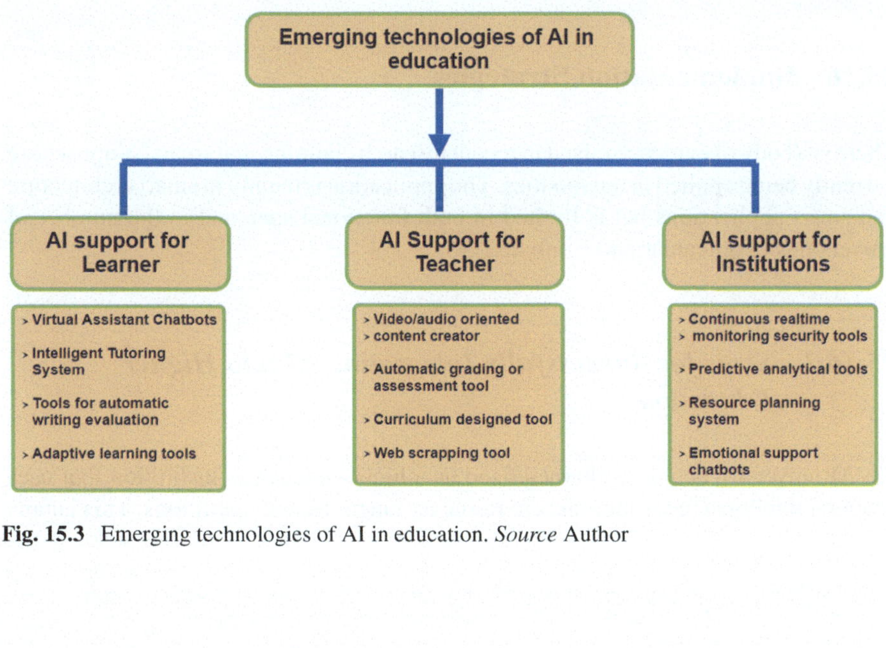

Fig. 15.3 Emerging technologies of AI in education. *Source* Author

Northern Arizona University can clarify this thought which formally announced AI AI-based smart campus in April 2022 while forecasting the upcoming development and demand fulfillment of the upcoming 10 years.

15.15.2 The Role of AI in Shaping the Future of Higher Education

Artificial Intelligence (AI) is the most powerful technological change in higher education, confronting the sector with unparalleled scholarly, ethical, and legal factors. AI not only mimics humans but also extend human ability of decision making to resolve complex problems, making the future of higher education intimately linked with AI.

Artificial intelligence (AI) applications in education are on the rise and have received a lot of attention in the last couple of years (Zawacki-Richter et al. 2019). On looking at the current impact of AI in higher education, it is so visible that AI is not departing soon. AI actually made us its fans and dependent on IT. On closed watch, it has been declared that education industry is growing enormously due to several factors like Adaptive learning, implementation of Augmented Reality, Improvise visualization of students, effective teaching tools like smart boards, visual aids, and more. Intelligent tutoring is hitting heights of popularity due to global and 24 * 7 available approach. These features are forcing us to have this cake sooner or later.

Even though we don't know exactly how artificial intelligence will develop in education, we can only speculate based on its current applications. Due to the rapid advancement of technology, the way artificial intelligence is used in education today may change. But in all we good say that AI has a great future ahead.

15.16 Implementation Strategies

There is a body of evidence raised in recent research claiming that smart campuses are currently being applied in universities. The application is mainly in smart architecture and smart applications but is limited in both functional span and in the number of universities (Yigitcanlar and Limb 2023).

15.16.1 Steps for Successfully Integrating AI into Higher Education

An AI university could be characterized as a higher education institution that uses artificial intelligence technologies to refine its functions and operations. This entails integrating AI across research, administration, teaching, and learning domains to bolster efficiency, effectiveness, and personalization (George and Wooden 2023).

Successfully integrating artificial intelligence (AI) into higher education requires careful planning, collaboration, and consideration of various factors. Here are steps that institutions can follow for successful AI integration.

A great success in any technology always lies on various parameters like fruitful planning, collaboration timely adaptation, and more. Same goes when integration of AI into higher education is required. well planned steps need to be adhered to for successful integration which could be as:

Needs Assessment and Goal Setting

- Before diving into implementation of new technology like AI in education it is must to identify associated challenges/opportunities. Also defining clear objectives and goals of integration of AI with education is must.
- This gives a clear perspective on which area requires transformation either learner, educator, or administrative part.

Create a Cross-Functional Team:

- Design a fantastic team comprehended with educators, administrators, IT specialists, and other stakeholders. Also, for attaining holistic approach for AI integration promotes collaboration between academia and IT departments.

Develop a Robust Infrastructure

A promising IT infrastructure is a demand of AI to support several AI-based applications and tools to implement in higher education. Researcher promotes investment in reliable network connectivity, computing capability, and data storage to bear the burden of powerful AI integration.

Data Management and Privacy

Clear stated policies and privacy regulations establishment and implementation of robust data security measures for sensitive information protection.

Educate and Train Staff

Higher education institutions must train their employees to meet the demands of educational institutions and digital transformation (Goulart et al. 2021). Educating and training direct stakeholders like students, teachers administrative persons becomes a mandate to make them familiarize with integrated tools, concepts and environment.

Choose Appropriate AI Applications

Against established goals and objectives, institutions are required to choose best fitted AI applications focusing on adaptive learning platform, intelligent tutoring for student success.

Pilot Programs and Test Implementations

Ensure small scale test to measure effectiveness of chosen AI application. Thereafter collecting feedback from user and adjustment in accordance is must.

Ensure Accessibility and Inclusivity

Keep a space to cater to the needs of different learner in terms of accessibility with their diverse learning styles, behavior, and special disabilities if any.

Encourage Collaboration and Interdisciplinarity

For the best result of integration of AI in education collaboration between different disciplines in academic is required along with several interdisciplinary project that involves educators and experts of technology.

Monitor and Evaluate

Regular assessment is a demand to read effectiveness of Integration towards established goals, For this generating metrics and key performance indicators is important at this point in time.

Collaboration Between Academia and Industry

Only theoretical studies don't promise better opportunities in future and great jobs. For looking into this consideration Higher educational institutes are collaborating with industry under their internship, training or such programs. These programs are intended to train students about new technologies to make them comfortable with such in their future. Academia–Industry collaborations have increasingly been acknowledged as mechanisms that craft opportunities for knowledge creation and technology exchange between the actors, leading to synergistic effects (Bhullar et al. 2019).

15.17 Conclusion

The integration of artificial intelligence (AI) in higher education is investigated in this research project, with a particular emphasis on student support and personalized learning. It emphasizes the application of AI technologies in education, including machine learning, natural language processing, and predictive analytics. The topic of AI's impact on resource allocation and administrative efficiency is also covered. It does, however, also address issues with employment displacement and ethics. The potential of AI to transform higher education and foster cooperation between academics and business is highlighted in this work's conclusion. Consideration has been given to the current situation of higher education as well as how artificial intelligence is changing conventional learning settings. It describes the principles behind AI technology and smart campuses as well as their advantages. Artificial

Intelligence (AI) technologies encompass machine learning, chatbots, virtual assistants, natural language processing, and predictive analytics. They improve resource allocation, administrative effectiveness, and teaching and learning. Concerns about ethics, diversity, accessibility, loss of employment, privacy, and legal ramifications are among the difficulties. It also showcases case studies and upcoming developments in the application of AI.

Recommendations:

Amazing results shown by Artificial Intelligence in collaboration with higher education systems open up opportunities for developing universities to incorporate AI to enhance the modern environment of education. AI caters to the needs of students and educators in an adaptive manner. A few of the recommendations for educational institutes for AI implementations are:

Technology	Reason	Tools/examples available
Adaptive learning platforms	Analysis of individual performance Tailored educational content Personalized learning	Surgent Knewton Fulcrum
Intelligent tutoring systems	Personalized support Real-time feedback and assistance Fosters effective learning environment	Electronix Tutor Algebra Tutor eTeacher EER-Tutor
Automated grading and assessments	Automation of grading of quiz, exams, and assignments Prompt feedback and results	mettl.com getapp.com exambuilder Flipgrid
Predictive analysis	Can be applied for students to predict performance and risk of failure Can be used by admin team for prediction of workforce, admission, potential risks	IBM Watson Studio RapidMiner Alteryx H20
Virtual classrooms	Chatbots, virtual assistance, automated systems to enhance experience for online learning	MOOC's Bootcamps
Facial recognition	For attendance For identifying suspicious personality To monitor students whose behavior reported to be violent in past	Buddy Punch Border Control Deep Face
Gamification	To enhance learning experience by playing game For motivation through rewards, points, etc.	Duolingo Greenlight Ambition Linkdin Peloton

(continued)

(continued)

Technology	Reason	Tools/examples available
Emotion recognition system	For students wellbeing Prediction of stress anxiety among students and workforce	

References

Ahmed V, Khatri MF, Bahroun Z, Basheer N (2023) Optimizing smart campus solutions: an evidential reasoning decision support tool. Smart Cities 6(5):2308–2346

Aluthman ES (2016) The effect of using automated essay evaluation on ESL undergraduate students' writing skill. Int J Engl Linguist 6(5):54–67. https://doi.org/10.5539/ijel.v6n5p54

Babić ID (2017) Machine learning methods in predicting the student academic motivation. Croat Oper Res Rev 8(2):443–461. https://doi.org/10.17535/crorr.2017.0028

Bearman M, Ryan J, Ajjawi R (2023) Discourses of artificial intelligence in higher education: a critical literature review. High Educ 86(2):369–385

Bezzina S, Dingli A, Pfeiffer A (2022) Leveraging gamification in education through artificial intelligence. https://doi.org/10.21125/inted.2022.2206

Bhullar SS, Nangia VK, Batish A (2019) The impact of academia-industry collaboration on core academic activities: assessing the latent dimensions. Technol Forecast Soc Change 145:1–11

García-Morales VJ, Garrido-Moreno A, Martín-Rojas R (2021) The transformation of higher education after the COVID disruption: emerging challenges in an online learning scenario. 12. https://doi.org/10.3389/FPSYG.2021.616059

George B, Wooden O (2023) Managing the strategic transformation of higher education through artificial intelligence. Adm Sci 13(9):196

Gheibi O, Weyns D, Quin F (2021) Applying machine learning in self-adaptive systems: a systematic literature review. https://doi.org/10.1145/3469440

Gligorea I, Cioca M, Oancea R, Gorski A-T, Gorski H, Tudorache P (2023) Adaptive learning using artificial intelligence in e-learning: a literature review. Educ Sci 13:1216. https://doi.org/10.3390/educsci13121216

Goulart AR, Liboni LB, Cezarino LO (2021) Qualification as a societal challenge and the role of higher education from a system approach. High Educ Skills Work Based Learn 11(5):1002–1019

Howard J (2019) Artificial intelligence: implications for the future of work. Am J Ind Med. https://doi.org/10.1002/ajim.23037

Jupalli TK, Reddy MST, Kondaveeti HK (2022) Artificial intelligence in higher education. https://doi.org/10.4018/978-1-6684-5400-8.ch001

Lai JWM, Bower M (2019) How is the use of technology in education evaluated? A systematic review. 133. https://doi.org/10.1016/J.COMPEDU.2019.01.010

Li X, Bergin C, Olsen AA (2022) Positive teacher-student relationships may lead to better teaching. Learn Instr 80:101581

Mathew AN, Rohini V, Paulose J (2021) NLP-based personal learning assistant for school education. 11. https://doi.org/10.11591/IJECE.V11I5.PP4522-4530

Ogunode NJ, Okolie KE, Chinedu R (2023) Artificial intelligence and tertiary education management. Electron Res J Soc Sci Hum 5(4):18–31

Palanivel K (2020) Emerging technologies to smart education. Int J Comput Trends Technol 68(2):5–16

Perc M, Ozer M, Hojnik J (2019) Social and juristic challenges of artificial intelligence. Palgrave Commun 5:61. https://doi.org/10.1057/s41599-019-0278-x

Raja R, Nagasubramani PC (2018) Impact of modern technology in education. 3. https://doi.org/10.21839/JAAR.2018.V3IS1.165

Sutjarittham T, Gharakheili HH, Kanhere SS, Sivaraman V (2019) Experiences with IoT and AI in a smart campus for optimizing classroom usage. IEEE Internet Things J 6(5):7595–7607

Tahiru F (2021) AI in education: a systematic literature review. 23. https://doi.org/10.4018/JCIT.2021010101

Talan T, Kalinkara Y (2023) The role of artificial intelligence in higher education: ChatGPT assessment for anatomy course. 7. https://doi.org/10.33461/uybisbbd.1244777

Tiwari R (2023) The impact of AI and machine learning on job displacement and employment opportunities

Tuomi I (2019) The impact of artificial intelligence on learning, teaching, and education: policies for the future. JRC science for policy report. European Commission

Turney CSM, Robinson D, Lee M, Soutar A (2009) Using technology to direct learning in higher education: the way forward? 10. https://doi.org/10.1177/1469787408100196

Wali AZ, Popal AW (2020) The emerging issues and impacts of technology in classroom learning. 15. https://doi.org/10.3991/IJET.V15I15.14175

Yigitcanlar T, Limb M (2023) The making of smart campus: a review and conceptual framework. 13. https://doi.org/10.3390/buildings13040891

Zawacki-Richter O, Marín VI, Bond M, Gouverneur F (2019) Systematic review of research on artificial intelligence applications in higher education—where are the educators? Int J Educ Technol High Educ 16(1):1–27

The manufacturer's authorised representative in the EU is Springer Nature Customer Service Centre GmbH, Europaplatz 3, 69115 Heidelberg, Germany. If you have any concerns regarding our products, please contact ProductSafety@springernature.com

Printed and bound by CPI Group (UK) Ltd, Croydon, CR0 4YY
01/10/2026
02225904-0017